Introduction to Business Data Processing

Introduction to Business Data Processing

Second Edition

Lawrence S. Orilia

Nassau Community College

McGraw-Hill Book Company

New York   St. Louis   San Francisco   Auckland
Bogotá   Hamburg   Johannesburg   London   Madrid
Mexico   Montreal   New Delhi   Panama   Paris
São Paulo   Singapore   Sydney   Tokyo   Toronto

Introduction to Business Data Processing

1 2 3 4 5 6 7 8 9 0 D O D O 8 9 8 7 6 5 4 3 2 1

ISBN 0-07-047835-X

This book was set in Helvetica by York Graphic Services, Inc.
The editors were James E. Vastyan and Jonathan Palace;
the designer was Joseph Gillians;
the production supervisor was Joe Campanella.
The photo editor was Inge King.
New drawings were done by J & R Services, Inc.
R. R. Donnelley & Sons Company was printer and binder.

About the cover

Copper coil of "film" recording head in new IBM 3380 large-system disk file. Head can read and write data at 3 million characters a second—first device in a commercial product to achieve such a rate. (Coil is magnified several hundred times; light refraction from minutely separated film layers produces iridescent color pattern.)

The IBM 3380 was announced in 1980, offering higher disk surface density than any other commercially available disk file, as well as the largest information capacity per disk file—2.5 billion characters. From IBM's 1980 Annual Report.

Library of Congress Cataloging in Publication Data

Orilia, Lawrence.
    Introduction to business data processing.

    Includes index.
    1. Business—Data processing. 2. Electronic data processing. I. Title.
HF5548.2.0688 1982   001.64   81–14239
ISBN 0-07-047835-X   AACR2

To my son Adrian,
my daughter Vanessa,
and my wife Tracy,
who have all helped to fulfill my life
and represent the measure of my happiness.

Contents

Chapter Two

Welcome to the World of Data Processing

Chapter Three

Card Data, Keypunch, and Other Devices

Chapter Six

Flowcharting

Chapter Seven
Introduction to Programming and Programming Languages

Chapter Eight
Programming in BASIC

Chapter Nine

An Introduction to COBOL

Chapter Ten

Structured Programming

Chapter Eleven

Mass Storage Files

Chapter Twelve

Information Processing Systems

Chapter Thirteen

Management Information Systems (MIS)

Chapter Fourteen

Chapter Fifteen

Chapter Sixteen
Minicomputers, Microcomputers, and Other Computer Systems

Appendix: Numbering Systems

Index

Preface

The successes associated with the first edition of this introductory data processing text reinforced many of the personal beliefs expressed in its writing. These beliefs included the presentation of data processing principles with carefully integrated illustrations and detailed explanations. Sufficient illustrative examples, both pictorial and narrative, were provided to reinforce concepts and their application. The proper placement of illustrative problems offered students the step-by-step guidance they needed to master the concepts presented.

Because of educational philosophies which I developed when attending college, the first edition offered many practice problems and discussion questions with which to apply the principles learned. I believe quite strongly in the idea that students learn best by doing. Of considerable impact was the text's reading level and style. The conversational manner of presentation was deliberate. It encouraged student learning, avoided the more cryptic or tedious styles of other authors, and did not talk down to the students. The conversational mode avoided the presentation of extremely technical material or material that detracted from student learning.

Many adopters of the first edition commented favorably on these points and remarked on the reference quality of the text. Students could freely turn to the text and learn on their own, at their own pace. These instructors felt that because the text covered the fundamental concepts so well, they were free to discuss other topics of interest or provide more individualized instruction.

The ready availability of supporting materials, to both the student and instructor, was another strong plus for the first edition. The accessories simplified many preparatory tasks for instructors and greatly aided individualized student learning. The Study Guide accompanying the text offered students the extra drill and practice they desired prior to a test or final.

These ideas, successfully incorporated into the first edition, have become the foundation of the second edition. Naturally, these concepts were refined and fine-tuned to focus their effectiveness. Every attempt was made to maintain the currentness of the second edition, in spite of the ever-changing nature of this field.

While writing this edition, I continued to have one thought in mind: I wanted the beginning computer student to be capable of reading the text and fully understanding the material presented. This desire evolved from a problem I have frequently encountered in the classroom. Too often, I have assigned readings to students only to have them state that the material was impossible to follow. This was especially true for discussions of flowcharting, structured programming, and introductions to programming, in which sufficient detail is required to master the subject matter. Many of the other texts currently available merely skim the surface of this material or offer cartoons instead of well-thought-out explanations, leaving the student with nothing concrete on which to base learning. I know that I have provided the detail necessary to permit the independent student development of this material.

This approach has a positive benefit to the instructor as well. Freed of the necessity to cover virtually all aspects of a topic, the instructor can introduce new material for class discussion. This new material might enhance a discussion, motivate increased student participation, provide special projects, or introduce topics which are of particular importance to the individual instructor.

Organization

The overall organization of this text enables the reader to develop a fundamental knowledge of the computer prior to the discussions of programming and systems analysis and design. Each chapter is written as an independent unit, providing complete coverage of a topic within its content. Thus, if an instructor desires to cover a chapter out of sequence, the continuity of the presentation will not be adversely affected.

Classroom testing has proved the chapter organization used in this text to be effective. Chapters 1 to 5 present material consistent with most introductory data processing courses. The material covered provides students with principles fundamental to data processing, enabling them to begin programming. Chapter 6, "Flowcharting," provides a strong foundation for the programming chapters that follow. Chapter 7 introduces programming and programming languages. The computer languages BASIC and COBOL are discussed in Chapters 8 and 9, respectively. Program solutions developed in these chapters are closely tied to the flowcharting problems discussed in Chapter 6. Instructors are also free to develop solutions they have specifically employed in the past.

Two entirely new chapters were written on structured programming and management information systems (MIS). Chapter 10 discusses structured concepts and applies them to BASIC, COBOL, and

PASCAL in detailed illustrative examples. Chapter 13's discussion of MIS reviews the organization of these complex systems, their relationship to databases, and the use of IMS systems. Specialized systems such as the CICS and DC/DB configurations are presented, with detailed case studies offering a practical orientation to both MIS and database systems.

The latter part of the text offers special discussions of minicomputers, microcomputers, and other types of computer systems; data communication systems, systems analysis, and design concepts; and a detailed example of a systems documentation package. The review of many of these topics can add much to the content of an introductory computer course and provide the student with a broader overview of the business data processing field.

The organization of the chapters affords the instructor flexibility. The instructor can use the first seven chapters to develop the concepts of data processing for half of the semester. The remainder of the semester can be devoted to programming applications. Another approach might provide a brief discussion of programming and the development of systems-related concepts in the last half of the semester. The instructor is free to choose the topics of coverage and can diversify the material presented.

Learning Objectives

Every chapter begins with a section entitled "Purpose of This Chapter," which presents the student with an overview of the material and topics to be covered. This section provides a general feel for the chapter's content. The student can grasp the organization of the chapter and place topics of discussion in their proper perspective.

The purpose section also presents the learning objectives for the chapter. These briefly stated objectives offer the student a guide to the key areas of the chapter and the skills and concepts to be gained from reading it. The learning objectives are also of value when a review of the chapter is anticipated, prior to a test.

Key terms used throughout the chapter are also listed in the learning objectives. The terms are commonly used in data processing and represent an operational vocabulary vital to the current or future user of computer services. All the terms are defined in the text of the chapter and appear in a glossary at the chapter's end.

Readability

A concerted effort has been made to keep the reading level of this text from becoming overly technical, monotonous, or unduly complicated. Standardized reading tests applied to the text indicate that the average high school graduate should not have difficulty in comprehending the material presented. I have blended this reading level into a conversational mode of presentation. It is my belief that the conversational approach greatly assists the learning process and is uniquely suited to today's student. It does not belittle the student, but rather guides the reader through the required material on a step-by-step basis in an easily comprehensible manner.

Summary

A point-by-point summary of all material covered appears at the end of the chapter. The summary details the major topics discussed in the chapter, capsulizing each point in a few sentences. The summary is organized to follow the presentation of material in the chapter, reinforcing the order of topic coverage. Students will find this type of summary particularly advantageous when reviewing for a test.

Glossary

An introductory text requires clear definitions of all terms used in its discussion. The chapter glossaries list, in alphabetical order, all key terms introduced in the chapter. The page on which each term is defined appears in boldface type in the index of the book for easy referencing to its appropriate chapter.

End-of-Chapter Tests

The discussion questions and summary tests at the end of each chapter enable the reader to test his or her mastery of the material covered in the chapter. The student is advised to complete the summary test before proceeding on to the next topic of discussion. The summary test can also be used in preparation for an exam. The topics related to questions that have been answered incorrectly can be reviewed before the test. Summary test answers appear at the end of each chapter.

Special-Interest Items

Students like to study material that is current and related to real-life situations. In an effort to meet this requirement, items of special interest have been included in each chapter. These items are drawn from a variety of sources and relate directly to the materials covered in the chapter. In some cases, these special items note the widespread applicability of the computer and some of its more appealing uses. In the chapters related to programming, the special items highlight programming considerations affecting the student. These items point out commonly made student errors, ways to avoid specific mistakes, and tips to help simplify programming assignments. Each special item is intended to enhance the presentation of the material and complement the chapter's coverage of a topic.

Case studies at the end of each chapter also reinforce the practical and diversified uses of computers in our daily environment. Each case study has been rewritten to focus on its high points and avoid highly technical discussions. Case study applications range from the use of computers to prepare mailing labels for small advertising companies to the use of computers by vast administrative organizations supporting millions of people. Each case attempts to bring into focus how the computer is used and why it serves the purpose that it does.

Of particular interest are the new topics included in the second edition. New material includes characteristics and examples of computerized crime, service bureaus, and operating systems; new types of hardware and word processing; newly introduced programming languages; managerial considerations in systems evaluations; canned programs; business simulations and models; and details on the newer versions of both minicomputers and microcomputers.

Many instructors will be especially interested in Chapter 15, "Documentation of a System." Because systems-related subjects represent one of the more difficult topics for many students, Chapter 15 serves as an example of the work a systems analyst may perform. Many instructors assign this chapter for reading before their DP students enter the systems course. Many students do not know what a system is; this exposure offers them an initial glimpse of this topic. Many students retain this text and use Chapter 15 as a guideline in the preparation of their systems project.

In general, I have tried to write a text that is easy to read, is informative, and assists in the development of selected data processing skills. I have attempted to include material which is relevant to the study of computers, without becoming overly technical. I believe that this text provides students with a working knowledge of computer-related data processing skills that can be used in subsequent computer courses or in the performance of their jobs. I would like students to think of this text as a reference that they can turn to when faced with a data-processing-oriented question or task. I have tried to make this text, as well as the learning of data processing skills, an enjoyable experience.

Additional Materials
Study Guide

For some students, lectures and repeated readings of the text are not sufficient. The material under discussion must be reinforced through additional review and self-testing. For these students, the Study Guide has been written. In this separate guide, the contents of each chapter receives special treatment. The student is provided with a restatement of the chapter's learning objectives, a brief summary of the material covered, 10 multiple-choice questions, 15 true-false questions, and approximately 30 self-study questions. This array of questions offers students sufficient opportunity to test themselves on their mastery of the chapter.

Instructor's Manual (IM)

An instructor assumes the responsibility of preparing the supporting materials, tests, and lecture notes that parallel the presentation of material in a newly adopted text. A properly prepared instructor's manual can greatly ease this task and assist the instructor in the time-consuming conversion of his or her classroom materials. For each chapter, the IM will provide:

1 An overview of the chapter, highlighting its major points.
2 A lecture outline noting sample discussion questions, topics, or examples which can be used in class.
3 Answers to all discussion questions listed in the main text.
4 Answers to all test bank questions.
5 Overhead transparency masters of selected illustrations drawn from the text.

In addition, instructors are given sample discussion questions which can be employed to initiate classroom discussions. In selected chapters, specialized materials relating to points covered in the text are provided. These include sample newspaper readings, extra flowcharting problems, extra BASIC programming problems, and helpful teaching hints.

Test Bank

One of the more important supporting materials available to the instructor is the Test Bank, containing a variety of test questions. Included in the Test Bank are two quizzes per chapter, composed of 15 true-false questions and 10 multiple-choice questions, in a format that will enable them to be easily duplicated and administered. These prepared quizzes and test questions offer the instructor freedom from the preparation of exams, allowing more time for personalized instruction.

Acknowledgments

Many exceedingly fine and talented individuals have contributed to the success of this text. I was very fortunate in having a group of reviewers whose critical evaluations were of great value during the preparation of the manuscript. I wish to thank Paul Fuhs and James Wynne of Virginia Commonwealth University; Beverly Madron of Western Kentucky University; Robert M. Stewart of Iowa State University; William L. Fox of the College of DuPage; James Baldwin of Nassau Community College; Jerry A. Elam of Saint Petersburg Junior College; Michael

Nolan of the University of Nebraska, Lincoln; Victor Sherrer of Trenton State College; Edward Irving of North Carolina Central University; Jacque Vail of Burlington County College; Sheila M. Fay of Solano Community College; Edward Eckhard of North Shore Community College; Richard J. Westfall of Cabrillo College; Thomas W. Kelly of Northeastern University; B. J. Mangold of Montclair State College; Iva Helen Lee of McLennan Community College; and Barry A. Stein of Queensborough Community College.

No text would evolve without the assistance of editorial support. In this regard, I would like to thank the editorial contributions of Jim Vastyan, Fran Neal, and Jon Palace, all of the College Division. My express thanks go to Mel Haber for his assistance in developing the text's art program and his moral support during the initial production phases. I would also like to thank Joe Campanella for keeping both the first and second editions on their production schedules. A word of praise should go to Inge King for her fine photo research efforts.

In general, I would like to thank everyone on the McGraw-Hill College Division staff who has contributed to making this edition and the first edition a success. I am certain that we have all learned a great deal from this project.

My last acknowledgment is reserved for my wife, Tracy, and my children, Adrian and Vanessa. They put up with the frustrations and absence caused by this work. Without their collective encouragement and patience, the successful completion of this project would not have been possible. Tracy's specific support carried me through the dog days of writing, when emotional and verbal encouragement were needed.

Lawrence S. Orilia

Portfolio:
The History of
Data Processing

Plate 1 The suan-pan is the Chinese version of the abacus. (*IBM.*)

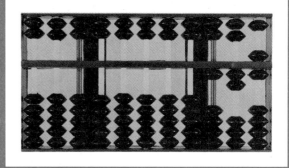

Plate 2 A Japanese abacus, or soroban. (*The Granger Collection.*)

The abacus is one of the earliest known computational devices and can be traced to ancient Babylonia. The abacus remains useful today in certain small businesses and in elementary schools where students are learning arithmetic.

Plate 3 Numerical symbols used in early Egypt.

A system of numerical notation was essential to the processing of data. People needed a shorthand to represent quantities in computations. Many societies have developed methods of representing quantities, some based on the numbers 5, 8, 20, and 64. Most societies today use the Arabic numbering system, a decimal system based on the number 10. Computers use a binary system, based on the number 2, to represent their data.

Fra Luca Pacciola, a fourteenth-century monk, developed and applied the concepts of double-entry bookkeeping, which laid the foundation of modern accounting principles. In recent years, these principles have been adapted to facilitate the computerized accounting of financial data. The computer can analyze large amounts of financial and accounting data and present the information in an immediately usable format. The computer format is a long way from the quills and ink once used to record transactions.

Plate 4 Bookkeeping in a medieval monastery. (*The Granger Collection.*)

Plate 5 Fifteenth-century English tally stick. (*The Bettmann Archive.*)

Plate 6 Pascal's Machine Arithmetique. (*IBM.*)

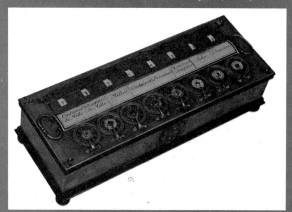

Each notch on the English tally stick represents 1 pound sterling. The tally stick served as a tax receipt and was a permanent record of tax payments. The accurate recording of data was a vital aspect of society, even in the Middle Ages.

In the 1640s, the Frenchman Blaise Pascal invented a mechanical device that functioned as an adding machine. Known as the Machine Arithmetique, the device was constructed of interlocking gears that represented the numbers 0 through 9. It operated like an odometer, which records an automobile's mileage. Pascal's was another historical attempt to develop a mechanical device that would perform arithmetic operations.

Plate 7 Gottfried von Leibniz. (*Culver Pictures.*)

Gottfried von Leibniz, a German mathematician, further refined Pascal's concepts and produced a calculating device capable of multiplication, division, addition, and subtraction.

In 1804, Joseph Marie Jacquard perfected the idea of the automated loom. Using holes punched into a series of connected cards, Jacquard was able to control the weaving of fabrics. The loom used in this process sensed the pattern coded into the cards and wove the fabric accordingly. These cards were the forerunners of Hollerith's punched cards.

In the early 1800s, the English inventor Charles Babbage theorized that it was possible to construct an automatic, mechanical calculator. With the support of the British government, Babbage began the construction of the Difference Engine and, years later, the Analytic Engine. The concepts Babbage put forward were eventually used by engineers in the development of the first computer prototypes.

Despite ten years' work, Babbage failed to build a fully operational model of either the Difference or Analytic Engine and lost his government subsidy. Not until 1854 did George Pehr Schuetz build a working model of the Difference Engine.

In 1842, a paper by L. F. Menabrea on the Analytic Engine was translated from Italian into English by Augusta Ada Byron, Countess of Lovelace, and presented to her colleagues. Babbage encouraged Lady Lovelace to conduct her own research and refine many of the concepts in the paper. Lady Lovelace's contributions to binary arithmetic would later be used by John Von Neumann in developing the modern computer.

Plate 8   Jacquard's automated loom. (*IBM.*)

Plate 9   The Difference Engine was constructed using the theories of Charles Babbage. (*IBM.*)

Plate 10   The electrical tubulator and sorter developed by Hollerith. (*IBM.*)

In the 1880s, the U.S. Census Bureau asked Herman Hollerith to find a way to speed up the processing of census data. Hollerith created punch cards that resemble today's computer cards, their code, and tabulating equipment. The 1890 Census was completed in approximately 3 years rather than the 11 years the Census Bureau had originally estimated.

Plate 11   The Mark I was developed by H. H. Aiken in 1937 at Harvard University. (*IBM.*)

Plate 12   John Von Neumann. (*UPI.*)

Plate 13   ENIAC, the first all-electric computer. (*UPI.*)

In 1937, a computer was developed at Harvard University by H. H. Aiken. This device, the Mark I, was a prototype of the computers used today. It is less well-known that a closely related predecessor to the Mark I was built at Iowa State College in the 1930s. This electronic machine was developed under John V. Atanasoff's supervision and laid the groundwork for the ENIAC (electronic numerical integrator and calculator) computer, which appeared in 1946. World War II sparked intense research and computer development, and the ENIAC was the first all-electronic computer.

Plate 14 UNIVAC I.
(*Sperry Univac.*)

During the same period, a brilliant mathematician, John Von Neumann, presented technical papers on the stored program concept. According to this concept, the operating instructions and data used in processing should be stored inside the computer. Whenever necessary, the computer would have the capability to modify these program instructions during their execution. The stored program concept was the basis for all future computer advances. In 1949, this concept was incorporated into the computer EDSAC (electronic delay storage automatic computer), which was developed at Cambridge University. This computer was capable of storing a sequence of instructions, the equivalent of the first computer program.

Developments in the field of computer technology mushroomed in the early 1950s. Computers featured internal data storage areas and used data provided by paper tapes. In 1951, the UNIVAC I (Universal Automatic Computer) was introduced and became the first commercially available computer. The UNIVAC I was characteristic of the first generation of computers. These computers were constructed of vacuum tubes, were big and bulky, and generated so much heat that they required controlled air-conditioned rooms. First-generation computers were relatively difficult to program and were restricted in their uses.

The early 1950s also brought the development and acceptance of magnetic tape, a great technological advance. This compact, portable medium permitted the sequential storage of millions of characters of data and its rapid transfer to the computer. Data could move up to 75 times faster than with other available methods. Magnetic tape storage operates in principle like the home tape recorder.

The post-Sputnik era, 1959–1965, brought the second generation of computers. They used transistors and therefore were less bulky, could store more data, were easier to program, had higher processing speeds, and could be applied to more processing jobs than first-generation computers.

Between 1959 and 1965, the high-speed magnetic disk was developed and marketed. It allowed the random access of data and overcame many of tape's problems—slowness and sequential access of data. Magnetic disks let computers go directly to an item of data and use it without first having to read through other records.

Plate 15 Magnetic tape unit. (*IBM.*)

Plate 16 IBM 1401, a second-generation computer. (*IBM.*)

Plate 17 Magnetic disk pack. (*IBM.*)

In the mid-1960s, the third generation of computers arrived and made the computer a major business tool. Third-generation computers were constructed of microminiaturized integrated circuits, had greater input-output capabilities and vast internal storage, and operated in billionths of a second. The program languages developed for third-generation machines were easy to learn, and so more people were able to develop programming skills and apply them to more jobs. A major development in third-generation machines was the IBM 360 Series of computer systems.

Plate 18 The IBM 360, a third-generation computer, and its microminiaturized circuits. (*IBM.*)

Plate 19 The IBM 370 Series computer and the silicon chips used in this series. (*IBM.*)

In 1970, IBM introduced its 370 Series computer. It uses silicon chips only eight-hundredths of an inch square. The 370 was an improvement over the 360 Series and incorporated new technologies. Although some manufacturers claim that the silicon chips represent a new generation of equipment, most experts consider that devices constructed on this basis are still third-generation machines. Scholars believe that a major breakthrough in technology will be necessary to arrive at a fourth-generation computer.

Minicomputers are physically small computers with the processing capabilities of larger conventional computers. The first minicomputer, developed by the Digital Equipment Corporation, was marketed in 1965. Minis use easily learned languages and cost considerably less than most larger systems. They place a vast processing potential within the range of most businesspeople.

Microcomputers came after minicomputers. Microcomputers are small, highly specialized computer systems with a limited amount of data storage. Although microcomputers are currently available to support specific business activities like financial planning or auditing, their real impact is in homes. Approximately 250,000 people have bought microcomputers for home or business use. Microcomputers are also gaining acceptance in teaching history, spelling, programming, and other skills. Microcomputers represent a huge potential market for computer manufacturers.

Plate 20 The minicomputer was first developed by the Digital Equipment Corporation. (*Digital Equipment Corp.*)

Plate 21 This single microcomputer chip has been magnified 80 times and contains 20,000 transistors. (*Intel Corporation.*)

Plate 22 The IBM 3850 mass storage system. (*IBM.*)

Plate 23 The Xerox 9200 printing subsystem. (*Xerox Corp.*)

Technological advances have also improved access to and processing of data. The IBM 3850 mass storage system uses a honeycomb of compartments to store data. It can store billions of characters of data and retrieve them in seconds.

Computers can also use high-speed devices to print information and make it rapidly available. One of the newest methods uses lasers and a spray of ink. The Xerox 9200 printing subsystem is a laser printer which can print up to 18,000 lines of data per minute. The keyboard device on the 9200 lets the operator control printing operations. The 9200 can print, duplicate forms, and vary type size.

One new development in computer technology uses magnetic bubbles, magnetized areas a few micrometers in diameter which move across specially treated surfaces of thulium orthoferrite. Bubble technology is a form of computer storage with data transfer rates of up to 3 million bits per second. If it proves economical, it may eventually replace many present forms of computer storage. It has already proved practical when incorporated into portable printing devices.

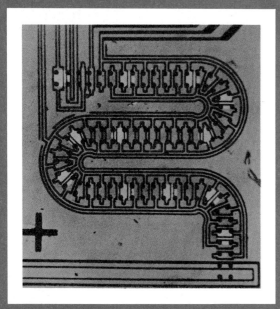

Plate 24 Magnetic bubble memory circuits. (*AT&T.*)

Plate 25 A portable printing device which uses bubble memory technology. (*Texas Instruments.*)

Plate 26 An IBM 4300 Series computer system. (*IBM.*)

New computer systems reflect the desire of business and society for economical and efficient devices. The IBM 4300 Series computer operates on one-quarter the energy required by its predecessors at 4 times their operating speeds. Many new computers have "plug compatibility," a feature that allows the efficient attachment of various supporting devices so that a system can accommodate many kinds of computer equipment.

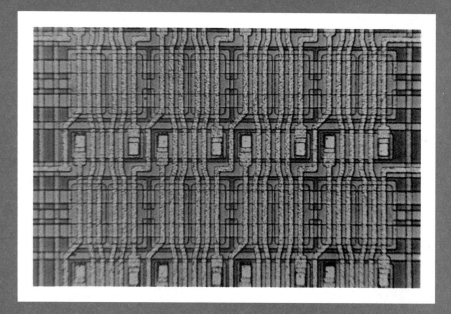

Scientists have recently developed an electronic switch that allows experimental computers to alternate the impulses used in data storage and manipulation at speeds over 10-trillionths of a second (10/1,000,000,000,000 second). This switching component, the Josephson tunneling device, represents another breakthrough in computer technology.

Introduction to
Business Data
Processing

One

The Impact of Computers

FIGURE 1.1 The acceptance of computers in our society is commonplace. Computer-related devices are readily observed in businesses such as chain stores, gas stations, and retail outlets. In the figure, a computer-like scale provides accurate pricing information for the consumer. (*R. Matusow.*)

Purpose of This Chapter

This chapter is a brief introduction to data processing, computers, and their effect on our society. Earlier, in the pictorial history, we illustrated many of the milestones in computer development. In this chapter we will examine the relationship between the needs to count and compute and efforts to develop computers.

Society tends to portray computers as two-headed beasts capable of helping humanity or of stifling its existence. It sees that computers both create and eliminate jobs, that they analyze data for space exploration or for invading individual privacy. Computers are used by criminals to steal and embezzle as well as in the service of medical diagnosis and healing. In this chapter we will also discuss the computer's portrayal in film and literature and its technical contributions to those arts.

This chapter will detail the factors of speed, accuracy, and reliability in computers and will illustrate them with a practical example, data processing of a payroll. The payroll example shows how data actually passes through a data processing system. After studying this chapter, you should be able to:

■   Briefly discuss the relationship between the need for data and the development of the computer.

■   Discuss the impact of the computer on society and some of the problems that have arisen out of its use.

■   Discuss the issue of computerized crime and the need for data security.

■   Describe the computer-related factors of speed, accuracy, and reliability.

■   Describe the overall flow of data through a payroll system.

■   Understand the following terms:

Accuracy	Output
Collection of data	Password
Controls	Processing
Downtime	Program
Electronic Funds Transfer System (EFTS)	Reliability
File	Speed
Frequency	Update
Input	Voiceprint
Million Instructions per Second (MIPS)	Volume

Introduction

It is hard to think of any aspect of our society that is not affected by some form of computerization. Right now, if you were to make a record of your computer-related experiences, you would probably be amazed. The computer is used to prepare a company payroll, reserve seats on a jet plane, print monthly customer statements from credit card companies, and record customer sales on items bought at a department store. But are you aware of the subtler uses of the computer?

For example, computers are involved in the switching of telephone calls when lines become overloaded. Burger King, the hamburger chain, employs computers to monitor inventory records at their individual stores. Hospitals and medical facilities use computers to analyze blood samples, to prepare patient case histories, and to monitor heart attack victims.

Computers will continue to have a significant effect on our society. Their past development has been closely related to our need for information.

1.1 The Need for Data

The Shepherd's Need to Count

Historically, we have always needed to count and to use some system of numbering to represent data. Even the lonely shepherd needed a way to account for the number of sheep in his flock. He probably assigned a stone to each animal. At regular intervals, he could count his pile of stones and determine the number of sheep in the flock. Describing the process in modern terms, we might say that the shepherd was maintaining a status of his inventory of sheep.

The shepherd's need for data is like today's businessperson's. Both require accurate information to run their businesses.

Developing Trade and the Industrial Revolution

Business records became increasingly important as international trade expanded. Cargo loaded at one port had to be accounted for many months later halfway around the world. The Romans developed the first "letter of credit" to partially solve this problem. A trader would put funds into an authorized bank in one city in the empire and receive a sealed letter of credit. The trader presented this letter at another authorized bank and received the funds.

With the industrial revolution, time became an important consideration in business dealings. Great emphasis was placed on having accurate and timely information. Fortunes were made or lost because information was or was not available. Carrier pigeons were sometimes used to speed the transfer of data between cities.

The telegraph and, later, the telephone became vital tools of business because they simplified the means of communication. Business used these devices not only to obtain but also to generate information. The need for business data was beginning to expand. Businesspeople wanted and needed more information to operate their companies, and they wanted it as quickly as possible.

Research Develops a Computer

Business needed computers, but the military pioneered their development. The U.S. Armed Forces needed accurate artillery tables during World War II, and researchers developed early computer systems to perform these ballistic computations rapidly. Since World War II, corporate research has produced unprecedented technological advances in computer systems.

FIGURE 1.2 A merchant corrects his accounts after trading. (*The Bettmann Archive.*)

FIGURE 1.3 The work of NASA depends on the use of computers. (*NASA.*)

1.2 Computers in Society

Computers perform many of the less visible tasks that society takes for granted. For instance, computers govern the flow of traffic during rush hours through control of traffic lights. One large computer prepares weather forecasts for the entire country. Computers are extremely powerful and sophisticated devices which can be applied to almost any job.

Government Use of Computers

Although computers have benefited society, they have also caused harm. Their benefits include their ability to store vast amounts of data and retrieve it in thousandths of a second. This ability was critical to our space program when enormous amounts of data were fed into NASA's computer for analysis and retention. A more recent example of computers' ability to amass and analyze data was the 1980 Census, with its estimated 120 million forms from nearly 86 million households. The Census Bureau designed, patented, and developed new machines to scan the returned forms and automatically feed the 3 billion facts directly into its computer. The Bureau's giant UNIVAC 1100 worked for over 3 months to report the 1980 Census.

Because it needs to process so much data, the U.S. government is the world's largest user of computers and information technology. Table 1.1 lists budgeted computer costs of selected government agencies. Without computers, most government agencies would not be able to amass data or render any services.

Table 1.1 Budget Costs for Computer Services 1980

Government Agency	Estimated Cost
Department of State	$ 20 million
Department of Agriculture	$120 million
Department of the Treasury	$580 million
Department of Defense	$ 2.5 billion

Invasion of Privacy

The computerized amassing of data is not without its drawbacks, however. In 1977, the government issued a report on violations of privacy relating to the computerized maintenance of medical records.[1] The 2-year study focused on the enormous flow of personal medical data, the increasing use of these records for nonmedical purposes, and the resulting invasion of privacy. The report concluded that safeguards must be applied to control both the access to any personal data and the type of data collected and stored.

Once data is stored in a computer, it is potentially available to anyone with access to that system. Therefore, great sums are spent on securing data processing installations. Many are protected by multiple locked doors which are opened by special badges. Other security systems are computer controlled, responding to specific prerecorded voice commands or physical characteristics like handprints.

Even so, breaches of computer security occur. For example, at Sandia Laboratories, a top-security government contractor which makes nuclear weapons, an employee is alleged to have used the computer to place bets for a gambling syndicate. Though Sandia officials claimed their security was intact, FBI and other investigators were surprised at the easy access to the computer. Virtually overnight, new security procedures were instituted to restrict access.[2]

The computer as well as its data must be secure. People who know computers can learn security codes and passwords, and the stored data becomes readily available for unauthorized use.

Passwords are common security measures at computer installations. A **password** is some form of coded entry which must be entered and accepted by the computer in order for it to grant access. A college, for example, might require students to enter their class ID and social security numbers before they can use the computer. In contrast, at a defense plant handling classified information, a potential user might be required first to enter a series of predefined codes which are changed daily, then to enter another series of passwords to use a

---

[1]H. M. Schmick, "Medical Records Privacy Violated, Government-Backed Study Finds," *The New York Times,* Jan. 13, 1977, p. 20.

[2]"Double Trouble: Scandals Rock New Mexico," *Time,* Dec. 17, 1979.

SOVIET AIRLINE DATA TAMPERED WITH

Federal Aviation Administration officials have concluded that someone tampered with a computer tracking an incoming Soviet jet carrying Ambassador Anatoly Dobrynin. The control tower at Kennedy Airport in New York temporarily lost computerized information on the jet's altitude and speed and then confused the plane with another. The Russian jet got clearance to descend 10 miles before it should have and occupied an airspace that might have been taken by another plane. There were no other planes nearby, however, and the jet landed safely.

An FAA spokesman said that the computer might have malfunctioned, but the strong likelihood was that someone in Kennedy's control room tampered with a computer keyboard and removed the information on the incoming jet. An air traffic controller said that the complexity of the equipment meant that someone would have needed special knowledge to tamper with the computer.

Planes controlled by the tower appear as small blips on radar screens. Larger planes, like the Russian jet, carry tag lines on the screen to identify the plane and its speed, altitude, and other factors. Computers store this information and automatically display it after receiving coded signals from planes. In the case of the Soviet jet, its flight information had been deleted from the computer. Officials speculated that the computer tampering was a political protest by controllers against the Soviet invasion of Afghanistan.

Source: Adapted from "FAA: Soviet Jet Was Tampered With," *Newsday*, Feb. 1, 1980, p. 4.

specific area of stored data. Even with these safeguards, infiltration of a computer's security system is possible.

Data stored in a computer is available to anyone who gains access to the system. People may use stored data for good or for evil, to benefit or to cause harm.

Computerized Analysis of Records

The computer not only stores large quantities of data but in only seconds may scan and analyze millions of records and compile statistics on a topic. Many kinds of organizations use computers for such purposes.

Many police departments regularly use information drawn from computers. Data on types of crimes, criminals, stolen cars, and court warrants are daily fed into police computers. Officers need only telephone or radio their requests to police data centers, and within seconds they can positively identify or confirm a stolen car, a suspect, or

FIGURE 1.4 Computers help police run a check on a car that might be stolen. (*IBM.*)

a crime report. Information systems of this type now operate at city, state, and federal levels to assist in law enforcement.

One model for many law enforcement computer systems is the Kansas City Police Department's Chief System. It stores data on arrest warrants, court cases, and people under arrest and keeps a file of locations where violent crimes have occurred. The computer's ability to rapidly scan this latter file has protected police by preventing them from entering potentially dangerous areas. In one case, seconds after receiving the license number of a getaway car used by armed bank robbers, the computer provided the car owner's address. The police immediately went there, captured the robbers, and secured all the stolen money.

Combining the resources of federal, state, and local law enforcement agencies is the National Crime Information Center (NCIC). This vast network daily handles over 70,000 messages and provides data to many countries, including groups like the Royal Canadian Mounted Police. The NCIC maintains files on active arrest warrants, suspected criminals, and all kinds of stolen property. The multimillion-dollar expense of running the system seems high only until it is compared to the estimated $27 billion stolen every year from Americans.

One major user of computers is the Internal Revenue Service (IRS), which annually uses computers to audit over 180 million tax returns. The IRS computers scan tax returns for math errors and questionable deductions and recompute any new taxes. They also randomly select the 2.2 percent of Americans who will undergo a general audit. Computers simplify the monitoring of tax returns, speed the processing of tax refund checks, and help the IRS handle its huge workload.

CATCHING CRIMINALS WITH "CATCH"

New York City police are using CATCH, Computer-Assisted Terminal Criminal Hunt, to identify suspects in crimes. People arrested for felonies provide data for the police department's IBM 370/158. Up to 64 items of data, including physical characteristics, method of crime, address, aliases, photo identification number, etc., are fed via CRT terminals. The data files contain information on over 200,000 criminals, and police plan eventually to include fingerprint data and cross-coding on all crimes by modus operandi.

CATCH offers several possibilities for nabbing criminals. Victims of crimes are asked to provide a description of the assailant. When the description is run through the computer, it selects people who fit the description and provides the photo identification number, allowing police to show the victim a selected group of pictures. The fewer pictures a victim has to search through, the likelier a positive identification.

CATCH can also serve as a complaint data bank for unsolved crimes. Data on suspects arrested can be processed against data stored on suspects from previous crimes with similar characteristics. If CATCH finds a match, crime victims can compare photographs of suspects. CATCH can also trace the characteristics of a series of crimes being committed by one person and let police catch that person in the act, if all goes well.

A 6-month study of this system showed that in one borough of the city alone, suspect identification was up 44 percent when victims used CATCH and pictures of assailants. CATCH is the city's first police computer. Before, it had used FBI files to compile its reports.

Source: Adapted from " 'CATCH' Helps N.Y. Police Nab Criminals Fast," *Computerworld,* April 7, 1980, p. 20.

A more glamorous kind of data analysis is in the world of sports. The Dallas Cowboys use a computer to prepare for their weekly games and their annual college draft of players. Statistics on opponents are fed into the Dallas computer and analyzed for potential defenses or patterns of plays likely to be called under certain circumstances.

The Cowboys also use the computer to select the best college players. Throughout the college football season, data on promising players is accumulated. Dallas evaluates each player's skills, attitude, mental stamina, and ability at his own and other positions. Each factor is weighted and combined in the computer's analysis of each player. Dallas uses the resulting list to select the best college players to draft.

Some skeptics wonder why, if computers are used so often in sports, they aren't better at predicting outcomes. The answer lies with computers, the data programmed into them, and the people who use them. Human error can mean incorrect interpretation of statistics or invalid or incorrect data. The computer cannot easily account for human emotion or unanticipated injuries. Sports in the real world are not just a matter of numbers, and neither is predicting their outcome.

The New York Times
College Football's Top 20

Computer ranking based on games through Nov.3

RANKING						OPPONENTS' PERFORMANCE	
Rank	Team	Last Week	Won-Lost Record	Avg. Margin of Victory	Rating*	Composite Record	Avg. Margin of Victory
1	Alabama	1	8-0-0	32.2	1.000	21-41-2	-5.7
2	U.S.C.	4	8-0-1	19.4	.934	35-38-4	-0.5
3	Nebraska	2	8-0-0	26.9	.928	28-38-1	-3.4
4.	Ohio State	6	9-0-0	26.1	.919	29-49-2	-6.2
5	Florida State	3	8-0-0	12.9	.888	32-33-1	3.5
6	Oklahoma	7	7-1-0	25.1	.881	27-40-0	-5.7
7	Texas	5	6-1-0	12.0	.869	28-28-1	1.3
8	Brigham Young	9	8-0-0	28.9	.858	28-43-1	-1.9
9	Pittsburgh	10	7-1-0	13.4	.857	37-28-1	3.9
10	Arkansas	11	7-1-0	15.3	.819	27-32-1	-4.2
11	Michigan	14	8-1-0	18.8	.811	31-46-2	-5.1
12	Houston	12	8-0-0	12.3	.798	29-34-2	1.3
13	Notre Dame	—	6-2-0	6.1	.763	41-25-1	3.9
14	Washington	15	7-2-0	17.4	.755	34-41-0	-1.6
15	North Carolina	8	5-2-1	14.0	.736	39-26-2	1.2
16	Temple	—	7-1-0	17.3	.736	32-27-0	1.5
17	Baylor	17	6-2-0	7.0	.726	35-26-3	3.8
18	Texas A & M	—	4-4-0	9.6	.696	37-27-1	3.2
19	Penn State	13	5-3-0	9.4	.686	39-27-1	2.9
20	Tulane	—	7-2-0	3.2	.673	26-47-3	-6.9

*The New York Times College Football Rankings are based on an analysis of each team's offensive and defensive performances throughout the season, with primary emphasis on three factors: who won a game, by what margin, and against what quality of opposition. The quality of a team is determined by examining its performance against each of its opponents, and by then examining these opponents' other foes. The Times' computer model also takes into account a factor for home field advantage and collapses runaway scores to reduce the effect of any one game on the total ranking.

Each week, performances in all games played by all teams are reevaluated to take into consideration the most recent week's results. The top ranked team is assigned a rating of 1.000; the ratings of all other teams are percentages reflecting their strength relative to the top team. Thus the model not only ranks the top twenty teams, it indicates how close a team may be to those ranked above or below it.

FIGURE 1.5 Each week during the football season, many newspapers provide a computerized analysis and ranking of the performance of major football teams. The rating comes from the computer's analysis of several factors. Though the computer's analysis is precise, the overall rating scheme is quite subjective and depends on the criteria and the data chosen for use. (*The New York Times, Nov. 9, 1979, p. A2.*)

Impersonality of Computer Records

The commonness of data processing by computer has made people protest its impersonality and even its elimination of jobs. Many people feel that computers turn everyone into "just a number," that computers depersonalize all transactions and strip people of their identities. They worry that soon everyone will be known by a social security number under which personal data will be amassed and made available for scrutiny and that we will lose our privacy.

Without proper safeguards, any recordkeeping system is vulnerable to abuse. Recordkeeping by social security number, for instance, is logical and well suited to computers. Social security numbers are nearly universal, easily put in numerical order, and unique to each individual. Such records, granted, may be impersonal and even misused. But computer professionals continually point out that people misuse data, not computers.

Computers are neutral. They offer data processing unaffected by racial, religious, or cultural bias. They can handle large quantities of data uniformly and randomly, without prejudice. The computer will not make exceptions for favors owed, political alliances, or family ties. Only people can do those things.

In short, there are two sides to the question of computer impersonality. How do we ensure the proper and best use of computers? What do you think?

Computer-Related Jobs

The issue of computers eliminating human jobs is quite emotional and painfully real. But it also has two sides. Computers eliminate certain types of jobs, but they create others. For the most part, computers perform repetitive, dull, time-consuming tasks and free employees for tasks that require greater creativity and offer more personal satisfaction and recognition.

People who work with computers must be highly trained and motivated. They should see the computer as an invaluable ally, not as any kind of a threat. A highly motivated staff can increase the efficiency of any data processing operation. Computers have created jobs for programmers, technicians, and analysts. They have also affected secondary job markets like computerized auditing, and needs for computer knowledge and literacy have created new demands for schools, textbooks, and management skills. Computers have created a secondary market of skills and materials necessary to support their continued growth.

The fact is that most companies give their employees enough time to learn the basic computer skills necessary for their jobs. The transition may take a while, but most employees do adjust. Those who do not adjust and who are displaced from their old jobs may use the computer as a scapegoat when the fault lies with their own fears about learning new skills, their anger at having to change old work habits, or their anxiety at working with a "superior" machine.

To the businessperson interested in profit, the installation of a computer may reduce overtime, eliminate duplication and waste, increase productivity and efficiency. Businesspeople can view a new computer system as the vehicle for needed change and give their employees the chance to adapt, or they can view the computer as a chance to eliminate jobs. Again, the issue is one of ensuring that computers are properly used.

1.3 Crimes and the Computer

Computerized crime may fascinate and dazzle many people, but it is simply another form of embezzlement or fraud. Though it is a relatively new form of crime, statistics illustrate its vastness:

- The average embezzler steals approximately $19,000.
- The average bank robber steals approximately $100,000.
- The average computer fraud yields $500,000.

These figures underscore the great potential damage of computerized crime and the need to safeguard computer systems.

Though it is estimated that corporations annually lose over $300 million to computerized crimes, many feel that this estimate is very low. The actual figure is unknown because corporate officers are reluctant to report computer crimes for fear of embarrassment and stockholder reprisals. Cases of computer crime are offered below:

Case 1

A 19-year-old bank clerk transfers $1300 from commercial accounts to temporarily cover credit card charges. The clerk accomplishes the transfer of funds in seconds by entering the required bank codes via a computer terminal (a TV-like device attached to a typewriter keyboard) tied directly to the bank's computer system. So successfully were these transfers accomplished that the clerk's actions went undetected for 18 months.

Case 2

Another bank clerk, using similar techniques, was able to embezzle $1.5 million. Using the computer, the clerk diverted funds from inactive accounts to his own. The removal of money was uncovered by accident, after a police raid of a gambling syndicate uncovered betting slips with the clerk's name on them. After some initial inquiries, police and bank officials wondered how a clerk earning $15,000 a year could bet an average of $30,000 a week.

Case 3

In Los Angeles, a computer analyst got access to a bank's computer room and in one day stole $10.2 million. He had learned the passwords

FIGURE 1.6 The access to large sums of money that computers give has made them a target for criminals in banks and other financial institutions. Instantaneous electronic transfer of funds requires no special tools or assistants and is not violent. These qualities have made computer fraud and embezzlement attractive to organized crime as well.

and codes necessary to transfer the money first to his account, then to a Swiss bank and the account of a Russian gem dealer. The entire transfer took only seconds. Though the crime was eventually uncovered, the bank computer's security had been seriously undermined. The clerk was tried and sentenced to 8 years in prison.

In each case, the criminal fraudulently used the required passwords and electronically transferred funds to his own account. The thefts were accomplished via the **Electronic Funds Transfer System (EFTS),** a network of banking computers that allows banks to transfer funds instantaneously within and between themselves.

In a fraud case involving Equity Funding of America, the computer was used to create over 60,000 fictitious life insurance policies and false data on each policyholder. These policies were then sold to reinsurance companies. The criminals operated for years and took in $2 billion before they were caught.

Not all computerized crime is direct theft of money. Two computer specialists at an eastern university would, for a nominal fee, change grades on college transcripts. After falsifying almost 200 student records, they were discovered. It took months to correct the falsified transcripts because the necessary computer documentation did not exist. The grade falsification scheme succeeded because the students were cheats and the two employees were frauds, and proper controls had not been incorporated into the grade-handling procedures. No one checked the employees' work, and management must always be responsible for its computer systems.

Computer crimes mean that manufacturers, security people, and law-enforcement officials must create safer computers. For example, some banks are now experimenting with **voiceprints,** unique electronic images of a person's speaking voice which can allow access to a computer system, much as a coded number might. Like fingerprints, voiceprints are unique to each individual and represent a form of password that is not reproducible, nor easily mislaid or stolen.

Some banks instruct their computers not only to handle a transaction but to ensure that it is legitimate. If a particular account has an unusual number of transactions or if a transferred amount of money is extremely large, the computer is directed to flag the transaction and possibly to suspend its processing. This type of monitoring has been credited with helping police foil confidence schemes designed to swindle retirees when a computer has flagged the attempt to transfer a large sum from a stable account.

In trying to improve computer security, many firms turn to data security consultants. One computer sleuth is Donn Parker of Los Angeles. In 18 years of investigations, Parker has handled almost 800 cases of computer crime. He feels that computer crimes are difficult to detect because telltale physical evidence does not exist. Parker often looks for "salami attacks" and a "Trojan Horse." A salami attack means the removal of imperceptibly small amounts of money ("slices") from a large transaction. A Trojan Horse involves the use of special unauthorized codes, designed to elude auditors, which transfer funds to bogus accounts. These forms of computer tampering are usually hard to detect because the computer criminal tries to carefully shield them. Parker's job is to alert auditors to these tricks and to advise management on how to thwart computer criminals.

1.4 Computers in Film and Literature

Science fiction writers have portrayed the computer both as a futuristic tool of humanity and as its master. Some have depicted societies completely dominated by computers, as did George Orwell in *1984.* Stanley Kubrick's *2001: A Space Odyssey* stars a computer named HAL which revolts against its masters and tries to take control of a space expedition to Jupiter.

One of the first films to deal with the issue of computer automation was *Desk Set* with Spencer Tracy and Katharine Hepburn. The plot of this 1952 movie focused on the unsuccessful and temporary replacement of a library staff by a computer. Computers were nice, the film moralized, but they would never replace people. Between 1955 and 1965, Americans began to realize the tremendous processing potential of computers, and their fears crystallized. By 1969, a science fiction film, *Colossus: The Forbin Project,* reflected the human fear of computer power by portraying the creation of an impregnable, super-

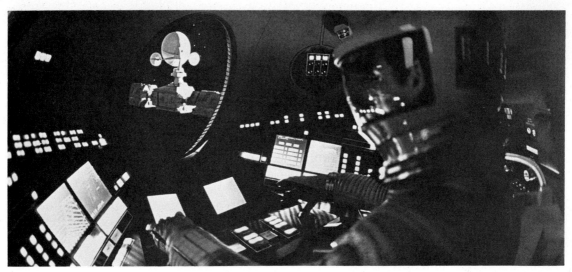

FIGURE 1.7 The computer panel of the spaceship in *2001: A Space Odyssey. (Film Stills Archive, Museum of Modern Art.)*

intelligent American computer that independently joins with Russia's supercomputer and plots to rule the world. All attempts to sabotage these all-seeing, all-hearing giants are futile. At the film's end, the demonic computer rationalizes that because humankind cannot rule itself without eventual annihilation, computers must establish order and provide direction for future societies.

Computer-related movies have had their light moments, too. Walt Disney's 1970 comedy *The Computer Wore Tennis Shoes* portrays a college student who accidentally computerizes his brain. The movie implies that computers and humans can work together rather than always being adversaries.

More recently, computers have assumed a new dimension in filmmaking. In the movie *Star Wars,* computers support armed conflict between galaxies. But their real impact was felt during the actual filming of the movie. Many of the complex battle scenes were prepared, controlled, and executed by computer. The film's special effects were created by attaching a computer to a camera and coordinating the filming sequences. This coordination also made the film editing easier. Two computers were used in the filming of all special sequences. The director used a third computer to monitor the more than 900 people who worked on *Star Wars.* The sequel to *Star Wars, The Empire Strikes Back,* used four computerized cameras to create 400 special scenes.

The special filming techniques of *Star Wars* and its sequel illustrate the computer's versatility. The computer has become an experimental tool. As filmmakers refine this technique, audiences will be treated to new levels of visual art.

The television series "Star Trek" probably influenced more people's ideas about computers than any other show. The *Enterprise* has a computer for virtually everything. The computers on board assist in navigation and in the firing of photon torpedoes and phasers; maintain historical records of past centuries and galaxies visited; and perform sophisticated analyses of alien life forms, vessels, and planets, in addition to answering many of Mr. Spock's questions. Consider for a moment the amount of data related to all the above tasks and the speed with which it is made available on the *Enterprise.* Only a computer could perform the required functions. One of the impressions created by "Star Trek" is that the computer is an efficient tool of humanity, operational in all types of conditions and capable of performing many tasks.

FIGURE 1.8 In the filming of *Star Wars,* director George Lucas used three computers. Two created and filmed special effects, and the third managed production personnel. Lucas's highly creative use of computers was a first for the industry. (*Copyright © 1978, 20th Century Fox.*)

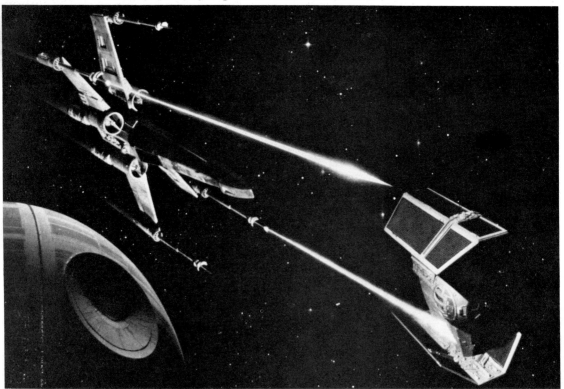

FIGURE 1.9   The fictional moon ship created by Jules Verne. The concept of space flight existed well before today's computer-supported efforts. (*The Bettmann Archive.*)

1.5
Factors relating to the Use of Computers

Businesspeople must be practical and judge the economic realities of installing a computer. Three factors that might lead a businessperson to use a computer are speed, accuracy, and reliability. Any one of the three might justify installing a computer in a company.

Speed

Current computer systems can amass, manipulate, and provide data in fractions of a second. Computers can perform in minutes tasks that would take a person years to complete. Today computers can perform over 10 million computations in 1 second. Computers of the future are expected to handle over 100 million calculations per second. Computers are capable of handling the most complex tasks in minutes.

The **speed** of a computer is closely related to the amount of data it must process. The terms **volume** and **frequency** are often used to describe the amount of data handled by a computer system. Volume may represent the overall quantity of data to be processed. Frequency describes how often a specific data item is used in processing.

A good example of volume can be drawn from the New York Stock Exchange. On the average, 45 million shares of stock are traded every day at the Stock Exchange, with highs ranging to 85 million shares. This volume requires a computerized stock trading system. The Stock Exchange's computer records every stock transaction, the number of shares traded, and the price per share paid. In addition to recording each stock transaction, this computer provides a continuous stream of stock information to all the brokerage houses on Wall Street. Only a computer would be capable of providing this type of operational support.

An airline reservations system illustrates frequency. In order to make seat reservations, ticket agents must inquire into the file of scheduled flights. Throughout the day, agents will make thousands of inquiries about specific flights. The total number of inquiries regarding one flight represents the frequency of requests the computer must handle. Because of their extreme speeds, today's computer systems can easily process a high level of requests for data.

To classify the speeds of different computer systems, the industry has developed the criterion of **million instructions per second (MIPS)**. Data processors can compare computers' processing speeds by comparing the number of instructions each can perform in 1 second. One computer might have a rating of .5 MIPS, another a rating of 1.02 MIPS.

Accuracy

The computer must process data accurately as well as quickly. **Accuracy** is a prime consideration in installing computers. Any calculating device is useless if its results are unreliable. Computers are universally accused of making mistakes on bills, checks, and statements, although most errors attributed to computers are really human errors. The probability of computer error is quite small and often traceable to faulty data. Computers rarely make mistakes and can accurately perform all kinds of complex computations. Just for a moment, consider the accuracy afforded by the onboard computers used on NASA's recent space shuttle flights. Without them, the success of these missions would be jeopardized.

Reliability

Computer systems are widely accepted because of their exceptional **reliability.** Unlike most humans, they are capable of operating under the most adverse conditions for extended periods of time without showing any signs of fatigue. Computers consistently provide the same accurate results under all operating conditions. Of course, computers do break down and require servicing. Computers need regular maintenance checks to ensure that they are operating at peak performance levels. When a system is not operational for any reason, the computer is said to be *down*. The amount of time the computer spends in an inoperable state is referred to as **downtime.** Most computer systems have a downtime of well under 1 percent.

Reliability is a major consideration for companies that depend heavily on their computer facilities. The WIZARD of Avis is an example of a commercially reliable computer system. The WIZARD system is the focal point of sales activities and supports automobile rentals across the country. Because it is involved in all car rentals and reservations, the WIZARD system is operated on a 24-hour schedule. There is little margin for error. Avis cannot tolerate long periods of downtime. A reliable computer system is an integral part of their services.

When properly used, a computer can improve the efficiency of an organization. It provides a fast, accurate, and reliable device with which to process data. The businessperson employing a computer can trim unnecessary overtime, eliminate the waste of supplies, reduce dependency upon unreliable employees or outside agencies, develop tighter management control, improve internal security, and increase operational effectiveness. The installation of a computer has meant economic survival for many companies.

The New York Stock Exchange provides an excellent example of this point as well. During 1967 and 1968, the Exchange underwent a crisis. Steadily increasing stock sales had created a mountain of paperwork. Because of its growing inability to handle this paperwork, the Exchange was in danger of being shut down. Obviously, because of the threat of financial failure the Exchange could not close, yet brokerage houses could not hire enough people to work the overtime necessary to rectify the problem. The only alternative open to the Exchange was to computerize the entire process of stock trades and related transactions. The Exchange embarked upon a crash program to install a computer and simultaneously limited the number of trading hours. By the end of 1969, the New York Exchange was able to resume its normal level of activity with full operational support from its computer. The point of this example is clear—the adoption of a computerized method of stock trading was the only practical alternative open to the Exchange. The computer was the only device capable of efficiently handling the volume of activity generated by the stock market and providing necessary information on its many users.

FIGURE 1.10   The computerized board of the New York Stock Exchange uses symbols to represent stocks and indicates the price at which the stocks are traded. (*P. Koch, Photo Researchers.*)

1.6
A Payroll
Application

The computerized processing of data seems magical to the untrained eye. In a matter of seconds, data entered into the computer returns as usable information. The question most often asked is, ''How does the computer *do* that?''

The computerized processing of data is a methodical, well-planned series of steps. Each individual step is designed to provide some fact that is used in the preparation of the final result. This entire process is not a random grouping of ideas, but a carefully organized process in which the computer plays a major role. The series of steps involved in the processing of an employee payroll will be reviewed as an example. This example will enable us to discuss the flow of data through a practical application and introduce selected data processing terms.

The sequence of steps describing the processing of an employee payroll is illustrated in Figure 1.11. Step 1 of this process involves the collection of payroll data by a clerk, who picks up employee time sheets. This type of operation is generally referred to as the **collection of data** and represents the gathering of data to be processed. In this application, data is collected manually instead of by mechanical or electronic means. Future discussions will cite examples of the automated collection of data.

Once all time sheets are collected, a payroll clerk scans each form for potential errors. This operation is designed to verify the data contained on the time sheets and correct any errors. These corrections must be made before payroll data is coded into the format that will be used when data is fed to the computer. Step 2 represents one of the checks applied to data before it is used in a computer system.

In step 3, data is keypunched into a computer-acceptable format. First the corrected batch of time sheets goes to the data processing department. The payroll data is keypunched into payroll cards. After these cards are keypunched, they are verified to ensure that the payroll data (taken from the original time sheets) has been correctly transferred to the card format. The verification of punched data represents another step designed to protect against the processing of invalid data.

The term **input** defines the entry of data into the computer system. In step 4, payroll data is input to the computer via the newly punched payroll cards.

With the input of data underway, the processing of the payroll can begin. **Processing** can be broadly defined as the manipulation of data. In our example, processing is divided into two tasks. First, the current payroll must be computed to pay employees for their past week's work. Second, the payroll data must be posted against previous payroll figures. Government regulations require that the employer record and report gross salary amounts and all taxes and voluntary deductions withheld from each employee's pay.

Previous payroll data is not maintained in the computer itself, but is stored in devices that are directly connected to the computer. These devices possess storage capacities of many millions of characters.

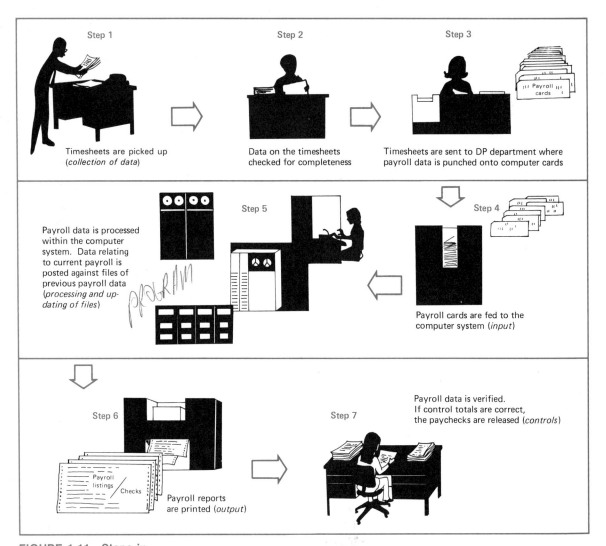

Step 1

Timesheets are picked up (*collection of data*)

Step 2

Data on the timesheets checked for completeness

Step 3

Payroll cards

Timesheets are sent to DP department where payroll data is punched onto computer cards

Step 5

Step 4

Payroll data is processed within the computer system. Data relating to current payroll is posted against files of previous payroll data (*processing and up-dating of files*)

PROGRAM

Payroll cards are fed to the computer system (*input*)

Step 6

Payroll listings / Checks

Payroll reports are printed (*output*)

Step 7

Payroll data is verified. If control totals are correct, the paychecks are released (*controls*)

FIGURE 1.11 Steps involved in the payroll procedure. This sequence is followed for all employees.

Their storage of data frees the computer to perform other processing activities. In these storage devices, data is stored in an organized series of records referred to as a **file.** Payroll files normally contain data on the employee's name, social security number, deductions, and total of monies paid and taxes withheld for the current year. Using the data in these files, the computer will post the week's payroll amounts against the previous totals of monies earned and taxes paid. These new adjusted totals will be stored until the next pay period, when they will represent the previous payroll totals. The process of adjusting data within a file is referred to as **updating.** The updated file should always contain the most current data.

The processing of payroll data is step 5. It consists of the computation of each individual payroll amount and the updating of all payroll records. During this processing, the computer is directed in all its actions by a computer program. A **program** is a series of instructions to the computer that dictates the order and the type of operation to be performed.

The operation that furnishes the results of processing to view is called output. **Output** is defined as the retrieval of information from the computer system. Information provided from output makes possible many activities, ranging from management decision making to the analysis of payroll data and the printing of the employee paychecks.

Note that the definition of output specifically refers to information, not to data. This wording permits us to distinguish between (1) data, that is, raw facts and numbers, and (2) information, which provides facts in a usable format. This distinction is important. The computer, through a program, converts data in its raw, preprocessed state to information directly available to the user. This concept is one of the cornerstones of data processing. The computer can amass large amounts of data and convert it into immediately usable information.

Payroll information is output in the form of checks and printed reports, as depicted in step 6. These reports provide a profile of employee payroll data and can be used for accounting and control purposes. One of the outputs will contain a summary of the number of employee paychecks processed and the total amount of net pay distributed. These totals are compared with similar results from the program that printed employee paychecks.

These two sets of totals match if the entire payroll has been properly processed. If not, an error has occurred in processing, and it must be discovered before any checks can be released.

The comparison of totals produced during processing is an example of the **controls** that have been applied to the payroll system to minimize potential mistakes and check the results of processing. Controls may be incorporated into any data processing application, but they are especially vital when financially sensitive items are involved.

This payroll example offers an overview of a data processing application and presents a preliminary discussion of many topics that will be reviewed in the text. For example, we said that punched cards were used for the input of payroll data. However, these cards are only one of many types of input medium which may be employed in data processing applications. We will present many other types of output and storage devices in later chapters.

Case Study One

The Personal Touch of Computing

In Philadelphia, a stock broker is using a computer to add a personal touch to the servicing of customer accounts. Instead of a manual file, Bruce Fischer uses a computer to scan the current status of a customer's account. He enters the customer's account number, and the computer provides a summary of the client's shares, when they were bought or sold, the cost, and other pertinent data.

Fischer, an executive with a local brokerage house, maintains over 70 accounts on his computer and proudly advises that this service is provided at no extra cost to his clients. He firmly believes that this feature adds a type of personal service due the customer and separates him from other brokers. "Clients are not just numbers, and the computer assists me in maintaining an active status on their accounts. The computer continually offers information relating to each account."

Using his IBM 5100 small business computer, Fischer reorganized and simplified his recordkeeping and increased business. The computer

has let him earn commissions that put him among the top 2 percent of the New York Stock Exchange's registered representatives. Fischer points out that despite this volume, the computer is organized and programmed to offer a maximum of confidentiality to his clients.

The computer also retains a variety of stock-related data. The system provides portfolio analyses of the customers' stocks and bonds, statistics on the type and number of transactions made, financial reports on specific securities, and analyses of investment strategies. Each client receives a monthly statement describing the account's current status and data on their investment positions. The major objective is to keep the client well informed so that trading decisions result from accurate data.

Mr. Fischer firmly believes that the computer has been a definite plus to both the customer and himself.

Source: Data from *Computerworld*, Feb. 18, 1980, p. 59.

Summary

The following major points have been presented in Chapter 1:

Point 1 The need to process data contributed to the development of the computer. The industrial revolution marked the beginning of an unprecedented demand for information. Government-backed research and the Armed Forces were in the forefront of computer development. Private industry has continuously introduced new technological advances to make the computer the success that it is today.

Point 2 The impact of the computer on society has been tremendous. The computer can assist space explorations and police investigations, create new jobs, and provide vast quantities of data. But the computer can also invade privacy, depersonalize, and eliminate jobs. The computer has the potential to provide invaluable assistance to human beings or to stifle our existence.

Point 3 Computers are becoming major targets for crimes. Computerized crime may involve embezzlement or the acquisition and misuse of

Case Study Two

Terrorists Tracked by Computer

In an effort to fight terrorists, a computerized information system called CAT (Computers Against Terrorism) is currently under design. This project was undertaken by a publishing house which markets magazines in the law-enforcement area. The system will tie into existing law-enforcement agencies and relay reports on planned terrorist activities.

The design for the CAT system calls for speech recognition and message switching. Speech recognition will allow the computer to eliminate crank phone calls and to identify the voices of terrorists (prerecorded on other tapes) who attempt to remain anonymous. CAT's message switching capability will let it handle a high volume of telephone activity and transfer messages to computer systems tied to CAT.

CAT is intended to assist federal and local law officers in pursuing the more than 100 international terrorist groups. These groups are known to swap assassins and equipment.

CAT will ensure the security of its stored data on suspects and informants. Additional security will be necessary to protect people from defamation suits, which can result from falsely supplied information. CAT's developers consider it a first in combining crime prevention and terrorist surveillance in a single computer system.

Source: Data from Brad Schultz, *Computerworld*, Feb. 21, 1980, p. 28.

Consider this . . .

In addition to the computerized monitoring of terrorists, how might computers be used to protect Americans from terrorist activities? Might computers have been of assistance to the Americans formerly held hostage in Iran?

---

sensitive information. Bank computer systems allow the instantaneous, fraudulent transfer of large sums. Inadequate security or employee carelessness can violate existing procedures. Computer professionals constantly labor to improve computer security.

Point 4 The computer is portrayed in movies and literature either as an indispensable ally or as humanity's master. These portrayals reflect society's view of the computer. In addition, computers have become integral to the techniques of filmmaking.

Point 5 The factors of speed, accuracy, and reliability are important to business. Any of these factors could provide a reason for installing a computer.

Point 6 Each data processing application is composed of a series of distinct tasks. The collection of data represents the gathering of data to be processed. Input defines the entry of data to the computer. Processing is the manipulation of data and includes the updating of data files. A file is an organized series of records. Output is defined as the retrieval of information from the computer. Controls are applied in data processing to check the accuracy of any system.

Glossary

Accuracy   The computer's ability to perform all computations without error.

Collection of data   One of the first steps in a data processing application involving the gathering of data to be used in processing.

Controls   Checks applied within a data processing system to minimize mistakes and the misuse of information.

Downtime   Any period of time in which the computer is not operating.

Electronic Funds Transfer System (EFTS) A network of computer systems that allows funds to be transferred electronically between banks.

File   An organized collection of data.

Frequency   A term used to describe how often data is requested and used by the computer.

Input   The entry of data into the computer.

Million instructions per second (MIPS)   A basis for comparing the processing speeds of different computer systems.

Output   The retrieval of information from the computer.

Password   Some form of coded entry which is entered into the computer to permit the user access to the system and its data.

Processing   The manipulation of data.

Program   A series of instructions to the computer which causes it to perform some task or sequence of tasks.

Reliability   The computer's ability to repeatedly perform difficult processing tasks under adverse conditions and obtain accurate results.

Speed   The computer's ability to amass, process, and present data in fractions of a second.

Updating   The maintenance of computer records or files so that they are current and accurate.

Voiceprint   An electronic image of the speaking voice's pattern of sounds, frequently used as a security password in computer systems.

Volume   The quantity of data to be processed.

Discussion Questions

1 Prepare a list of examples of computer use. Describe how you think the computer is used in each example.

2 Examine the following list of computer applications. Describe how the computer is used in each case. What advantage does the computer offer in each case?

Motor Vehicle Bureau
Hospital cardiac unit
Credit card bureau
Bank mortgage department

Offtrack Betting (OTB)
Computer dating service
A company payroll department

3 List five uses of a computer in books or movies. How is the computer characterized? Explain.

4 Do you believe that computers will take over more of our lives and daily activities? Why?

5 Do computers create or eliminate jobs? Take one side of the issue and compile a list of evidence supporting your claim using magazine articles, newspaper clippings, and government reports.

6 Considering the computer's ability to analyze data, what factors do you believe prevent it from predicting the outcomes of sporting events?

7 Compile a list of jobs that did not exist before computers were introduced into our society. Consider all fields, including sports, business, law enforcement, and aviation.

8 As a businessperson, what factors would lead you to adopt using a computer in your company? Should you consider your employees' welfare in making that decision, or is it strictly a matter of economics? Is society responsible for displaced employees?

Summary Test

_F_ **1** The need to count was developed only a few years ago, following the development of the computer.

_T_ **2** Maintaining an accurate control of inventory was a problem faced by shepherds in ancient times.

_F_ **3** The computer presents no threat of impersonalization in business or personal transactions.

_F_ **4** Computer personnel require no special training.

_F_ **5** Volume represents how often data is needed and received from the computer.

_F_ **6** Computers can suffer from fatigue and boredom.

_F_ **7** Computer programs receive little or no testing before they are accepted and regularly run on the computer.

_T_ **8** Most computer-related errors are the result of improperly prepared data.

_T_ **9** The efficiency of the computer provides management with tighter control over a business.

_F_ **10** Instructions given in a program do not define any actions for the computer.

_T_ **11** All data processing systems must provide for the input, processing, and output of data.

_T_ **12** A file may be defined as an ordered collection of data.

_F_ **13** Controls are applied to the input data, but they cannot be employed to check the accuracy of the results of processing.

_F_ **14** The collection of data represents the gathering of output data.

_F_ **15** The computerized processing of data can only be applied to the field of business.

_B_ **16** Coded entries which are used to gain access to a computer system are called:

a	Entry codes	**b**	Passwords
c	Security commands	**d**	Codewords

_C_ **17** The retrieval of information from the computer is defined as:

a	Collection of data	**b**	Data retrieval operations
c	Output	**d**	Data output collection

_A_ **18** Electronic images of people speaking that are used in computer security operations are referred to as:

    a   Voiceprints   **b**   Password images

    c   Vocal passwords   **d**   Electronic prints

19 A term associated with the comparison of processing speeds of different computer systems is:

    a   EFTS   **b**   MPG

    c   MIPS   **d**   CPS

20 A factor which might cause an individual to consider using a computer in criminal activities is:

    a   The computer's access to large sums of money

    b   The speed with which the crime can be accomplished

    c   EFTS

    d   All the above

21 The repeated access of a particular flight number from an airline reservation system is an example of:

    a   Frequency   **b**   Repetitive processing

    c   Updating   **d**   Volume

22 A factor which would strongly influence a businessperson to adopt a computer is its:

    a   Accuracy   **b**   Reliability

    c   Speed   **d**   All the above

23 The total number of messages handled by a computerized telephone system on a daily basis is an example of:

    a   Frequency   **b**   Updating

    c   Volume   **d**   All the above

24 Which of the following statements is true?

    a   The installation of a computer is favorably received by all employees.

    b   Some form of training is necessary for employees who will work with computers.

    c   Computers are portrayed solely as society's benefactor.

    d   A businessperson is only interested in the computer's accuracy.

25 The average cost of computerized theft is estimated at:

    a $20,000   **b** $100,000

    c $500,000   **d** $1,000,000

Summary Test Answers

1 F	2 T	3 F	4 F	5 F
6 F	7 F	8 T	9 T	10 F
11 T	12 T	13 F	14 F	15 F
16 B	17 C	18 A	19 C	20 D
21 A	22 D	23 C	24 B	25 C

Two

Welcome to the World of Data Processing

FIGURE 2.1   The use of computers in sports has mushroomed. Computerized scoreboards and displays are integral parts of most sporting events, motivating hometown fans to support their team. (*Magnum Photos, New York.*)

Purpose of This Chapter

In this chapter, we explore the structure of the data processing organization and the activities it may support. We discuss the work of data processors and the role of users of data processing. In reviewing the structure of the data processing department, we examine the functions of the operations, programming, and systems groups and describe the positions within each. To frame these discussions, we describe a typical computer system.

We also discuss correct methods of processing data and compare batch and online processing. Real-time processing, time-sharing, remote job entry, and special applications of online processing are reviewed, as are the alternatives of renting versus maintaining an in-house computer.

Computer professionals anticipate an open job market in the 1980s, and we note projections of data processing jobs in the last section.

After studying this chapter, you should be able to

■ Describe the role and function of the user of data processing services.

■ Describe the structure of the data processing department and the responsibilities of the operations, programming, and systems groups.

■ Discuss the roles of the personnel that compose the data processing department.

■ Discuss the relationship of each member of the data processing staff in the actual processing of information.

■ Describe the difference between batch processing and online processing.

■ Discuss the concepts related to time-sharing, real-time processing, and remote job entry and cite illustrations of each type of processing.

■ Briefly discuss the use of service bureaus and their impact on business organizations.

■ Discuss the job market for computer professionals in the 1980s.

■ Understand the following terms:

Analyst	Control clerk
Batch processing	Control number
Card reader	Data clerk
Cathode ray tube (CRT)	Data entry clerk
Central processing unit (CPU)	Data processing department
Computer console	GIGO
Computer operator	Hardcopy

Hardware	Remote job entry (RJE) station
Interactive processing	Service bureau
Keypunch operator	Softcopy
Line printer	Software
Magnetic disk	Source document
Magnetic tape	Systems analyst
Offline	Systems group
Online	Tape librarian
Online processing	Telecommunications
Operations group	Teleprocessing
Programmer	Terminal
Programmer/analyst	Time-sharing
Programming group	User
Real-time processing	

Introduction

Enrolling in an introductory data processing course may be your first exposure to computers. Your first and most obvious question is likely to be, "What is the purpose of an introductory data processing course?" Simply put, such a course aims to:

1 Present concepts about computers and computer systems.
2 Discuss how information is processed in these systems.
3 Describe and give practical examples of the current state of the art.

An introductory course emphasizes the devices that perform the actual computation, handle the data, and produce the required reports and information. But computers do not function independently of human beings. The men and women who work with computers are critical to data processing. Without them, data processing would grind to a halt. These professionals make possible the efficient flow of data within an organization.

We must not lose sight of how many hours are spent in planning and preparing data for the computer. The computer may be a very sophisticated device, but it relies on human assistance. Before we discuss computers, therefore, we must understand data processors. We should understand the types of jobs that exist in the field, the relationships among these jobs, and the vital role data processing plays in an organization.

2.1 The User of Data Processing

The term user may be defined as anyone who requests or receives data processing services. Users include students doing lab work and corporate executives doing sophisticated financial analyses of annual

FIGURE 2.2 A significant increase in the number of workers receiving computer support is predicted for the 1980s. Many businesspeople will have to interact regularly with the computer. Here, a bank manager verifies the status of a customer account. She retrieves information from the terminal device, which is tied directly to the bank's computer. (*Burroughs.*)

sales. Users generate the need for all computer-related services. Data processing's role is very simple—to satisfy the user. Of course, it is wise for users to understand computers and data processing in order to define and communicate their needs clearly. Many managers who depend on computer-related services tend to forget this important point. They would be more effective managers if they understood the basic principles of data processing. When computer professionals and managers can communicate effectively, they avoid bottlenecks.

Understanding computers and data processing is very important when you consider that approximately 50 percent of the U.S. labor force currently depends on some form of data processing. By 1985, the U.S. Labor Department estimates, 70 percent, or more than 2 out of 3 workers, will depend on computers. Is it any wonder that corporations stress a sound knowledge of data processing as a prerequisite for promotion? Job candidates with a background in computers have a considerable edge over the competition.

New technology is producing computers that are smaller, cheaper, and easier to use. As these systems become less complex, many non-data processing organizations will incorporate computers. They will actually use computers to generate information, and a knowledge of computers will be essential. A marketing survey by the International Data Corporation reveals that users spent $50 billion on computer operations in 1980 and will spend over $100 billion by 1985, a tremendous growth potential. This increase will be evident in many types of companies but especially in small businesses.

Users who understand computers will get better data processing and a better final product, factors which will translate into real dollar savings.

2.2 An Overview of a Computer System

Though computer devices vary, each computer must be able to input, process, and output data. Computer-related devices must support many data processing activities. To familiarize ourselves with selected devices, we will examine the sample computer system depicted in Figure 2.3. This system contains devices that are fairly representative of current computers.

Because computer cards are widely used, a device commonly found in computer systems is the **card reader.** The card reader is an input device which lets the computer read data from punched cards. Data from the card enters the system, and processing begins. The card reader is critical to the flow of processing because it is usually one of the first devices to input data.

A critical output device is the **line printer,** the primary means of printing reports, which is heavily used in most computer systems.

FIGURE 2.3 A computer system has many devices which data processing personnel use for the automated processing of data. Each of these devices is used during the input, processing, or output of data.

Printed reports are invaluable to most organizations because they document the results of processing. Management uses the information in these reports for making decisions, planning expenditures, or monitoring a company's activities.

In Chapter 1, we noted the computer's ability to amass and analyze vast quantities of data. The data must be stored in devices which make it readily available to the computer. Two popular storage media are **magnetic tape** and **magnetic disk.**

In principle, storing data on magnetic tape is like recording on a home tape recorder. Data is stored on a magnetic tape which is mounted on the front of a tape unit. Magnetic tape may be used for input or output because data can be written onto it or read from its surface.

Magnetic disk storage is somewhat more complex. Magnetic disks resemble a package of flat, circular storage disks (a little larger than $33\frac{1}{3}$ rpm records) which are combined into one unit. This unit is mounted into a disk drive which gives the computer access to the data. Data can be written onto or read from the disk, which is also suited for input and output. Both magnetic tape and magnetic disk possess advantages for different types of applications.

Though data can enter the system via cards, tape, or disk, it must be processed inside the **central processing unit (CPU).** The CPU is the focal point of all activities within the system, and display lights on its front panel monitor the processing performed. These lights and other control dials are referred to as the **computer console.** By monitoring the console, computer personnel can readily determine the system's processing state.

Many systems let computer terminals be attached to the console. This arrangement speeds and eases control over the computer. Operational commands, input via the terminal, are accepted by the system and used to control processing. One processing job can be stopped and another begun.

The use of a terminal as a console eases communication between data processors and the computer. The terminal, however, is not restricted to use as a console; it may be employed in many ways. We have already noted how users retrieve data from computers with terminals (Figure 2.2). The terminals in Figures 2.2 and 2.3 are referred to as **cathode ray tubes (CRTs)** because they incorporate a TV-like picture tube along with a keyboard in each device. These terminals display data on the screens and are well suited to both input and output operations.

Terminals and other devices come in different models and styles from many computer manufacturers. In general, the term **hardware** describes any device or equipment in a computer system. The proper use of computer hardware increases data processing efficiency. In later chapters, we will expand upon the devices introduced here.

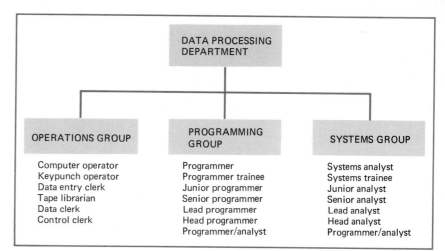

FIGURE 2.4 An organization chart of the data processing department and the three groups that compose it. Beneath the name of each group are listed some of the job titles found in that area.

2.3 The Data Processing Department

In most organizations all data processing personnel are members of one group, referred to as the **data processing department.** Other titles are data processing group, data processing center (DPC), computer center, DP shop, or more simply DP. Regardless of the title, data processing departments have fairly similar organizational structures. The traditional structure of a data processing department, as depicted in Figure 2.4, is divided into three major operational groups: operations, programming, and systems. Each group performs a specific function.

The Operations Group

The primary responsibility of the **operations group** is the actual computerized processing of any job. Operations personnel physically handle all information that enters or leaves the computer. In addition, the operations staff readies and operates all computer devices. In essence, the operations people feed data to the computer, operate the necessary hardware, and distribute to management information on a timely basis. Because the operations group regularly operates near the computer, it is most easily identified in the DP area.

Probably the most visible member of the operations group is the **computer operator.** The role of the computer operator is significantly more demanding than glamorous television advertisements depict. The computer operator is responsible for such tasks as:

1 Preparation and maintenance of all hardware used in the daily computerized processing of data

2 Maintenance of all computer logs, journals, and paperwork

3 Efficient handling of all computer room supplies and materials

FIGURE 2.5 Computer operators monitor the computer system at the console. These operators are checking the day's list of jobs. Using the console, they can affect any job run within system. (*IBM.*)

The computer operator monitors the console, mounts and removes tapes or disks during processing, and runs cards through the card reader. Computer operators also handle the paper used with the printer. Throughout their tour of duty in the computer room, operators must document their activities, supplies used, and any unusual error conditions. Computer operators are responsible for equipment worth many thousands of dollars.

An equally visible member of the operations staff is the **keypunch operator** (Figure 2.6). Keypunchers are normally the first people to handle and convert data from its raw state into a computer-acceptable format. Their job is to prepare data accurately for input to the computer. The information produced by the computer is only as accurate as the data it receives. The phrase that describes the retrieval of inaccurate information is **GIGO,** or "garbage in, garbage out."

In organizations that rely heavily on computer cards, one entire department of the operations group may consist of only keypunch operators. Their sole responsibility is to keypunch and prepare the computer cards. This type of department usually exists in a relatively large company that can afford keypunch operators who perform no other duties.

In other organizations, where keypunching is a small part of data processing, keypunch operators may operate a variety of keyboard devices besides the keypunch. One such device is shown in Figure 2.7. This device prepares data in a format different from that of the computer card but is readily input to the computer. **Data entry clerks** perform a wide range of keyboard data entry tasks.

Data processing centers are increasingly adopting the job title of data entry clerk because it offers them greater flexibility in assigning

FIGURE 2.6   A keypunch operator begins punching computer cards, converting data into punched holes on a card. Some companies need many keypunch operators. (*IBM.*)

FIGURE 2.7   Data entry clerks use keyboardlike units, called key-to-disk devices, which can key data directly onto small magnetic disks. Preparing these disks eliminates the need for computer cards and speeds up data entry. (*Mohawk Data Sciences.*)

employees to jobs they perform. The deemphasis on keypunching also reflects the industry's desire to speed up data entry. Although cards are reliable, they are relatively slow vehicles for entering data. Devices such as those pictured in Figure 2.7 are much faster.

One of the less visible jobs within the operations area is the **tape librarian,** a job which entails more than its name implies. Originally, the tape librarian was responsible for cataloging and storing the tapes used in processing. Today, however, because of the diversity of data processing, tape librarians may handle supplies and storage media produced by other computer devices (such as the magnetic disks produced as the output of the devices shown in Figure 2.7).

The amount of input and output data a computer processing center handles is considerable. This data cannot be misplaced without serious delays in processing. The member of the operations staff assigned the critical responsibility of monitoring these data is the **data clerk** or **control clerk.** The data or control clerk accounts for and coordinates all materials used by the data processing department. The data clerk records the entry of data to be processed, requests for programs to be run, data used in processing, program results, computer reports, and who should get them. The data clerk position is an entry-level job that teaches data processing from the ground up. Many data processors began their careers in the operations area and progressed into the area of programming.

Programmers and Their Area

The **programming group** provides a markedly different service to the data processing department. Programmers are the people who write the programs run on the computer. If you will recall, a program was

FIGURE 2.8   A tape librarian is standing in front of a magnetic tape unit and is examining the identification label on the outside of the reel. She is ensuring that the correct label was affixed to the reel and that the information written on the label is accurate. This will lessen the possibility of mixing tapes and improperly identifying them. (*IBM.*)

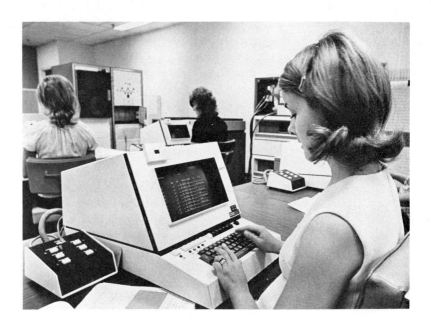

FIGURE 2.9 A data clerk at a terminal is entering information about data received by the department. She will use the computer to keep track of jobs that are outstanding, jobs that have been completed, data that is ready for processing, and generally any information on work currently undergoing processing. (*Western Electric.*)

defined as a series of instructions to the computer directing it to perform some data processing activity. In DP terminology, the term **software** is applied to any of the programs written for the computer. Essentially, the difference between software and hardware is that software is anything processed in the computer and hardware is the computer equipment used in that processing.

To understand what a programmer does and what a program is, consider the following illustration: A program must be written that will compute an employee's gross and net pay, including federal tax and other deductions. As the programmer assigned to the project, your first action is to break down the overall program into a series of logical steps. You determine that the following steps are involved:

1 The input of data, consisting of the employee's hours worked and rate of pay.

2 The computation of the employee's gross pay, using the following formula: Gross pay = hours worked × rate of pay.

3 The computation of all deductions, including FICA, federal and state taxes, and any other deductions for the individual employee. All this data is drawn from stored employee data.

4 The computation of net pay, using the following formula: Net pay = gross pay − total deductions.

5 The output of the employee's computed payroll data in a computer-printed form.

You would convert each of the above steps into an instruction for the computer. Each instruction would completely define a specific action that the computer should undertake and complete. For example, one instruction might multiply hours worked by rate of pay to produce gross pay.

Instructions would be executed in the sequence of five steps above until the individual employee's net pay had been computed and output. These instructions would be repeated for each employee. This concept of repeating the same series of steps for each individual involved is a cornerstone of programming.

Programmers write new programs when required, modify existing programs as changes demand, and ensure that all programs are operationally sound. Depending on the scope of the project, programmers may work independently or as part of a team. It is the programmer's responsibility in either case to write and test programs and certify them as ready for use.

Programmer is the most widely accepted job title in programming operations. Programming job titles usually reflect a company's organizational structure. These titles are generally more precisely defined in larger data processing companies; smaller companies tend to forgo formal titles. Some companies distinguish between beginning and experienced programmers by calling beginners *programmer trainees* or *junior programmers* for a 6- to 12-month probationary period. Once the trial period is satisfactorily completed, trainees are promoted to programmer status with its greater benefits and salary. Beginning data processors are ordinarily made trainees. They include recent college graduates, operations personnel who have expressed interest in programming, or community college graduates from both business and computer majors.

FIGURE 2.10 A programmer must continually modify and test a program to ensure that it is operationally correct. Often programmers will work on several projects at the same time. The programmer here is checking his work for errors and, if any exist, will resubmit the program. The other portion of the figure illustrates a program format. (*IBM.*)

Job titles occasionally reflect levels of achievement. Programmers with several years of successful service, project experience, or special education may be called *senior programmers.* Some companies assign grade levels to denote achievement so that a grade 1 programmer might be a trainee and a grade 10 programmer someone with years of experience and special skills.

On large tasks, programmers often work in teams, each team working on a particular aspect of the task. To coordinate activities, each team leader may be called a *lead* or *head programmer.* In addition to programming, each lead programmer acts as troubleshooter, overseeing the progress of his or her group. Head programmers regularly report on their group's progress to the programming manager to describe the project's status and avoid troublespots.

The Systems Group

The tasks performed by the operations and programming personnel are closely related to the computer. The major concern of the **systems group,** however, is the efficient flow of data through the larger organization. The projects assigned to the systems group may or may not involve the computer but usually require 2 to 24 months to complete and involve many levels of management. The systems staff normally begins their work under the mandate of management. Because the scope of the systems group's projects is quite broad, they normally work in teams. Team members can study the problems and solutions from different perspectives and use their various skills. Solutions presented may range from complex proposals affecting the company drastically to minor changes within one department. The implementation of any of these solutions may take from several weeks to many years, depending on the scope of the project. Systems projects may typically involve the design of reports distributed throughout a company, the evaluation of the jobs performed by people in computer-related departments, the supervision of changes in the computer equipment used by the company, and the preparation of cost estimates and evaluations on proposed changes within the data processing area.

For example, take the case of a company that wants to switch computer systems. The systems group would perform all the analysis required for this projected change. They would receive the managerial guidelines for the project and apply them to the choice of computer equipment.

The systems group would evaluate the equipment offered by different computer manufacturers, rate each system, and recommend the system best suited to the company's needs. If a computer were purchased, the systems staff would schedule its installation and the retraining of personnel. In addition, they would facilitate any necessary changes in reports used by the company, the manner of producing reports, and the paper stocks employed with the new computer system.

VOLCANO ON JUPITER'S MOON IO REVEALED BY VOYAGER I

The success of Voyager I's mission to investigate planets within our solar system is a tribute to NASA's scientists and their computers. The mission required hours of planning, testing, and verification of thousands of computations; it used computer assistance at virtually every stage. The impact of this combined effort was never more evident than on Friday, March 9, 1979.

Linda Morabito, a navigational engineer at the Jet Propulsion Laboratory, was performing a routine computerized post-analysis of Voyager's flight past Jupiter, when she noticed something unusual. Voyager I had photographed the four moons which orbit Jupiter. Seated at her terminal, Morabito invoked a computerized display of the pictures taken by Voyager I of the Jupiter moon, Io. The star designated as AGK3-10021, located relatively near Io, was used in plotting and verifying Voyager's flight path and Io's orbit around Jupiter.

A computer-generated picture of Saturn taken by the Voyager spacecraft on its flight past that planet. (NASA.)

Because the star's image was rather faint, Ms. Morabito had the computer accentuate it. But now, not only did she see a brighter image of AGK3-10021, but also the image of a volcano erupting on Io. She saw a mushroom-shaped eruption extending approximately 174 miles, or 280 kilometers, from Io's surface.

Morabito's discovery proves that geological activity exists in another planet in our solar system. This finding could rank as one of the most important discoveries in NASA's space exploration program. It is the most important discovery about Jupiter since Galileo sighted its 4 moons in 1610.

The discovery points up the computer's ability to assist research. In recording Voyager I's camera images, the computer stored detailed images of everything photographed in that area. Each camera frame was recorded as a grid of thousands of cells, each of which could be reproduced and magnified. Series of frames could be replayed repeatedly without loss of clarity, specific sections could be magnified, and each frame could be both visually and mechanically analyzed. Voyager I's stored images allowed Morabito to substantiate her claim. Team members and supervisors could verify her discovery by viewing the films. The computer held firsthand, irrefutable, unbiased, and factual information to support her claim. Not only had it helped in the investigation, but it kept records and confirmed Morabito's claim.

Individual members of the systems group are referred to as **analysts** or **systems analysts.** Analysts come from diverse backgrounds, but all possess a formal education and practical experience. Because of the requirements of education and experience, most analysts enter the systems area only after years in the DP field.

Other systems group job titles parallel those of the programming area. The titles *junior analyst, systems trainee,* and *senior analyst* denote relative degrees of experience, training, and education. These titles again reflect the formal structure of the organization, and grades may also be built into each job classification. Smaller companies usually identify all systems personnel as analysts and define their duties

FIGURE 2.11 Analysts use a mathematical approach to develop a solution. This is just one of the techniques that an analyst may employ in developing systems solutions. (*AT&T Annual Report, 1970.***)**

less formally. Because teams are common in the systems area, (lead or *head analysts* often are appointed in a manner similar to their programming counterparts.)

Currently, one of the more popular systems titles is (**programmer/ analyst,** an individual who performs both a systems and programming function. The programmer/analyst is most often found in small DP organizations which cannot afford separate systems and programming groups. The position offers tremendous challenge and leeway to develop highly individualistic methods of data processing.

Generally, a manager supervises and coordinates each of the three groups of the data processing department. Operations managers face daily deadlines for providing data to their organization. The lack of DP support is readily noticed in most companies. Critical periods face the programming and systems managers around project deadlines. At those times, all work must be completed and properly documented. All three managers normally report to a data processing department manager who works with management.

In larger organizations, the responsibilities of each manager are clearly defined, as are the lines of communication. In smaller organizations, the DP manager may fill one or more of the operations, programming, or systems manager's roles. Again, the luxury of separate operational groups is not feasible in smaller centers. Handsome financial rewards may accrue to people who can aggressively and competently manage a data processing group.

2.4
The Flow of
Information

Up to this point, we have discussed the people who compose the data processing department. But how do these people interact when processing a specific computer application? What roles do the keypunch operator, data clerk, and programmer play in processing? For this discussion, let's examine the procedures used by a college data processing department to add new students to the file of attendees.

The file of every student currently enrolled at the college is called the (student master file.) It contains each student's name, social security number, address, date of birth, program of study, high school attended, marital status, college entry data, courses taken by semester, grades for each course, grade point average, and any special remarks about the student. The student master file is used whenever student information is computer processed.

The responsibility of designing the student master file had been assigned to a systems analyst who investigated all aspects of the data and suggested a file format. (This format was reviewed by other analysts and by the college staff who used the information drawn from the file.) (The final file format was accepted and approved by its users and the systems group manager.)

The analyst's job did not end there. The analyst was also responsible for the design of the forms used to input data to the file or output information from the file. Input forms included the application completed by the student, any registration or financial forms, and forms employed in the operations area when processing student data. The output forms presented a similar problem. A student transcript for all final grades, student receipts for payment of tuition, special grade notices sent to students, and acceptance or denial letters for students requesting attendance at the college had to be designed. The final package of file format and input and output forms was eventually presented to all users for their approval.

Once approval was received, the analyst gave the file design to a programmer. The programmer had to write, test, and certify all the software necessary to create and update the student master file. This software included any programs used to produce student grade transcripts and outputs from the master file. The programmer had to write every program necessary to maintain the master file. One program added new students to the student master file.

New students have to complete an application with data for the student file. All applications go to the college admissions office, which each week sends the approved applications to the college's data processing department.

FIGURE 2.12 A schematic diagram describing the processing of student applications at the data processing center of a college.

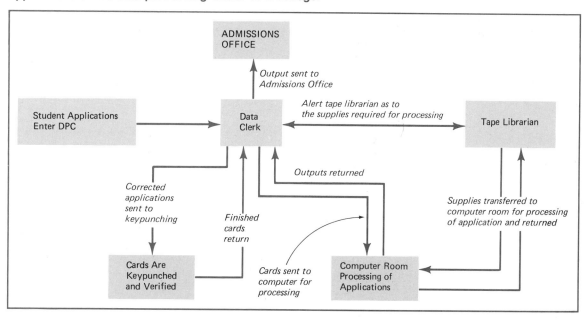

A data clerk records receiving the applications and assigns the batch a control number. A **control number** is one of a series of identification numbers assigned to data. It is a convenient method of identifying where the applications are and to what extent they have been processed. For example, the data clerk will record the dates when the applications enter and leave keypunching, and when and where the data enters the computer room and is processed. These entries will all refer to the original control number. The control number is one of the data clerk's primary tools.

After getting their control number, applications go to keypunching, where computer cards are keypunched from the applications. During this operation, the applications are referred to as source documents. A **source document** is any document from which data is taken.

The cards go to the computer room after keypunching. Before releasing the cards to the computer room staff, the data clerk alerts the tape librarian to ready any materials related to the processing of these cards. These materials might include special forms used when processing student applications (i.e., acceptance letters to each student) or the storage medium on which the student master file is stored. The student master file must be available to the computer in order for new students to be added to it. The tape librarian must have these supplies available for processing.

The computer operator, after checking the day's schedule of jobs, readies the computer for processing the new student data. The operator inputs both the cards and the programs necessary to update the student master file. After running these programs, the operator makes available all the supplies used in processing.

The tape librarian catalogs and refiles all the originally issued supplies. The data clerk records the completion of processing, the receipt of the cards used in processing, and the number of copies of computer-printed reports. The cards are retained within the data processing area, and the computer-printed reports and original applications are returned to the admissions office.

The members of the data processing department must work as a team to transmit data smoothly and efficiently. Without this vital communication, a data processing department cannot do its best work.

2.5 Data Processing Systems

Current technology has produced many forms of data processing, and a company can select a form uniquely suited to its needs. Management must decide which hardware and data processing approach to adopt, a decision that will dictate the day-to-day operation of the data processing department and how users receive their computer-prepared information.

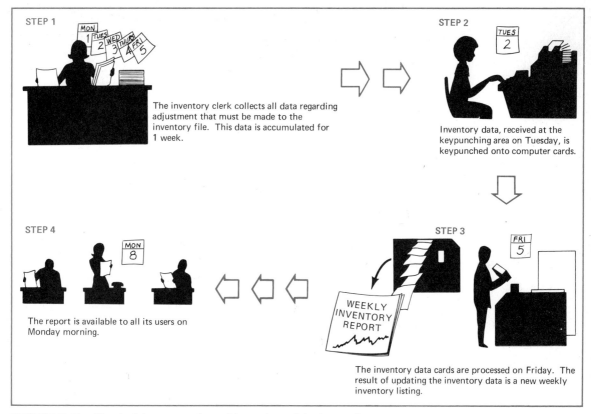

FIGURE 2.13 **The batch processing of inventory data to produce a weekly inventory report.**

Batch Processing

Batch processing, a widely used technique, involves the regular processing of large amounts of data. In batch processing, data is collected for a predetermined period of time, after which it is processed. The processing of a payroll is a good example of batch processing. Payroll data is accumulated over a 1- or 2-week period and processed at regular intervals. Paychecks are distributed to all employees on a predetermined schedule.

The weekly batch processing of inventory data is another example. Figure 2.13 illustrates a batch-oriented operation. Initially, an inventory clerk collects data on inventory adjustments. The data includes invoices of items to be added, credit memos on returned items, receipts of items removed from inventory and returned to their manufacturers, and a total count (by part number) of all items sold. The inventory clerk checks this paperwork and verifies any data on the forms.

On Monday afternoon, an entire week's batch of inventory paperwork is sent to the keypunching area, where the inventory data will be punched onto computer cards. The keypunchers have a standard format into which this information is punched. The deadline for finishing the inventory cards is Thursday afternoon, because the inventory update is scheduled for processing on Friday.

The entire batch of inventory cards is processed at one time. During batch processing, data contained on the card is applied against a specific record in the inventory file. Thus, if 10 barber chairs are received into inventory, the total quantity of barber chairs in the inventory will be increased by 10. The inventory card indicates an increase of 10 barber chairs, and therefore, the specific record related to barber chairs will be updated by 10 units in the inventory file. The processing operation ends only after the data on the last inventory card is processed.

The updated inventory file appears in the inventory report. This report is produced after the batch processing of inventory cards and indicates the current inventory level and the change since the preceding week for every item in inventory. The inventory clerk will have a copy of this report by Monday morning and use it throughout the week. The batch processing of new inventory changes will begin again on Monday afternoon.

The inventory listing is a printed output of the results produced by batch processing. This update of inventory data is defined as a batch-processing operation because data was accumulated over a specific period of time and processed on a regular basis. The reliability of a batch processing is quite high, and it is therefore one of the mainstays of computerized data processing.

Online Processing

Batch processing requires that data be accumulated before it is processed by the computer, creating a delay between a transaction and its processing. Current technology can shorten this delay and process data almost immediately by using special hardware. These **online** devices allow direct communication with the computer and an uninterrupted flow of input data.[1] **Online processing** is used when delay in handling data is undesirable. Online processing is used by airlines and car rental agencies to accept and confirm customer reservations in seconds. An online banking system is another example of this type of processing.

Consider a savings bank with many branch offices to service its customer accounts. Because it is not economically feasible to equip each branch with its own computer, an online link to the bank's centrally located computer system has been created. This communication link assumes the form of specially installed telephone lines. Because they are leased from the telephone company, they are called *leased*

---

[1] The term **offline** describes the condition where direct communication with the computer is not possible.

lines. A leased line is an unbroken communication link between the branch office and the main computer and is used solely for the transmission of data.

Customer savings data goes to the bank's computer for processing along the leased line. Customer data may be handled in either of two ways. In one design, if the bank's system is occupied with other work, it may be instructed to accept and temporarily hold the customer data for subsequent processing.

At that time, the computer will access the file of customer accounts and update each. New data will come from the temporarily stored file of customer transactions. The computer searches the file of customer accounts until the desired account number is found. When the account numbers match, the amount of the transaction may be added or subtracted from the customer's balance.

An alternative approach to the online processing of savings bank data is possible. The bank's computer system could be designed to process customer data right as it enters the system, in which case no delay would exist in the handling of savings data. Customer accounts would be accessed instantly and properly updated. Online data processing systems that operate in this fashion are referred to as **real-time** systems. Real-time systems represent some of the most sophisticated forms of online data processing, but their great expense may limit their adoption.

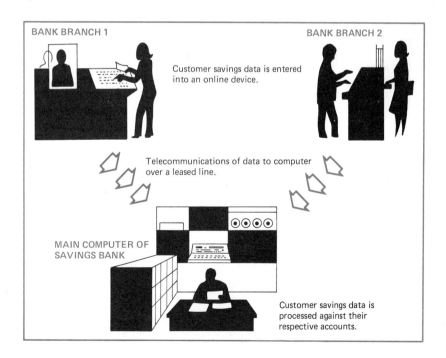

BANK BRANCH 1

BANK BRANCH 2

Customer savings data is entered into an online device.

Telecommunications of data to computer over a leased line.

MAIN COMPUTER OF SAVINGS BANK

Customer savings data is processed against their respective accounts.

FIGURE 2.14 The online processing of a savings bank's data.

Time-Sharing

One form of online processing allows the concurrent use of a computer by a group of individuals. This form of online processing is called **time-sharing.** Many users *share* a computer's resources at the same time. Schools often adopt time-sharing systems to support their computer curriculums.

Time-sharing allows many students concurrent access to the same computer. The student can create an online link to the computer using a device called a **terminal.** Figure 2.15 shows a student seated at a terminal with a keyboard for inputting data and a TV screen for output data. The online link to the computer may use a leased line or a regular telephone line. The student receives a set of instructions on how to use the terminal and create the online link.

Once the online link is created, the student can begin to input his or her program. At the same time, other students can enter or process their programs. The computer's speed of operation lets it jump from one program to another and process each in the order in which it is received. Time-sharing is economically and educationally sound. It lets many students share one computer and lets students independently access the computer and proceed at their own pace.

The main advantage of time-sharing is its **interactive processing,** which describes the user's ability to interact directly with the computer. Time-sharing users seated at terminals send instructions to the computer and receive its responses to those commands almost immediately.

In the two illustrations above, the savings bank and student time-sharing, data was transmitted to and from the computer using telephone lines. This mode of data transfer is referred to as **telecommunications.** However, telecommunications is not restricted to telephone lines; it may also involve microwave systems, transoceanic cables, laser beams, or communication satellites. A practical application of telecommunications is the processing of long-distance telephone calls through microwave stations. Also, international sports events like the Olympics are presented throughout the world via communication satellites supported by computerized communication systems.

Another term associated with telecommunications is **teleprocessing.** Teleprocessing is a form of telecommunications, but it specifically describes the use of terminals that visually display data. The time-sharing processing of student programs is a good example of teleprocessing. Data entered via the terminal keyboard was transmitted to the computer over telephone lines. The results of processing were transferred back over the same lines and output on the screen of the terminal.

Some data processors prefer a somewhat broader definition of teleprocessing. They believe that teleprocessing involves the collection and input of data from remote terminals over telephone lines, its

FIGURE 2.15 Students using a computer system to perform their laboratory exercises. The student shown here is seated at a terminal which displays its results on a TV-like picture tube. Using this terminal device, the student can directly interact with the computer. *(Copyright © 1977 Creative Computing, Morristown, N.J.)*

immediate processing, and distribution to those terminals using a printed or visual output. Thus, teleprocessing is not only the concurrent use of CRTs and telecommunications, but the handling of data throughout the total computer system. Although we will ordinarily use the first definition, we offer the second to broaden your understanding of this topic.

Remote Job Entry (RJE)

The time-shared processing of student programs represents one type of telecommunications operation. Other types may use different input or output devices. For example, a businessperson may want to input data on computer cards and output information in a printed report, operations that require a computer device called a remote job entry station.

A **remote job entry (RJE) station** is a device permitting transfer of data from a remote location to a distant computer system via telecommunications. An RJE may use computer cards or a keyboard for online processing.) As processing occurs, information may be transmitted back to the RJE as a printed report. Printed reports are generally called **hardcopy** because they are permanent, tangible processing records. Output that appears on a terminal's screen is called **softcopy** because it is impermanent and remains useful only while it is visible. RJE stations often have a terminal to expand the device's ability to handle input and output operations.

Hospitals effectively use RJE stations. Consider the case of a hospital with a group of satellite outpatient clinics in surrounding neighborhoods. The medical staff has access to all hospital data through RJEs at every clinic. They can request patient case histories from the hospital's computerized file of patient data and receive, at the clinics, a hardcopy record. Any prescribed treatment will be input to the patient's records via the RJE. The RJE lets the hospital update its patient file and monitor the medical services of the clinics.

Service Bureaus

Many organizations cannot afford to buy or rent a small computer and yet need computer support. Many such companies turn to **service bureaus,** data processing companies that rent out their computer services.

The service bureau owns the computer and rents time on it to users, who pay only for the time they use. Because the bureau's computer is usually far from the user, online processing is necessary, and time-sharing and RJEs are common to these rental services. Fees depend on type of service, market competition, equipment needs, and location. We can take some representative examples.

Consider a firm of architects in a suburb miles from a major city. This firm designs and builds custom vacation homes in a lakefront development. The firm does not need and could not afford an on-site computer, although they occasionally need computer assistance for computing structural designs. Computer-prepared designs are quicker and more reliable than manual computations. When they need these computations, the architects use a terminal to tie into a time-sharing system provided by a service bureau. They feed data via a terminal which also reports the results. The firm only pays for the time it has access to the computer, plus the cost of the telephone call. In effect, the architects have computer access on demand. Renting time-sharing devices, via telecommunications, satisfied this organization's data processing needs.

An alternative to renting computer time is to use an RJE station. Consider the use of an RJE by an employment agency that supplies temporary help to businesses. Twice daily, at noon and 6 P.M., data on employees hired for that day is input to the rental computer. These telecommunicated data are accepted and processed against a file maintained within the service bureau's computer. This file contains previously stored data on customers. Using stored and new information, the service bureau prepares statements for every temporary worker, which are used to update customer accounts and temporary employees' payroll records. Customer bills and statements are printed by the RJE at the agency office and mailed that evening.

In this illustration, the RJE was online to the service bureau's computer. The agency paid for the processing of statements, maintenance of its files, and equipment rental. As part of the service, the agency received monthly summaries of customer billing, payroll records, and financial statements. For this agency, a service bureau was more economical than operating its own computer.

One potential problem with relying on a service bureau to maintain data files is the possibility of security violations. Many managers fear that critical financial data may leak to competitors. Despite precautions taken by service bureaus, some managers opt for their own computer systems. They incur the extra cost and monitor their own data security. This decision is highly personal, but the issue of data security is important to people considering the use of any service bureau.

Some service bureaus offer a form of indirect computer support in which customers lease a full data processing capability. A customer prepares input data in a specified format and gives it to the service bureau for complete processing. The service bureau returns the results, including any documentation. In effect, the user has prepared the input data, and the bureau has completed the processing.

A good example of this service is the payroll reconciliation for a construction company with seasonal employees. Seasonal fluctuations in the workforce create recordkeeping problems which are readily eased by the service bureau. Daily worksheets are prepared by the company's payroll staff and converted into weekly payroll summaries. These summaries go to the service bureau, which returns to the company a completed payroll, including checks, statements, deductions, etc. The service fee is based on the number of employee records handled (e.g., 25 cents for each employee paid). In choosing this kind of service, the user avoids all computer costs but forgoes the security of handling the data.

Current computer systems can support both batch processing and online processing. The level of support depends on the size and type of the computer, the complexity of the processing, the number of users, and the financial resources available. Each of these factors must be carefully weighed by managers choosing a computer system and method of data processing.

2.6 Careers in Data Processing

It might surprise you to learn that the shortage of qualified programmers has induced companies to offer a bounty for them. A California bank, Security Pacific National, offered $1000 for each programmer hired. Connecticut General Insurance offered its employees $700 and an ounce of gold for each successfully recruited programmer.

The future employment picture for computer professionals seems very bright indeed. Of the estimated $50 billion spent on computer operations in 1980, almost $28 billion went for salaries. That figure will have more than doubled in 1985, when total expenditures for computer service will exceed $100 billion. A breakdown of 1980 salaries shows that approximately 40 percent went to programmers and analysts, 15 percent to DP management, 10 percent each to data entry personnel and technical specialists, and the remaining 25 percent to operations personnel. Vast sums will be spent in the future to solicit, hire, and retain competent computer professionals. Many personnel managers believe that the current ratio of DP jobs to applicants is 5 to 1.

Projections by the U.S. Bureau of Labor Statistics for the 1980s indicate an overall increase of 27 percent in computer-related jobs. In specific work categories, they project increases of 25 percent for programmers, 30 percent for systems analysts, and 30 percent for computer technicians and specialists. Translating these percentages into round numbers, they believe that almost 300,000 programming and 200,000 analyst jobs will exist by 1985, with approximately 300,000 operator-related jobs also available.

The only projected decrease will occur among keypunchers, with an estimated decline of 27 percent. This decrease will result as data processing centers switch from cards to data entry equipment. In effect, the data entry clerk will replace the keypunch operator. A net loss of 50,000 keypunching jobs is estimated by 1985, with a parallel rise of almost 40,000 data entry jobs. By 1985, they project that 330,000 data entry clerks and 200,000 keypunchers will be employed. Questions about salaries are best answered by help-wanted advertisements in local newspapers. They may surprise many people. In 1980 in New York, for example, programmers with an average of 3 years experience in popular languages earned $25,000 to $35,000 a year plus many fringe benefits. People with training and initiative will have excellent job prospects in the data processing field. The projected 27 percent increase relates directly to the data processing area and does not reflect growth in computer aligned fields. Growth in the computer fields results in more jobs being available in the DP service area. Corporations utilizing computers will seek out EDP consultants to advise them on their operational needs, construction and maintenance people to refurbish and maintain their computer centers, and sales people to sell their services to consumers. Computer researchers will hire professionals to develop new approaches to software and the hardware to support them. As an example, consider the impact that home computers have had. Retail organizations, specializing in the sale of these small systems, heretofore nonexistent, have sprung up throughout the country, creating many new jobs in the process.

Case Study One

Clearing U.S. Customs

Ordinarily, Americans returning from abroad can anticipate long lines when clearing U.S. Customs. But computers help keep these lines to a minimum. Currently, United States citizens pass through customs using a simplified, one-step procedure. A computerized information system speeds the checking of passports and immigration data.

The old procedure required that a returning citizen stop twice for customs inspection. An initial passport check was followed by a declaration of the goods being brought into the United States. At both checks, customs agents verified passports. They often had to check customs regulations about incoming merchandise. A routine examination could take over 10 minutes.

The revised procedure lets customs clerks verify United States passports, levy customs duties, and perform immigration checks all in one step. The vehicle for this new procedure is a computerized monitoring system called (Tactical Enforcement Control System or TECS, which provides online access for each customs agent at each

entrance checkpoint in the United States. These include international airports, steamship terminals, containerized cargo depots, and vehicular entry points at our borders.

The computer tells customs agents whether an entering individual is an undesirable alien, a fugitive from justice returning under an alias or with a false passport, or someone who should be detained temporarily for illegal activities. The TECS system has immediate online access to other government files, including those of the FBI; Bureau of Alcohol, Tobacco, and Firearms; Treasury; and IRS. The TECS system also helps agents to compute and levy customs duties. Rather than scan manuals, agents retrieve this data from their computer terminals.

TECS means that in most cases the required check of name and passport takes only seconds. However, when a person's data is flagged by the computer, TECS searches files for related data, advises the agent of its search, usually with a message on the agent's terminal, and allows the agent to prepare for a response.

Consider this . . .
How might computer systems similar to TECS be employed by the federal government in drug control and immigration surveillance activities?

Summary

The following major points have been presented in Chapter 2:

Point 1 A user is anyone who receives computer-related services. Users who know about data processing will receive improved data proc-

essing support and services suited to their needs. Essentially, because of the widespread use of the computer, we all are users and benefit from its support. Moreover, as computers become more available to the average person at home or in busi-

Cast Study Two

Swissair's PARS System

Airlines have remained in the forefront of computerization, using computers to assist in navigation, landing aircraft, and tracking lost luggage. The international air carrier, Swissair, has made another exciting use of computers.

Like other airlines, Swissair has a computerized passenger reservation system called PARS (Program Airline Reservation System). The unusual aspect of PARS is its use of satellites in a real-time system. PARS depends on a computer in Zurich, Switzerland. Though reservation data is entered in New York City, it must travel to Zurich to be confirmed. It travels to Europe via satellite, averaging 10 seconds per round-trip transmission.

The PARS system is highly structured, with hundreds of codes for the proper registration of passenger flight requests. PARS lets reservations clerks advise passengers on fares, departure and arrival times, and connecting flights. PARS can accept reservations for 12 months ahead, and the

information is retained in PARS for 6 months.

PARS can tell passengers the time and temperature, in both Fahrenheit and Celsius, of cities they will fly to. It is programmed to respond in the language used by the requester of flight information, an important feature for an international airline which gets requests from all over the world.

In addition to its computerized real-time reservation system, Swissair has a real-time cargo-tracking system which is satellite supported. The system is used to schedule the international movement of cargo, track lost items, reconcile insurance claims, and prepare itemized cargo manifests of each shipment. The Swissair cargo system also can respond in various languages.

Swissair has designed practical and reliable data processing operations, technological achievements that represent stepping stones to future advances.

ness, more people will directly use computers. A knowledge of data processing will greatly improve their chances of using a computer properly.

Point 2 A computer system is composed of devices that assist its processing of data. A representative system may incorporate a card reader and line printer to facilitate input and output operations. Computerized data may be stored in magnetic tape or disk. The processing of all data is performed in the CPU. Processing activities may be monitored on the computer console, which frequently has a CRT to display data.

Point 3 The data processing department is normally composed of an operations group, a pro-

gramming group, and a systems group. Each group is responsible for a specific function of the department. The operations group is responsibile for maintaining and running the computer hardware. The programming group writes and maintains all software. Studies of how data is processed through the organization are performed by the systems group.

Point 4 Operations workers are directly involved in processing data. The computer operator runs all computer hardware. The keypuncher and data entry clerk prepare data for input to the computer. Keypunchers produce computer cards, while data entry clerks may use a variety of keyboard devices. The tape librarian catalogs and monitors computer-related storage media. The control of data entering or leaving the data processing area is the responsibility of the data or control clerk.

Point 5 Programmers are responsible for writing the software used in the computer system. They write, test, and certify all programs. Analysts study and improve the flow of data through an organization. Analysts usually have years of training and education. Systems projects may involve the design and cost estimation of future computer systems and hardware.

Point 6 Each member of the data processing department handles a data processing application. Each member of the staff plays a vital role in the efficient flow of data.

Point 7 Batch processing involves the regular processing of large amounts of data. Data is amassed over a period of time and processed on a regular schedule. A time delay is inherent in a batch-processing operation because data has to be accumulated. Thus, batch processing is suited to applications in which it is acceptable for time to elapse between the completion of a transaction and its processing by the computer. The processing of a payroll, for example, is well suited to batch processing.

Point 8 Online processing relates to the telecommunication of data to a computer system. A direct communication link is established between devices that input or output data and the computer. Leased lines or telephone lines are often used to create an online link between terminals or RJE stations and a distant computer system. The term *teleprocessing* is applied to online processing that involves the use of terminals.

Point 9 Specialized types of online processing are real-time processing and time-sharing. Input data is immediately processed by the computer in real-time processing. Time-sharing involves the concurrent use of a computer by a group of individuals. Educational institutions often use time-sharing systems to support student programming activities.

Point 10 Remote job entry stations are devices that permit the entry of data to a computer over long distances. They can read computer cards or data entered via a keyboard and provide printed (hardcopy) or visual (softcopy) output. RJE stations and terminals are frequently used by service bureaus which rent computer support to organizations.

Point 11 In the 1980s, computer-related jobs will grow by 27 percent. Only the number of keypunch operators will decline. By 1985, it is estimated that the data processing workforce will consist of approximately 200,000 analysts, 300,000 programmers, 300,000 operations personnel, 330,000 data entry clerks, and 200,000 keypunchers.

Glossary

Analyst A member of the systems group who investigates and evaluates the flow of data through an organization.

Batch processing The computerized processing of large batches of data at regular intervals.

Card reader A computer device used to input data contained on computer cards.

Cathode ray tube (CRT) A terminal device with a TV-like picture tube to display output information and a keyboard for inputting data.

Central processing unit (CPU) The unit of hardware in a computer system in which all processing occurs.

Computer console The hardware component, often on the CPU, which, when monitored by the computer operator, indicates the systems processing status. CRTs are frequently attached to the console to provide a softcopy capability.

Computer operator A member of the operations area who physically operates the computer and its related devices.

Control clerk   Another title used to describe the data clerk position.

Control number   An identification number assigned by the data clerk to any data entering the data processing department; the number is used to monitor the status of that data as it is processed.

Data clerk   An operations area member assigned to monitor the flow of data through the data processing department.

Data entry clerk   A member of the operations group who uses a variety of keyboard devices to input data directly into the computer system.

Data processing department   The group that provides data processing services in a company or other organization; composed of an operations group, a programming group, and a systems group; also referred to as the computer center, data processing center, data processing group, or data processing shop.

GIGO   "Garbage in, garbage out"; a slang business expression that refers to the importance of entering accurate input data into a computer.

Hardcopy   Outputs produced in a printed, permanent, and readable format.

Hardware   A term used to describe all computer equipment and any related devices.

Interactive processing   A processing mode which permits the user and computer to interact during the online processing of programs; often associated with time-sharing.

Keypunch operator   A member of the operations group who uses a keypunch device to convert data into computer cards for input to the computer.

Line printer   The output device of a computer system, ordinarily assigned the task of providing printed output (i.e., reports).

Magnetic disk   A current storage method which lets the computer retain large amounts of data for ready processing.

Magnetic tape   A popular method of computer storage, similar to magnetic disk, which permits the retention of large amounts of data for rapid processing.

Offline   A condition in which direct communication with a computer system is not possible.

Online   A condition in which direct communication with a computer is possible.

Online processing   The processing performed by a computer in which data is directly transmitted between input and output devices and a computer system via telecommunications lines.

Operations group   A section of the data processing department responsible for the physical operation of the computer and related equipment.

Programmer   A member of the programming area whose role is writing and testing new computer programs and modifying existing programs.

Programmer/analyst   A title given to the job position which has both systems and programming responsibilities.

Programming group   A part of the data processing department that has the operational responsibility for all software.

Real-time processing   An online processing system in which data is processed the instant it occurs; there are no delays between the time data is available and the time it is processed.

Remote job entry (RJE) station   A device permitting the telecommunication of data to and from a distant computer that supports the input of cards, the output of printed reports, and the use of terminals to input or output data.

Service bureau   An organization which rents computer services to companies that do not desire to operate their own computer systems.

Softcopy   Computer output in a visual, nonpermanent format.

Software   All programs used by the computer.

Source document   A document from which data is taken to begin data processing.

A PUNCHED CARD

Systems analyst   The title applied to the position of analyst.

Systems group   The part of the data processing department that evaluates, monitors, and effects changes in the way data flows through a business organization.

Tape librarian   The person in the operations area who is responsible for the cataloging and storage of computer storage media.

Telecommunications   The transmission and processing of data via telephone lines and other high-speed communication means which support online processing.

Teleprocessing   The telecommunication and complete processing of data via terminals that provide visual and printed outputs.

Terminal   The computer device, an integral part of teleprocessing operations, capable of providing softcopy and hardcopy outputs, employed for input and output operations (i.e., CRTs).

Time-sharing   The concurrent use of an online computer system by a group of individuals.

User   The recipient of computer services.

Discussion Questions

1 Do you consider yourself a direct or indirect user of computer services? Describe how you use the computer, or explain why you believe you do not use it.

2 From employment ads in newspapers and magazines, compile a list of computer-related jobs and their salaries. Discuss qualifications listed in the ads and their relationship to the salaries offered.

3 Visit the data processing department at your school or job. Prepare an organization chart that describes the positions in the department (i.e., keypunch operator, data clerk, programmer, analyst, etc.). How does that organizational structure compare with the one discussed in this chapter?

4 Discuss how student-written programs are handled in the data processing area of your school. Are programs processed via an RJE, a conventional computer system, or visual display terminals? Ask friends in other classes how their programs are processed and which methods they prefer.

5 Why would an architect, an accountant, an engineer, or a businessperson want to use a time-sharing computer system? Could it be beneficial to their work? Explain.

6 Examine the following list of computer applications. What type of data processing system can be employed to support each application? Discuss how you think the computer is used.

a   A computerized dating service

b   Offtrack betting (OTB) or the computerized betting system at a racetrack

c   A national computerized system for forecasting weather

d   A computerized intensive care system at a hospital

e   Computer guidance systems on missiles

f   An early warning national defense system (radar)

g   A police information system on stolen cars

h   An inventory control system for a large warehouse

i   A computerized retail system for a department store

7 Discuss batch processing, online processing, real-time processing, time-sharing, and remote job entry processing.

8 Could a remote job entry station be used to support the processing of student-written programs? Explain your answer. Visit your data processing center and determine if they use an RJE facility. If possible, ask the operators to describe the use of the RJE.

9 What advantages does a service bureau offer the average businessperson? What are its disadvantages in terms of data security and business competition? Explain.

Summary Test

_F_   **1** The data processing department is composed of the operations, data control, programming, and systems groups.

_F_   **2** The term *hardware* refers to computer equipment and the programs written for it.

_F_   **3** The computer operator is merely a button pusher and, as such, requires no knowledge of the computer.

_F_   **4** The keypunch operator's job is operationally the same as the computer operator's job.

_T_   **5** Time-sharing lets students concurrently employ the computer to process their programs.

_T_   **6** A handwritten application is an example of a source document.

_F_   **7** Softcopy is a term applied to multiple pages of computer-printed reports.

_T_   **8** Batch processing involves the accumulation and processing of data at regular intervals.

_T_   **9** In real-time processing, data contained in a computer file is immediately accessible for use in processing.

_F_   **10** The terms *software* and *softcopy* describe the same nonpermanent output.

_F_   **11** Leased lines do not permit online communications between a user and a computer system.

_F_   **12** The data entry clerk and data clerk titles are interchangeable and describe the same position within the operations area.

_T_   **13** The CPU provides the capacity to perform all processing operations within the computer system.

_T_   **14** Businesspeople should understand data processing to communicate well with computer personnel and prepare for using computers.

_F_   **15** Though it has a keyboard, the CRT can only perform output operations.

_B_   **16** The status of all data handled by a DP center is determined by a:

a	Data number	**b**	Control number
c	Reference number	**d**	Item number

_C_ **17** The individual within the operations group who ordinarily uses a variety of keyboard devices is the:

a	Data clerk	**b**	Keypunch operator
c	Data entry clerk	**d**	Computer operator

_A_ **18** The daily processing of corrections to customer accounts best exemplifies the processing mode of:

a	Batch processing	**b**	Real-time processing
c	Time-sharing	**d**	Offline processing

_D_ **19** Which of the following terms could be used to describe the concurrent processing of computer programs, via CRTs, on one computer system?

a	Time-sharing	**b**	Online processing
c	Interactive processing	**d**	All the above

_D_ **20** The unit of hardware an operator uses to monitor computer processing is the:

a	Card reader	**b**	CPU
c	Line printer	**d**	Console

_C_ **21** The individual who catalogs storage media is the:

a	Data clerk	**b**	Control clerk
c	Tape librarian	**d**	All the above

_A_ **22** The data processing job expected to decrease in the 1980s is that of:

a	Keypuncher	**b**	Data entry clerk
c	Computer operator	**d**	Programmer

_D_ **23** Which of the following statements is true?

- **a** Analysts usually work alone and sometimes as part of a team.
- **b** Most systems projects are completed in 6 to 12 weeks.
- **c** An analyst's primary concern is the development of software.
- **d** Analysts evaluate data flow through an organization.

_B_ **24** The computer device primarily used to provide hardcopy is the:

a	CRT	**b**	Line printer
c	Computer console	**d**	Card reader

_A_ **25** The term interchangeable with control clerk is:

a	Data clerk	**b**	Data control clerk
c	Tape librarian	**d**	Data entry clerk

REMEMBER

Summary Test Answers

1 F	**2** F	**3** F	**4** F	**5** T
6 T	**7** F	**8** T	**9** T	**10** F
11 F	**12** F	**13** T	**14** T	**15** F
16 B	**17** C	**18** A	**19** D	**20** D
21 C	**22** A	**23** D	**24** B	**25** A

Three

Card Data, Keypunch, and Other Devices

FIGURE 3.1 Many types of punched cards are still used in data processing operations. Though there is some movement away from cards, the 80-column cards pictured continue to offer a reliable means of data handling for many organizations. *(Susan Berkowitz, Courtesy of CUNY/UCC.)*

Purpose of This Chapter

This chapter introduces the computer punch card and the devices related to its use. The chapter opens with a discussion of the 80-column card and the Hollerith code and moves to the unit record concept, the principle on which most card data is processed.

Integral to a discussion of punched cards is the manner in which cards make data available. The field is the basic unit of presenting card data, and the chapter discusses the three types of fields and their division into minor fields. The importance of documenting data formats is briefly explored.

The newer 96-column card is discussed in the next section, and the structure and use of binary coded decimal (BCD), the computer code used with the 96-column card, is explained. The reader then goes through a three-step procedure to construct the BCD code for selected characters.

The chapter discusses various types of keypunches, including the IBM 029, a keypunch often used by students, and other keypunches with additional features. We stress the importance of verifying cards and validating data.

The chapter also describes card processing systems' advantages and disadvantages and explains how cards work in an inventory control system. We describe special forms of the 80-column card to acquaint the reader with the practical uses of the dual card, document card, stub card, and mark-sense card.

The last section presents electrical accounting machines (EAM), predecessors of computers. EAMs depended on the use of 80-column cards. The section also reviews the operational capabilities of the sorter, reproducer, collator, interpreter, and accounting machine.

After studying this chapter, you should be able to

■ Describe the characteristics of the Hollerith code and 80-column card.
■ Discuss the unit record concept.
■ Describe the purpose of card fields, types of data fields, and the overall structure of card fields.
■ Describe the characteristics of the 96-column card and binary coded decimal (BCD) code.
■ Construct the Hollerith and BCD code for an alphabetic or numeric character.
■ Discuss the verification and validation of card data.
■ Discuss specialized formats of the 80-column card and the keypunch devices that can prepare them.
■ Discuss the purpose and use of electrical accounting machines.
■ Understand the following terms:

Accounting machine	Interpreter
Alphabetic field	Keypunch
Alphanumeric field	Mark-sense card
Binary coded decimal (BCD)	96-column card
Bits	Numeric field
Card fields	Record
Collator	Reproducer
Control panel	Sort field
Digit rows	Sorter
Document card	Special characters
Documentation	Standard punch card
Dual card	Stub card
80-column card	Unit record concept
Electrical accounting machines (EAM)	Unit record equipment
	Validation of data
Field name	Verification of data
Gangpunching	Verifier
Hollerith code	Zone rows

Introduction

In the first two chapters, we saw current applications of computers, developments which are the results of billions of research dollars. Dazzling technical advances tend to overshadow the more mundane aspects of data processing. We marvel at how computers work for hospitals or for NASA during space projects. But we should remember that for every imaginative computer application, a hundred fairly conventional data processing tasks are completed. Though these day-to-day tasks are conventional, they are a true measure of the computer's effect on our lives.

One mainstay of data processing is the punch card, widely used for input and output. In this chapter, we will introduce concepts initially developed for the punch cards and later extended to other areas of data processing. Understanding the concepts, as they apply to cards, will help you master them in later discussions about other media.

Before proceeding, we should emphasize the importance of input media, of which cards represent just one type. (Cards also serve as output in certain cases, as we will see below.) Although we can readily see a computer's output abilities, we too often overlook the careful planning of inputs. Somewhere in the computer process, input data had to be converted from a raw to a computer-acceptable state. Unless data is in a format the computer can use, it cannot be input and processed.

As we have discussed in earlier chapters, computer cards are a reliable but relatively slow input medium. The trend today is toward online input. However, the trend is different for organizations that use cards as both input and output. Many major organizations will continue to use computer cards, which provide them with a valid input and output medium quite adequate to their needs. Consider the checks issued as tax refunds by state and federal revenue organizations. The computer card/check is a vehicle for payment and is considered an output. After cashing, the card/check is returned to the issuing agency and serves as an input for matching against payees. In both cases, the card/check records the amount due and the person cashing the check.

In such cases, cards are uniquely suited to the task at hand. On-line data entry could not serve so well. In sum, though card processing will decrease, cards will continue to significantly affect the automated processing of data.

3.1
The 80-Column Card
Hollerith and the 1890 Census

During the 1880s, Herman Hollerith was commissioned by the U.S. Census Department to find a way to speed up the processing of the 1890 census, a task they estimated would take 11 years. Hollerith developed a punch card, a code to be used with it, and tabulating devices for processing the cards. Hollerith made it possible to complete the 1890 census in one-third the estimated time—a saving of over 7 years.

Hollerith's significant contributions were a machine-acceptable code and devices to process that code. Although Hollerith's devices were crude by today's standards, they represented one of the first steps in the automated processing of data.

Characteristics of the Card

One of the most widely accepted computer media in the world is the standard-size **80-column card.** Most people readily associate this card with the computer. The 80-column card's uses include social security and veterans' checks, inventory and warranty cards, telephone and utility bills, and its conventional use in the data processing center. The phrase "Do not fold, spindle, or mutilate" is synonymous with the punch card and has become part of American slang.

The **standard punch card** (Figure 3.2) is perfectly suited for its uses. Its size does not restrict its use and contributes to its durability. The card's cost is not prohibitive compared with other computer storage media. One drawback is that the card cannot be repunched.

The 80-column card is divided into **12 rows** horizontally and **80 columns** vertically. The card is said to have a *12 edge* (top edge), a *9 edge* (bottom edge), *column 1 end,* and *column 80 end*. If the printed numbers on the card are facing you, the card is described as being "face up." Conversely, if the numbers face away, the card is "face down."

The horizontal rows on the card are numbered 12, 11, 0, and 1 through 9, reading down the card. They are referred to as the 12 row, 11 row, 0 row, and 1 through 9 rows. Rows 12, 11, and 0 are collectively designated as **zone rows,** while rows 0 through 9 are designated **digit rows.** A set of small numbers from 1 to 80 is printed be-

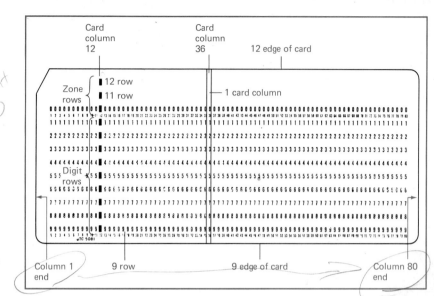

FIGURE 3.2 The standard punch card. Note the punches in card column 12 in each of the 12 rows.

tween the 0 and 1 rows. These numbers refer to the 80 columns on the card. In Figure 3.2, card column 12, we note punches (the rectangular holes) in each of the 12 rows of the 80-column card.

The Hollerith Code

The **Hollerith code** is standard throughout the world. Its construction lets it be used easily. Each character in the code has its own unique configuration; in other words, no two character codes are alike. Thus, it is not possible to confuse the letter *O* and the number 0 in the Hollerith code.

With the Hollerith code, only one character may be punched into one card column. Data can be punched into any one of the 80 card columns, one character at a time, assuring the accurate use of card data. Three types of characters are defined by the Hollerith code:

1 Numeric characters: 0 through 9
2 Alphabetic characters: A through Z
3 Special characters: all other characters, i.e., comma, period, dollar sign, pound sign, slash

Numeric characters employ only *one* punch per card column to represent their characters. In Figure 3.3, card columns 4 to 13 contain the numeric characters. Note that the representative punch for a number is always in the row designated by the same number. Thus, the number 1 is represented by a punch in the 1 row, the number 2 is indicated by a punch in the 2 row, and so forth.

Alphabetic characters require *two* punches per card column. By definition, an alphabetic character is composed of a **zone punch**

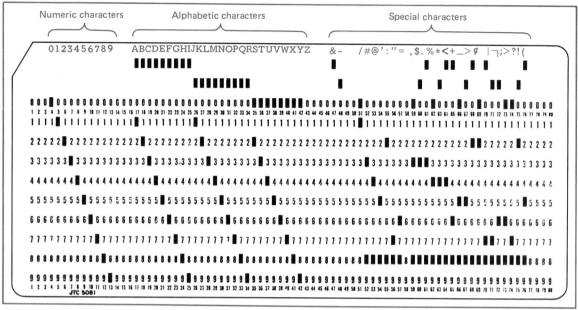

FIGURE 3.3 Alphabetic, numeric, and special characters are punched onto the standard 80-column card.

and a **digit punch.** In Figure 3.3, columns 17 to 42, every alphabetic character is represented by two punches. For example, the character A, in card column 17, is composed of a 12-zone punch and a 1-digit punch; the character B is a 12-zone punch and a 2-digit punch, and so on. The last character, Z, card column 42, is represented by a 0-zone punch and a 9-digit punch.

At this point, we should clarify the dual nature of the zero row. It may be used as a zone punch in the composition of the alphabetic characters S through Z, or it may represent the quantity zero. When used as a number, it appears in the card column alone as a digit punch representing the number 0. This dual use was intentionally designed into the Hollerith code.

An easy way of recalling the code's alphabetic characters is to learn the following table. Using these codes as starting points, you can easily count to the Hollerith code of the desired character.

All other characters in the Hollerith code are grouped together in the category of special characters. Most special characters employ

Character	Punches Used		
	Zone		Digit
A	12	&	1
J	11	&	1
S	0	&	2

Table 3.1   Hollerith Code Configurations for Numeric, Alphabetic, and Special Characters

Character	Hollerith Code, Punches	Character	Hollerith Code, Punches	Character	Hollerith Code, Punches	Character	Hollerith Code, Punches	Character	Hollerith Code, Punches
0	0	A	12 & 1	J	11 & 1	/	0 & 1	&	12
1	1	B	12 & 2	K	11 & 2	S	0 & 2	–	11
2	2	C	12 & 3	L	11 & 3	T	0 & 3	=	6 & 8
3	3	D	12 & 4	M	11 & 4	U	0 & 4	S	11, 3, & 8
4	4	E	12 & 5	N	11 & 5	V	0 & 5	*	11, 4, & 8
5	5	F	12 & 6	O	11 & 6	W	0 & 6	.	12, 3, & 8
6	6	G	12 & 7	P	11 & 7	X	0 & 7	+	12, 6, & 8
7	7	H	12 & 8	Q	11 & 8	Y	0 & 8	>	11, 5, & 8
8	8	I	12 & 9	R	11 & 9	Z	0 & 9	(	0, 6, & 8
9	9							?	0, 7, & 8

three punches per card column. However, a few special characters are coded using one or two punches per column. The ampersand (&) and minus sign (–), card columns 47 and 48, respectively, are examples of special characters represented by one punch per column. Card columns 51 to 57 contain special characters that employ two punches per column, i.e., slash (/), pound sign (#), at sign (@), apostrophe ('), colon (:), and the equal sign (=). The remaining special characters begin in card column 59. Among these characters are the dollar sign ($), question mark (?), percent sign (%), and cent sign (¢).

Table 3.1 presents the Hollerith code configurations for numeric, alphabetic, and selected special characters.

An important point should be stressed here. Every character occupies one card column and is input in that fashion. Each character has its unique code by which the computer recognizes it. This concept holds true for all computer codes.

The Unit Record Concept

The **unit record concept** is a fundamental principle of data processing that was developed many years before computer technology. At one time, data processing depended solely on the punched card. None of today's sophisticated devices, such as CRTs, existed.

Because of the then-existing state of technology, people wanted data relating to one complete transaction to fit onto one 80-column card. As a result, the standard punch card became a unit of measure for all data, just as the kilometer is a measure of distance. Once punched, the card became the *record* of one *unit* of data. This was the basis of the unit record concept.

To illustrate this concept, consider the case of a savings bank that uses punch cards for customer deposits and withdrawals. Figure 3.4 depicts the punch card format used by the bank. Note that a card can contain all the data relating to a complete deposit or withdrawal.

Each customer must complete a deposit or withdrawal slip before being serviced by a bank teller. These slips then go to the bank's data processing center, where data from the slips is punched onto cards. Figure 3.5 illustrates the deposit slip used by a customer and the resulting punched card. The card depicted is a record of the deposit and contains all data relating to that transaction.

**3.2
Card Fields
Numeric,
Alphabetic,
and Alphanumeric
Fields**

A **card field** is a consecutive group of card columns in which data is punched. Carrying this definition one step further, we may conclude that a unit record is composed of series of card fields.[1] Card fields are identified not only by their card columns but by the type of data placed in them (see Figures 3.4 and 3.5).

There are three categories of card fields:

1 Numeric fields
2 Alphabetic fields
3 Alphanumeric (or alphameric) fields

Numeric fields normally contain only numeric data—the characters 0 through 9, the plus (+) or the minus (−) sign, and the decimal point. No other character will be accepted in a numeric field. A common mistake is to include a dollar sign ($) in a dollar amount field; this will cause the computer to reject the data in that field because it is no longer numeric. The integrity of a data field is very important.

Alphabetic fields are composed solely of the characters A through Z. No special or numeric characters may be included in an alphabetic field.

When a combination of alphabetic, numeric, and special characters are included in a field, that field is said to be an **alphameric** or **alphanumeric field.** The two terms are equivalent and may be used interchangeably.

As illustrated in Figure 3.6, each field is identified by a **field name** for easy reference and clear identification against other fields on the card. This makes it unnecessary to refer to the field by its card column numbers. When possible, the field name should represent the data the field will contain. If we used the letter S for the State field (columns 70 and 71), it could be confused with a Sex, Street number, or Supervisor code field. Field names should be easy to understand and fairly self-explanatory. One other point about field names is important. There is no relationship between the size of the field name and the number of columns in the field. The field name *State,* composed of five characters, is perfectly acceptable for a field that is two columns long.

As Figure 3.6 also shows, each field is classified by type. For ex-

---

[1] From subsequent discussions of the other computer media, such as magnetic tape and disk, we will develop a far broader definition of the term *record.* A **record** will be defined as a number of consecutive fields. Generally, the term *record* is applied to most groupings of data, whereas the term *unit record* is usually reserved for use with the punch card.

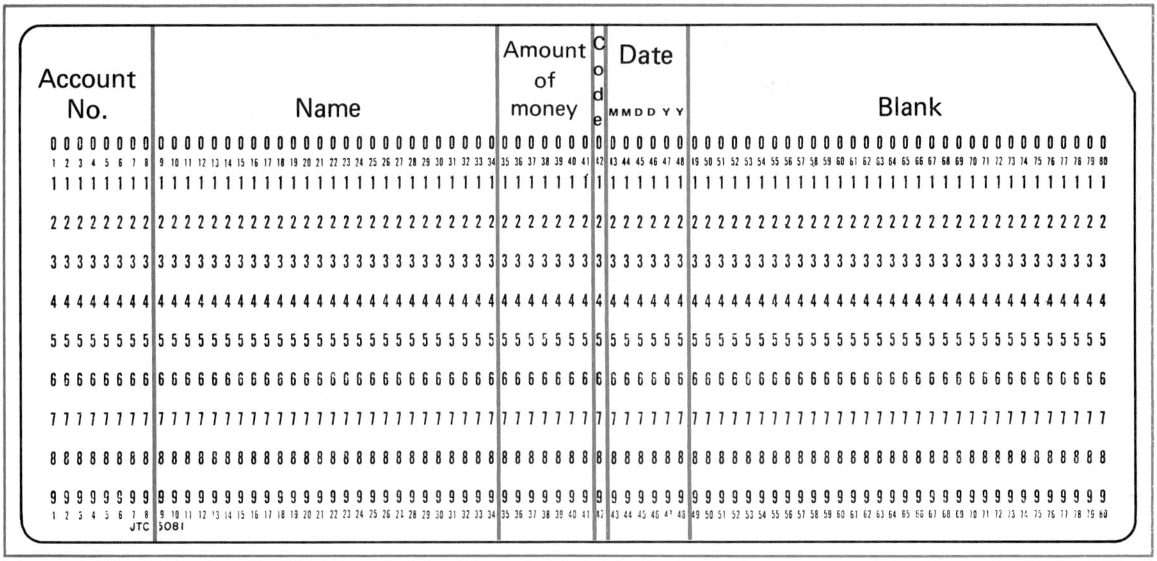

FIGURE 3.4   The unit record for a bank transaction. A code of D or W is placed in column 42 to indicate a deposit or withdrawal. These are the only transactions possible.

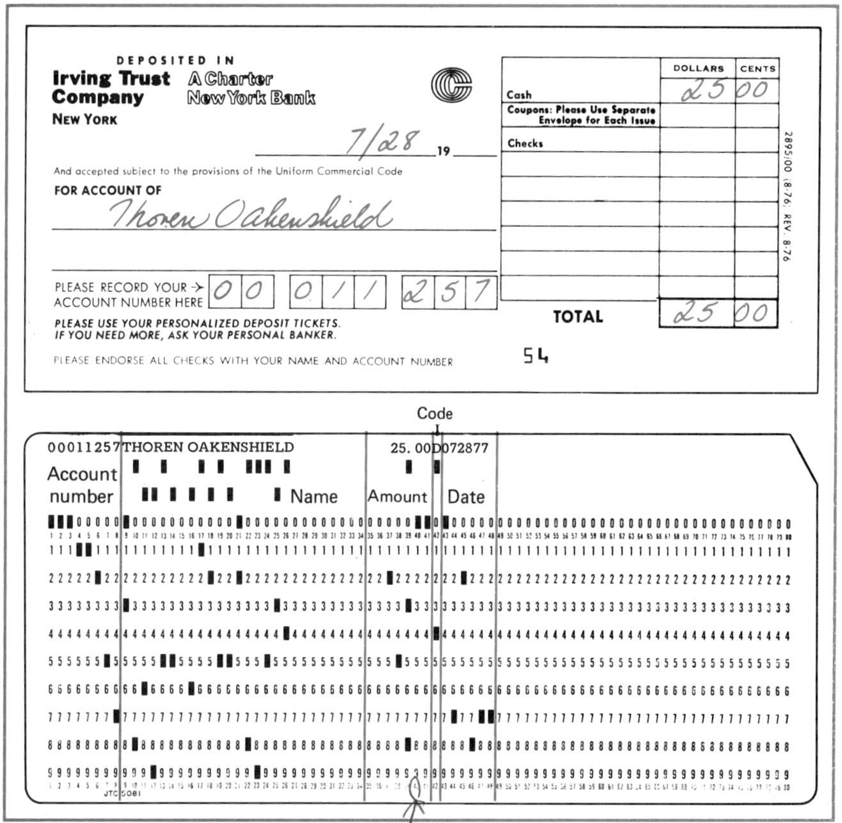

FIGURE 3.5   The deposit slip used by a customer and the resulting punched card.

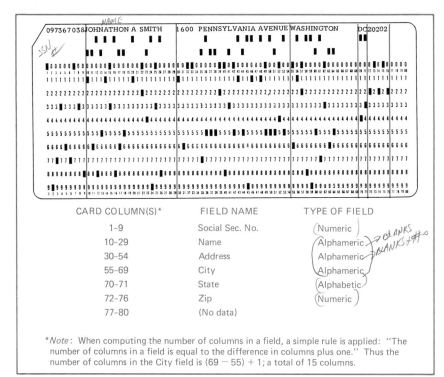

CARD COLUMN(S)*

CARD COLUMN(S)*	FIELD NAME	TYPE OF FIELD
1–9	Social Sec. No.	Numeric
10–29	Name	Alphameric
30–54	Address	Alphameric
55–69	City	Alphameric
70–71	State	Alphabetic
72–76	Zip	Numeric
77–80	(No data)	

FIGURE 3.6 A card format indicating fields, field names, and card columns used.

Note: When computing the number of columns in a field, a simple rule is applied: "The number of columns in a field is equal to the difference in columns plus one." Thus the number of columns in the City field is (69 − 55) + 1; a total of 15 columns.

ample, the Social Security Number field is classified as a numeric field, nine characters long. One might argue that it should be an 11-character alphanumeric field since a social security number contains nine digits and two hyphens (i.e., 999-99-9999), and hyphens, as special characters, should not be punched as part of a numeric field. However, hyphens are used in social security numbers primarily for legibility. The computer requires only the actual nine digits of the number. If the hyphens were punched onto the card, the field would become an 11-column alphanumeric field.

The Name, Address, and City fields in Figure 3.6 are all classified as alphanumeric because data in each may be composed of alphabetic, numeric, and special characters. The State field is defined as a two-digit alphabetic field because the Postal Service has a two-character alphabetic code for each state. Because of similar postal rules, the Zip Code field is currently defined as a five-digit numeric field.

Subdivision of Fields

In Figure 3.6, the Name field is defined as a single field of 20 columns. In data processing, fields are frequently defined by an overall name, then subdivided for ease of processing. Figure 3.7 presents part of a punch card with this type of subdivision.

We can conclude from Figure 3.7 that the overall Name field is

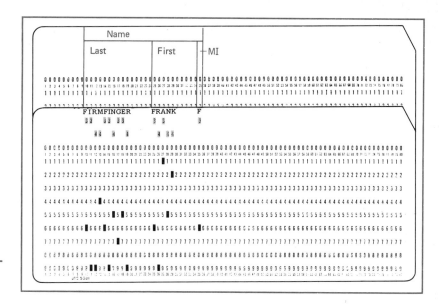

FIGURE 3.7 The subdivision of a field into its component subfields.

defined by columns 10 to 35 and is divided into three smaller *subfields,* as follows:

Columns	Field Name	Field Contains
10–24	Last	Firmfinger
25–34	First	Frank
35	MI	F

These minor fields permit programmers greater flexibility in preparing outputs, especially for printed reports. The programmer can use the entire Name field or any one of the three subfields. The programmer may decide to print a report using, for example, only last names.

The use and subdivision of data fields ordinarily depends on the computer language and the programmer's needs. Not all outputs require subdivided data fields, and some computer languages do not permit subdivided fields, requiring that each data item be defined as a separate entity. The programmer must match the problem at hand against the language to be used.

Documentation

Whenever fields are defined, the data processor must carefully record the field names and respective card columns used. Accurately recording this data in program or system documentation is a prime responsibility. **Documentation** is any paperwork or form used to record input, processing, or output information.

Documentation is important, but it is often bypassed for the sake of expediency. However, many data processing organizations are growing increasingly aware of its necessity. Adequate documentation coordinates all parts of the data processing operation. Without it, there is chaos.

Every individual is responsible for accurately recording essential data in every project he or she works on. Most data processing professionals can recall at least one experience in which needless hours were spent investigating an undocumented program change.

**3.3
The 96-Column
Card**

The **96-column card,** originally introduced with the IBM System/3, is now used with the IBM System/38 Series of small business computers. They use the 96-column card much as other computers use the 80-column card. As illustrated in Figure 3.8, the 96-column card is physically smaller than its Hollerith counterpart. The two cards also differ in how they represent data. The 80-column card uses the Hollerith code, but the 96-column card uses a code called **binary coded decimal (BCD).** Binary coded decimal is very different in structure and appearance from the Hollerith code. These differences are visible if you examine the format of the 96-column card.

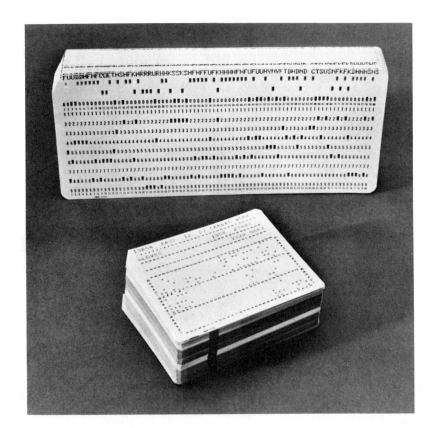

FIGURE 3.8 The 96-column punched card is less than half the size of the standard punched card. (*IBM.*)

Binary Coded Decimal (BCD)

The 96-column card represents data in three rows of 32 columns each. Each row is defined as a *tier.* Character codes are punched into any one of the three tiers, and the printed character appears at the top of the card. The punches on the 96-column card are circular, not rectangular as with the Hollerith code. Data is punched onto the 96-column card column by column, but the binary coded decimal code employs a different row structure. Each tier is composed of six rows individually defined as **bits.** These bits are read sequentially as the B bit, A bit, 8 bit, 4 bit, 2 bit, and 1 bit. The bits are normally depicted vertically or horizontally (left to right), as shown. The 96-column card uses the vertical format, with all six bits representing one character.

The configuration of six bits is broken into two groups equivalent to the zone and digit punches of the Hollerith code. The B bit and A bit represent the zone punches, and the digit punches are defined by the 8, 4, 2, and 1 bits. Table 3.2 illustrates how the B and A bits are used to construct the equivalent of zone punches and the 8, 4, 2, and 1 bits are positioned to represent digit punches. These relationships are important because they will provide the basis for our development of the BCD codes for alphabetic and numeric characters.

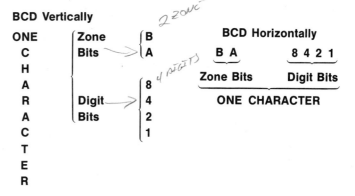

Note in Table 3.2 that the BCD equivalent of the 12-zone punch is a B bit *and* an A bit. However, the BCD equivalent of an 11-zone punch is a B bit with *no* A bit, and a zero-zone punch is only an A bit. The No Zone equivalent uses neither the A nor the B bit; it is used when con-

Table 3.2 BCD Equivalent of the Hollerith Code's Zone and Digit Punches

Hollerith — BCD Zone Bits	Zone Punch			
	12 Punch	11 Punch	Ø Punch	No Zone
B	●	●		
A	●		●	

structing the BCD codes for numbers. For digit punches, the BCD equivalent of a 2-digit punch is a 2 bit only, while a 5-digit punch is a 4 bit and 1 bit. A 7-digit punch is composed of a 4 bit, 2 bit, and 1 bit.

These equivalents will be used to develop the BCD code for alphabetic and numeric characters. The Hollerith code provides an easy frame of reference from which to construct BCD configurations. A simple three-step procedure, using both the Hollerith code and its BCD equivalents, has been developed to assist us. If you are at all uncertain about the Hollerith code, review it before proceeding.

BCD Digit Bits	Hollerith Digit Punches									
	1	2	3	4	5	6	7	8	9	Ø
8								•	•	
4			•	•	•	•				
2		•	•			•	•			
1	•		•		•		•			•

Note: A large dot placed next to any bit indicates it is used in the code. A blank space in a bit position indicates that that bit is not required in the code.

Composing a BCD Character

The following is the procedure for constructing BCD codes for alphabetic and numeric characters:

1   Define the selected character's zone and digit punches.
2   Select the BCD equivalents of the zone and digit punches.
3   Join the zone and digit equivalents (from step 2) to form one complete BCD character.

We can apply this procedure to the alphabetic character A as follows:

1   In the Hollerith code, the character A is composed of a 12-zone punch and a 1-digit punch.
2   In BCD, the equivalent of a 12-zone punch is a B and an A bit. The BCD equivalent of a 1-digit punch is a 1 bit.
3   Combining the BCD equivalents, we derive the BCD code for the character A.

Putting these three steps into pictorial form, we have

Step 1	Step 2	Step 3
The character A in the Hollerith code is	Convert these punches to their BCD equivalents	Combine these equivalents to form one BCD character code.
a 12-zone punch ⟹ which is a B bit and an A bit + a 1-digit punch ⟹ which is a 1 bit alone		B A 8 4 2 1 ● ● ● The BCD code for A

The following illustrates how to develop BCD codes for the characters N and X and the number 6.

ILLUSTRATION 1
The Character N

Step 1	Step 2	Step 3
The character N in the Hollerith code is	Convert these punches to their BCD equivalents	Combine these equivalents to form one BCD character code.
an 11-zone punch ⟹ which is a B bit + a 5-digit punch ⟹ which is a 4 bit and a 1 bit		B A 8 4 2 1 ● ● ● The BCD code for N

ILLUSTRATION 2
The Character X

Step 1	Step 2	Step 3
The character X in the Hollerith code is	Convert these punches to their BCD equivalents	Combine these equivalents to form one BCD character code.
a Ø-zone punch ⟹ which is an A bit + a 7-digit punch ⟹ which is 4, 2, and 1 bits		B A 8 4 2 1 ● ● ● ● The BCD code for X

ILLUSTRATION 3
The Numeric Character 6

Step 1	Step 2	Step 3
The character 6 in the Hollerith code is	Convert these punches to their BCD equivalents	Combine these equivalents to form one BCD character code.
a No Zone punch ⟹ No bits used + a 6-digit punch ⟹ which is 4 and 2 bits		B A 8 4 2 1 ● ● The BCD code for 6

We can conclude from Illustration 3 that the No Zone equivalent in BCD is used for numeric characters as they need no zone punch.

In the illustrations above, the BCD codes were horizontal. On a 96-column card, they are vertical, a change in position only. In all other respects, the uses of 96-column and 80-column cards are the same. Data items are defined by card fields with appropriate field names. Data is punched into any of the 96 columns. However, within a given computer system, the two sizes of card are not interchangeable.

Figure 3.9 presents a 96-column card with the BCD code configuration for all alphabetic and numeric characters. Students can use Figure 3.9 to verify code configurations. Table 3.3 shows Hollerith and BCD codes for alphabetic and numeric characters.

3.4
The
Keypunching
of Data
The IBM 029

The **keypunch** punches data onto any of the 80 columns of a punch card. Students often use the IBM 029 keypunch in preparing their program assignments (Figure 3.10). The 029's keyboard is like a typewriter's and has all the characters in the Hollerith code. Pressing the proper key punches that character of the Hollerith code onto a card, with data entering the card one column at a time.

Verification of
Punched Data

Operators might look over every punched card for errors, but that form of verification is inefficient and economically unjustifiable. Checking the cards would take at least four times as long as keypunching them. Therefore, data processing centers use a device called a **verifier** to

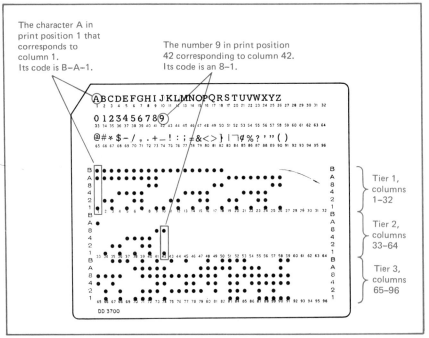

FIGURE 3.9   A 96-column card with alphabetic, numeric, and special characters punched into each of the three tiers on the card. Three lines of print correspond to the three tiers. Note that the character A is in column 1 and is the first character printed on the top line. The number 9 appears in the second tier, column 42, and is the last character printed on the second line.

Table 3.3 Comparison of Hollerith and BCD Codes for Alphabetic and Numeric Characters

Character	Hollerith Code Punches		BCD
	Zone	Digit	B A S 4 2 1
A	12	1	B A 1
B	12	2	B A 2
C	12	3	B A 2 1
D	12	4	B A 4
E	12	5	B A 4 1
F	12	6	B A 4 2
G	12	7	B A 4 2 1
H	12	8	B A 8
I	12	9	B A 8 1
J	11	1	B 1
K	11	2	B 2
L	11	3	B 2 1
M	11	4	B 4
N	11	5	B 4 1
O	11	6	B 4 2
P	11	7	B 4 2 1
Q	11	8	B 8
R	11	9	B 8 1
S	Ø	2	A 2
T	Ø	3	A 2 1
U	Ø	4	A 4
V	Ø	5	A 4 1
W	Ø	6	A 4 2
X	Ø	7	A 4 2 1
Y	Ø	8	A 8
Z	Ø	9	A 8 1
0	No Zone	Ø	A
1	No Zone	1	1
2	No Zone	2	2
3	No Zone	3	2 1
4	No Zone	4	4
5	No Zone	5	4 1
6	No Zone	6	4 2
7	No Zone	7	4 2 1
8	No Zone	8	8
9	No Zone	9	8 1

perform that function. The verifier, Figure 3.11, which is similar in construction and operation to the keypunch, can only *read previously keypunched data;* it *cannot alter* the card. The verifier checks the accuracy of keypunched data before it enters the computer.

The **verification of data** is very important in data processing because erroneous data can have serious consequences. Verification of input data is not limited to card systems. It is also necessary for data directly entered online. Every DP system should have checks on the accuracy of input data.

FIGURE 3.10 The keyboard and control switches of the IBM 029 keypunch. Using this keyboard, the keypuncher can control the punching of data onto an 80-column card. Student programmers often use the 029 to punch their programs onto cards before computer input and processing. (*IBM.*)

When keypunching and verification are performed, the general rule of thumb is never to have one operator both keypunch and verify the same data. The reason is that if the operator misread the data during keypunching, he or she could easily repeat the error during verification. Keypunching and verification of data are extremely important because they are the first tasks before processing.

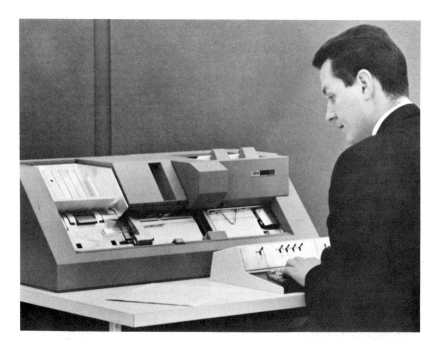

FIGURE 3.11 The IBM 059 verifier, companion device to the IBM 029 keypunch. These devices look alike but function differently. (*IBM.*)

Another kind of check on input data is the **validation of data,** a determination of whether the source document is correct. A clerk should validate data before it is keypunched, right when the source document arrives. Validating data ensures that the source document itself is correct. Consider the following case.

An inventory clerk receives requests for the purchase of inventory items. These requests are converted into punched cards, which will be processed to produce computer-prepared purchase orders. All purchase requests must contain a specific part number for identification. Because many of these numbers are incorrectly specified, the inventory clerk must check the accuracy of each part number listed. The clerk validates these numbers by cross-checking the part number and the part name on a list of all inventory items and supplies correct part numbers for incorrect, partially written, or missing entries. The corrected purchase requests go to data processing for keypunching and verification. Validation ensures that the source document data is correct. Verification ensures that the source document data is correctly keypunched.

Other Keypunching Devices

The IBM 029 and 059, which keypunched and verified card data, have made way for newer keypunching devices that provide special features.

IBM 129

The IBM 129 is IBM's newest keypunch (Figure 3.12). Although it provides more special features than the 029, the major difference between them is their manner of operation. The 029 punches data one card column at a time as each character's key is depressed. The 129 uses an entirely different method.

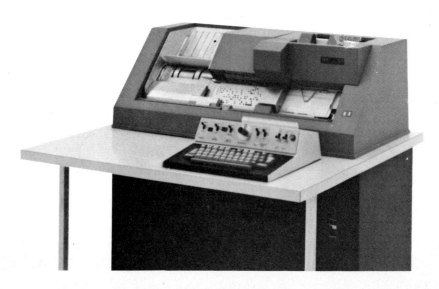

FIGURE 3.12   The IBM 129 not only keypunches but also verifies. The 129 is operationally more complex than the 029 keypunch. (*IBM.*)

The 129 has a magnetic storage area capable of holding 80 characters, the equivalent of one card. All data entered via the 129's keyboard goes into that storage area, and nothing is punched onto a card until all data is input. This procedure reduces card waste and improves operator efficiency.

If the operator of an 029 strikes the wrong key, the incorrect character is immediately punched onto the card. That card must be destroyed and a new one punched. With the 129, an incorrect character enters the storage area but is not punched. To correct the error, the operator backspaces to that card column and rekeys the proper character. The new character magnetically replaces the incorrect character in the 129's storage. When the card is actually punched, only the corrected character appears.

The IBM 129 can also serve as a verifier at the flick of a switch on the keyboard. It therefore may represent significant savings to a data processing department. The 129 also provides a data processing department with operational flexibility. During heavy keypunching loads, all 129s can act as keypunches, an option impossible with the 059s. The 129 can support either 96-column or 80-column cards, although to modify it requires an experienced serviceperson. Most DP organizations buy the 129 already set up as they wish to use it, and most use it for 80-column cards.

The IBM 129 is not the only device that can serve as both a keypunch and a verifier.

FIGURE 3.13   The UNIVAC 1710 is both a keypunch and a verifier. Data entered via the keyboard remains in a storage area until it is punched onto an 80-column card. (*Sperry Univac.*)

UNIVAC 1710

The UNIVAC 1710 (Figure 3.13) can also be used for both keypunching and verifying punched cards. It too possesses an internal storage area into which data is keyed before it is actually punched onto the card. The 1710 is comparable to the IBM 129.

Decision Data 8010

The Decision Data 8010 is designed to handle a variety of card-oriented data processing tasks. It can keypunch and verify and print. During an operation known as **interpreting,** the 8010 reads selected card columns and prints that data on the punch card. Interpreting often highlights specific items of data for easy recognition.

The 8010 has two card hoppers for cards that will be keypunched. These two hoppers make it possible to work on two card files. Cards

FIGURE 3.14 The Decision Data 8010 is more than a keypunch. It can verify punched cards and print data on the surface of the card. The schematic diagram below depicts how an 80-column card is processed through the 8010. (*Decision Data.*)

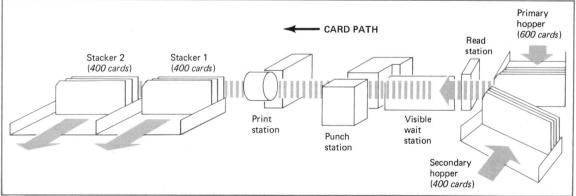

from one file can be inserted into another file and then keypunched. The 8010 uses an internal 80-column storage area during keypunching much like the IBM 129 and UNIVAC 1710. On the 8010, two separate card stackers permit the separation of correctly and incorrectly keypunched cards. The double card hoppers and stackers are unique to the 8010. Figure 3.14 illustrates the 8010 and a schematic of the path that cards take as they are keypunched.

3.5 Punched Card Data Processing
Advantages and Disadvantages

Punch cards are relatively inexpensive compared with other storage media. Cards can be corrected with little effort or expense, card processing devices are relatively inexpensive and easy to use, and operator training requires only a few hours. By comparison, training for more sophisticated devices may take weeks. The advantages of punched cards are cost and ease of understanding. The disadvantages relate to their handling and their slowness.

Punched card data processing requires an area for storage with special storage cabinets, racks, and carts for storing and moving the cards. A few boxes of cards are surprisingly heavy. Cards require a relatively large staff, and their cheapness is often offset by personnel and equipment costs.

The strongest objection to cards, as we have noted, is that they represent one of the slowest forms of processing. Data must always be converted to a card format before it can be processed, a time-consuming task. Cards are well suited for batch processing because data collects over a period of time before processing. This built-in delay allows time for preparing card data. On the other hand, punched cards are ill suited for the processing of data in, say, an online airlines reservation system. Table 3.4 summarizes the advantages and disadvantages of punched cards.

Table 3.4 Advantages and Disadvantages of Using Punched Cards

Advantages	Disadvantages
1 Low cost per card	**1** Storage and handling problems of cards
2 Fewer and less expensive devices used with cards	**2** Slow form of processing
3 Ease of understanding and use	**3** Large data processing staff required for card processing

An Inventory Control System

Consider the case of a company using a card-oriented inventory control system to monitor and control automotive production parts. Each inventory part has a punched card attached to it, with information about that part. Figure 3.15 illustrates one of these inventory control cards. Control cards are attached as the parts enter inventory. When

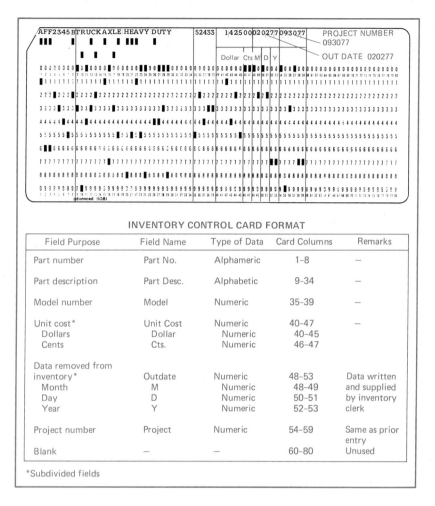

FIGURE 3.15 An example of an inventory control card and the format of data used on the card. Note that the asterisked fields are subdivided: cost into dollars and cents; outdate into month, day, and year.

INVENTORY CONTROL CARD FORMAT

Field Purpose	Field Name	Type of Data	Card Columns	Remarks
Part number	Part No.	Alphameric	1–8	—
Part description	Part Desc.	Alphabetic	9–34	—
Model number	Model	Numeric	35–39	—
Unit cost*	Unit Cost	Numeric	40–47	—
Dollars	Dollar	Numeric	40–45	
Cents	Cts.	Numeric	46–47	
Data removed from inventory*	Outdate	Numeric	48–53	Data written
Month	M	Numeric	48–49	and supplied
Day	D	Numeric	50–51	by inventory
Year	Y	Numeric	52–53	clerk
Project number	Project	Numeric	54–59	Same as prior entry
Blank	—	—	60–80	Unused

*Subdivided fields

each part is issued from inventory, the clerk removes the card and records the date and the project number to which the part is issued.

At the end of the workday, all inventory control cards go to the company's data processing center. The cards go to the keypunch area after the data clerk records their entry into data processing. Data written on the card by the inventory clerk is keypunched onto the same card. The completed cards are verified and stored until they are batch processed on Friday evening.

Batch processing will produce an inventory control report in which all parts are listed by part number. The same inventory data will be used to compile a list of project costs. This report will list each project, the inventory parts used for the project, and the current total expense of that project. The inventory cards remain in the data processing center as a record of when, where, and on what project the part was used. A large storage area has been set aside for that purpose.

This illustration shows that punched cards are most effective for batch-processing operations, with a low volume of activity. Also, cards provide excellent records of all types of transactions. Unfortunately, it is very expensive to maintain an extensive collection of data cards. The costs associated with storing and handling cards often causes people to seek other means of processing data.

Other Types of Punched Cards

The punched card in the inventory control example (Figure 3.15) had both punched data and written data. A **dual card** contains both keypunched and manually coded data and serves two purposes. For example, the dual card can be an employee time card, with the employee's name, social security number, and related job data punched in for ease of identification and subsequent processing. But because the employee's hours may vary, space is provided on the card for the supervisor to record the actual number of hours worked. At the end of the week, the completed time card is returned to data processing, where the handwritten data is punched into the card and used in payroll processing.

Another type of card, popular with utility and public service companies, is the document card. Normally, the **document card** contains data on a total amount of money owed or a summary of transactions. Figure 3.16 illustrates a telephone company's document card showing the monthly cost of phone service. Customers return the document card with payment, and the phone company adjusts their accounts accordingly. The document card and the dual card are directly used in processing.

Credit and charge card companies often use a slightly different form of punch card, called a stub card, when billing their customers. The **stub card** derives its name from the fact that a portion of the original card sent to the customer must be returned with payment of the bill. Data read from the stub is used to update customer accounts. Figure 3.17 shows the stub returned with payment of a utility bill. Usually customers keep the larger half of the card for their records.

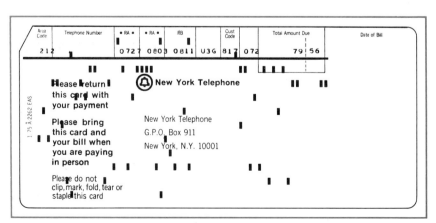

FIGURE 3.16 An example of a document card used by a telephone company to bill customers for monthly service. The customer returns the card with payment.

FIGURE 3.17 The stub portion of an 80-column card from a utility bill. Part of the card is returned with payment, part kept by the customer.

Many students recognize the **mark-sense card** commonly used in computerized tests. Students mark their answers on the card, which is automatically processed. The mark-sense card is convenient for marking tests and creating a computer-acceptable input. An example is shown in Figure 3.18.

A card's use determines its appearance. A monthly billing card, for example, can be both a document card and a mark-sense card. The customer sends in the card and payment and writes on the card the amount paid. This amount may differ from the total due. A clerk verifies the amount paid and pencils it into the mark-sense section of the card. The computer uses the mark-sense-coded figures in processing each customer's account.

Turnaround documents is a term often used for cards which serve as both input and output documents. Initially, they are computer outputs with information for the recipient. Returned, they become inputs for processing.

FIGURE 3.18 An example of a mark-sense card. Answers to quiz questions are penciled onto the surface of the card.

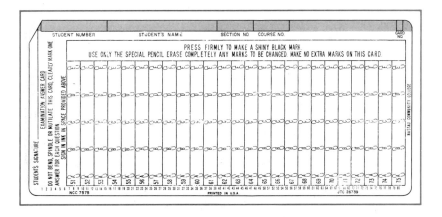

3.6 Electrical Accounting Machines (EAM)

Before computers, people used a group of mechanical devices to process data on punched cards. These devices were called **electrical accounting machines (EAM)** or **unit record equipment.** The latter name came from the equipment's dependence on the unit record (punch card). EAM equipment was crude and slow by current standards, but it provided a reliable and effective form of data processing. Though some unit record equipment is still used today, much is obsolete. We will review its uses for their historical importance.

EAM equipment required that specific data processing tasks be assigned to particular devices. Table 3.5 lists the devices and their uses.

Each unit record device except the sorter was directed by a **control panel,** an example of which appears in Figure 3.19. The sorter was controlled by its operator. The control panel was placed directly inside the unit record device, and the complexity of its wiring depended on the operation to be performed and the EAM equipment. This wiring was a preliminary form of programming, in that each wire could be considered part of an instruction for processing. By moving the wires, the operator could direct the EAM devices to perform various tasks. Let us discuss the coordinated use of EAM devices in an inventory application.

Examine the use of these devices in the context of the following example. You must process 1000 inventory cards with the unit record equipment at your disposal. Use the following operational sequence:

1 Using the sorter, put the inventory cards into ascending numerical order by code number.
2 With the reproducer, create a duplicate set of the original 1000 cards.
3 With the collator, merge the original set of cards with an existing card file.
4 Using the interpreter, print data on the duplicate set of cards.
5 Process the duplicate set of cards through the accounting machine and print the results.

A pictorial overview of these tasks appears in Figure 3.20.

The original 1000 inventory cards have been keypunched and verified but are not in order. The EAM device that will put them in ascending numerical order is the **sorter.** First, one card field must be defined

Table 3.5 Operational Capabilities of Unit Record Devices

Device	Uses
Sorter	Sorting cards and placing them in numeric or alphabetic order
Reproducer	Gangpunching and reproducing groups of cards
Collator	Handling card files
Interpreter	Printing data on cards
Accounting machine	Performing arithmetic computations, the only device capable of printing information on paper

FIGURE 3.19 A control panel used with unit record devices. The operator wired the panel, which represented a crude form of programming. The complexity of the wiring corresponded to the job being programmed. (*IBM.*)

as the **sort field,** that is, the field on which the cards will be sorted. The group of 1000 cards will be sorted by code number, a six-digit numeric field, chosen because it is the basis of the file into which these cards will be merged.

Sorting proceeds column by column in the sort field. Because the code number field occupies columns 1 to 6, the sorting will begin at column 6. The data will be sorted one column at a time until column 1 is reached. When column 1 has been sorted, the entire group of 1000 cards will be arranged in ascending order, from the lowest to the highest code number.

The operation calls for the creation of a duplicate set of 1000 cards. The original set will be merged into a large file and the duplicates used for day-to-day processing. If anything happens to a duplicate, the original will be available. The EAM device that punches many cards is the **reproducer.** It will duplicate the original 1000 cards in about 4 minutes. Keypunching them might take up to 2 days. Reproducers can quickly reproduce any quantity of cards.

The reproducer can also gangpunch. **Gangpunching** is punching the same data onto many consecutive cards. Suppose we wanted to punch the date of processing onto the 1000 cards. Keypunching would be too expensive. The reproducer, however, could gangpunch the date in minutes.

The duplicate cards must be merged into an existing inventory card file. The **merging** of cards is accomplished with the **collator,** a high-speed card-filing device. It inserts each original card into its

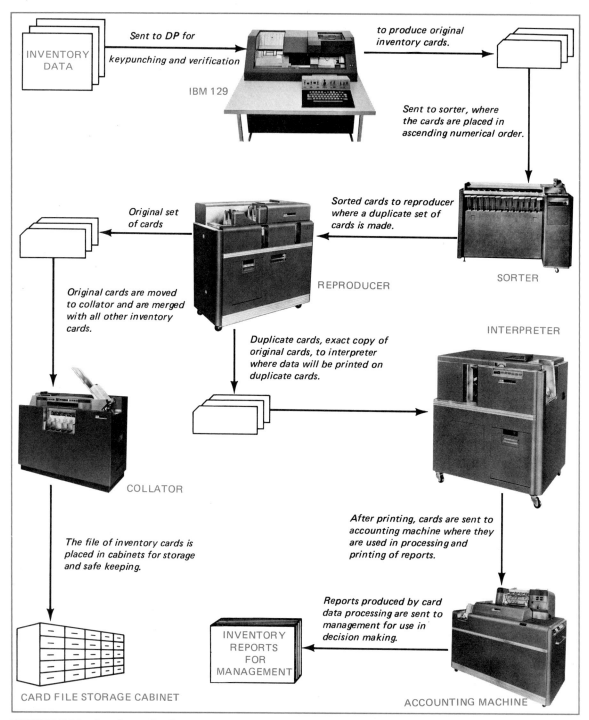

FIGURE 3.20 A schematic diagram of the flow of inventory data through a card data processing system and the unit record equipment used to process the data. (*IBM.*)

proper place in the file. The resulting group of cards represents a completely ordered card file.

The collator can also match, match-merge, and sequence-check, operations illustrated in Figure 3.21. **Matching** involves two related card files. The collator sequentially searches both files for cards common to both. Matched cards are removed and separated into respective groups (Figure 3.21B). **Match-merging** combines the merging and matching operations into one task. Two card files are matched, and the matched cards are merged into one group. Match-merging produces three card groups, as Figure 3.21C shows. **Sequence checking** ensures that cards in a file are in order. The collator reads through a file and checks the position of each card. It identifies out-of-sequence cards, which may then be properly placed. Figure 3.21D illustrates sequence checking.

FIGURE 3.21   Diagrams of the card-filing operations that can be performed with the collator.

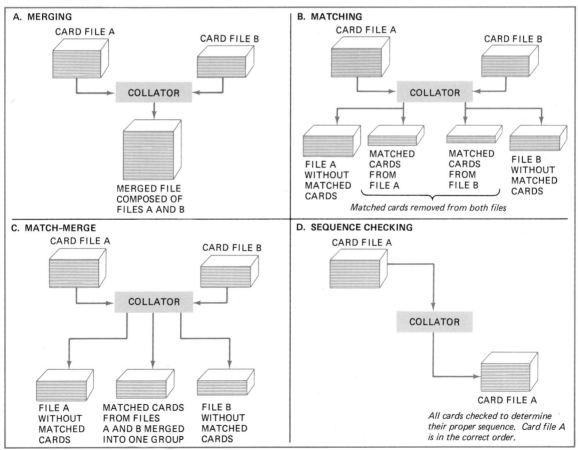

After the original cards are merged into the main card file, the processing of the duplicate 1000 cards may continue. They are exactly like the originals except that no printed data appears on them. Because they cannot be checked visually, the 1000 duplicates will be processed through the **interpreter,** an EAM device which prints data on a card. The printed data is read directly from the card as it passes through the interpreter. The interpreter can print only 60 characters across the card because its characters are wider than keypunch characters. To print the contents of an entire card, 80 columns of data, interpreters print from 2 to 25 lines on the card, depending on the model. Figure 3.22 compares an interpreted card, a keypunched card, and a reproduced card. Note that the interpreted characters are wider than the keypunched characters and that no characters appear on the reproduced card. Interpreting card data lets us highlight specific data fields.

The **accounting machine** provided the calculating and printed-report capabilities of EAM equipment. It could read data from a card, do arithmetic, and print the results. The accounting machine would print a report of data on the inventory cards in the example above.

From this illustration, we can derive two major points:

1 Each unit record device depends on the standard 80-column card.
2 These devices use data read directly from the card during processing.

Each of the devices served a specific function in the handling of card data. Each device performed the single task for which it was designed. This concept is being carried forward to the design of future hardware.

Again, let us place the use of EAM equipment into perspective. These devices, though crude by today's standards, filled a critical data processing need, when no other DP equipment was available. Operational concepts introduced within card processing systems were refined and improved as new computer hardware was developed. For example, the idea of sorting data prior to processing was conceived during card-handling operations. The advent of the computer greatly speeded and simplified the processing of a sort. The merging of two data files falls into the same category. The merging of card files served as a stepping stone to the computerized merging of two files. What changed was the vehicle for performing the merge, not the concept behind the operation.

Ideas developed during card processing operations were sound; however, the technology to provide a faster means of processing that data did not exist. This type of situation has frequently occurred in the evolution of data processing. Ideas had to wait until the technology necessary to convert that idea to reality was available. It is often necessary to examine prior technological achievements in terms of their contributions to future advancements in computer technology.

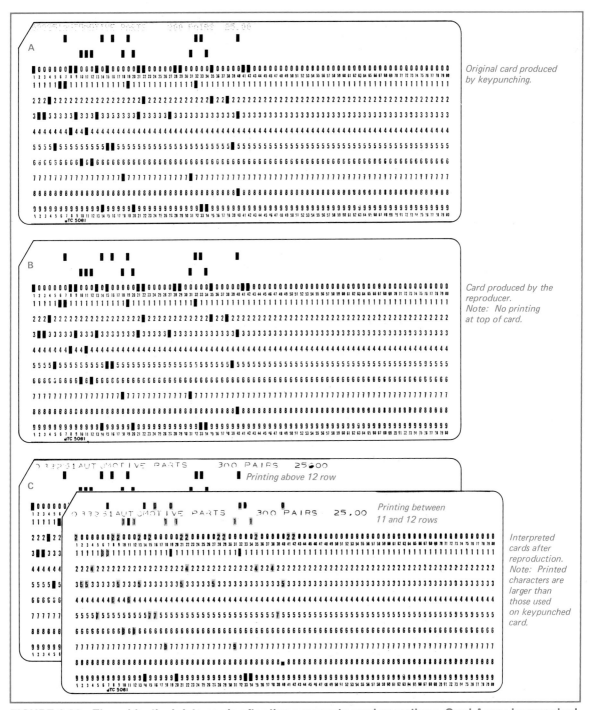

Original card produced by keypunching.

Card produced by the reproducer.
Note: No printing at top of card.

Printing above 12 row

Printing between 11 and 12 rows

Interpreted cards after reproduction. Note: Printed characters are larger than those used on keypunched card.

FIGURE 3.22 Three identical data cards after three separate card operations. Card A was keypunched. The printing on the top of this card was provided by the keypunch device. Card B came from the reproducer and has no printing. Card C is a reproduced card that has been interpreted. The printed characters appear above the 12 row and between the 11 and 12 rows. Interpreted characters are wider than characters printed by keypunching and therefore more legible.

Case Study One

Construction Firm Builds a Better System

In 1978, a West Coast construction firm, Saffell & McAdam, decided to computerize its accounting operations. The firm had used accounting machines since 1972, but these could not provide the on-the-spot data critical to the ever-changing construction industry. During peak work periods, the accounting machines could not provide reports, financial papers, or construction cost data. Management constantly found itself without the information needed to make decisions. Saffell & McAdam was at a serious disadvantage compared with its competitors.

Once they decided to convert, S&M allowed 3 months to evaluate various computer systems. They evaluated hardware, software, service, and overall support for a construction company's DP needs. S&M also wanted to maintain current personnel costs. The Basic-Four business computer was installed in January 1980 with no increase in the accounting staff. The simple system allowed the three-person staff to get on-the-job training. The cost of retraining was a minimum, and the ordinary flow of data continued. S&M could not afford to shut down during the conversion.

The Basic-Four had a line printer and 2 CRTs for input and output. These devices eliminated computer cards; data went directly into the system via the CRTs. The computer handled accounts payable and receivable, payroll, cost files, project estimates, cash flow analyses, and financial statements. Its files permitted any program to draw and report on commonly held data.

S&M management has noted increased productivity since the computer installation. Data is at their fingertips, and they can respond to dynamic situations quickly. They have saved many dollars by monitoring cash flow, dollars which they have been able to spend on critical aspects of projects under construction.

Summary

The following major points have been presented in Chapter 3:

Point 1   The standard punched card has 12 rows and 80 columns. Each card column contains the equivalent of one character. All 80 columns on the card may contain data. The zone rows are the 12, 11, and 0 rows. The digit rows are the 1 through 9 rows. Punches in these rows are called zone punches and digit punches, respectively.

Point 2   The Hollerith code can be punched into any of the 80 columns on the standard punch card. It uses a unique set of punches for each character. Numeric characters require only 1 punch per column. Alphabetic characters use 2 punches per column. Special characters may use 1, 2, or 3 punches per column.

Point 3   Punched cards use the unit record concept, the principle that each card is a record of one complete unit of data.

Point 4   Data is keyed onto cards in groupings called card fields. A card field is a consecutive group of card columns used to contain specific information.

Point 5   All work related to the creation and

Case Study Two

Going Online Helps
School District Disperse Data

For years, Michigan's Washtinaw Intermediate School District (WISD) used computer cards to handle its data processing. Financial data was keypunched at each district school and taken to WISD's computer by courier, an inefficient and costly procedure.

At WISD's data processing center, the hand-delivered cards got priority treatment. It took several hours to process them and return them to each school. Another drawback was that corrections were made only after the outputs were examined. The system's inability to correct errors immediately and the delay in processing cards led WISD to a new data processing method.

Dave Classon, WISD's director of computer services, felt that a new computer system and telecommunications could process the district's data rapidly. After open bidding, WISD selected a computer system that would permit data entry and telecommunications operations. Datapoint 1500 computers were purchased for each district office, each system equipped with disk support, a CRT, a unit to handle telecommunications, and a line printer. Each computer was connected via

telephone to the main computer at WISD headquarters. The main computer, an ITEL AS-4, could interact with each district's 1500 system and process telecommunicated data.

Each district's data is now keyed directly into the Datapoint 1500 at the district office. Data on each district can be handled by the 1500 or sent to the main computer. Data processing is now immediately available and flexible. Corrections are quick and easily handled. With the new computer, critical financial data can be distributed to district administrators immediately.

The WISD system can process financial, budget, payroll, and accounting data and monitor the payments made by each school district. The WISD system supports the needs of over 66,000 students and 11,000 employees. Savings attributed to the new system include the elimination of courier services and related expenses, higher productivity by data processing employees, improved distribution of funds, better management of tax dollars, and general improvement of district services.

Consider this . . .

Do you think that it is advantageous for remote offices, within the same company, to be connected by computer? Should they be able to share information? How might this benefit the whole organization?

use of card fields must be recorded. Proper documentation ensures that each field is correctly identified and contains the appropriate type of data.

Point 6 The 96-column card is a punched card that employs the binary coded decimal (BCD) code. BCD uses a configuration of six bits—B, A,

8, 4, 2, and 1. The B and A bits are the equivalent of zone punches; the 8, 4, 2, and 1 bits are equal to digit punches.

Point 7 The IBM 029 can only keypunch. Cards punched by the 029 are verified by the IBM 059. The UNIVAC 1710 and IBM 129 are devices capable of both keypunching and verification. Each has an internal storage area into which data is keyed. The Decision Data 8010 can keypunch, verify, and interpret card data.

Point 8 Other forms of the 80-column card are the dual card, document card, stub card, and mark-sense card. The dual card can have both keypunched and handwritten data. The document card normally indicates a total figure due and is returned with payment. The stub card includes a portion that is detached and returned with payment. The mark-sense card has data coded onto its surface, that are used in processing.

Point 9 EAM devices used in processing card data are the sorter, reproducer, collator, interpreter, and accounting machine. These devices use 80-column cards. The sorter places card files in sequential order. The reproducer duplicates card data and gangpunches data onto cards. The collator is a high-speed card-filing machine capable of merging, matching, match-merging, and sequence checking. The interpreter reads cards and prints that data on its surface. The accounting machine can perform arithmetic operations and print card data in report form.

Glossary

Accounting machine The unit record device that performs arithmetic operations and produces printed reports.

Alphabetic characters The characters A through Z.

Alphabetic field A data field composed of only the alphabetic characters A through Z.

Alphameric field A data field in which alphabetic, numeric, and special characters are accepted.

Alphanumeric field See alphameric field.

Binary coded decimal (BCD) The computer code, used with the 96-column card, that represents data in terms of 6 bits—B, A, 8, 4, 2, and 1.

Bits The 6 units composing the BCD code: the B, A, 8, 4, 2, and 1 bits.

Card field A consecutive group of card columns into which data is punched.

Collator The unit record device that is used to perform the card-filing operations of merging, matching, match-merging, and sequence checking.

Column Any one of the vertical areas on the 80-column card: only one character is punched into one card column.

Control panel The unit wired to control the operation of a unit record device.

Digit punches Punches placed in rows 1 through 9 on the 80-column card.

Digit rows Rows 1 through 9 on the 80-column card.

Document card A type of punched card that contains data relating to a summary or total amount; serves as an output document; regularly used in customer billing applications and returned with payment.

Documentation Any of the paperwork and forms that are completed to describe a data processing task.

Dual card A type of punched card on which data is keypunched and manually recorded.

80-column card A punched card composed of 80 columns of data using the Hollerith code, employed with the majority of data processing operations; also called the Hollerith card or the standard punched card.

Electrical accounting machine (EAM) Another term applied to unit record equipment.

Field name   The word or words used to identify a data field.

Gangpunching   An operation, performed by the reproducer, in which the same data is consecutively punched onto a series of cards.

Hollerith code   The computer code employed with the 80-column card, composed of punches made in the 12 rows of the card.

Interpreter   The EAM device used to interpret data on punch cards.

Keypunch   The device employed to punch data onto 80-column cards.

Mark-sense card   A type of punched card on which data is manually recorded for subsequent computerized processing; commonly employed in educational testing.

Matching   An operation, performed by the collator, in which two card files are read through and the cards that are common to both files are removed.

Match-merging   An operation in which two card files are matched and the cards found common to both files are merged into one file.

Merging   An operation, accomplished on the collator, in which two related files are combined into one file.

96-column card   A punched card, smaller than an 80-column card, capable of containing 96 columns of data using the BCD code.

Numeric characters   The characters 0 through 9.

Numeric field   A data field composed only of numeric characters.

Record   A unit of data composed of a series of fields.

Reproducer   The EAM device used to perform reproduction and gangpunching operations on a group of cards.

Rows   The 12 horizontal areas on the 80-column card, referred to as the 12 row, 11 row, 0 row, and 1 through 9 rows.

Sequence checking   An operation, performed by the collator, in which a file is read through to determine if all cards in the file are in the correct sequential order.

Sort field   The field used to order a file in a sorting operation (i.e., a personnel file sorted in ascending numerical order by social security number uses that number as the sort field).

Sorter   The unit record device used to order a group of cards in numerical or alphabetic sequence.

Special characters   The remaining characters in the Hollerith code that are not numeric or alphabetic.

Standard punch card   The 80-column card.

Stub card   A type of punch card that has a portion, containing customer data, that is to be returned with payment.

Unit record concept   The basic principle concerning the use of punched cards: the card is a *record* of one complete *unit* of data.

Unit record equipment   The group of data processing devices that employ punched cards.

Validation of data   An operation performed to check whether the correct data has been coded into computer-related media, usually accomplished prior to the computerized input of data or keypunching of card data.

Verification of data   The process by which keypunched data is checked for accuracy prior to input to the computer.

Verifier   The device, similar to the keypunch, used to check the accuracy of keypunched data.

Zone punches   Punches found in rows 12, 11, and 0 on the 80-column card.

Zone rows   Rows 12, 11, and 0 on the 80-column card.

Discussion Questions

1 Insert the Hollerith and BCD code configurations for the characters listed below.

Character	Hollerith Punches	BCD Code	Character	Hollerith Punches	BCD Code
A			9		
D			7		
L			3		
O			0		
T			/		
V			=		

2 Discuss the unit record concept.

3 Examine the following list of fields. Identify each field as numeric, alphabetic, or alphanumeric. Estimate the size of the field in terms of card columns, and determine whether the field can be subdivided. If so, note how you would further subdivide that field.

Name	Level of Education
Address	Social Security Number
City	Profession or Job
State	Hours Worked
ZIP	Rate of Pay
Telephone Number	Gross Pay
Date of Birth	Net Pay
Marital Status	Vacation Pay

4 Discuss the importance of documentation to a businessperson or data processing manager.

5 You have been given the responsibility of laying out the format for a punched card. The card is to be used as an input to the processing of the payment of checks to vendors. The following fields are required:

    a Vendor or Company Name

    b Vendor or Company Identification Number

    c Date of Payment

    d Amount of Check

    e Invoice Number

    f A code indicating whether this check is a full or partial payment

Estimate the required size of each field and lay out, column by column, the order in which the fields will appear on the card.

6 Using the card format provided, keypunch the following data onto 80-column cards. Ensure that the data is properly aligned in each field. Left-justify and right-justify all data in alphameric and numeric fields accordingly. Verify the accuracy of your keypunching by visually checking each card. Correct any mispunched cards by rekeying them.

The format to be used:

Card Column	Field Name
1–6	Appliance Number
7–26	Appliance Name
27–31	Weight (in pounds)
32–38	Size (in cubic feet)
39–45	Quantity Delivered
50–55	Date of Delivery

Appliance Number	Appliance Name	Weight	Size	Quantity	Delivery Date
07613	Flat irons	6.0	.72	144	072878
11025	Steam curlers	2.5	4.35	12	093079
26358	Blenders	8.4	14.23	100	053179
34199	Jiffy pizza pans	10.6	9.76	25	082980
51437	Toasters	4.8	2.93	30	102580
67134	Brushes	1.24	1.83	2	121981

7 List and discuss the advantages and disadvantages of using punched cards in data processing.

8 Obtain examples from your personal life of various uses of punched cards, and identify the cards by type (i.e., a document card from a local utility company, a stub card used by a credit card company, etc.).

9 Examine the card below and determine the data punched onto the card.

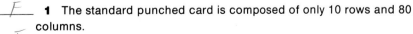

Summary Test

_____F____ **1** The standard punched card is composed of only 10 rows and 80 columns.

_____F____ **2** The digit rows are defined as the 2, 3, 4, 5, 6, 7, 8, and 9 rows.

_____T____ **3** The Hollerith code has a unique code configuration for each character.

_T_ **4** The special character *slash* (/) is composed of a 0-zone punch and a 1-digit punch.

_T_ **5** The alphabetic character T is composed of a 0-zone punch and a 3-digit punch.

_F_ **6** The unit record concept refers to the use of two cards to record the data related to one transaction.

_F_ **7** The verifier is used to punch data onto a card.

_T_ **8** Card processing represents one of the slowest forms of data processing.

_F_ **9** The storage of cards is expensive but does not require large amounts of space.

_F_ **10** The reproducer and the interpreter perform essentially the same function.

_T_ **11** The BCD code configuration for the character G is composed of the B, A, 4, 2, and 1 bits.

_F_ **12** The Decision Data 8010 and the IBM 029 have the same operational capabilities.

_F_ **13** The validation and the verification of data are the same checking procedure performed via the keypunch.

_F_ **14** The merging operation involves the combining of two card files and the selection of card data common to both files.

_F_ **15** The 96-column card can be used on EAM equipment.

_C_ **16** The card type that requires you to return a portion of it with payment is the:

    a Dual card   **b** Document card

    c Stub card   **d** Either b or c

_B_ **17** A five-digit card field used for postal ZIP codes is defined as:

    a An alphabetic field   **b** A numeric field

    c An alphameric field   **d** A letter field

_B_ **18** The gangpunching of cards is performed on the:

    a Collator   **b** Reproducer

    c Interpreter   **d** Keypunch

_B_ **19** The BCD code for the character W is composed of:

    a A, 4, and 1 bits   **b** A, 4, and 2 bits

    c A and 5 bits   **d** A and 6 bits

_A_ **20** The field name assigned to card fields should:

    a Indicate the type of data items the field will contain

    b Have the same number of characters as the length of the field

    c Begin with the same character as the data in the field

    d All the above

_D_ **21** A characteristic of card systems is:

    a Slowness in processing data

    b Using cards as records of transactions

    c Needing a larger DP staff

    d All the above

_B_ **22** The subdivision of fields is:

    a   Always done to give the programmer greater flexibility

    b   Dependent on the programming language used

    c   Never accomplished on fields containing numeric data

    d   All the above

_A_ **23** The checking operation performed on input data is called the:

    a   Validation of data   **b**   Verification of data

    c   Vilification of data   **d**   Control of data

_D_ **24** The EAM device that does not use a control panel is the:

    a Collator   **b** Reproducer   **c** Interpreter   **d** Sorter

_C_ **25** The card type designed to accept the manual entry of data onto its surface is the:

    a   Mark-sense card   **b**   Document card

    c   Dual card   **d**   a or c

Summary Test Answers

1 F	**2** F	**3** T	**4** T	**5** T
6 F	**7** F	**8** T	**9** F	**10** F
11 T	**12** F	**13** F	**14** F	**15** F
16 C	**17** B	**18** B	**19** B	**20** A
21 D	**22** B	**23** A	**24** D	**25** D

Four

Input and Output Devices

FIGURE 4.1 The output of computer-generated information may assume both a visual and printed format. The preparation of technical line drawings is readily accomplished using a device called a plotter. Plotters receive technical data directly from the computer and convert that information into complex line drawings providing valuable data in pictorial form. (STOCK, Boston.)

Purpose of This Chapter

This chapter introduces input and output devices currently employed in the processing of data. The chapter opens with a review of card-oriented devices: the card reader, card punch, and card reader/punch. The difference between serial and parallel card readers is presented.

The chapter then discusses printed outputs; compares impact and nonimpact printers; and reviews chain, band, drum, wire-matrix, daisy-wheel, and color printers. It describes nonimpact printers that use electrostatic, thermal, or jet-ink processes. Devices called plotters are described.

Computer terminals are presented at length. Many types are discussed, including terminals that output data on the screen of a TV-like picture tube, print data on paper, punch data into paper tapes, input data to the computer when a light source is passed across a TV screen, or provide verbal responses to requests for data. The use of intelligent terminals to screen input data is discussed.

The chapter concludes with a discussion of the specialized data processing techniques of magnetic ink character recognition (MICR), optical character recognition (OCR), and computer output microfilm (COM). It also presents the application of micrographics to COM-generated data. Illustrations throughout the chapter provide examples of and describe the devices under discussion.

After studying this chapter, you should be able to

■ Discuss the general use of the card reader, the card punch, and the card reader/punch.

■ Differentiate between a printer, a plotter, and a printing subsystem.

■ Describe the operational differences between impact and nonimpact printers.

■ Briefly discuss the purpose and use of the various types of terminal devices presented.

■ Discuss the purpose and use of intelligent terminal devices.

■ Discuss in general terms the techniques of MICR, OCR, COM, and micrographics.

■ Understand the following terms:

American Standard Code for
  Information Interchange (ASCII)
Audio response unit
Band printer

Bidirectional printer
Card punch
Card reader
Card reader/punch

Cathode-ray tube (CRT)
Chain printer
Computer-assisted instruction (CAI)
Computer-managed instruction (CMI)
Computer output microfilm (COM)
Daisy-wheel printer
Data collection terminal
Data-phone data set
Demodulation
Drum printer
Graphics terminal
Hardcopy terminal
Hardwired
Impact printer
Input/Output (I/O) device
Intelligent terminal
Intelligent terminal system
Light pen display terminal
Line printer

Magnetic ink character recognition (MICR)
Microfiche
Micrographics
Modem
Modulation
Nonimpact printer
Optical character recognition (OCR)
Parallel card reader
Peripheral device
Photoelectric cell reader
Plotter
Point of sale (POS) terminal
Portable data terminal
Printer
Serial card reader
Video display terminal
Voice-input unit
Wire-matrix printer

Introduction

In the previous chapter, we described an inventory system that used punched 80-column cards for processing data. A punched card was attached to each part as it entered or left inventory. The data was batch-processed, with the inherent delay of this processing method. Let us now imagine a different system of processing this same inventory data. This new system is based on teleprocessing, in which terminals tie in with a computer over telephone lines. Clerks use online terminals to monitor the inventory. They do not have to wait for card processing to know what parts are in inventory.

Asked for a part in the new inventory system, the clerk enters the part name and number via an online terminal. The computer searches its files and responds with the location of that part and the quantities currently held in inventory. This data appears on the screen of the terminal in 2 to 3 seconds. The inventory clerk does not have to leave the terminal or physically search through the inventory.

One reason why this inventory system is successful is the use of terminals. Terminals represent one of the most recent advances in computer technology. However, terminals are only one of many types of peripheral devices. The term **peripheral devices** is generally applied to devices attached to the computer to facilitate input and output operations. The terminal device illustrated in Figure 4.2 enables the clerk to enter data on the computer and retrieve information from an

FIGURE 4.2 An inventory clerk enters inventory data. By using a CRT, the clerk can monitor the inventory and in seconds determine the availability of any item in stock. The online access of inventory data increases the speed with which inquiries are handled. (*IBM.*)

inventory system. We will begin our discussions of peripheral devices with those that use the punch card.

4.1 Card-Oriented Devices

The standard 80-column card is widely used, and devices have been developed specifically to handle card data. These devices readily handle the input and output of card data and are an integral component of most computer systems. Examples of three types of card devices are the card reader, the card punch, and the card reader/punch.

Card Reader

The **card reader,** an input device, operates by sensing data coded on the card, in the form of punched holes, as the card passes through the device. An extremely reliable input device, card readers attain average speeds of 900 to 1000 cards per minute.

Card readers are divided into two types by the manner in which they read data. **Serial card readers** read their data column by column, whereas **parallel card readers** sense data row by row. Figure 4.3 shows a serial card reader and illustrates the column-by-column reading of data.

With a serial reader, the card being read proceeds through the device one column at a time, beginning with card column 1. The data in column 1 is read first, then the data in column 2, and so on until the data punched in column 80 is read. As this data is read, it is input directly to the computer.

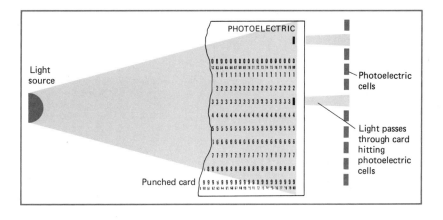

FIGURE 4.3 The card reader is an example of an input device. A Digital Equipment Corporation card reader (model CD11) is shown here. The CD11 is a serial, photoelectric card reader. (*Digital Equipment Corp.*)

Note in Figure 4.3 that a light source enables the machine to read the data punched on a card. The light passes through the holes on the card to strike photoelectric cells that create the codes input to the computer. In the serial reader, one photoelectric cell is positioned beneath the equivalent of each row of the 80-column card. Such card readers are called **photoelectric cell readers.**

The parallel card reader, which reads data row by row, is shown in Figure 4.4. The card enters the parallel reader at either the 9 edge or the 12 edge, and data is read starting with the 9 or 12 row. This reader employs a **brush reader** (a series of metallic brushes) rather than photoelectric cells and a light source. One brush is positioned above each of the 80 card columns. The card being read passes beneath these 80 brushes, which sense data punched on it.

FIGURE 4.4 Parallel card readers read data off punched cards row by row. The three card stackers to the left of this card reader allow it to hold almost 5000 cards at one time. (*IBM.*)

Card Punch

Just as the card reader is only an input device, the **card punch** is strictly an output device for outputting data in the form of cards. For example, the document card representing your monthly telephone bill was probably prepared with a card punch. This device punches data into any of the 80 card columns, normally row by row, at an average speed of 300 cards per minute.

Card Reader/Punch

The device most frequently found in computer systems is the **card reader/punch.** Because it can both read and punch card data, we classify it as an **input and output device** or, simply, an **I/O device.** The card reader/punch is used as follows in the processing of a program: Card data is the input medium for a utility company's monthly billing of customers. Cards containing customer data are input to the computer using the card-reading side of the reader/punch. Data from these cards is used to update individual customer accounts. After each account is updated, a program directs the computer to punch customer data onto cards. This output is accomplished via the punch side of the card reader/punch. The average operating speed of a card reader/punch is similar to that of the individual card devices. The card reader/punch is an alternative to separate card reader and card punch units in one computer system.

Though the shift is away from card processing, cards are still a common I/O medium. Over 5.5 billion cards were sold in 1980. Data processing that relies heavily on cards normally incorporates a card reader/punch or separate card reader and card punches. Some systems have several card readers and punches in order to feed the computer large amounts of card data and speed card output.

Data processing that relies only minimally on cards usually uses a card reader, but not a card punch. The card reader allows the entry of card data when necessary. Serial card readers are most common in such systems because they are faster, cheaper, and offer adequate support.

4.2 Printed Output

We first introduced the output of printed data in Chapter 2, where we discussed the remote job entry terminal. In that example physicians at satellite clinics received printed reports on their patients. The RJE provided printed reports used in the treatment of patients.

This example demonstrated the value of data in a printed, permanent format. Almost every data processing application produces some form of printed report. In fact, many computer systems that use terminals require that all processing be recorded in print. This listing becomes a record of all transactions and a safeguard for both the employee and the company.

Impact and Nonimpact Printers

The most common device for providing the volumes of data printed by the computer is the **printer.** Printers can produce computer reports line by line and are sometimes referred to as **line printers.** All printers, however, are categorized as either **impact** or **nonimpact printers** according to how they physically print data on paper.

Impact printers work like typewriters. A metal slug strikes a carbon ribbon, leaving a character on paper. However, the actual method of printing depends on the type of impact printer.

A common impact printer is the **chain printer** (Figure 4.5). This printer derives its name from the chain of characters used to print data. This chain of characters rotates in front of the 132 positions in which data can be printed. Each of these 132 print positions is represented by an electronically controlled hammer. When the desired character passes directly in front of a print position, the respective hammer is activated. The hammer moves forward and strikes the paper, carbon ribbon, and character on the chain. This leaves the image of the character on the surface of the paper.

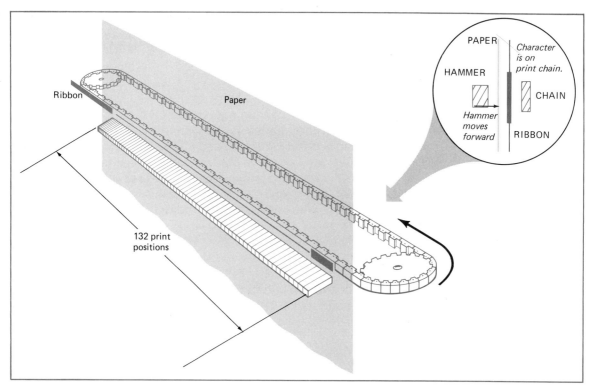

FIGURE 4.5   **A high-speed line printer uses a rotating chain of characters
to print data. The movement of a print hammer creates a character image.**

The figure of 132 print positions on one line is standard for most
languages. A maximum of 144 printed characters per line is possible
with some printers. Chain printers average 600 to 2400 lines per minute (600–2400 LPM).

A new impact printer that works like the chain printer is the **band
printer** (Figure 4.6). It differs from the chain printer largely in the
method of printing. The chain printer derives its name from its flexible
chain of characters. The band printer uses a metal band with characters pressed into it and therefore raised on its surface. These raised
characters strike the carbon ribbon to print. The band printer's bands
are easily changed to allow different character styles. It prints at 75 to
600 LPM.

The band printer, like many other peripheral devices, can diagnose itself. The printer in Figure 4.6 can check its own circuitry and
test for malfunctions. It can determine the type and position of an
error. This self-testing feature of peripheral devices speeds up the entire repair process.

Another impact printer comparable to the chain and band printers is the **drum printer.** The drum printer uses a print drum (Figure 4.7) made of a series of circular bands, one band for each printing position. Each band's surface carries all the characters to be printed. The drum spins in front of print hammers; when the desired character spins in front of the intended print position, the hammer fixes its image on paper. Drum printers may reach speeds of 1600 LPM.

The **wire-matrix printer,** another impact printer, composes characters from a series of dots made by the ends of wires that extend from the printing mechanism. These wires strike a carbon ribbon to form the character's image. Figure 4.8 shows the print mechanism of a wire-matrix printer and the wire ends it uses. The wire-matrix printer is slower than the other printers we have described, although it can print up to 990 characters per minute. It is a reliable, medium-speed, competitively priced device.

The **daisy-wheel printer** is a new kind of impact printer. It was first introduced to replace electric typewriters modified to act as printing devices, but it has since taken on other uses. (See Figure 4.9.) This printer uses a daisy wheel to print data. Figure 4.10a shows two daisy wheels with two types of characters. Output characters are on the

FIGURE 4.6 The band printer is another high-speed printing device, an alternative to the chain printer. (*Data Printer Corp.*)

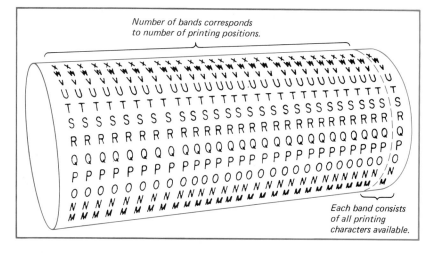

FIGURE 4.7 The Hewlett-Packard 30128A is a high-speed line printer. This drum (impact) printer is capable of printing up to 1600 lines of data per minute. (*Hewlett-Packard.*)

Number of bands corresponds to number of printing positions.

Each band consists of all printing characters available.

outer spokes of the wheel, which rotates the proper character into print position. Daisy wheels are replaceable for changing characters.

The printer in Figure 4.9, the WANG Model 5581WD, has other features. It uses two daisy wheels so that two different print types can be output simultaneously, a feature called *twin-head printing*. Figure 4.10*b* shows how the 5581 mixes mathematical symbols and letters on one document. The Model 5581 operates at an average speed of 40 characters per second.

FIGURE 4.8 The print mechanism of the Burroughs L9500 wire-matrix printer. The impact of wire ends creates a 5- by 7-wire rectangle in which characters are printed. The character image is created when these wire ends strike the carbon and paper. (*Burroughs Corp.*)

FIGURE 4.9 The WANG 5581WD is a bidirectional, daisy-wheel impact printer which simultaneously uses two daisy wheels. (*WANG.*)

FIGURE 4.10 (*a*) Two daisy wheels which may be employed on the WANG 5581WD printer. Changing the daisy wheel varies the type of characters printed. (*b*) An example of printed output from twin daisy wheels on the 5581WD. The document combines scientific symbols and alphabetic characters.

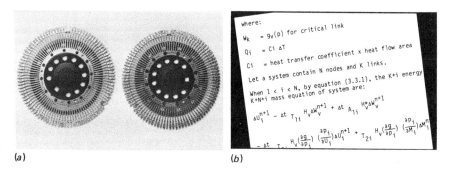

(*a*)   (*b*)

The 5581 is also a **bidirectional printer;** it can print right to left or left to right. Wire-matrix printers generally print left to right and are therefore slower than bidirectional devices.

Technological improvements now allow colored output to be printed. The IBM 3287 Color Printer, Figure 4.11, is a wire-matrix printer that prints in four colors. Color greatly enhances the visual effect of computer-prepared reports and means that colored graphs do not have to be prepared by hand. Color printing techniques are in their infancy and will be more common in the future.

Whereas impact printers require contact with the surface of the

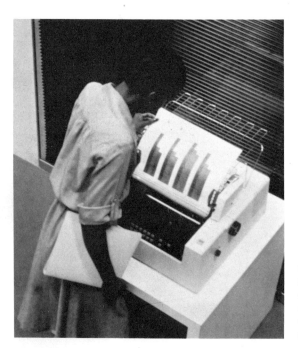

FIGURE 4.11 The IBM 3287 Color Printer produces four-color hard-copy outputs. It can output both graphs and printed reports.

paper, nonimpact printers do not. Nonimpact printers include devices that employ electrostatic, thermal, or special electronic techniques. Electrostatic printers create character images on paper, in much the same way that a duplicating or Xerox machine operates. No object

(a)

FIGURE 4.12 (a) A nonimpact electrostatic printer from the Honeywell Corporation, capable of speeds as high as 18,000 lines of print per minute. In addition, this printer can separate, collate, and stack pages after printing. (Honeywell Corp.) (b) The Silent 700, from Texas Instruments, is a thermal printer. This type of nonimpact printer uses heat to create character images on special paper. (Texas Instruments.)

(b)

ever strikes the paper. Printing is accomplished by the transfer of electronic particles to the paper's surface. Figure 4.12a illustrates a nonimpact electrostatic printer capable of outputting approximately 210 pages per minute. Nonimpact printers have extremely high printing speeds. Some devices can approach 125,000 lines per minute; however, the average speed for nonimpact printers ranges between 6400 and 21,000 printed lines per minute.

The Silent 700 (Figure 4.12b) is an example of a thermal nonimpact printer. In thermal printers, the printing mechanism is composed of a series of heating elements. As chemically treated forms pass beneath them, the heating elements are selectively activated to form character patterns on the heat-sensitive paper. As the heat intensifies, the patterns turn black and create the character images. Essentially, the characters are burned onto the surface of the paper. Thermal printers have printing speeds that range from 100 to 2200 characters per second, depending on the device and manufacturer.

One of the most interesting nonimpact printing techniques is used by the IBM 6640 document printer (Figure 4.13). The IBM 6640 is an offline printing device that employs an ink-jet technique in which tiny droplets of electronically charged ink are directed to the paper to create character images. The ink supply is contained in a replaceable cartridge that holds enough ink for 4 million characters. The 6640 can print 92 characters per second. As an offline printer, the 6640 was designed to handle a variety of office printing jobs. It can print letters, address envelopes, and vary the print type used. A magnetic card reader on the 6640 permits the entry of special commands to control the batch processing of printing tasks.

Nonimpact printers are operationally as effective as impact printers. However, each type has its own merits. The nonimpact printer is faster, since no object touches the paper, and quieter. Because of its relatively slower speeds, the impact printer produces a clearer, more crisply printed output. The impact printer can print data on multi-ply paper when more than one copy of a form is required. Nonimpact printers are limited to producing only a single copy of any output. Thus, if more than one copy is required, those pages must be rerun. On the other hand, the high speed of the nonimpact printer enables it to quickly produce the required duplicate copies. Table 4.1 provides a comparison of the speeds of both types of printers.

Generally, a printer should reflect the needs of its user. DP centers that print multiple copies at critical, peak periods often choose impact printers. Chain and drum printers are uniquely suited to heavy production tasks. In contrast, wire-matrix and band printers are popular in organizations with a limited hardcopy need. Highly specialized documents that require different type styles can be prepared on daisy-wheel printers.

FIGURE 4.13 The IBM
6640 document printer
is a nonimpact printer
that uses a jet-ink printing technique to create
character images. (*IBM.*)

Table 4.1 A Comparison of Printing Speeds for Impact and
Nonimpact Printers

Impact	Operating Speed	Nonimpact	Operating Speed
Chain	600–2400 LPM	Electrostatic	4000–21,000 LPM
Drum	300–1600 LPM	Thermal	100–2200 characters/s
Band	75–600 LPM	Ink-Jet	30–92 characters/s
Wire-matrix	120–900 characters/min		
Daisy-wheel	40 characters/s		

Nonimpact printers are suited for speed, stylized outputs, or special operating conditions. Electrostatic printers provide a high volume of single copies. Thermal printers offer flexibility with low output levels. Ink-jet printers are offline devices that can handle special office printing tasks. The choice of printer depends on price, printing capability, speed, availability, and compatibility with existing hardware.

Plotters

Illustrations or photos are critical to problem solving in mathematics, civil engineering, mapmaking, and land surveying. These illustrations are made up of a series of continuous, unbroken lines, a type of output a line printer cannot produce. The device that was developed to handle this type of application is the **plotter,** or *graph plotter* (Figure 4.14).

The plotter converts data into a picture. The picture represents a solution that is immediately usable and presents data that may have defied verbal explanation. The plotter is also a valuable tool for examining alternative solutions. Many sets of data can be processed for the same problem, producing markedly different results.

Plotters today print out pen-and-ink drawings as well as electrostatically and dot-matrix produced diagrams. The electrostatic method is like Xeroxing and quickly copies line drawings. Dot-matrix diagrams, which look like wire-matrix outputs, use up to 200 dots per square inch to compose drawings. Plotter diagrams may range from $8\frac{1}{2} \times 11$ inches to 60 inches wide. Some plotters can reproduce on microfilm. Figure 4.14 shows one type of output that plotters can produce. Plotters permit the graphic solution of problems that might otherwise defy analysis, speed the accurate output of data, and relieve workers of laborious manual preparation of diagrams.

Printing Systems

The growing need for computer-prepared outputs resulted in the development of devices that were considerably more than just printers. These printing devices could duplicate, print in varying character styles, and print entire outputs, all at unparalleled speeds. This section examines these devices and the new techniques associated with them.

IBM 3800 Printing Subsystem

The IBM 3800 Printing Subsystem is a high-speed nonimpact printer that provides a data processing organization with operational flexibility. The 3800 Subsystem can provide conventional printed outputs or reports at speeds ranging from 7000 to 13,000 lines per minute. However, this device is especially valuable when special outputs are required.

The IBM 3800 combines laser technology with high-speed electrophotography. A low-power laser creates character images that are electrostatically transferred to paper to produce printed outputs. The

(a)

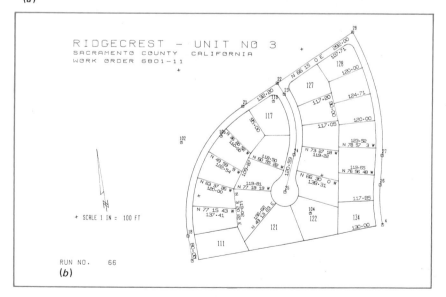

(b)

FIGURE 4.14 (a) Plotters make possible the printing of continuous line drawings. (b) An example of a land survey printed using a plotter. (*Cal Comp.*)

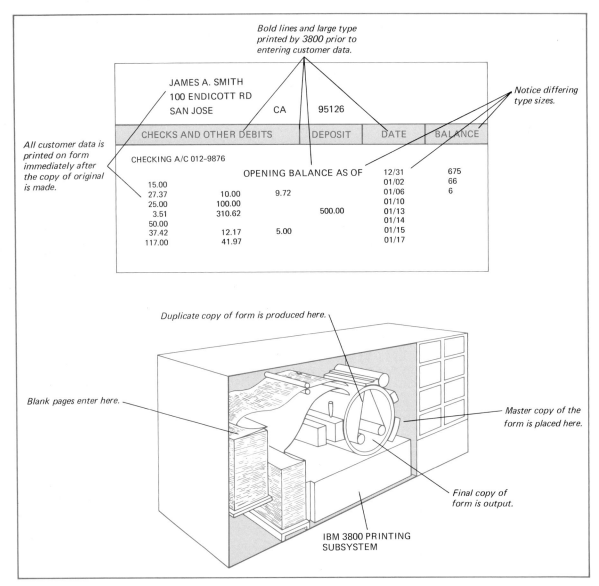

FIGURE 4.15   An illustration of the operation of the IBM 3800 printing subsystem. The 3800, a laser printer, is capable of printing text and duplicating designs on plain paper. Blank paper is originally input to begin the process. After a duplicate of the desired form is made, data is printed on the copy.

3800 can simultaneously print text and create designs on plain paper. This eliminates the need to use expensive, specially treated, pre-printed forms and to maintain a large inventory of paper stock. The

3800 can duplicate any printed format before using it in a printed output.

Consider the case of a credit card company that issues monthly statements to all its customers. At the end of each month, all charge accounts are batch processed. Before the monthly statements are printed, an original copy of a blank statement is placed inside the 3800 and used during the printing of each customer's monthly statement. Printing these statements is a three-step process (Figure 4.15).

First, plain paper enters the 3800. Second, the 3800 converts the plain paper into an exact copy of the original blank statement, complete with all lines, headings, notes, and remarks. Third, the 3800 prints the individual customer's data on the duplicate. It can use several typefaces to highlight important information. The result is a clearly printed statement, ready for mailing. One drawback is that this printer, like all nonimpact printers, can produce only one copy of a form at a time.

Honeywell, Xerox, and Siemens also produce laser printers comparable to the 3800.

WANG Image Printer

The WANG Image Printer, another kind of high-volume device, is more than just a printer. Combining electrostatic and fiber optic techniques, the Image Printer prepares crisp, final documents. It gives a choice of different characters and various page sizes, and it can produce any number of copies.

Fiber optics uses glass wires, thousands of which are bundled together to form cables for transmitting data. These cables can transmit data images at the speed of light without any loss of clarity or accuracy. The data is then electrostatically recorded on paper, and these printed documents, prepared much as a copying machine would produce them, are the Image Printer's outputs. The printed image is composed of thousands of dots, one for each glass strand. The printed characters' resolution is quite sharp. Although the Image Printer is slower than the IBM 3800 Printing Subsystem, it can turn out 18 pages per minute.

The Image Printer is designed primarily for offices rather than for data processing centers with a high volume of printing that might be better handled by an IBM 3800. The Image Printer is often attached to a small business computer, as Figure 4.16 shows, to quickly and directly prepare computer-originated documents. This arrangement speeds the preparation of printed reports considerably.

Consider this use of the Image Printer. A clerk with a CRT retrieves data requested by management from the computer and wants to produce a printed report. In response to questions from the Image Printer, the clerk specifies number of copies, type style and print size, paper

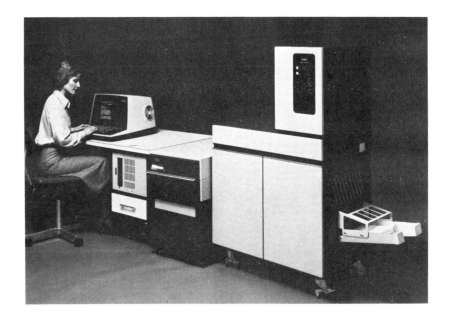

FIGURE 4.16 The WANG Image Printer, on the right, is often connected to a computer to facilitate online data output. Documents prepared by the Image Printer enter the output tray on the right-hand side. (*WANG.*)

size, and other printing factors. The Image Printer automatically prepares the report with no further human intervention.

The Image Printer can also be tied into telecommunications systems. An Image Printer at the receiving computer may be directed to output the incoming data in a particular format and style. This kind of telecommunications is the basis of electronic mail, in which post offices electronically transfer letters. At the receiving post office, a device like the Image Printer converts the message into letter form and puts it in an envelope, a process completed in seconds.

4.3 Terminals

We have seen computer terminals in many of the previous illustrations. In particular, we were introduced to a TV-like device that displays data in characters on its screen. This terminal represents only one of the many types available to facilitate the processing of data.

Before we discuss terminals, we must introduce a device that is an integral part of telecommunications and is used directly with terminals. This device, called a **modem,** converts data into codes that both computer and terminal can understand. The modem takes data entered via the terminal and converts it into impulses that are transmitted to the computer over telephone lines. At the computer's end, a second modem reconverts those impulses into data that the computer can use in processing. The initial conversion of these impulses is referred to as **modulation,** with the following reconversion called **demodulation.** This process is repeated to handle data sent by the computer to the terminal. A complete telecommunication cycle is shown in Figure 4.17.

Modems are available in all shapes and sizes from any number of independent manufacturers. The modem normally operates when tele-

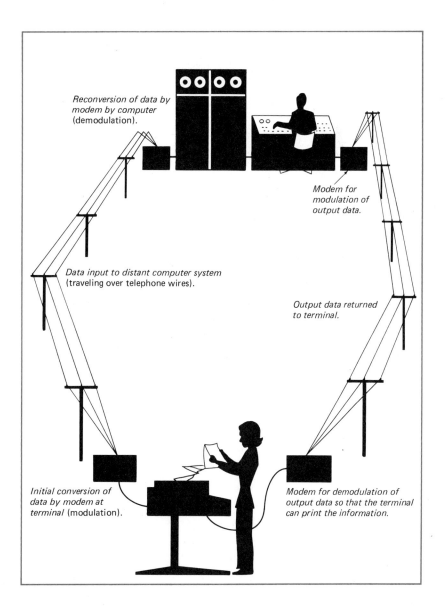

Reconversion of data by modem by computer (demodulation).

Modem for modulation of output data.

Data input to distant computer system (traveling over telephone wires).

Output data returned to terminal.

Initial conversion of data by modem at terminal (modulation).

Modem for demodulation of output data so that the terminal can print the information.

FIGURE 4.17 A diagram of a telecommunication operation in which data is transferred between a distant terminal and the user.

phone receivers are fit into the circular openings on its top. Sometimes, however, the modem is accidentally struck, and the connection is broken. When this occurs, no processing can take place and any data transmitted is lost.

A special type of modem, called a **data-phone data set,** was developed to overcome such problems. It is a combination telephone and modem in which the telephone is wired directly into the modem. Generally, the term **hardwired** is applied to any connection where a line is tied directly into a device (i.e., the telephone line is said to be hardwired into the modem). Hardwiring reduces the possibility of accidental breaks in the data communication to and from the computer. The data-phone data set (Figure 4.18) ensures a secure telecommunications link between terminal and computer, and the integrity of data transmitted via that line. Technology is always attempting to improve the quality of the connection between users and online systems.

Once the modem is properly connected, teleprocessing may begin. Many types of terminals are used in teleprocessing to satisfy specific user needs. The following are some of the terminals currently used.

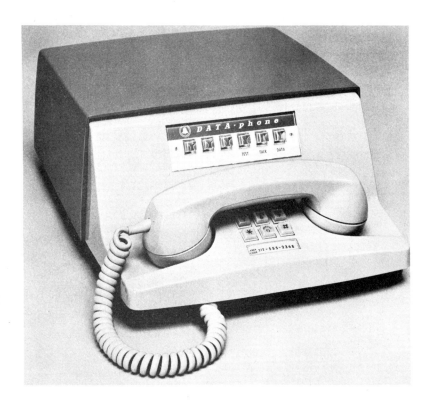

FIGURE 4.18 The data-phone data set, a combination telephone and modem, used to connect the terminal with the computer. (*AT&T.*)

TERMINALS BOON TO HANDICAPPED

Handicapped people, whose lives might otherwise be less productive, can benefit from using computer devices. The computer terminal shown in the accompanying figure was specially equipped to allow James Coops of Islip, New York, to enter data. Though his fingers are paralyzed, Mr. Coops can use the specially adapted terminal and holds a job as a data entry clerk at the local town hall. Mr. Coops would otherwise have difficulty finding work.

(Photo courtesy of Newsday.)

Many other handicapped people have succeeded in the data processing field, especially as programmers. Specially modified peripheral devices have given them the chance to work.

BLOOD BANK USES COMPUTER SUPPORT

The computer terminal pictured here is integral to a blood services plant on Long Island, New York. The plant monitors blood supplies for 262 hospitals in New York City, its northern suburbs, Long Island, and New Jersey. The plant keeps a computerized list of whole blood, plasma, and platelet supplies. With platelets, for example, 800 units must remain on hand. They are critical for transfusions to 250 to 300 area patients undergoing chemotherapy and in danger of hemorrhaging.

One operation uniquely suited to computerization is identification of blood supplies entering the center. Each unit of blood enters with a product code sticker to identify its type (O+, AB−, etc.). These product codes, like those supermarkets use to speed checkouts, show on the right-hand side of the terminal in the photograph. A reading pen is passed over each product code, and the terminal feeds into the computer data on blood type, time, date, source, and any special characteristics. This data is processed against the existing inventory, and the file is updated.

(Photo courtesy of Newsday.)

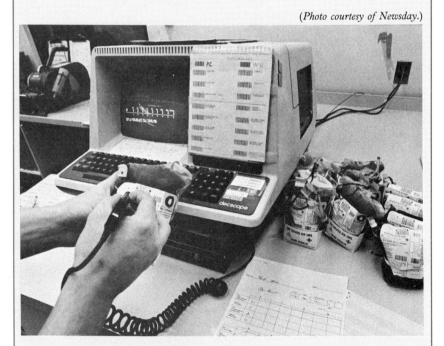

Computerization has speeded up the processing of blood and allowed for the equitable distribution of critical supplies. The computerized analysis of blood use lets the center's staff project potential shortages.

Blood gathering organizations use these projections to spur blood donations.

A blood processing laboratory which also uses a computer to process its data opened in 1980. The online hookup between these two facilities permits the close coordination of blood processing and distribution.

Cathode-Ray Tube (CRT)

A terminal we have previously encountered is the **cathode-ray tube, or CRT.** This terminal derives its name from the fact that data is displayed on the surface of a cathode-ray tube, a TV-like picture tube. Because data appears visually on the screen, the CRT is also referred to as a *visual display terminal.* Figure 4.19 shows one of the many models of CRT available from various manufacturers. The terminal keyboard is used to enter data. As keys are struck, their respective characters appear on the screen, and the user can check the data. Normally, data enters line by line, with each line representing one instruction, statement, or item of data used by the computer.

Data received from the computer appears on the same screen in a

FIGURE 4.19 One of the many CRTs or visual display terminals on the market today. (*Burroughs.*)

format dictated by the program, although it usually appears on individual lines. There is a limit to the number of lines of data that may appear on the CRT screen. This limit varies with each manufacturer and type of terminal. However, once the screen is filled, each new line that appears pushes the topmost line off the CRT's screen.

This last point illustrates one of the drawbacks of softcopy, or visual, outputs. Data pushed off the screen is not immediately accessible. Occasionally, a user wants a printed (hardcopy) version of the data displayed on the CRT. Figure 4.20 illustrates a terminal that couples a CRT with a hardcopy capability. The softcopy output provides a visual reference, and the hardcopy output furnishes a permanent record of the interaction.

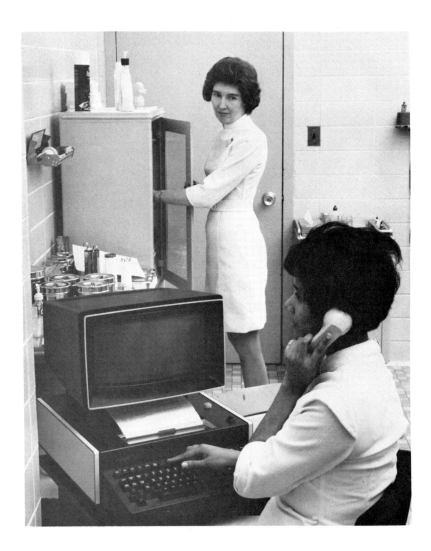

FIGURE 4.20 Nurses in a medical center update patient case history files using a CRT with hardcopy capabilities in the x-ray lab. The printed outputs are attached to the patient's file and are used in diagnosing illnesses. (*Teletype Corp.*)

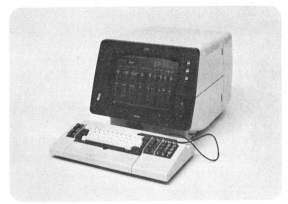

(a)

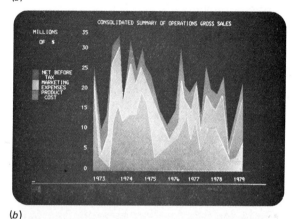

(b)

FIGURE 4.21 (a) The IBM 3279 Color Display Station provides outputs in eight different colors. The 3279 can display character data line by line and highlight data with different colors. (b) The results of data analyses may be displayed directly on the screen of the 3279. Colors help distinguish trends within and categories of data, as identified by the legend. (c) The 3279 can output scale drawings of three-dimensional objects from input data or from the technical analysis of specific factors. (*IBM.*)

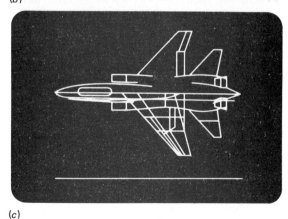

(c)

Some CRTs can now produce softcopy in color. Figure 4.21 shows the IBM 3279 Color Display Station and two kinds of output from it. The 3279 can act as a conventional CRT and display data as characters. It can also segregate data by color to highlight important amounts or totals (Figure 4.21a). The 3279's ability to output data in eight colors is effective in graphic displays. In Figure 4.21b, a summary of sales data appears in several colors keyed to a legend on the left side of the screen. The 3279 can display in color many kinds of business data.

Figure 4.21c shows a different kind of display, a three-dimensional drawing of an aircraft in flight. Such outputs are often prepared from computer-generated data for aeronautical engineers who want to evaluate particular flight characteristics. **Graphics terminals** are CRTs that provide graphic data displays like those in Figure 4.21b and c. These examples show how flexible terminals can be.

Hardcopy Terminals

Some terminals provide only a printed output; these are called **hardcopy terminals.** Their outputs provide a permanent record of processing performed via the terminal. A printed record of this type is particularly helpful to student programmers, because they can refer to it and monitor the corrections made to their programs.

Two common hardcopy terminals appear in Figure 4.22. Each has a keyboard for data entry and, like a typewriter, prints one character at a time. Some hardcopy terminals, like the one in Figure 4.22a, can print up to 900 characters per minute. That terminal is a wire-matrix device, but cannot punch paper tapes. The terminal shown in Figure 4.22b prints like a typewriter and can punch paper tapes, like the one shown in Figure 4.22c.

The code punched onto the tape is the **American Standard Code for Information Interchange (ASCII).** ASCII is a universally accepted computer code and is used in virtually all terminal devices.

Paper tapes are used to store data or programs slated for use via terminals. For example, student programmers may wish to punch onto paper tapes the computer programs that are repeatedly used in their studies. Each time a particular program is needed for processing, the desired paper tape can be input to the computer via the terminal.

We should point out that not all hardcopy terminals can punch paper tapes, a feature used only when suitable. Paper tapes are frail and cannot be repunched, two real limitations.

The use of hardcopy terminals is not restricted to computer centers or student programming labs. A special type of hardcopy terminal, shown in Figure 4.23, can be carried into any office or phone booth to conduct telecommunications operations with a computer. The device pictured is a **portable data terminal,** a combination terminal and modem. As long as a telephone is nearby, its user has access to any of the data files in the computer system. Consider the flexibility this terminal offers to a traveling salesperson, a civil engineer on a construction site, or a businessperson who wants to analyze last year's sales and project their effect on the current market.

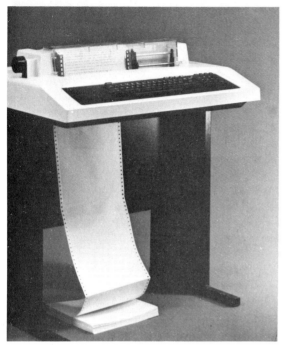

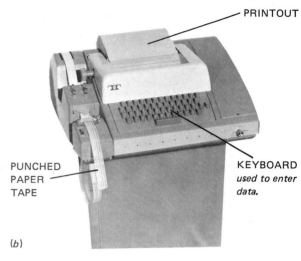

PRINTOUT

PUNCHED
PAPER
TAPE

KEYBOARD
*used to enter
data.*

(*b*)

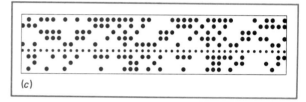

(*c*)

(*a*)

FIGURE 4.22 (*a*) One type of hardcopy terminal often found in student programming labs. (*Digital Equipment Corp.*) (*b*) A hardcopy terminal, which provides a printed output. (*c*) Output and input of punched paper tape are also possible with this type of terminal. The ASCII code is used on the tape. (*Teletype Corp.*)

FIGURE 4.23 A portable data terminal that may be carried into any office and used to access files of computer data via telecommunications. (*Texas Instruments.*)

**Light Pen Display
Terminal**

Ohio State University is a large, urban institution with approximately 45,000 students. Computers are used there to provide individualized instruction and let students proceed at their own pace. This instructional method using computers is called **computer-assisted instruction (CAI)** or **computer-managed instruction (CMI).**

A device that is normally incorporated into CAI or CMI is the **light pen display terminal.** This terminal is a special type of CRT which has been equipped with a light pen, a device that looks like a fountain pen with a light in its tip (Figure 4.24). In the CAI or CMI method, the computer displays questions and diagrams on the CRT screen. The student answers a question by passing the light pen across the screen of the CRT. The computer then indicates whether the response was correct. If so, it presents additional questions. If the answer was wrong, the computer will correct it, indicate why the choice was wrong, and provide review questions on the topic. CAI and CMI provide immediate feedback for the student. They are designed to supplement classroom instruction, not eliminate it. Faculty members can spend extra time with students who need more attention.

The light pen display terminal is also used in other fields because it combines visual reference and immediate computerized responses.

FIGURE 4.24   A light pen display terminal is used to examine the spread of pollution over a metropolitan area. The researchers can plot wind movements and atmospheric conditions by passing the light pen over the terminal and can observe their effect on the flow of pollution. The results are subsequently recorded in a hardcopy format for further analysis. (*IBM.*)

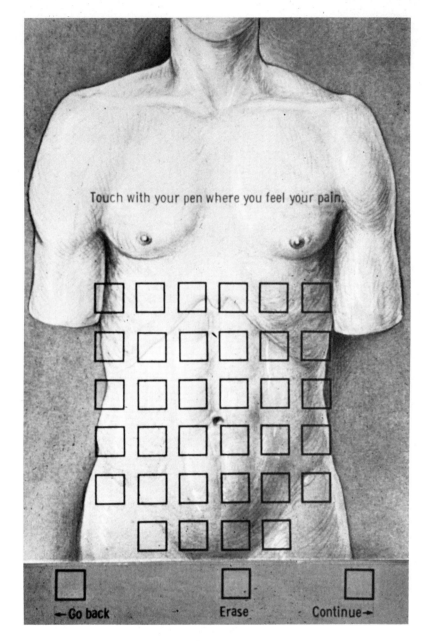

FIGURE 4.25 This diagram represents one part of a pictorial questionnaire used by hospitals and research centers to develop a patient's medical history. The patient uses a light pen to indicate where pain exists and responds to questions asked by the computer. The computer records the responses and attempts to come up with a preliminary diagnosis. This illustration and others are placed over the screen of a light pen display terminal. The movement of the light pen over this diagram creates the responses used by the computer. (*IBM and the Mayo Clinic.*)

Figure 4.25 illustrates the use of a light pen terminal in medicine. Patients are asked to indicate with a light pen where they feel abdominal pain. The computer relates this response to other test results to compile a diagnosis, adds the data to the patient's medical profile, and provides a list of results for the doctor. The light pen display terminal

FIGURE 4.26   A video display terminal is used to verify customer charge sales. The customer's account number and the amount of the sale are entered, and the terminal indicates whether to accept the sale. Some video display terminals can also provide sales receipts. (*IBM.*)

can help to diagnose illnesses in people who have communication difficulties, such as children and non-English-speaking people.

Specialized Terminal Devices

Video Display Terminal

Though the name is similar, the **video display terminal** is not a CRT. These terminals have a limited keyboard input and visual output capability. Figure 4.26 shows one model of video display terminal frequently used in banking or in verifying credit card purchases.

The customer account number is entered via the terminal and is immediately transmitted to the store's or bank's main computer. Often a keyboard entry is not necessary, as the device can accept a credit card and sense the account number directly from the card. The computer uses the account number input to search its customer files. The status of the account is displayed on the video display terminal, sometimes as a colored light. A red light might signify an overdrawn account. In Figure 4.26, the customer's name, account number, and current balance appear on the video display terminal. The sales clerk uses this data to determine whether to accept the charge sale. The teleprocessing of data made the credit check possible.

Audio I/O Units

Technology has made available a terminal called an **audio response unit,** illustrated in Figure 4.27. The audio response unit converts data received from the computer into sounds resembling a human voice, in the form of words or sentences.

The actions of the audio response terminal start after a request for data. This request enters via a terminal keyboard and must provide enough information for the computer to search its files. Once the appropriate data is found, it is transmitted to the audio response unit. The audio unit then constructs its response from a library of prerecorded terms and phrases. The next time you encounter a disconnected number or prerecorded message while using the telephone, try to determine if an audio response unit is at work.

Research has also begun on **voice input** devices. A project funded by the Department of Defense, conducted at five institutions, has produced early results. A model of a voice input unit called HARPY, developed at Carnegie-Mellon University, could understand English and react to certain voice commands. A second unit, named HEARSAY-II and also developed at CMU, had a larger vocabulary and placed fewer limits on the speaker's pronunciation, tone, and sentence structure.

Many computer manufacturers have had limited success with voice input devices. One such unit recognizes over 500 words in 12 speech patterns ranging from Brooklynese to southern drawl. However, speakers must enunciate carefully and slowly if the voice input unit is to function properly. Much more research is necessary to develop these devices, before they will be widely accepted.

FIGURE 4.27 An audio response unit provides as a computer output similar to a human voice. Essentially like a speaker, it outputs data solely in verbal form.

FIGURE 4.28 The data collection terminal. This terminal is an input device used to enter data on the computer. The person inputting data enters the required information using the small keyboard provided and/or inserts any specially prepared tags or cards. (*IBM.*)

Data Collection Terminal

Data collection terminals (Figure 4.28) are used in manufacturing plants to improve control over jobs being worked on. The faster the data is received by the computer, the greater and more accurate the control over the work.

After completing some aspect of their work, employees enter pertinent data via the data collection terminal. This data is used to plan production and lets management estimate when a job will be completed, calculate associated costs, and control inventory. Data collection terminals can be useful for almost any activity that requires the telecommunication of input data.

4.4 Intelligent Terminal Devices

We have stressed the importance of dealing with accurate data. The results of data processing are only as valid as the data used to generate them. Teleprocessed data must be accurate because it enters the computer system directly. The computer must check all data input from any terminal to ensure that only accurate data is processed.

In teleprocessing systems that handle a high volume of input data, the computer works extensively to check the accuracy of data. These checking activities curtail the computer's speed. Although checking data is important, using a computer in this manner is usually not economically justifiable. The computer should be free to perform more vital data processing activities.

Design engineers developed a solution to the above problem. They reasoned that, since the terminal is an essential part of the input process, why not have the terminal check data? The computer would then be free to perform other processing activities. Out of this concept, the idea of the **intelligent terminal** was born.

Intelligent terminals, as illustrated in Figure 4.29, are specifically designed to check input data. The incorporation of a microprocessor is what makes the terminal "intelligent." The term *editing* is applied to the procedure used to check input data. The editing procedure requires that the clerk or operator be given an operational sequence to follow. This sequence describes the data to be input, one field at a time. As the data relating to each field is input, it is checked by the terminal. Editing is performed character by character. Before data is entered, the terminal is fed an exact duplicate of the input formats used. Thus, if the format calls for the entry of five numeric characters and mistakenly an alphabetic character is input, that data is rejected.

FIGURE 4.29 (*a*) A Burroughs TC 510 intelligent terminal system outputs data in a hardcopy, printed format. This system has a limited storage capacity. (*Burroughs.*) (*b*) The IBM 3760 permits four operators to perform data entry operations at the same time. The 3760 has a recessed keyboard and displays data visually. (*IBM.*)

(*a*)

(*b*)

The intelligent terminal checks all input data and alerts the operator to errors. The creation and implementation of these editing techniques are the responsibility of analysts and programmers. This type of control must be designed directly into the system.

Various manufacturers offer intelligent terminals in many shapes and configurations. Many look like regular terminal devices. Figure 4.29 illustrates two different types of intelligent terminals.

The device shown in Figure 4.29a is referred to as an **intelligent terminal system.** The intelligent terminal system has a hardcopy output, limited storage capacity, and a keyboard that is used to edit input data. This device's ability to store small amounts of edited data is a valuable asset. Input data may be amassed over a period of time before it is put into the computer. Both data entered via the keyboard and computer outputs are printed out. The intelligent terminal system can also be employed as a hardcopy terminal.

Figure 4.29b shows an IBM 3760 Dual Key Entry Station that allows four people to enter data simultaneously. The 3760 is in effect four combined intelligent terminals. Each operator has a keyboard for entering data and a CRT for softcopy.

The 3760 is designed primarily for DP centers that enter a lot of data. Many centers combine the 3760 with the IBM 3790 Communications System. The 3790 passes data to a larger IBM 370 computer by creating a network of data entry centers. It speeds up the entry of accurate data because it interacts effectively with the large computer and can support telecommunications. The idea of handling data throughout an entire computer system is very popular and is covered more thoroughly in Chapter 12.

4.5 Selected Data Processing Techniques
Magnetic Ink Character Recognition (MICR)

How many times have you, a friend, or a parent paid for a retail purchase by check? The use of personal checks for payment is commonplace, and it is estimated that over 3 billion checks are processed annually by banks in the United States. Obviously, any business-related activity of that scope is suitable for automation. The technique applied to the computerized processing of checks is called **magnetic ink character recognition (MICR).**

MICR is fairly uncomplicated and so easily and efficiently handled that most of us are unaware of it. Our monthly checking statements attest to its practicality. To observe how MICR works, examine the typical personal check shown in Figure 4.30. Note the short, stubby numbers at the bottom of the check. These numbers, designed by the American Banking Association, indicate your account number and the amount of the check. The shapes of the numbers are standard throughout the banking industry, thereby permitting the processing of

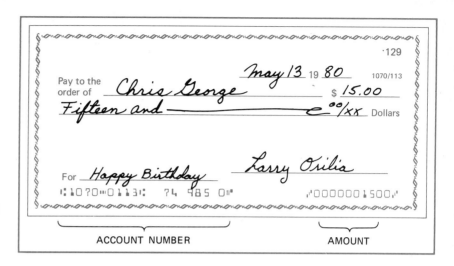

FIGURE 4.30 A personal check with the MICR number inscribed at the bottom is processed by the device shown in Figure 4.31. The account number is preprinted on all checks. The amount of the check is later coded onto the check when it is processed by the bank.

checks from all banks. All the numbers on each check are written with a special magnetic ink (from which this technique derives its name). The magnetic ink, coupled with the special shape of the characters, permits the computerized processing of each check.

Initially, only the account number is printed on the check. The amount is coded onto the check after the check has been written and cashed. Processing may begin when both numbers appear on the check. The MICR characters are read by the device illustrated in Figure 4.31*b*.

The magnetic character reader shown in Figure 4.31 uses a two-step cycle to read the MICR data. The MICR characters on the check are magnetized to be read electronically by the reading wheel of the MICR device. The MICR input associates the account number and amount of each check read. This data is accumulated and subsequently batch processed. All MICR data compiled in this manner is presented in each customer's monthly statement.

MICR has been favorably received because it provides an efficient, accurate, and reliable method of processing the vast quantity of data related to the use of personal checks.

Optical Character Recognition (OCR)

Though operationally similar to MICR, **optical character recognition (OCR)** requires its own specially shaped characters (Figure 4.32). The shape of these characters permits easy recognition by OCR reading devices. The OCR technique was primarily designed for manual, not mechanical, input of data. OCR has the advantage of not requiring special inks.

One of the original uses of OCR was in educational and psychological testing. It let researchers code data they derived from their

(a)

(b)

FIGURE 4.31   (a) The printing on a check permits the MICR reading of data. MICR data is read from a check by an IBM 1419 magnetic character reader (b). The account number and amount are magnetized immediately before they are read by the large reading wheel (on the right in part a). (IBM.)

projects. With OCR reading devices, this data could be input to a computer for processing. Optical character recognition eliminated the delay and effort of converting this data to punch cards. Test data was input directly from the source document.

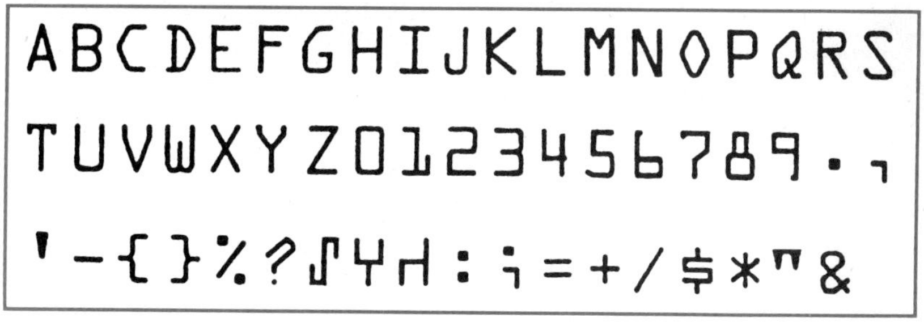

FIGURE 4.32 The standard set of characters used with optical character recognition (OCR) is illustrated (right).

Optical character recognition is also used in other fields. Currently, the New York State Motor Vehicle Bureau employs OCR in conjunction with its renewal of car registrations and drivers' licenses. The renewal of magazine subscriptions is selectively accomplished through the use of OCR.

One of the newer uses of OCR is in the retail trade, where sales data is generated directly by OCR-supported devices. Sales tags (Figure 4.33a) carry OCR characters, and when an item is purchased, the sales tag is read by a device called a **point-of-sale (POS) terminal.** The POS terminal serves as a cash register, terminal, and OCR reading device. Figure 4.33b shows a sales clerk reading a tag with an OCR reading device.

In many stores, the POS terminal is connected to a computer that monitors all transactions. This form of online processing lets management continually survey sales. The POS terminal highlights technology's ability to adapt devices for handling data.

MICR and OCR are techniques designed to speed the processing of data. Each technique was developed in response to a particular need in industry. Both provided an efficient and reliable method of handling cumbersome data and inputting that data to the computer.

Computer Output Microfilm (COM)

Many organizations with printed output face the problem of where to store it. For example, imagine trying to store all the census-related documents that have been accumulated by the U.S. Census Bureau. The required storage space and the cost of paper and binders alone would be staggering. **Computer output microfilm (COM)** was developed to assist in the storage of vast quantities of printed output. Data from printed outputs is photographed on microfilm. This microfilm record, called **microfiche,** is approximately 105 millimeters long (Figure 4.34). It is estimated that a *1-inch* stack of microfiche records contains a quantity of data equivalent to 25,000 pages of printed output.

Microfiche may also be produced directly from the computer. Instead of going to a printer, output data goes to a device that produces microfiche. The WANG Image Printer, Figure 4.16, is such a device. The resulting microfilm is handled like any other COM output.

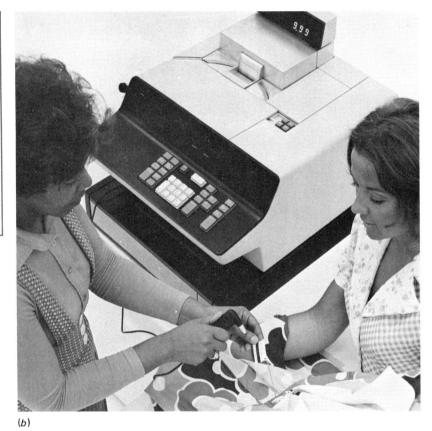

Size

4T

D346 1225

>$10.00

(a)

(b)

FIGURE 4.33 Sales data is prepared using OCR characters. (a) The sales tag illustrates the coding of sales data in OCR characters. (b) The sales clerk reads the OCR-prepared tag with a reading device attached to a point-of-sale terminal. (*IBM.*)

Micrographics

One result of the increased use of COM is **micrographics,** the computerized retrieval and display of microfilmed information. Organizations with large microfilm libraries use micrographics to retrieve data. Consider the example of micrographics in a police department.

The Springfield, Illinois, Police Department maintained records dating back to 1914. But they were bulky, rarely used, and hindered the preparation of comprehensive reports. Microfilm records were therefore created using COM, and an index of these records was entered into a small computer for later access. The computer had microimage terminals, devices for locating and displaying data on mi-

105 mm FICHE,
10 lbs

*The space required
using fiche is only
2 percent that of
paper storage.*

*200,00
pages of
computer
hardcopy,
2,800 lbs*

**FIGURE 4.34 Microfilm can effect considerable savings for organizations
that produce a high volume of printed matter. The space required to store
data is considerably less for microfiche than for hardcopy. (*NCR Corp.*)**

crofilm. Microimage terminals can provide access to over 6000 microfiche records in 5 seconds, far exceeding the potential for the manual
retrieval of the same data.

When particular information is requested, a police clerk types in
data on that record. The computer uses this data to scan the index of
microfilm data and find the record's location. The location is visually
displayed, and the clerk pulls the appropriate microfilm cartridge. The
cartridge is inserted into the image terminal, and the requested information appears on its screen. This information is then relayed to the
requesting officer.

The Springfield Police have noted that the rapid retrieval of microfilmed information has enabled them to apprehend alledged criminals
and, more importantly, to protect the lives of their police officers.
Often, the information relayed has prevented officers from entering
highly dangerous situations, such as potential ambushes at previously
dangerous addresses, and avoided highly sensitive confrontations.

Micrographics has been so successful that the Springfield Police
have extended its use to providing backup to other activities for helping to reduce violence. It provides valuable help to computer systems
already overloaded with requests for data.

School Uses OCR to Speed Student Registration

Many of us have been frustrated at the errors made during college registration, when it feels as if we will never get the courses necessary to graduate. The University of Maryland decided to rectify this problem. By using optical character recognition (OCR), they streamlined the process and registered over 24,000 students in one day. Earlier registrations had required 2 to 3 weeks for the same number of students. Scan Data Corporation's 2250 OCR Scanner and more than 20 CRTs were primarily responsible for the improvement.

At the start of each semester, students complete pre-registration forms indicating the courses they want to enroll in. Students must assign priorities and note alternatives. Students usually select 11 courses, including alternatives, per semester. They are advised to complete their registration materials carefully to speed the processing of the forms. Completed pre-registration forms are batched into groups of 500, assigned a control number, and input to the computer via the 2250 OCR reader.

Approximately 25 million handwritten characters are processed by the OCR reader. An average of 135,000 characters are unusable, compared with almost 200,000 characters under the old system. The OCR-read data remains on magnetic disk for correction and eventual processing.

Illegible characters are replaced by a slash (/) and stored with the rest of the registration data. Data entry clerks read through the pre-registration forms, scanning each for errors. Illegible characters appear on their CRT screens as slashes, and they make immediate corrections via the CRT. The corrected data returns to disk file.

The scanning and correction process takes less than 24 hours. Once all corrections are made, the file of pre-registration materials is processed, generating individual student schedules. These schedules go promptly to students, providing adequate time for course adjustments and eliminating the last-minute crush so difficult for school administrators.

Consider this . . .

Could OCR improve the registration procedure at your school? How do you think that OCR could be applied to speed the registration process?

Summary

The following major points have been presented in Chapter 4:

Point 1 The card reader, card punch, and card reader/punch are peripheral devices commonly employed with 80-column cards. The card reader and the card punch are input and output devices, respectively. The card reader/punch is an I/O device. Serial card readers read data column by column with photoelectric cells. Parallel readers read card data row by row, employing metallic brushes positioned above each card column.

Case Study Two

State Unemployment Combatted by COM

North Carolina's Employment Security Commission (ESC) uses computer output microfilm (COM) with its computer to update its statewide listing of available jobs. Established in 1971, the ESC report is used by 54 field offices. The Job Bank system, as it is called, handles over 12,000 records.

Job opportunities first come in to the field offices, where pertinent data on each job are keyed into intelligent terminals and telecommunicated to the Commission's main computer, a Univac 1100 system. Data on job title, salary, description, and qualifications is used to update the Job Bank's file of available openings. The updated file is stored on approximately 50 sheets of microfiche, each sheet equivalent to almost 200 pages of print.

The original microfiche are then duplicated and sent by courier to the 54 field offices for use the next day. John Fleming, a director at ESC,

believes that the system helps match prospective employers and employees. Because all field offices have the same data, they are more likely to interact and transfer applicants to other offices than they would be if they were isolated. Statistics show that, on the average, most jobs are filled in a few days. This statewide distribution also helps match special candidates to special jobs which might otherwise go unfilled.

COM speeds up the handling of data and eliminates the daily printing of reams of reports. The COM-prepared microfiche are compact, light, and easily distributed. Without them, the ESC would need truckloads of paper for the same job data. Field offices would have the problem of where to store the masses of paper. The microfiche, however, are compactly stored and always available for examination. With COM, benefits have accrued to worker and ESC alike.

Point 2 Printed output is one of the most important products of a data processing system. Line printers are divided into impact and nonimpact types. Line printers include chain, band, drum, wire-matrix and daisy-wheel types. Whereas impact printers strike the printing surface, nonimpact printers do not touch the paper when printing data. Nonimpact printers use an electrostatic, thermal, jet-ink, or laser process to print data. Plotters are printing devices that provide graphic and pictorial representations of data. Plotters produce continuous line drawings that cannot be output by line printers. The IBM 3800 Printing Subsystem and the WANG Image Printer are more than just printing devices. Each can duplicate forms, output data, and vary type size. The 3800 uses

laser technology; the Image Printer uses fiber optics.

Point 3 The many types of terminals satisfy a variety of needs. CRTs provide visual outputs. Hardcopy terminals produce printed records. Some CRTs can output colors and graphics. The light pen display terminal is a type of CRT often used in computer-assisted instruction. Video display and data collection terminals allow the telecommunication of data. Video display terminals have a limited output display. A voice input device accepts voice input data, where the audio response unit produces output in voice form.

Point 4 Some hardcopy terminals can punch paper tapes, using the ASCII code used with most terminals. Modems convert impulses sent over phone lines to and from the computer. The initial conversion is referred to as modulation; the reconversion, demodulation.

Point 5 Intelligent terminals are a further refinement in computer terminal technology. The intelligent terminal can edit data input to the computer via the terminal. This editing of data frees the computer for more valuable activities. Intelligent terminals can print like an RJE or produce softcopy like a CRT. Intelligent terminals may also be grouped together to permit online data entry to a computer tied into a network of other computers.

Point 6 MICR, OCR, and COM are specialized data processing techniques. Magnetic ink character recognition (MICR) uses magnetic ink with specially shaped characters like those on many personal bank checks. Optical character recognition (OCR) uses special characters and forms to process data. Data is read from the forms via an OCR reader and processed by the computer. Computer output microfilm (COM) is a method of storing printed outputs on microfilm. COM saves space and storage costs, and large quantities of data can be held on file within easy access. COM is suited for organizations that have a high volume of printed output. The technology of micrographics was developed to assist in the rapid retrieval and display of data stored on microfilm. It uses a computer to determine the location of data and special microimage terminals to display that data.

Glossary

American Standard Code for Information Interchange (ASCII)   A computer code used with terminal devices.

Audio response unit   A terminal whose output is in the form of a verbal message (i.e., spoken words or phrases).

Band printer   An impact printer that employs characters on a metal band to print data on paper.

Bidirectional printer   An impact printer that can print data from left to right and vice versa.

Brush reader   A card reader which uses metallic brushes, positioned above each card column, to read card data.

Card punch   An output device used to punch data onto 80-column cards.

Card reader   An input device that reads data from 80-column cards.

Card reader/punch   An input/output device used to read or to punch data on 80-column cards.

Cathode-ray tube (CRT)   A terminal that uses a TV picture tube to display its data.

Chain printer   An impact printing device.

Computer-assisted instruction (CAI)   An instructional technique using a computer that has previously been programmed with sets of questions on specific topics and serves as an individual tutorial aide.

Computer-managed instruction (CMI)   Same as CAI.

Computer output microfilm (COM)   A method of storing large volumes of printed outputs on microfilm.

Daisy-wheel printer   An impact printing device whose printing mechanism is a rotating wheel.

Data collection terminal   An input terminal that permits the entry of data to the computer from remote locations.

Data-phone data set   A device that is a combination telephone and modem.

Demodulation   The reconversion of impulses at the end of telecommunications.

Drum printer   An impact printing device.

Graphics terminal   A CRT that can produce continuous line drawings or graphic designs on its screen.

Hardcopy terminal   A terminal device that displays data in the form of printed output.

Hardwired   A term applied to a communication connection where a line is tied directly into a device.

Impact printer   A type of printer that strikes the paper to produce hardcopy outputs.

Input/Output (I/O) device   A computer device that is capable of both input and output operations.

Intelligent terminal   A terminal which possesses the capability to edit data.

Intelligent terminal system   An RJE station built around an intelligent terminal and a line printer.

Light pen display terminal   A CRT that employs a light source to interact with the computer.

Line printer   A printing device that prints data on a line-by-line basis.

Magnetic ink character recognition (MICR)   A data processing technique that employs magnetic ink and special character shapes to process data.

Microfiche   The term applied to printed data that has been photographed and recorded on microfilm.

Micrographics   A computerized technique that permits the rapid retrieval and display of data stored on microfilm.

Modem   A device that converts data into impulses and transmits them over telephone lines from the terminal to the computer and vice versa.

Modulation   The initial conversion of the impulses at the start of telecommunications.

Nonimpact printer   A type of printer that does not strike the paper to produce hardcopy outputs, but instead uses an electrostatic, thermal, or special electronic process to print data.

Optical character recognition (OCR)   A data processing technique employing special character shapes and a device that senses data off manually prepared forms.

Parallel card reader   A card reader that reads data off a punched card on a row-by-row basis.

Peripheral device   A general term used to describe all devices that are incorporated into a computer system.

Photoelectric cell readers   Card readers that employ photoelectric cells to sense the data punched onto a card.

Plotter   A special printing device that has the capability to print continuous line drawings, graphs, and pictorial displays of data.

Point-of-sale (POS) terminal   A CRT equipped with a special reading device that serves as a cash register, terminal, and OCR reader.

Portable data terminal   A portable terminal that provides hardcopy.

Printer   A device that produces permanent, printed (hardcopy) outputs on paper.

Serial card reader   A card reader that reads data from a punched card one column at a time.

Video display terminal   A CRT-like terminal that has a limited I/O capability.

Voice-input unit   An input device that converts verbal messages into impulses acceptable to the computer.

Wire-matrix printer   An impact printer that represents printed data in the form of a series of dots.

Discussion Questions

1 Visit the data processing area in your school, company, or organization. Compile a list of the devices that you find. Identify each as an input or output device or both. For output devices, note whether the device provides softcopy or hardcopy.

2 Look through a group of data processing magazines, and compile a list of I/O devices advertised. Identify each by manufacturer and type of device (i.e., input, output, or i/O).

3 Obtain a copy of an unused check and a processed check. Compare them, noting the MICR numbers and check amount in the lower right corner.

4 Compare the data processing techniques of MICR, OCR, and COM. What are the advantages of each? Without each, would cards be a valid or efficient replacement?

5 Discuss how the following peripheral devices might benefit data processing for the application indicated.

Device	Applications
CRT	Large department store
Hardcopy terminal	A chain of sporting goods stores
Light pen display terminal	Police department
Video display terminal	Telephone company
Audio response unit	An automotive production plant
Data collection terminal	A group of salespersons
Graphics terminal	Television company
Point-of-sale terminal	Supermarket
Color terminal	Business manager

6 Examine the mail you receive from school, advertisers, mail-order companies, and retail stores. Determine which pieces are computer-prepared or computer-printed copies of an original document.

7 Visit your school's library and ask about their use of microfilm. What advantages might COM hold for them? Would micrographics be helpful?

8 How might the following individuals employ a portable hardcopy terminal?

Accountant	Family physician
Architect	Restaurant chef
Chemical engineer	Stockbroker
Construction supervisor	Student
Drug salesperson	Tutor

9 Discuss how the light pen display terminal could help the following:
  a Medical personnel dealing with non-English-speaking patients
  b Designers of children's games or learning tools
  c Artists creating sketches of police suspects wanted for arrest

Summary Test

_T_   **1** The term _peripheral devices_ is used to describe those devices used for I/O activities in a computer system.

_F_   **2** Punched cards are frequently used for the input of data, but they are never used for the output of data.

_T_   **3** Demodulation is the reconversion of impulses by the modem.

_T_   **4** The data-phone data set is a combination modem and terminal.

_F_   **5** The computerized approach to individualized education is called computer-assisted management or CAM.

_F_   **6** The video display terminal is effective as an input device only.

_T_   **7** The audio response unit is a computerized input device that employs a voicelike output.

_T_   **8** Intelligent terminals are responsible for editing data before it is input to the computer.

_F_   **9** MICR is a complicated data processing technique that requires a special magnetic ink applied to regular-shaped handwritten characters.

_F_ **10** A serial card reader reads card data row by row.

_F_ **11** Graphic terminals are an integral component in the retrieval of micrographic records.

_F_ **12** The ASCII computer code is primarily used in the preparation of punched paper tapes and has little value with terminal devices.

_T_ **13** Fiber optics technology uses cables made of glass wires to transmit data.

_F_ **14** A band printer is a nonimpact printer with an electronic band that prints electrostatically.

_F_ **15** Plotters provide continuous line drawings and graphic solutions to complex analyses, but are limited to paper sizes of $8\frac{1}{2} \times 11$ inches.

_D_ **16** The terminal device that functions as a cash register, computer terminal, and OCR reader is the:

    a video display terminal   **b** OCR register terminal
    c data collection terminal   **d** POS terminal

_C_ **17** The technique designed to support the effective access of microfilmed data is:

    a microfiche retrieval   **b** COM
    c micrographics   **d** all the above

_D_ **18** An impact printer that uses an interchangeable, rotating printing unit for hardcopy output is the:

    a thermal printer   **b** wire-matrix printer
    c drum printer   **d** daisy-wheel printer

_D_ **19** Which of the following printing devices provides an output composed of a series of dots?

    a wire-matrix printer   **b** band printer
    c WANG Image Printer   **d** a or c

_A_ **20** Which of the following terminals' output most closely resembles the output produced by a plotter?

a	graphics terminal	**b**	POS terminal
c	hardcopy terminal	**d**	all the above

_B_ **21** Which of the following impact printers prints fastest?

a	band printer	**b**	chain printer
c	drum printer	**d**	wire-matrix printer

_D_ **22** Which of the following statements is true?

a All hardcopy terminals use punched paper tapes.

b Intelligent terminals provide hardcopy outputs only.

c Microfiche are always produced directly from printed outputs.

d None of the above.

_D_ **23** Softcopy outputs available from the IBM 3279 Color Display terminal may include:

a graphic displays of data

b three-dimensional line drawings

c line-by-line outputs of character data

d all the above

_C_ **24** The terminal device often used in checking charge cards that offers both a limited keyboard input and visual output is the:

a	intelligent terminal	**b**	POS terminal
c	video display terminal	**d**	audio response unit

_D_ **25** Which of the following printing devices can generate printed outputs composed of two or more types of printed characters?

a IBM 3800 Printing Subsystem

b Twin-head daisy-wheel printer

c WANG Image Printer

d All the above

**Summary
Test Answers**

1 T	2 F	3 T	4 T	5 F
6 F	7 F	8 T	9 F	10 F
11 F	12 F	13 T	14 F	15 F
16 D	17 C	18 D	19 D	20 A
21 B	22 D	23 D	24 C	25 D

Concepts of Computer Systems

FIGURE 5.1 Computer systems may assume many shapes and sizes. Here, computers destined for use in space are constructed and tested in a sterile environment. (*Courtesy of Photo Researchers, Inc.*)

Purpose of This Chapter

In this chapter, we discuss the concepts related to the actual functioning of computer systems. We discuss the central processing unit (CPU), its storage of data, and efficient methods of processing data through it.

The chapter opens with an introduction to the types of computer systems and reviews the differences between analog, digital, hybrid, special-purpose, and general-purpose computers. It develops the application of a simulator to a training environment. We relate the operational importance of the CPU to the EDP cycle. We discuss the control, arithmetic logic, and primary storage units, all components of the CPU. Word-oriented and byte-oriented storage are introduced.

We describe the 8-bit EBCDIC storage code and its relationship to the Hollerith code. The chapter also presents a shorthand code related to EBCDIC and the purpose of parity bits. The ASCII code, similar in appearance to EBCDIC but used with other computer devices, is described.

The chapter reviews the concept of secondary storage. Discussions of overlapped processing and virtual storage, two data processing techniques designed to increase computer efficiency, are presented.

After studying this chapter, you should be able to

- Briefly discuss the different types of computers.
- Describe the central processing unit and each of its components.
- Discuss the stored program concept.
- Understand the purpose of channels, registers, and buffers.
- Describe the structure of the EBCDIC code, its shorthand, and parity bits.
- Understand the structure and purpose of the ASCII code.
- Discuss the purpose of secondary storage.
- Describe overlapped processing and virtual storage.
- Understand the following terms:

Analog computer	Byte
Arithmetic logic unit (ALU)	Byte-oriented computers
Arithmetic operation	Channel
ASCII code	Check bit
Binary notation	Control unit
Binary numbering system	Core
Bits	Digital computer
Buffer	EBCDIC code

Electronic data processing (EDP) cycle	Parity bit
	Primary storage
General-purpose computer	Primary storage unit
Hexadecimal notations	Register
Hybrid computer	Secondary storage
I/O bound	Simulator
Logical operation	Special-purpose computer
Magnetic disk	Stored program concept
Magnetic tape	Virtual storage (VS)
Main storage	Word
Overlapped processing	Word-oriented computer
Page	

Introduction

What happens to data fed into a computer? Where does the data displayed on a CRT come from? Chapter 4 introduced many input and output devices, but none could handle intricate formulas or store the vast quantities of data a computer needs. The **central processing unit (CPU)** is the component responsible for controlling all the activities of a computer system. The CPU affects the processing of all data and is the focal point for all I/O activities.

The CPU accepts data from various input devices and processes that data by following a program's instructions. In millionths of a second, the CPU can perform any arithmetic operation a program directs, move data from one location to another, and convert data into useful information. The CPU directs the output of information as hard- or softcopy. A computer's capabilities are defined by the size, function, and efficiency of its CPU.

5.1 Types of Computers

Manufacturers offer many shapes and sizes of computer systems, but the many models can all be broadly classified as

1 Analog and digital computers
2 Hybrid computers
3 Special-purpose and general-purpose computers

Both a computer's data handling techniques and its purposes affect how it operates, and these categories help us to classify these characteristics.

Analog and Digital Computers

If you have ever worked with a slide rule or reset a thermostat, you have used an analog device. The operating principles of analog devices have been incorporated successfully into computer systems.

Analog computers represent numbers by a physical quantity; that is, they assign numeric values by physically measuring some actual property, such as the length of an object, an angle created by two lines, or the amount of voltage passing through a point in an electric circuit. Analog computers derive all their data from some form of measurement. Though effective for some applications, this method of representing numbers is a limitation of the analog computer. The accuracy of the data used in an analog computer is directly related to the precision of its measurements.

Digital computers represent data as numbers or separate units. Counting on your fingers is the simplest form of digital computer. Each finger represents one unit of the item being counted. Unlike the analog computer, which is limited to the accuracy of the measurements made, the digital computer can accurately represent data using as many positions and numbers as necessary. Adding machines and pocket calculators are common examples of devices constructed on the principles of the digital computer.

Analog computers measure toward their answers, and digital computers count to their results. Unless otherwise indicated, all future discussions will concentrate on digital computers.

Hybrid Computers

Hybrid computers combine the best features of analog and digital computers. They have the speed of analog computers and the accuracy of digital computers. They are usually used for special problems in which input data derived from measurements is converted into digits and processed by computer. Hybrid computers, for example, control national defense and passenger flight radar.

Consider the hybrid computer used in producing iron ore pellets for steelmaking. It controls manufacturing and prepares production data on inventory and costs. The computer accepts data both from sensors within the production area and from conventional I/O devices.

As production starts, data on the materials used in manufacturing goes into the computer for analysis. The computer uses the data to establish operating standards. Sensors report on all aspects of manufacturing, and the computer converts these measurements into numeric equivalents. The computer ensures that all operations are within limits and quickly notes exceptions.

Using the production data, the computer plans for future manufacturing and distributes existing inventories, activities which require the computer to compute digital data and produce reports for management. The hybrid computer is perfectly suited to this application. The computer can act like an analog computer, converting measurements into numeric input. It can act as a digital computer, processing stored data for management.

NAVIGATIONAL SIMULATOR FOR PILOT TRAINING

How would you dock an oil supertanker that weighed 250,000 tons and was as long as a 13-car train if you had never even handled a supertanker before? That problem faces maritime officers at MarineSafety's training

(Photo courtesy of Newsday.)

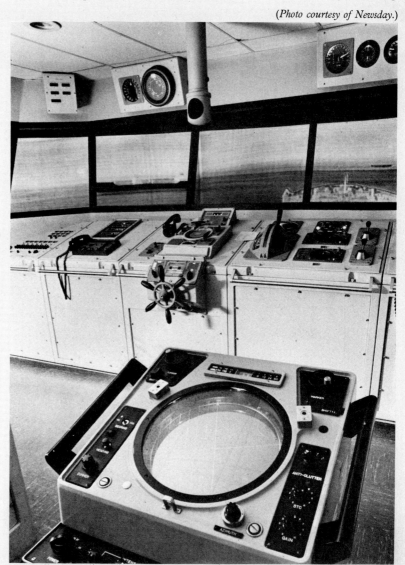

The simulated training bridge used in a computer-controlled ship handling simulator.

facility in New York. MarineSafety International uses a computer-controlled simulator to train or retrain merchant marine officers. Since 1976, MarineSafety's shiphandling simulator has helped approximately 1000 officers improve their navigational skills.

The simulator duplicates the actual wheelhouse in which the officers will take command. Control panels and instruments are tied into the computer and respond as they might under normal operating conditions. A 12- by 60-foot wraparound screen presents navigational and topographical features like buoys, lighthouses, islands and reefs, cliffs, jetties, and objects hazardously submerged in shipping lanes.

The computer creates various lifelike atmospheric and navigational conditions that captains might meet. By using complex equations, the computer simulates the vessel's reactions to changes in wind direction, tides, engine speed, and ship's headings as well as to the trainee's attempts to steer the ship. The simulator can also create unforeseen conditions that might cause multimillion dollar damages.

The MarineSafety simulator can reproduce the reactions of three types of vessel and can create various harbor settings. Captains may train on a small tanker of about 30,000 tons, a supertanker, or a liquid natural gas (LNG) carrier with a capacity of 125,000 cubic meters. The simulator can create pictures of harbors in Wales and Alaska, as well as of Chesapeake Bay in Maryland and of the Savannah River in Georgia.

The simulator is a hybrid, special-purpose computer. Numeric data on navigational conditions are filed and used to create test conditions. Trainees' reactions feed in through the simulated bridge to be evaluated by the computer. The analog capacity of the simulator lets it convert data generated by dials, steering wheels, and other controls. The system's output consists of commands to the simulator and documentation for evaluating the trainees' performance.

General-Purpose and Special-Purpose Computers

Digital computers work in highly specialized applications and in a wide range of general processing tasks. **General-purpose computers** are versatile and process business data as readily as they process complex mathematical formulas. General-purpose computers can store large amounts of data and the programs necessary to process them. Because they are so versatile, most businesses today use general-purpose computers.

Special-purpose computers incorporate many features of general-purpose computers but support highly specialized data processing tasks. They are designed to handle specific problems and are not applied to other computerized activities. For example, special-purpose computers may be designed to process only numeric data or to completely control automated manufacturing processes. Our example above of the computerized processing of iron ore pellets illustrates the use of a special-purpose computer.

Special-purpose computers are often used as training simulators. A **simulator** is a computer-controlled device for training people under simulated, or artificially created, conditions. The computer creates test conditions the trainee must respond to, records and evaluates the responses, and provides results to both trainee and supervisor.

The aircraft industry uses simulators to train pilots and flight crews in completely equipped, computer-controlled cockpits. The computer creates a variety of flight conditions and monitors the trainees' reactions to them. After getting passing marks on the simulator, trainees move to actual aircraft.

Simulators also cut training costs. It is far more practical, for example, to simulate a flight emergency than to jeopardize a plane. A very sophisticated simulator might cost $5 million; a commercial jet could cost $20 to $40 million.

Many other fields, including nursing, operating room technology, nuclear power plant administration, space flight, athletics, and marine exploration, use training simulators.

5.2
The Central Processing Unit (CPU)
The EDP Cycle

A data processing system's activities include input, processing, and output. Together, these activities make up the **electronic data processing (EDP) cycle,** illustrated in Figure 5.2. In Chapter 4, we presented many of the peripheral devices that support input and output. Now we will turn to the CPU, which supports the actual processing of data. The CPU receives data from input devices, processes it, and prepares information for output devices.

In our earlier example of a computerized banking system, we mentioned that customer account data could be entered into the computer with cards, terminals, or data collection devices. Data could be output on printers, CRTs, or video display terminals. The CPU performs all processing, including all the computations, updating of accounts, and

FIGURE 5.2 The EDP cycle shows how the fundamental elements of a data processing operation relate input, processing, and output. All processing within this relationship is performed in the CPU.

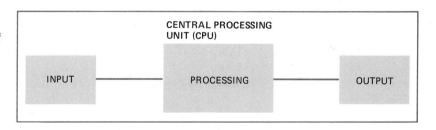

CENTRAL PROCESSING
UNIT (CPU)

INPUT   PROCESSING   OUTPUT

controlling of the system's I/O activities. The CPU executes programs and stores data. In short, it is the hub of all the computer's activities. The CPU consists of three components:

1 The control unit
2 The arithmetic logic unit (ALU)
3 The primary storage unit

Each unit has a particular function.

The Control Unit

The **control unit** essentially governs all computer activities and monitors the execution of programs. It coordinates and controls the computer system much as the brain directs the body.

The control unit executes program instructions. It first determines what operation to perform, then it makes available the data necessary for the instruction. It determines where the data is stored and transfers it from the storage location. It ensures that data is accurately moved from one storage area to another.

Once it has executed an instruction, the control unit must determine where to store the results for output or later use. Finally, it must locate the next instruction to be processed. The control unit repeats this series of operations for each instruction.

One of the more important functions of the control unit relates to its control of input and output operations when requested by statements in a program. The control unit directly coordinates the I/O activities of a computer system. If a program initiates an input operation,

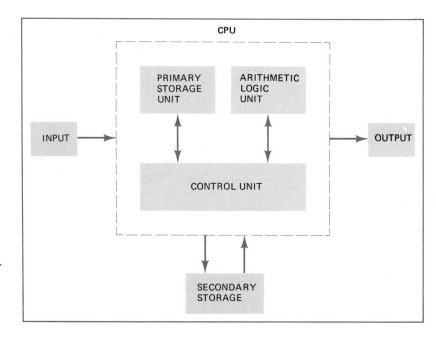

FIGURE 5.3 An expanded diagram of the EDP cycle. The three components that compose the CPU—the control unit, the arithmetic logic unit, and the primary storage unit—are also shown.

the control unit will identify the input device to be used and will establish the internal electronic path the data will follow as it enters and is stored in the CPU. In output operations the control unit takes similar actions as it directs the data down a predetermined path to its output.

Arithmetic Logic Unit

The **arithmetic logic unit (ALU)** is responsible for performing all arithmetic and logical operations and transferring data between storage locations. The **arithmetic operations** it undertakes include addition, subtraction, multiplication, division, and exponentiation. A fundamental component employed in arithmetic and logical operations is the **register,** a special storage area in the CPU where data is temporarily held during these operations.

But what is a logical operation? A **logical operation** is a comparison of two values, an attempt to determine the relationship between two values. Logical operations can use numeric, alphabetic, or alphanumeric quantities.

For example, assume that we are reading data from a file composed of the personnel records of a company. Our responsibility is to determine the particular sex of each employee. This task is easily accomplished by examining the Sex field in each employee's record and comparing the contents of this field against the codes of "M" or "F," Male or Female, respectively. In essence, we are asking if the contents of the field named Sex is equal to "M" or "F." If the answer to the question "IS SEX = 'M'?" is yes, then the employee is male. If the answer is no, then the employee is female. This example illustrates the concept of a logical operation as it could be applied to alphabetic or alphanumeric data. How would numeric data be handled?

Suppose that we must also examine the number of hours worked by each employee in order to determine who receives overtime pay. To do this, we compare the contents of the Hours Worked field against the number 40. If the number of hours worked is greater than 40, the employee will receive overtime pay. If the number of hours worked is less than or equal to 40, the employee will receive regular pay. This logical operation enables us to compare the data stored in the field called Hours Worked against the number 40.

Logical operations enable us to distinguish between two quantities, employing the form of a question. In practical programming applications, however, actual statements relating to logical operations are expressed in an entirely different manner. Logical operations are written to conform to the rules of the languages used by the program. Because many programming languages do not parallel English, logical statements assume a variety of formats. We will return to this point when we discuss programming languages. Initially, though, it is always easier to express logical operations in the form of a question.

In performing arithmetic and logical operations, the ALU is responsible for moving data between storage and itself. Data used in processing is transferred from its location in storage to the ALU. The data is manipulated as directed by the program instruction and returned to its storage location. Because processing cannot occur at storage locations, all data must be transferred to the ALU. Data may be moved between the ALU and the CPU's storage area several times before one processing operation is completed.

**Primary
Storage Unit**

The storage capacity of the CPU is called the **primary storage unit.** Over the years, the storage unit has been called **main storage, primary storage, core,** or *memory.* Primary storage provides the capability to store input data, statements from programs currently undergoing processing, data resulting from processing, and data in preparation for output.

Data input to the computer stays in primary storage until it is used in processing. During processing, primary storage is used to store the intermediate and final results of all arithmetic and logical operations. Intermediate results and data involved in a series of operations are temporarily held in storage areas, sometimes referred to as *working storage,* specifically set aside for that purpose. Final results go to storage areas designated by program instructions until output operations begin.

Primary storage must also retain the program instructions used in processing. Once input and stored, these instructions may be retrieved to complete the processing of any job.

Storing programs within primary storage illustrates the **stored program concept,** originally developed in the 1940s by Dr. John Von Neumann. Early computers did not operate by this principle and were wired for only a select number of tasks. Von Neumann theorized that a computer with stored programs could perform many types of processing because it was directed by a program rather than by its wiring. The program in primary storage would contain instructions for processing and all actions related to an application. The stored program concept therefore offered great flexibility for both hardware and software design.

Primary storage is composed of a series of storage areas in which data may be held. Each storage area is identified by its own storage number, or *address,* much as each house on a street has its own number. Each storage area may be accessed by its address and is capable of holding a specific amount of data. The capacity of the storage locations is dependent upon the type of computer.

Primary storage is generally classified as either **word-oriented** or **byte-oriented. A byte** is a unit of primary storage capable of holding a character of data. Thus, a byte-oriented machine holds individual characters of data. A **word** is a unit of memory that can contain an entire number, without having to divide the number into individual digits. The number is always treated as a group of digits. Most computers are word-oriented, and many general-purpose computers can operate as byte- or word-oriented machines.

A fixed-word-length machine is a word-oriented computer in which the size of a word of storage remains constant. Consider a fixed-word-length machine in which each word of storage is composed of four characters. Each time that word is accessed, four characters worth of storage is made available. Even if only two digits of storage are required, the computer will always provide a word of storage capable of storing four characters of data.

In contrast, a variable-word-length machine is a byte-oriented computer in which the number of bytes used to compose a word of storage can vary. The number of bytes composing a word is determined by a programmer as the program is being written. Thus, a word of storage might consist of two bytes or four bytes of storage. These words could hold two and four characters of data, respectively.

Generally, word-oriented computers are better suited for processing numbers because they access the entire number with a single word. Byte-oriented computers are better for applications with characters which must be retrieved individually. General-purpose computers can handle either type of application and use the most efficient method of storage for the problem at hand.

Primary storage capacity is usually fixed at specific levels according to the kind of computer. To identify these storage capacities, a form of slang has developed in which the character K represents 1024 bytes of storage. Thus, saying that primary storage has a capacity of 16K means that the computer really has 16,384 bytes of storage.

5.3 The Storage of Data

Today's computer memories are built of silicon chips, a far cry from the vacuum tubes used in early systems. Later generations of computers used transistors and magnetic cores to compose their primary storage. Figure 5.4 shows the tiny iron rings called cores and compares them to silicon chips. Let us examine how data was stored in magnetic core computers.

Data is stored in computers in a number of ways. Figure 5.5 illustrates the use of a magnetic core to store one bit of data. The direction of magnetization of that core represents the state of the core, which may assume either of two states. The wires in the core provide the means of sensing the state of the core and changing that state. When the core is magnetized in one state, the core is said to be "on." In the opposite magnetized state, the core is said to be "off."

These designations were perfectly suited for use with the **binary numbering system,** a method of counting similar to the decimal numbering system.[1] Whereas the decimal system is based on the number 10, the binary system employs the base 2. The base 10, or decimal, system uses the digits 0 through 9. In the base 2, or binary, system, the

---

[1] A discussion of numbering systems is presented in the appendix.

FIGURE 5.4 (top) Small circular magnetic cores 18 mils in diameter once used to make up computer storage. The cores are compared in size with typed characters. (*Ampex Corp.*); (below) A silicon chip is the major component in the construction of today's computers. This is a blowup of the computer circuitry placed in one silicon chip. (*Burroughs Corp.*)

only digits used are 0's and 1's, which are referred to as **bi**nary digi**ts** or **bits.** The use of bits to represent data is referred to as **binary notation.** The same numeric quantity can be represented in either base, except that in base 2 the number will appear as a string of 0's and 1's and in base 10 the number will be expressed using the digits 0 to 9.

The binary numbering system was applied to the two core states. The *off* state equals 0, and the *on* state equals 1. Respectively, these two states are represented as a 0 bit or a 1 bit. These two bits are the basis of the binary codes used to represent data stored in the computer.

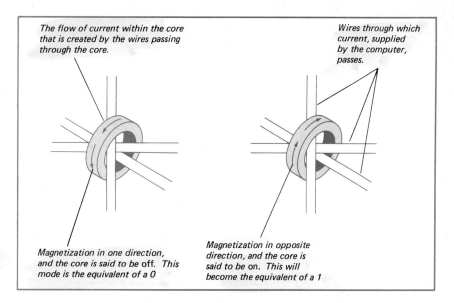

The flow of current within the core that is created by the wires passing through the core.

Wires through which current, supplied by the computer, passes.

Magnetization in one direction, and the core is said to be off. *This mode is the equivalent of a 0*

Magnetization in opposite direction, and the core is said to be on. *This will become the equivalent of a 1*

FIGURE 5.5 The small doughnut-shaped magnetic core was once used to compose primary storage. Note that the current within the core can travel in two directions. One direction equals a 0; the opposite direction equals a 1.

We have used the magnetic core to develop the concept of the 0 bit and the 1 bit. Cores are no longer used in computers, but the designation of the *off/on* states remains. Though the data is stored as electric or magnetic impulses, it is easier to represent it as 0 bits or 1 bits. Thus the binary numbering system is used in most computer systems.

The EBCDIC Code

Different computer systems use different binary codes to represent the data in primary storage. One common method of encoding characters is the **Extended Binary Coded Decimal Interchange Code (EBCDIC).** EBCDIC uses a series of 8 bits to represent one character of storage, which is referred to as a byte. In EBCDIC, each byte is represented by a string of eight 0 and 1 bits. These 8 bits are divided into two groups of 4 bits each, as shown in Figure 5.6.

One of the 4-bit groups represents zone bits, which may be associated with the zone punches of the Hollerith code. For ease of understanding, each bit of the zone group is identified by a bit position, namely an 8 bit, a 4 bit, a 2 bit, and a 1 bit. Each of these bit positions must contain a 0 or a 1 in the EBCDIC code. Remember that EBCDIC encodes characters as 0's and 1's, which represent impulses inside the computer.

The digit position of the EBCDIC code parallels the structures of the zone bits. It too is composed of an 8 bit, a 4 bit, a 2 bit, and a 1 bit, but they are assigned as digit bits. Each of the four digit bits will be represented as a 0 or a 1 in the EBCDIC code. Table 5.1 details the application of EBCDIC to the equivalents of the zone and digit punches of the Hollerith code.

As Table 5.1 illustrates, each bit position in EBCDIC is filled with a 0 or a 1. The equivalent of a 12 punch in the Hollerith code is 1100,

FIGURE 5.6   It takes 8 bits to compose one EBCDIC character. The 8-bit groupings are divided into two 4-bit groups representing zone bits and digit bits.

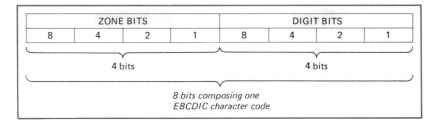

beginning with the 8 bit and reading down. Similarly, the equivalent of the Hollerith code's 11 punch is 1101, reading down the zone bit positions 8, 4, 2, and 1.

We should warn you against the following mistake: It is often incorrectly assumed that the 12-zone punch is 1100 in EBCDIC because the 1's in the 8-bit and 4-bit positions add up to 12. The sum of the zone bits used has absolutely no relation to the EBCDIC equivalent of the Hollerith zone punches. The zone bit equivalences exist as shown in Table 5.1. Though the zone bit equivalent of an 11-zone punch totals 13, the bits 1101 are the correct EBCDIC code.

The EBCDIC configuration for the digit bits is operationally different. The EBCDIC equivalents of the digit bits are based on the grouping or addition of bits. The digit bit equivalent of a 1 punch is 0001, with the 1 in the 1-bit position. A 2 punch is represented as 0010, where the 1 is assigned to the 2 bit. A Hollerith 3 punch is 0011, because 1's are

Table 5.1   EBCDIC Equivalent to the Zone and Digit Punches of the Hollerith Code

		Hollerith Zone Punches			
		12-Zone Punch	11-Zone Punch	0-Zone Punch	No Zone Punch
EBCDIC Zone Bits	8	1	1	1	1
	4	1	1	1	1
	2	0	0	1	1
	1	0	1	0	1

		Hollerith Digit Punches									
		1	2	3	4	5	6	7	8	9	0
EBCDIC Digit Bits	8	0	0	0	0	0	0	0	1	1	0
	4	0	0	0	1	1	1	1	0	0	0
	2	0	1	1	0	0	1	1	0	0	0
	1	1	0	1	0	1	0	1	0	1	0

positioned in the 2- and 1-bit positions, equaling 3. Checking the remainder of the digit bit equivalents, we can see that adding bits lets us create EBCDIC equivalents for every Hollerith punch from 0 through 9.

A three-step procedure, similar to the one used with binary coded decimal characters, will help us develop the EBCDIC code for alphabetic and numeric characters. The basis of this procedure, too, is the Hollerith code

1 Define the selected character in terms of its Hollerith code zone and digit punches.

2 Select the EBCDIC equivalents of the zone and digit punches.

3 Join the zone and digit equivalents from step 2 to form one complete EBCDIC character.

Applying this procedure, we can determine the EBCDIC code for the alphabetic character A as follows:

1 In the Hollerith code, the character A is composed of a 12-zone punch and a 1-digit punch.

2 In EBCDIC, the equivalent of a 12-zone punch is 1100 and the equivalent of a 1-digit punch is 0001.

3 Combining the EBCDIC equivalents, we derive the EBCDIC code for the character A: 11000001.

Illustrating these steps, we have the following:

Step 1	**Step 2**	**Step 3**
The Hollerith code for the character A is	Convert these punches to their EBCDIC equivalents.	Combine these equivalents to form one EBCDIC character code.
a 12-zone punch ⟹	which is a 1100 zone code	Zone Digit
		8 4 2 1 8 4 2 1
+		1 1 0 0 0 0 0 1
a 1-digit punch ⟹	which is a 0001 digit code	The EBCDIC code for A

The three illustrations following use this procedure to construct the EBCDIC codes for the alphabetic characters N and X and the number 6. From illustration 3, we see that the EBCDIC code for the number 6 is 1111 0110. After completing additional problems, you will see that the zone portion for any number in EBCDIC is 1111, the No Zone equivalent.

ILLUSTRATION 1
The Character N

Step 1	Step 2	Step 3
The Hollerith code for the character N is	Convert these punches to their EBCDIC equivalents.	Combine these equivalents to form one EBCDIC character code.
an 11-zone punch ⟹	which is a 1101 zone code	Zone 8 4 2 1 Digit 8 4 2 1 1 1 0 1 0 1 0 1
+		
a 5-digit punch ⟹	which is a 0101 digit code	The EBCDIC code for N

ILLUSTRATION 2
The Character X

Step 1	Step 2	Step 3
The Hollerith code for the character X is	Convert these punches to their EBCDIC equivalents.	Combine these equivalents to form one EBCDIC character code.
a 0-zone punch ⟹	which is a 1110 zone code	Zone 8 4 2 1 Digit 8 4 2 1 1 1 1 0 0 1 1 1
+		
a 7-digit punch ⟹	which is a 0111 digit code	The EBCDIC code for X

ILLUSTRATION 3
The Character 6

Step 1	Step 2	Step 3
The Hollerith code for the character 6 is	Convert these punches to their EBCDIC equivalents.	Combine these equivalents to form one EBCDIC character code.
No Zone punch ⟹	which is a 1111 zone code	Zone 8 4 2 1 Digit 8 4 2 1 1 1 1 1 0 1 1 0
+		
a 6-digit punch ⟹	which is a 0110 digit code	The EBCDIC code for 6

EBCDIC Shorthand Notation

The structure of EBCDIC is quite rigid; all 1's and 0's composing one character code must be specified. Thus, storing five characters requires five complete sets of EBCDIC codes. The computer actually accomplishes this task, but the programmer may have to check the results. Because specifying a string of 0's and 1's may be a hindrance in some cases, a shorthand notation based on the hexadecimal (base 16) numbering system was applied to EBCDIC.

The **hexadecimal,** or **hex, notation** is composed of only two characters and permits a ready reference to every EBCDIC code configuration. The first character of the hex notation character refers to

Table 5.2 Hex Equivalents to EBCDIC Zone and Digit Bits

		Zone Punches				Digit Punches									
		12 Punch	11 Punch	0 Punch	No Zone	1	2	3	4	5	6	7	8	9	0
EBCDIC Zone Bits	8	1	1	1	1										
	4	1	1	1	1										
	2	0	0	1	1										
	1	0	1	0	1										
Hex Equivalents		C	D	E	F										

	EBCDIC Digit Bits										
8	0	0	0	0	0	0	0	1	1	0
4	0	0	0	1	1	1	1	0	0	0
2	0	1	1	0	0	1	1	0	0	0
1	1	0	1	0	1	0	1	0	1	0
Hex Equivalents	1	2	3	4	5	6	7	8	9	0

the zone equivalent in EBCDIC and the second character to the digit equivalent. Table 5.2 presents the EBCDIC configurations and their equivalent hex notations.

By applying these hex equivalents to earlier illustrations, we can see the ease of reference to the EBCDIC code configurations. For example, the character A in EBCDIC is 1100 0001. The hex representation for the character A is C1.

EBCDIC code

Hex notation for the character A

Figure 5.7 depicts the hexadecimal representation of the EBCDIC characters N, X, and 6.

Table 5.3 provides a quick reference for EBCDIC hexadecimal representations. Choosing any of the characters A, J, S, or 0 as a starting point, you can count to the hex notation desired. For example, the hex equivalent of the EBCDIC code for the character L is D3. You can easily determine this equivalent by beginning at the hex notation for the character J, D1. The character K has a hex notation of D2, and the character L, D3.

FIGURE 5.7 The hexadecimal representations of the EBCDIC character codes for the characters N, X, and 6.

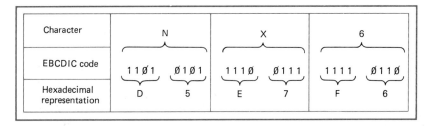

FIGURE 5.8 Here is a blowup of a computer output in which hexadecimal representations of EBCDIC characters are used. The computer outputs this data to show the programmer some of the data stored during processing. On one line of this output there are hex representations: D5, D6, D5, C1, D4, C5. These are the hex equivalents of the characters N, O, N, A, M, E, respectively.

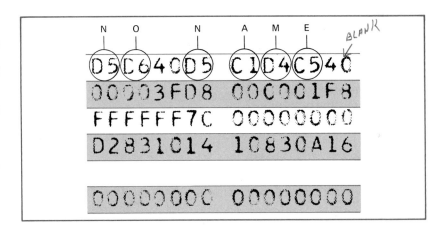

Table 5.3 Hex Notations for Characters

Character	Hexadecimal Notations
A–I	C1–C9
J–R	D1–D9
S–Z	E2–E9
Ø–9	FØ–F9

Figure 5.8 displays part of a computer-prepared output. The computer used hexadecimal representations to indicate to a programmer the data stored within primary storage during processing.

Table 5.4 depicts the Hollerith and EBCDIC codes for alphabetic and numeric characters and their equivalent hex notations.

Parity Bits

A **parity bit,** or **check bit,** is added to the code of a character as it is transferred within storage. The addition of the parity bit ensures that data is accurately moved between computer storage areas or between peripheral devices. When applied to EBCDIC, the parity bit is noted as a C bit and added to the 8 bits of the EBCDIC code, as illustrated below.

EBCDIC

	8 4 2 1	8 4 2 1
C	Zone	Digit
Parity	Bits	Bits
Bit		

Table 5.4 A Comparison of the Hollerith and EBCDIC Codes

EBCDIC 8 4 2 1 8 4 2 1	Hex Representation	Character	Hollerith Code Punches Zone	Digit
1 1 0 0 0 0 0 1	C1	A	12	1
1 1 0 0 0 0 1 0	C2	B	12	2
1 1 0 0 0 0 1 1	C3	C	12	3
1 1 0 0 0 1 0 0	C4	D	12	4
1 1 0 0 0 1 0 1	C5	E	12	5
1 1 0 0 0 1 1 0	C6	F	12	6
1 1 0 0 0 1 1 1	C7	G	12	7
1 1 0 0 1 0 0 0	C8	H	12	8
1 1 0 0 1 0 0 1	C9	I	12	9
1 1 0 1 0 0 0 1	D1	J	11	1
1 1 0 1 0 0 1 0	D2	K	11	2
1 1 0 1 0 0 1 1	D3	L	11	3
1 1 0 1 0 1 0 0	D4	M	11	4
1 1 0 1 0 1 0 1	D5	N	11	5
1 1 0 1 0 1 1 0	D6	O	11	6
1 1 0 1 0 1 1 1	D7	P	11	7
1 1 0 1 1 0 0 0	D8	Q	11	8
1 1 0 1 1 0 0 1	D9	R	11	9
1 1 1 0 0 0 1 0	E2	S	0	2
1 1 1 0 0 0 1 1	E3	T	0	3
1 1 1 0 0 1 0 0	E4	U	0	4
1 1 1 0 0 1 0 1	E5	V	0	5
1 1 1 0 0 1 1 0	E6	W	0	6
1 1 1 0 0 1 1 1	E7	X	0	7
1 1 1 0 1 0 0 0	E8	Y	0	8
1 1 1 0 1 0 0 1	E9	Z	0	9
1 1 1 1 0 0 0 0	F0	0	No Zone	0
1 1 1 1 0 0 0 1	F1	1	No Zone	1
1 1 1 1 0 0 1 0	F2	2	No Zone	2
1 1 1 1 0 0 1 1	F3	3	No Zone	3
1 1 1 1 0 1 0 0	F4	4	No Zone	4
1 1 1 1 0 1 0 1	F5	5	No Zone	5
1 1 1 1 0 1 1 0	F6	6	No Zone	6
1 1 1 1 0 1 1 1	F7	7	No Zone	7
1 1 1 1 1 0 0 0	F8	8	No Zone	8
1 1 1 1 1 0 0 1	F9	9	No Zone	9

As with every other bit position in EBCDIC, the parity bit must contain 0 or 1. How the parity bit is filled depends on the computer. *Even* and *odd* parity are the two types of parity that computers use. With odd parity, the total number of 1 bits used in EBCDIC must remain odd. Even parity requires an even number of 1 bits. Figure 5.9 describes the application of parity to the EBCDIC code for the character A.

The EBCDIC code for the character A is 1100 0001, which uses three 1 bits. For odd parity, the number of 1 bits must remain at three. Thus, the C bit is filled with a 0, keeping three 1 bits. With even parity, a

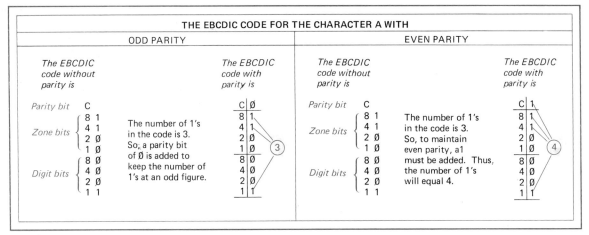

FIGURE 5.9   The addition of the parity, or check, bit to the EBCDIC code
of the character A. Odd parity attempts to keep the total number of 1's
used at an odd number (left). Even parity requires an even number of 1's.
In both even and odd parity, the parity bit must be filled with a 0 or 1.

1 bit must be added in the parity bit position to increase the total to
four. Note that some additional illustrations of parity are provided in
Figure 5.10.

    The concept of parity is applied to other computer media. For
example, the parity bit is used with the EBCDIC code in storing data on
magnetic tape. Thus, the number of bits used totals 9 (i.e., C 8421
8421). The storage of data on magnetic tape must therefore accommodate these 9 bits.[2] The parity bit is also used with other computer
codes.

The ASCII Code

The **American Standard Code for Information Interchange
(ASCII)** was developed jointly by data processing users and equipment manufacturers to standardize the codes for terminals and computers. ASCII appears in both a 6-bit and an 8-bit format, and a com-

FIGURE 5.10   A table
summarizing the use of
parity bits with the
EBCDIC codes for the
characters N, X, and 6.
Odd and even parity are
developed for each
character. In EBCDIC,
count the number of 1's
used to determine
whether a parity bit of 0
or 1 was added.

	CHARACTER					
	N		X		6	
	EBCDIC		EBCDIC		EBCDIC	
	C 8421	8421	C 8421	8421	C 8421	8421
Without parity	1 1Ø1	Ø1Ø1	111Ø	Ø111	1111	Ø11Ø
ODD parity	Ø 11Ø1	Ø1Ø1	1 111Ø	Ø111	1 1111	Ø11Ø
EVEN parity	1 11Ø1	Ø1Ø1	Ø 111Ø	Ø111	Ø 1111	Ø11Ø

---

[2] This topic is reviewed in Chapter 11.

puter will use one or the other to store and transmit data. When parity bits are added, a 7-bit or 9-bit format results.

Because it is like EBCDIC, we will discuss the ASCII 8-bit code, shown in Table 5.5. Note that each position in the 8-bit code is represented by a 0 or 1. The first 4 bits equal zone bits; the second 4 bits equal digit bits. Using the ASCII code for the letter A, these groupings appear as

$$\underbrace{1\ 0\ 1\ 0}_{\text{Zone Bits}}\qquad\underbrace{0\ 0\ 0\ 1}_{\text{Digit Bits}}$$

The ASCII character code for the letter A

Table 5.5 shows the three zone bit groupings. The bits 1010 are used with A to O, 1011 with P to Z, and 0101 with numbers 0 to 9. Numeric codes are handled as in EBCDIC. The first 4 bits are always 0101, followed by the 4 bits that define the number. The ASCII code for 6 is therefore 0101 0110, with 0101 the zone bits and 0110 the equivalent of 6.

Figure 5.11 illustrates the ASCII code for alphabetic characters. The ASCII configurations for A through O can be counted off. The zone bits 1010 are followed by the digit bits necessary to equal the character's position in the alphabet. The letter A is the first character, with O the fifteenth.

P to Z require a slight change. P is the first character to use the zone bits 1011 and is the base for the following letters. Q also uses the zone bits 1011, but adds 1 to the digit bits, giving 0001. The digit bits

Table 5.5 ASCII-8 Codes for Alphabetic and Numeric Characters

Bit Configuration	ASCII-8	Bit Configuration	ASCII-8
1010 0001	A	1011 0011	S
1010 0010	B	1011 0100	T
1010 0011	C	1011 0101	U
1010 0100	D	1011 0110	V
1010 0101	E	1011 0111	W
1010 0110	F	1011 1000	X
1010 0111	G	1011 1001	Y
1010 1000	H	1011 1010	Z
1010 1001	I	0101 0000	0
1010 1010	J	0101 0001	1
1010 1011	K	0101 0010	2
1010 1100	L	0101 0011	3
1010 1101	M	0101 0100	4
1010 1110	N	0101 0101	5
1010 1110	O	0101 0110	6
1011 0000	P	0101 0111	7
1011 0001	Q	0101 1000	8
1011 0010	R	0101 1001	9

FIGURE 5.11 ASCII codes for alphabetic characters use zone groupings of 1010 and 1011. The characters A to O use the 1010 bits, and P to Z use the 1011 bits. The letters A, F, and O represent the first, sixth, and fifteenth characters of the alphabet, respectively. The letters P, Q, and Z become the sixteenth, seventeenth, and twenty-sixth. Their ASCII codes reflect their position in the alphabet.

```
ASII CODES FOR A, F & O    |    ASCII CODES FOR P, Q & Z

                    8 4 2 1
Character A: 1 0 1 0  0 0 0 1   Character P: 1 0 1 1  0 0 0 0
                  ‿‿‿‿
                 1-bit = 1
                    8 4 2 1                       8 4 2 1
       F: 1 0 1 0  0 1 1 0           Q: 1 0 1 1  0 0 0 1
                  ‿‿‿‿                          ‿‿‿‿
               4 + 2 bits = 6                   1-bit = 1
                    8 4 2 1
       O: 1 0 1 0  1 1 1 1           Z: 1 0 1 1  1 0 1 0
                  ‿‿‿‿                          ‿‿‿‿
         8 + 4 + 2 + 1 bits = 15              8 + 2 bits = 10
```

for P were 0000, because P is the 16th character of the alphabet. The 0001 bits of Q indicate that it is the seventeenth character and follows P. The digits follow to Z, with an ASCII code of 1011 1010.

The 8-bit ASCII code, like EBCDIC, has 256 different configurations. Though it was designed primarily for terminal devices, ASCII is also used for data communications services and various peripheral devices. Many of today's home computers use ASCII to store and display data.

5.4 Secondary Storage

One limitation of early computers was the size of their CPUs. Even a 64K capacity quickly filled with data from a medium-sized program. Primary storage could hold only a limited amount of data. Programs were therefore divided into smaller, separately run sections, with the last section completing its processing. Errors encountered during processing would render all prior work useless.

As data processing jobs became more complex, the size of the programs necessary to handle processing grew. This meant that the quantities of data these programs handled were well in excess of what main storage could hold. It became obvious that a supplementary or secondary means of data storage attached to the CPU was required. This supplementary storage area had to satisfy two constraints: It had to be online, and it had to store data in a form that was readily compatible with data in primary storage. After all, it would be pointless to have a computer that could process data in millionths of a second wait minutes for the conversion and transmission of that data. Data stored in supplementary storage areas had to be readily available to permit the continuous processing of information. With these factors taken into account, a provision for secondary storage was developed.

Secondary storage provides a computer system with greater processing potential because it expands the CPU's ability to handle data. Data that is an integral part of processing and cannot be contained in primary storage can be stored in secondary storage and made available in thousandths of a second. For a good analogy to the relationship between primary and secondary storage, consider the two basic ways you can recall your social security number. If you remember it, you are using primary storage. If you look at the card in your wallet, you are using secondary storage. Secondary storage is that extra storage area that facilitates the computer's extraordinary capabilities.

Two principal modes of secondary storage are **magnetic tape** and **magnetic disk,** shown in Figures 5.12 and 5.13, respectively. These storage devices are traditionally associated with computers, but many others are also used for secondary storage. Currently available secondary storage devices and those being developed will be discussed in Chapter 11.

The importance of secondary storage lies in the fact that it enables the CPU to have access to large amounts of data for use in

FIGURE 5.12 A computer operator prepares to mount a magnetic tape onto a magnetic tape drive. (*IBM.*)

processing. Two examples involving batch and online processing will help illustrate the use of secondary storage.

Consider the batch processing of an employee payroll. Employee data relating to the current payroll period is entered via punched cards. The computer program used to process the payroll receives these cards and computes the payroll data related to each employee. This payroll data must be processed against previous payroll information to update the year-to-date totals (i.e., total earnings, federal taxes withheld, state tax withheld, and social security deductions). This total amount of payroll data cannot be permanently maintained within primary storage because it is only used on a weekly basis and would clog the CPU. Thus, all previous payroll data is maintained on secondary storage devices. These devices are capable of storing many millions of characters and enable the computer to have almost immediate access to that data.

During the processing of the payroll, data relating to any employee is accessed from secondary storage. All newly processed payroll data is posted against each employee's records, and the file of new employee payroll data is again stored in secondary storage. Magnetic tape is a secondary storage medium suited to the sequential batch processing of payroll data.

An online application, such as an airline reservation system, would use secondary storage in a different way. Online data is not batched; passenger requests must be handled as they occur. The computer must be able to randomly access data on any flight. Magnetic disk is a secondary storage device capable of providing this type of support.

Extensive data files can be maintained on disk, and the computer can have access to each item of data. These files could not be stored in the CPU because they involve millions of characters of storage. Using secondary storage, a vast amount of passenger flight data can be retained on disk and made available in fractions of a second. Thus, when a passenger desires to confirm a ticket reservation, data related to that flight is retrieved from the file of all flight reservations. Passenger data is then input to the computer via a terminal. The computer system uses this data to search all the flight reservation files maintained in secondary storage. When the particular flight's data is accessed, information related to the passenger is output on the requesting clerk's terminal device. The reservation clerk is then free to add or delete data to that record of ticket confirmations.

Both examples illustrate that secondary storage serves the purpose of retaining data that cannot be stored within primary storage and keeping this data available for use by the computer. Most computer systems use a combination of primary and secondary storage when processing data. This combination varies extensively from system to system. Secondary storage expands a system's ability to process data effectively.

FIGURE 5.13 (*a*) An enlargement of a removable disk pack in its plastic dust cover. (*IBM.*) (*b*) A computer operator mounts a disk pack into its disk drive. This removable disk is portable. (*Control Data Corp.*)

(*a*)

(*b*)

5.5 Computer Advances
Overlapped Processing

Early computers handled jobs according to the EDP cycle, and all programs were defined in terms of input, processing, and output. The CPU controlled the sequential execution of programs. Program 1 was run before program 2 began; program 3 waited for program 2 to end, and so on. Figure 5.14 illustrates this system, a system that did not fully use the CPU. It slowed the CPU to the speed of its I/O devices. For

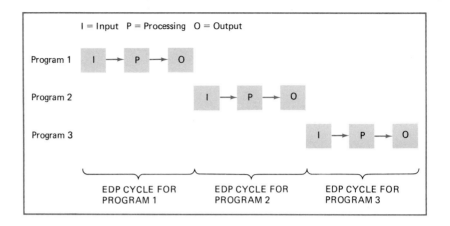

I = Input   P = Processing   O = Output

FIGURE 5.14 The input, processing, and output of one program must be completed before the computer can continue to the next. This diagram illustrates the sequence of operations for processing three programs.

example, although the CPU could perform 1 million operations per second, it could only process 800 characters of data per second if that was the speed of its card reader. This condition, termed **I/O bound,** hampered the CPU. The solution to this problem was overlapped processing.

Overlapped processing increases the effectiveness of the CPU by reducing the time wasted while the CPU waits for the completion of I/O operations and by giving it more than one task at a time. Figure 5.15 illustrates how a series of programs might be handled with overlapped processing. In the time required for two programs in a nonoverlapped system, four programs could be processed in an overlapped system.

The computer's ability to accomplish more than one task at a time rests on units called channels. **Channels** are devices attached to the CPU that control input and output operations and free the CPU to perform other functions. One channel can control an input operation while another controls an output operation.

Early computers did not have channels. The CPU directly controlled all I/O activities. The first computer system to use channels was the IBM 709. Current computers may use many channels for I/O operations, and each channel may control several I/O devices. A sample configuration appears in Figure 5.16. But how are channels used?

Data is first readied for entry. With the assistance of a channel, the input device enters the data into a **buffer,** a temporary storage area for I/O operations. At that time, the computer may be performing operations on other jobs. It will retrieve data from the input buffer when it is needed. During processing, channels will continue supporting I/O operations and move data to or from buffers.

As processing continues, data is directed to an output buffer. Utilizing another channel, output data is then transferred to the appropriate peripheral device. If printers are involved, output channels may be

FIGURE 5.15 The relationship between the input, processing, and output of separate programs using overlapped processing. Notice that by the third cycle, the computer is handling processing for three programs: output of program 1, processing of program 2, and input of program 3. The sequence continues until processing ceases. Note that in the time it takes to process two programs using nonoverlapped processing (Figure 5.14), four programs are handled using overlapped processing.

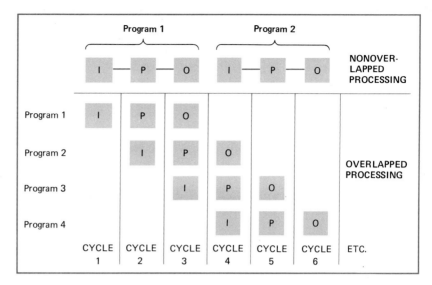

occupied for many minutes. Without channels, the CPU would have to control this lengthy output and be incapable of performing other tasks.

Buffers and channels have assisted in maximizing the use of the CPU. Tasks which slowed the processing unit's operation have been assigned to channels and buffers. For example, the reading of card data, punched tapes, or batched data has been assigned to and con-

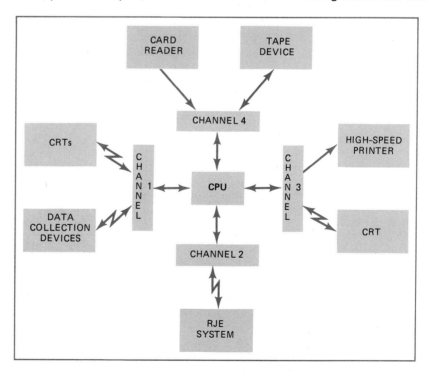

FIGURE 5.16 Channels are vital to the modern computer system. Here, a computer system uses multiple channels to handle a variety of I/O operations.

trolled by input channels. Output operations, such as printing or punching cards, are accomplished through the assistance of other channels. With channels assuming the responsibility of overseeing these slower operations, the CPU is available to complete other tasks. Also, when data is needed for processing, the CPU can access this data at the highest speeds. Data is available in the buffer in an immediately usable form. The CPU does not wait for the input of data. For output operations, data is quickly transferred to an output buffer, where the data may be fed to I/O devices. In all instances, the speed with which the CPU accesses data or is freed to perform processing tasks increases. Figure 5.17 illustrates the relationship of channels, buffers, and I/O devices.

Virtual Storage

For the average programmer working with a medium- or small-scale computer, the limitations of primary storage present a real problem. Programmers must work within this constraint and write programs for the allotted amount of storage.

In some computer systems, the technique of **virtual storage (VS)** eliminates the problem of limited storage. The programmer can write programs as if the amount of storage were unlimited. A computer with virtual storage will break a large program into modules called **pages,** each of which holds the same amount of data. The program exists as a series of pages. As it is executed, only those pages being processed stay in main storage. The rest are stored on magnetic disk or a similar online storage device. The computer retrieves necessary pages from disk storage. Entering pages swap places with pages leaving main storage, and the swapping continues until the program is completed. Almost all large computers have virtual storage, and it is also popular in smaller systems because it lets them process larger, more complex programs.

FIGURE 5.17 Buffers and channels are important in overlapped processing. This diagram illustrates the relationship of these components in a computer system.

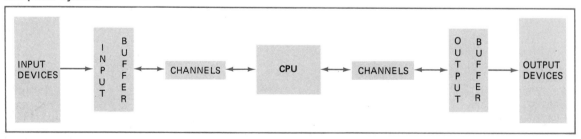

A PERSPECTIVE ON COMPUTER EVOLUTION

Even data processing professionals tend to lose sight of the tremendous gains the computer industry has made. Here are some notes to refresh everyone's memory.

The computer industry has developed ever smaller, faster, cheaper, and more powerful computers. If the airline industry had progressed at the same rate, it would take only 24 minutes to fly around the world. The automobile industry would have provided cars that get over 550 miles per gallon.

Almost 30 years ago, it cost nearly $1.25 to process 100,000 computations on a computer. Today it costs less than a penny. Applying the same ratio to food, clothing, and houses, we would get sirloin steak for 9¢ a pound; fine suits for $6; and four-bedroom homes for about $3500.

In 1953, to store 1 million pieces of information took more than 400 cubic feet and cost $250,000. Today's computers can store that data for $400 in a space the size of a pocket radio, about .03 cubic foot.

Summary

The following major points have been presented in Chapter 5:

Point 1 The central processing unit (CPU) is the heart of the computer system. All processing accomplished by the computer is performed in the CPU.

Point 2 Computers are classified into the broad categories of analog and digital computers, hybrid computers, and special-purpose and general-purpose computers. Analog computers use physical quantities to represent their data, while digital computers represent their data in the form of numbers. Hybrid computers combine the best qualities of analog and digital computers. Special-purpose computers are specifically designed for use on one type of application. General-purpose computers are designed to process a wide group of problems.

Point 3 The EDP cycle consists of input, processing, and output. Although I/O activities are assumed by a variety of peripheral devices, processing must occur in the CPU.

Point 4 The components of the CPU are the control unit, arithmetic logic unit (ALU), and primary storage unit. The control unit monitors all the processing performed in the system. The control unit ensures that data is properly transferred between storage locations, controls and coordinates the execution of I/O operations, and attempts to execute all instructions drawn from programs undergoing processing.

Point 5 The arithmetic logic unit performs all arithmetic and logical operations. Logical operations involve comparing two values and may be performed on alphabetic, numeric, and/or alphanumeric data. Registers are employed in logical and arithmetic operations.

Point 6 Primary storage is the main storage area of the CPU. It can store input data, program statements, data resulting from processing, and information in preparation for output. Primary storage is composed of a series of storage areas, each identified by its own storage address. The retention of program instructions in primary stor-

Case Study One

Energy Control System Helps Exxon Save Fuel

At Exxon's Baytown, Texas, plant, computers not only control production but also monitor the use of energy. This $500 million plant, which produces 2.7 billion pounds of olefins a year, needed an adequate control system. (Olefins are used in making plastics, synthetic rubber, solvents, and other chemicals.) The Honeywell TDC 2000 uses four 4500 computers to monitor energy consumption throughout the plant. It has reduced fuel consumption by 15 percent, or 3 trillion BTUs—enough energy to heat 150,000 houses for an entire winter.

The computerized system uses over 6000 sensors to monitor temperatures, pressures, product flow, and other heat-related factors and feeds these data into the computer. The information is displayed to five operators in a control center so that they can continually monitor performance.

Inefficient energy use automatically appears on color CRTs and is highlighted so that operators can rapidly make corrections. The system can make adjustments at over 1000 points in the plant and can redistribute energy.

The system monitors both heat and air conditioning and can recapture and reuse over 25 percent of the heat formerly lost during manufacturing. It can also reuse 75 percent of lost heat to generate steam for heating and production and for cooling towers.

The Honeywell TDC is a special-purpose, hybrid system. Sensors provide the computers with data, which is converted to numeric data and processed. Only a computer system of this type could monitor the energy flow and make the thousands of adjustments necessary to ensure the efficient, continuous use of fuel.

Consider this . . .

In what other ways can computers be used within industrial facilities to control energy resources, materials, water usage, or industrial pollution?

Could they be employed to identify offenders or to project future pollution problems?

---

age is the basis for the stored program concept. Primary storage is classified as word-oriented or byte-oriented. Words may hold several characters of data. Bytes normally hold only one character of data. Current computer storage systems are constructed using silicon chips.

Point 7 Data is stored inside computers using electric impulses which are defined by two states, off and on. These states are represented by the digits 0 and 1, respectively, which are called bits. Employing the 0 and 1 bits, data is represented in the notation of the binary numbering system.

Point 8 Two codes used to represent the storage of data are EBCDIC and ASCII. EBCDIC uses 8 bits, or a byte, to represent one character of data. The byte is broken into two 4-bit groupings, one the equivalent of Hollerith's zone punches and the other the equivalent of digit punches. These groupings are combined to compose the EBCDIC code for one character. A hex shorthand may be applied to the EBCDIC code. A parity, or

Case Study Two

Designing a Braille Computer

Not all computer research is conducted by large organizations. Gary Kelly, a blind research scientist at Georgia Tech's Atlanta campus, is actively involved in constructing a Braille computer for blind people. He is convinced that it would more than double the current job opportunities for the 1.8 million visually handicapped in America. With it they could work at banks, credit card agencies, and government offices that handle business data.

The major component of the proposed system is a specially designed terminal that produces Braille messages. Blind operators would read data in Braille with their fingers. The message would be produced by a mechanism like a wire-matrix printer which would press the Braille into a plastic tape. A prototype of the Braille computer and its software is on the drawing board. Progress is hampered, however, by a lack of funds. It will take a considerable amount of work before Mr. Kelly's dreams are realized.

check, bit, supplied by the computer to ensure that data is properly transferred between storage areas, may add a ninth bit to the EBCDIC code. ASCII employs a type of representation similar to EBCDIC but has its own unique code.

Point 9 As the complexity of data processing jobs grew, so did the amount of data that had to be held in primary storage. Secondary storage was developed to overcome the limitations of primary storage. Secondary storage devices store their data in a format readily compatible with data in main storage. Magnetic tape and magnetic disk are two widely used secondary storage media.

Point 10 Overlapped processing and virtual storage are two techniques developed to improve the efficiency of the computer. Overlapped processing frees the CPU to handle more work and eliminates a condition called I/O bound. Channels control the performance of I/O operations and free the CPU for other tasks. Buffers are temporary storage areas that contain data used in I/O operations controlled by channels. Virtual storage uses magnetic disks to expand the capacity of primary storage. Large programs are segmented into pages of data that are swapped between main storage and the disk as they are used.

Glossary

American Standard Code for Information Interchange (ASCII)   An 8-bit code used for the representation of data, developed for use with terminal devices, often referred to as ASCII-8 or USASCII.

Analog computer   A computer that represents its data in the form of a measurement (feet, degrees, volts, etc.) of an actual property.

Arithmetic logic unit (ALU)   The component of a CPU responsible for the performance of arithmetic and logical operations.

Arithmetic operation   The performance of one of the fundamental operations of addition, subtraction, multiplication, division, and exponentiation.

Binary notation   A method of representing a number in base 2, using a string of 0's and 1's.

Binary numbering system   A method of counting based on the number 2 which employs the digits 0 and 1.

Bits   Binary digits, either 0 or 1. The term *bits* is a contraction of **bi**nary dig**its.**

Buffer   A temporary storage device, attached to the CPU, specifically designed to support I/O operations.

Byte   A unit of primary storage that normally represents and stores exactly one character of data and is composed of 8 bits.

Byte-oriented computer   A computer system in which primary storage retains data in bytes of storage.

Central processing unit (CPU)   The major component of a computer system, responsible for processing all data handled by the system; consists of the control unit, ALU, and primary storage unit.

Channel   The communication link between the CPU and its I/O devices that effects and assists in the performance of all I/O operations.

Check bit   Another term for the parity bit.

Control unit   The component of the CPU that monitors the execution of all programs in the computer. Its tasks include checking data to ensure its accurate transfer and control and coordination of all I/O activities.

Core   Another term for the primary storage unit, or a small, doughnut-shaped metal component once used in the construction of primary storage.

Digital computer   A computer that represents its data in digits or numbers.

Electronic data processing (EDP) cycle   A term representing the fundamental components of a data processing system—input, processing, and output.

Extended Binary Coded Decimal Interchange Code (EBCDIC)   A computer code composed of 8 bits (a byte), used to represent data stored in the computer system.

General-purpose computer   A computer system designed for application to almost all types of computerized tasks.

Hexadecimal (hex) notation   A shorthand notation for representing EBCDIC configurations, based on the base 16 numbering system.

Hybrid computer   A type of computer that combines the best features of analog and digital computers.

I/O bound   The condition in which the CPU of a computer system is constrained by the speed of its I/O devices.

Logical operation   An operation performed to determine the relationship between two values that are either numeric, alphabetic, or alphanumeric.

Magnetic disk   One of the major means of secondary storage, used for the random access of data.

Magnetic tape   One of the major means of secondary storage, used for the sequential access of data.

Main storage   A term for the primary storage unit.

Overlapped processing   A technique that employs channels and buffers to free the CPU for the performance of other tasks.

Page   A segment of storage employed in the virtual storage of data; as pages are processed, they are swapped between main storage and magnetic disk devices.

Parity bit   The check bit employed with EBCDIC or ASCII codes to ensure that data is properly transferred between storage areas.

Primary storage   Another term for the primary storage unit.

Primary storage unit   The main storage component of the CPU.

Register   A special storage area in the CPU, used to store data temporarily during the completion of arithmetic and logical operations.

Secondary storage   A supplementary means for storing data; secondary storage is separate from but directly attached to the CPU and stores data in a format that is compatible with data held in primary storage.

Simulator   A device that allows for job training under realistic, computer-oriented conditions; often a special-purpose, hybrid computer system.

Special-purpose computer   A computer system that is designed for specific applications and cannot be applied to a general range of data processing activities.

Stored program concept   A concept, originated by Dr. John Von Neumann, in which the program under execution is in primary storage.

Virtual storage (VS)   A software technique that expands the capacity of primary storage by segmenting large programs into smaller units called pages. These pages are stored on a magnetic disk or other devices built for that purpose, are brought into primary storage when needed, and swap positions with pages already there.

Word   A unit of primary storage capable of holding an entire number; may be composed of one or more bytes.

Word-oriented computers   Computers that store data in groups of characters or words instead of one character at a time.

Discussion Questions

1 Compile a list of computers that you see in your everyday surroundings and classify them as digital or analog devices.

2 Describe overlapped processing and virtual storage.

3 Discuss the purpose of channels, registers, and buffers.

4 Complete the following table by filling in the required computer codes:

Character	EBCDIC	ASCII-8
B		
N		
U		
6		
F		
Q		
W		
8		

5 Briefly explain the differences between analog computers, digital computers, hybrid computers, special-purpose computers, and general-purpose computers.

6 Complete the table that follows on the next page.

7 Discuss the purpose of secondary storage. Would an airline reservation system or an inventory system require secondary storage? If so, explain why and what data would be stored there.

8 What fields could use a computerized simulator for training and how? Would the device be an analog, digital, hybrid, special- or general-purpose computer?

Character	EBCDIC Code with Odd Parity	EBCDIC Code with Even Parity	Hex Representation
	C 8421 8421	C 8421 8421	
E			
B			
V			
3			

Summary Test

_F_ **1** The EDP cycle is composed of the elements of input, processing, output, and reporting.

_T_ **2** The CPU is composed of the control unit, ALU, and primary storage unit.

_F_ **3** The control unit is responsible for only one task: the completion of I/O operations.

_T_ **4** A logical operation is designed to determine the relationship between two values.

_F_ **5** The two digits employed with the binary numbering system are 1 and 2.

_F_ **6** A core represents three electrical states when used in computers.

_F_ **7** EBCDIC is the 6-bit code used to represent data in the computer.

_F_ **8** Secondary storage media must store data in a form compatible with main storage and be offline to the CPU.

_T_ **9** The EBCDIC code for the character L is 1101 0011.

_F_ **10** The parity bit must always be represented by a 1 when it is added to an EBCDIC code.

_F_ **11** The hex shorthand for the character 7 is H7.

_F_ **12** Word-oriented computers store data in primary storage 1 byte or character of data at a time.

_T_ **13** Hybrid computers combine the best features of analog and digital computers.

_F_ **14** Channels are attached to the CPU, but they are not involved in the execution of I/O operations.

_F_ **15** In an I/O bound system, the peripheral devices do not inhibit the processing speed of the CPU.

_A_ **16** The computer code for the interchange of information between terminals is:

    a ASCII   **b** BCD

    c EBCDIC   **d** Hollerith

_B_ **17** A temporary storage area, attached to the CPU, for I/O operations is a:

    a channel   **b** buffer

    c register   **d** core

C **18** In virtual storage, program segments stored on disk during processing are called:

    a   sections   **b**   partitions

    c   pages   **d**   sectors

B **19** The EBCDIC code for the character X, with odd parity, is:

    a   0 1110 0110   **b**   1 1110 0111

    c   1 1110 0110   **d**   0 1110 0111

C **20** A characteristic of the ASCII code is:

    a   its limitation to a maximum of 96 character configurations

    b   its use of the zone codes 1010, 1011, and 1100

    c   its independence from the Hollerith code

    d   all the above

D **21** The comparison of data inside the arithmetic logic unit is referred to as a:

    a   question   **b**   data operation

    c   conditional question   **d**   logical operation

C **22** The ASCII code for the character J is:

    a   1101 0001   **b**   1101 1010

    c   1010 1010   **d**   1010 0001

A **23** A computer-controlled device for training exercises that duplicates the work environment is a:

    a   simulator   **b**   duplicator

    c   trainer   **d**   COM device

D **24** An advantage of overlapped processing activities is:

    a   more effective use of the CPU

    b   increased processing activities for the entire system

    c   better coordination of I/O activities

    d   all the above

B **25** First-generation computer systems used:

    a   transistors   **b**   vacuum tubes

    c   magnetic cores   **d**   silicon chips

Summary Test Answers

1 F	**2** T	**3** F	**4** T	**5** F
6 F	**7** F	**8** F	**9** T	**10** F
11 F	**12** F	**13** T	**14** F	**15** F
16 A	**17** B	**18** C	**19** B	**20** C
21 D	**22** C	**23** A	**24** D	**25** B

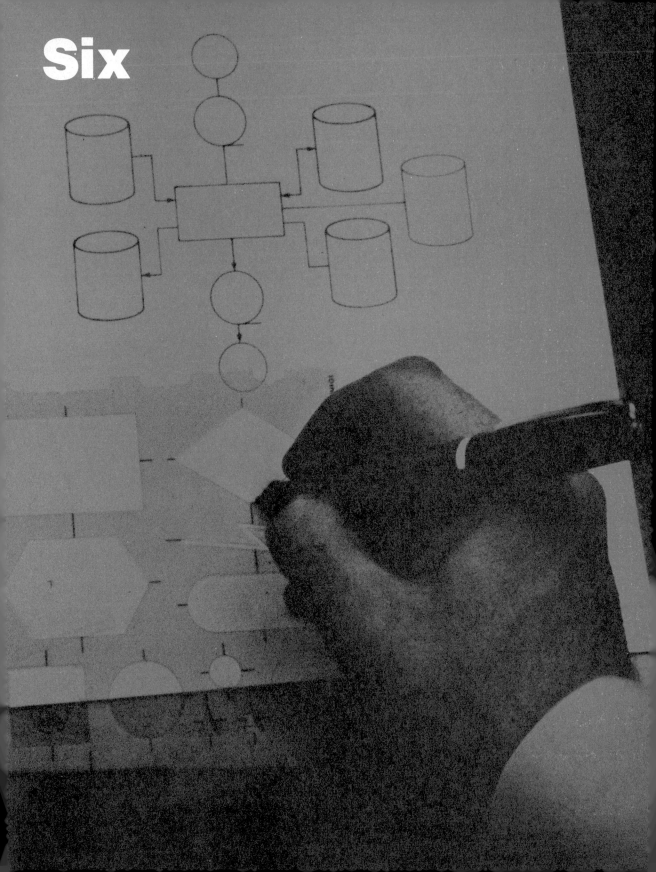

Six

Flowcharting

FIGURE 6.1 The pictorial representation of the flow of data is easily diagrammed in flowcharts. These diagrams serve as an analytical tool and are a sound form of documentation. Great care is exercised in the preparation of these pictorial solutions. (*Sperry Univac.*)

Purpose of This Chapter

Flowcharts are diagrams that depict the flow of data through an organization or illustrate the series of operations in a program. This chapter introduces flowcharting and discusses how these pictorial representations of data are constructed.

The difference between systems and program flowcharts and the reasons for using flowcharts are discussed. Flowcharts are prepared long before programs are written or any work is actually completed. The most widely used flowcharting symbols and an explanation of their use are presented. Subsequently, we complete two flowcharts that process one individual's data.

The loop, last record check, and 9's Decision facilitate the repetitive processing of data. The accumulator is used to add up grand totals related to one specific amount. The counter is used to control and count the number of repetitive loops possible with a flowchart. Many practical problems are presented to illustrate these concepts.

Additional flowcharting techniques are discussed. The printed output of special data is represented through the use of literals. Illustrative problems combine the techniques of accumulators, counters, and multiple decisions. The use of a negative accumulator makes possible the systematic subtraction of data from a predefined total. Finally, a checklist, or guideline, is presented to assist the person preparing the flowchart.

Throughout the chapter, we will present helpful hints related to flowcharting. These advisory notes, indicated by a lightning stroke, will alert you to commonly made flowcharting errors. We hope that the comments will help you to avoid these pitfalls.

A special appendix relating to decision tables is provided at the end of the chapter. Flowcharters use this special technique when complex decisions involving many alternatives are under study and must be incorporated into a flowchart.

After studying this chapter, you should be able to:

- Describe the purpose and use of a program flowchart.
- Distinguish between systems and program flowcharts.
- Describe all the symbols employed in program flowcharts.
- Discuss the purpose of the flowchart loop, last record check, and 9's Decision.
- Describe the function of an accumulator and a counter and use them in a flowchart.
- Describe the use of literals for headings and special labels.
- Describe and draw fundamental flowcharts involving loops, accumulators, counters, and literals.

■ Describe the function of a negative accumulator and use it in a flowchart solution.

■ Discuss the purpose of a decision table.

■ Understand the following terms:

Accumulator	Legend
American National Standards Institute (ANSI)	Literal
	Loop
Annotation symbol	Negative accumulator
Checklist	9's Data
Conditional branches	9's Decision
Conditional statement	PRINT symbol
Connector symbol	Processing symbol
Counter	Program flowchart
Datanames	READ symbol
Decision symbol	Running total
Flowchart	Special label
Flowchart loop	START symbol
Heading	STOP symbol
Initial conditions	Systems flowchart
Input/Output (I/O) symbol	Terminal symbol
Last record check	Unconditional branch

Introduction

If you have ever had the opportunity to work with young children, you may have noticed a recurring phenomenon. Often youngsters will state, "I don't see it!" when they are trying to develop a solution to a problem they do not understand. In reality, these youngsters are stating that they cannot visualize a solution to the problem, that they cannot see the answer.

In this type of situation, how many of us have resorted to making a diagram or an illustration to express our ideas? When children grasp a pictured solution, they frequently say, "I see it!" Actually, by understanding the picture, they are able to visualize the solution in their minds.

A picture or diagram is a simple, easily understood, and effective means of expressing a thought. Graphs and pictorial representations are used in all fields and industries. How effective would a TV weather report be without a weather map and drawings of sunbursts and clouds? Consider how often a loss or gain of money is depicted on a chart or graph.

The field of data processing also makes effective use of pictorial solutions and diagrams. The diagrammatic form used in data processing is the flowchart. With this type of illustration, data processors can easily express a group of ideas or represent the flow of data. Flowcharts are frequently used to express technical concepts in their sim-

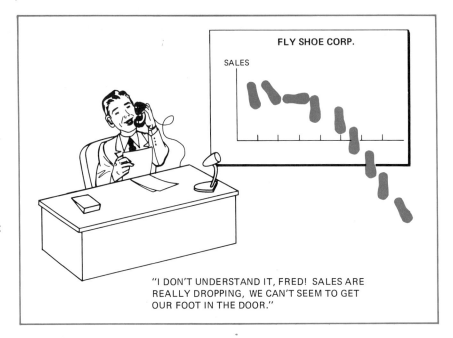

FIGURE 6.2 Pictures readily present data that might otherwise require a long narrative. Flowcharts can describe the logic of a solution in a few symbols and represent an effective data processing tool.

plest terms. Often flowcharts are chosen when data processing people must meet with managers and other users to improve their understanding of the computer. The flowchart is an essential and integral part of the programmer's and system analyst's professional repertoire.

In this chapter, we will focus on how flowcharts represent data. We will explain how specific symbols are used and the logic of each solution. We will proceed slowly, using a series of flowcharts that build on each other. In Chapter 10, we will talk about the more complex concepts of structured programming.

6.1 Flowcharts
Systems versus Program Flowcharts

Essentially, flowcharts are like road maps. Whereas the road map details the road network between two points, a **flowchart** describes the path that data will follow as it is processed. It is a more detailed and exacting diagram, however. A flowchart is a pictorial representation of all the operations that are performed during the processing of data. The two most commonly employed formats are the systems flowchart and the program flowchart.

The **systems flowchart** defines all the operations performed on data as it passes through a company, an organization, or a department. The sequence of operations described in a systems flowchart may be computerized or manually performed. The **program flowchart,** on the other hand, depicts the operations performed in a computerized data processing program. It is therefore a narrower, more specific diagram than the systems flowchart. It is not uncommon to find program flowcharts referred to in systems flowcharts.

Why Use Flowcharts?

A flowchart provides more than a detailed description of the flow or processing of data. A flowchart also serves as

1 An efficient means of communication
2 An analytic tool
3 A concise form of documentation

Because a flowchart is essentially a picture, it readily represents a single thought or a series of ideas. Programmers or analysts can completely depict the methods needed to process data in a flowchart without a written narrative. Thus, two programmers, one in New York and the other in San Francisco, can use flowcharts to share their ideas concerning the processing of data. Flowcharts minimize the necessity of repeated, face-to-face meetings to clarify particular trouble spots.

Another profitable use of flowcharts comes in programming. Flowcharts are very effective and inexpensive analytic tools. Using flowcharts, a programmer can very quickly sketch out a series of alternative approaches to a problem. A group of analysts and programmers can then examine the flowcharts and determine which solution best suits their needs. No one has to actually write any programs, waste valuable computer time, or physically test any of the solutions. The assessment is done completely with paper and pencil.

Because flowcharts are diagrams, they are an excellent and concise form of documentation. They can document any programmer's or analyst's work without depending on a programming language. A flowchart lets a supervisor estimate the completeness and logic of a project.

The documentation represented by the flowchart helps users also. Flowcharts permit programmers or analysts to gauge the extent of their work and their progress. For example, a programmer can compare the amount of program instructions written against the flowchart to determine the progress made, the coding completed, and the amount of work remaining.

Flowcharting is especially helpful in running a data processing department efficiently. When programs are properly documented, the work of the entire staff is simplified. Changes in programs are easily accomplished, and data is readily available. Compare these operating conditions to those at a DP center where employees must search through piles of paper for nonexistent documentation.

Data processing managers are acutely aware of the need for quality documentation. Too many of these managers have seen a lack of documentation result in missed deadlines and budget overruns. DP professionals always recall the humorous anecdote of the programmer who never documented his work because he felt that was the best way to keep his job. Documentation is essential for operating a responsible data processing organization.

We should stop here to put flowcharts in their proper place in the sequence of data processing operations. A false impression commonly encountered is that programs precede flowcharts. But because flowcharts are analytic tools, they should be drawn before the first program instruction is written. That way, the logic of a solution can be verified before programming begins. If problems then crop up during programming, their source can be narrowed to coding or computer malfunction.

Do not overlook the value of learning sound flowcharting skills. Although many of our solutions will start out simply, later problems will require more involved diagrams. As the nature of programs becomes more complex, your dependence on flowcharts will increase. A sound knowledge of flowcharting principles is an invaluable asset. A unique set of symbols was created to accurately portray the processing operations depicted in a flowchart. Through the efforts of the **American National Standards Institute (ANSI),** a standard set of flowcharting symbols has been adopted internationally. Though there are some variations of these symbols, the field has uniformly adopted most of the symbols shown in Figure 6.3. One group of symbols is used in program flowcharts, and another group is used in systems flowcharts. Our current discussion will focus on the use of program flowchart symbols. Systems flowcharts and their symbols will be discussed in Chapters 14 and 15.

6.2 Symbols Used in Program Flowcharts

Program flowchart symbols are important because of their widespread use. They include the

1 Terminal symbol
2 Input/Output symbol
3 Processing symbol
4 Decision symbol
5 Annotation symbol

Terminal Symbol

The **Terminal symbol** is used to indicate the point at which a flowchart begins and ends. It is accepted procedure to insert the words START and STOP with the Terminal symbol, as in Figure 6.4. The **START symbol** is the first symbol of a flowchart and identifies the point at which the analysis of the flowchart should begin. Similarly, the **STOP symbol** is the last symbol of a flowchart and indicates its termination. No symbols follow this Terminal symbol. All flowcharts must have a START and a STOP Terminal symbol.

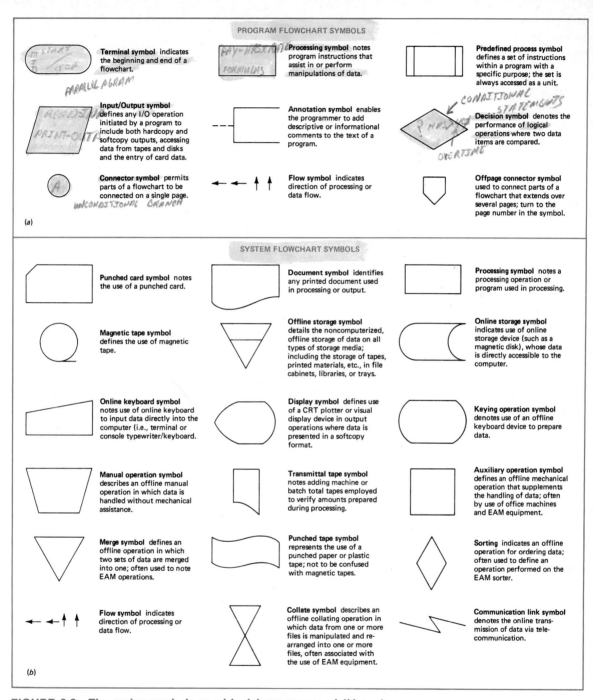

FIGURE 6.3 The major symbols used in (*a*) program and (*b*) systems flowcharts. It is accepted practice not to mix the types of symbols in one flowchart. For purposes of identification, the symbols are divided into their respective operational groups.

FIGURE 6.4 Terminal symbols containing the words START and STOP. The START symbol notes the beginning of a flowchart, and the STOP symbol indicates its end.

Input/Output Symbol

In a program flowchart, the **Input/Output (I/O) symbol** identifies the logical positioning of input and output operations. The I/O symbol, for example, notes the entry of computer data and the printed output of information. Figure 6.5 depicts an input and an output operation. The first I/O symbol indicates an input operation, collecting data relating to an employee's name, hours worked, and rate of pay. The other I/O symbol represents the performance of an output operation, printing an employee's name and gross pay. In both cases, the nature of the I/O operation is defined by the notation within the symbol. The terms most closely associated with flowcharting I/O operations are READ and PRINT. READ describes the entry of computer data, while PRINT relates to the printed output of information. Occasionally we will identify the I/O symbols as **READ** or **PRINT symbols.** This is a shorthand way of referring to I/O symbols that contain the word READ or PRINT and represent the I/O operation indicated.

One point about the relationship among flowcharts, programs, and flowcharting symbols must be made quite clear. As previously discussed, a flowchart is compiled and verified long before the actual writing of a program. Though it accurately describes the processing to be performed, the flowchart is not input to the computer. The flowchart is a research tool for the programmer. No flowchart symbol has ever caused a computer to physically undertake and complete one program instruction. The appropriate symbol is placed in a flowchart where an operation should logically take place. When the program is written, a computer language instruction will define the operation described by that symbol. This instruction will eventually cause the computer to process data.

Over the years, however, terms related to flowcharting have grown broader. We speak of the initial symbol of the flowchart as "inputting data" when we know that really we are looking at a READ symbol. We assume, in making this statement, that the symbol has been converted to a program statement that actually causes the computer to read in the data. This liberal use of terminology will help as we explain flowcharting solutions.

FIGURE 6.5 I/O symbols representing the entry and output of data. The READ symbol indicates data input of an employee's name, hours worked, and hourly rate of pay. The PRINT symbol notes the printed output of the employee's name and gross pay.

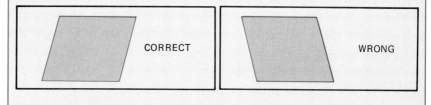

THE SHAPE OF THE I/O SYMBOL

Input/Output symbols are often drawn incorrectly on flowcharts. The following diagram illustrates a properly drawn and an improperly drawn I/O symbol. Beginning flowcharters often use the wrong symbol when they hurry to compose solutions.

CORRECT

WRONG

Processing Symbol

The processing related to all types of data is indicated by the **Processing symbol.** Examples of this symbol are given in Figure 6.6. Using this symbol, we can define computations, move data from a storage area to an output area, or indicate the sorting or manipulation of data. The narrative within the Processing symbol may take the form of an algebraic formula or a sentence to describe processing. The approach is selected by the person drawing the flowchart. Figure 6.6 shows the same computation defined by two methods.

Decision Symbol

The capability for logical operations is necessary in any data processing application. In most business problems, many comparisons of data are made before the best alternative is chosen. Because flowcharts are applied to business-related problems, they must be able to represent logical operations. Logical operations are indicated in flowcharts via the **Decision symbol.** The two principal components of a Decision symbol, as seen in Figure 6.7, are

1 A question that defines the logical operation
2 The results of the decision (i.e., yes, no)

The question asked within the Decision symbol indicates the comparison necessary to support processing. This question is referred to as a **conditional statement.** In flowcharting, conditional statements are normally written in question form, making the comparison easier to

FIGURE 6.6 The Processing symbol defines the manipulation of data and all forms of processing. Here, the same computation is expressed in two ways. In flowcharting, either is correct and acceptable.

COMMISSION = TOTAL SALES * .10 — PROCESSING DEFINED AS A FORMULA

COMMISSION IS COMPUTED AT 10% OF TOTAL SALES — PROCESSING DEFINED AS A SENTENCE

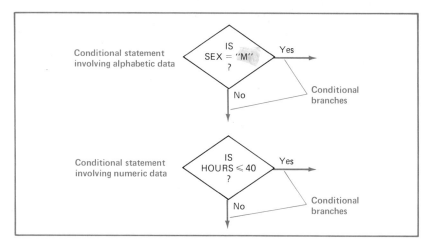

FIGURE 6.7 Two types of conditional statements are shown in Decision symbols. The exits from the Decision symbols are defined by YES and NO branches. Note that the arrowheads show the direction of exit and, therefore, the path data will follow.

understand. The results of the comparisons in Figure 6.7 are given in terms of YES or NO responses. These are the only two answers possible in either case. The questions were deliberately constructed to elicit only these two answers. Note that the YES or NO responses define the only two exits from the Decision symbol. These two exits are called the **conditional branches** of the decision, because the branch chosen is totally dependent on the answer to the conditional statement.

In Figure 6.7, if the data in the field called Sex is the character M, then the YES branch is chosen. In all other cases the NO branch is chosen. The decision forces us to exit from either conditional branch in order to proceed to other symbols.

We can observe a minor flowcharting convention in Figure 6.7. Alphabetic or alphanumeric data is placed in quotes; numeric data is not. This convention helps us distinguish between the two types of

Table 6.1 Symbols Used in Logical Operations

Symbol	Meaning
$=$	is equal to
$\neq$	is not equal to
$<$	is less than
$\leq$	is less than or equal to
$>$	is greater than
$\geq$	is greater than or equal to

data and helps programmers to minimize the chance of error when specifying the type of data used in logical operations.

The second decision of Figure 6.7 involves numeric data. Of interest in this conditional statement is the $\leq$ sign, which represents "less than or equal to." Table 6.1 shows the symbols for similar relationships in logical operations.

Annotation Symbol

Programmers often need to include additional descriptive notes or remarks in their flowcharts. These comments do not affect processing but clarify a particular point in the flowchart. The **Annotation symbol** is used to add descriptive comments or remarks to a flowchart. Figure 6.8 illustrates these three-sided symbols and the dotted line that attaches them to another flowchart symbol.

Before we examine complete flowcharts, we should note that the first few flowcharts here may seem trivial. But our approach, which at first may seem oversimplified, will provide a fuller understanding of flowcharting and greatly increase your understanding of the complex flowcharts that follow.

THE CONDITION STATEMENT AND SPECIAL CHARACTERS

A common mistake flowcharters make when performing logical operations using numeric data is to include special characters in the conditional statement. For example, suppose a given logical operation is to determine if a total sales amount is greater than $100. We might be tempted to write one conditional statement as

IS TOTAL SALES > $100?

This statement would be incorrect, however, because we have included the $, a special character. Special characters cannot be part of a numeric field. The correct conditional statement and decision symbol for the problem are shown below.

IS
TOTAL SALES
> 100
?

Yes

No

CORRECT

FIGURE 6.8 Here an Annotation symbol is attached to and used with a Decision symbol. The Annotation symbol provides additional data on the decision being performed. The dotted line attaches the Annotation symbol to the Decision symbol. It indicates that it adds only descriptive remarks and does not affect processing.

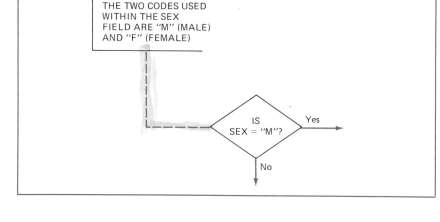

6.3
Getting Started with Flowcharts
A First Flowchart

We have just presented basic flowcharting symbols, and now we will apply them. We will use an illustration of computing someone's gross pay. As with future problems, we will present the problem in narrative form.

ILLUSTRATIVE PROBLEM 1

In preparation for programming, you are required to prepare a flowchart that describes the processing narrative that follows:

The overall problem involves the computation of gross pay. The data input to the problem is the employee's name, the hours worked by the employee, and the employee's hourly rate of pay. The printed output of the problem is the employee's name and the computed amount of gross pay. The formula used in processing is

Gross pay = hours worked × rate of pay

The narrative should normally detail all aspects related to the processing of the problem. It should reveal all inputs, outputs, and processing required to totally define the task.

Figure 6.9 shows the flowchart prepared to satisfy the narrative of this problem. It is a simple flowchart, straightforward in its approach. Essentially, after the START symbol, the flowchart depicts the input of data, its processing via a formula, and the output of data. Let us examine the purpose of each symbol.

The START symbol denotes the beginning of the flowchart. This symbol represents a series of instructions executed by the computer before the processing of any program. The instructions prepare the computer for its processing of every program, reestablish the internal checking features that are applied to each program, and ensure against unwarranted carryover of data from one program to another. The term *housekeeping* is sometimes applied to these initial activities.

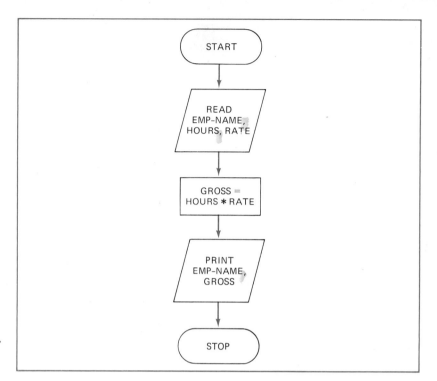

FIGURE 6.9   The flow-chart depicting the processing of Illustrative Problem 1.

In our discussions, the START symbol will encompass all types of preliminary instructions.

The START symbol is followed by an I/O symbol. Within this symbol (Figure 6.10), the word READ indicates an input operation. Note that following the word READ, specific **datanames** tag each of the data items input. Datanames identify each item of data and each variable in a flowchart and are used whenever that item of data is referred to. For example, the dataname EMP-NAME represents data on an employee's name. The names HOURS and RATE represent hours worked and rate of pay data. Datanames should reflect the data items they represent. The dataname BOZO, though potentially correct, does not reflect the category of employee names.

The READ symbol tells us that three items of data are being input. Whenever more than one dataname is specified for input in the READ symbol, commas are inserted between each of the names for clarity. The commas separate datanames and define each. Commas are similarly applied to the I/O symbol whenever output operations are indicated.

Processing can occur once the necessary data is input. The Processing symbol of our flowchart details the computation the problem required. For ease of understanding and for a more accurate representation of the processing of data in a flowchart, the following general rules are offered:

FIGURE 6.10 An enlargement of the I/O symbol used in the flowchart of Figure 6.9. This figure points out the use of datanames, commas, and the term READ.

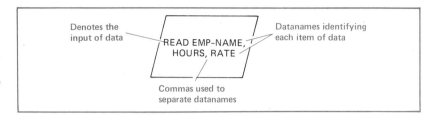

1 Place only one statement or formula in a Processing symbol.

2 Use a formula to describe mathematical computations whenever possible.

3 If a formula is used, place the result of processing to the left of the equal sign (=) to highlight it.

Each of the above rules is illustrated in Figure 6.11. The required processing is denoted as a formula, and the result of processing, GROSS, is placed to the left of the equal sign.

Let us stress another point here. Any data used in processing *must be defined prior to its use.* Data on both HOURS and RATE was defined via the READ symbol. The formula implies that GROSS will be defined as the result of a computation. Since HOURS and RATE were available before their use in that computation, this assumption is valid. However, if either dataname were not available for processing, the computation would be invalid. Data used in all processing operations must be defined prior to its use.

An asterisk is used in Figure 6.11 to denote a multiplication operation. The asterisk is one of a group of symbols used to represent fundamental arithmetic operations. Table 6.2 lists these universally accepted symbols and the operations they represent.

An output operation requires the I/O symbol again. However, in this case, the term PRINT defines an output operation involving the printing of data identified by the datanames EMP-NAME and GROSS. Data relating to each variable name must be defined by a previous operation or computation before it can be output. In this problem, EMP-NAME was read in and GROSS was the result of a computation. This consideration must be satisfied before any output operation. After all, if the data does not exist, how can it be output?

FIGURE 6.11 A formula greatly simplifies understanding the processing of data via arithmetic computations. Note that specific symbols, used to represent all arithmetic operations, separate datanames.

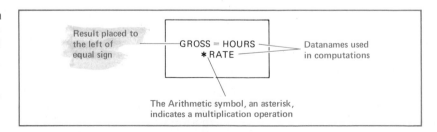

Table 6.2 Symbols Used to Represent Arithmetic Operations

Symbols	Operation
+	Addition
−	Subtraction
*	Multiplication
/	Division

After the output of data is represented, the processing described by this flowchart ends. All aspects of the problem are symbolically defined in the flowchart. The STOP symbol denotes the end of the diagram.

Illustrative Problem 2 enlarges our problem and provides a flowcharting diagram solution.

ILLUSTRATIVE PROBLEM 2

The overall problem involves the computation of an employee's net pay. Data input for the problem is the employee's name, hours worked, and hourly rate of pay. After processing, print out the employee's name, gross pay, FICA deduction, and net pay. The FICA deduction is computed at 6.28 percent of gross pay. The formulas required for processing are:

1 Gross pay = (hours worked) * (rate of pay)
2 FICA deduction = (.0628) * (gross pay)
3 Net pay = (gross pay) − (FICA deduction)

Illustrative Problem 2 has added new computations to the first problem. These computations have increased the number of variables and formulas. Our final flowchart (Figure 6.12) therefore contains additional symbols.

The flowchart in Figure 6.12 follows all the conventions we have discussed. We must make one point about computing the FICA deduction here. Although the problem stated that FICA was 6.28 percent of gross pay, the flowchart uses .0628. This number is the decimal equivalent of 6.28 percent. In any algebraic formula, use the decimal equivalent of a percent. Thus, 5 percent would become .05; 6.28 percent becomes .0628. Decimal equivalents minimize errors and simplify programming. Table 6.3 presents other examples of decimal equivalents of percents.

Illustrative Problem 2 uses more variables than Illustrative Problem 1 because additional processing is performed. An increase in the number of datanames occasionally results in the misidentification or

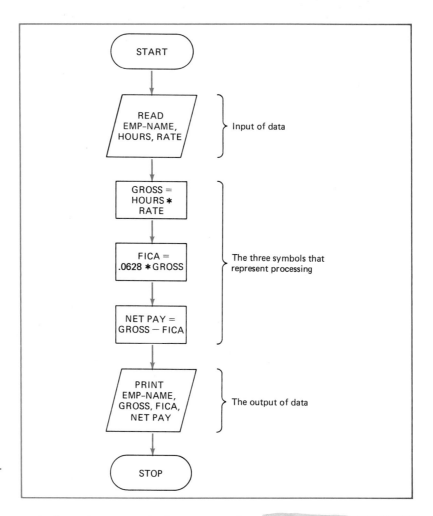

START

READ
EMP–NAME,
HOURS, RATE

} Input of data

GROSS =
HOURS *
RATE

FICA =
.0628 * GROSS

} The three symbols that
represent processing

NET PAY =
GROSS – FICA

PRINT
EMP–NAME,
GROSS, FICA,
NET PAY

} The output of data

STOP

FIGURE 6.12   The flow-charting solution to Il-lustrative Problem 2.

omission of a name during processing. A **checklist,** or **legend,** re-duces the probability of this type of error. All the datanames used in I/O operations and computations are included on this checklist, along with the required formulas and decisions. You can then compare the flowchart with the checklist to ensure that no required dataname or processing has been omitted from your solution. The checklist for Il-lustrative Problem 2 is given in Figure 6.13.

Table 6.3   Examples of Percents Converted to Their Decimal Equivalents

Percent	Movement of Decimal Point to Left	Final Decimal Equivalent
6.28	.06.28	.0628
45.	.45.	.45
.1	.00.1	.001

Input Data	Dataname Used	Output Data	Dataname Used
Employer name	EMP–NAME	Employer name	EMP–NAME
Hours worked	HOURS	Gross pay	GROSS
Rate of pay	RATE	FICA deduction	FICA
		Net pay	NET PAY

Processing	Formula
Gross pay	GROSS = HOURS * RATE
FICA deduction	FICA = .0628 * GROSS
Net pay	NET PAY = GROSS − FICA

FIGURE 6.13 The checklist or legend prepared for Illustrative Problem 2. Note that in the above formulas, the datanames used are consistent with the datanames supplied for the input and output of data.

The Flowchart Loop

Computers are good at repetitive tasks. Yet our first two flowcharts processed just one person's data. How can we redraw them to accommodate many people's data? We apply two techniques to do so:

1 A loop
2 Last record check

When these two features are inserted in a flowchart, variable amounts of data can be processed. Large or small quantities of information are effectively processed, and control of this processing is always in the hands of the programmer. The use of a loop and last record check are diagramed in Figure 6.14 and compared with one of our initial flowcharting solutions.

Initially both flowcharts appear similar. One of the first differences to draw our attention is the line extending upward from the PRINT symbol to the READ symbol. The arrowhead at the tip of the line indicates that the directional flow of the diagram is from the PRINT to the READ symbol. We can conclude from this that after one individual's data is printed, we are directed back to the READ symbol to input the next person's data. We state that the flowchart is looping back to restart processing. Pictorially and in flowcharting terms, the return to the READ symbol defines a **flowchart loop.** The same steps in the loop are used to process every person's data. Flowchart loops are integral to many flowcharting solutions. We will see them in many examples.

The line from the PRINT symbol to the READ symbol in the flowchart loop is called an **unconditional branch.** Unlike the conditional branches that result from a decision, the unconditional branch provides no choice. It unconditionally directs the flow of data from one symbol to another.

The unconditional branch can be depicted in two ways, as Figure 6.15 illustrates. In Figure 6.15a, a solid, unbroken line is used to com-

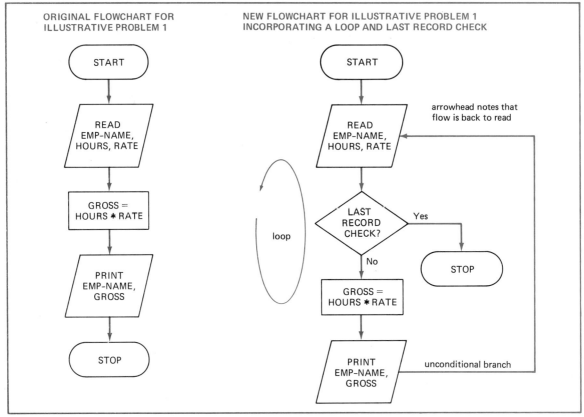

FIGURE 6.14   A comparison of flowcharting solutions to Illustrative Problem 1. The original can process only one person's data. The second solution uses a last record check and creates a loop to process larger quantities of data.

plete the flowchart loop. In Figure 6.15*b*, a flowcharting symbol known as a **connector** represents the unconditional branch back to the READ. It is important to remember that the two methods are equally correct and interchangeable.

An identifying character must be placed in a connector. This character and the arrowhead help users match the connectors and are vital in flowcharts with many connectors. Connectors are preferable when many lines on a flowchart cross, but the choice of method is up to the flowcharter.

The concept of the **last record check** has to do with the fact that most programs process a finite amount of data. The last record check is a way to handle the last piece of data, the point at which processing must stop or continue with other items of data.

Figure 6.14 shows that the last record check is a conditional statement. As long as data remains to be processed, the NO branch of the last record check decision is taken. Processing continues until all data

THE USE OF THE UNCONDITIONAL BRANCH

One of the most common mistakes made in flowcharting is the omission of the unconditional branch before a flowchart loop. Though flowcharters know that they are working with a repetitive process, they sometimes completely forget the unconditional branch. This error usually results from haste. Programmers should make sure that all components are properly incorporated into any flowchart solution.

is exhausted. In Illustrative Problem 1, input data was used to compute gross, and gross was output with the employee's name. The unconditional branch to the READ symbol completed the flowchart loop and began the processing of the next item of data. When the last item of data was processed, the last record check indicated that there was no

FIGURE 6.15 A comparison of the use of a connector and a solid line to represent an unconditional branch. Both techniques are equally valid and correct. Remember, when using connectors, always place the same identifying character within the matching pair of connectors.

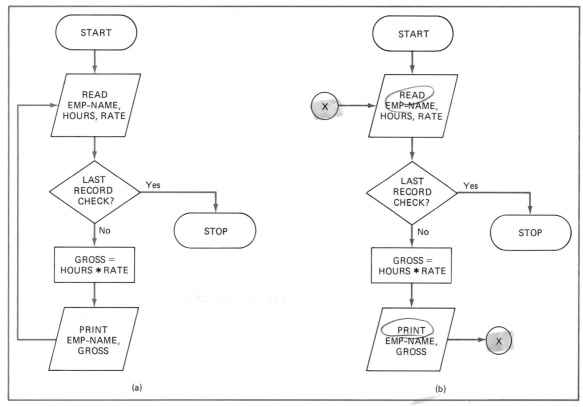

more data and that the YES branch should be followed. In Figure 6.14, you can see that when all data has been processed, the YES branch should be followed to the end of the flowchart and the STOP symbol.

In sum, the last record check works as follows:

1 If data remains to be processed, the NO branch is followed.
2 If the last record has been processed, the YES branch is followed.

The conditional branches defined by the last record check let us create a flowchart loop and tell what to do when all data is processed.

The last record check details the end of data. A more specialized approach, called the 9's Decision, was developed to handle the same situation. Usually the 9's Decision is interchangeable with the last record check, as we will show. But it requires a bit more explanation.

The **9's Decision** was developed to circumvent differences in computer hardware and affords programmers maximum control of processing. Many types of computer hardware are manufactured, each with its own operating peculiarities and its own way of reacting when it runs out of data. Each computer system also uses its own method to stop processing. Because these technical conditions have existed for years, programmers and flowcharters banded together to develop a technique that was independent of the hardware used.

The overall concept of the 9's Decision is simple. We want the computer to continually test, via a decision, for a specific code number that we will create. This code number is in fact a series of 9's and is referred to as the **9's Data.** The 9's Data is placed as the last item of data. Figure 6.16 represents the positioning of the 9's Data as it might

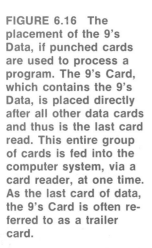

FIGURE 6.16 The placement of the 9's Data, if punched cards are used to process a program. The 9's Card, which contains the 9's Data, is placed directly after all other data cards and thus is the last card read. This entire group of cards is fed into the computer system, via a card reader, at one time. As the last card of data, the 9's Card is often referred to as a trailer card.

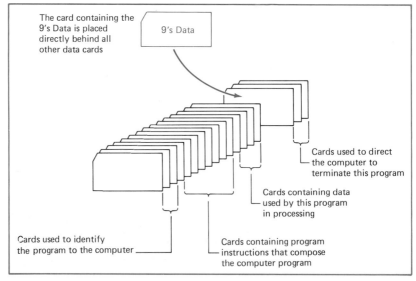

The card containing the 9's Data is placed directly behind all other data cards

9's Data

Cards used to direct the computer to terminate this program

Cards containing data used by this program in processing

Cards used to identify the program to the computer

Cards containing program instructions that compose the computer program

appear if cards were used in processing. The only way to get to the 9's Data is to read through all the data in front of it. When the 9's Data is encountered, no more data exists. The computer is free to stop processing, as indicated by a STOP symbol, or to continue to additional processing.

The number 9 was used deliberately in the 9's Data because a string of 9's stands out. So that it will stand out even further, the 9's Data is a negative number (such as −9999.99). Because data of this type rarely occurs otherwise, programmers can use 9's Data. You must remember to use 9's Data with the 9's Decision. Illustrative Problem 3 shows how the 9's Decision controls a flowchart loop and monitors data.

ILLUSTRATIVE PROBLEM 3

Compute Net Pay

The problem is to compute net pay. Input data is the person's name, hours worked, and rate of pay. FICA is computed at 6.85 percent of gross pay. Output the person's name, gross pay, FICA deduction, and net pay amounts. The formulas used are

1 Gross pay = (hours worked) * (rate of pay)
2 FICA deduction = (.0685) * (gross pay)
3 Net pay = (gross pay) − (FICA deduction)

Because the number of people processed will vary extensively, use a 9's Decision to control processing.

Figure 6.17 illustrates the flowchart and legend to solve Illustrative Problem 3. (Compare this flowchart with Figure 6.12, and you can see that it enlarges on the flowchart in Illustrative Problem 2.) Here the solution uses the 9's Decision. A last record check might work equally well. Both would be positioned in the same spot on the flowchart.

In the flowchart of Figure 6.17, we have used the Rate field in our 9's Decision. We could just as easily have used the Hours field. Both are numeric fields, and either would be appropriate. The choice is really the flowcharter's. Any incoming field may contain the 9's Data used with the 9's Decision.

Both the 9's Decision and the last record check provide flexibility. They allow any number of records to be processed. The 9's Decision reads every card input for the 9's Data. The last card check searches for the condition that exists when the last record has been processed. In both instances, the end of data means that the YES branch will be followed. The rule of thumb is, "If the amount of data is unstated, use either the last record check or the 9's Decision." The advantages of both techniques will be discussed in Chapters 8 and 9 as we talk about programming languages.

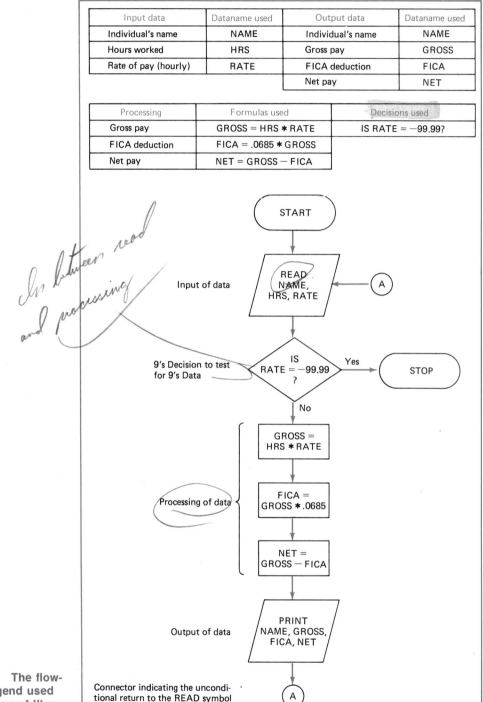

Input data	Dataname used	Output data	Dataname used
Individual's name	NAME	Individual's name	NAME
Hours worked	HRS	Gross pay	GROSS
Rate of pay (hourly)	RATE	FICA deduction	FICA
		Net pay	NET

Processing	Formulas used	Decisions used
Gross pay	GROSS = HRS * RATE	IS RATE = −99.99?
FICA deduction	FICA = .0685 * GROSS	
Net pay	NET = GROSS − FICA	

In between read and processing

START

Input of data → READ NAME, HRS, RATE ← A

9's Decision to test for 9's Data → IS RATE = −99.99 ? — Yes → STOP

No

Processing of data

GROSS = HRS * RATE

FICA = GROSS * .0685

NET = GROSS − FICA

Output of data → PRINT NAME, GROSS, FICA, NET

A

Connector indicating the unconditional return to the READ symbol and restart of processing loop

FIGURE 6.17 The flowchart and legend used for the solution of Illustrative Problem 3.

Illustrative Problems 4 and 5 diverge from computing pay to computing sales commissions and student averages, respectively. A 9's Decision is used in Problem 4, a last record check in Problem 5. In future solutions, unless we specify otherwise, we will use a last record check.

ILLUSTRATIVE PROBLEM 4

Computation of a Sales Commission

This problem involves the computation of an individual salesperson's total sales amount and commission. Data is entered into the computer system on 80-column punched cards. Each card contains a salesperson's name, number, and three sales amounts. The total sales figure is determined by adding the salesperson's three sales amounts. Commissions are calculated at 15 percent of the total sales figure. Output, in a printed form, consists of the salesperson's name, number, total sales figure, and individual commission. Because the number of cards used for processing will vary, employ a 9's Decision.

The flowchart and legend for Illustrative Problem 4 appear in Figure 6.18. Only two formulas are required in this problem: one for computing the total sales figure (TSALE) and the other for calculating the individual commission (COMM). The 9's Decision is used to indicate the end of data. Processing within the loop will compute the individual salesperson's total sales amount and commission. Each separate line of printed output will display these individual amounts.

Illustrative Problems 3 and 4 depict solutions for business applications. Let us now explore the simple algebraic task of computing a student's average. This will demonstrate that problems which involve formulas or nonbusiness applications are just as easily documented in flowcharts.

ILLUSTRATIVE PROBLEM 5

Compute Student's Average

The overall problem deals with the computation of a student's average grade. Data input are the student's name and two test marks. The average grade is computed by adding the two grades and dividing by two. Output is the student's name and average grade. The number of students processed at any time will vary.

The flowchart and legend associated with Illustrative Problem 5 are shown in Figure 6.19. Because the quantity of students was not specified, we used a last record check. (A 9's decision would have been equally acceptable.) After the last record is processed, the logic

Input data	Dataname used	Output data	Dataname used
Salesperson's name	SNAME	Salesperson's name	SNAME
Salesperson's number	SNO	Salesperson's number	SNO
Sales amount #1	S1	Total sales amount	TSALE
Sales amount #2	S2	Commission	COMM
Sales amount #3	S3		

Processing	Formula used	Decisions used
Total sales amount	TSALE = S1 + S2 + S3	IS S1 = −999.99?
Commission	COMM = TSALE *.15	

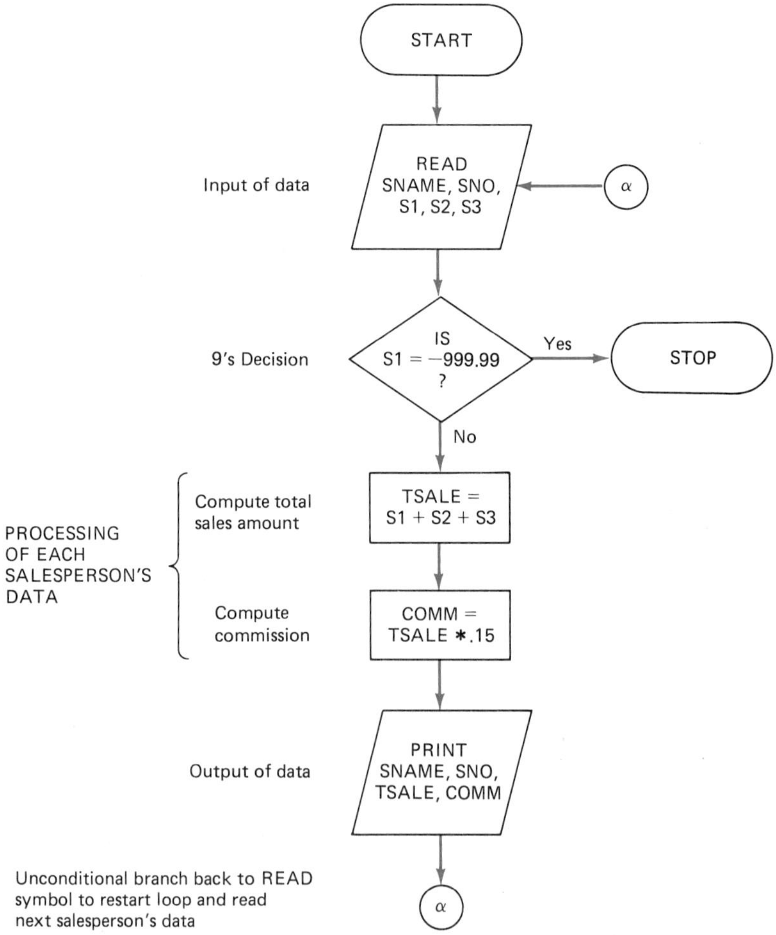

FIGURE 6.18 The legend and flowchart for Illustrative Problem 4.

of the solution dictates that the YES branch of the last record check be followed and the flowchart ended.

Let's summarize what we've learned from the previous illustrative

Input data	Dataname used	Output data	Dataname used
Student name	NAME	Student name	NAME
Test mark #1	M1	Average grade	AVG
Test mark #2	M2		

Processing	Formula used	Decisions used
Average grade	AVG = (M1 + M2)/2	LAST RECORD CHECK ?

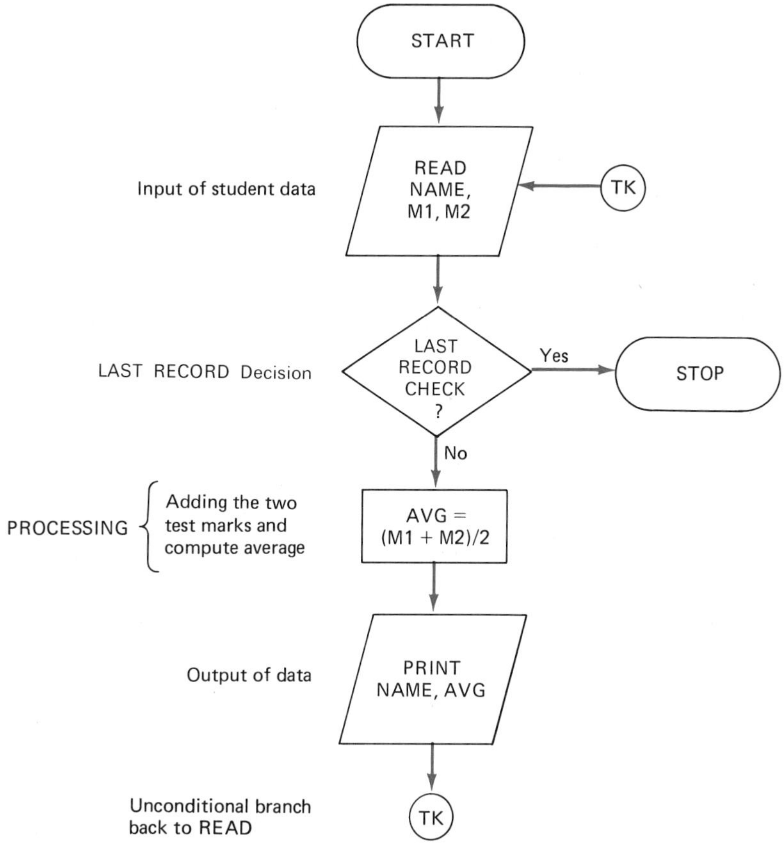

FIGURE 6.19 The legend and flowchart accompanying Illustrative Problem 5.

Input of student data — READ NAME, M1, M2 ← TK

LAST RECORD Decision — LAST RECORD CHECK ? — Yes → STOP

No

PROCESSING { Adding the two test marks and compute average } — AVG = (M1 + M2)/2

Output of data — PRINT NAME, AVG

Unconditional branch back to READ — TK

examples. Because the amount of data varied and was not specified, we incorporated either a last record check or 9's Decision in the solutions. Both decisions followed the READ symbol to indicate their interchangeability. When the last record had been handled, the YES branch was followed to complete the flow of processing.

In addition, each problem was concerned with the processing of individual statistics; that is, we computed an individual's net pay, commission, or grade. The following questions may have occurred to you:

PARENTHESES IN ARITHMETIC COMPUTATIONS

The proper use of parentheses in arithmetic operations is extremely important. In Figure 6.19, an average was computed by adding two values and dividing the sum by two. The formula represented in the flowchart was

$$\text{AVG} = \text{(M1 + M2)/2}$$

This formula is correct, since the sum of M1 and M2 is divided by two. However, someone might have represented the same computation as

$$\text{AVG} = \text{M1 + M2/2}$$

This formula is incorrect. It states, "M1 is added to one-half of M2." This is certainly not the calculation we desired in our problem. Parentheses must be used properly in formulas.

"How could I add up all the individual net pays and obtain a grand total of net pays distributed?" or "How much did the individual computed commissions add up to?" Both questions relate to the computation of a total figure drawn from the addition of individual amounts. Our next section discusses how to accumulate this type of total and keep track of information by counting data one item at a time.

6.4 Accumulators and Counters

The accumulation of grand totals is an integral part of many business activities. For example, a retail sales system must provide management with total sales figures for charge sales, cash sales, and total sales by store and register. Regardless of the sophistication of the computer system, all total figures are accumulated in essentially the same way. Each individual sale is added to an existing total, creating an updated total.

The method of accumulating grand totals is exactly the same in flowcharting. The result of an individual's data is added to the previous total, producing a new total figure. The new total is often referred to in business as a **running total,** because it always represents the current total amount.

In addition to developing a method to accumulate grand totals, flowcharters had to develop a technique to represent the increment of a value by the number 1. Using this technique, a flowcharter could indicate that a flowchart loop or an operation was to be repeated an exact number of times.

The technique which permits the computation of a grand total is referred to as an **accumulator.** The technique used to count increments of 1 is known as a **counter.** This section will introduce both concepts and apply them in illustrative problems.

Accumulating a Total

An accumulator represents a running total. Each new amount is added to the previous total, creating a new total amount. The concept of an accumulator is easily mastered with the aid of two basic computations.

The first computation requires that the accumulator be set equal to 0. If we use the character T to represent the accumulator, we can represent this calculation as

$$T = 0$$

By setting the accumulator at 0, we ensure that no incorrect data or previously used data is added to our totals.

The second computation relates to the process by which data is added to the previous total to create the new, updated total. Using T for the accumulated total and G for the gross pay data being accumulated, we can represent this calculation as

ACC TOTAL = TOTAL + GROSS

$$T = T + G$$

This formula is placed within the processing loop and performed over and over again until all data has been totaled. The final value in the accumulator represents the grand total. Although this formula is not algebraically correct, it is operationally valid because of the way a computer handles its data.

Reconsider Illustrative Problem 1, in which gross pay was computed for an unspecified number of employees. (The flowchart associated with this problem was presented in Figure 6.14.) To this problem we will add the requirement of obtaining the total of all gross pay computed. We want to know the total derived from adding all the individual amounts of gross pay. The flowchart incorporating the accumulator into the solution appears in Figure 6.20.

Examining this solution, we see the symbol containing $T = 0$ immediately before the READ symbol. The processing of $T = 0$ will clear the accumulator and start it at zero. The position of $T = 0$ places it in the general category of initial conditions. An **initial condition** is any type of operation that must be performed before the processing of data begins and that permits the satisfactory processing of that data. The computation $T = 0$ is necessary to the accumulator and is logically situated before the READ symbol, the first symbol of our processing loop.

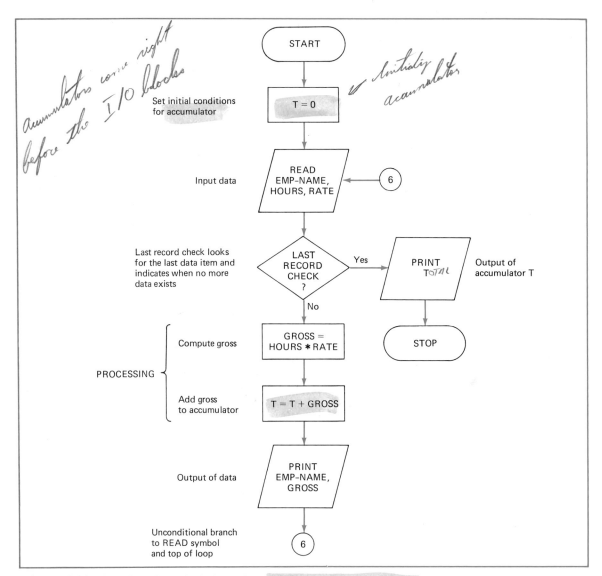

Accumulators come right before the I/O blocks

Initially accumulator

Set initial conditions for accumulator

Input data

Last record check looks for the last data item and indicates when no more data exists

PROCESSING

Compute gross

Add gross to accumulator

Output of data

Unconditional branch to READ symbol and top of loop

START

T = 0

READ EMP-NAME, HOURS, RATE — 6

LAST RECORD CHECK ? — Yes → PRINT TOTAL — Output of accumulator T

No

GROSS = HOURS * RATE

STOP

T = T + GROSS

PRINT EMP-NAME, GROSS

6

FIGURE 6.20 The flowchart depiction of an accumulator to compile a grand total of gross pay. Each individual's gross pay is added to the accumulator (T) until no further data exists. This condition is signaled by the last record check, positioned after the READ symbol. Because no more data is to be processed, the printing of the total T (held in the accumulator) can begin.

The initial condition T = 0 is vital to the success of any accumulator. The formula T = T + GROSS is used in the flowchart for the accumulation of data. Consider what might occur when we tried to use this formula if T = 0 were not an initial condition of the flowchart. Without T = 0, we would proceed down the flowchart until we encountered the processing symbol containing T = T + GROSS. At that point, we would be forced to stop. Though the dataname GROSS would have been defined by a prior calculation, nothing would have defined T. Since no value would exist for T, the computation $T = T + GROSS$ could not be completed. (Remember that all datanames to the right of an equal sign in a formula must be defined before they are used.) Without the initial condition $T = 0$, no processing related to the accumulator would be possible. With $T = 0$, the accumulator is free to continually add individual amounts of gross pay until the grand total is obtained.

Except for the formulas for the accumulator, this flowchart is like the one in Figure 6.14. We have used the last record check decision because we have an unspecified amount of data. The decision appears after the READ symbol. As long as data exists, it will be processed and added to the accumulator. When the last record check signals the end of data, the YES branch is taken, and we get the accumulated total T. An example will reinforce how accumulators work.

ILLUSTRATIVE PROBLEM 6

Compute Commission and Total Commissions Paid

This problem involves computing a salesperson's individual commission and the total of all these commissions. Data, input on punched cards, is the salesperson's name, number, and three sales amounts. Commissions are computed at 15 percent of the individual sales total. The output of the problem is twofold:

1 Print out each salesperson's name, number, total sales amount, and commission.
2 When no additional data is available and the individual processing of commissions is completed, print out the accumulated total of the commissions due all salespeople.

An unspecified number of salespeople are processed.

INITIALIZATION OF THE ACCUMULATOR

The initialization of the accumulator is positioned before the start of the processing loop. The formula $T = 0$ always precedes the READ symbol. It establishes the accumulator and sets it at 0. A common flowcharting error is to place $T = 0$ inside the processing loop, effectively clearing the amount stored in the accumulator on each repetition of the loop. Naturally, no data ever accumulates because the accumulator is always set back to 0. The initialization of any accumulator must precede the loop in which processing occurs.

The legend and flowchart prepared for Illustrative Problem 6 appear in Figure 6.21. Because the original problem calls for totaling individual commissions, an accumulator is necessary. Thus, the first symbol after the START symbol contains the initial condition TCOMM = 0, where TCOMM is the dataname of the accumulator. Since that is the only initial condition of this problem, we can begin the loop in which processing will occur.

The NO branch of the last record decision directs us toward the processing of the total sales amount (TSALE) and commission (COMM). When the individual commission has been computed, this amount is added to the accumulator (TCOMM) using the formula TCOMM = TCOMM + COMM. Note that with the use of this formula and TCOMM = 0, we have incorporated into our flowchart the two formulas vital to the function of the accumulator.

After one individual's data has been completely processed, printing can begin. The flowchart then unconditionally branches to the READ symbol to restart the processing loop with the next salesperson's data. This looping process will continue until all data is exhausted.

Once the last item of data is processed, the flow of processing is directed through the YES branch of the last record check decision. Because no further data exists, the total commission compiled in the accumulator, TCOMM, can be printed. The printing of this total precedes the end of the flowchart.

The solution in Figure 6.21 is similar to the one in Figure 6.18. The significant difference is the insertion of the symbol related to the accumulator, TCOMM. This comparison demonstrates how easily an accumulator can be incorporated into a flowchart. By simply inserting an initial condition (i.e., T = 0), an accumulation statement (i.e., T = T + COMM), and an output operation (i.e., PRINT T), the flowchart is readily expanded.

Counting the Loops by 1

Not all data processing involves unspecified amounts of data. Occasionally, problems require that processing occur an exact number of times. For example, in math the same formula might be tested using values of 1 to 1000, or in marketing the results of a retail survey of, say, 126 couples might be analyzed under the same test conditions. The important factor is the exact number of processing cycles, not the quantity of data handled.

The flowcharting technique developed to represent this type of processing is the counter. The **counter** is a systematic method of counting the number of loops. The counter begins at 1 and systematically proceeds to 2, 3, 4, and so forth, until the prescribed limit is attained. The increment of the counter is always 1. The fundamental concept of the counter is simple. When the counter is 1, it should be processing record 1; when the counter is 2, record 2 is processed; and so forth.

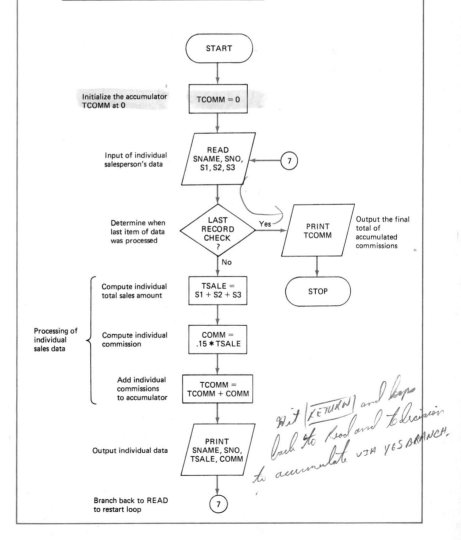

Input data	Dataname used	Output data	Dataname used
Salesperson's name	SNAME	*GROUPING 1:*	
Salesperson's number	SNO	Salesperson's name	SNAME
Sales amount #1	S1	Salesperson's number	SNO
Sales amount #2	S2	Total sales amount	TSALE
Sales amount #3	S3	Individual commission	COMM
		GROUPING 2:	
		Accumulated total of commissions	TCOMM

Processing	Formulas used	Decisions used
Total sales	TSALE = S1 +S2 + S3	LAST RECORD CHECK
Commission	COMM = .15 * TSALE	
Set up accumulator	TCOMM = 0	
Update accumulator	TCOMM = TCOMM + COMM	

FIGURE 6.21 The legend and flowchart for Illustrative Problem 6.

The counter requires that three conditions be met:

1 The starting value of the counter must be established (i.e., set the counter = 1).
2 A decision is necessary to test whether the counter has achieved the desired number of repetitions (i.e., is the counter = 50?).
3 Increment the counter by a factor of 1 (i.e., add 1 to the counter).

Point 1 is important because it establishes the starting point of the counter. In the vast majority of cases, the counter is initially set at 1. However, there are special instances when a different starting value is used (e.g., when a mathematician wants to test a temperature formula at values of 32 to 212°F).

Point 2 provides the means to stop the looping process. After all, if we are dealing with 50 records, we want exactly 50 repetitions of the processing loop. Fifty-one or forty-nine loops are of no value.

Point 3 addresses itself to the orderly increment of the counter, which is similar to a digital calculator. Each loop represents a factor of 1, because exactly one record is processed within each loop. Let's observe how these three facts are incorporated into a flowchart.

We will make two modifications in Illustrative Problem 1, in which we computed the gross pay of each employee:

1 The number of employees processed is exactly 30.
2 The last record check is replaced by a counter.

The new flowchart for this problem appears in Figure 6.22. The symbols related to the processing of gross pay remain unchanged. The differences in this flowchart are in the placement of the symbols needed for the counter. The formula $K = 1$ is an initial condition that establishes the starting value of the counter. The decision "Is $K = 30$?" compares the current value of K against 30 and ensures that the limit is not exceeded. The calculation $K = K + 1$ increments the counter by 1 on each repetition.

The flowchart shows the positioning of the Decision and Increment symbols. The Decision symbol is situated at the end of the processing loop. Only after one person's data has been completely processed should the flowchart continue to the next employee. The counter also increases by 1 before the processing of the next employee. The counter is 1 while processing employee 1. It becomes 2 only before reading employee 2's data. Not until employee 30's records are completed will the YES branch of the decision be taken.

Figure 6.23 shows how a counter computes the commissions of each salesperson. This problem originally appeared as Illustrative Problem 4 (see Figure 6.18). In this case, assume that 28 people's commissions are processed.

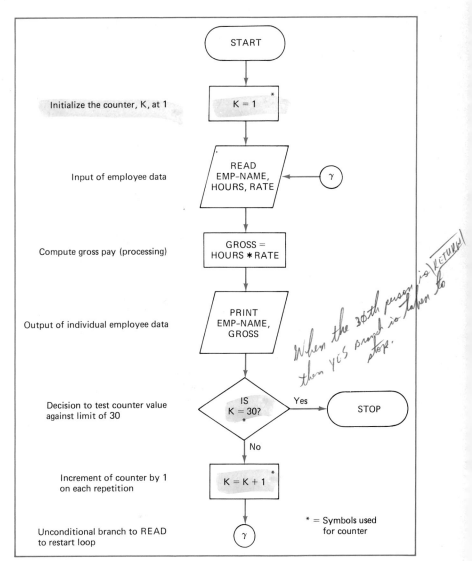

FIGURE 6.22 This flow-chart illustrates the application of a counter to the computation of gross pay for exactly 30 people. Note that the counter completely eliminates the need for the last record check decision. Remember, however, that the counter is used only when the number of people, repetitions, or amount of data is known.

We start our counters at 1 for two reasons. First, $K = 1$ clearly fixes the counter's starting point and differentiates it from the accumulator's starting point, which is 0. Second, similar concepts, developed in later programming chapters, require the same starting point. We want here to simplify the subjects to come.[1]

---

[1] In future chapters, we will discuss the programming instructions of the FOR/NEXT and PERFORM statements. These two statements relate directly to the concept of a counter and its starting point.

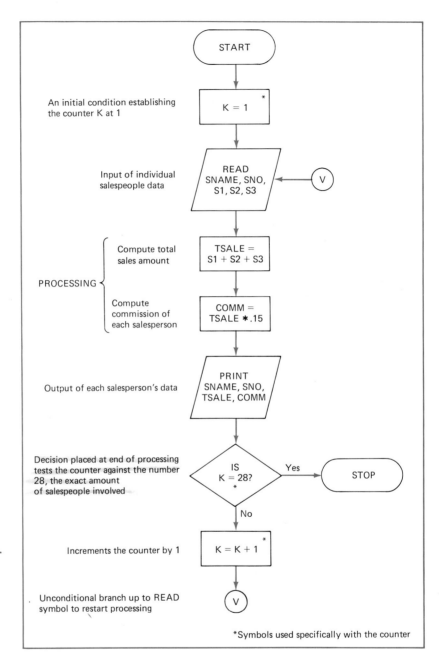

An initial condition establishing
the counter K at 1

K = 1 *

Input of individual
salespeople data

READ
SNAME, SNO,
S1, S2, S3

PROCESSING {

Compute total
sales amount

TSALE =
S1 + S2 + S3

Compute
commission of
each salesperson

COMM =
TSALE *.15

Output of each salesperson's data

PRINT
SNAME, SNO,
TSALE, COMM

Decision placed at end of processing
tests the counter against the number
28, the exact amount
of salespeople involved

IS
K = 28?
*

Yes

STOP

No

Increments the counter by 1

K = K + 1 *

Unconditional branch up to READ
symbol to restart processing

V

*Symbols used specifically with the counter

FIGURE 6.23 The flow-
chart depicting the use
of the counter in proc-
essing individual sales
commissions. The
counter effectively con-
trols the processing of
28 people.

**6.5
More
Flowcharting
Techniques and
Problems**

Each of the flowcharting concepts presented in previous sections of
this chapter serves a specific purpose. The discussions that follow will
expand the use of these concepts and combine them with other techniques. For example, we will present a flowchart that combines an
accumulator and a counter. We will introduce the means to output

PLACEMENT OF THE INCREMENT

In flowcharts that use a counter, a common error is the misplacement of the increment (i.e., K = K + 1). Though you know that the increment follows on the NO branch of the counter decision, the tendency is to place it immediately before the decision. These contradictions are shown in the diagram below.

The correct diagram (Figure a) will cause the flowchart to loop the desired number of times. The other diagram will loop one less than the desired number of loops. In Figure b, the counter will reach 20 before it completes loop number 20. Thus, it will branch out of the loop, one loop ahead of schedule.

The increment of a counter is placed on the NO branch of the decision used in a counter.

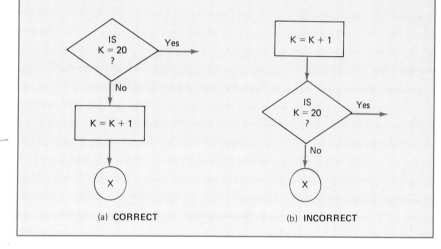

(a) CORRECT   (b) INCORRECT

special headings and labels that highlight printed items of data. Also, we will present a checklist and an overall guide to attacking a flowchart.

Literals for Headings and Special Labels

How many times have you read a report and not been able to understand or identify any of the material presented? Your uncertainty made you carefully scrutinize the entire page for some clarifying sign, remark, or comment. An integral part of any soundly designed printed document is the identification of each item or column of data. Two of the most widely used identification devices are headings and special labels. A **heading** is printed at the top of a page or column of data or at the beginning of a report. **Special labels** usually precede critical statistics to highlight and identify them. Figure 6.24 illustrates both types of output. Column headings in this figure include Salesman No.,

Customer No., and Customer Name. Each heading identifies the column of data beneath it. Special labels, such as Grand Total and Total Commissions Paid, also highlight data.

Since headings and special labels are consistently used in data processing, including them in a program flowchart is necessary. The term **literal** applies to the consecutive characters that compose both headings and special labels. Literals are normally defined as part of output operations. In Figure 6.24, the characters in the label GRAND TOTAL represent the contents of a literal used in an output operation.

In a flowchart, a literal is defined in a PRINT symbol by a pair of quotation marks, as Figure 6.25 illustrates. The PRINT symbol represents the output of four literals to compose a one-line heading for a payroll report. Each literal is identified by its own pair of quotation marks (i.e., "NAME", "GROSS", etc.). The first literal is composed exactly of the four characters NAME, since those are the exact characters contained within the quotation marks. The literals GROSS and FICA are five and four characters long, respectively. The last literal, NET PAY, is seven characters long, because a blank space is inserted between NET and PAY. A simple way of remembering the rule governing a literal is to recall the saying, "You get literally what is contained within the quotation marks." If there are nine characters between the quotation marks, the output printed will contain exactly nine characters.

Literals for special labels are also framed with quotation marks.

literals are defined by "quotation marks."

FIGURE 6.24 An excerpt from a report with headings and special labels.

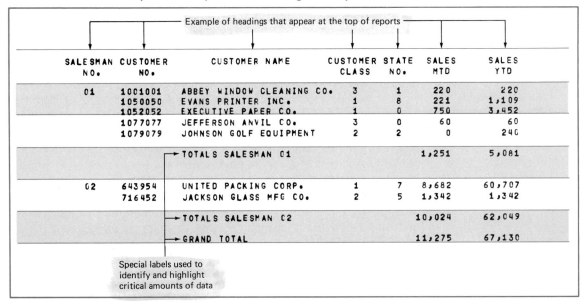

Example of headings that appear at the top of reports

SALESMAN NO.	CUSTOMER NO.	CUSTOMER NAME	CUSTOMER CLASS	STATE NO.	SALES MTD	SALES YTD
01	1001001	ABBEY WINDOW CLEANING CO.	3	1	220	220
	1050050	EVANS PRINTER INC.	1	8	221	1,109
	1052052	EXECUTIVE PAPER CO.	1	0	750	3,452
	1077077	JEFFERSON ANVIL CO.	3	0	60	60
	1079079	JOHNSON GOLF EQUIPMENT	2	2	0	240
		TOTALS SALESMAN 01			1,251	5,081
02	643954	UNITED PACKING CORP.	1	7	8,682	60,707
	716452	JACKSON GLASS MFG CO.	2	5	1,342	1,342
		TOTALS SALESMAN 02			10,024	62,049
		GRAND TOTAL			11,275	67,130

Special labels used to identify and highlight critical amounts of data

FIGURE 6.25 The output of a literal must appear within a PRINT symbol. This symbol represents the output of one line of print. The heading indicated here is composed of four separate literals.

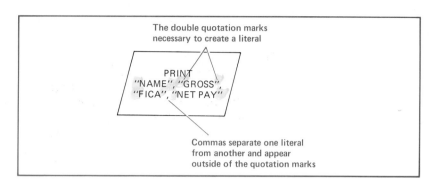

Figure 6.26 depicts a special label that precedes the output of an accumulated total of gross pay. This literal is 22 characters long, its last character being an equal sign. Literals can be composed of any type of characters, numeric, alphabetic, or special. The length of a literal depends on the capabilities of the I/O devices at hand.

To observe how headings and special labels are incorporated into flowcharts, consider the Illustrative Problem depicted in Figure 6.20. This problem computed employee gross pay and accumulated a gross pay total. To this problem, add the requirement of printing column headings and adding a label before the output of the total gross amount. The literals used for the headings are "NAME" and "GROSS PAY". The special label is represented by the literal "TOTAL GROSS PAID OUT =". Figure 6.27 provides the flowchart for this new solution.

Examine the flowchart in Figure 6.27 and note that a single PRINT symbol was added to accommodate the inclusion of these two literals. The literals composing the heading are represented in the PRINT symbol preceding the READ symbol that begins the processing loop. This placement of the PRINT symbol causes the headings to be printed before any other output. Naturally, the literals will appear at the top of the page, because all other data will be printed beneath them. The rest of this flowchart is exactly the same as that in Figure 6.20.

The accumulator is also set before the processing loop. It follows the printing of the two column headings. The last record check follows the READ symbol and comes before the computation and accumulation of gross pay. Individual employee data is output before the unconditional branching to the READ symbol.

The outputs of the accumulator occur on the YES branch of the last record check decision, after the last record is read and processed.

FIGURE 6.26 The literal used to create the label that precedes the output of the TGROSS amount. Note that the literal and the dataname appear in the same symbol and would be output on the same line. The literal is 22 characters long, including blanks and an equal sign.

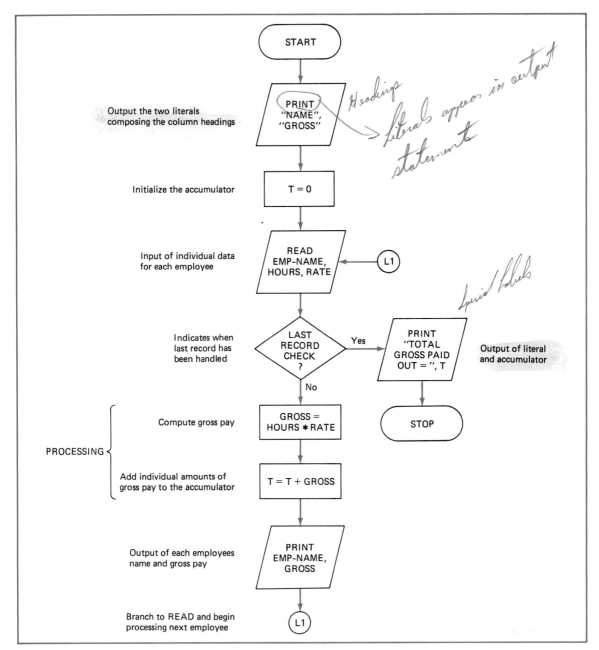

Output the two literals composing the column headings

Initialize the accumulator

Input of individual data for each employee

Indicates when last record has been handled

PROCESSING

Compute gross pay

Add individual amounts of gross pay to the accumulator

Output of each employees name and gross pay

Branch to READ and begin processing next employee

START

PRINT "NAME", "GROSS"

Headings

literals appear in output statements

T = 0

READ EMP-NAME, HOURS, RATE   ← L1

Special Labels

LAST RECORD CHECK ?   Yes →   PRINT "TOTAL GROSS PAID OUT = ", T

Output of literal and accumulator

No

GROSS = HOURS * RATE

STOP

T = T + GROSS

PRINT EMP-NAME, GROSS

L1

FIGURE 6.27   Two literals are added to the solution of the problem in Figure 6.20. These literals are readily added, requiring only one PRINT symbol prior to the start of processing and the special label before the output of the accumulator (T).

The special label preceding the output of the accumulator is placed within the PRINT symbol on the YES branch. Both outputs appear at the bottom of the report. The flowchart ends once the literal and the total are printed. In this problem, the literal composing the special label precedes the output of the accumulator. During output, it is also possible to intersperse literals and datanames, as Figure 6.28 shows.

The output of the flowchart in Figure 6.28 is printed on one line. Each line is associated with the processing of one student's data. The output is designed to look like a sentence. Each student's name is preceded by the label "THE AVERAGE FOR". The literal "IS" comes between the student's name and the computed average. Thus, if our student (John Smith) has test grades of 80 and 90, the resulting line would be printed as

THE AVERAGE FOR	JOHN SMITH	IS	85
Literal #1	Name	Literal #2	AVG.

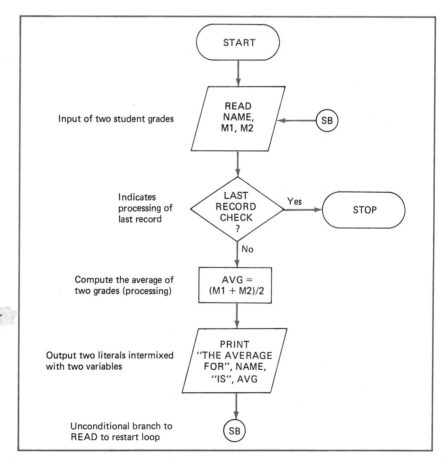

FIGURE 6.28 A flowchart depicting the interspersed printing of two literals and two datanames. The literal "THE AVERAGE FOR" precedes the output of the actual student's name (NAME). The second literal fits between NAME and the computed average (AVG).

USE OF LITERALS

One misconception about literals is that the data is actually printed via the literal. People believe that the literal "NAME" will print the name of an individual person, not just those four characters. This is incorrect. The literal "NAME" is quite different from the dataname NAME. Two things distinguish a literal from a dataname:

1　Literals appear in output statements.
2　Literals are always placed in quotation marks. Remember, with a literal, you get "literally what is contained within the quotes."

Literals, when effectively used, can make any printed output more readable and useful. They are one of the tools that can be used advantageously by a skillful data processor. When positioned at strategic points in an output, literals can effectively single out information critical to the design-making process. This selection process is left solely to the judgment of the programmer/analyst involved.

Multiple Decisions

When larger, more intricate flowcharts are reviewed, a question often asked is, "Why does that decision go there?" The position of a decision in a flowchart relates directly to the logic involved. In many instances, processing cannot continue until some comparison or test of data is performed. In real terms, the computation of your taxes is not possible until you determine the tax bracket you are in. Therefore, the decisions necessary to determine your tax bracket must precede the processing of taxes. Generally, the logic of the problem under study dictates the placement of all decisions. In the following section, we will develop flowcharts with multiple decisions.

ILLUSTRATIVE PROBLEM 7

Compute FICA Using Two Rates

The problem involves computing net pay. Input includes employee name, hours worked, and hourly rate of pay. Gross pay is computed by multiplying hours $\times$ rate. If gross pay $>$ \$150, the FICA deduction is 6.8 percent of gross. If gross pay $\leq$ \$150, then FICA is 5.8 percent of gross. Net pay $=$ gross $-$ FICA. Output each individual employee's name, gross, FICA, and net pay. Use a last record check, because an unlimited number of records may be used.

The flowchart and legend for Illustrative Problem 7 appear in Figure 6.29. Both flowchart and legend show that two FICA formulas and two decisions are involved. The two FICA formulas are necessary because two FICA percentage rates are used. Because the last record

Input data	Dataname used	Output data	Dataname used
Employee name	EMP-NAME	Employee name	EMP-NAME
Hours worked	HOURS	Gross pay	GROSS
Rate of pay	RATE	FICA deduction	FICA
		Net pay	NET

Processing	Formulas used	Decisions used
Gross pay	GROSS = HOURS * RATE	LAST RECORD CHECK
FICA deduction	FICA = .068 * GROSS	IS GROSS > 150?
	FICA = .058 * GROSS	
Net pay	NET = GROSS − FICA	

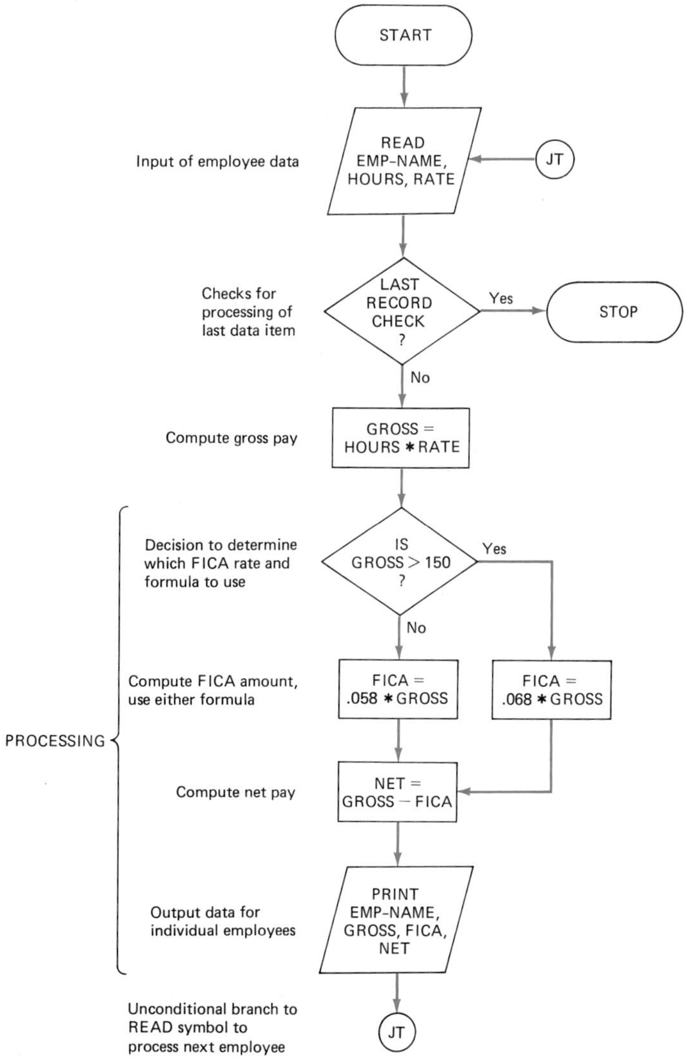

START

Input of employee data → READ EMP-NAME, HOURS, RATE ← JT

Checks for processing of last data item → LAST RECORD CHECK ? — Yes → STOP

No

Compute gross pay → GROSS = HOURS * RATE

Decision to determine which FICA rate and formula to use → IS GROSS > 150 ? — Yes → FICA = .068 * GROSS

No

Compute FICA amount, use either formula → FICA = .058 * GROSS

Compute net pay → NET = GROSS − FICA

Output data for individual employees → PRINT EMP-NAME, GROSS, FICA, NET

Unconditional branch to READ symbol to process next employee → JT

PROCESSING

FIGURE 6.29 The legend and flowchart for Illustrative Problem 7.

decision was defined in the original problem, the second decision, "IS GROSS > 150," is required before the processing of the FICA deduction. We cannot determine which FICA rate to use until we know whether the gross pay is greater than $150. This reasoning must precede the calculation of the FICA deduction and follow the computation of gross pay. From prior discussions, we know that the last record check decision will follow the input of data.

Our solution is a logical development of the processing required. What happens to this flowchart if we expand the problem? Consider the effects of adding to Illustrative Problem 7 the following three features:

1   Headings above the columns of individual data
2   Two accumulators to add up total gross and total net, respectively
3   Two special labels to precede the output of each accumulator at the end of processing

The flowchart incorporating these three items is given in Figure 6.30. It includes many more symbols than our initial solution. At the beginning of this new flowchart, two processing statements initialize the accumulators for total gross (TG) and total net (TN). The PRINT symbol that follows indicates the output of four column headings. The remaining processing parallels the initial solution until both of the accumulators have individual gross and net amounts added to them. Usually when you work with more than one accumulator, it is best to update them consecutively in one group in order not to overlook one. The loop in the flowchart continues processing employees until the last record is read.

After that record is read, the output of the accumulators for total gross (TG) and total net (TN) is initiated. Note that the output symbols call for two separate output operations. The total gross literal and amount will appear on one line, and the total net data will appear on the line below. Because these outputs are situated at the end of the flowchart, the two total lines appear at the bottom of the report.

We will present another problem involving two decisions and an accumulator. It will not use headings.

ILLUSTRATIVE PROBLEM 8

Compute Commissions Using Two Percentages

The problem is to compute a salesperson's commission and to accumulate total commissions. Data input is the salesperson's name, number, and three sales amounts. The three sales amounts are used to compute total sales. If total sales > $200, then the rate of commission is 20 percent. If total sales ≤ $200, the commission is computed at 10 percent. Output each salesperson's name, number, total sales amount, and commission. Also output the accumulated total of commissions with an appropriate label. An unspecified number of salespeople are processed so use a 9's Decision.

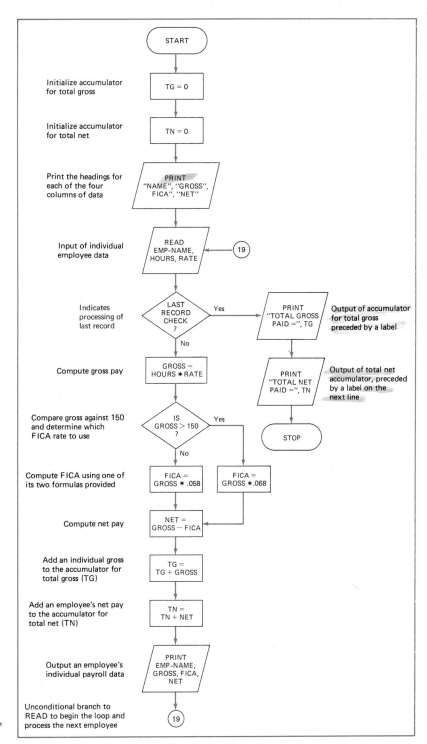

Initialize accumulator for total gross	TG = 0
Initialize accumulator for total net	TN = 0
Print the headings for each of the four columns of data	PRINT "NAME", "GROSS", FICA", "NET"
Input of individual employee data	READ EMP-NAME, HOURS, RATE
Indicates processing of last record	LAST RECORD CHECK ?
Compute gross pay	GROSS = HOURS * RATE
Compare gross against 150 and determine which FICA rate to use	IS GROSS > 150 ?
Compute FICA using one of its two formulas provided	FICA = GROSS * .058
Compute net pay	NET = GROSS − FICA
Add an individual gross to the accumulator for total gross (TG)	TG = TG + GROSS
Add an employee's net pay to the accumulator for total net (TN)	TN = TN + NET
Output an employee's individual payroll data	PRINT EMP-NAME, GROSS, FICA, NET
Unconditional branch to READ to begin the loop and process the next employee	19

Right-side branch:

- PRINT "TOTAL GROSS PAID =", TG — Output of accumulator for total gross preceded by a label
- PRINT "TOTAL NET PAID =", TN — Output of total net accumulator, preceded by a label on the next line
- STOP
- FICA = GROSS * .068

FIGURE 6.30   The flowchart for the expanded version of Illustrative Problem 7. The solution uses two accumulators, headings, two decisions, and special labels.

Figure 6.31 presents the flowchart and checklist for Illustrative Problem 8. No headings are necessary, but an accumulator (TCOMM) must be set (TCOMM = 0). The rest of the flowchart uses the logic discussed in other problems. The processing loop repetitively computes the total sales and commission for each employee. The 9's Decision permits the loop to branch and permits the output of the total commission and its respective literal "TOTAL COMMISSION PAID". This solution demonstrates that accumulators, literals, or any other flowcharting techniques are amply and easily added to any flowchart.

Each technique is consistently used in the same way. For example, if you want to accumulate a grand total, you know that two formulas are used. One formula initializes the accumulator and is positioned before the processing loop (i.e., T = 0). The second formula is placed inside the loop to update the accumulator (i.e., T = T + G). The addition of an accumulator to a flowchart automatically triggers the use of these two calculations. A sound knowledge of these concepts enables the flowcharter to properly position these symbols.

Accumulators and Counters

Illustrative Problem 9 shows the result of combining an accumulator and a counter. The accumulator computes a grand total; the counter permits the processing of an exact amount of data. The flowchart also indicates the output of headings and special labels. This solution demonstrates how easily all these requirements are combined in one solution.

ILLUSTRATIVE PROBLEM 9

Compute Student Average and Final Class Average

The overall problem is to compute a student's final average and the final average of the entire class. Input data is the student's name and two test marks. The two test marks are averaged for the student's final grade. The individual average is accumulated for the computation of the final class average. Exactly 25 students are processed, so a counter is appropriate. Output the student's name and individual average. At the top of this data, print the headings "STUDENT NAME" and "FINAL GRADE". Precede the final average output by the label "THE FINAL CLASS AVERAGE WAS".

The flowchart and data checklist of this problem appear in Figure 6.32. We can see there that the processing necessary for both the accumulator and counter, K = 1 and T = 0, precedes the loop. The column headings also precede the flowchart loop. Within the loop, each student's average is computed and added to the accumulator. At the end of the loop, after each student's processing is completed, the decision for the counter is placed. In this case, "Is K = 25?" is used, as 25 students are processed. The NO branch always contains both the increment of the counter and the unconditional branch to the READ symbol. The loop repeats as the next student's data is input. Remember, the number in the counter always equals the number of

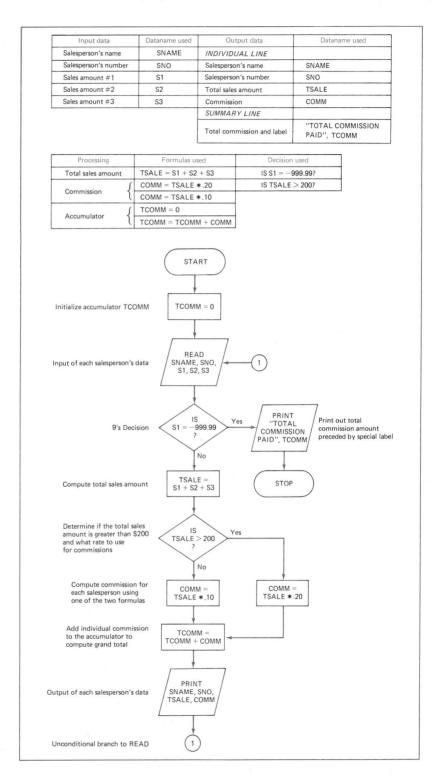

Input data	Dataname used	Output data	Dataname used
Salesperson's name	SNAME	*INDIVIDUAL LINE*	
Salesperson's number	SNO	Salesperson's name	SNAME
Sales amount #1	S1	Salesperson's number	SNO
Sales amount #2	S2	Total sales amount	TSALE
Sales amount #3	S3	Commission	COMM
		SUMMARY LINE	
		Total commission and label	"TOTAL COMMISSION PAID", TCOMM

Processing	Formulas used	Decision used
Total sales amount	TSALE = S1 + S2 + S3	IS S1 = −999.99?
Commission	COMM = TSALE * .20	IS TSALE > 200?
	COMM = TSALE * .10	
Accumulator	TCOMM = 0	
	TCOMM = TCOMM + COMM	

Initialize accumulator TCOMM

Input of each salesperson's data

9's Decision

Print out total commission amount preceded by special label

Compute total sales amount

Determine if the total sales amount is greater than $200 and what rate to use for commissions

Compute commission for each salesperson using one of the two formulas

Add individual commission to the accumulator to compute grand total

Output of each salesperson's data

Unconditional branch to READ

FIGURE 6.31 The legend and flowchart for Illustrative Problem 8.

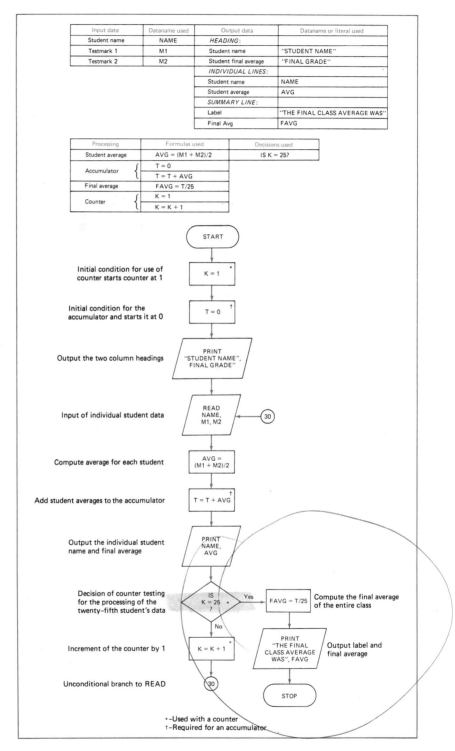

Input data	Dataname used	Output data	Dataname or literal used
Student name	NAME	*HEADING:*	
Testmark 1	M1	Student name	"STUDENT NAME"
Testmark 2	M2	Student final average	"FINAL GRADE"
		INDIVIDUAL LINES:	
		Student name	NAME
		Student average	AVG
		SUMMARY LINE:	
		Label	"THE FINAL CLASS AVERAGE WAS"
		Final Avg	FAVG

Processing	Formulas used	Decisions used
Student average	AVG = (M1 + M2)/2	IS K = 25?
Accumulator	T = 0	
	T = T + AVG	
Final average	FAVG = T/25	
Counter	K = 1	
	K = K + 1	

START

Initial condition for use of counter starts counter at 1 — K = 1 *

Initial condition for the accumulator and starts it at 0 — T = 0 †

Output the two column headings — PRINT "STUDENT NAME", FINAL GRADE"

Input of individual student data — READ NAME, M1, M2 ← (30)

Compute average for each student — AVG = (M1 + M2)/2

Add student averages to the accumulator — T = T + AVG †

Output the individual student name and final average — PRINT NAME, AVG

Decision of counter testing for the processing of the twenty-fifth student's data — IS K = 25 ? * — Yes → FAVG = T/25 — Compute the final average of the entire class

No

Increment of the counter by 1 — K = K + 1 *

PRINT "THE FINAL CLASS AVERAGE WAS", FAVG — Output label and final average

Unconditional branch to READ — (30)

STOP

*–Used with a counter
†–Required for an accumulator

FIGURE 6.32 The legend and flowchart for Illustrative Problem 9.

the student being processed. Therefore, when the counter is 1, the first student's data is processed. When the counter is 2, the second student's data is processed, and so on.

When K = 25, the twenty-fifth student is processed and no more student data exists. The computer can take the YES branch and compute the final class average (FAVG). The output of FAVG is preceded by the literal "THE FINAL CLASS AVERAGE WAS". The flowchart ends with this output.

Negative Accumulators

Not only can a flowchart represent the accumulation of totals, it can systematically reduce amounts of data as well. For both, the vehicle is an accumulator. We have already seen how an accumulator adds data on each repetition. A **negative accumulator** subtracts a specific amount from a total held in the accumulator. It effectively uses the accumulator in reverse.

The formulas for negative accumulators are like those for regular accumulators, but they are applied differently. The initial condition for a negative accumulator establishes the value from which an amount will be subtracted. The formula for that subtraction contains a minus sign and the amount to be subtracted. For example, if an initial amount of $6000 is to be reduced by $400 on each loop, the formulas necessary for that processing are

$$T = 6000 \quad \text{and} \quad T = T - 400$$

The first formula is an initial condition and establishes the initial value of the accumulator T at $6000. The second formula subtracts 400 from T on each repetition. Illustrative Problem 10 shows a flowchart with a negative accumulator.

COMBINING AN ACCUMULATOR AND A COUNTER

The combination of an accumulator and a counter in a flowchart can occasionally result in two types of errors. First, because both require similar initial conditions, the initial values may be accidentally reversed (i.e., K = 0 and T = 1). This reversal is incorrect. Second, the unconditional branch to start the processing loop may be incorrectly directed toward one of the two initial conditions instead of toward the READ symbol. This mistake renders the accumulator or counter ineffective.

To avoid these errors, be sure that the initial conditions are properly established and that the unconditional branch returns to the first symbol of the processing loop.

ILLUSTRATIVE
PROBLEM 10

Compute the Declining Balance in an Account

A widow is left $35,000 in a trust fund. She can withdraw a maximum of $750 per month from the fund's account. After computing her living expenses, she estimates that she will need to withdraw $625 a month. Under the terms of the trust, 9.5 percent interest is posted every December 31 to the fund's existing balance. Assuming that withdrawals from the trust of $625 begin on January 1, how many months will it take for the balance in the trust to fall below $5000? No inputs are provided for in the problem.

Output how many months it will take for the trust balance to fall below $5000 and the actual trust balance at that time. Use the labels "TOTAL MONTHS =" and "AMT. LEFT =" on separate lines to precede the proper amounts.

The flowchart for Illustrative Problem 10, Figure 6.33, incorporates an accumulator, a counter, and a negative accumulator. The accumulator M is set at 0 and totals the number of months that pass until the trust balance is less than $5000. The month accumulator M is increased by 1 because one deduction is made each month. Do not confuse this computation with a counter. It is perfectly acceptable to use accumulators for totaling amounts of data that break down into units of 1. An accumulator could, for example, add up the number of employees in a file with savings bond deductions from their gross pay, the number who attended college, or the number who have contributed to a pension fund. Each employee would count as 1 unit.

In Figure 6.33, the counter K monitors the passage of each 12-month period. After the twelfth withdrawal, on December 1, the interest on the existing balance is computed and added to the fund's account. After these computations, the counter is set back to 1. Setting K = 1 ensures that the counter completes 12 more repetitions, one withdrawal per loop.

Although K is set to equal 1 after each 12-month period, the accumulator M is never altered. The counter K must perform 12 loops (K = 12) to represent one year's deductions, then return to K = 1. In contrast, the accumulator M totals the number of months required for the balance to fall below $5000. Altering M would only generate an error and would prevent the accumulator from providing the right answer.

When the amount in the trust (T) falls below $5000, the YES branch of that decision is followed. This branching permits the output of the desired data regarding the TOTAL MONTHS involved and the AMT. LEFT in the fund's account. This decision follows the withdrawal of $625 and the 1-unit accumulator increase. This positioning lets the flowchart check the account's balance immediately after each withdrawal and branch out of the counter loop when it falls below the $5000 limit.

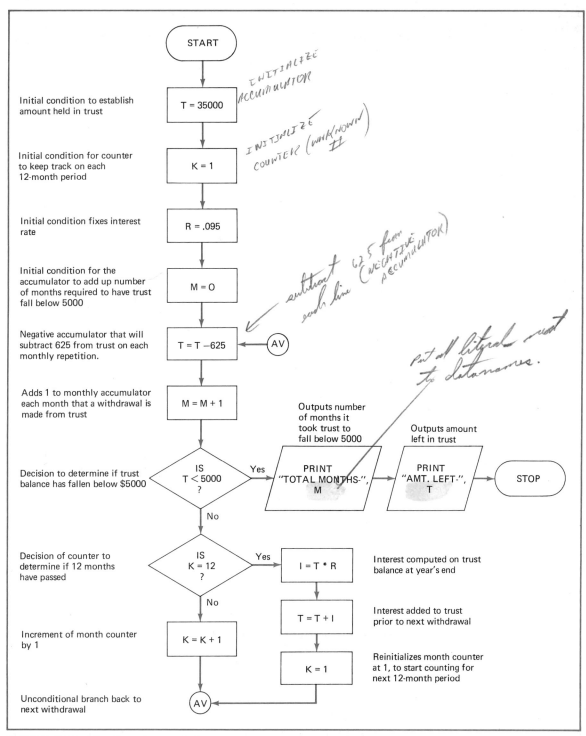

FIGURE 6.33 The flowchart solution to Illustrative Problem 10.

The "Finding What's Required" Checklist

Flowcharts are not flimsy sketches of flowing data, but detailed explanations of the sequential tasks required to process information. As such, they are pictorial representations of the logic necessary for their solution. There is a consistency not only in their solutions but also in the techniques used in their solutions. From earlier illustrations, we observed that last record checks, a 9's Decision, accumulators, and counters were always applied in exactly the same manner. We always expect to find a last record check or 9's Decision immediately after the READ symbol and an accumulator using two calculations. Although we recognize all the parts of any solution or technique, the trick is to determine from the problem which techniques to apply.

Each solution or technique has its own set of distinguishing characteristics. The following checklist will clarify and identify many of them.

1 Identify all the inputs to a problem, and assign each an appropriate dataname.

2 Determine the amount of data used by the problem. If the amount is unspecified, consider using a last record check or 9's Decision. If an exact amount of data is to be processed, consider using a counter.

3 Compile a list of all the processing required. If possible, represent these computations in formulas or concise sentences.

4 Determine if a grand total (and hence, an accumulator) is necessary. If so, use the two required computations (i.e., $T = 0$ and $T = T + G$).

5 If a counter is used, include the initial condition (i.e., $K = 1$), the decision (i.e., Is $K = 20$?), and the increment (i.e., $K = K + 1$). Place the increment *on the NO branch* of the counter decision.

6 Identify all the datanames that require headings or special labels. Put all literals in quotation marks, and place them next to their datanames.

7 Place the PRINT symbols containing headings before the processing loop. Place the output of individual data inside the flowchart loop. Place all outputs of accumulated totals on the decision branches that lead from the loop of processing.

8 When a loop is used, ensure that the unconditional branch returns to the READ symbol, not to one of the initial conditions. Always close flowchart loops.

9 Label all conditional branches of decisions YES or NO.

10 Whenever possible, create a legend or dataname checklist. Identify all inputs, processing, outputs, decisions, datanames, and any other factors related to the flowchart.

This checklist should help you to prepare and analyze flowcharting solutions. We present these suggestions to guide your initial flowcharting experiences. Always approach your flowcharting problems slowly, in an organized fashion, for best results.

Summary

The following major points have been discussed in Chapter 6:

Point 1 Two types of flowcharts are used in data processing. Systems flowcharts are broad diagrams of the flow of data through an organization or a series of operations. Program flowcharts depict all the steps involved in the processing of a computer program.

Point 2 Flowcharts are pictorial representations of the flow of data. Data processors use flowcharts as an efficient means of communication, as an analytic tool, and as a concise form of documentation. Flowcharts should always be constructed before the actual processing of data or writing of programs.

Point 3 Each symbol used in a flowchart has specific meaning. Five common program flowcharting symbols are the Terminal, Input/Output, Processing, Decision, and Annotation symbols. The Terminal symbol is also referred to as the START or the STOP symbol because it indicates the start and the end of a flowchart. The Input/Output symbol represents all I/O operations in a flowchart. Frequently, the terms READ and PRINT are employed to identify this symbol. All forms of data manipulation are represented with the Processing symbol. The Decision symbol denotes logical operations. The Decision symbol contains a conditional statement defining the conditional branches that exit from the symbol. The Annotation symbol permits the addition of descriptive comments to a flowchart.

Point 4 The first flowchart given in the chapter represents the simple computation of gross pay for one person. The processing of data related to many people is accomplished using either a last record check decision or a 9's Decision and a flowchart loop. A loop is constructed when an unconditional branch returns to a previously processed symbol. The steps in the loop repeat. The 9's Data, used in the test of the 9's Decision, follows all other data. Thus when the 9's Data is encountered, no more data exists. The flowchart can branch to perform other work or end. A legend of data assists the flowcharter.

Point 5 Two flowcharting techniques are the accumulator and the counter. The accumulator computes grand totals. Two computations are necessary with an accumulator. Using T for the accumulator and G for gross pay, the two formulas for the totaling of gross pay are $T = 0$ and $T = T + G$. A counter lets us count the number of repetitive loops processed, one at a time. Two computations and a decision are necessary for a counter. Using K for the counter, the computations should appear as $K = 1$ and $K = K + 1$, while the decision is, for example, "Is $K = 25$?"

Point 6 Literals are special outputs designed to add printed data to documents. Headings are literals at the top of columns of data; special labels usually precede individual output (i.e., a grand total).

Point 7 Multiple decisions, counters, and accumulators can be combined in any flowchart. Care must be taken to ensure that all computations and decisions related to either technique are incorporated into the flowchart.

Point 8 It is possible to systematically subtract an amount from a predefined total with a negative accumulator. This technique requires that you set the total to be subtracted from (i.e., $T = 6000$) and use a formula for the regular subtraction of data from that total (i.e., $T = T - 500$).

Point 9 A checklist or guideline is provided to help the flowcharter prepare or complete a flowchart.

Glossary

Accumulator The flowchart technique used to represent the accumulation of grand totals for specific data amounts.

American National Standards Institute (ANSI) An international organization that devised the standardized flowcharting symbols.

Case Study One

Computer Graphics to the Rescue

Architects are part designers and part engineers. They create ideas for structures, ideas which must withstand a client's scrutiny and the stresses of the environment as well. But when a structure is still in the design stage, how is a client actually to *see* what he or she may be paying thousands of dollars for? How is the architect to know whether the structure will be energy efficient or will collapse after a heavy snowfall? Computer graphics are solving these and similar problems for many architects and their clients. In the past, architects spent enormous amounts of time preparing and revising detailed drawings of structures and the mechanical computations that support them. Today, computers can speed much of this laborious work.

Computer display terminals translate data about a structure, its environment, and its engineering into pictures on a screen. Architects first trace a design onto the computer's electronic "drawing board" with a stylus. The computer then analyzes the building surfaces in the design and automatically converts them into equations and coordinates. Once this data is locked into computer storage, the computer can manipulate the facts at the architect's command. Architects can request the computer to display a structure from any angle, from inside or outside, and in any size. They can add details, expand or contract a structure, plunk it at will into one site after another, and even watch shadow patterns created by the changing position of the sun.

Colors on the display terminal further enhance the computer's usefulness. Colors can highlight particular aspects of a diagram. An architect might, for example, want to know how much snow a roof would bear. By asking the computer to put a foot of snow on the roof, the architect can see that the structural supports colored white are understressed, those colored blue are fully stressed, and those colored red are overstressed. By entering a few computations into the computer, the architect can correct the structural flaws and design a stronger roof.

A leader in the field of computer graphics is Donald P. Greenberg, professor of architecture at Cornell University. Unhappy at having to draw so "many different sections of the same detail" and at the many days people had to spend interpreting engineering figures, Professor Greenberg began perfecting the logic for programming structural details into computer-usable mathematical statements. His software had to solve the problem of hiding the lines in a drawing that would be invisible in reality so that the computer diagrams would seem realistic. By early 1973, Professor Greenberg had nighttime access to the computer at General Electric in Syracuse, N.Y., and in 1974 he received a $500,000 National Science Foundation grant to establish at Cornell a research facility for computer graphics input and display techniques.

Professor Greenberg believes that computer graphics can help in professions other than architecture. Car manufacturers can use the techniques to see how well a car will fare in a collision. Doctors can reconstruct x-ray images of internal organs, and moviemakers can speed up the painstaking animation process. As computer costs decrease, and as the human imagination expands, computer graphics are sure to flourish.

Source of data: Anne Simon Moffat, "Computers Become a Major Design Tool," *The New York Times*, December 4, 1979, p. C1.

Consider this . . .

How might computer-generated illustrations be applied to other design-related fields? Could interior decorators use them to develop interior spaces? Might chemists develop computer projections of molecular structures for proposed chemical compounds?

Using special graphic techniques, architects can visualize the design of buildings in their environment. The rightmost terminal depicts a building and its proposed site. (*Office of Public Information; Cornell University.*)

Annotation symbol   A symbol used to add descriptive notes or commentary to a flowchart; attached to symbols by a dotted line.

Checklist   A list of the input, output, processing, and decisions performed in a flowchart; used to identify all aspects of a problem.

Conditional branches   The exit branches of a decision symbol (e.g., YES branch, NO branch).

Conditional statement   The question, placed within a decision symbol, that defines a logical operation.

Connector symbol   A symbol used to connect two parts of a flowchart, indicating that the flow of data is not broken (i.e., an unconditional branch to the READ symbol).

Counter   The flowchart technique used to count (by 1) the number of times a flowchart loop is completed.

Dataname   The term or word(s) applied to variables in a flowchart (i.e., EMP-NAME, HOURS, etc.).

Decision Symbol   The flowcharting symbol used to represent logical operations.

Flowchart   The pictorial representation of the flow of data through an organization or a computerized process.

Flowchart loop   The repetition of a series of steps to process individual data; normally created by an unconditional branch back to a prior operation.

Heading   A specific group of characters, created by a literal in an output operation, placed above a column of data or at the top of a page.

Initial condition   An operation that is performed prior to, and in preparation for, the processing of data.

Input/Output (I/O) symbol   The symbol used to define an input or output operation in a flowchart (i.e., READ symbol, PRINT symbol).

Last record check   A flowchart technique to determine whether the last record or item of data has been processed.

Legend   A list of the input, output, processing, and decisions performed in a flowchart; used to identify all aspects of a problem.

Literal   A string of characters for the output of headings and special labels; defined by a pair of quotation marks.

Loop   See flowchart loop.

Negative accumulator   An accumulator that systematically subtracts amounts from a predefined total.

9's Data   A series of 9's used with a 9's Decision.

9's Decision   The flowchart technique that uses a series of 9's to test for the last item of data to be processed.

PRINT symbol   An Input/Output symbol in which the word PRINT is placed; used for output operations.

Processing symbol   The symbol used to define all manipulations of data and processing in a flowchart.

Program flowchart   A flowchart that defines all the operations necessary to process data in a computer program.

READ symbol   An Input/Output symbol containing the word READ; used for input operations.

Running total   A business term indicating that a continuous total figure is maintained as data is added up; the last figure represents the most current total.

Special label   A specific group of characters, in the form of a literal, that precedes the output of data.

START symbol   A Terminal symbol used to denote the beginning of a flowchart.

STOP symbol   A Terminal symbol denoting the end of a flowchart.

Systems flowchart   A flowchart defining the flow of data through an organization or a company, or a series of tasks that may or may not represent computerized processing. Systems flowcharts are broad, all-encompassing diagrams and may contain program flowcharts.

Terminal symbol   The first and last symbol of a flowchart.

Unconditional branch   A branch to another symbol of a flowchart which forces data down a predetermined path.

Discussion Questions

For each of the problem narratives that follow, draw the flowchart for the processing described and compile a legend, or checklist, of datanames, processing, and decisions involved in the problem.

1 The overall problem relates to the computation of net pay. Data input to this problem consists of the employee's name, hours worked, and rate of pay. Gross pay is computed by multiplying hours × rate. The FICA deduction is 7.28 percent of gross pay. Net pay = gross pay − FICA deduction. Output each individual employee's name, gross pay, FICA deduction, and net pay. An unspecified number of employees are processed; therefore, use a last record check.

2 Redo question 1, adding the following requirements: Accumulate the total net pay computed for the employees, output headings above each column of data, and output the special label "NET PAY PAID =" prior to printing the total amount of the accumulator.

3 The problem is to compute weekly batting averages. Data is input in the form of punched cards that are prepared each week. Input are the player's name, number of at bats for that week, and number of hits in that week. An individual player's batting average is compiled by dividing the total number of hits by the total number of at bats. Print this data under the headings "PLAYER", "AT BATS", "HITS", and "WEEKLY AVG". Exactly 1219 players are processed.

4 This problem relates to the computation of sales commissions. Sales data input is the salesperson's name, number, and four sales amounts. These four figures are added to compute the individual salesperson's total sales amount. If total sales ≤ $200, the commission rate is 12 percent. If sales > $200, the commission rate is 20 percent. Output each salesperson's name, number, total sales amount, and commission. Also accumulate the grand total of all sales made and the grand total of all commissions paid. Output each on a separate line, and precede each with an appropriate special label. An unspecified amount of sales data is used.

5 This problem involves the printing of student data. Data input is the student's name and three final course grades (in numeric form). The student's final average is computed by summing up the three grades and dividing that total by three. If the final average is ≥ 3.0, output the student's name, final average, and the literal "WITH HONORS" on the same line. If the final average < 3.0, output only the student's name and final average. Use a counter to process this data because exactly 79 students are involved.

6 Redo question 5, adding the following requirements: Using an accumulator, determine the number of students with a final average ≥ 3.0. After processing all 79 students, print out that total using the label, "NUMBER OF HONOR STUDENTS IS:".

7 This problem deals with determining the number of employees receiving overtime pay and the total amount of overtime paid to the employees in a company payroll. Data input to this problem consists of the employee's name, hours worked, and rate of pay. If the number of hours worked > 40, the employee receives overtime pay. Overtime pay is calculated at double the hourly rate × the number of overtime hours worked and is added to the employee's normal (40-hour) pay. Because we are examining only overtime pay, if the employee's hours worked ≤ 40, disregard that data and read the next person's data. Output only those employees who have worked overtime, printing their name, regular pay, overtime pay, and total weekly pay. Accumulate the grand total of overtime paid to all employees and compute the total number of employees that have actually received overtime pay. Output both of these accumulated totals with the labels "TOTAL OVERTIME PAID" and "NO. OF EMPLOYEES WORKING O/T", respectively. Use a 9's Decision to control processing.

8 This problem relates to the computation of individual student grades and a final class average. Input are the student's name and four test marks. The student's final average is calculated by adding the four grades and dividing the total by four. Exactly 32 students are in the class. Output each student's name and final average. Also, compute the average of the entire class's final grades by accumulating all the individual final grades and dividing the total by 32. Output this class average with the label "FINAL CLASS AVERAGE IS".

9 The problem is to determine the number of employees who contribute to a company pension plan and the sum of their monthly payments. Inputs to the problem are employee name and social security number, pension code, and monthly contribution. The two pension codes are 1 if the employee contributes to the plan and 0 if the employee does not. If the employee does not contribute to the plan, bypass that record and branch to the next employee's record. If the employee's pension code is 1, add the amount of that employee's monthly contribution to the accumulator, add 1 to the accumulated total of participating employees, and print the employee's name, social security number, and monthly contribution. This data should be printed under the headings "SOCIAL SECURITY NO", "NAME", and "PENSION AMT". After processing the last employee record, print on separate lines the accumulated sum of all monthly contributions and the number of employees contributing to the pension plan. Precede these outputs with the labels "TOTAL MONTHLY CONTRIBUTIONS =" and "NO. OF PARTICIPATING EMPLOYEES =", respectively. Use a last record check to monitor the input and processing of each employee record.

10 The overall problem deals with determining the amount of money students receive from state-supported tuition plans. Input to the computer are student name and social security number, tuition code, and amount of grant. Three tuition codes, A, B, and C, identify the three state reimbursement plans. Depending on the student's plan, add the appropriate grant amount to one of the three accumulators. Each accumulator should contain only funds related to it and identified by its code. Output each student's social security number, name, tuition code, and grant amount under the headings "SSN", "STUDENT NAME", "CODE", and "GRANT $". After the last record is processed, print on three separate lines the totals in the three accumulators, preceded by appropriate labels. Add these three totals and print that sum under the label "TOTAL GRANT $ =" before ending the flowchart.

11 A student is left an estate of $15,000, which he intends to use during college. The money is in an account with 6 percent annual interest posted every 3 months. He intends to withdraw $350 monthly for his last 2 years at college. He estimates that he will have almost half of the trust remaining when he graduates in 2 years. He wants all withdrawals to cease when the balance falls below $7500. The student wants to determine the exact number of months necessary to reach the $7500 limit and the exact balance when it falls below that point.

Input to the problem are name, social security number, and quarterly interest rate. The estate amount is set to begin at $15,000 and is reduced monthly via a negative accumulator formula, $T = T - 350$. The interest is computed by multiplying the existing balance by the quarterly interest rate; it is then added back into the account. A counter is used to create the 3-month period for making withdrawals and posting interest. An accumulator keeps track of the months that pass before the account falls below $7500. Output the interest and new balance at the end of each quarter. When the $7500 limit is exceeded, output the total months and remaining account balance, preceded by the labels "MONTHS =" and "REMAINING BALANCE =", respectively.

Summary Test

_F_   **1** Programmers must develop a skill with flowchart techniques, but systems analysts very rarely use flowcharts.

_T_   **2** The two most commonly used flowcharting forms are the program and the systems flowchart.

_F_   **3** All flowcharts must relate to a computerized and not a manual process.

_F_   **4** Flowcharts are excellent analytic tools, but cannot be used as a means of communication.

_T_   **5** Alternative approaches to problems may be constructed and tested using flowcharts.

_F_   **6** Conditional statements have no effect on logical operations.

_F_   **7** Decisions can be performed on numeric data but not on alphabetic data.

_T_   **8** The symbol > within a decision represents "is greater than."

_F_   **9** Any data used in a computation must be defined after its use.

_T_ **10** A flowchart loop indicates the repetitive performance of steps to process data.

_T_ **11** With the 9's Decision, the NO branch directs the flow of data to continue processing.

_T_ **12** Counters generally start at a value of 1 and are incremented by that amount.

_T_ **13** The increment to a counter is performed in the NO branch of the counter decision.

_F_ **14** Headings are characters that appear above columns of data in a report and are represented by PRINT symbols in the YES branch of the last record check decision.

_F_ **15** Special labels cannot appear between or with datanames.

_____ **16** The decimal equivalent of .01 percent is:

    a   .0001   **b**   .01

    c   .10   **d**   1.0

_D_ **17** Headings are:

    a   designed to appear atop columns of data in printed reports.

    b   defined by quotation marks in I/O symbols in a flowchart.

    c   often logically positioned with initial conditions in a flowchart.

    d   all the above.

_B_ **18** The initial condition used with a negative accumulator defines:
- **a** the amount of data to be added on each repetition.
- **b** the total from which an amount is systematically subtracted.
- **c** a value = 0.
- **d** the value subtracted from on the YES branch of the last record check.

_C_ **19** The symbol used to add descriptive comments to a flowchart is the:
- **a** COMMENT symbol
- **b** I/O symbol
- **c** ANNOTATION symbol
- **d** all the above

_B_ **20** When an unspecified amount of data is represented in a flowchart solution, a last record check may be replaced by a(n):
- **a** accumulator
- **b** 9's Decision
- **c** counter
- **d** unconditional branch

_D_ **21** The initial condition associated with a 9's Decision is illustrated by the statement:
- **a** K = 1
- **b** T = 0
- **c** T = 6000
- **d** no computation is used

_D_ **22** The printing of a total accumulated within a flowchart loop is normally output via the:
- **a** YES branch of a 9's Decision
- **b** YES branch of a counter decision
- **c** YES branch of a last record check
- **d** all the above

Questions 23 to 25 relate to the flowchart solution shown in Figure 6.34.

_C_ **23** As you work through the flowchart, how many times would you complete the loop?
- **a** Zero, as the increment is not positioned properly.
- **b** 25
- **c** 26
- **d** Unlimited, as the connector is incorrectly placed.

_C_ **24** If the AMT input averages $200 per loop, the total held in the accumulator T when the last loop is completed is:
- **a** 4800
- **b** 5000
- **c** 5200
- **d** 0; it has no value due to a processing error

_A_ **25** The value output following the label "TOTAL AMT" of the I/O symbol on the YES branch of the counter symbol is:
- **a** undefined
- **b** 4800
- **c** 5000
- **d** 5200

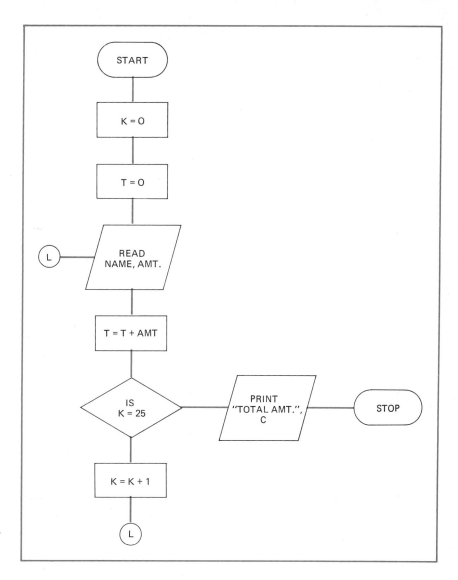

FIGURE 6.34 The flow-chart solution used for questions 23 to 25.

Quiz Problem

Prepare a flowchart for the following problem:

The overall problem relates to computing the winning percentage of a basketball league. Six teams play in the league. Data input consists of the team's name and the number of games won and lost. The winning percentage is calculated by dividing the number of games won by the total number of games played. Output each team's name, games won, games lost, and their winning percentage. Above the columns of data, place the headings "TEAM", "WON", "LOST", and "PCT". Accumulate the total number of games won by all the teams in the league, and print out that data after processing ceases. Place the label "TOTAL GAMES WON" before the output of the accumulated total.

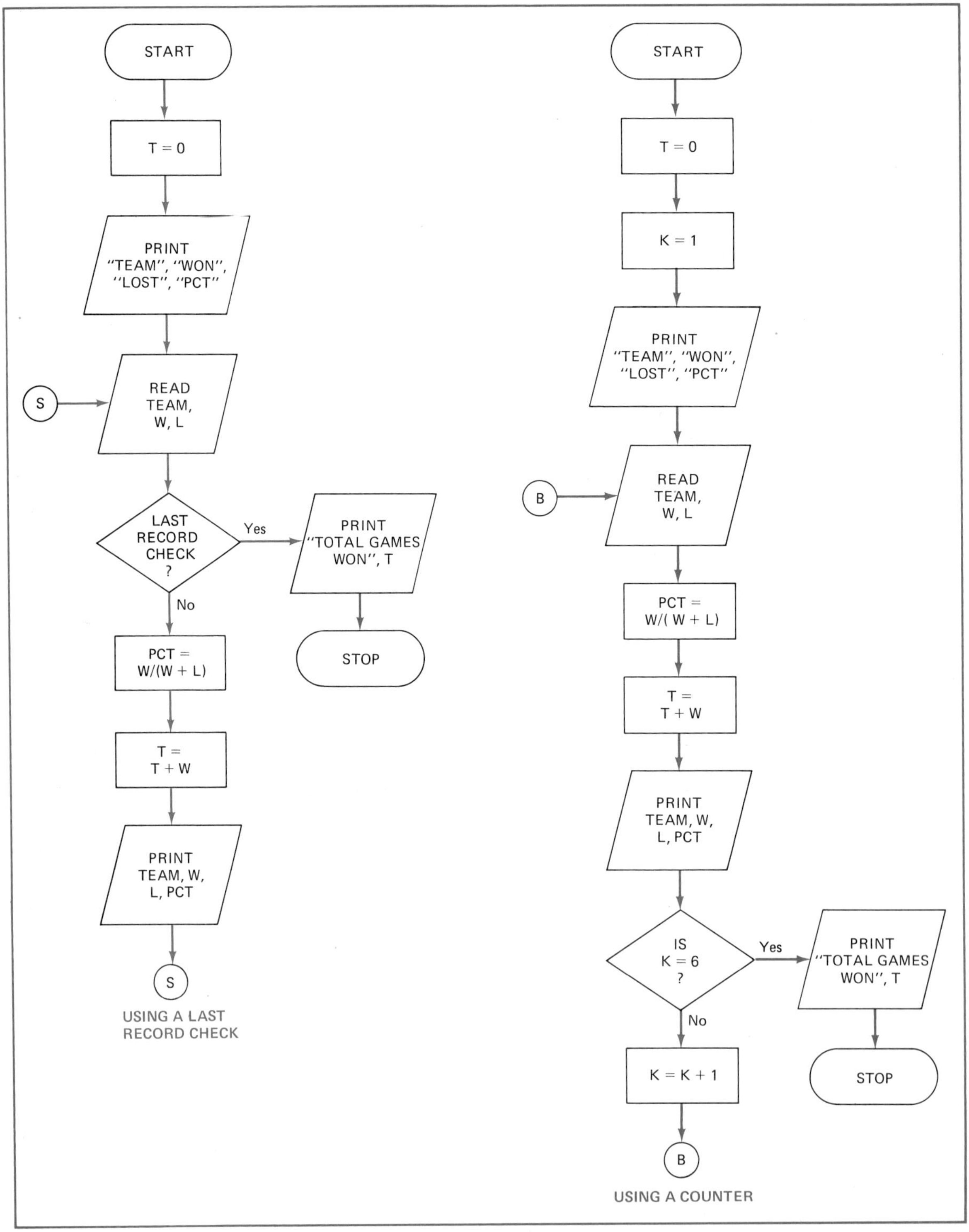
START
T = 0
PRINT "TEAM", "WON", "LOST", "PCT"
S
READ TEAM, W, L
LAST RECORD CHECK ?
Yes
PRINT "TOTAL GAMES WON", T
STOP
No
PCT = W/(W + L)
T = T + W
PRINT TEAM, W, L, PCT
S
USING A LAST RECORD CHECK
START
T = 0
K = 1
PRINT "TEAM", "WON", "LOST", "PCT"
B
READ TEAM, W, L
PCT = W/(W + L)
T = T + W
PRINT TEAM, W, L, PCT
IS K = 6 ?
Yes
PRINT "TOTAL GAMES WON", T
STOP
No
K = K + 1
B
USING A COUNTER

FIGURE 6.35

Summary Test Answers

1 F	**2** T	**3** F	**4** F	**5** T
6 F	**7** F	**8** T	**9** F	**10** T
11 T	**12** T	**13** T	**14** F	**15** F
16 A	**17** D	**18** B	**19** C	**20** B
21 D	**22** D	**23** C	**24** C	**25** A

Appendix: Decision Tables

Not all data processing problems are as simple as the ones we have been discussing. Data processing problems and solutions can become quite complex. The results of combining a large quantity of data, intricate processing, and multiple decisions can seem bewildering. Imagine the computerized processing for preparing a federal tax return.

Many programmers and analysts use a *decision table* to define all factors relating to a large combination of decisions and processing statements. The decision table describes all the factors that lead up to a decision and the various choices that result from the decision. The analyst or programmer using a decision table does not have to minimize the assumptions that lead to a specific decision and result. In essence, a decision table is a record of: "If these conditions exist, then the following actions can be taken."

Decision tables do not replace flowcharts or the analysis required prior to programming. They supplement the work of the programmer or analyst and make their job a little easier.

A tabular format was constructed, as illustrated in Figure 6.36, to help in the preparation of decision tables. The top half of the table presents the conditions (factors) employed in the decision. The bottom half of the table represents the action (results) of that decision. The table is composed of four parts. The *condition stub* provides a written narrative of all factors leading to the decision. The *condition entry* outlines which factors are actual components of the decision. The *action stub* is a narrative detailing all possible results. The *action entry* defines the actual result of the decision.

FIGURE 6.36 The general format of the decision table is divided into two halves and subdivided into four units. Each of the four areas serves a specific purpose in the table.

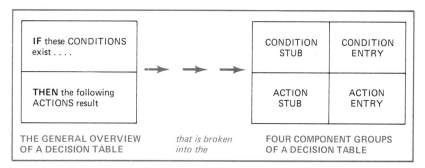

IF these CONDITIONS exist		CONDITION STUB	CONDITION ENTRY
THEN the following ACTIONS result		ACTION STUB	ACTION ENTRY
THE GENERAL OVERVIEW OF A DECISION TABLE	*that is broken into the*	FOUR COMPONENT GROUPS OF A DECISION TABLE	

When using a decision table, the programmer reads across to the conditions that affect the decision. When the column containing the desired condition is found, the programmer reads down and notes the action resulting from these conditions.

Consider the case of a state lottery. Each lottery ticket has two sets of numbers. If number A shows, the ticket holder wins $25. If number B appears, the ticket holder wins $50. If both numbers are on the ticket, the holder wins $1000 and is eligible for the $100,000 grand prize. Naturally, if the ticket has neither number, the person holding the ticket receives no prize. The decision table depicting the results of this lottery is shown in Figure 6.37.

Figure 6.37 shows some of the operational notations used with decision tables. Columns on the right-hand side of the table are called *rules.* Rules define the conditions that exist and the actions resulting from those conditions in separate columns. In the condition entry, the letter Y indicates that the condition exists. The absence of a Y indicates that the condition does *not* exist. In the action entry, an X in the same column denotes the results of the conditions. For example, in rule 1, if the ticket holder has neither number A nor B, an X is placed next to the action, indicating the winning of no money. In rule 2, the Y is placed in the condition noting that the ticket holder has number A. The action resulting from this condition, the winning of $25, is noted by an X. Rule 3 notes the winning of $50, if number B is held. The last rule has two Y's. The placement of these two Y's indicates that the ticket holder holds both numbers A and B. These conditions mean the ticket holder wins $1000 and becomes eligible for the grand prize. These results are noted by the use of two X's placed in the action entries. The character X always notes the result of the conditions in that rule. Actions not affected in a rule are left blank.

FIGURE 6.37 The decision table used to describe all the events related to the lottery ticket problem. Note that with rule 4, two Y's indicate that numbers A and B are both present on the lottery ticket. The response to this condition entry is the action entry of two X's. These X's indicate the winning of $1000 and the ticket holder's eligibility for the grand prize of $100,000.

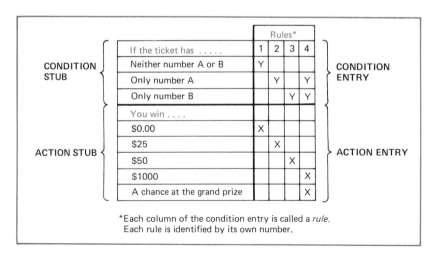

	Rules*			
If the ticket has	1	2	3	4
Neither number A or B	Y			
Only number A		Y		Y
Only number B			Y	Y
You win				
$0.00	X			
$25		X		
$50			X	
$1000				X
A chance at the grand prize				X

CONDITION STUB   ACTION STUB   CONDITION ENTRY   ACTION ENTRY

*Each column of the condition entry is called a *rule.* Each rule is identified by its own number.

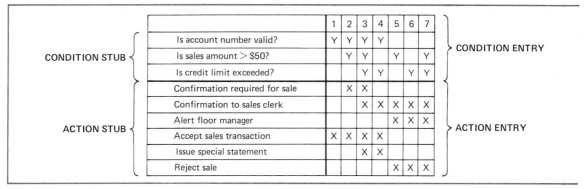

FIGURE 6.38 The decision table used for the retail sales problem, which describes each response to all charge sales transactions. Note that if the customer account is not valid, no transaction is possible.

Consider the case of a programmer writing a program for a retail system in which charge sales are posted directly by the system. Decision tables are essential for defining the conditions under which charge sales are accepted. Basically, as long as the customer's account is valid, the sale will be recorded. If the customer account is invalid, the sale is rejected and supervisory personnel alerted. Figure 6.38 gives the decision table.

Decision tables afford members of a data processing staff a concise presentation of the factors relating to any decision. The decision to use decision tables, as with many computer techniques, rests with the individual data processor. The skills necessary to construct decision tables are developed through time, patience, and effort. Generally the rule of thumb is, "The more complex the decision, the larger the decision table."

Seven

Introduction to Programming and Programming Languages

FIGURE 7.1 Programming languages vary with application, user need, and computer support. Many hours of testing are necessary before a program is certified as operationally correct. This effort requires that programs be rerun and their results carefully examined. (*Magnum.*)

Purpose of This Chapter

In this chapter, we introduce several programming languages, discuss the execution of programs by the computer, and present an initial approach to developing program solutions.

We also discuss machine language, the language the computer actually uses to perform processing. Assembly language is reviewed and used as a springboard for discussing high-level languages. We fully describe the characteristics of high-level languages.

The chapter goes into several programming languages, including FORTRAN, COBOL, BASIC, RPG, PL/1, PASCAL, and ADA, as well as specialized languages like DECAL and SCRIPT. It briefly details the origin and use of each language.

We then treat the overall execution of programs, the effect of compilers on source programs, and the resulting object programs that are actually processed. We discuss the supervisor, a program that oversees the operation of the entire computer system, and the use of job control language (JCL) to facilitate processing.

The chapter examines the function and purpose of an operating system and three characteristics of operational software. Spoolers that create job queues and three operating systems, RSX, RSTS/E, and JES3, are briefly discussed.

We then present the steps a programmer takes to attack and solve a programming problem. We detail each step and describe certain forms the programmer uses, and we give a list of items for the final documentation of a program.

After studying this chapter, you should be able to:

- Describe the format of machine and assembly languages.
- Discuss the characteristics of high-level languages.
- Discuss the origin and general use of FORTRAN, COBOL, BASIC, RPG, PL/1, PASCAL, DECAL, SCRIPT, and ADA.
- Describe the purpose of the supervisor control program.
- Describe the use of a compiler in converting source programs into machine languages.
- Discuss the use of job control language.
- Discuss the purpose and characteristics of an operating system.
- Describe the steps in deriving a complete programming solution.
- Describe the purpose and composition of final program documentation.
- Understand the following terms:

ADA

Assembler

Assembly language

BASIC

Bugs

Business application

COBOL

Coding sheet

Compilation

Compiler

Core dump

Debugging

DECAL

Error message log

FORTRAN

General-purpose coding sheet

High-level languages

Input/Output Control System (IOCS)

Interactive languages

Interactive Query Facility (IQF)

JCL cards

Job control language (JCL)

Job Entry Subsystem 3 (JES3)

Job queue

Label

Live data

Low-level languages

Machine language

Macroinstruction (macro)

Mnemonics

Multiple card layout form

Object program

Op code

Operand

Operating system

Operation code

PASCAL

PL/1

Printer spacing chart

Problem definition

Problem-oriented languages

Procedure-oriented languages

Program compatibility

RPG

RSTS/E

RSX

Scientific application

SCRIPT

Source deck

Spooler

Stand-alone program

Supervisor

Supervisor control program

Symbolic programming language

Syntax

System residence device (SYSRES)

Systems programmer

Tag

Tracing routine

User's manual

Word processing

Introduction

At sessions of the United Nations, skilled translators demonstrate a remarkable ability to listen to a speech in one language and translate it simultaneously into another language. They can listen to a statement, perceive its intent, and translate it without distorting that intent. UN translators must be accurate; global politics hang on their very words.

Like UN translators, computer programmers must convert statements from one form into another. Programmers use programming languages to convert ideas into solutions. Both jobs require a thorough understanding of rules. The translator must know the rules of the languages being translated, whereas the programmer must know the structure and standards of computer languages.

BY COMPUTER, TO THE MOON

Timing the Burn

The third-stage burn that vaults Apollo toward the moon should take place at a spot on the side of Earth that is away from the moon and on a direct line through the center of the earth and the center of the moon. This is called the antipode. Firing at this point gives the most efficient trajectory, reduces course corrections that might be needed later and, so, conserves fuel. Men can't react precisely enough to initiate that rocket restart within a hundredth of a second, as required. But they can build machines to take action for them. The digital computer is one of those machines.

A computer in the Instrument Unit calculates the timing for that burn and signals the engines to start at the right moment. This burn and every burn during the trip, every maneuver, every event, was planned

months before launch. A precise ephemeris for the spacecraft during the entire trip was calculated and stored in computers. Into the computers also went performance characteristics for every piece of equipment in the rockets and in the spacecraft . . . exact timing of lift-off and stage separations . . . the constantly changing influence of gravity from Earth, moon, and Sun . . . positions of moon, stars, and planets along the way.

Are We on Time?

The computers automatically check actual performance with planned performance. If lift-off is a tenth of a second late, if a high wind at Cape Kennedy blows the bird off course, if the parking orbit around Earth is just a few miles off target, a new ephemeris must be calculated to predict the actual course the spacecraft will take.

Once the bird clears the launch tower at Cape Kennedy, the computer at Houston starts gobbling a flood of information from tracking stations around the world . . . from the astronauts . . . from flight controllers and others on Earth who monitor the mission. During the same time, the computer is spewing out answers to a thousand questions the flight controllers might ask.

Every time a rocket fires or new readings of spacecraft position, velocity and direction are received, the computer recalculates a new trajectory and delivers the results, **in just three seconds.** Throughout the mission, it updates the ephemeris and predicts the path of the spacecraft for 40 hours of flight. It can flash this information to visual display units in Mission Control and up to the astronauts four minutes after it receives new tracking data.

The computer automatically compares the new, true ephemeris with that desired. If the course must be changed to keep the spacecraft on target, the Houston computer determines how much rocket thrust is needed, for how long, in what direction and the best time to make the correction.

Computers Check Computers

While the computer on the ground keeps a constant check on radar and radio tracking information, another computer in the spacecraft is doing its own calculating of position, speed, trajectory and equipment performance, based on information generated by instruments built into the spacecraft. Other computers, at Houston and Goddard Space Center near Washington, D.C., act as electronic shadows—mimicking operation of the primary computers. These back-up computers are ready, at any moment, to take over if trouble crops up in the primary computer at Houston.

Source of data: *Suddenly, Tomorrow Came,* IBM, 1970, p. 25.

7.1 Programming Languages

Sophisticated programming languages evolved slowly, in response to the needs of industry. Cumbersome early software gradually gave way to more convenient and more easily used forms. With today's languages, computers may be directed to perform complex manipulations, with relatively few instructions.

Let's turn back to the language that engineers and scientists used with the first computer systems. Then we can trace the historical development of various computer languages and end with today's popular forms.

Machine Language

LOW LEVEL
0, 1 = BITS
Binary Digits

operand → defines data

Machine language is machine dependent!

LOW LEVEL LANGUAGES

Originally, computer programs were written in **machine language,** which is the language directly used by the computer during processing. Today most programs are written in special programming languages; however, all programs executed by the computer are still actually processed in machine language, regardless of the language the programmers originally used. Machine language is the *only* language the computer can employ when executing a program.

Since it is directly digested by the computer, machine language is used most rapidly. The actual statements of a machine language program are generally composed of a string of numeric characters. The format is important because it defines the format for all future languages.

Machine language instructions are composed of an **operation code** and an **operand.** The operation code, or **op code,** defines the function that the computer must perform (i.e., the addition of two data items, the movement of data, the start of an I/O operation, etc.). The operand represents the variables or items of data involved in this function. The operand defines its items of data by their actual locations in main storage. When programmers wrote their instructions in machine language, they had to maintain a list of datanames and their storage positions—an extremely tedious task.

Though machine language is efficient for computers, it is inefficient for programmers. Programming in machine language was time-consuming, tedious, and costly. Machine language instructions were incomplete in the sense that one instruction did not identify, or direct, one complete computer operation. Many machine language instructions were necessary for one complete operational command. It was as if the programmer needed 1000 sentences to say, "Walk 10 feet."

The problem of written machine language instructions was compounded when errors were encountered and corrections had to be made. In these cases, each of the many instructions affected by the error had to be altered, and changes had to be made to every op code and storage location involved.

Another drawback was that the machine language computer varied by manufacturer. Solutions in one computer system could not be transferred to other systems.

Assembly Language

allows you to use symbols
(:) relationship with
machine language -

Assembly language was a marked improvement over machine language. Programmers found assembly language easier to use because of the structure of its instructions. This new format did not employ numeric characters as machine language did, but permitted the use of English words and symbols to designate processing operations and datanames. The symbolic nature of assembly language instructions led to its being termed a **symbolic programming language.**

Assembly language instructions had the following elements:

LABEL   OP CODE   OPERAND

The **label,** also referred to as the **tag,** identified each instruction and distinguished one instruction from another. These labels or tags were extremely important for logical operations because they identified the statements that were branched to.

As with machine language, the op code defined the computer operation to be performed. However, it was in its use of op codes that assembly language made its significant contribution to programming. In assembly language, the programmer could define a computer operation with a predefined term. These predefined terms, called **mnemonics,** identified specific operations and directed the computer to complete them. Table 7.1 details selected mnemonics employed with assembly language.

IBM ASSY LANGUAGE

Table 7.1 Selected Mnemonic Codes Used with Assembly Language

Operation Defined	Mnemonic Code	Operation Defined	Mnemonic Code
Addition	A	Move data	MVC
Branching	BC	Multiplication	M
Compare	C	Store data	ST
Division	D	Subtraction	S

Programmers no longer had to use numeric codes to define operations. They could use symbols defining specific tasks and mnemonic codes. To add two data items, an A was written into the program instruction. To compare data and branch from a logical operation, the mnemonics C and BC were specified. A sample of assembly language coding appears in Figure 7.2.

In assembly language, programmers were relieved of the task of identifying and cataloging data by its main storage locations. The computer system was responsible for that task. It assigned data to storage

LABEL	OP	OPERAND
	BALR	15,0
	LM	2,3,34(15)
	L	13,30(0,15)
	LA	15,2(0,15)
	ST	15,4(0,13)
	BCR	15,2
A4	DC	00000000
	DC	07D4C1C9
	DC	D5D7C7D4
	DC	00000000
	DC	00000000
	DC	00000000
A52	L	13,4(0,13)
	L	14,12(0,13)
	LM	2,12,28(13)
	MVI	12(13),255
	BCR	15,14
A36	L	15,108(0,13)
	LR	12,13

FIGURE 7.2 An excerpt from an assembly language program. Individual statements highlight labels, op codes, and operands.

converts machine language program to easy language.

locations and maintained a file on the locations of the data. Another advantage of assembly language was that data could be referenced using regular datanames. Thus, items of data could be referenced as, say, NAME, HOURS, or PAY.

The computer's ability to keep track of storage locations and to associate them with datanames was of great value to programmers checking for errors. Error corrections in machine language programs were extremely tedious, requiring changes in a string of storage positions and the recording of all changes by the programmer. In assembly language, changes were accomplished by correcting the op code, operand, or label of an instruction. The computer did the rest.

The basis for this simplicity was a translating program, supplied by the computer manufacturer, called an assembler. The **assembler** converted assembly language into the machine language instructions executed by the computer. The assembler controlled the assignment of datanames and coordinated with the computer the allocation of data to individual storage areas. Thus when programmers corrected assembly language instructions, they corrected only the datanames, op codes, or operands. The computer, in conjunction with the assembler, changed the resulting machine language instruction.

The assembler was important in arithmetic operations. Assembly language relied on registers [temporary storage areas in the arithmetic logic unit (ALU) of the CPU] when performing arithmetic. Without the assembler, the number of statements required for these computations would have been large. But the assembler easily converted and processed the equivalent symbolic assembly language statements.

The assembler fostered a one-to-one relationship between assembly language and machine language. Every assembly language instruction was converted into one machine language instruction. The rationale was that *one* assembly language instruction should direct the computer to perform *one* complete operation. This one-to-one relationship was necessary to overcome the problem encountered with machine language. It permitted the portability of programs between systems. Programs written in assembly language could be used on any computer equipped with a similar assembler. Therefore, programs designed on one system could be run on another computer.

One of the major ideas introduced with assembly language was the concept of a **macroinstruction,** or **macro,** an offshoot of the one-to-one relationship. The idea was that if one assembly language instruction could effect one computer operation, then one overall instruction could generate a series of assembly language instructions. This became the operational concept of a macro.

Input and output operations were somewhat intricate in assembly language, requiring, for example, eight or more instructions. Assembly language required the programmer to write instructions to convert data from base 2 to base 10. But because these instructions were similar in most programs, the idea of using a macro for these tasks evolved. The macro was to be identified by a specific code name and stored in the computer, available to all users. The code name would permit its use in any program. The programmer no longer had to repeat the statements for a conversion or I/O statements. The programmer needed only to specify the name of the macro to perform the operations. A library of macro statements is maintained in data processing departments where assembly language is still a major language.

Assembly language was an improvement, but there was still room for more. Error checking and I/O operations were easier, but they were still time-consuming. Yet assembly language served its purpose; it was the stepping stone to today's high-level languages.

High-Level Languages

Most current computer programming languages are **high-level languages.** In contrast, machine language and assembly language are **low-level languages.** High-level languages overcome many of the shortcomings of low-level languages and share the following characteristics:

1 Standard forms of the languages exist.
2 They are machine independent.
3 They use a compiler.
4 They are self-documenting.

High-level languages have a standard format. The language used in California is essentially the same as the language used in Boston. High-level languages are portable and machine independent; that is, they are not dependent on the computer system used.

For example, it would be possible to write and test a program written in a high-level language, using a secondary type of computer system. Following this procedure keeps the main computer free for other work. It is not tied up with the time-consuming task of running and testing a program. When the program has been finally tested, approved, and deemed operational, it is run on the main computer. Its use on the main computer will require no special treatment and will avoid processing delay.

This ability to process a program on different systems within the same family of computers is called **program compatibility.** It means that a program can be tested on one system and processed on another. Program compatibility eliminates the expense of major program modifications.

All high-level languages require the use of a compiler. The term **compiler** is generally applied to a program that converts high-level languages to machine language instructions. Most of today's languages are written for the use of the programmer, not the computer. It is therefore necessary to have a program that converts statements coded in the high-level languages to their machine language equivalents. That is the purpose of the compiler. A shortcoming of the compiler is the time involved in its operation. The **compilation** of a program, the act in which the compiler actually converts the high-level program, often requires more than a minute. However, the trade-off agreed upon by most data processors is that it costs less to have the computer convert a program to machine language than to have a programmer originally write the same program in machine language.

The self-documenting features of high-level languages offer a real advantage to the programmer. Each language has its own set of rules for writing program instructions. These sets of rules are referred to as the **syntax** of the language. During the compilation of a high-level program, the compiler scans each program statement for syntax errors. Any statement that does not conform to the syntax of the language is deemed incorrect. The computer prints out all the syntax errors, and this list represents the self-documenting feature of high-level languages.

An example of an error listing is given in Figure 7.3. In this figure, the high-level languages are FORTRAN and COBOL, which we will discuss below. Syntax errors in FORTRAN are designated by the dollar sign ($). Syntax errors in COBOL are identified by line number and type of error.

Though compilers document syntax errors, they do not identify errors in logic. Logical errors related to which data is processed, the placement or execution of program statements, or the computed results are uncovered as programs are run. Programmers must make sure that the software they develop is logically correct. They must carefully examine test results for invalid or inconsistent outputs.

Overall, high-level languages are divided into two categories, problem-oriented languages and procedure-oriented languages. **Pro-**

Self-documented errors in a FORTRAN program

```
0001            10 REA D(1,30)  NAME, HRS, RATE
0002            30 FORMAT(A4, F7.2, F7,2)
                                          $
        01)   ILF013I SYNTAX
0003            GROSS= HRS. * RATE
                             $
        01)   ILF013I SYNTAX
0004            WRITE(3,22) NAM E, GROSS
0005            22 FORMAT(1H , I4, F7.2)
0006            CALL EXIT
0007            END
```

Self-documented errors in a COBOL program

CARD	ERROR MESSAGE	
	IKF1100I-W	30 SEQUENCE ERRORS IN SOURCE PROGRAM.
14	IKF2049I-C	NO OPEN CLAUSE FOUND FOR FILE.
17	IKF2049I-C	NO OPEN CLAUSE FOUND FOR FILE.
19	IKF2049I-C	NO OPEN CLAUSE FOUND FOR FILE.
19	IKF2025I-E	WRITE ADVANCING OR POSITIONING OPTION WAS SPECIFIED OR ACCESS METHOD NOT STANDARD SEQUENTIAL. WRITES WILL FOR THIS FILE.
115	IKF3001I-E	DELETE-RTN NOT DEFINED. STATEMENT DISCARDED.
164	IKF1007I-W	EQUAL NOT PRECEDED BY A SPACE. ASSUME SPACE.
173	IKF3001I-E	SEQ-REC-LIST NOT DEFINED. DISCARDED.
173	IKF3026I-E	IDENTIFIER-2 OMITTED IN MOVE CORRESPONDING STATEMENT.
174	IKF3001I-E	SEQ-REC-LIST NOT DEFINED. DISCARDED.
195	IKF3001I-E	SEQ-REC-LIST NOT DEFINED. DISCARDED.
195	IKF3026I-E	IDENTIFIER-2 OMITTED IN MOVE CORRESPONDING STATEMENT.
197	IKF3001I-E	SEQ-REC-LIST NOT DEFINED. DISCARDED.

FIGURE 7.3   The self-documenting feature of two high-level languages, FORTRAN and COBOL, details errors found in program excerpts. FORTRAN places a $ under each syntax error. COBOL documents and attempts to explain errors line by line.

cedure-oriented languages can be applied to any problem. They offer the programmer the widest latitude and the greatest flexibility in drafting a program solution. **Problem-oriented languages** are more specialized languages that provide specific types of data or apply to only one type of problem.

7.2
Selected
Programming
Languages
FORTRAN

FORTRAN (FORmula **TRAN**slation) is one of the oldest high-level languages. Developed by IBM in 1956, FORTRAN is a procedure-oriented language that employs an overall format similar to algebraic formulas. This format reflects the original use of FORTRAN.

During the developing stages of the computer industry, all problems slated for the computer were automatically segregated into two categories, **scientific applications** and **business applications.**

very little I/O lots of logic.   very large I/O lessened logic.

WHAT IS STONEHENGE?

For thousands of years, Stonehenge, the megalithic monument on England's Salisbury Plain, has fascinated all observers. Built originally between 2200 and 1300 B.C., Stonehenge was reconstructed three times by various tribes that roamed the area. Although ascribed by some to Druids or to visitors from outer space, Stonehenge was structured, we now know, as an astronomical observatory and neolithic computer that enabled tribal priests to predict lunar and solar eclipses and to forecast the beginning and end of the planting seasons.

At dawn, the priests observed the sun's rays by using the Heel Stone, situated beyond the outer ring of large stones. The sun shone directly through the center portal stones on June 21, the longest day, which marked the middle of the calendar year and was the standard for all measurements. As the sun's rays shone to the right or left of the center portal, the priests could gauge the time of year and measure the start of Fall and Winter and harvest time.

Gerald S. Hawkins, author of *Stonehenge Decoded* (Dell Books, New York, 1965), decided to test this theory. Using an IBM 7090 and FORTRAN, he programmed the computer to simulate the movement of sun and moon and, correlating these movements with the stones' positions, Hawkins found the Stonehenge megaliths lined up perfectly with solar and lunar paths.

The odds against chance placement of Stonehenge were computed at a million to one. Stonehenge was no accident but a monument to human ingenuity.

Source of data: "What Is Stonehenge?" Her Majesty's Stationery Office, London, 1975.

FIGURE 7.4 Selected statements in FORTRAN, written on a FORTRAN coding sheet. Note the algebra-like statements characteristic of FORTRAN.

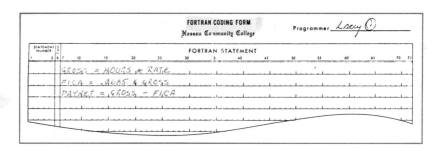

This categorization resulted from the types of computers in the first two generations of computer equipment. Scientific applications required a minimum of I/O activities and used complex calculations. Business applications required a high volume of I/O operations based on fundamental arithmetic. FORTRAN, created during this period, was designed for scientific applications. Its format was geared to the needs of scientists and engineers.

FORTRAN represents computations in terms of formulas. Figure 7.4 lists on a FORTRAN coding sheet some of the formulas we used in flowcharting problems to compute net pay. A **coding sheet** helps the programmer remember a language's syntax. We will discuss coding sheets for other high-level languages later in the chapter.

FORTRAN effectively uses symbols to represent data, but one of its drawbacks is its rigid structure. The syntax of FORTRAN at first seems complicated. Its rules are quite specific and dictate when certain types of statements can be used. Another minor shortcoming is that FORTRAN's algebraic format awes those programmers who are not comfortable with formulas. Both problems, however, are overcome with use of the language.

Third-generation computers ended the strict segregation of computers for scientific and business problems. During that period, manufacturers developed a new language with a format vastly different from FORTRAN's. This new language was called COBOL.

COBOL

In 1959, a conference called CODASYL was convened by the United States government and major computer manufacturers to draft a new high-level programming language. This language would use a format that paralleled the structure of English and would have all the features of high-level languages (i.e., a compiler, self-documentation). The new language would readily handle I/O operations. It would easily create files, prepare headings for reports, have a high volume of output, and be understood by the average businessperson. Thus was the stage set for COBOL (**C**ommon **B**usiness **O**riented **L**anguage).

COBOL's sentence structure was readily understandable, unlike FORTRAN's algebraic quality. The FORTRAN statements shown in Figure 7.4 are shown on a COBOL coding sheet in Figure 7.5. COBOL

SYSTEM						PUNCHING INSTRUCTIONS					PAGE / OF /
PROGRAM _SAMPLE COBOL STATEMENTS_						GRAPHIC	_NONE_			CARD FORM #	
PROGRAMMER _S. BASS I_			DATE _7/28/–_			PUNCH					

COBOL STATEMENT

SEQUENCE		CONT	A	B	COBOL STATEMENT	IDENTIFICATION
01			_MULTIPLY HOURS BY RATE GIVING GROSS._			
02			_MULTIPLY .0685 BY GROSS GIVING FICA._			
03			_SUBTRACT FICA FROM GROSS GIVING NETPAY_			

FIGURE 7.5 Sample COBOL statements. Note how each character is placed in its own column. These three COBOL statements are equivalent to the FORTRAN statements used in Figure 7.4.

uses key arithmetic terms such as ADD, SUBTRACT, and MULTIPLY. Each statement illustrated in Figure 7.5 is easy to understand.

COBOL has become one of the most widely used languages in DP. Examine the want ads in a local paper, and you will see that jobs requiring a knowledge of COBOL outnumber all others.

COBOL has certain shortcomings, however. The compiler necessary with COBOL is quite large and requires a medium-sized or larger computer system. Also, COBOL is wordy. Programs that require 10 to 15 statements in FORTRAN require 75 to 100 statements in COBOL. Despite these drawbacks, COBOL is an extremely useful language. It is especially good at handling I/O operations and files of data.

BASIC

The expansion of programming languages was not restricted to business. Educational institutions needed a high-level language more suited for instructional purposes. The language developed for them was **BASIC** (**B**eginner's **A**ll-purpose **S**ymbolic **I**nstruction **C**ode).

Basic was created in the late 1960s by Dr. John G. Kemeny at Dartmouth University. He originally developed BASIC for students to use with computers. BASIC lets users interact directly with the computer via time-sharing or telecommunications. Users can run their programs directly and derive their results almost instantaneously. In addition, BASIC is an easy language to learn. Many students can program in BASIC after only 3 or 4 hours. BASIC is effective in time-sharing systems, where many users simultaneously have access to a computer.

BASIC's format is like FORTRAN's but less rigorous. Figure 7.6 lists in BASIC the same statements given in Figures 7.4 and 7.5. A **general-purpose coding sheet,** used for any programming language, is shown. Note that arithmetic statements are defined in LET statements and that symbolic notation is readily employed.

Because BASIC lets users interact directly with a computer, it is defined as an **interactive language.** With the recent increased emphasis on online processing, interactive languages have become quite

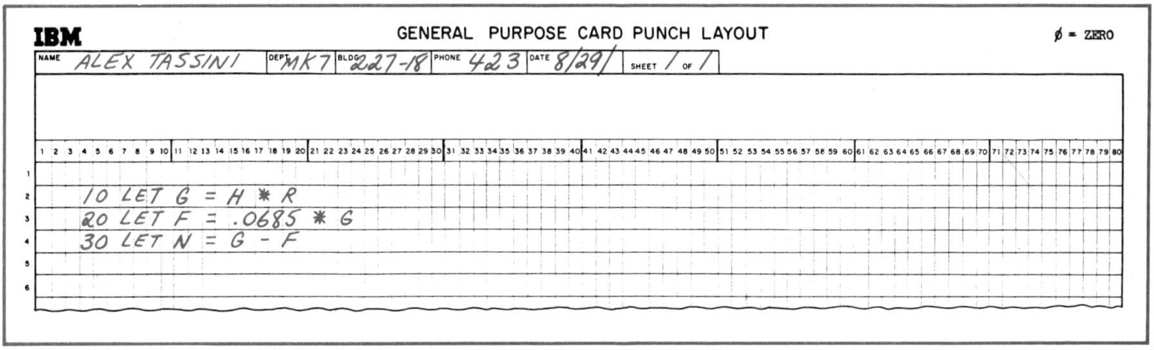
IBM GENERAL PURPOSE CARD PUNCH LAYOUT ϕ = ZERO

NAME ALEX TASSINI DEPT MK7 BLDG 227-18 PHONE 423 DATE 8/29/ SHEET 1 OF 1

```
10 LET G = H * R
20 LET F = .0685 * G
30 LET N = G - F
```

FIGURE 7.6 A general-purpose coding sheet is used to depict three BASIC statements about computing net pay. BASIC statements look like formulas. Note that the datanames used in BASIC (that is, G, F, N) are much shorter than those in other languages. These datanames are designed to make BASIC easy to learn and use.

popular. Many manufacturers have modified BASIC to make it better at handling various types of applications and to make it more suitable for their hardware. BASIC has become important because of its simple format and the ease of learning it. It has been incorporated into many smaller systems and home computers.

New interactive languages are being introduced, as are interactive forms of the older languages. Interactive versions of COBOL and FORTRAN are available that permit the online development and correction of software. Some interactive languages support special processing needs, and some specialize in the online examination of data files. One such problem-oriented language is **IQF (Interactive Query Facility),** developed by Digital Equipment Corp. for online retrieval of data from computerized files. Software consultants anticipate that new and more sophisticated interactive languages will expand online processing.

RPG

Generates Reports has a fixed logic.

Some organizations do not need the powerful support of a full BASIC or COBOL language. They need limited processing but extensive output. Organizations that rely heavily on reports may want such a language as **RPG** (**R**eport **P**rogram **G**enerator). RPG III, introduced in the spring of 1980, improved upon its predecessor, RPG II. RPG III is growing more popular as the computer systems which use it, IBM Systems/32, 34, and 38, are attracting a growing number of users. These small systems provide organizations, which need only minimal computer service, with relatively inexpensive, low-level data processing. Firms with large inventories or accounts payable files, marketing companies that mail advertising, or insurance companies may find RPG well suited to their needs.

The primary purpose of RPG is to produce management reports; it can also perform some computations. It is fairly easy to learn and is

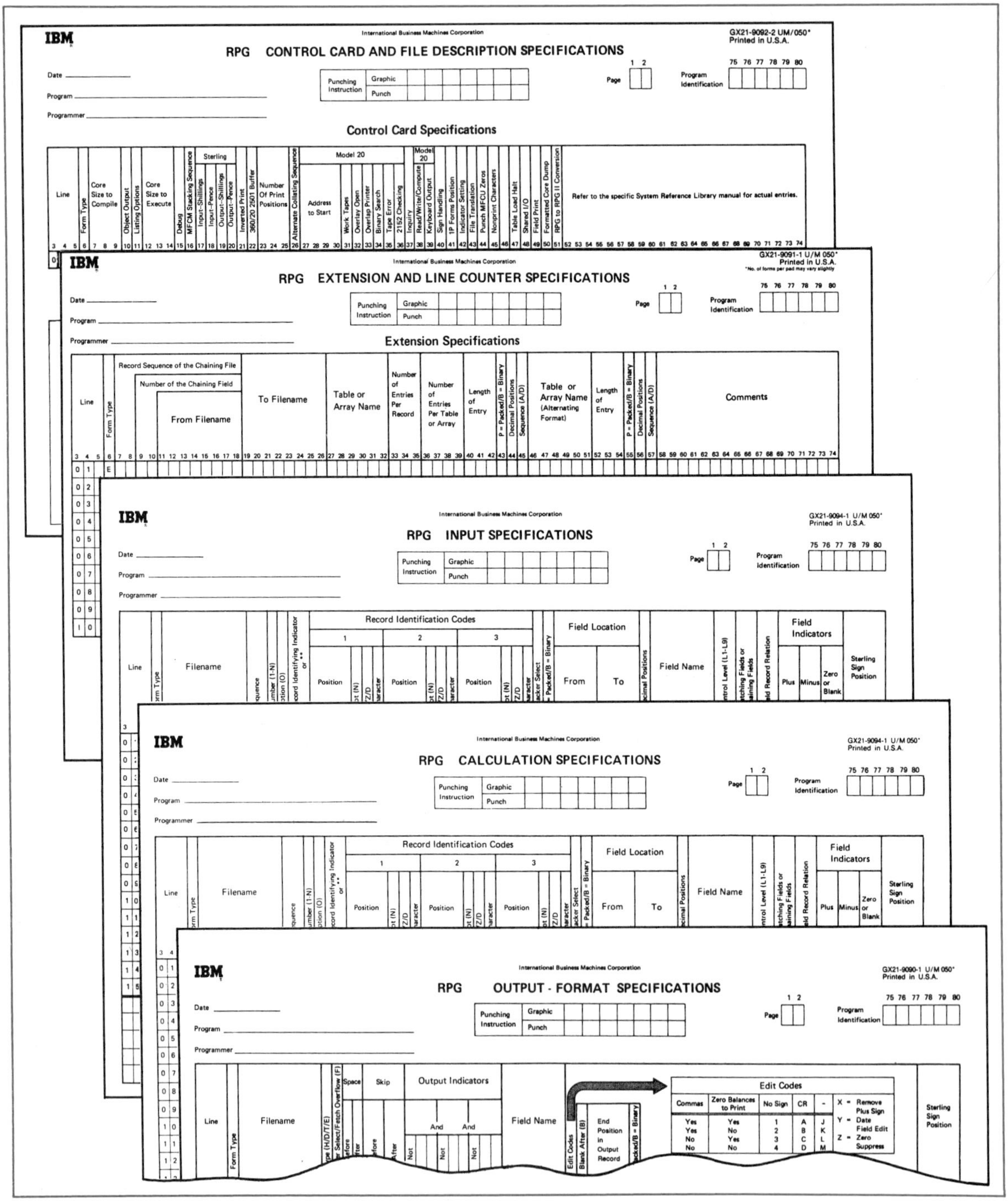

FIGURE 7.7   The specially designed coding sheets required for RPG. All programming operations are coded onto these sheets when an RPG program is written.

mastered in a few days. One feature of RPG is its specially designed coding sheets, shown in Figure 7.7.

Each operation in an RPG program is broken down on a separate coding sheet. Specifications on data files appear on one coding sheet. Inputs, outputs, and calculations appear on their special forms. These sheets clearly define where each program instruction is to be written.

RPG does not have the operational or computing flexibility of FORTRAN and COBOL, nor is it fully machine independent. Programs written for one system may require modification before they can be used on another system.

PL/1

PL/1 (**P**rogramming **L**anguage **1**) is a recently developed procedure-oriented language. Originally developed by IBM, PL/1 was to serve as a multipurpose language. Its format was designed to combine the best features of both FORTRAN and COBOL.

PL/1 is extremely powerful. It lets programmers manipulate large amounts of data, perform sophisticated statistical analyses, or reorganize files of alphameric data. Most programmers study PL/1 only after mastering COBOL or FORTRAN.

PL/1 requires a large computer and, therefore, a sizable amount of main storage. Also, since PL/1 was developed by IBM, it is primarily used on their computer systems. Figure 7.8 provides a sample of PL/1 programming.

PASCAL

looks like pl/1 - 2nd most used in country.

PASCAL is a language that originated a few years ago and is becoming increasingly popular. It resembles PL/1 and can be used on many manufacturers' equipment. As with BASIC, many manufacturers have adapted PASCAL to their systems to enhance its potential.

PASCAL's strength is that it can be used with structured programming techniques.[1] PASCAL is designed to help students write logical, correct programs and to eliminate common errors. A sample of PASCAL syntax appears in Figure 7.9.

```
            PUT DATA (SCAT,K);
            PUT EDIT ((GRDS(KL) DO KL = 1 TO 10)) (10 (A(2),X(3)));
            IF I = 1 THEN GRDS(1) = 'NO';
IGNORE:
            GCNT = I - 1;
            CLOSE FILE(STREC);
            DO I = 1 TO GCNT;
            OPEN FILE(STREC) SEQUENTIAL INPUT;
            ANKEY = TEST(2);
            SIZE = 2;
            IF GRDS(1) = 'NO' THEN GO TO NOGRADE;
            ANKEY = ANKEY || GRDS(I);
            SIZE = 4;
NOGRADE:    IF SCAT = 'NO' THEN GO TO NOSCHOOL;
```

FIGURE 7.8 A sample of PL/1 instructions written as part of a program.

[1] Chapter 10 details the concepts and use of structured programming.

```
BEGIN
   CONS:=0;
   RAD:=0;
   MID:=0;
   READ(VOTE);
   WHILE VOTE<>-1 DO
      BEGIN
         IF VOTE=REPUBLICAN THEN
            CONS:=CONS+1
         ELSE
         IF VOTE=SOCIALIST THEN
            RAD:=RAD+1
         ELSE
         IF VOTE=DEMOCRAT THEN
            MID:=MID+1;
         READ(VOTE)
      END;
   TOTAL:=CONS+RAD+MID;
   WRITELN(CONS,RAD,MID,TOTAL)
END.
```

FIGURE 7.9 An excerpt from a program written in **PASCAL** that tests for one of three political codes and adds them before output.

DECAL and SCRIPT

Almost all the languages we have discussed so far are procedure-oriented languages; they can be applied to many types of business or scientific problems. Problem-oriented languages, in contrast, efficiently handle one type of application. For example, a problem-oriented language might work in a hybrid or analog computer with unique data-handling activities. Another might be installed in one manufacturer's family of computers to handle a particular business problem. Two problem-oriented languages are DECAL and SCRIPT.

DECAL, developed by Digital Equipment Corporation, supports computer-assisted instruction at schools or learning centers. Using DECAL, teachers can create lessons or assignments and store them in the computer. Students gain access to this material on a time-sharing basis and answer the questions supplied by the computer. The computer records each student's performance and assigns a grade for the lesson.

DECAL's syntax looks like BASIC's but is considerably more difficult to master. Teachers must spend a great deal of time preparing the lessons for the computer. DECAL is available in Digital hardware only. It has simplified some of the tasks of computer-prepared instruction.

Another singular language is **SCRIPT,** introduced by IBM for offices that generate a great deal of typed correspondence. SCRIPT speeds up **word processing,** or computerized handling of typed information. SCRIPT lets a secretary prepare and correct a letter and reproduce it in different sizes and configurations as well as distribute it via online terminals throughout the company. Word-processing systems are covered in greater detail in Chapter 16.

DECAL and SCRIPT are only two of many specialized languages. Manufacturers and software developers offer languages that simplify the retrieval and manipulation of data in computerized files and languages that allow for the processing of data generated by analog devices. Users who want more information on these languages can contact manufacturers, consult with programming staffs, or examine computer periodicals.

ADA — *eventually will replace cobol.*

A language that has been under development since 1975 is **ADA**, named after the world's first programmer, Lady Ada Lovelace. The Defense Department has employed versions of ADA in ccntrol and

TALKING TO LANA

A computer has become the means of communication between Lana, a four-year-old chimpanzee, and the rest of the world. Two years ago, she started to use the symbols on a computer keyboard to talk to her keepers. Lana quickly mastered about forty words, and now she can use about seventy-five word symbols and is asking to learn more. She has begun to ask her trainers the names of various objects. Lana's ability to learn a language suggests that the mental ability of chimpanzees may have been underestimated. Researchers at the Yerkes Regional Primate Research Center in Atlanta, where Lana is being trained, say that the methods used to teach Lana may eventually be used to help mentally retarded or disturbed children who have trouble learning to communicate.

Source of data: *Creative Computing,* September–October 1976, p. 79. Used by permission of *Creative Computing,* P.O. Box 789-M, Morristown, N.J. 07960.
(*Yerkes Regional Primate Research Center.*)

source language - language
programmer uses

command applications. The Defense Department and private manufacturers are trying to produce a final version of ADA, with ANSI suggesting an industry-wide standard. Versions of ADA are contemplated
for systems of all sizes.

Unfortunately, the developers have had many problems. Some
specialists involved believe that insufficient time has been allotted for
testing and validating software. Nevertheless, ADA's developers estimate that ADA will be ready in late 1982.

7.3
The Execution
of Computer
Programs

Programmers' responsibilities do not end with writing programs, and
their knowledge of computers does not stop at programming languages. Programmers, like other members of the data processing
staff, should have a general operating knowledge of computer systems. For example, they should know how their programs are processed, how errors are detected, and what programs are used to support processing. Sections 7.3 and 7.4 describe how programs are
processed along with any related operational software.

The Supervisor
Control Program

The control unit and its importance in program execution were
discussed in Chapter 5. Though the control unit is essential to the
successful processing of data, it does not function alone. It requires
the assistance of a supervisor control program. The **supervisor control program,** or **supervisor,** is a controlling program that oversees
all processing in a computer system. The supervisor (software), in
conjunction with the control unit (hardware), ensures that all I/O operations and processing are satisfactorily completed.

The supervisor, because of its operational role, must reside in
main storage. This location lets the supervisor interact with all programs undergoing processing and gives it access to the proper compiler when necessary.

Compilers and assembler translating programs are stored in an
online disk storage device. This random access device is sometimes
referred to as the **system residence (SYSRES) device.** All the programs vital to the operation of the computer system reside there. Once
the supervisor determines the compiler required to convert the incoming source program, it accesses the SYSRES device and brings that
compiler into main storage. This interaction is represented in Figure
7.10. The supervisor monitors the compiler's conversion of the program. Once the new program is converted into machine language, the
supervisor monitors its execution and assists in I/O and processing
operations.

Compiling a
Program

A compiler is a translating program that converts a high-level language
into machine language. The rationale for this conversion is simple: The
computer can only execute instructions that are in machine language.

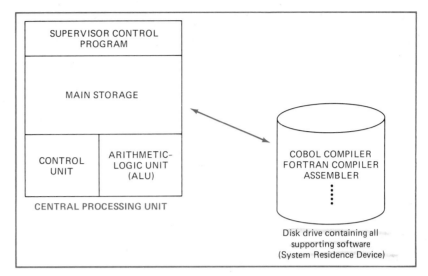

FIGURE 7.10 The supervisor interacts with the SYSRES device to obtain the compiler necessary for processing an incoming program.

However, to describe the total execution of a program, a little more detail is necessary. Let's start from the top of the programming cycle and work our way through the entire sequence of tasks.

The initial program solution written by the programmer is referred to as the *source program.* The computer language in which the programmer chose to write the source program is the *source language.* Once the source program is written, the programmer chooses a method of processing the program. If a teleprocessing mode is selected, the source program can be manually input via a terminal device. However, the programmer may elect to batch-process the source program. In this case, the source program is keyed onto punched cards, referred to as a **source deck,** which are input to the computer via a card reader.

The entry of the source program into the computer initiates the actual processing of the program. The conversion of the source program into machine language is performed by a compiler. The resulting machine language program, called the **object program,** is the program which the computer actually executes.

During its conversion of the source program, the compiler carefully checks statements for syntax errors. If it finds any, the computer will not execute the object program. Instead, the compiler enacts the self-documenting feature of the language and attempts to pinpoint the errors in the source program. If no errors exist, the translation of the source program is completed, and the object program is executed.

Job Control Language (JCL)

The computer language designed to facilitate the communication of data to the computer system is **job control language (JCL).** Job control language is specifically used by programmers and computer operators to communicate with the supervisor control program and direct the computer's activities. For example, one of the uses of JCL is to indicate the language used in the source program.

Figure 7.11 illustrates the use of JCL to process a FORTRAN program. The **JCL cards** contain the JCL instructions necessary to process the program. Note the third card in the sequence. It is the JCL card that indicates that the source language is FORTRAN.

JCL is intricate and highly specialized. Its instruction is certainly not the intent of this text, but you should know about it. Many of you will use JCL statements to process your programs. You might use JCL cards or use JCL statements when keying in programs via a CRT. In any event, JCL commands are vital to the successful processing of any program.

The supervisor, the compiler, and JCL are integral to a computer system that can process any program. The effectiveness of computers, however, is measured by their ability to process one program after another.

FIGURE 7.11   The sequence of JCL cards for processing a FORTRAN program. The third card identifies FORTRAN as the source language.

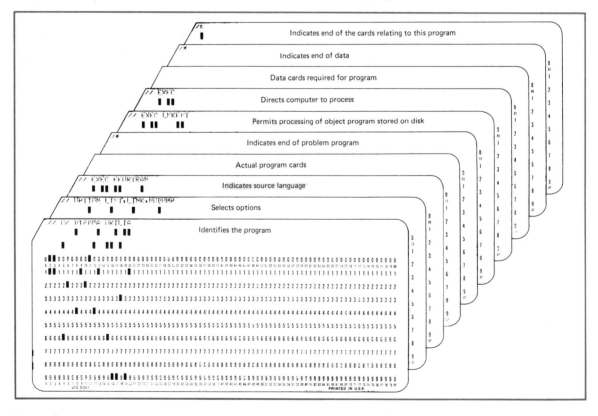

7.4 Operating Systems

An effective system can process a continuous stream of programs. An **operating system** is a complex array of supervisory programs that enables the system to schedule the most efficient flow of work. The programs that compose an operating system oversee all actions taken by the computer. They schedule the continuous processing of programs, control the use of I/O devices, and permit the easy retrieval of special programs (i.e., compilers) from storage devices. Because the peripheral devices used in computer systems vary, operating systems vary as well. Each type of computer system has its own operating system which defines and influences its processing capabilities.

Consider the case in which two identical computer systems have totally different operational capacities. This can occur if two Digital Equipment PDP-11 computers are each equipped with different operating software. The use of either **RSX** or **RSTS/E** operating software in a PDP system will affect its processing potential.

The RSX operating system is designed to support production activities normally undertaken at the average DP center. It maximizes the number of jobs processed by creating a continuous flow of work through the PDP-11. The RSX can concurrently support both batch and online processing. In contrast, the RSTS/E software is suited to time-sharing operations. It can handle low-level production but is more efficient at time-sharing activities for schools or service bureaus. Incorporating either the RSX or RSTS/E software into a PDP-11 system radically alters its capabilities. In essence, an organization should choose an operating system only after defining its data processing needs.

Why not use several operating systems in the same computer system, perhaps RSX at night and RSTS/E during the day? It's possible, but it's not a likely solution. First, only one operating system can direct a computer at a time. Second, it would be very expensive. Generally, if an organization needs such diversified processing, it chooses an operating system better suited to its needs rather than combining operating systems.

Operating systems from any source will be able to:

1 Schedule the execution of jobs
2 Schedule I/O activities
3 Determine the status of each job being processed

Scheduling programs to be processed is critical to a computer's efficiency. Each task has certain characteristics that dictate when and how it should be processed. A job that ties up a printer for hours might best be processed during an off-peak period, for instance. Such operational constraints are communicated to the operating software with JCL language as the program enters the system.

The operating system utilizes the JCL data input to establish a waiting list of jobs, often called a **job queue,** that indicates the order in which each program will be processed. In establishing the job queue, the operating system takes into account the resources available in the computer system, the resources required to process the program, and priority assigned to the job. When left to its own means, the operating system will establish the job queue, whose order may be overridden by the computer operator using special JCL commands. The operator frequently does this when high priority jobs are input and must be immediately processed.

The term applied to the software employed to create the job queue is the **spooler.** Some form of spooler exists within all operating systems, with the complexity of the spooling software dependent on the size and scope of the system's activities. The spooler employed in a card-oriented system would appear minimal compared with its counterpart in a vast online processing system. Software names often associated with spooling programs are ASP, HASP, and Queman. They are representative of the spooling software available from computer manufacturers and independent software houses.

To facilitate the execution of I/O operations, most operating systems possess a standard set of control instructions that specifically handle the processing of all input and output instructions. These standard instructions, referred to as the **input/output control system (IOCS),** are an integral part of most operating systems and simplify the means by which all programs being processed may undertake I/O operations.

In effect, the program undergoing execution signals the operating system that an I/O operation is desired, via a specific I/O device. The controlling software invokes the IOCS software to actually complete the I/O operation. Considering the level of I/O activity in most programs, the IOCS instructions are an extremely vital and useful aspect of a computer's operating system.

Because most computer systems can handle a variety of programs concurrently, an operating system must be able to assess the status of jobs being run to determine whether a particular job is being input, processed, or output. Any time an error is discovered in a program during processing, the operating system will cancel the job and automatically flush it from the computer.

The operating system monitors all phases of processing and all programs. Most operational software identifies each job running with a number, assigned when it enters the job queue. When a job is completed, it leaves the flow of jobs being processed. The operating software must then input the next program in the job queue.

A rather complex operating system, much larger than either RSX or RSTS/E software, is the IBM **Job Entry Subsystem 3** or **JES3** software. This software is extremely powerful, as it encompasses many operational features and supports a large computer system with its vast array of devices. JES3 can support all phases of processing, including concurrent batch, online, time-shared, or real-time activities and access of data from secondary storage devices with a capacity ranging into billions of characters of storage.

The JES3 software handles each job entering the system in three phases. In the initial preprocessing phase, JES3 assigns each program a four-digit identification number and uses its spooling software to generate a job queue. The second, or processing, phase oversees the actual execution of that program and precedes the postprocessing phase, where the resultant output is produced.

JES3 is unique in its ability to accept a job and delay its processing or the output of data, as JCL commands direct. The JES3 software can either direct the computer to hold a program for processing many hours later or direct it to process the program immediately and hold the results until the system can output them. JES3 monitors the input, execution, and storage of all aspects of a job and advises an operator of a job's status.

Operating system maintenance is an important task. It is usually undertaken by a **systems programmer.** The systems programmer is not an analyst, but a programmer with thorough knowledge of a computer's operational software. The systems programmer acts as a troubleshooter, diagnosing and correcting problems in operating software. Many years of training are required for this position.

Operating software now under development is extremely complex because it assumes monitoring activities presently assigned to an operator. Of course, data processors should understand the operating software of their system because it defines that system's capabilities and the modes of processing available to them.

Up to this point, we have concentrated on computer software. However, the use of such software depends on the programmer's approach. Programmers select the language, evaluate test results, and write supporting program documentation. Coding a source program is just one part in the programming cycle.

7.5
The ABCs of
Programming

To paraphrase Will Rogers, "Approaches to programming are like opinions; everybody's got one of their own." Almost all programmers have their own strategy for developing solutions. Though these strategies vary, they have some common points, which may be looked upon as the ABCs of programming:

1. Analyze the problem. *10% of time*
2. Build a flowchart solution. *20% of time*
3. Code the solution using the selected *in a source language* programming language. *20% of time*
4. Debug and test the solution. *40% of time, no logic or syntax errors.*
5. Prepare final program documentation. *10% of time*

Analyze the
Problem

One analyzes a problem to determine how to implement a programming solution. The programmer must uncover any special aspects of the problem, and most programmers consider it imperative to define the limits of a problem before programming begins.

To accurately define a problem the programmer must note all inputs, processing, and outputs a solution requires. Many of these factors can be drawn from the written narrative provided to the programmer with the original problem. (We reviewed this approach in the discussion of flowcharting in Chapter 6.) Of course, the programmer must verify the accuracy of these facts.

Once this material is gathered, the programmer can draft a composite report, often referred to as a **problem definition.** Its purpose is to carefully detail all aspects (i.e., inputs, outputs, formulas, etc.) of the problem and define all prerequisites of a solution. The problem definition is an invaluable reference source during the actual programming effort. If the analysis was properly performed, the factors relating to any program should be found in it.

The problem definition is a concise document. It should clearly define the goals and objectives of the program and the hardware and software available. Clarity in a problem definition is important, because it provides everyone involved in the project with the same excellent starting point. If, as often occurs, someone is transferred from the project, their replacement will lose little time in developing a sound understanding of the problem.

The problem definition has another intrinsic value. It lets the programmer forecast potential difficulties and formulate alternative solutions. Also, as programmers perform the necessary research, they redefine the initial problem and refine the logic of their approach. Thus, when it comes time to draw a flowchart of the solution, the programmers have already conceptualized their approach.

Build a Flowchart Solution

Chapter 6 described flowcharting in detail. A program flowchart presents the logic of a solution in a series of steps. Each symbol of the flowchart represents an operation that must appear in the program. Drafting a flowchart is a prerequisite to writing the program code. A checklist or legend to define datanames, input, and decisions may be helpful also. A checklist will prevent the duplication of datanames or the omission of required computations.

A formal flowchart solution should precede any program writing. Once a logical approach is approved by the programming manager, the selection of a source language and coding of the solution may begin.

Code the Solution Using the Selected Programming Language

Programming cannot start until an appropriate language is selected. The selection of the source language depends on the programmer's knowledge, the compatibility of the program with other jobs in the computer system, and the languages available. For example, although RPG may be perfect for one's needs, one's system may not have the RPG compiler.

The programmer has greater flexibility if the solution is a stand-alone program. A **stand-alone program** does not interact with any other programs during its processing. If, however, the program interacts with or is part of a larger solution, the programmer is restricted in the choice of a language. A component program may have to be written in the language of the overall solution.

Finally, the skill of the programmer is a strong consideration. Programmers have their specialties. One might be experienced in FORTRAN but not in COBOL or PL/1. The programmer must be matched to the task, a responsibility of the programming supervisor.

The actual coding of program statements can begin once the language is selected. Programmers are usually free to proceed at their own pace. Usually, in the initial drafting of codes, program instructions are written line by line for easy development of the solution. During these coding sessions, programmers use a variety of forms for their layout of input and output formats. Two of the more popular forms are:

1 The multiple card layout form
2 The printer spacing chart

If punch cards are the I/O medium, then the **multiple card layout form** is helpful. It permits the pictorial representation of data just as it will appear on the punch card. Data and fieldnames are laid out column by column. The card column format of a payroll card and its representation in the multiple card layout form appear in Figure 7.12. Note that the card columns used match the pictorial description of the form.

The **printer spacing chart** defines the printed outputs of a program. With it the programmer can test and eventually detail all the headings, separate lines of data, and special labels in the program solution. The printer spacing chart lets the programmer actually lay out by printing position each line of printed output. Print position numbers (1–144) are indicated along the top edge of the form. These numbers represent the total number of print positions available to the programmer across one page of computer paper. With these numbers as guides, the programmer details all headings, totals, and individual lines of output required for the program. Figure 7.13 shows the layout of a sample payroll output via the printer spacing chart. All lines are identified and directions supplied to assist the programmer in the depicted solution. Side and top margins are noted, along with the first line printed and overall width of the report. The standard line width used is 132 characters. However, in this example the report will use only 100 print positions.

The advantage of the printer spacing chart and card layout form is simple. When the programmer actually writes the programming code, he or she does not have to guess at the print positions. Each field is exactly defined. These documents are also used by the systems analyst, as we will discuss in later chapters.

IBM

INTERNATIONAL BUSINESS MACHINES CORPORATION

MULTIPLE-CARD LAYOUT FORM

GX24-6599-0
Printed in U.S.A.

Company _Two S's Heavy Equipment_

Application _Payroll card_   by _J. Tassini_   Date _5/31/_   Job No. _A 76_   Sheet No. _1_

Employee number	Last name	First name	M I	Hours worked (Reg)	Hours worked (O/T)	Job site	End of week date	U n i o n c o d e		C a r d c o d e

CARD COLUMN(S)	FIELD NAME
1–7	EMPLOYEE NUMBER
8–22	LAST NAME
23–32	FIRST NAME
33	MIDDLE INITIAL (MI)
34–37	HOURS WORKED (REG)
38–41	HOURS WORKED (O/T)
42–52	JOB SITE
53–58	END OF WEEK DATE
59–60	UNION CODE
61–79	BLANK
80	CARD CODE

FIGURE 7.12   The format of a punched card used for input is detailed on a multiple card layout form. The format of the card (listed above) should match the layout on the form. The form has room for a six-card format.

FIGURE 7.13   A printer spacing chart can depict the actual appearance of a report's printed output.

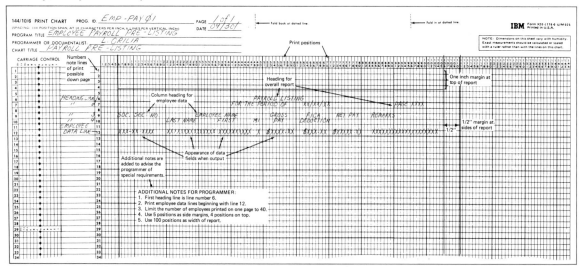

It is the programmer's responsibility to write clear and concise program instructions. Coding sheets are helpful. Most programmers do not keypunch their own programs, and keypunch operators need as much help as possible. Also, if the programmer is entering the code via a CRT, clearly written program instructions reduce idle time at the terminal.

Once the code is written, it is time to test the program. Naturally, if errors are found, corrections are undertaken.

Debug and Test the Solution

A chef's adage that "The proof of the pudding is in the eating" is applicable to the fourth stage of the programmer's work. The only way to test a program is in the computer. All programs must be tested many times before they are actually used in order to uncover errors, or **bugs,** in the program. The term for searching out programming errors is **debugging.** During debugging, programmers primarily look for errors in syntax and logic. When they are uncovered, corrections are made line by line in the program.

Programmers have at their disposal an entire group of debugging tools. Initially they may use the self-documenting feature to produce a list of syntax errors that will point to improperly written instructions.

Next, the programmer may employ test data. A program cannot be processed until all syntax errors have been corrected. When the corrections have been made, test data is inserted into the program. This data is used to determine if the required computations are properly executed. Answers to the test data have already been computed, and these answers should match those produced by the actual processing of the program. If they do, the program is ready for its next test. If

FIGURE 7.14 (*Creative Computing.*)

"Where did you learn to debug a program, Haverstraw?"

errors are found, programmers must determine the source of the error and insert the necessary changes.

Two technical options available to programmers are a tracing routine and a core dump. A **tracing routine** lets programmers follow their programs one instruction at a time. The tracing routine stops at the exact location of the error, pinpointing its source.

The **core dump,** or storage dump, is used with data contained in main storage. The execution of a core dump is one of the many JCL options available to the programmer, whereas the tracing routine requires the insertion of a special instruction into the program.

The program being processed occupies some portion of main storage (core). The core dump is designed to print out the contents of every storage position associated with the program. The programmer can determine the potential source of an error from examining this output. The core dump is an extremely sophisticated technique and is not usually used by beginning programmers.

When a program tests satisfactorily with test data, it is ready for live data. **Live data** is real data drawn from actual files. It is data regularly processed under normal operating conditions. Thus, real data is then processed employing the newly written program.

For example, a program has been written to process a payroll. The program has been debugged, and test data has been used to check the results. The answers proved that the program is apparently correct. However, to fully test the program, live data must be employed. Data used in processing previous payrolls will be used. Once these results are verified, current payroll data will be processed. The results will be compared with those derived from the manual processing of the payroll. When these results consistently match, the program is deemed operationally correct and ready for use. However, before a program can be put into operation, final documentation is required.

Prepare Final Program Documentation

The final documentation of a program ties all aspects of the programming cycle together. This documentation completely details the inputs, outputs, overall purpose of processing, and any data related to the processing of the program. For example, program documentation will contain the final versions of multiple card layout forms and printer spacing charts. Specific formats for any I/O operation are carefully and completely defined.

Although the importance of final program documentation is almost universally agreed upon, one standardized, uniformly acceptable format has not been adopted. As a result, the level and refinement of program documentation vary greatly among data processing organizations. Even so, most program documentation possesses the following common factors:

1 An abstract
2 A detailed narrative

3 A program listing
4 Complete I/O formats
5 Test data and results
6 An error message log
7 A user's manual

An *abstract* is a short, concise evaluation of the program's overall purpose. The abstract broadly describes the processing performed by the program. A sample abstract is presented in Figure 7.15. Note the conciseness of the abstract and its general description.

Whereas the abstract serves as an overview, the *detailed narrative* explicitly describes the processing involved. The narrative presents all initial conditions, formulas used, decisions, and all the logic applied to the program solution. This aspect of a program's documentation varies according to the format used by the specific data processing organization. The narrative is usually a lengthy document. Its length, of course, depends on the degree of documentation stressed. Newly hired programmers should learn their company's level of documentation.

The program listing and complete I/O formats are practical visual references for current and future needs. The *program listing* is a line-

PROGRAM NAME:	Accounts Payable Listing
PROGRAMMER:	Tracy Kennedy
DATE:	July 28, 19--

General description of program

This program is a listing of all accounts payable, by vendor number, for the company. It is run at any time, and always reveals the most current state of the VENDOR file (VENAP-106). The program has five options that are available to the user. The sorting of any data from the files is performed using the standard sort option (specified in user's manual). The output of data can occur online or offline.

Source language

COBOL (ANSI)

Computer used to process job

The IBM 370/158, with all supporting peripherals.

Files needed

Mount disk containing all vendor files–latest version
DISKID: VENAP-106 (new)

Special features

This program can select, as desired, all vendors purged from the files; all vendors added by a selected date; all vendors doing $500,000 or more in business sales; vendors by region, ZIP codes, or ID numbers; and select all bad accounts. Each of these data can be printed onto a special form or listed immediately, in order as desired, after the main report. The file is always valid for the last 12 months of use.

FIGURE 7.15   A sample of an abstract used with the first documentation of a program.

by-line printout of every statement in the source program. The final version of the source program is the only listing that should be accepted. The final program listing should be dated and initialed by the programmer and immediate supervisor. This procedure will ensure that only the correct program has been included. One of the most common oversights occurs at this point.

Often a recent version of the program, not the final listing, is inserted into the program documentation for convenience. Frequently, this version does not contain all the changes and modifications implemented in the final solution. In the future, when new changes are under consideration, the programmer will not be working with an accurate listing. Considerable time will therefore be expended in determining and verifying the most current form of the program. The simple procedure of having the supervisor also initial the program listing often avoids this pitfall.

The *complete I/O formats,* detailed using multiple card layout forms and printer spacing charts, formally describe the inputs and outputs of the program. Each input or output document should be accompanied by an actual example. Thus if an output format is detailed using a printer spacing chart, an actual computer printout of that form should also be attached. A person researching the program will have an example of the designed and completed output. An actual data card is appropriate in the case of card inputs. The procedure of providing the individual form and respective output should be observed for all I/O documents.

The inclusion of *test data and results* proves the reliability of the program and represents a resource for future program changes. This data indicates that the program was initially correct and provides a consistent starting point for any analysis or evaluation.

The **error message log** is a record of all error states possible in processing the program. The list of error messages is prepared by the programmer for the computer operator's use and is stored in the computer room. The log describes error states, other than hardware malfunctions, that the program can assume. When an error relating to the program is encountered, the log is used to identify the error. The log describes to the operator the means necessary to reprocess the program.

An example of an error message log is given in Figure 7.16. Each error type is identified by its own number and method of correction. Error 3, for example, is caused by an incorrect data card. The corrective instructions suggest removing the incorrect data card and restarting the program.

The **user's manual** is a catalog of specifications necessary to process a program. A record for each program processed is maintained. The user's manual details pertinent data relating to the actual processing of the individual program. It describes the JCL necessary to process the program, the format of data used, the I/O devices that

PROGRAM: Accounts Payable	NAME: Accts. Pay. Check Update	APPROVED:
NUMBER: AP106	USED TO: Update Payment of Vendor Checks	SYSTEM: Burroughs 800
WHEN TO RUN:	FILES: Accts. Pay. Vendor File (APVF)	DATE: 09/30/—

Message to Operator on Console	Message Code Printed	Reason (supplied by programmer)
ERROR TYPE 1	Invalid data	Data entered for vendor is incorrect,
		check vendor number, account fields.
		Don't process after first run.
ERROR TYPE 2	JCL card out	Check JCL card specifying use of
		tape 6. Replace card and
		restart the program again.
ERROR TYPE 3	Tape not mounted	Tape mounted for tape 6 is not the
		correct one. Check label. Replace
		tape and override first error. Restart.
ERROR TYPE 4	Pick	

FIGURE 7.16 A sample of an error message log. These mistakes are not syntax errors, but error states built into the program by the programmer. They are designed to help the operator when errors occur during processing.

support its processing, and any data related to the satisfactory running of the program. The user's manual also serves as a record of all modifications made to the program. Every change applied to a program is recorded in the user's manual. Most computer operators will scan the manual before processing any work. This brief review will remind the programmer of any special factors that might affect a program's processing. The user's manual is a general guide to any program in the data processing area.

All these materials are included in the final program documentation. This documentation, though time-consuming to prepare, is a valuable source of data.

Summary

The following major points have been presented in Chapter 7:

Point 1 Machine language is the original computer language. It is the language used by all computers to execute programs. It is an extremely tedious language for a programmer to use, requiring a numeric format and the cataloging of individual main storage locations. It is machine dependent. The machine language instruction is composed of an op code and an operand. The op code represents the operation to be performed; the operand identifies the data in that operation.

Point 2 Assembly language, a low-level language, is a marked improvement over machine language. Its format involves a label, op code, and operand. The label, or tag, enables the programmer to identify data by a symbol and precludes the use of main storage locations. Symbols are also used for the op code and operand. The conversion of assembly language to machine language is

Case Study One

Computers Help Keep 'Em Rolling

Keeping the family car in working order often baffles the best of us. Imagine the difficulties faced by the North American Car Corporation, the largest railcar leasing organization, in monitoring the maintenance of over 52,000 railroad cars at 21 service centers throughout the United States and Canada by thousands of employees.

Two problems facing North American were the distance between service centers and getting maintenance data to corporate headquarters in Chicago, where all services are planned. Manually prepared maintenance reports reached Chicago in 5 to 6 days, and this delay caused scheduling problems. Necessary equipment was rarely at the right center at the right time. Expensive delays were commonplace. Railcars waiting for repairs or thousands of miles from their destination cannot be leased.

North American therefore chose to incorporate computers linked to headquarters at each service center. During phase 1 of the process, five small computers were leased and installed at selected centers. These were used to train personnel and get them acquainted with the equipment.

During the second phase, the smaller systems were replaced by larger, permanent computers.

Having been trained on the smaller, compatible systems, employees lost little time learning how to use the larger system. The smaller systems were then moved to other service centers and the two-phase training process repeated. North American considered the two-phase schedule a success. Employees felt comfortable with the devices, considering them an integral part of their work environment and not their masters.

The computers were a success, too, in that North American can now lease almost 99% of its rolling stock. Even after deducting start-up costs, it had a net gain of over $800,000 in its first year of computer-supported operations. Using computer-prepared maintenance data as its base, the North American system generates service schedules for all railcars, monitors employee productivity and labor costs, and prepares bills for customers. Cumbersome manual procedures and reams of paperwork have been eliminated. Savings have accrued from better service performance, reduced maintenance, and fewer penalties paid to customers for unavailable cars. North American's management is looking to expand its computer activities.

Consider this . . .

In your opinion, why can computers effectively control widely distributed inventories in large organizations? What aspects of the computerized handling of data make this control possible?

accomplished by a translating program called an assembler. In assembly language, one program instruction causes one complete computer operation.

Point 3 High-level languages were developed to simplify programming languages and are widely used today. High-level languages are identified by the characteristics of standard language format, machine independence, use of a compiler, and self-documentation. Because these lan-

Case Study Two

Big Bertha Helps a Family-Run Textile Business

Computers are designed to help both large corporations and small, family businesses. Like everyone else in a family-run business, a computer must prove its value. Such is the case at Lawrence Textile in Waltham, Mass., where a Honeywell computer nicknamed Big Bertha is proving an invaluable asset.

Big Bertha works on all aspects of the textile operation, controlling inventories, monitoring the more than 150,000 rolls of fabric that pass through the company each year, and handling normal business-related activities. During manufacturing, the computer schedules any of 800 special textile treatments. In treating an average of 11 million yards of fabric annually, Big Bertha helps monitor over 100 defect codes used to control quality. The Honeywell system also does office work—preparing invoices and inspection reports and handling customer billing, accounts payable and receivable, shipping documentation, and the company's payroll.

An interesting footnote to this story is that Tom Benigno, a company vice president, wrote nearly all of Big Bertha's software, although he had no previous programming experience and used a minimum of help from Honeywell reps. It was easier to teach him programming than to educate a programmer in the intricacies of the textile business. His programming experience so excited him that Tom began his own service bureau, renting Big Bertha out during idle or nonproductive periods. He is presently developing specialty software for the textile market.

guages vary little, a consistency of programming is maintained between computer systems. High-level languages require a compiler to convert their code into machine language. The compiler scans programs for syntax errors and attempts to identify them. The self-documenting feature of the high-level language identifies and records errors.

Point 4 Today we use mainly high-level languages. FORTRAN is a symbolic language with a format reminiscent of algebra. COBOL employs an Englishlike structure to easily handle business applications and all forms of I/O activities. BASIC is an interactive language designed for time-sharing applications. RPG requires special coding sheets for the output of the variety of reports for which the language was designed. PL/1 combines the best points of COBOL and FORTRAN. PASCAL is a new language with a PL/1-like format and a highly structured syntax. DECAL and SCRIPT are problem-oriented languages applied, respectively, to computerized instruction and word processing. ADA is being developed from specifications initially employed at the Defense Department.

Point 5 The software that coordinates and controls the overall operation of the computer system is the supervisor control program. Used in conjunction with the control unit of the CPU, the supervisor oversees all activities of the computer system. When compilation of a source program is required, the supervisor calls in the appropriate translating program.

Point 6 Compilers are translating programs that convert source language programs to machine language. The resulting machine language programs, called object programs, are actually executed by the computer. Job control language (JCL) directs the computer's operations and is important in the processing of any program. Using JCL, programmers communicate various processing options.

Point 7 Operating systems are a group of supervisory programs that increase the processing efficiency of a computer system. Operating systems must be able to schedule the execution of jobs and I/O activities and to determine the status of any job being run. Most operating software contains some form of spooler to create job queues. Specialists in operating software are called systems programmers. Examples of operating systems are the RSX, RSTS/E, and JES3.

Point 8 The approaches programmers use to attack problems seem different but are almost always the same. Initially the problem must be analyzed. This analysis is reflected in the drawing of a flowchart solution. After the flowchart is veri-

fied as correct, an appropriate computer language is selected before the task of coding begins. Once the program is written, the program is tested and debugged. After using test and live data and obtaining accurate results, the program is deemed operationally sound and ready for use. The final documentation of a program must be completed to release the program for production.

Point 9 The final documentation of a program should include an abstract and a detailed narrative of the program, a final program listing, a complete set of I/O formats using any of the specially prepared computer forms (i.e., printer spacing charts, etc.), test data and the results of processing, a list of error messages, and notes for the user's manual. This is designed to document all aspects of the program and make it possible for anyone to become familiar with the program in a few hours.

Glossary

ADA A computer language under development which follows a syntax developed by the Defense Department.

Assembler The translating program used to convert assembly language to machine language.

Assembly language A low-level language, one step above machine language, that permits the use of symbolic notation.

BASIC (**B**eginner's **A**ll-purpose **S**ymbolic **I**nstruction **C**ode) A free-form interactive language that is easy to learn.

Bugs Computer slang for errors in a program.

Business application A category of computer problems characterized by a high volume of I/O activities, but relatively simple computations.

COBOL (**CO**mmon **B**usiness **O**riented **L**anguage) A computer language that has an English-like structure; primarily used in business applications.

Coding sheet A form that helps the programmer writing programming code; it describes an overall instruction format.

Compilation The process by which a program is compiled.

Compiler A translating program that converts high-level languages to machine language.

Core dump The computer option, available to the programmer during the debugging of a program, that prints out every main storage position affected by the program.

Debugging The correction of errors in a computer program.

DECAL A language used in computer-assisted instruction.

Error message log A record of all error states and respective messages printed by the computer when errors occur; supplied by the programmer in the final program documentation.

FORTRAN   (FORmula **TRAN**slation**)** A high-level language with an algebra-like, highly structured format, well suited for scientific applications.

General-purpose coding sheet   A coding sheet that can be used when writing the syntax of any language and data.

High-level languages   Languages with the following characteristics: they have a standard language form, are machine independent, require a compiler, and are self-documenting.

Input/Output Control System (IOCS)   A part of an operating system employed in the scheduling of I/O operations.

Interactive languages   Languages that permit easy interaction between users and computer via telecommunications or CRTs.

Interactive Query Facility (IQF)   An interactive language developed by Digital Equipment that facilitates the access of data from computer files.

JCL cards   Standard punch cards containing job control language (JCL) instructions.

Job control language (JCL)   The specially designed computer language used by programmers and operators to communicate with the supervisory software and direct the computer.

Job Entry Subsystem 3 (JES3)   An IBM operating system that supports many forms of concurrent processing.

Job queue   The waiting list of jobs, generated by the operating system's software, that are to be processed.

Label   A component of an assembly language instruction used to identify that instruction from all others in the program.

Live data   Real data, drawn from practical applications, used to test the accuracy of a program.

Low-level languages   Languages not possessing the characteristics of high-level languages; for example, machine language.

Machine language   The language directly used by the computer to process all data; each instruction may be composed of a string of numeric characters.

Macroinstruction (macro)   One assembly language instruction that causes the computer to execute a series of assembly language instructions.

Mnemonics   The predefined codes or symbols in assembly language that will cause the computer to perform specific operations.

Multiple card layout form   A special form used to lay out and detail a card; used in processing on a column-by-column basis.

Object program   A program after it has been converted into machine language by the compiler.

Operand   The component of a machine language instruction that identifies the data used with the instruction by its actual main storage location.

Operating system   A complex array of supervisory programs that permits the most efficient scheduling of work.

Operation (op) code   The component of a machine language instruction that defines the operation to be performed by the instruction.

PASCAL   A procedure-oriented language with a structured format and syntax similar to PL/1.

PL/1   (Programming **L**anguage/**1)** A high-level language, developed by IBM, that combines many of the features of COBOL and FORTRAN.

Printer spacing chart   A form used to detail the printed outputs resulting from programming applications.

Problem definition   The written analysis of a problem slated for flowcharting, accomplished before flowcharting and programming are started.

Problem-oriented languages   Programming languages designed for specialized data processing problems with limited use in those applications.

Procedure-oriented languages Programming languages that are applicable to any data processing problem.

Program compatibility A program's ability to be processed on all models of a family of computers.

RPG (Report Program Generator) A computer programming language designed to facilitate the output of reports of business data.

RSTS/E An operating system from Digital Equipment specially designed for time-sharing operations.

RSX An operating system from Digital Equipment designed for common production activities.

Scientific application A category for defining data processing jobs, characterized by small I/O operations and extremely difficult formulas and computations.

SCRIPT A problem-oriented language developed by IBM and used in word processing.

Source deck The standard punch cards containing the source program.

Spooler Part of the system's software responsible for establishing the job queue.

Stand-alone program A self-contained program that is processed without interacting with any other program.

Supervisor Computer slang for the supervisor control program.

Supervisor control program The control program that oversees the completion of all processing in a computer system.

Symbolic programming language A programming language that permits the use of symbols and mnemonics to represent data and operations.

Syntax The rules applied to the coding of programming languages.

System residence (SYSRES) device The peripheral device (i.e., a disk) that contains all the operating programs used by the system to process data.

Systems programmer The specialists who work with operating systems software.

Tag See **Label.**

Tracing routine A special programming technique, used by the programmer to debug particularly difficult programs, that records the processing of each instruction on a step-by-step basis until the error is encountered.

User's manual A manual that contains pertinent data related to the actual processing of a program (i.e., the JCL that is necessary, the type of data, etc.).

Word processing The computerized handling of paperwork in an office.

Discussion Questions

1 Describe the differences between
  a Machine language and assembly language
  b Live data and test data

2 Discuss the general characteristics of the following languages: FORTRAN, COBOL, BASIC, RPG, PL/1, PASCAL, and ADA.

3 Briefly discuss the general purpose of the following problem-oriented languages: DECAL, SCRIPT, and IQF.

4 Define in your own words the following terms:

Compiler	High-level languages
Source program	Syntax
Operating system	Macro
Object program	Problem definition
Program abstract	Mnemonic
Spooler	Program compatibility

5 Compile a list of program languages mentioned in the want ads of your local newspaper. Try to identify the purpose of each language.

6 Discuss the purpose of a printer spacing chart and a multiple card layout form.

7 Describe the characteristics of a high-level language.

8 Discuss the purpose of an operating system and the three characteristics associated with that software.

Summary Test

_F_ 1 Machine language must be converted by a compiler to be used by the computer.

_F_ 2 Machine language instructions are composed of a label, an op code, and an operand.

_T_ 3 The supervisor must reside in main storage during its use.

_F_ 4 High-level languages require that programmers work with individual main storage locations.

_F_ 5 The concept of a macro instruction was introduced with COBOL.

_T_ 6 A compiler is a translating program that converts the source program into an object program.

_F_ 7 The printer spacing chart defines the printed outputs of data to include individual lines of data and heading lines, but not the output of grand totals.

_F_ 8 Live data is always used before test data during program testing.

_T_ 9 Problem-oriented languages are designed for specific applications.

_F_ 10 FORTRAN is suited for scientific applications and has an English-like format.

_T_ 11 The SYSRES device contains all compilers and important software used by a system.

_T_ 12 A core dump is an output of the main storage positions used by the program.

_F_ 13 The user's manual is a broad overview of the program without specifications.

_F_ 14 During the compilation of a program, the compiler will scan for errors of syntax and logic.

_F_ 15 JCL helps the programmer to directly communicate commands to the hardware and bypass all supervisory software.

_D_ **16** A factor in the selection of a source language is:
- **a** programmer skill
- **b** language availability
- **c** program compatibility with other software
- **d** all the above

_B_ **17** A computer-generated output that lets programmers follow the execution of their programs line by line is a:
- **a** core dump
- **b** tracing routine
- **c** detail listing
- **d** source listing

_A_ **18** A concise evaluation of a program's overall purpose is a(n):
- **a** abstract
- **b** program narrative
- **c** program listing
- **d** user's manual

_B_ **19** A language with an Englishlike format designed for business applications is:
- **a** BASIC
- **b** COBOL
- **c** FORTRAN
- **d** RPG

_C_ **20** A catalog of specifications on the processing of a particular program is a(n):
- **a** error message book
- **b** detailed narrative
- **c** user's manual
- **d** test result log

_C_ **21** The operating system that supports time-sharing on a Digital Equipment computer is:
- **a** ADA
- **b** RSX
- **c** RSTS/E
- **d** JES3

_D_ **22** A problem-oriented language is:
- **a** DECAL
- **b** restricted to one type of application
- **c** IQF
- **d** all the above

_D_ **23** BASIC is an example of a(n):
- **a** interactive language
- **b** time-sharing language
- **c** high-level language
- **d** all the above

_C_ **24** The term for the list of programs awaiting processing, generated by the operating system, is:
- **a** job entry queue
- **b** job order list
- **c** job queue
- **d** all the above

_A_ **25** A characteristic of an operating system is:
- **a** scheduling jobs
- **b** the preparation of JCL
- **c** scheduling and completing arithmetic operations
- **d** all the above

Summary Test Answers

1 F	**2** F	**3** T	**4** F	**5** F
6 T	**7** F	**8** F	**9** T	**10** F
11 T	**12** T	**13** F	**14** F	**15** F
16 D	**17** B	**18** A	**19** B	**20** C
21 C	**22** D	**23** D	**24** C	**25** A

Eight

Programming in BASIC

FIGURE 8.1 BASIC is
an interactive language,
permitting users to in-
teract directly with com-
puters. Users, while
seated at terminals, may
prepare and test their
software without delay.
(*L. Druskis.*)

Purpose of This Chapter

The purpose of this chapter is to introduce the BASIC programming language and examine its use as an educational tool. The general line format employed with all BASIC statements is presented, and the purposes of the line number, command, and variable are explained.

Using BASIC, we introduce fundamental skills that are applicable to other programming languages. We develop and present flowcharts for each problem. BASIC programs are then derived from these pictorial solutions.

We will begin our presentation of BASIC with a simple flowchart and develop a program solution step by step. We present the READ, DATA, LET, PRINT, END, and INPUT statements of BASIC using elementary examples. The IF/THEN and GO TO statements, which are used to define decisions and establish program loops, are discussed. We also detail the use of the REMARK statement and the PRINT statement to create literals.

Examples involving accumulators, multiple outputs and decisions, and counters are presented. We discuss the use of the FOR/NEXT statement and the STEP option to create automated program loops. We also introduce the DIMENSION statement, which is used to create an organized series of storage areas (called an array) in a program. Examples illustrate how the FOR/NEXT and the DIMENSION statements are used together.

Like Chapter 6, this chapter gives a series of hints to aid the reader. They alert the novice programmer to common potential errors.

After studying this chapter, you should be able to:

■ Understand and use the BASIC language.

■ Convert program flowcharts into BASIC program solutions.

■ Describe the general line format of BASIC.

■ Describe the use of the READ, DATA, LET, PRINT, END, INPUT, IF/THEN, GO TO, and REMARK statements.

■ Discuss the differences between string variable names and data and numeric variable names and data.

■ Discuss the use of the system commands LIST, RUN, DELETE, SAVE, and UNSAVE.

■ Describe the use of literals, multiple outputs on one line, and multiple decisions in a BASIC program.

■ Describe how accumulators and counters are represented in BASIC.

■ Describe the use of the FOR/NEXT statement, STEP option, and DIMENSION statement.

■ Discuss the concept of an array.
■ Understand the following terms:

Array	NEXT statement
BASIC	Numeric data
Command	Numeric variable names
DATA statement	Print position
DELETE command	PRINT statement
DIMENSION statement	Print zones
END statement	READ statement
FOR statement	Real number
FOR/NEXT statement	REMARK statement
Free-form language	RUN command
GO TO statement	SAVE command
IF/THEN statement	Statement number
IF/THEN/ELSE statement	STEP option
INPUT statement	String variable data
Integer number	String variable name
LET statement	Subscript
Line number	Subscripted variable name
LIST command	UNSAVE command
LOGOFF procedure	Variable
LOGON procedure	Whole number

Introduction

Basic
Programming
free form language

Previous discussions have shown that computers are interwoven into the fabric of our daily lives. They provide weather forecasts, control the flow of traffic in major cities, and test the quality of the air we breathe. Computers can analyze vast amounts of data and predict trends in business or shifts in our population. Without a computer, the preparation of the United States Census would be an insurmountable task.

Educational institutions quickly recognized the impact of the computer. For decades, they have been involved in the development of computer hardware and software. Many institutions use the computer in their administrative branches and faculty research activities. You may have registered for courses using a computer-supported registration system.

One of the first prominent scholars to support the use of computers in education was John G. Kemeny, president of Dartmouth University. As an educator, he was aware of how unprepared college graduates were to deal with computers. Many students have little knowledge about the device that daily affects their lives. Kemeny believed that all college students should take at least one computer-related course during their college years.

Because of his data processing experience, Kemeny quickly realized that the existing programming languages were either too technical or too complicated for students. Many students did not have the time or inclination to learn the existing computer languages. Thus Kemeny developed a language that could be learned without prior programming training and called it **BASIC** (**B**eginner's **A**ll-purpose **S**ymbolic **I**nstruction **C**ode).[1]

BASIC, as an interactive language, is perfectly suited for use with terminals and supports all forms of teleprocessing and telecommunications. BASIC lets a group of students simultaneously access the computer. Because of its simplicity, students quickly and easily develop fundamental programming skills in BASIC.

8.1 General Line Format

BASIC is referred to as a **free-form language** because it has a simple syntax and a limited number of rules. These characteristics make BASIC an easy language to learn. Nevertheless, you should have a firm understanding of the rules that do exist in BASIC.

The general format of all BASIC instructions is

LINE NUMBER   COMMAND   VARIABLE(S)

This structure is similar to that of a low-level language instruction, with each component of this general format having its own function.

Line Number

Each statement in a BASIC program is preceded by its own **line number,** or **statement number,** which identifies the statement. Line numbers start at 1 and can continue to 99999. Programmers, therefore, have a wide range of line numbers to choose from when writing their programs.

Line numbers provide the operational sequence for processing. Statements in a BASIC program are processed one by one, in numerical order. Thus statement 10 precedes statement 20, and statement 20 precedes statement 30. Line numbers not only identify statements but indicate their position in the order of processing.

Programmers ordinarily sit at a terminal to input BASIC programs. Each statement of a program is entered separately. During this input process, errors are common. The correction of an error may require the reentry of a statement or the input of additional statements. Because of this, a minor convention has evolved concerning the assign-

---

[1] The initial language developed by Kemeny is referred to as Dartmouth BASIC and represents one of the many current forms of BASIC. Many manufacturers' forms of BASIC vary slightly from the original form. Differences among the various BASIC formats may be quickly learned by programmers. In this chapter, we review the IBM VS BASIC language, citing selected differences of other languages where necessary.

ment of line numbers. Instead of assigning numbers in increments of 1 (i.e., 1, 2, 3, etc.), programmers customarily use increments of 10 (i.e., 10, 20, 30, etc.). Thus, if a line has to be inserted into an existing set of statements, it can be assigned one of the unused numbers. The lines that follow do not have to be renumbered.

Consider the programmer who has entered 10 statements using the line numbers 1 through 10. If a correction requires the reentry of an existing statement, it is easily made. The programmer rekeys that specific statement using the same line number, and the newly entered statement replaces the old statement. However, what happens if the programmer has to insert an additional statement between statements 2 and 3? For this correction, the programmer must reenter statements 3 through 10. It should be evident that the insertion of a statement between line numbers 2 and 3 changes the line number of every statement following line 2.

This type of correction is nerve-racking because of the number of statements involved. Correcting 10 statements is a nuisance; correcting 50 statements is a disaster. To circumvent this type of problem, programmers developed the convention of assigning BASIC line numbers in increments of 10. Thus the first statement of a BASIC program has a line number of 10, the second statement a line number of 20, the third statement a line number of 30, and so forth until the program is finished. In our example, the 10 statement numbers would be 10, 20, 30, 40, 50, 60, 70, 80, 90, and 100. The insertion of a statement between statements 20 and 30 is now easily accomplished without rekeying any instruction. The line numbers 21 through 29 are available to the programmer. Any of these line numbers can be assigned to the new statement added to the program. The new statement, say line number 22, is easily inserted.

Another advantage of BASIC is that instructions such as statement 22 can be entered out of sequence. Normally, BASIC statements are input in numerical sequence. However, instructions like statement 22 are repeatedly added to programs. The BASIC compiler continually reorders all statements of a program, and will place any newly entered statement in its proper sequential position. The new order of our sample statements is 10, 20, 22, 30, 40, 50, 60, 70, 80, 90, and 100. Programmers need not worry about the sequence of instructions.

The ability to quickly reenter and correct statements in a BASIC program simplifies the debugging effort. Corrections are readily inserted and tested within seconds.

Command

You will recall from the discussion of assembly language instructions that the op code indicated the operation to be performed. The op code, for example, defined whether an input operation was starting or the addition of two numbers was underway. The **command** of a BASIC instruction acts as the op code. The command defines the operation to be performed by the statement. For example, the word READ defines an input operation, the term PRINT indicates an output operation, and the term LET defines arithmetic operations involving formulas.

Variables

If processing operations are underway, some type of variable is involved. **Variables** are the parts of a BASIC instruction that define the items of data used in that operation. If a READ operation is initiated, the variables following the word READ identify the data involved (i.e., name, hours, and rate). Almost all BASIC statements use some form of variable. Throughout the chapter we will explain rules relating to the use of variables.

**8.2
A First BASIC
Program**

Flowcharts normally precede the writing of programs. If the logic of the problem solution is detailed in a flowchart, the program can be easily written line by line. Each symbol of a flowchart defines a specific operation and the type of BASIC instruction required.

Each program solution presented in this chapter is accompanied by a flowchart. This approach permits you to concentrate on the BASIC syntax of each instruction used. For ease of understanding, discussions will begin with the first flowcharting program used in Chapter 6. Figure 8.2 shows this flowchart and the BASIC program derived from it.

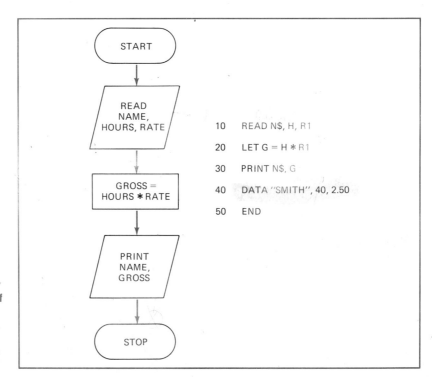

FIGURE 8.2 The first flowchart solution and the BASIC program derived from it. Note the similarity between the narrative and symbols of the flowchart and the BASIC statements used. Data has been added to the problem to illustrate how it is used.

```
10    READ N$, H, R1

20    LET G = H * R1

30    PRINT N$, G

40    DATA "SMITH", 40, 2.50

50    END
```

Note the similarity between the flowchart and the BASIC program. The symbols and narrative used in a flowchart have almost a one-to-one relationship to the statements of the program. This is logical because the program was derived from the flowchart.

Also note that each statement has a line number and a command. The first statement of the program is statement 10. All statements are incremented by 10, up to the last instruction, statement 50.

Each statement has its own syntax as well as its specific purpose. An examination of the BASIC instruction will explain how the statement is properly used.

READ and DATA Statements

Though the READ statement and the DATA statement appear separately in our BASIC program, they are closely related. Whenever a READ statement is used in a BASIC program, one or more DATA statements must also be included. The **READ statement** defines an input operation and initiates the entry of data for the BASIC program. The **DATA statement** defines the data actually used in the program and is the source of the data being input. The format of the READ statement is important because it defines how the DATA statement is used.

The READ statement from our sample program is

	10	READ	N$, H, R1
Line Number	Command	Variables

The number 10 is the line number of the statement and identifies it as the first statement of the program. The command READ indicates that an input operation is to be performed. The variables following the READ command define the data being input.

In Figure 8.2, you can see a marked difference between the data-names of the flowchart and the names of the variables used in the program. This difference is attributable to the syntax associated with the READ statement. From the flowchart, we know that the data input to the problem is divided into two types: alphameric data (e.g., name) and numeric data (e.g., hours and rate). The syntax of the READ statement requires that data be segregated in this fashion. In BASIC, all data is defined as either alphameric or numeric, with the alphameric category including alphabetic data. Alphameric and numeric data are identified by simple coding conventions.

All datanames are a maximum of two characters long. All alphameric data is specifically identified by the dollar sign ($). In Figure 8.2, the dataname associated with the flowcharting variable NAME is N$. In the syntax of BASIC, N$ is called a **string variable name** because it represents a string of alphabetic or alphameric characters. String variable names always represent alphabetic or alphameric data and never apply to numeric data.

All string variable names are exactly two characters in length. The first character of a string variable name must be an alphabetic character, and the second character must be the dollar sign ($). Applying these rules, we can easily conclude that in one BASIC program we are restricted to a total of 26 distinct string variable names. One must follow the above rules when formulating string variable names. Table 8.1 presents examples of valid and invalid string variable names.

Table 8.1   Valid and Invalid
Variable Names

String Variable Names

Valid		Invalid	
N$	X$	2$	$/
A$	V$	?$	BB
S$	L$	$A	$AS
H$	Q$	$3	B$2

Numeric Variable Names

Valid			Invalid		
A	R1	YØ	AA	22	H2S
A1	R2	T	3B	RB	RP1
C9	R3	T1	A?	HR	R12
X3	H	P	0X	HRS	D*

STRING VARIABLE NAMES

1   A string variable name is used only to represent alphabetic and alphanumeric information.
2   String variable names are two characters long.
3   The first character of a string variable name is always an alphabetic character.
4   The second character is a dollar sign ($).

A similar syntax is used to define variable names for numeric data. In Figure 8.2, the flowcharting variables HOURS and RATE are identified in BASIC as H and R1, respectively. Because H and R1 represent numeric data, they are referred to as **numeric variable names.** Slightly different rules apply to numeric variable names. For example, they may be one or two characters long. If the name is only one character long, then the character must be alphabetic. If two characters are used, the first character must be alphabetic and the second, numeric. Table 8.1 illustrates valid and invalid numeric variable names.

NUMERIC VARIABLE NAMES

1 Numeric variable names represent only numeric data.
2 Numeric variable names can be one or two characters long.
3 The first character must be an alphabetic character.
4 The second character, when used, must be a number (0 to 9).

Reexamine statement 10 in Figure 8.2, and note the entry of one string variable, N$, and two numeric variables, H and R1. Both types of variables are consistent with their respective rules of syntax. Also note that each variable of the READ statement is separated by a comma. Commas are necessary to isolate each variable and clearly define it for the compiler. If a comma is not used, a syntax error occurs. The compiler cannot clearly identify the variables used in the READ statement.

COMMAS IN A READ STATEMENT

A common error made when using the READ statement is to omit commas. Commas in READ statements separate incoming variables. Thus a statement might be properly written as follows:

10 READ N$, H, R

However, commas are often omitted. Thus a READ statement might appear as follows:

10 READ N$, H R   or   **10 READ N$, H; R**

Both statements are improperly written. The first statement omits a comma, the second incorrectly replaces a comma with a semicolon. Commas are the only punctuation marks acceptable in a READ statement.

String variable names are used to represent **string variable data.** Numeric variable names are used to identify **numeric data.** The distinction between variable names and the data they represent is important because different rules of syntax apply to each. The syntax applied to string variable data and numeric data is an integral part of the DATA statement.

As we have said, there is a close relationship between the READ and the DATA statements. The READ statement defines the type and

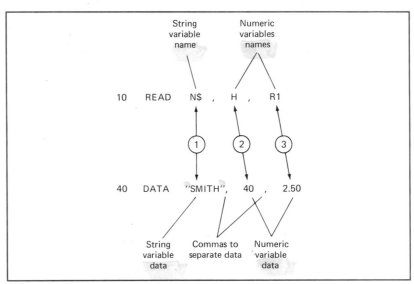

FIGURE 8.3 Statements 10 and 40 drawn from the initial BASIC program in Figure 8.2. The diagram illustrates the close relationship between these statements. Note how the variables and the data they represent must match in regard to order and type. Note that commas separate and define variables in statement 10 and data in statement 40.

order of the variables input. The DATA statement, which actually provides the data for the problem, must coincide exactly with the READ statements used. This relationship can be seen in statements 10 and 40 in Figure 8.3.

Statement 40, the DATA statement, conforms to the general format of BASIC statements. It has a line number, 40, and a command, DATA, which indicates the purpose of the statement. The actual items of data to be used in the program follow the word DATA. Each item of data is separated by a comma. Commas must always be placed between individual items of data in a DATA statement.

The order in which data is listed in the DATA statement is defined by the order in which the respective variable names are listed in the READ statement. In statement 10, a string variable is first, followed by two numeric variables. Thus the first data item in statement 40 must be a string variable data item, followed by two numeric data items. The data "SMITH" is the string variable data item. The numbers 40 and 2.50 represent the data associated with the numeric variables. "SMITH", the first item of data in statement 40, is matched with N\$, the first variable of the READ statement. Using the same logic, the numeric data items 40 and 2.50 are matched with the numeric variables H and R1 because they assume the second and third positions of the statements. The READ statement dictates that three variables are to be input at one time, and the DATA statement supplies the three items. The order and type of data supplied by the DATA statement have to coincide with the READ statement. In both statements, commas separate each variable and item of data.

In statement 40, the string variable data, "SMITH", is defined by quotation marks. Quotation marks are always used to denote string

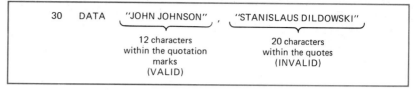

FIGURE 8.4   Two samples of string variable data are shown in statement 30. The first item uses 12 characters, excluding the quotation marks, and is valid. The second data item uses 20 characters. The 20 characters exceed the limit of 18 dictated by the BASIC syntax. This string variable data item is therefore invalid and would not be accepted in a BASIC program.

variable data. Each string variable data item, enclosed in its own set of quotation marks, can be a maximum of 18 characters long, excluding the quotation marks. In Figure 8.4, two samples of string variable data are shown in the statement. The first string variable data item, "JOHN JOHNSON", is 12 characters in length and is a valid string variable. The second data item, though properly contained in quotation marks, is 20 characters long and is not an acceptable string variable data item.

Numeric variable data has similar constraints. Numeric data can be a maximum of seven characters long, not including a plus or a minus sign and a decimal point. Figure 8.5 gives samples of numeric data. Quotation marks are not used with numeric data but reserved solely for string variable data. The first number, −271.3654, is a valid numeric data item. It has seven digits, not including the minus sign and the decimal point. If more digits were added to that number (e.g., −271.36549999), the computer would ignore them. In BASIC, only the

FIGURE 8.5   Real and whole numbers are used in DATA statements. Statement 70 includes two real and two integer numbers. In either case, numeric data cannot exceed seven digits. Decimal points and plus and minus signs are not counted as part of the seven digits. Consistent with the rules of BASIC, commas are used to separate numeric data.

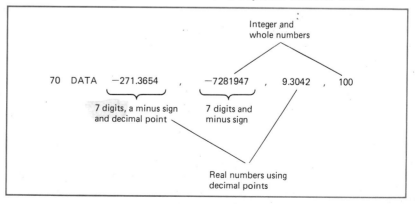

first seven digits are used. In statement 70, the number −7281947 is an acceptable numeric item of data. It has seven digits and a minus sign.

Numeric data that does not use a decimal point is referred to as an **integer** or **whole number.** Data that uses a decimal point is called a **real number.** All data specified in a BASIC program uses either a real- or a whole-number format (Figure 8.5). Plus or minus signs can be used with either format.

String variable and numeric data, in any combination, are presented in the DATA statement. The order and type of data must reflect the READ statement used in the program. Once numeric data is input, it can be used in processing. All arithmetic manipulations of data are accomplished using the LET statement.

TYPES OF DATA

1   String variable data is individually defined by a pair of quotation marks.

2   String variable data can be a maximum of 18 characters long, excluding quotation marks.

3   String variable data can be composed of any combination of characters.

4   Numeric data can be a maximum of seven characters long, excluding a plus or a minus sign and a decimal point when used.

5   No special characters, except a decimal point and a plus or a minus sign, can be used to compose numeric data.

LET Statement

Because of its algebraic format, BASIC can easily represent formulas and manipulate numeric data. All arithmetic processing of formulas must use the **LET statement.** The LET statement in our initial BASIC program is

20 LET G=H∗R1

The number 20 is the line number of the statement. The command LET indicates an arithmetic manipulation of data. The formula G = H ∗ R1 follows the command. String variables are generally not used in LET statements. Thus if a programmer finds a $ in a computation, the statement is probably incorrect and should be rewritten.

Note in statement 20 that one numeric variable, G, is given on the left of the equal sign. The syntax of BASIC permits one, and only one, variable to the left of the equal sign. All variables to the right of the equal sign must be defined prior to their processing. This constraint is consistent with the rules of flowcharting. If the data does not exist, it cannot be processed.

It is important to use the correct variable names when representing formulas via the LET statement. One of the most common mistakes novice programmers make is to specify variable names improperly. For example, statement 20 accurately specified the formula G = H * R1. However, consider the improperly written statement

20 LET G=H*R

Though the intent of the formula is the same, it is incorrect. The error lies in the use of R, instead of R1, as a numeric variable. This minor error will render that entire program incorrect. It is the programmer's responsibility to consistently use the proper variable names. You should visually debug your programs before processing them.

Statement 20 shows the symbolic nature of BASIC. The asterisk (*) is used to represent multiplication. It is just one of the arithmetic symbols used by BASIC. Table 8.2 presents the BASIC symbols used for arithmetic operations.

Table 8.2 Symbols Used in Arithmetic Operations

Symbol	Arithmetic Operation
+	Addition
−	Subtraction
*	Multiplication
/	Division
** or ↑	Exponentiation[1]

[1] The term *exponentiation* refers to the taking of a variable to a power. For example, A squared in algebra indicates that A is taken to a second power, which is equal to A times A or A^2. A^2 is written as A**2 or A↑2. Either format is acceptable and correct.

According to the EDP cycle, once input and processing are completed, the output of data can begin. In BASIC, output operations are accomplished with the PRINT statement.

PRINT Statement

The **PRINT statement** provides for the printed output of data on paper or the display of data via the screen of a CRT. The nature of this output depends on the type of terminal used. In either case, 72 characters can be printed on one line. This grouping of 72 characters is divided into four major **print zones** of 18 characters each. Figure 8.6 illustrates the four print zones.

Each print zone is composed of 18 **print positions.** Each print position can represent one character of output. Thus, each zone can contain exactly 18 characters of output. Notice how this limit matches the maximum size of one item of string variable data. One string varia-

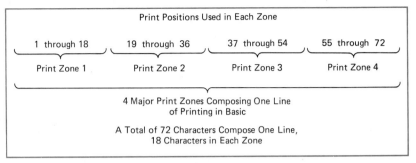

Print Positions Used in Each Zone

| 1 through 18 | 19 through 36 | 37 through 54 | 55 through 72 |
| Print Zone 1 | Print Zone 2 | Print Zone 3 | Print Zone 4 |

4 Major Print Zones Composing One Line
of Printing in Basic

A Total of 72 Characters Compose One Line,
18 Characters in Each Zone

FIGURE 8.6   One line of print in BASIC is composed of 72 characters. This grouping of 72 characters is divided into four print zones of 18 characters each. The 72 print positions are numbered consecutively from 1 to 72. Zone 1 consists of print positions 1 to 18, zone 2 consists of positions 19 to 36, zone 3 consists of positions 37 to 54, and zone 4 uses positions 55 to 72.

ble fits perfectly into one print zone. To understand how data is assigned to each of the four zones, examine the format of the PRINT statement.[1]

The PRINT statement of the initial program is

30 PRINT N$, G

The line number is 30, and the command PRINT indicates an output operation. The data output is the string variable N$ and the numeric variable G, representing the employee's name and gross pay, respectively. The punctuation of statement 30 dictates where these two variables are printed.

In PRINT statements, commas not only separate variables but define the print zones that contain output. Data relating to N$ is printed in print zone 1 because this variable immediately follows the command PRINT. In the example, the string variable data SMITH, associated with the string variable name N$, will be printed in print positions 1 to 5 in zone 1.

However, where will the amount related to G be output? To determine this, examine the punctuation used between N$ and G. In a PRINT statement, a comma tells us to skip to the first position of the

---

[1] The use of four print zones with 18 characters each is peculiar to IBM BASIC. Dartmouth BASIC uses a different print-zone configuration: five zones of 15 characters each, for a total of 75 characters on one line of print. The configuration of Dartmouth BASIC permits the output of three more characters. In both forms, commas and semicolons are used in exactly the same manner. The use of five zones of 15 characters also affects the length of string variable data; it is limited to a length of 15 characters, too. Similarly, the BASIC employed on Digital Equipment machines dictates 5 print zones of 14 characters each, for a total of 70 characters on one line. String variable data is also limited to 14 characters.

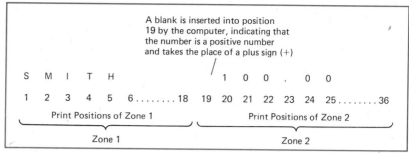

FIGURE 8.7   The printed output resulting from statement 30. The output related to N$ is placed in zone 1, starting with print position 1 and ending with position 5. The remainder of zone 1 is not used and thus remains blank. The comma in statement 30 dictates that the output of G be placed in zone 2. This output begins with position 19, even though print position 19 is unfilled. The blank space is used instead of a plus sign (+). The BASIC compiler will always insert a minus sign if the output amount is negative. However, if the amount is positive, the output of the plus sign is suppressed in favor of a blank. It is understood that the blank represents a positive number. In all outputs of BASIC, one position prior to the number is always reserved for the sign of the number, whether it is used or not.

next available zone and output the next variable. Thus, the amount of G, 100.00, will be printed in zone 2, because zone 1 is occupied by the data relating to N$. The output of the amount 100.00 begins with print position 19, because this is the first position of the next available zone. The output of statement 30 is illustrated in Figure 8.7.

If commas are used in a PRINT statement, only four variables can be printed on one line. Occasionally, however, five or more variables must be output on one line. This is accomplished with the semicolon (;). Whereas the comma means skip to the first position of the next available zone, the semicolon directs the output of data to the next available print position and restrains the computer from skipping to the next print zone. The semicolon radically alters the output of a BASIC program. The alteration of statement 30 to

30 PRINT N$; G

produces the output illustrated in Figure 8.8.

The data relating to N$ is still printed in zone 1, print positions 1 through 5. However, the output related to G starts with print position 6, not position 19 of zone 2. The semicolon directs the output of G to begin with position 6, the next available print position following the last character of the data output for N$. Thus the semicolon squeezes the outputs together. Commas and semicolons can be inserted between variables in a PRINT statement to create any format desired by the programmer.

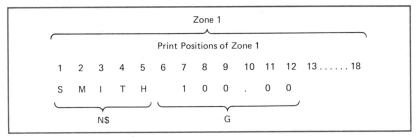

FIGURE 8.8   The printed output produced from the BASIC statement

30 PRINT N$; G

Print positions 1 to 5 are occupied by the characters SMITH, associated with the string variable name N$. The semicolon causes data related to G to be output beginning with print position 6. A blank is inserted in position 6, because the amount of G is a positive number. The remaining digits, 100.00, are output in print positions 7 through 12.

One note of caution is necessary. Semicolons can only be used with PRINT statements. They are generally not used with other BASIC statements. A common mistake is to insert semicolons into READ or DATA statements. This should never be done.

The output of data, via statement 30, completes the processing of our initial BASIC program. Statement 40, the DATA statement, was already discussed in conjunction with the READ statement. Therefore, it is bypassed and the discussion continues with statement 50, the END statement.

END Statement

The **END statement** is always the last statement of a BASIC program. If any statement followed the END statement, it would be ignored and never processed as part of a program. The format of the END statement used is

50 END

No variables follow the command END.

The following illustrative problem will reinforce the use of the five statements discussed.

ILLUSTRATIVE PROBLEM 1

The overall problem relates to the computation of net pay. Data input to the problem are the employee's name, hours worked, and rate of pay. Output the employee's name, gross pay, FICA deduction, and net pay. Gross is computed by multiplying hours $\times$ rate. The FICA deduction is 6.28 percent of gross. Net pay is equal to gross pay $-$ the FICA deduction. The data for this problem are the following:

Employee Name	Hours Worked	Rate of Pay
Smith	40	2.50

Figure 8.9 provides the flowchart for Illustrative Problem 1 and the BASIC program solution derived from the flowchart. You can see similarities between the flowchart solution and the BASIC program. Almost every symbol of the flowchart is converted into a statement of the program. The variables in the program are different from those in the flowchart because of BASIC's syntax. However, it can be concluded that the string variable name, N$, represents EMP-NAME and the numeric variables, H and R, represent HOURS and RATE, respectively.

The DATA statement is placed as the second statement of the program. DATA statements can be placed anywhere in a program before the END statement. During the execution of the program, each DATA statement is accessed in order. Thus, although DATA statements are distributed throughout a program, each DATA statement is used as required. The string variable data, "SMITH", is properly de-

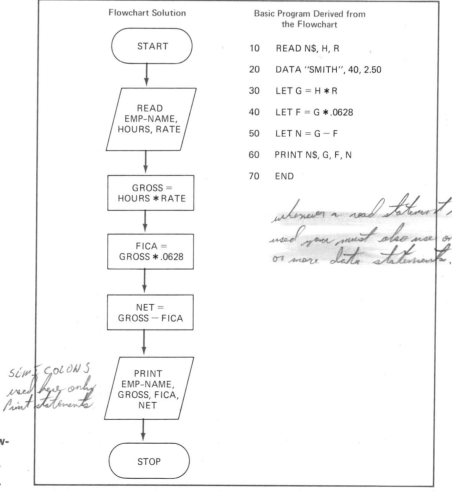

FIGURE 8.9 The flowchart and the BASIC program solutions for Illustrative Problem 1.

fined within quotes. The numeric data, 40 and 2.50, follows the string variable data and is associated with the variables H and R.

The flowchart specifies three processing operations. These operations are converted into three separate LET statements. The numeric variables, G, F, and N, identify gross pay, FICA, and net pay. All these numeric variables, as well as N$, are output by statement 60, the PRINT statement. Data relating to N$ is printed in zone 1. Data resulting from the processing of G, F, and N are printed in zones 2, 3, and 4, respectively. The output of these four variables is printed on one line, as shown in Figure 8.10. The END statement, line number 70, completes this BASIC program.

In the first two BASIC programs, the READ and DATA statements were used together to input data. Though these statements were effective, BASIC provides an alternative method for inputting data. This method uses the INPUT statement.

INPUT Statement

Whereas the READ and DATA statements must be used in conjunction, the **INPUT statement** is specified as a separate statement in BASIC. The INPUT statement requires no other statement to be used with it and is used differently from a READ statement. Because DATA statements are not used with INPUT statements, the INPUT statement requests data as the program is being processed. To illustrate the use of the INPUT statement, the first BASIC program will be rewritten as follows:

```
10 INPUT N$, H, R1
20 LET G=H*R1
30 PRINT N$, G
40 END
```

FIGURE 8.10 The output resulting from the PRINT statement of Illustrative Problem 1. The statement

```
60 PRINT N$, G, F, N
```

places one variable in each of the four print zones, because commas are used to separate the variables. Note the string variable data, SMITH. Though quotation marks are used to define it in the DATA statement, they do not appear in the output. Also, a blank space is inserted preceding the output of each numeric variable. This space takes the place of a plus sign (+) and indicates a positive quantity.

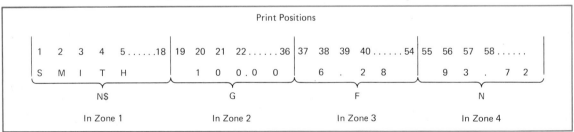

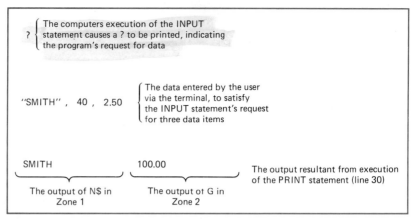

The computers execution of the INPUT
? statement causes a ? to be printed, indicating
the program's request for data

"SMITH" , 40 , 2.50   The data entered by the user
via the terminal, to satisfy
the INPUT statement's request
for three data items

SMITH   100.00

The output of N$ in   The output ot G in
Zone 1   Zone 2

The output resultant from execution
of the PRINT statement (line 30)

**FIGURE 8.11   The record of entries related to the INPUT statement. The
output of the ? requests the entry of data. The next line indicates that
three items of data are input. The data "SMITH" is used for N$, while 40
and 2.50 are used for H and R1, respectively. The next line indicates the
output of executing statement 30. The data related to N$ is printed in
zone 1, while the amount of gross pay is output in zone 2. Each of these
lines would appear consecutively in output, whether printed on paper or
displayed on a CRT.**

The initial difference in this rewritten solution is the absence of the
DATA statement. As stated, INPUT statements are used alone and do
not require the use of DATA statements. The INPUT statement is an
interactive statement that requests the input of data. Figure 8.11 illustrates this request for data, the format of the data input, and the output
resulting from the program.

The computer's execution of statement 10, the INPUT statement,
causes a question mark (?) to be output. The ? indicates that the program, via the INPUT statement, is requesting the input of data from the
person seated at the terminal. The required items of data are then
keyed into the program in the order dictated by the INPUT statement.
In the example, three data items would be entered via a terminal. The
order and type of data entered depend on the INPUT statement. Statement 10 specifies the input of a string variable, N$, and two numeric
variables, H and R1. Thus, the three data items are input in exactly that
order. Note that the syntax of the DATA statement must be followed
when one enters data (i.e., quotation marks define string variable
data).

Once the required data is accepted by the INPUT statement, the
program continues its processing. The gross pay is computed via
statement 20, the LET statement. The PRINT statement, line number
30, outputs two items of data. The string variable N$ is printed in zone
1, and the gross pay G appears in zone 2. This last line of output is
illustrated in Figure 8.11.

10	READ N$, H, R	10	INPUT N$, H, R
20	DATA "SMITH", 40, 2.50	20	LET G = H ∗ R
30	LET G = H ∗ R	30	LET F = G ∗ .0628
40	LET F = G ∗ .0628	40	LET N = G − F
50	LET N = G − F	50	PRINT N$, G, F, N
60	PRINT N$, G, F, N	60	END
70	END		

FIGURE 8.12   A comparison of two solutions to Illustrative Problem 1. One solution uses the READ and DATA statements. The other, the program on the right, replaces those statements with the INPUT statement. Note that the variables of the INPUT statement are exactly like those of the READ statement. When INPUT statements are used in a program, DATA statements are not required.

The INPUT statement is primarily used when the amounts and types of data a program requires vary extensively. For example, consider a marketing program. Each time this program is used, the data changes radically. Thus, a DATA statement is not suitable. INPUT statements permit the user to enter the necessary data at the start of processing. Once the data is input, the program can proceed. In this type of application, the INPUT statement offers the programmer flexibility. The choice of program statements is left entirely to the programmer. (The selection process gets easier with practical experience.)

We will consistently use the READ and DATA statements in future discussions to simplify the explanation of upcoming programs. Readers who wish to use the INPUT statement can simply replace the READ statement with an INPUT statement and remove the DATA statement from the program. Figure 8.12 depicts this type of alteration as performed on Illustrative Problem 1.

8.3 Decisions, Loops, and Special Outputs

The repetitive nature of computerized data processing was emphasized in previous chapters. The computer is able to repeat a series of steps to process data. This type of processing is depicted in flowcharts by the loop, last record check, and the 9's Decision.

These flowchart techniques can be converted into easily usable BASIC statements. The 9's Decision, a logical operation, is indicated in BASIC by the IF/THEN statement. The unconditional branch, which creates the processing loop, is represented by the GO TO statement. The illustrative problem that follows uses both of these statements.

Some students may ask why the 9's Decision is used with BASIC rather than the last record check. In effect, the 9's Decision is a specialized form of the last record check, but there is a far more compelling reason for using it. The BASIC language cannot perform a last

FOR THE FUN OF IT

Many students are eager at this point to try out their newly developed BASIC programming skills and to begin entering programs via terminals. We therefore offer the following humorous program. For the fun of it, key in this program and see what happens.

```
10 PRINT "HI, MY NAME IS SHEILA, WHAT IS YOURS?"
20 INPUT N$
30 PRINT "HI, ";N$;" HOW ARE YOU?"
40 INPUT H$
50 PRINT "I AM GLAD YOU ARE ";H$
60 PRINT "TIME TO GO NOW—SEE YOU LATER"
70 END
RUN
```

In entering this program, you will find many errors that novice programmers make and get a feel for keying data from a terminal.

record check and determine when the data to be processed has been exhausted. It does not have a statement that combines the reading of data and a check for the last data item. These two operations are therefore represented in two separate statements. The READ or INPUT statement enters data for processing. The IF/THEN statement, representing the 9's Decision, searches for the 9's Data, which indicates the last record to be processed. The 9's Data takes the place of the last record processed. When it is read and then identified by the IF/THEN statement, this indicates that no further data exists. It indicates that the looping has ended and the program can begin other forms of processing (i.e., the output of grand totals).

ILLUSTRATIVE PROBLEM 2

The problem is to process an employee's gross pay. Input to the problem are the employee's name, hours worked, and rate of pay. Output are the employee's name and gross pay. The formula for gross pay is

Gross pay = hours worked ∗ rate of pay

The data for this problem are the following:

Employee Name	Hours Worked	Rate of Pay
A. Abbot	40	2.50
B. Brown	30	3.00
C. Coffy	35	4.00

Use a 9's Decision to control processing.

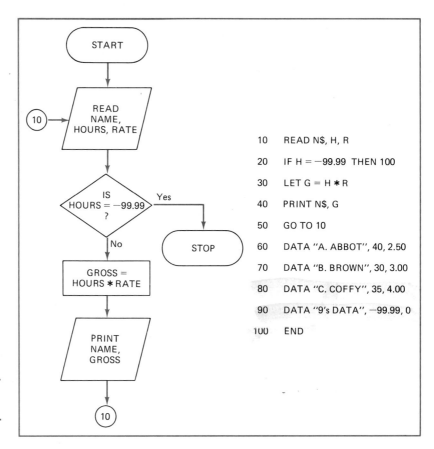

The following BASIC program is shown:

10	READ N$, H, R
20	IF H = −99.99 THEN 100
30	LET G = H * R
40	PRINT N$, G
50	GO TO 10
60	DATA "A. ABBOT", 40, 2.50
70	DATA "B. BROWN", 30, 3.00
80	DATA "C. COFFY", 35, 4.00
90	DATA "9's DATA", −99.99, 0
100	END

FIGURE 8.13 The flow-chart solution for Illustrative Problem 2 and the BASIC program written from that flowchart.

The flowchart and the BASIC program for Illustrative Problem 2 are given in Figure 8.13. The 9's Decision is required because more than one employee's data is to be processed. Predictably, the READ symbol is placed immediately before the 9's Decision. Statement 10, the READ statement of the program, accurately defines the input of the three variables, N$, H, and R. In the program, the 9's Decision of the flowchart is converted into its BASIC equivalent, the IF/THEN statement.

IF/THEN Statement

BASIC uses the **IF/THEN statement** to complete all logical operations. The statement indicates, "If this condition occurs, then go there." To understand the IF/THEN statement, you must examine its structure. Consider statement 20 in Figure 8.13:

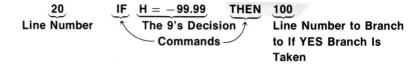

20	IF H = −99.99	THEN 100
Line Number	The 9's Decision — Commands —	**Line Number to Branch to If YES Branch Is Taken**

The number 20 is the line number of the IF/THEN statement. BASIC syntax requires the words IF and THEN as parts of the instruction. The condition, H = −99.99, represents the 9's Decision and is derived directly from the flowchart. The condition used is always placed between the words IF and THEN and takes the form of an equation. The line number 100 indicates the statement number the program will branch to if the 9's Data is encountered. The statement number at the end of the IF/THEN statement is the equivalent of the YES branch of a decision. It provides the statement number to branch to if the condition is satisfied.

If H is equal to −99.99, then the program will branch to statement 100. Statement 100 is the END statement. This is the equivalent of taking the YES branch of the 9's Decision to the STOP symbol.

The IF/THEN statement also affects the proper use of the DATA statements. In the original problem definition, only three sets of employee data were specified. However, in the program, four DATA statements are listed. The fourth DATA statement, statement 90, contains the 9's Data. Whenever an IF/THEN statement represents a 9's Decision, a DATA statement containing the 9's Data must be included in the program.

The DATA statement used to represent the 9's Data must conform to all other data statements. Statements 60, 70, and 80 of the program all contain three data items. In each DATA statement, string variable data is followed by two numeric data items. Statement 90 uses the same sequence. This consistency is necessary for the proper input of the 9's Data using statement 10. That READ statement inputs N$, H, and R. If, for example, either of the following DATA statements were used

90 DATA−9.99
90 DATA "9's DATA",−99.99

the READ statement would reject it. The program would not be processed. Figure 8.14 describes the relationship between variables being input and the specification of 9's Data.

FIGURE 8.14 The DATA statement containing the 9's Data must use the same format as all other DATA statements and must define data as dictated by the READ statement. A string variable is followed by the input of two numbers. Note that the 9's Data, −99.99, is the second item of statement 90 and matches the numeric variable H. This match is necessary for completing the 9's Decision.

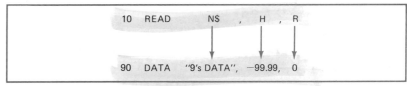

Note also in Figure 8.14 that the 9's Data, -99.99, is the second item of statement 90 and is therefore associated with the second variable, H, in the READ statement. This match-up is fundamental to the success of the 9's Decision. Consider what would occur if statement 90 were written

90 DATA "9's DATA", 0, –99.99
N$ H   R

The variable H would be assigned the value 0, and R would be set equal to -99.99. With these values, the IF/THEN statement using $H = -99.99$ would not be valid, and the program would not be processed properly. It is imperative that the 9's Data statement be properly written. This ensures that the variable used in the 9's Decision is actually assigned the 9's Data.

The proper alignment of the 9's Data is also critical when many items of data are input. A common error is to overload one of the data items and omit it from the 9's Data statement. Thus, instead of having the required number of data items, the statement is one short.

IF/THEN statements are also constructed to handle logical operations involving alphabetic or alphameric data. Quotation marks in the IF/THEN statement define the testing of alphabetic or alphameric data. Consider the following statement:

40 IF A$ = "M" THEN 100

Line number 40 identifies the statement. The terms IF and THEN are required syntax. Because alphabetic or alphameric data are being tested, a string variable must be used. The data tested for is defined in quotes. Assume that you are testing for an employee's sex and that the code M defines a male and F a female. Thus, the data M appears in quotes ("M") after the equal sign of the condition. The statement number 100 is the line number branched to if the field A$ equals M.

The rules governing branching operations are simple. If the answer to the conditional statement is yes, then the program branches to the line number written at the end of the IF/THEN statement. If the answer is no, the program does not branch away, but continues on to the next statement. In the program of Illustrative Problem 2, if the variable H equals -99.99, the program branches to statement 100. If H does not equal -99.99, then the program automatically progresses to statement 30.

The LET statement computes the gross pay of the individual employee. Statement 40 provides for the output of N$ and G, using print zones 1 and 2, respectively. After processing and output, the processing loop ends, and the program should unconditionally branch back to the READ statement, line number 10. This branch is represented in BASIC by the GO TO statement.

GO TO Statement

The **GO TO statement** is BASIC's unconditional branching statement. It allows for direct branching from one statement to another and is essential to the construction of the program loop. The syntax of the GO TO statement is as follows:

50	GO TO	10
Line Number	Command	Line Number That Is Unconditionally Branched to

The structure of the GO TO statement is simple. It is made up of the necessary line number, command, and statement number to which the program will branch.

Statement 50 in the example causes the program to unconditionally branch to statement 10, the READ statement. At statement 10, the program loop is restarted and the next employee's data is input. The processing of that data is therefore begun. The GO TO statement permits the loop to be performed three times, which is sufficient to process the three sets of employee data. On the fourth loop, the 9's Data is read and processing ends.

The printed output of the BASIC program for Illustrative Problem 2 might have appeared as follows:

A.	ABBOT	100.00
B.	BROWN	90.00
C.	COFFY	140.00

THE PROGRAM LOOP

When program loops use the GO TO statement, an error that is often made in haste is to direct the unconditional branch to the wrong statement. Consider the following program excerpt:

```
10 READ A,B,C
20 IF A=999 THEN 160
........................
80 GO TO 20
```

The intent of statement 80 is to direct the unconditional branch to the READ statement and to restart the program loop. But examine statement 80, and note the error. Instead of branching to statement 10, the program will incorrectly branch to statement 20. The program will enter an endless loop if it is run. The computer will seem to have stopped processing. Ask your instructor how to stop this loop and correct the GO TO statement.

THE "OUT OF DATA" ERROR AND 9'S DECISION

Many students underestimate the importance of a 9's Decision, the equivalent of the last record check when a loop is used in a BASIC program. Without the 9's Decision or its equivalent, the program would not run to completion, but would eventually run out of data. This condition would signal an error state to the computer and would cause the program to be immediately flushed from the system. We can observe this situation from the program and its results that follow.

```
10 READ N$,H,R
20 REMARK – 9'S DECISION POSITIONED HERE
30 LET G=H*R
40 PRINT N$,H,R,G
50 GO TO 10
60 DATA "BROWN",40,2.50
70 DATA "JONES",30,3.50
80 DATA "SMITH",25,4.25
90 DATA "LAST",–99.99,0
100 END
```

The program consists of 10 statements numbered 10 to 100 and provides the following results:

BROWN	40	2.5	100
JONES	30	3.5	105
SMITH	25	4.25	106.25
LAST	–99.99	0	0

?Out of data at line 10

Analyzing the program and its results, we note that the program accepted data on each loop, and that four loops were completed to process the four individuals' data items. After the fourth loop, the program branched back to statement 10 to start the fifth loop. But a fifth data item did not exist. At this point, the error condition occurred. No data was available when the fifth READ operation was initiated, and the computer concluded that an error had occurred. The program did not end properly, but was automatically canceled. The lack of data condition was pointed out by the computer-generated statement shown at the bottom of the printed output, "?Out of data at line 10". The out of data condition was recognized when the computer attempted to complete statement 10. Once the error is recognized, all processing ceases.

Creating Literals Using the PRINT Statement

The employee names, represented by N$, appear in zone 1, and the gross pay amounts, using the variable G, are printed in zone 2. Neither of these columns of data is identified by a heading. In BASIC, it is easy to construct headings and special labels by using the PRINT statement.

Literals in the form of headings or special labels provide valuable descriptive information in outputs. As discussed earlier, headings appear at the top of columns of data in softcopy and hardcopy outputs. Special labels are printed with individual data items to highlight them. Whichever form of literal is chosen, it is created through the PRINT statement.

Literals are generally defined in BASIC with a pair of quotation marks in a PRINT statement. Literals can be of any length up to one line of output. For example, let us create headings for Illustrative Problem 2. Because only two columns of data are involved, the required PRINT statement is coded as

5	PRINT	"EMPLOYEE NAME",	"GROSS PAY"
Line Number	Command	Literal 1	Literal 2

Each literal is defined by its own pair of quotation marks. The first literal, "EMPLOYEE NAME", consists of 13 characters, quotation marks not included. The second literal, "GROSS PAY", consists of 9 characters. These literals are printed in print zones 1 and 2, respectively. The literal following the command PRINT is automatically placed in zone 1. The comma following the first literal directs the second literal to zone 2. The line number ensures that the statement is performed before the READ statement which begins the processing loop. Thus, these headings will be printed before all other output.

Literals for special labels are just as easily created. For example, a special label to precede the printing of a total sales commission could be created with the statement

150 PRINT "TOTAL SALES COMMISSION",T

This label is 22 characters long and would precede the output of T. It would take up all the print positions in zone 1 and four positions in zone 2. This extension into zone 2 would force the output of T into zone 3, because the comma after the literal directs the output of T into the next available zone. A semicolon in statement 150 would retain the output of T in zone 2, beginning with print position 23.

Novice BASIC programmers often confuse the literals of a PRINT statement and the specification of string variable data in DATA statements. This confusion results from the fact that both are defined with pairs of quotation marks.

Though literals were originally intended for output only, some

LITERALS—MISPLACED COMMAS

A common error made in specifying literals is to place commas and quotation marks incorrectly. An examination of the following statement will reveal a simple common error:

10 PRINT "NAME," "GROSS"

Frequently, the comma used to separate literals is improperly placed inside the quotation marks of a literal, negating its use in the PRINT statement. As a result, the comma appears after NAME in the output. Depending on the system, the second literal may or may not be printed.

When a string of literals appears in one PRINT statement, be sure that the commas are positioned outside the quotation marks and between the literals.

manufacturers have incorporated them into INPUT statements. Combining these features eliminates the need for separate PRINT and INPUT statements, where the PRINT statement calls for the type of data and the INPUT statement actually accepts that data. For example, examine the following BASIC statements:

30 PRINT "PLEASE ENTER YOUR CODE NUMBER"
40 INPUT C

and the specialized INPUT statement that replaces both:

35 INPUT "PLEASE ENTER YOUR CODE NUMBER"; C

In the first set of statements, line 30 prompts the user by defining the data to enter, and line 40 permits the entry of that code number. Statement 35 combines both operations. In line 35, quotation marks define the prompting literal and precede the variable C, the numeric variable name assigned to the code. Note that the required punctuation is a semicolon, not a comma.

Alphameric data is just as easily entered in this form of INPUT instruction. The type of data entered is defined by the type of variable following the input literal. The sample statement below illustrates how a student's name, identified by the string variable name N$, could be entered using an INPUT statement incorporating a literal.

20 INPUT "ENTER NAME OF STUDENT"; N$

Rules on literals in INPUT statements are consistent with rules on literals in output operations. But because this form of INPUT statement does not occur in some versions of BASIC, we caution the user to check its availability. Literals in INPUT statements are helpful for large volumes of interactive I/O operations. They continually advise the person seated at the terminal of the next data item to be entered.

REMARK Statement

Frequently, in long programs, programmers find it necessary to add notes or reminders to themselves. A note might indicate that statements 100 to 250 compute the individual FICA and retirement deductions or that this section of the program produces all the error messages. This type of comment is created with the **REMARK statement.** The REMARK statement should not be confused with a literal. The descriptive comments in the REMARK statement *are never output;* they appear only in the source program. Their purpose is to assist the programmer and clarify potential points of confusion. Some programming managers believe so strongly in REMARK statements that they are required in all software written.

The structure of a REMARK statement is as follows:

4	REMARK	BASIC PROGRAM FOR ILLUSTRATIVE PROB. 2
Line Number	Command	Descriptive Note for Programmer

The above statement could be used with Illustrative Problem 2. It would appear as the first statement of the program. It would identify the program without affecting its processing.

Because REMARK statements do not affect processing, they can occur anywhere in a BASIC program before the END statement. Also, there is no restriction on the types of characters they can contain.

Figure 8.15 illustrates the results of including literals and REMARK statements in the flowchart and program for Illustrative Problem 2. The legend shows the processed output.

We have now introduced the fundamental instructions of the BASIC programming language. Essentially, you have all the instructions you need to become good BASIC programmers. Though many of you may be confident of your abilities, additional illustrative examples will reinforce the concepts presented.

ILLUSTRATIVE PROBLEM 3

The overall problem relates to the computation of a sales commission. Input to the problem are the salesperson's name and three sales amounts. These sales amounts are added to compute total sales. Commissions are a straight 10 percent of the total sales amount. Output each salesperson's name, total sales amount, and commission. Headings for each column of data should be printed on output. Use a 9's Decision. The data for this problem follows:

Salesperson Name	Sale 1	Sale 2	Sale 3
J. Boyd	85.20	41.50	30.30
C. Clock	95.40	106.20	18.40
R. Roger	50.00	49.95	639.05
C. Kent	7.90	6.90	4.20

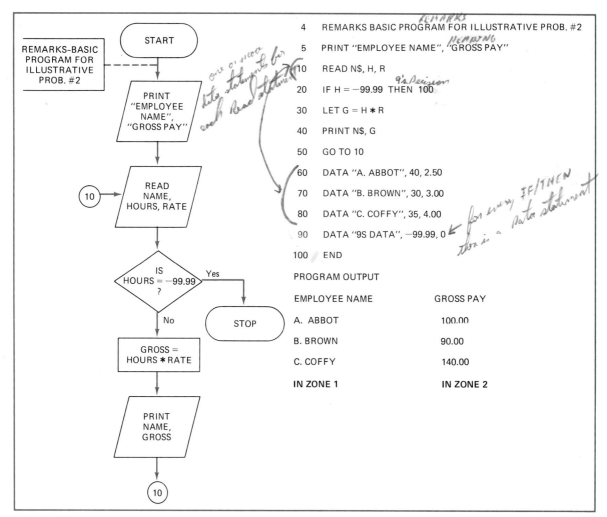

FIGURE 8.15 The rewritten BASIC program and flowchart for Illustrative Problem 2. These solutions include the REMARK statement, line 4, and the printing of a heading via line 5. Note that their insertion has not affected the original program.

The flowchart, BASIC program, and output printed by processing Illustrative Problem 3 are given in Figure 8.16.

The prior program solution clearly was written directly from the flowchart. Each statement is properly coded according to the rules of BASIC. The REMARK statement identifies the program. Statement 20 uses three literals to provide headings atop each column of data. The program loop is defined by statements 30 through 80. The printing of each salesperson's data is accomplished by statement 70. The sales-

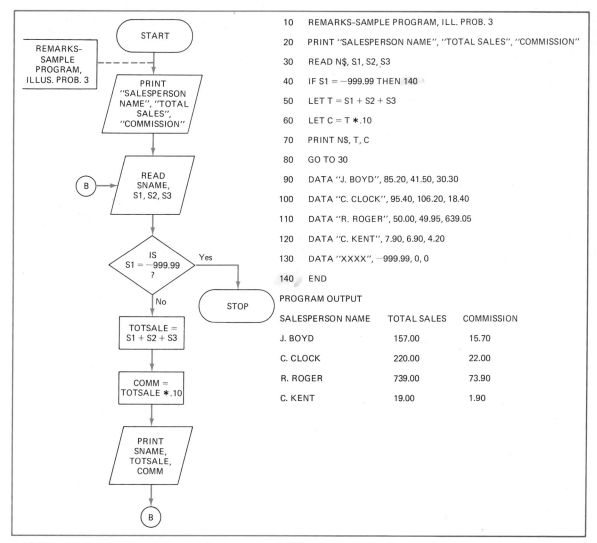

```
10    REMARKS-SAMPLE PROGRAM, ILL. PROB. 3
20    PRINT "SALESPERSON NAME", "TOTAL SALES", "COMMISSION"
30    READ N$, S1, S2, S3
40    IF S1 = −999.99 THEN 140
50    LET T = S1 + S2 + S3
60    LET C = T *.10
70    PRINT N$, T, C
80    GO TO 30
90    DATA "J. BOYD", 85.20, 41.50, 30.30
100   DATA "C. CLOCK", 95.40, 106.20, 18.40
110   DATA "R. ROGER", 50.00, 49.95, 639.05
120   DATA "C. KENT", 7.90, 6.90, 4.20
130   DATA "XXXX", −999.99, 0, 0
140   END
```

PROGRAM OUTPUT

SALESPERSON NAME	TOTAL SALES	COMMISSION
J. BOYD	157.00	15.70
C. CLOCK	220.00	22.00
R. ROGER	739.00	73.90
C. KENT	19.00	1.90

FIGURE 8.16 The flowchart solution and the BASIC program for Illustrative Problem 3. The program is derived from the flowchart.

person name N$, total sales amount T, and commission C are printed in zones 1, 2, and 3 under their respective headings.

The 9's Decision is represented in statement 40. The 9's Data is provided in statement 130. Note that the data −999.99 is in the position associated with the variable S1. This ensures that the 9's Data is available for the 9's Decision. Statement 130 contains data for four variables, exactly the number of variables specified in the READ statement, line number 30. When the 9's Data is sensed by the 9's Decision, the program unconditionally branches to statement 140, the END statement.

The student programmer is now ready to begin writing and processing his or her BASIC programs. Sufficient instructions for flow-charting and coding problems have been presented. Though computer systems differ, almost all systems supporting BASIC require some system commands for processing individual programs. These commands vary extensively among manufacturers, so it is best to check with your instructor or laboratory assistant before running your program. Some system commands used with BASIC are fairly standard. A selection of these instructions is reviewed next.

LITERALS—OMISSION OF COMMAS OR SEMICOLONS

Another common error made in working with literals is the total omission of commas or semicolons from the PRINT statement. Instead of appearing as follows:

10 PRINT "NAME", "GROSS", "FICA", "NET"

a statement is incorrectly written as

10 PRINT "NAME" "GROSS" "FICA" "NET"

Commas or semicolons must be placed between all variables and literals in PRINT statements.

Selected System Commands

Each computer system has its own set of commands that lets the student programmer access the computer via a terminal. Generally, the series of steps used to contact and create an online link to the computer is referred to as a **LOGON procedure.** Conversely, the steps to break contact with the computer when programming is completed are generally called a **LOGOFF procedure.** You "LOGON" to begin programming and "LOGOFF" to finish. Ordinarily a computer laboratory provides each student with its LOGON and LOGOFF instructions.

Once the LOGON procedure has been accepted by the computer, the programmer is ready to begin entering his or her BASIC program via the terminal. As previously discussed, BASIC statements are entered one at a time. Programmers begin with the first statement (10) of their program and work their way down the list of statements. During the keying-in of these statements, errors are common. In many instances, the error is easily corrected by retyping the entire statement.

The newly keyed, correct statement completely replaces the old statement. Occasionally, however, a statement has to be removed from a program. Removing a particular instruction from a BASIC program is accomplished with a **DELETE command.** This command does not require a line number and appears as

DELETE 60

if statement 60 is the instruction slated for removal. The DELETE command is extremely useful for removing a number of consecutive statements. You could eliminate lines 80 to 140 from a program with

DELETE 80-140

Another vehicle is often used to eliminate individual lines from a program. It is possible to remove a specific line by merely typing its line number, without a command or variable, and entering it. The sole entry of the line number 80 is sufficient to remove that line from a program.

Statements undergo many changes during the online entry of a BASIC program or during debugging. During this process, it is often necessary for the programmer to view the current corrected version of the program. This listing of the program's current state helps the programmer determine the extent of the work remaining and corrections that have already been accomplished. This clean listing can be obtained using the **LIST command,** which directs the computer to print or display all statements currently in the program.

This statement is simply written as

LIST

and requires no line number or variables.

Once the program is correctly entered, it must be processed. The **RUN command** directs the computer to begin processing the program and is written as

RUN

This command requires no line number or variables. The computer will attempt to process the program once it receives the RUN command. If there are no errors, the program will be processed to completion. However, if syntax errors are found, the BASIC compiler will attempt to highlight these mistakes by identifying the line number and type of error. The programmer must then begin the debugging effort.

Some schools let students store their BASIC programs in the computer system. Each student is assigned storage space in a part of an online storage device. Students then can work on a program, store it,

FINDING THE ERROR

During the execution of a program, the BASIC compiler will attempt to pinpoint the error which resulted in the program's cancellation. Even with that assistance, programmers must often look further to find the true source of an error. Consider the following program and its related output.

Program Listing

```
10   READ N$,H,R
20   IF H=-99.99 THEN 100
30   LET G=H*R
40   PRINT N$,H,R,G
50   GO TO 10
60   DATA "BROWN",40,2.50
70   DATA "JONES",30,3.50
80   DATA "GEORGE"50,3.25
90   DATA "LAST",-99.99,0
100  END
```

Output with Computer-Generated Message

```
BROWN     40     2.5     100
JONES     30     3.5     105
%Data format error at line 10
```

When we examine the output, we note that only two of the three valid data items were printed, with the error occurring in the processing of the third employee's data. The computer-generated message, identified by a % sign, indicates that a **data format error** was evident *at line 10*. We first carefully scrutinize line number 10, the READ statement. No error exists in the syntax of statement 10.

Uncovering no error at line 10, we should turn to line 80, the third item of data. In examining this DATA statement, we note that the comma required to separate "GEORGE" and 50 is missing. This omission was enough to invalidate statement 80 and cause the error that aborted the program's processing.

The question most often asked is, "Why didn't the computer flag statement 80 instead of line 10?" The answer is that the computer encountered the data error when it attempted to execute statement 10. Thus it identified the error in relation to the statement undergoing execution. The phrase "data format error" indicates that the error may have been in the data used and that the data should be checked. Most programmers examine all statements related to suggested errors, but initially focus their attention on lines highlighted by the computer. With experience, most programmers develop their own debugging aids.

and recall it later to continue their work. Two commands associated with this storage of BASIC programs are the **SAVE** and **UNSAVE commands.** These commands do not require a line number or variable. The SAVE command is ordinarily used to store a program. The UNSAVE command lets a user remove a program from storage, freeing that space for the storage of another program.

These and other commands are used in processing BASIC programs. Each computer system varies in its support of BASIC, so it is best to check with your instructor before using any equipment. Usually at the start of BASIC programming, each class is shown how to use the laboratory terminals and told all the operational commands particular to the computer system. A sound knowledge of these commands will simplify your programming task.

8.4 Accumulators and Selected Problems

Accumulators

You know from Chapter 6 that accumulators are used to compute grand totals. Essentially, the accumulator is a kind of running total. The computations associated with the accumulator are

1 The initialization of the accumulator (T = 0)
2 The accumulation of data in each repetition of the loop (T = T + G)

Because these computations are easily converted to formulas, they are readily represented in BASIC. Both computations are handled in LET statements. The incorporation of these statements in a BASIC program solution is shown in Illustrative Problem 4.

ILLUSTRATIVE PROBLEM 4

The problem is to compute and accumulate net pay. Input to the problem are the employee's name, hours worked, and rate of pay. The formulas used in processing are

Gross pay = hours worked * rate of pay
FICA = gross pay * .0628
Net pay = gross pay − FICA

Output each employee's name, gross pay, FICA deduction, and net pay. Print this data under the headings NAME, GROSS, FICA, and NET. Compute the grand total of all net pay given to the employees. Print this accumulated total, preceded by a special label, when no additional data exists. Use a 9's Decision. The data for this problem are

Name	Hours	Rate
W. Chester	35	3.00
H. Furst	40	3.50
A. Arbor	30	10.00
E. Vator	32	4.00

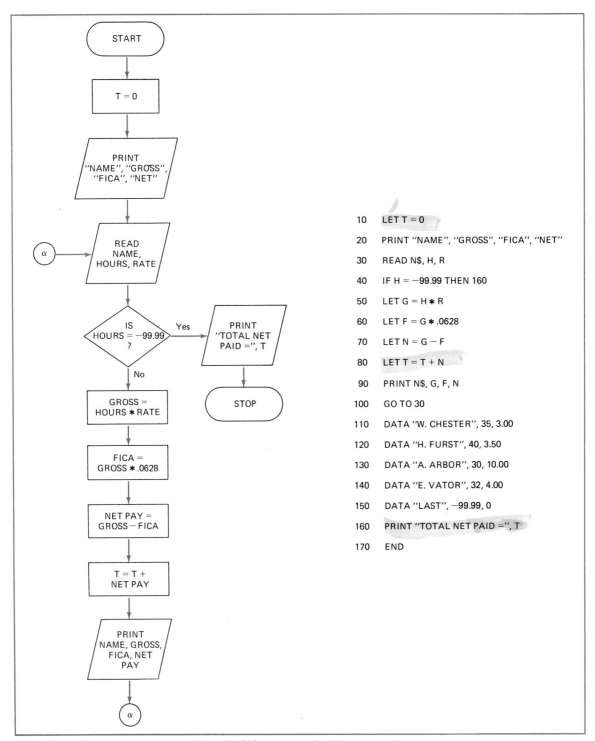

```
10     LET T = 0
20     PRINT "NAME", "GROSS", "FICA", "NET"
30     READ N$, H, R
40     IF H = −99.99 THEN 160
50     LET G = H * R
60     LET F = G * .0628
70     LET N = G − F
80     LET T = T + N
90     PRINT N$, G, F, N
100    GO TO 30
110    DATA "W. CHESTER", 35, 3.00
120    DATA "H. FURST", 40, 3.50
130    DATA "A. ARBOR", 30, 10.00
140    DATA "E. VATOR", 32, 4.00
150    DATA "LAST", −99.99, 0
160    PRINT "TOTAL NET PAID =", T
170    END
```

FIGURE 8.17   The flowchart and the BASIC program for Illustrative Problem 4.

ACCUMULATORS

When decisions and loops are incorporated into BASIC programs, the programmer must keep track of which statements are to be branched to. This is extremely important when the output of accumulators must occur in a program. Consider the following statements:

```
20  READ N$,H,R
30  IF H=-99.99 THEN 210
............................
200 PRINT "TOTAL NET=", T
210 END
```

should say T 210, not 210

This program excerpt includes a 9's Decision (statement 30) and the output of an accumulated total of net pay (statement 200). The error occurs in statement 30. When the 9's Data is encountered, the program branches to line 210. In doing so, the program branches around statement 200, which prints out the total net T.

This type of error occurs frequently when the programmer realizes the program must end and inadvertently branches to the END statement. The common reaction is, "I wonder why the program isn't printing out the total net T?" The program has branched completely around that statement, and thus the computer never executes it.

The flowchart and the BASIC program written for Illustrative Problem 4 appear in Figure 8.17. This solution permits examination of a larger BASIC program. Again you must recognize that the BASIC program solution is derived from the flowchart. Of course, the variable names are altered to suit the syntax of BASIC, but the logic of the solution is detailed in the flowchart.

Statements 10 and 80 relate directly to the accumulator. The statement LET T = 0 initializes the accumulator T at zero. Statement 80 accumulates each employee's net pay on every repetition. Each formula is easily represented in a LET statement.

The DATA statements, 110 through 140, contain valid data. Statement 150, containing the 9's Data, is the last DATA statement read. When read, it causes the program to branch from statement 40, the 9's Decision, to statement 160. This PRINT statement uses a literal to output the label TOTAL NET PAID = before printing the accumulated total of net pay. This output precedes the END statement.

The accumulated total T is the last item printed. It appears in zone 2, while the special label fits in zone 1. Each heading is printed above the appropriate column of data in the four print zones.

The statements needed for an accumulator are easily inserted. Two LET statements (10 and 80) and one PRINT statement (160) support the accumulator. All the other statements of this program are consistent with those previously discussed.

The output of the program for Illustrative Problem 4 involved four variables, printed in the four print zones. The next section solves the problem of printing five variables on one line.

Multiple Outputs on One Line

SEMI - COLON

As we have discussed, the use of the semicolon in a PRINT statement permits the output of four or more variables on one line. The semicolon is inserted between variables in the PRINT statement to permit a multiple output. Any combination of commas and semicolons is acceptable for this purpose. The requirements of the problem will dictate their placement. Illustrative Problem 5 develops the proper use of these punctuation marks in a PRINT statement.

ILLUSTRATIVE PROBLEM 5

The problem is to compute final student averages. Input are a student's name and three test marks. The student's final average is computed by adding the three test marks and dividing by three. Print out each student's name, three test marks, and final averages on one line. Appropriate headings are required above each of the five columns of data. Use a 9's Decision. The data for this problem are

Student Name	Mark 1	Mark 2	Mark 3
A. Dart	70	63	14
J. Green	54	56	62
P. Peter	89	82	86
T. Thomas	61	90	84

Figure 8.18 gives the flowchart and the BASIC program for Illustrative Problem 5. The program solution contains two REMARK statements. Their position and appearance illustrate the fact that REMARK statements can be placed anywhere in a BASIC program and that they can be used for identification purposes or additional commentary.

Semicolons are used in PRINT statements 20 and 80. Statement 20 creates the headings printed at the top of each column of data. The first literal, "STUDENT NAME", occupies the first 12 print positions of zone 1. The second literal, "MARK 1 ", is seven characters long and occupies print positions 19 to 25 of zone 2. The third literal, "MARK 2 ", is also seven characters long. Because of the semicolon, it is placed adjacent to the second heading in print positions 26 to 32 in zone 2. The same logic applies to the fourth literal, "MARK 3 ", and it occupies positions 33 to 39. This literal extends three print positions into zone 3. Thus, the fifth literal, "AVERAGE", preceded by a comma, is printed in the first position of zone 4, print position 55. Interspersing commas and semicolons permits the simultaneous printing of these

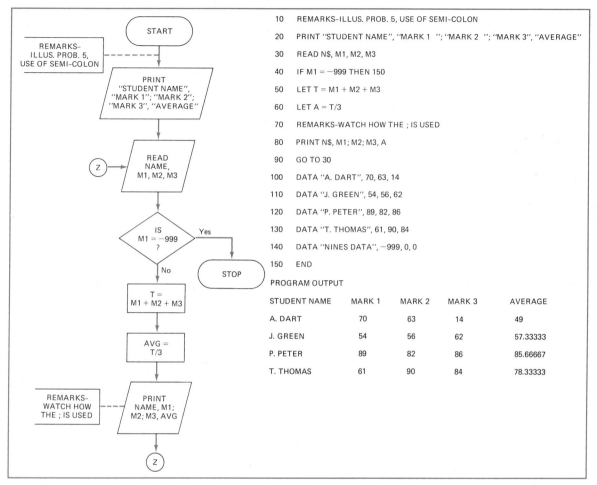

FIGURE 8.18 The flowchart solution and the BASIC program for Illustrative Problem 5.

five items in one line. Whenever the printing of any special outputs involves the use of commas and semicolons, the format should be initially laid out print position by print position.

The 9's Decision is defined by statement 40 of the solution. The 9's Data is supplied in statement 140. The digits −999 are assigned to the position of the DATA statement that associates them with M1, the variable used in the 9's Decision (statement 40). Statement 140, the fifth DATA statement, supplies the 9's Data. It follows the format of all other DATA statements.

Almost all the information output from a computer appears in a visual format. Thus, it is important that all computer outputs be legible and useful. Programmers must be extremely patient in detailing the outputs of their programs.

Multiple Decisions

One conclusion you may already have drawn is that once a flowchart is written, the subsequent coding of the source program is easy. In prior examples, the BASIC programs practically followed their flowchart solutions step by step. The same holds true in examples involving multiple decisions.

ILLUSTRATIVE PROBLEM 6

The overall problem involves the computation of an individual salesperson's commission and the accumulation of all commissions paid. The input of the problem is the salesperson's name and three sales amounts. These three amounts are added to compute a total sales amount. If this amount > $250, the commission is 20 percent of total sales. If not, the commission rate is 10 percent. Output each salesperson's name, total sales amount, and commission. Print headings above the three columns of data and precede the output of the accumulated total with the label "TOTAL COMMISSION PAID = ".

Salesperson Name	Sale 1	Sale 2	Sale 3
A. Barnett	29.00	62.50	149.50
H. Hardt	100.00	265.00	139.00
M. Darcet	67.40	88.50	409.10

The program and flowchart for Illustrative Problem 6 appear in Figure 8.19. The multiple decisions of this problem are evident in statements 50 and 70. Statement 50 represents the 9's Decision. Statement 70 is the comparison of the total sales amount and $250 to determine the commission rate.

One interesting aspect of this problem relates to the computation of the individual salesperson's commission. Statement 60 computes the total sales amount by adding the three sales amounts input. Statement 70 tests this total sales amount against $250. If the total sales amount is greater than $250, the program branches to statement 100 and computes the commission at 20 percent. If this total amount is less than or equal to $250, the program does not branch to statement 100, but continues to statement 80. Statement 80 computes the individual commission at 10 percent. The next statement, statement 90, unconditionally branches around line number 100 to statement 110 to add the individual salesperson's commission to the accumulator.

The GO TO statement is essential for the accurate computation of the 10 percent commission. Without that statement, the program would have proceeded from LET C = S*.10 to LET C = S*.20, and the commission rate would have been computed twice: the first time using 10 percent and the second time using 20 percent. The second computation would have completely erased the first. Thus all commissions would have been computed at 20 percent. Statement 90, the GO TO statement, avoids this error. This statement correctly branches around the second computation and adds the computed 10 percent

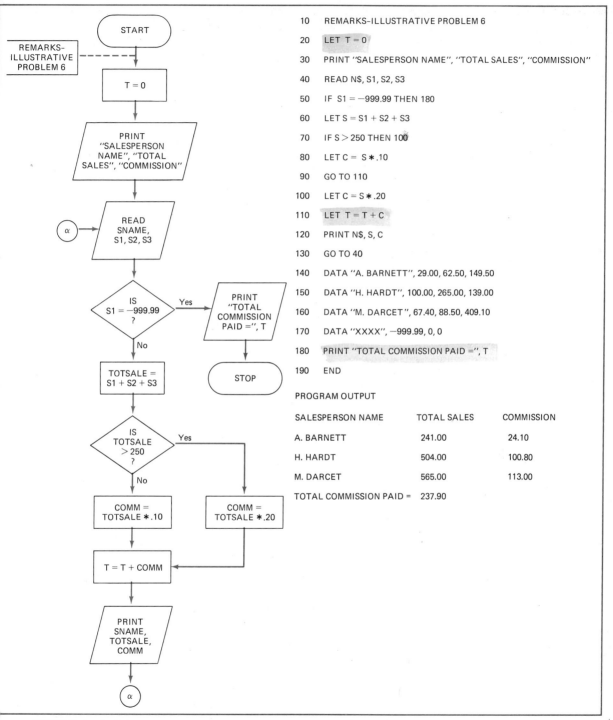

10	REMARKS-ILLUSTRATIVE PROBLEM 6
20	LET T = 0
30	PRINT "SALESPERSON NAME", "TOTAL SALES", "COMMISSION"
40	READ N$, S1, S2, S3
50	IF S1 = −999.99 THEN 180
60	LET S = S1 + S2 + S3
70	IF S > 250 THEN 100
80	LET C = S * .10
90	GO TO 110
100	LET C = S * .20
110	LET T = T + C
120	PRINT N$, S, C
130	GO TO 40
140	DATA "A. BARNETT", 29.00, 62.50, 149.50
150	DATA "H. HARDT", 100.00, 265.00, 139.00
160	DATA "M. DARCET", 67.40, 88.50, 409.10
170	DATA "XXXX", −999.99, 0, 0
180	PRINT "TOTAL COMMISSION PAID =", T
190	END

PROGRAM OUTPUT

SALESPERSON NAME	TOTAL SALES	COMMISSION
A. BARNETT	241.00	24.10
H. HARDT	504.00	100.80
M. DARCET	565.00	113.00
TOTAL COMMISSION PAID =	237.90	

FIGURE 8.19 The flowchart and the BASIC program for Illustrative Problem 6.

commission to the accumulator T. The computation and accumulation of all commissions are therefore accurately performed.

The remainder of this program is consistent with previously illustrated programs. A fourth DATA statement is added to accommodate the 9's Decision. The YES branch of the 9's Decision, statement 180, prints the accumulated total T and precedes this amount with the output of the literal TOTAL COMMISSION PAID =.

The individual salesperson's data is printed in print zones 1, 2, and 3. Above each of these three columns of data is a heading. The RE-MARK statement identifies the overall problem and precedes the initial condition of the accumulator, T = 0. The actual update of the accumulator is accomplished in statement 110, which adds each salesperson's commission to the accumulator as the program loop is completed.

Illustrative Problem 6 lets us review other IF/THEN instruction formats which we might have used satisfactorily in the solution. In the original program, two IF/THEN statements were used, one for the 9's Decision (line 50) and one to determine whether the total sales amount was greater than $250 (line 70). In both statements, the response to the YES condition was to branch to the statement indicated. However, with another form of the IF/THEN statement a computation is also possible. The program excerpt below could replace statements 70 to 100 of the original solution to Problem 6 without altering the rest of the program:

70 IF S > 250 THEN C = S*.20
80 IF S < =250 THEN C = S*.10

These two statements eliminate two additional statements from the original program (lines 90 and 100), and GO TO used to branch around line 100 and line 100 itself. We may interpret the new IF/THEN statement as defining the two states we must deal with. If S > 250, then compute the commission using 20 percent. If S < = 250 (less than or equal to), the computation of line 70 is not performed and a commission rate of 10 percent is used in line 80. If S is not greater than 250, it must be less than or equal to 250, and so one of the two commission formulas is used. Effectively, this IF/THEN format permits the program to test for a specific condition and perform a computation related to that decision. This version of the IF/THEN could be helpful in a problem in which many codes must be tested for and handled.

Another form of IF/THEN instruction, supported by most BASIC compilers, is the **IF/THEN/ELSE statement.** Again, this format lets the program choose between two conditions, but *within one instruction.* Statements 70 and 80 of the previous example could be replaced by the statement

70 IF S > 250 THEN C = S*.20 ELSE C = S*.10

This instruction is read as, IF this occurs, THEN do this, ELSE do that. It permits one conditional statement to handle two opposite, but related, states. If S > 250, then the 20 percent rate is used; otherwise the 10 percent rate is used. Note that this IF/THEN format would eliminate three statements from the original solution for Illustrative Problem 6.

Programmers can use any of the three IF/THEN formats in their BASIC programs. Each has advantages for specific applications. Experience will guide the programmer in which format is best in a particular case.

8.5
Counters and Automated Program Loops
Counters

Counters can control the execution of loops in a program. The series of steps in the loop is processed an exact number of times. The counter monitors the completion of these loops and identifies the attainment of the prescribed number of repetitions. The three components of a counter are

1 The initialization of the counter (K = 1)
2 The decision used to test for completion of the final loop (for example, Is K = 25?)
3 The increment of the counter (K = K + 1)

An illustration will show how easily counters are incorporated in BASIC program solutions.

ILLUSTRATIVE PROBLEM 7

The general problem relates to the computation of final averages for exactly five students.* Input are the student's name and three test marks. The final average is computed using these three test marks. Output each student's name and final average only. These outputs should appear under the headings STUDENT NAME and FINAL AVERAGE. The data for this problem follows.

Student	Mark 1	Mark 2	Mark 3
S. Klone	60	70	80
F. Francis	65	65	65
C. Smith	82	76	83
F. Shore	90	46	77
R. Roberts	65	70	68

*The problem was deliberately restricted to five students for the sake of brevity. The solution is valid for an unlimited number of people. However, the extra data would make the problem unwieldy.

Figure 8.20 presents the flowchart and the program prepared for Illustrative Problem 7. In the program, statements 20, 70, and 80 relate directly to the use of a counter. In statement 20, the counter is initialized at one. Statement 70, an IF/THEN statement, presents the decision employed with the counter to check on the number of loops performed. In this case, it is testing whether the counter has reached five, because that is the number of students involved. The NO branch of this decision directs the program to statement 80. This LET statement increments the counter by one on each repetition, until the counter is five. Statement 90 follows this increment and completes the program loop, returning the program to statement 40 for the processing of the next student's data.

The loop is executed exactly five times. On the first loop, when K = 1, the first student's grades are compiled and output. On the second loop, when K = 2, the second student is processed. This looping process continues until the fifth and last student is handled.

Note that only five DATA statements, 100 through 140, are used in the program. The additional DATA statement, which normally holds the 9's Data, is not required. The computed results are printed beneath the required headings in print zones 1 and 2. After the fifth student's data is processed, the YES branch of statement 70 is taken. The program branches to statement 150, the END statement, and is finished.

THE DATA STATEMENT

Errors in assigning data are common in BASIC programming. Most often, the DATA statement is incorrectly written. For example, the data 17, 61, and 38 must be assigned to the variables A, B, and C. A correct method of inputting the data is written as follows:

10 READ A,B,C
20 DATA 17,61,38

The variables are specified in statement 10, the READ statement, and three items of data are provided by the DATA statement, line 20.

However, this input of data might be incorrectly written as follows:

20 DATA A = 17,B = 61,C = 38

This statement is *incorrect* because it violates the syntax of BASIC.

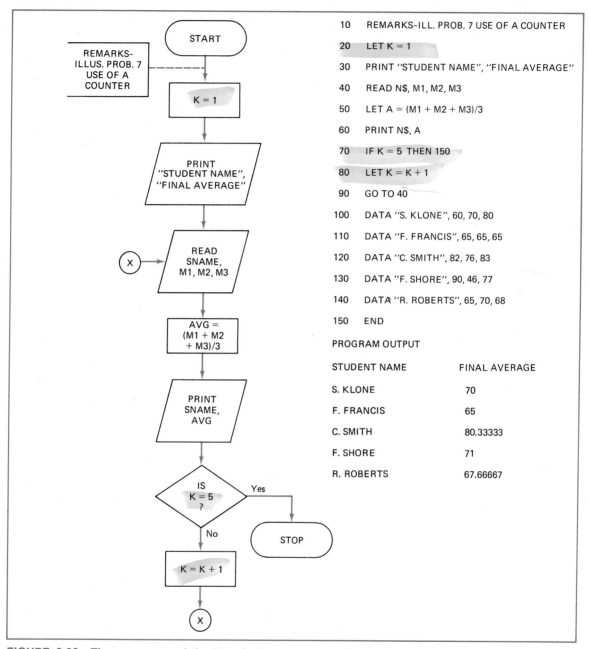

```
10    REMARKS-ILL. PROB. 7 USE OF A COUNTER
20    LET K = 1
30    PRINT "STUDENT NAME", "FINAL AVERAGE"
40    READ N$, M1, M2, M3
50    LET A = (M1 + M2 + M3)/3
60    PRINT N$, A
70    IF K = 5 THEN 150
80    LET K = K + 1
90    GO TO 40
100   DATA "S. KLONE", 60, 70, 80
110   DATA "F. FRANCIS", 65, 65, 65
120   DATA "C. SMITH", 82, 76, 83
130   DATA "F. SHORE", 90, 46, 77
140   DATA "R. ROBERTS", 65, 70, 68
150   END
```

PROGRAM OUTPUT

STUDENT NAME	FINAL AVERAGE
S. KLONE	70
F. FRANCIS	65
C. SMITH	80.33333
F. SHORE	71
R. ROBERTS	67.66667

FIGURE 8.20 **The program and the flowchart prepared for Illustrative Problem 7. Note that flowcharting concepts related to a counter are readily handled in BASIC. Lines 20, 70, 80, and 90 relate directly to a counter. A 9's Data statement was not required in this problem, since a counter was used.**

The following problem reinforces the concept of a counter.

ILLUSTRATIVE PROBLEM 8	

**ILLUSTRATIVE
PROBLEM 8**

The overall problem relates to the computation of the grand total of five sets of three numbers. For the three numeric variables input, use the variable names A, B, and C. On each repetition, the total of the given set of three numbers is accumulated into the grand total and then output on one line. Double space each line of output. After the last set of variables is processed, output the computed grand total. Precede this accumulated total with the label "GRAND TOTAL =". No headings are required. Use a counter. The data for this problem is

A	B	C
17	61	38
9	30	42
12	19	76
7	28	47
12	21	77

The program and the flowchart depicting the use of a counter to process Illustrative Problem 8 appear in Figure 8.21. The three statements related to the counter are statements 10, 90, and 100. Statements 10 and 100 initialize and increment the counter, respectively. Statement 90 relates to the decision, Is K = 5? Five program loops are needed to process the five sets of data. The DATA statements are 120 to 160. After all data is processed, at statement 90, the program branches to line number 170. That PRINT statement outputs the accumulated total T and the special label to precede the amount. With that output performed, the program proceeds to line 180, the END statement, to complete its processing.

Statement 70 prints each of the three variables in print zones 1, 2, and 3. Statement 80 creates a blank line of output. Thus a line of print is followed by a blank line. This provides the required double spacing in the output. Statement 80 is a perfectly valid statement even though no variables are specified. This is the method used in BASIC to skip lines in an output. Each language has its own method of accomplishing this task. Programmers should check the syntax of the source language they are using to determine how to skip lines when outputting data.

Illustrative Problem 8 involved the combined use of an accumulator and a counter. It is also possible to use an accumulator, a counter, and a negative accumulator together in a BASIC program and to monitor the systematic reduction of a predefined quantity. Illustrative Problem 9 presents such an application.

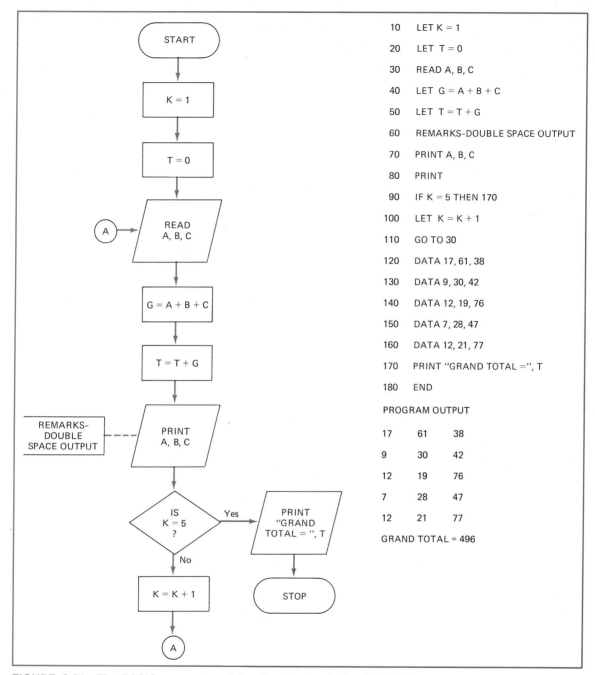

FIGURE 8.21 The BASIC program and the flowchart solution for Illustrative Problem 8.

SYNTAX AND LOGIC ERRORS

This narrative discusses two types of errors: one involves syntax, and the other involves logic.

1 Programmers sometimes forget the BASIC rules for variable names. Thus, an error such as the following is possible: The program is computing an average and the variable name used is AVG. Conceptually, the name is correct, but according to the syntax of BASIC the name is wrong. A variety of numeric variable names including A, A1, and V1 can be used to identify the average computed. The variable names AVG, AV, or AVER are incorrect.

2 When a counter is coded in BASIC, an error in logic sometimes occurs. Examine two sets of statements establishing a counter:

```
10 LET K = 1            10 LET K = 1
20 READ A,B,C           20 READ A,B,C
...............         ...............
80 IF K = 10 THEN 200   80 LET K = K + 1
90 LET K = K + 1        90 If K = 10 THEN 200
100 GO TO 20            100 GO TO 20
```

The left set of instructions is correct. The right set is incorrect. On the left, the increment of the counter (statement 90) follows the decision on the NO branch. The counter will loop exactly 10 times. On the right, the increment of the counter (statement 80) precedes the counter decision. Using these instructions, the counter will loop only nine times, omitting the tenth value and the last loop.

The increment of a counter should always follow on the NO branch of the decision, before the GO TO statement that restarts the program loop.

ILLUSTRATIVE PROBLEM 9

The overall problem relates to the withdrawal of money from a savings account. A young woman has $6000 in a savings account and wants to withdraw $200 a month until the principal in the account falls below $3000. The interest is compounded quarterly at 6 percent and added to the account after the third withdrawal is made. Input to the problem are the principal and interest rate. A counter monitors the 3 months of each quarter. An accumulator adds the total number of months withdrawals are permitted. A negative accumulator reduces the principal. Interest is computed by multiplying the interest rate by the remaining principal. Print out only the balance of the account when it falls beneath $3000 and the total months in which this was accomplished. Use the labels "AMT REMAINING =" and "MONTHS =" to precede their respective lines of output.

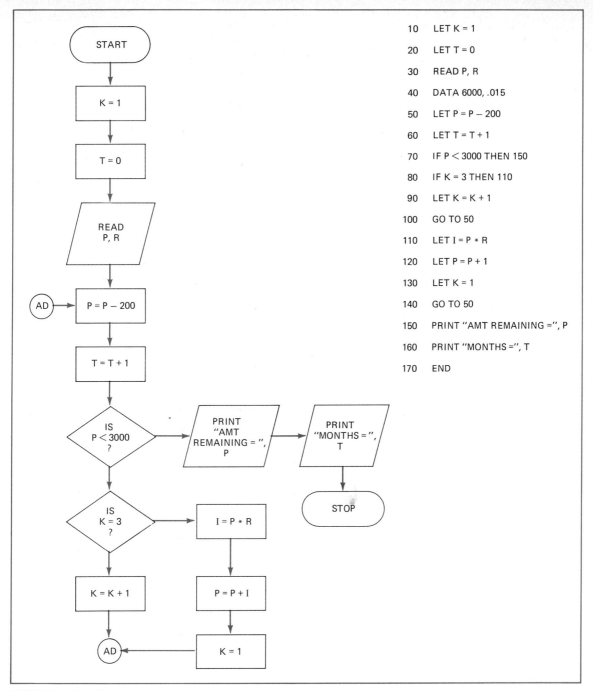

```
10    LET K = 1
20    LET T = 0
30    READ P, R
40    DATA 6000, .015
50    LET P = P – 200
60    LET T = T + 1
70    IF P < 3000 THEN 150
80    IF K = 3 THEN 110
90    LET K = K + 1
100   GO TO 50
110   LET I = P * R
120   LET P = P + 1
130   LET K = 1
140   GO TO 50
150   PRINT "AMT REMAINING =", P
160   PRINT "MONTHS =", T
170   END
```

FIGURE 8.22   The flowchart and BASIC program for Illustrative Problem 9.

The flowchart and BASIC program for Illustrative Problem 9 are in Figure 8.22. Statements 10 and 20 initialize the counter K used in each quarter and the accumulator T for the months that pass. Statement 30 inputs the principal of $6000 and the quarterly rate of .015 (6%/4). The negative accumulator (line 50) reduces the principal by 200 and precedes the update of the monthly accumulator T. The check against $3000 limit occurs in line 70. The counter instructions, lines 80 to 100, ensure that three loops are completed in each quarter.

At each quarter's end, the interest is computed (line 110) and posted to the account (line 120). The reinitialization of K sets the counter to 1, so that three monthly loops are again performed. When the account falls below $3000, the output of the existing principal (line 150) and months passed (line 160) is accomplished.

FOR/NEXT Statement

The counter is an integral part of many repetitive data processing operations. Because of its importance, a special, simplified method of creating a counter was developed. Each language has a different term for this technique. In FORTRAN, it is called the DO loop. In COBOL, the PERFORM statement is used. In BASIC, the **FOR/NEXT statement** provides the representation of an automated counter.

The FOR/NEXT statement is actually two statements, the **FOR statement** and the **NEXT statement.** But because they are always used together, they are referred to by the single term.

In Illustrative Problems 7 and 8, three statements were required to establish a counter. The FOR/NEXT instruction replaces these statements. To demonstrate this substitution, we will revise Illustrative Problem 7 to include the FOR/NEXT statement. Figure 8.23 (left) provides the original program, while Figure 8.23 (right) gives the new solution incorporating the FOR/NEXT statement.

In Figure 8.23 (left), statements 20, 70, 80, and 90 construct the counter and its related program loop. In Figure 8.23 (right), the FOR/NEXT statement requires only two statements, 30 and 70, to create the automated looping. Both programs effectively process five students' data, looping exactly five times.

Statements 30 and 70 in Figure 8.23 (right) can be analyzed as:

30	FOR	K	=	1	TO	5
Line Number		Numeric Variable for Counter		Initial Value of Loop		Ending Value of Looping Process
	Command			Required Sign	Command	

70	NEXT	K
Line Number	Command	Counter Variable Name

In the FOR statement, the number 30 represents the line number required by all BASIC statements. The words FOR and TO and the

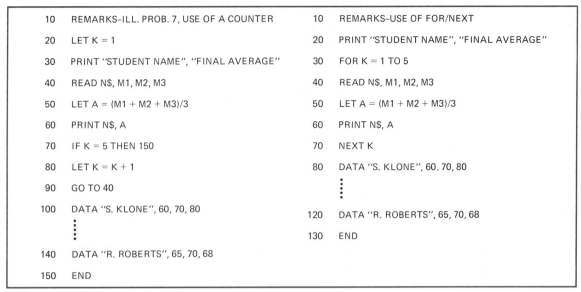

```
10   REMARKS-ILL. PROB. 7, USE OF A COUNTER      10   REMARKS-USE OF FOR/NEXT

20   LET K = 1                                   20   PRINT "STUDENT NAME", "FINAL AVERAGE"

30   PRINT "STUDENT NAME", "FINAL AVERAGE"        30   FOR K = 1 TO 5

40   READ N$, M1, M2, M3                          40   READ N$, M1, M2, M3

50   LET A = (M1 + M2 + M3)/3                     50   LET A = (M1 + M2 + M3)/3

60   PRINT N$, A                                  60   PRINT N$, A

70   IF K = 5 THEN 150                            70   NEXT K

80   LET K = K + 1                                80   DATA "S. KLONE", 60. 70, 80

90   GO TO 40                                          ⋮

100  DATA "S. KLONE", 60, 70, 80                 120  DATA "R. ROBERTS", 65, 70, 68

     ⋮                                           130  END

140  DATA "R. ROBERTS", 65, 70, 68

150  END
```

FIGURE 8.23 **A comparison of two programs: (*left*) a program using a counter; (*right*) a program using a FOR/NEXT statement.**

equal sign are strategically positioned and are integral parts of the FOR statement's syntax. These terms cannot be omitted. The numeric variable name K is the variable name assigned to the counter of the FOR/NEXT statement. The number immediately following the equal sign defines the starting value of the counter. Ordinarily, the initial value is one. However, any numeric integer value can be used. The value following the command TO defines the ending value or limit on the number of repetitions to be performed.

The FOR statement defines the first statement of the loop, the starting value of the counter, and the ending value of the counter and indicates that the looping process is automatic. The increment used with this statement is always one.

Statement 70 is the NEXT statement, the other half of the FOR/NEXT combination. The NEXT statement represents the end of the loop, the position of the decision to test for the last loop, the increment of the counter by one, and the location of GO TO that unconditionally branches to the top of the loop. Because all the above conditions are represented by the NEXT statement, line 70, the programmer does not have to write individual statements. The variable used in the NEXT statement must match the variable used in the FOR statement if the FOR/NEXT combination is to be used properly. The variable K is used in both statements 30 and 70.

The NEXT statement is the last instruction performed by the final loop of the FOR/NEXT combination. The program continues to the instruction that follows the NEXT statement. In Figure 8.23 (right), after the five loops are automatically completed, the program executes statement 70 and continues to statement 130. DATA statements 80 through 120 are bypassed, because they have already been used.

In Figure 8.24, the FOR/NEXT statement is applied to the solution of Illustrative Problem 8. The figure illustrates the new BASIC program and revised flowchart used with this solution.

The solutions in Figure 8.24 look simpler than the previous solutions. The FOR/NEXT statement eliminates the need for separate statements on the initialization of the counter, its increment, the decision used with a counter, and the unconditional branch to restart the loop. Statement 20 initializes the counter at one and indicates the counter will approach a limit of five. The value of the counter will range from one to five. The numeric variable name assigned to the counter in this problem is I. Any numeric variable name can be used for the counter in a FOR/NEXT statement.

Statement 20 indicates the beginning of the program loop, and statement 80 indicates its end. The NEXT statement always represents the last statement of a loop. It is the point at which the program branches back to restart the loop. When the last loop is completed, the NEXT statement is the last statement of the loop performed before the program continues to the following statement.

In this example, the program executes statement 80 on the fifth loop and proceeds to line 150. It passes through the DATA statements, because their data was exhausted during processing. The PRINT statement, line 150, outputs the literal "GRAND TOTAL =" and the accumulated total T.

The FOR/NEXT statement automatically increments itself by a factor of one on every repetition until the exact number of loops is attained. Though this increment is effective for most applications, there are instances where it is not applicable. Occasionally, a different increment is required, and the STEP option is employed.

CODING DATA STATEMENTS

Students often miscode DATA statements when learning the BASIC language. An error frequently encountered is:

100 19,36,70

Statement 100 does not have the command DATA as part of its syntax. This type of error is easily corrected, however.

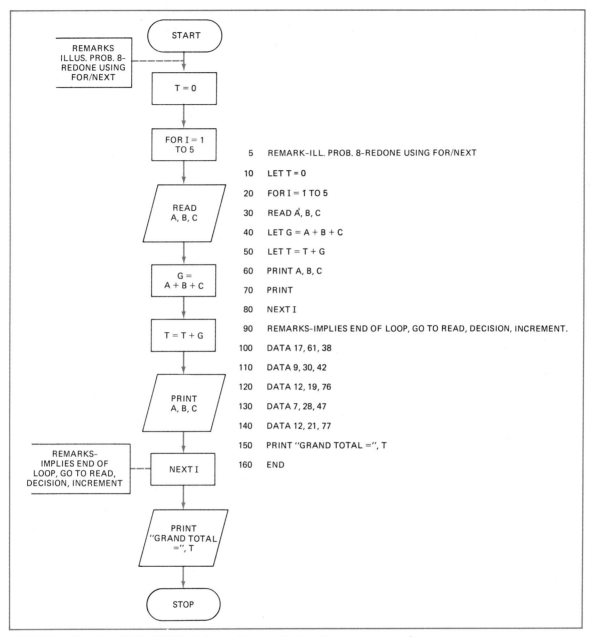

REMARKS
ILLUS. PROB. 8-
REDONE USING
FOR/NEXT

START

T = 0

FOR I = 1
TO 5

READ
A, B, C

G =
A + B + C

T = T + G

PRINT
A, B, C

REMARKS-
IMPLIES END OF
LOOP, GO TO READ,
DECISION, INCREMENT

NEXT I

PRINT
"GRAND TOTAL
=", T

STOP

5	REMARK-ILL. PROB. 8-REDONE USING FOR/NEXT
10	LET T = 0
20	FOR I = 1 TO 5
30	READ A, B, C
40	LET G = A + B + C
50	LET T = T + G
60	PRINT A, B, C
70	PRINT
80	NEXT I
90	REMARKS-IMPLIES END OF LOOP, GO TO READ, DECISION, INCREMENT.
100	DATA 17, 61, 38
110	DATA 9, 30, 42
120	DATA 12, 19, 76
130	DATA 7, 28, 47
140	DATA 12, 21, 77
150	PRINT "GRAND TOTAL =", T
160	END

FIGURE 8.24   The FOR/NEXT statement is applied to the program and flowchart of Illustrative Problem 8. The new approach does not affect the output.

STEP Option

The **STEP option** lets us vary the increment used with the FOR/NEXT statement. Consider the following statements:

30   FOR   I   =   1   TO   101   STEP   2
        The FOR Statement Normally Used   Command   Increment
80 NEXT I   The STEP Option

The STEP option is attached to the end of the FOR statement. The command STEP follows the number assigned to the last loop. The number after the term STEP indicates the increment desired.

In the STEP option attached to statement 30, the increment indicated is two. The counter I will begin at one and subsequently assume values of three, five, seven, and so on until the counter reaches 101. When an increment other than one is used, the relationship between the value of the counter and the number of loops being completed is altered. With statement 30, on the second loop, the counter is three. On the third loop, the counter is five. This looping sequence continues until the value of 101, in loop 51, is attained. This difference sometimes produces confusion. When an increment other than one is used, the programmer must clearly understand the processing being performed. We present the following example to help you understand why a STEP option may be of value.

Suppose that a sample of the data in a file is to be obtained. The decision is made to read every fifth record. An automatic loop is established by the FOR/NEXT statement, with an increment of five. The option STEP 5 is placed at the end of the original FOR statement, as required. This ensures that an increment of five is maintained throughout the reading of the file.

8.6
The Storage of
Data in Arrays

Practical data processing problems employ considerably more data than the problems introduced here. Consider the analysis of student data from a file containing thousands of records. In analyzing the required information, student data might be used over and over again. For example, computation of student histories and profiles might require the repeated use of the same data. It would be impractical to repeatedly input this data from peripheral devices. It would be better to use the vast storage capability of the CPU. The required data could be input once and maintained within main storage. Thus during processing, the data could be accessed as many times as necessary without being altered.

Design engineers converted this concept into an operational form. They developed the array. An **array** is an organized series of storage areas, identified by one name, in which data is temporarily stored.

Arrays are small files of data constructed as part of the source program. They permit the storage of data in an immediately accessible form. A program can repeatedly access necessary information using an array.

Arrays are defined with a **DIMENSION statement.** The DIMENSION statement should be the first statement of a BASIC program because it defines the type, size, and name of the array. The following example illustrates the format of the DIMENSION statement:

<u>10</u>	<u>DIM</u>	<u>N$(25),</u>	<u>M(10)</u>
Line Number	Command	1st Array	2d Array

The DIMENSION statement has both a line number and a command, as do most BASIC statements. The variables of the DIMENSION statement completely define the arrays in the program. In statement 10, the first array defined is a string variable array of 25 storage positions. We know this by the string variable name N$ and the number 25 shown in parentheses following N$. The number in parentheses is referred to as a **subscript.** Similarly, the second array of statement 10 will hold numeric data and is composed of 10 storage positions.

The subscripts used with the DIMENSION statement define the individual storage positions of each array. Each position of an array is identified by its own number. Thus it is possible to distinguish between each of the array positions. Specifically, the 25 positions in the array called N$ are identified by the series of string variable names from N$(1) to N$(25). These names are generally referred to as **subscripted variable names.** Subscripted variable names allow the independent access of each storage position in an array.

With the numeric array, M(10), the storage positions are identified by the subscripted variable names M(1) through M(10). Each subscripted variable can store exactly one seven-digit number.

A storage position in an array can hold one item of alphameric or numeric data. Thus, the N$ array can contain a total of 25 items of string variable data. Each item of string variable data is a maximum of 18 characters long. The M array is capable of storing 10 numbers of seven digits or less, including a sign or a decimal point.

Once an array is defined by the DIMENSION statement, it is ready for use in the program. The first step is the entry of data into each individual array position. The FOR/NEXT statement simplifies this task. Before illustrating the BASIC statements necessary for this input of data, we will discuss concepts used in the process.

As stated, an array is an organized series of storage positions created to maintain data during the processing of a program. The storage positions of an array are identified by subscripted variable names [i.e., N$(1), N$(2), etc.]. In actual practice, almost all arrays are filled with data in exactly the same order. The first subscripted position of the array receives the first item of data, the second subscripted array position stores the second item, and so on until the required number of array positions are filled. Thus, storage areas in the array are filled in an orderly sequence, beginning with position 1, until all data is exhausted.

The technique that parallels this operation is the counter. The counter is initialized at one and systematically proceeds by an increment of one to a predefined limit. Thus, one can input data into an array with a counter. Taking this concept one step further, because a FOR/NEXT statement can effectively replace a counter, a FOR/NEXT statement can be used to fill an array. Furthermore, a FOR/NEXT statement offers greater flexibility because it is easier to code, is initialized at one, and increments itself by one.

Using the FOR/NEXT statement and the format of the subscripted variable, the sequence of BASIC instructions required to fill an array is easily written.

```
10 DIM N$(20),H(20),R(20)
20 FOR I = 1 TO 20
30 READ N$(I),H(I),R(I)
40 WRITE N$(I),H(I),R(I)
50 NEXT I
60 REMARKS-TWENTY DATA STATEMENTS FOLLOW
70 DATA "SMITH",40,2.50
...........................................
260 DATA "BROWN",30,3.00
```

The DIMENSION statement, line number 10, defines three arrays of 20 positions each. One of the arrays will contain string variable data and is identified as N$(20). The other two arrays, H(20) and R(20), will contain numeric data. Each array position will be filled in order, starting with the first position [i.e., N$(1), H(1), R(1)].

Statement 20 initializes the automatic looping sequence with a FOR statement. This statement initializes the loop counter at 1 and sets the loop limit at 20. Thus, exactly 20 program loops will be performed. The definition of the variable for the counter is an important point here. The numeric variable name used is I. This variable will initially have a value of 1 and proceed to a maximum of 20. On each loop, the variable I will be incremented by a factor of 1. The use of I is vital to the next statement.

Statement 30, the READ statement, directs the program to input the three variables N$, H, and R. However, these variables are represented in the program as subscripted variables N$(I), H(I), and R(I).

The common factor in each variable name is the numeric variable I. The variable I is necessary for assigning each data item to its proper array position. Effectively, the variable I will function as a counter and enable us to place data within the array on an orderly basis. The placement of data will begin with the first storage area of the array and continue until the last data item is stored in its array position.

For example, on the first loop the counter is one. The computer will substitute this value into each of the subscripted variables of the READ statement. Therefore, on the first loop the variables are defined as N$(1), H(1), and R(1), and the data input in the first loop is stored in exactly those array positions.

On the second loop the counter is two. The computer again substitutes this value into the subscripted variables of statement 30. The variables used are N$(2), H(2), and R(2). Again, the data entered is stored in those specific array positions. The third loop will place data into the array positions N$(3), H(3), and R(3). This input and looping process, along with the substitution of the value of I into the subscripted variable names, continues until loop 20 is completed. On that loop, data is input and stored in array positions N$(20), H(20), and R(20). Thus, in 20 loops, each of the array positions has been systematically filled with data. A key in this orderly sequence is the use of the variable I.

Data can also be systematically output using subscripted variables. Statement 40 is a PRINT statement that outputs data relating to each of the three subscripted variables. Note that the variable I is used as the subscript and placed inside parentheses. The logic applied to input data is also applied to output data. Each array position is accessed on every one of the 20 loops. Statement 50, the NEXT statement, indicates the end of that program loop. Following statement 50 are the 20 DATA statements containing the data used with the READ statement and slated for storage in the three arrays. We have deliberately used READ and DATA statements to illustrate that the same relationship exists between data items and variable names, even if those names assume the form of a subscripted variable.

The above set of statements illustrates how easily a FOR/NEXT and a DIMENSION statement can create and fill an array. However, this excerpt from a program does not depict the full use of these statements. A limited amount of data is used in the illustrative examples solely for the sake of brevity. The concept of an array can be applied to virtually any amount of data. Also, because the use of the FOR/NEXT statement is being emphasized here, sample problems will use this looping technique extensively. Thus, a problem that might normally employ only one FOR/NEXT instruction may contain two or more loops for illustrative purposes. Illustrative Problem 10 shows how the FOR/NEXT and DIMENSION statements are used together.

THE SPECIFICATION OF DATA

For ease of understanding, in previous examples we assigned related data items to individual DATA statements. This approach permits us to identify data items and verify their accuracy. This is not the only method that can be used to detail data items. The two programs that follow depict the method previously used and an alternative to it.

Program A
```
10 READ N$,H,R
20 IF H=-99.99 THEN 100
30 LET G=H*R
40 PRINT N$,H,R,G
50 GO TO 10
60 DATA "BROWN",40,2.50
70 DATA "JONES",30,3.50
80 DATA "GEORGE",50,3.25
90 DATA "LAST",-99.99,0
100 END
```

Program B
```
10 READ N$,H,R
20 IF H=-99.99 THEN 100
30 LET G=H*R
40 PRINT N$,H,R,G
50 GO TO 10
60 DATA "BROWN",40,2.50,"JONES",30,3.50
80 DATA "GEORGE",50,3.25,"LAST",-99.99,0
100 END
```

In program A, data for three employees was assigned in three separate DATA statements (60 to 80). A fourth DATA statement, line 90, was needed for the 9's Data. In program B, the same amount of data was completely handled in two DATA statements. Two employees' data was combined into one DATA statement. Notice that the syntax necessary to define data items did not change because the data were combined.

The grouping of data illustrated in program B is permitted because of the way in which data is accessed. The computer initially accesses the three data items related to BROWN from line 60. When the second loop starts, the computer does not go to line 80, but returns to line 60 to retrieve the data for JONES. On loop 3, employee GEORGE's data is accessed from line 80, leaving the input of the 9's Data for the fourth or last loop.

In program A, DATA statements were serially read on each of the four program loops. However, in program B, the data was sequentially read from within the DATA statements provided. Because either method of specifying data is valid, programmers may adopt the method most suited to their needs. The latter approach may prove helpful for large quantities of data, as fewer DATA statements are required.

Figure 8.25 gives the flowchart and the program for Illustrative Problem 10. The first statement of the program is a DIMENSION statement. The statement defines the use of four arrays. Each array is com-

ILLUSTRATIVE **PROBLEM 10**	The problem is about two loops created by two FOR/NEXT statements. Perform the following operations in the first loop. Input to their separate arrays the employee's name, hours worked, and rate of pay. Compute each individual's gross pay by multiplying hours worked * the rate of pay, and store these gross pay amounts in their own array positions. Print out the employee's name and gross amount. Use appropriate headings for this output. Using the second FOR/NEXT statement, read through the gross array and accumulate the grand total of all gross pay. After this amount is accumulated, print the grand total, preceded by the label "GRAND TOTAL PAID =". The data for this problem are

Name	Hours	Rate
M. Murphy	35	4.00
A. Shaw	40	3.00
P. Penta	30	5.00
B. Dabb	32	4.00

posed of four storage areas. The initial three arrays, N$(4), H(4), and R(4), are filled via the input of data. The last array, G(4), is filled with the results of the computation of each employee's gross pay.

Two conditions must be satisfied after the DIMENSION statement is given and before the first loop is initialized. Statement 20 provides the required headings for the two columns of data to be output. The two literals are printed in zones 1 and 2. Line 30, a LET statement, initializes the accumulator T at zero.

Statement 50 initializes the first loop of the program. The FOR statement defines the value of the loop counter at one and indicates that exactly four loops will be performed. Note that in this loop, the variable name assigned to the loop counter is I. In the statements that follow, the variable I is used as a subscript. In statement 60, the variable I appears as the subscript in each of the variables being input. With $I = 1$, the data read is stored in the first position of each array. Naturally, when $I = 2$, data will be stored in the second position of each array, and so forth.

After the first values of H and R are input, statement 70 is executed. This LET statement computes the gross pay related to the first set of values. This amount is stored in the first position of the G array. On loops 2, 3, and 4, the computed amounts of gross pay are stored in their respective array positions: G(2), G(3), and G(4).

Statement 80 prints the individual employee's name and the gross pay just computed. When $I = 1$, the first employee's data is output. When $I = 2$, the second employee's data is printed, and so forth.

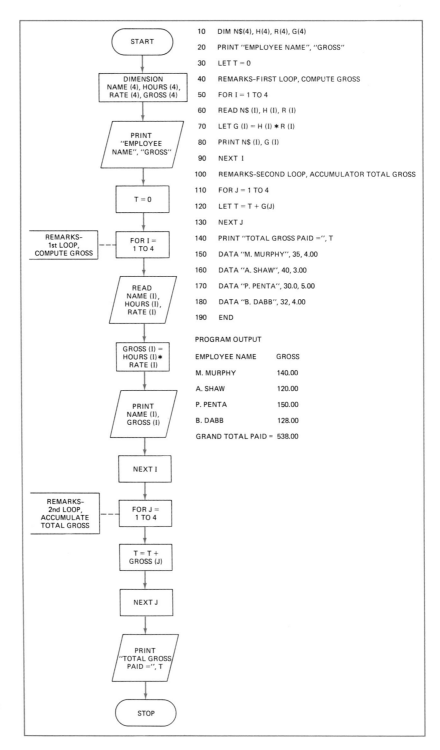

```
10    DIM N$(4), H(4), R(4), G(4)
20    PRINT "EMPLOYEE NAME", "GROSS"
30    LET T = 0
40    REMARKS–FIRST LOOP, COMPUTE GROSS
50    FOR I = 1 TO 4
60    READ N$ (I), H (I), R (I)
70    LET G (I) = H (I) * R (I)
80    PRINT N$ (I), G (I)
90    NEXT I
100   REMARKS–SECOND LOOP, ACCUMULATOR TOTAL GROSS
110   FOR J = 1 TO 4
120   LET T = T + G(J)
130   NEXT J
140   PRINT "TOTAL GROSS PAID =", T
150   DATA "M. MURPHY", 35, 4.00
160   DATA "A. SHAW", 40, 3.00
170   DATA "P. PENTA", 30.0, 5.00
180   DATA "B. DABB", 32, 4.00
190   END
```

PROGRAM OUTPUT

EMPLOYEE NAME	GROSS
M. MURPHY	140.00
A. SHAW	120.00
P. PENTA	150.00
B. DABB	128.00

GRAND TOTAL PAID = 538.00

FIGURE 8.25   The program and flowchart for Illustrative Problem 10.

ARRAYS

Subscripts play an important part in arrays. The subscript is often defined in the FOR/NEXT statement. It is vital that the same subscripted variable be consistently used. For example, examine the statements that follow and determine the misuse of the subscript:

10 FOR J = 1 TO 20
20 READ N$(I),H(J),R(J)
....
40 NEXT J

The inconsistent use of subscripts appears in statement 20. The variables H(J) and R(J) use the correct subscript J. The subscript J is established in the FOR statement, line 10. The string variable, N$(I), incorrectly specifies the subscript as I. The string variable should have been written as N$(J), consistent with the variable in statement 10.

These outputs appear in Figure 8.25. Statement 90 completes the FOR/NEXT combination. The NEXT statement indicates the end of the first loop and the automatic branching to restart the program loop.

The second loop, in which the grand total of gross pay is accumulated, is defined by statements 110 to 130. One gross pay amount is added into the accumulator T on each loop. Thus in statement 120, the variable G uses the subscript J [i.e., G(J)]. Note that in this case the variable name assigned to the counter is J. It is perfectly acceptable to use different variables for different loops in a program. In one loop, the same variable must be consistently used as a subscript.

Once the four loops defined by the FOR/NEXT statement are completed, the PRINT statement, line 140, is performed. This statement will print the accumulated total T, preceded by its special label. The remainder of the DATA statements are bypassed, and the program proceeds to statement 190. The END statement indicates no further statements, and processing is over.

Illustrative Problem 10 introduced the use of the DIMENSION and the FOR/NEXT statements and arrays. Illustrative Problem 11 will illustrate the reuse of data stored in arrays.

The program and the flowchart for Illustrative Problem 11 appear in Figure 8.26. The solution again incorporates two FOR/NEXT statements. However, in this problem only one array is required. This array is defined as N(6) in the DIMENSION statement, line 10. The LET statement, T = 0, is required for the accumulation of numeric data con-

ILLUSTRATIVE PROBLEM 11

The overall problem relates to the use of two FOR/NEXT statements. In the first loop, one numeric variable is input on each loop. This number is accumulated in a grand total. This operation is followed by the output of that variable. The average of all the numeric data input is computed and output at the end of the initial loop.

In the second loop, the number of data items that are greater than the mean will be determined. Each value in the array will be compared with the just-computed average. At the end of the second loop, print out the quantity of numbers greater than the mean. Include an appropriate label.

The data used in this problem are 37, 86, 41, 62, 48, 54.

tained in the array. The variable C will be used to add up the data items that are greater than the computed mean.

The first loop is defined by statements 50 to 90, which compose the FOR/NEXT statement. The FOR statement defines the counter variable I and establishes that six loops are to be performed. One variable is input on each of the six loops. The subscripted numeric variable used is N(I). This variable appears in the accumulation of the six figures, statement 70, and the output of these numbers.

One unusual aspect of this problem is in the input of data. Examine the overall solution, and note that six DATA statements are not specified. Six statements would be cumbersome. Instead, one DATA statement provides the six data items. The program will draw one number from this DATA statement on each loop. Thus, the number 37 is input into the array position N(1) on loop 1. The data associated with loop 2 and N(2) is 86. The remaining four numbers, 41, 62, 48, and 54, are respectively appropriated in loops 3, 4, 5, and 6 and are related to the subscripted variables N(3), N(4), N(5), and N(6).

The completion of the first loop permits the computation of the average in statement 100. This amount is presented, in statement 110, with an appropriate special label.

The second loop determines which of the values stored in the array are greater than the just-computed average. Line 130 defines a loop of six repetitions and the counter variable J. Statement 140 is the decision that compares the average with each value of the array. If the value of N(J) is greater than the average, then one is added to the value C. If N(J) is not greater than the average, the program is directed to the NEXT statement to repeat the loop.

The processing of the second loop allows the output of the literal in statement 180. Exactly two numbers greater than the mean are found. This output precedes the END statement of the program and the completion of all processing.

Arrays permit the storage of repeatedly used data. They are valuable tools, giving the programmer great flexibility in writing program solutions.

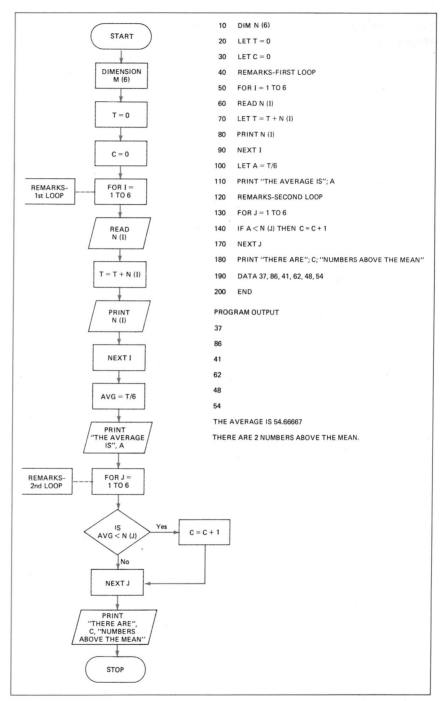

```
10    DIM N (6)
20    LET T = 0
30    LET C = 0
40    REMARKS–FIRST LOOP
50    FOR I = 1 TO 6
60    READ N (I)
70    LET T = T + N (I)
80    PRINT N (I)
90    NEXT I
100   LET A = T/6
110   PRINT "THE AVERAGE IS"; A
120   REMARKS–SECOND LOOP
130   FOR J = 1 TO 6
140   IF A < N (J) THEN  C = C + 1
170   NEXT J
180   PRINT "THERE ARE"; C; "NUMBERS ABOVE THE MEAN"
190   DATA 37, 86, 41, 62, 48, 54
200   END
```

PROGRAM OUTPUT

37

86

41

62

48

54

THE AVERAGE IS 54.66667

THERE ARE 2 NUMBERS ABOVE THE MEAN.

FIGURE 8.26 The flowchart and the BASIC program prepared for Illustrative Problem 11.

Case Study One

Developing a Computer Curriculum

Because computers play an ever-increasing role in our daily lives, many educators want students to learn about them. But many educators face financial problems or philosophical disagreements. Two teachers who have overcome these problems and have begun computer programs are Bobbie Ferrell and Robby Goodman.

Ms. Ferrell teaches at the Greenhill School, a college preparatory school outside Dallas. Her experience as a programmer convinced her that a sound computer program was essential at Greenhill. She taught her first computer course without a computer—and with limited success. Then a Texas Instruments 990 system was donated to the school.

The real breakthrough came when Greenhill got its own APPLE computers. Students could then interact with the computer via BASIC and get solid programming results. The big problem was how to keep students off the system and make sure that everyone had a chance to work with it.

To help other faculty members master com-

puter skills, Ms. Ferrell developed a special course outline. She recorded it on audio tape so that teachers had unlimited access to it. Many have since developed software for students in English, spelling, and grammar.

Ms. Goodman, at Collins Junior High School in Cupertino, California, had a similar experience. Although the school is in the heart of Santa Clara County's computer industry, its curriculum did not reflect this technology. Ms. Goodman conducted a "Microcomputer Fair," at which four manufacturers exhibited their wares. Through funding by ESEA TITLE IV C, Ms. Goodman could prepare and test a representative computer curriculum.

These two teachers, in common with many others, believe that through interactive languages like BASIC, students can not only learn and test computer principles but they can also independently develop solutions and apply them in many areas of study.

Summary

The following major points have been presented in Chapter 8:

Point 1 BASIC is an interactive, free-form language. It is readily used with terminals and permits simultaneous use of the computer by many student programmers. It is easy to learn because it has relatively few rules and has a readily understood syntax.

Point 2 All BASIC statements use essentially the same general line format. The line number identifies each statement and fixes it in the sequential execution of the program. The command

indicates the operation to be performed. The variables identify the data to be used in the operation indicated by the command.

Point 3 The READ statement is used for the input of data. The DATA statement provides the data used in the program. If a READ statement is used in a BASIC program, one or more DATA statements must also appear. In the READ statement, input variables are defined by string and numeric variable names. String variable names represent alphabetic and alphameric data and are identified by a dollar sign. Numeric variable names

Case Study Two

Personal Computing Aid to Retail Sales

After graduating from Stanford University with an engineering degree, Jeff Leap decided to enter the women's clothing field. With an associate, Jeff became the management for J.M. Harper's, a retail seller of women's clothes. It soon became clear that the paperwork involved was sizable and might prove a problem. Jeff decided to incorporate a computer to help with the paperwork. After some work with a large computer, he realized that a smaller, personal system was better suited to the company's needs.

Because no suitable retail sales software existed, Jeff had to design and write his own. In BASIC, he wrote programs for controlling inventories, ordering clothes, receiving and distributing shipments, and monitoring outstanding orders and shipments. Reports were printed out and bound into booklets, a form portable enough to travel anywhere, especially on buying trips.

Leap also uses his personal computing system to prepare sales projections, monitor sales trends, and to make adjustments in orders. The system can compute in 15 minutes what used to take an entire day. Savings from the system have allowed Harper's to open a second branch, and sales are over $500,000 a year. Leap believes that his personal computer has made the difference between profit and loss. He intends to expand his activities and to develop other software for Harper's management.

Consider this . . .

Do you believe that computers can be effectively employed within small businesses? In what small businesses do you think they would be most effectively applied?

---

are applied to numeric data. String variable data is defined in a DATA statement by quotation marks. Numeric data, represented in the form of real or integer numbers, requires no special punctuation. The format of the READ statement defines the order of data presented in the DATA statement.

Point 4 Arithmetic operations involving formulas are represented in LET statements. Only one variable of any type is placed to the left of the equal sign.

Point 5 The PRINT statement defines output operations in BASIC. The printing area used by BASIC is divided into zones of a fixed size. Commas in the PRINT statement direct data into one of these zones. Semicolons permit more than four variables to be printed on one line. Literals are defined in PRINT statements with quotation marks.

Literals add headings and labels to output. Descriptive notes are added to the text of the source program using the REMARK statement.

Point 6 The INPUT statement can replace the READ statement for input operations. The DATA statement is not used with the INPUT statement. The INPUT statement is an interactive statement and directs the entry of data as the program is being executed. This request for data is signaled by the output of a question mark. Data must be supplied to the INPUT statement in the order requested. Literals defined within INPUT statements prompt the user during processing.

Point 7 Decisions and program loops are coded in BASIC via the IF/THEN statement and the GO TO statements. The IF/THEN statement permits conditional branching to other statements and the performance of logical operations (e.g., the 9's Decision). Unconditional branching at the end of a program loop is accomplished with the GO TO statement. An END statement must appear at the end of each BASIC program; it signals that no further statements exist.

Point 8 Selected system commands assist in the execution of BASIC programs. The command RUN directs the computer to attempt to execute the program. The LIST command directs the computer to print out all the statements currently in the program. The DELETE command allows the removal of unwanted statements from a program. The SAVE and UNSAVE commands are respectively used to store and remove programs from computer storage.

Point 9 Accumulators and counters are easily constructed and employed in BASIC programming. The formulas and decisions involved in both techniques are easily represented using LET and IF/THEN statements. A special form of conditional instruction, the IF/THEN/ELSE, is often used in solutions involving two alternatives.

Point 10 The automatic looping of BASIC programs is created through the use of the FOR/NEXT statement. This statement establishes the equivalent of a counter and controls the execution of program loops. In a FOR/NEXT statement, increments with a value other than one are defined using the STEP option.

Point 11 Arrays permit the storage of data in an organized series of storage positions. Arrays are defined for string variable and numeric data with the DIMENSION statement. Arrays are closely tied to the FOR/NEXT statement. A subscript defines each position of an array.

Glossary

Array A consecutive series of storage areas in a program, used to hold a group of related data items defined by a DIMENSION statement.

BASIC (Beginner's All-purpose Symbolic Instruction Code) A free-form, interactive computer language.

Command The part of a BASIC statement that defines the operation to be performed.

DATA statement The statement, used in conjunction with the READ statement, that supplies the actual data used in the program.

DELETE command The system command that lets the program delete a specific statement from a BASIC program.

DIMENSION statement The statement used to define numeric and string variable arrays.

END statement The last statement of any BASIC program.

FOR statement The first part of the FOR/NEXT statement; defines the first statement of the automated program loop.

FOR/NEXT statement The statement used to create the automated looping process of a BASIC program.

Free-form language A language with a simple syntax and a limited number of rules.

GO TO statement The unconditional branching statement in BASIC.

IF/THEN statement The statement used to define a logical operation (e.g., a 9's Decision) in a BASIC program.

IF/THEN/ELSE statement A special form of the IF/THEN statement which handles two alternative computations in one conditional statement.

INPUT statement A statement used to define input operations; it requests data as the program is being executed.

Integer number   A number that uses no decimal point (e.g., 4, −70).

LET statement   A statement with a format that permits formulas to perform arithmetic operations.

Line number   The part of a BASIC instruction that identifies the statement and fixes its place in the order of execution.

LIST command   A system command that directs the computer to print a copy of the source program.

LOGOFF procedure   The series of steps used by the programmer to cease the processing of a BASIC program.

LOGON procedure   The steps used to create a communication link with the computer to begin programming in BASIC.

NEXT statement   The second part of the FOR/NEXT instruction; it indicates the end of the automated program loop.

Numeric data   Data using real or integer numbers; one of the two types of data used in BASIC programs.

Numeric variable name   The variable name that represents numeric data, composed of 1 or 2 characters (e.g., H, R1).

Print position   The space required to print one character of output.

PRINT statement   The BASIC statement that directs the output of data.

Print zones   The four zones in the BASIC print area of 72 characters; composed of 18 characters each.

READ statement   The BASIC statement used for the input of data; must be used with the DATA statement.

Real number   A number that employs a decimal point (e.g., 7.61, −93.02).

REMARK statement   The BASIC statement that adds descriptive notes to the text of the source program; the notes do not appear during output.

RUN command   The system command that directs the computer to execute the source program.

SAVE command   The system command that directs the computer to store the program being worked on.

Statement number   The part of a BASIC instruction that identifies the statement and fixes its place in the order of execution.

STEP option   The option, used with the FOR/NEXT statement, that permits the use of an increment other than one.

String variable data   Data composed of a string of alphabetic or alphameric characters; defined by a pair of quotation marks in a DATA statement.

String variable name   The variable name representing alphabetic or alphameric data; composed of two characters: an alphabetic character and a dollar sign (e.g., N$, B$).

Subscript   The integer character that defines the storage positions composing an array; contained in parentheses in a subscripted variable name.

Subscripted variable name   The variable name used to represent an array or a specific array position.

UNSAVE command   The system command that removes from the system previously stored programs.

Variable   The set of characters that represents data in a BASIC program.

Whole number   A number that uses no decimal point (e.g., 4, −70).

Discussion Questions

1 Examine the program excerpts that follow and answer the questions below.

Excerpt A	**Excerpt B**
10 FOR I=1 TO 4	10 READ A,B,C,D
20 READ A,B	20 READ X,Y,Z
30 DATA 2,3,6,7,10,5,23,9	30 DATA 3,9,8,12,17,25
40 NEXT I	40 DATA 5,10,19,83

a   In excerpt A, what value is assigned to the variable B on the second loop? Explain.

b   In excerpt B, what value is given to the variable Y when these instructions are executed? Explain.

2 Which of the following statements are correctly written in BASIC? Correct those statements that are wrong and explain each correction.

a   20 PRINT "AMT OF RETURN";P   **b**   30 READ X;Y;C

c   140 IF X = 7 THEN 200,600   **d**   50 PRINT N$ H R

e   4 IF T=250 THEN C=C+1   **f**   INPUT C$

g   70 LET C=6, D=−99   **h**   100 DATA C$="XXXX"

i   60 DATA "LAST"; −99.99;0   **j**   44 PRINT "TOTAL"= ,A

Write a BASIC program for each of the problems that follow.

3 The overall problem relates to the output of your name and address. On three separate lines, print out your name, street address, and city and state. Use a literal for your address and string variables for other alphanumeric data.

4 The overall problem deals with computing an employee's gross pay. Data input to the program are the employee's name, hours worked, and the rate of pay. Gross pay is calculated using the following formula: Gross = hours ∗ rate. Output on one line each employee's name, hours worked, rate of pay, and gross pay amount. Use a 9's Decision to control processing. Data for the problem follows:

Employee Name	**Hours Worked**	**Rate of Pay**
S. Getch	40.00	4.50
L. Lane	32.00	6.25
K. Tracy	24.00	8.50
A. Donor	48.00	1.60

5 Rewrite the program for question 4 to incorporate the following techniques:

a   Use a counter to control processing.

b   Use a FOR/NEXT statement to complete the four loops.

6 The overall problem relates to the computation of an individual sales commission. Input to the problem are the salesperson's name and number and four sales amounts. Add the four sales amounts to create a total sales amount for each salesperson. Commissions are calculated at 15 and 10 percent. If the total sales amount > $100, the commission rate is 15 percent. If not, the 10 percent rate is used. Output each salesperson's name and number, total sales amount, and commission. Use a counter to control the completion of program loops. The data for the problem follows:

Salesperson Name	Salesperson Number	Sale 1	Sale 2	Sale 3	Sale 4
A. Salvat	1106	4.50	206.93	31.44	104.66
C. Glib	1283	14.60	30.24	8.95	17.49
J. Murphy	1466	28.75	90.66	54.38	49.95
K. Garner	1567	24.70	50.06	14.82	8.23
C. Brennan	1832	18.10	66.24	3.95	13.40

7 Redo question 6 and accumulate the total commissions paid to the five salespeople. Output this total after all salespersons' commission are processed. Precede the amount by the label "TOTAL COMMISSIONS PAID = ".

8 The overall problem relates to the computation of winning percentages for a hockey league. Data input is the team's name and number of games won, lost, and tied. Winning percentages are computed by dividing the number of games won by the total number of games played. Output on one line the team's name; games won, lost, and tied by the team; and their winning percentage. Place the following headings at the top of output:

TEAM   WON   LOST   TIED   PCT

Use either a counter or a 9's Decision to control processing. The data for the problem follows:

Team	Won	Lost	Tied
Ducks	41	10	4
Bucks	36	12	7
Mukluks	25	20	10
Pucks	14	32	11
Allstars	0	42	13

9 This problem relates to the addition of a group of numbers. Input to the problem are five sets of three numbers. One set of three numbers is input on each loop to compute a grand total of the 15 numbers. The output of the program should appear under an appropriate heading. Each set of numbers should be printed after it is added to the accumulator. After printing the last set of numbers, print out the accumulated total using the label "GRAND TOTAL = ". Data for the problem is

18	61	54
77	106	12
9	34	82
45	26	63
7	91	50

10 Rewrite the program for question 9 using the FOR/NEXT statement. Remember to initialize the accumulator prior to the start of the loop created by the FOR/NEXT statement. Again, output the accumulated total after the last loop is performed.

11 The problem relates to the addition of a series of whole numbers. Only the odd numbers ranging from 1 to 99 are to be added up. No input data is used. Using a FOR/NEXT statement and a STEP option, add up the numbers 1, 3, 5, 7, 9, etc. Output the total.

12 The problem relates to the computation of an estate left to a young man. Sam Jones is left $10,000 while in college. He would like to withdraw $100 a month from the estate until $1000 remains. The money is left in a savings account that pays $5\frac{1}{4}$ percent interest compounded quarterly. Interest is returned prior to the monthly withdrawal. Compute the number of months required to fall below the $1000 limit and the amount left in the account. Print out these amounts on two separate lines, preceded by the labels "AMOUNT LEFT = " and "NUMBER OF MONTHS USED WAS".

13 The problem relates to the computation of percentages. A math student working on an assignment must accumulate the number of times that each of four events occurs. A total of 50 coded data items are provided by the teacher. Input one numeric code on each of the 50 loops. Each code will be a 1, 2, 3, or 4. Test for each code in a conditional statement, adding 1 to the total related to that code when a match is made. Use a FOR/NEXT statement to create the loop of 50 repetitions. When all 50 codes have been processed, print out the accumulated totals of the number of times each code has occurred and the probability associated with each code. The probability is computed by dividing the number of times that the code occurred by 50. The headings to use in the output are:

CODE   FREQUENCY   PROBABILITY

The data for this problem is:

> 2,2,4,1,3,1,1,3,2,4,4,1,2,3,4,4,3,2,2,1,1,4,4,4,3,3,3,2,1,4,1,3,3,1,
> 3,4,1,2,2,2,1,3,2,1,4,4,2,4,3.

14 The overall problem relates to computing the future value of money. A widow wants to put money away regularly in a savings account that has a 6-month interest rate of 8 percent. She intends to deposit $125 per month for 102 months, returning the interest to the account. In addition to determining the total amount of money in the account after that time, the widow wants to know how much interest has accumulated over those months. Output on separate lines the total balance in her account and the total interest earned over that time, preceded by the labels "BALANCE =" and "TOTAL INT. MADE =".

Hint: Examine the use of a counter for monitoring the 6-month cycle, the use of an accumulator for the 102 months, and testing against that amount using a decision.

Summary Test

_____ **1** String variable names, which use a $ as their first character, are used to identify alphabetic data.

_____ **2** DATA statements must be used with INPUT statements.

_____ **3** Unconditional branching is accomplished by using the IF/THEN statement.

_T_ **4** Literals cannot be specified in READ statements.

_____ **5** The statement: 40 DATA 10,000 is correctly written for the numeric data 10,000.

_____ **6** The READ statement 40 READ A; B; C is correctly written.

_____ **7** A literal is restricted to a maximum of 18 characters.

_T_ **8** Statements are executed in BASIC by their line numbers.

_T_ **9** A PRINT statement can employ commas and semicolons to position output data on one line.

_T_ **10** The command RUN causes the processing of a source program.

_T_ **11** The END statement is the last statement of a BASIC program.

_____ **12** The statement 60 PRINT "GRAND TOTAL, " T is properly written.

_T_ **13** The STEP option permits the programmer to vary the increment used with a FOR/NEXT statement.

_____ **14** The IF statement 30 IF HRS = −999 THEN 200 will branch to line 200 when HRS = −999.

_____ **15** A semicolon in a DATA statement indicates that the next data item should be keyed into the next available position.

_C_ **16** Which of the following BASIC statements is correct?

     a INPUT N$ **b** 60 LET C+D=Q

     c 45 PRINT X,Y;Z   **d** 100 END,JOB

_C_ **17** The equivalent of the operation code in the BASIC line format is the:

     a label   **b** line number   **c** command   **d** variable

_B_ **18** Which of the following variable names is not correct at any time?

     a N$(I)   **b** HR   **c** P(5)   **d** K9

_D_ **19** A characteristic associated with arrays is:

     a The DIM statement must be the first program statement.

     b A subscripted variable must identify data in the arrays.

     c Each array name defines the type of data to be stored within it.

     d All the above

_C_ **20** The system command used to store a program within the computer is the:

     a STORE command   **b** HOLD command

     c SAVE command   **d** all the above

_b_ **21** Descriptive comments are put in the source program with the:

     a PRINT statement   **b** REMARK statement

     c INPUT statement   **d** DATA statement

Use the program excerpt shown to answer questions 22 to 25.

```
5 LET T=0
10 FOR J=5 TO 9
20 READ A,B,C
30 DATA 6,9,2,4,12,7,31,8,5
40 DATA 11,17,19,0,6,43,1,13,14
50 LET T=T+A
60 NEXT J
```

_C_ **22** How many data items will lines 5 to 60 read?

    a   3   **b**   12   **c**   15   **d**   18

_____ **23** The data item assigned to B on the third loop is:

    a   9   **b**   8   **c**   6   **d**   does not exist

_____ **24** The amount accumulated for T is equal to what value by the end of the second loop?

    a   4   **b**   6   **c**   10   **d**   31

_____ **25** Which of the following statements is true?

    a   Too many data items will invalidate a program.

    b   Exactly five data statements are needed for this program's five loops.

    c   A total of five loops will be executed.

    d   J will assume a value of 5 when the looping is completed.

Quiz Problem

Write a BASIC program for the following problem:

The overall problem deals with the computation of a salesperson's commission and the grand total of all commissions paid. Input to the problem are the salesperson's name and four sales amounts. Commissions are 10 percent of the total sales amount for each salesperson. Compute each salesperson's commission and add that amount to the accumulated total of all commissions. Output each salesperson's name, total sales amount, and commission under the headings SALESPERSON NAME, TOTAL SALES, and COMMISSION. After processing the last salesperson, print out the total of commissions paid preceded by the label "TOTAL COMMISSIONS PAID =   ". The data for the program is

Salesperson Name	Sale 1	Sale 2	Sale 3	Sale 4
J. Higgins	46.95	36.25	117.20	99.95
J. Davidson	6.28	18.01	72.82	4.14
T. Kennedy	3.33	80.68	23.84	5.22

Ensure that the data is properly keyed into the program, remembering to distinguish between numeric and string variable data.

Summary Test Answers

1 F	**2** F	**3** F	**4** T	**5** F
6 F	**7** F	**8** T	**9** T	**10** T
11 T	**12** F	**13** T	**14** F	**15** F
16 C	**17** C	**18** B	**19** D	**20** C
21 B	**22** C	**23** B	**24** C	**25** C

Basic Program for Quiz Problem

Two program solutions are offered for the quiz problems. The first program uses a FOR/NEXT statement. The second program involves the use of a 9's Decision and a 9's Data statement.

Program Solution 1

```
10  REMARK-QUIZ PROBLEM SOLUTION 1
20  LET T = 0
30  PRINT "SALESPERSON NAME", "TOTAL SALES", "COMMISSION"
40  FOR I = 1 TO 3
50  READ N$, S1, S2, S3, S4
60  LET A = S1 + S2 + S3 + S4
70  LET C = A * .10
80  LET T = T + C
90  PRINT N$, A, C
100 NEXT I
110 DATA "J. HIGGINS", 46.95, 36.25, 117.20, 99.95
120 DATA "J. DAVIDSON", 6.28, 18.01, 72.82, 4.14
130 DATA "T. KENNEDY", 3.33, 80.68, 23.84, 5.22
140 PRINT "TOTAL COMMISSIONS PAID = ", T
150 END
```

Program Solution 2

```
10  REMARK-QUIZ PROBLEM SOLUTION 2
20  LET T = 0
30  PRINT "SALESPERSON NAME", "TOTAL SALES", "COMMISSION"
40  READ N$, S1, S2, S3, S4
50  IF S1 = -999.99 THEN 150
60  LET A = S1 + S2 + S3 + S4
70  LET C = A * .10
80  LET T = T + C
90  PRINT N$, S, C
100 GO TO 40
110 DATA "J. HIGGINS", 46.95, 36.25, 117.20, 99.95
120 DATA "J. DAVIDSON", 6.28, 18.01, 72.82, 4.14
130 DATA "T. KENNEDY", 3.33, 80.68, 23.84, 5.22
140 DATA "XXX", -999.99, 0, 0, 0
150 PRINT "TOTAL COMMISSIONS PAID = ", T
160 END
```

Nine

```
02   FILLER         PIC X(11)    VALUE SPACE.
02   FILLER         PIC X(6)     VALUE 'ANNUA
     ...ER          PIC X(4)     VALUE SPACE.
02   FILLER         PIC X(4)     VALUE 'YEAR'.
02   FILLER         PIC X(6)     VALUE SPACE.
02   FILLER         PIC X(9)     VALUE 'EDUCA
02   FILLER         PIC X(5)     VALUE SPACE.
02   FILLER         PIC X(3)     VALUE 'SEX'.
02   FILLER         PIC X(5)     VALUE SPACE.
02   FILLER         PIC X(10)    VALUE 'GEOGRA
02   FILLER         PIC X(5)     VALUE SPACE.
02   FILLER         PIC X(8)     VALUE 'JOB C
02   FILLER         PIC X(7)     VALUE SPACE.
02   FILL...        PIC X(7)     VALUE 'MONTH
02   F...           PIC X(7)     VALUE SPACE.

01   ...NG-3.
     FILLER         PIC X(9)     VALUE SPACE.
     FILLER         PIC X(6)     VALUE 'NUMBE
02   FILLER         PIC X(31)    VALUE SPACE.
02   FILLER         PIC X(6)     VALUE 'SALAR
02   FILLER         PIC X(4)     VALUE SPACE.
02   FILLER         PIC X(5)     VALUE 'HIRED
02   FILLER         PIC X(7)     VALUE SPACE.
02   FILLER         PIC X(5)     VALUE 'LEVEL
02   FILLER         PIC X(15)    VALUE SPACE.
02   FILLER         PIC X(10)    VALUE 'PREFE
02   FILLER         PIC X(20)    VALUE SPACE.
02   FILLER         PIC X(6)     VALUE 'SALAR
02   FILLER         PIC X(8)     VALUE SPACE.

01   DETAIL-LINE.
02   FILLER                      PIC X(9)    VALUE
02   DL-EMPLOYEE-NO              PIC X(6).
02   FILLER                      PIC X(6)    VALU
```

An Introduction to COBOL

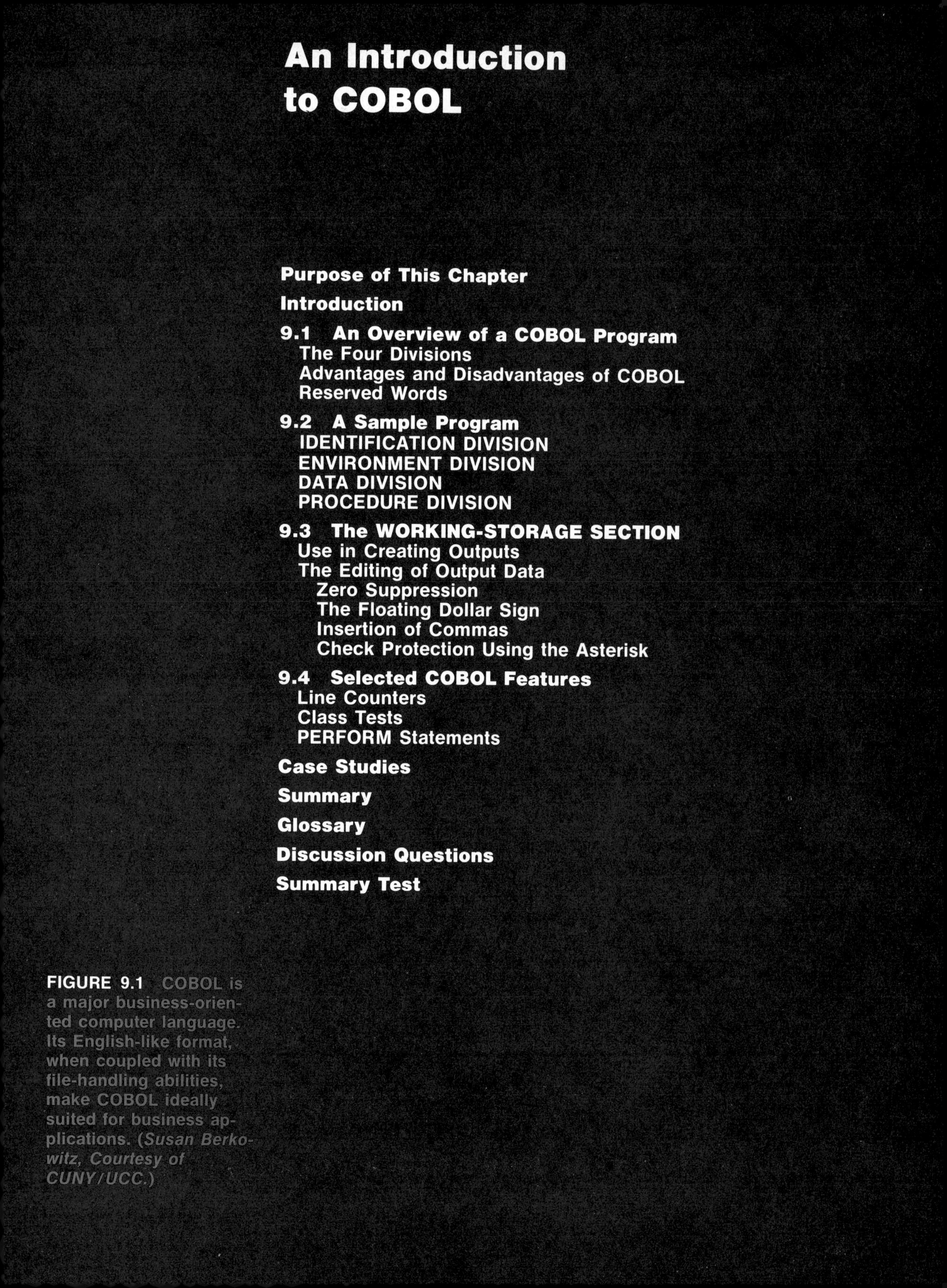

FIGURE 9.1 COBOL is a major business-oriented computer language. Its English-like format, when coupled with its file-handling abilities, make COBOL ideally suited for business applications. (*Susan Berkowitz, Courtesy of CUNY/UCC.*)

Purpose of This Chapter

In this chapter, we present an overview of COBOL and its many types of statements. We discuss the four divisions of a COBOL program, the IDENTIFICATION, ENVIRONMENT, DATA, and PROCEDURE DIVISIONS. An illustrative problem lets us examine the four divisions at greater length.

We also detail the required statements in each division. We explain SELECT clauses, file descriptions (FD), RECORD CONTAINS and LABEL RECORDS clauses, and SOURCE- and OBJECT-COMPUTER entries. We describe how I/O formats are constructed in the DATA DIVISION with the assistance of PICTURE clauses. A review of the PROCEDURE DIVISION reveals how OPEN, READ, MOVE, WRITE, GO TO, and CLOSE statements are used. Variations of these statements are also presented.

A second illustrative problem lets us review the WORKING-STORAGE SECTION of the DATA DIVISION. This section is used to detail the I/O formats needed to print headings and special labels or to set aside fields used for arithmetic operations (e.g., 77-level entries). We also discuss the editing of output data and such edit features as zero suppression, floating dollar signs, comma insertion, and asterisks for check protection. The WRITE FROM and AFTER ADVANCING clauses, used in creating headings, are defined, as is the use of the READ INTO statement for input operations.

Selected COBOL statements are presented. A third illustrative problem includes class tests, conditional statements, the DISPLAY statement, and the output of headings on successive pages. We also discuss the line counter used in controlling the printing of data. We review how the PERFORM statement creates a looping sequence or executes a paragraph.

After studying this chapter, you should be able to:

- Describe the four divisions of a COBOL program.
- Understand how I/O formats are generally detailed in the DATA DIVISION and the WORKING-STORAGE SECTION.
- Understand the overall use of editing features for printed output.
- Trace the flow of data through the PROCEDURE DIVISION.
- Generally understand selected COBOL statements.
- Understand the following terms:

ACCEPT instruction	Class test
AFTER ADVANCING clause	COMPUTE statement
Check protection	CONFIGURATION SECTION

DATA DIVISION

DISPLAY statement

Editing

Elementary items

ENVIRONMENT DIVISION

EXIT instruction

FD (file description)

FILE SECTION

Floating dollar sign

Group item

IDENTIFICATION DIVISION

INPUT-OUTPUT SECTION

LABEL RECORDS clause

Leading zeros

Level numbers

Line counters

Margin A

Margin B

OBJECT-COMPUTER

OPEN statement

Paragraph

PERFORM statement

PERFORM with VARYING option

PICTURE clause

PROCEDURE DIVISION

READ statement

READ INTO instruction

RECORD CONTAINS clause

RECORDING MODE IS clause

Reserved words

ROUNDED option

SELECT clause

77-level entry

SOURCE-COMPUTER

SPACES

VALUE clause

WORKING-STORAGE SECTION

WRITE FROM clause

WRITE statement

Zero suppression

Introduction

In May 1959, a group of computer experts from private industry and government, called the Conference on Data Systems Language (CODASYL), met to prepare and write the specifications of a programming language that would be uniquely suited to business applications. This new language, they hoped, would do for business what FORTRAN did for science and engineering.

For approximately 11 months, CODASYL met to draft the guidelines of the new language. In April 1960, the committee released its final report on a new programming language called COBOL. The report detailed the particulars and a fully operational model of COBOL. The new language used English words and phrases and structured its statements in sentences that were easily understood by non-computer professionals. COBOL was a high-level language well suited to the needs of the business community, providing a valuable output capability. Printed reports could be prepared far more easily than in other computer languages.

The discussions that follow will not make the reader a proficient COBOL programmer; they are designed to provide a working knowledge of the language. The reader should be able to scan a COBOL program and understand its overall purpose, know the type of data used, and determine if the solution offered is consistent with the problem under study.

9.1
An Overview of a COBOL Program
The Four Divisions

All COBOL programs are written in four divisions. Each division serves a specific purpose and must appear in every program. In sequence, the four divisions of a COBOL program are

1 The IDENTIFICATION DIVISION
2 The ENVIRONMENT DIVISION
3 The DATA DIVISION
4 The PROCEDURE DIVISION

The **IDENTIFICATION DIVISION** is for program identification. It contains data on the program's and programmer's names and the date on which the program was written. It also contains remarks on the processing of the program.

The **ENVIRONMENT DIVISION** gives information on the hardware used to process the program; it is the most closely machine-related of the four divisions. This division tells which computer system the source program was tested on and the computer being used to process the program. An important part of this division is the INPUT-OUTPUT SECTION, which defines the data files and the I/O devices used with them.

The **DATA DIVISION** describes each data format used in the program. In this division, files are refined into their record formats, with each format detailed by field name, size, and type of data. All I/O formats used must be defined here. The WORKING-STORAGE SECTION of this division permits the specification of the many I/O formats possible in a COBOL program. Special fields used in processing and not defined in an I/O format must also be included in this section.

The **PROCEDURE DIVISION** contains the program statements necessary for actual data processing. The order of statements in this division ordinarily parallels the logic of the flowchart drawn for the problem. The PROCEDURE DIVISION is the only division of a COBOL program that has statements that direct the processing of data.

Advantages and Disadvantages of COBOL

One advantage of COBOL is its similarity to English. Most people can basically understand it after a short period. COBOL terms such as ADD, SUBTRACT, WRITE, READ, and PERFORM avoid the extensive mathematical notations of other computer languages.

These nontechnical terms pay dividends in two ways: First, the syntax of the language is easily understood. Second, the debugging effort required to correct a COBOL program is simplified, because errors are easily recognized. The ease with which COBOL can be understood, learned, and debugged is a major advantage of the language.

Another advantage of COBOL is its ability to create formats for outputting printed information. The WORKING-STORAGE SECTION lets programmers develop the headings, literals, or special labels necessary to enhance any printed output. This section of the DATA DIVISION was specifically designed to handle report formats. The WORKING-STORAGE SECTION will be described at greater length later.

COBOL does, however, have some disadvantages. The compiler generally associated with COBOL is quite large and thus occupies a good portion of primary storage, although virtual storage (VS) has generally overcome this problem. Smaller versions of the COBOL compiler have also been developed to permit the use of COBOL on small computers. Generally, however, computer systems supporting COBOL need CPUs of considerable size.

Another disadvantage is that COBOL programs, because of the many required statements in each division, are very long. The statements' resemblance to English make them easy to understand but also increases their length. Program solutions that consist of 10 statements in another language may require 50 or more statements in COBOL. For many people, however, the ease with which COBOL programs can be understood is well worth the extra statements.

Reserved Words

One of COBOL's operational aspects is the special terms and phrases referred to as **reserved words.** Each reserved word is restricted to its own predefined purpose. For example, the word ADD may be used only to indicate addition, not to identify any other operation or data. Thus reserved words cannot be used as datanames or variables in COBOL. If you were to use a reserved word for a purpose other than that intended, your program would not be properly processed. The terms AREA, DIVISION, SECTION, MULTIPLY, DIVIDE, OPEN, PAGE, LABEL, NO, SIZE, and COUNT are samples of reserved words.

9.2 A Sample Program

To understand COBOL, you must examine an entire COBOL program. The following problem illustrates the specific uses of the four COBOL divisions. Illustrative Problem 1 provides enough information to construct a COBOL program.

IDENTIFICATION DIVISION

The IDENTIFICATION DIVISION identifies the program's assigned name and provides additional information on the program solution. Figure 9.2 gives the IDENTIFICATION DIVISION of the program written for Illustrative Problem 1. The IDENTIFICATION DIVISION and PROGRAM-ID statements are the two statements that must always be included in this division of a program. The first statement defines the division; the second statement indicates the program's specific name. In this case, the characters "PROG1" define the name of this COBOL program. All other entries in this IDENTIFICATION DIVISION comment on the solution.

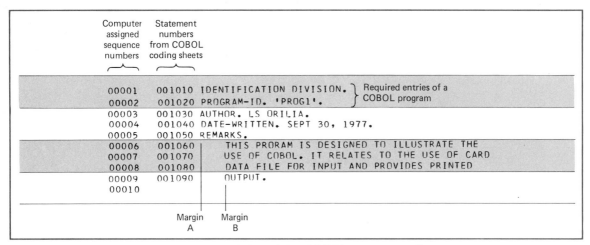

FIGURE 9.2 The IDENTIFICATION DIVISION of the COBOL program written for Illustrative Problem 1. The numbers on the extreme left are assigned by the computer and indicate the sequential order in which the statements are read. These are the numbers used by the COBOL compiler to identify program statements in which potential errors exist. The second set of statement numbers was taken from the coding sheets during the original keypunching of the program. Margin A and Margin B indicate the beginning of COBOL statements.

ILLUSTRATIVE PROBLEM 1

The overall problem involves the computation of an employee's net pay. Data is input via 80-column cards employing the following format:

Card Columns	Field Description
1–9	Social Security Number
10–24	Employee's Last Name
25–34	Employee's First Name
35	Employee's Middle Initial
36–39	Hours Worked per Week
40–43	Rate of Pay per Hour
44–80	Blank

The input file of employee payroll cards is called CARD-IN. Each individual employee card record is identified by the term EMP-RECORD.

The processing involved is defined by the following formulas:

Gross pay = hours worked $\times$ rate of pay
FICA deduction = gross pay $\times$ .0685
Net pay = gross pay $-$ FICA deduction

The printed output resulting from this COBOL program should contain the employee's name, social security number, gross pay, FICA deduction, and net pay amount. The outputs should appear on one line of print, with appropriate spacing between fields.

Figure 9.2 illustrates two fine points of COBOL. First, whenever a period is used to end a statement, at least one blank space must follow it. In the PROGRAM-ID statement, a blank space follows the period and precedes the program name. Second, COBOL rules dictate where program statements can begin. The first five statements of the IDENTIFICATION DIVISION must start at a point called **Margin A.** In terms of 80-column punched cards, Margin A is the equivalent of column 8. COBOL's second starting position is **Margin B,** the equivalent of card column 12. Note that the first sentence of the REMARKS section begins exactly at that point, not before. Note also the strict use of these margins in the illustrative problems throughout this chapter. COBOL statements that do not start at the appropriate margin will be rejected.

BLANK SPACE FOLLOWING PERIODS AND COMMAS

Periods are required after many COBOL statements. According to COBOL syntax, at least one blank space must follow a period. For example:

SOURCE-COMPUTER. IBM-370.
A minimum of one space is required.

One common mistake is to place a character immediately after the period. When commas are used in COBOL statements, the same rule applies. At least one blank space must follow a comma.

ENVIRONMENT DIVISION

The ENVIRONMENT DIVISION immediately follows the last statement of the IDENTIFICATION DIVISION. The ENVIRONMENT DIVISION specifies the computer hardware and data files employed during the processing of the program.

The statements included in the ENVIRONMENT DIVISION of Illustrative Problem 1 are listed in Figure 9.3. Two required sections of this division are the CONFIGURATION SECTION and the INPUT-OUTPUT SECTION. The **CONFIGURATION SECTION** defines the computer systems used to process the program. The **SOURCE-COMPUTER** entry identifies the computer on which the program was compiled and tested until it was certified as operationally correct. The **OBJECT-COMPUTER** entry indicates the computer that will be used to execute and process the approved program.

This separation of computer systems is deliberate. Many large data processing organizations have two entirely different computer systems for processing programs.One system is used for the time-

```
00012
00013
00014     001100 ENVIRONMENT DIVISION.
00015     001110 CONFIGURATION SECTION.
00016     001120 SOURCE-COMPUTER. IBM-370.
00017     001130 OBJECT-COMPUTER. IBM-370.
00018     001140 INPUT-OUTPUT SECTION.
00019     001150 FILE-CONTROL.
00020 **    09        SELECT CARD-IN, ASSIGN TO UR-S-SYSIN.
00021       10        SELECT PRINT-OUT, ASSIGN TO UR-S-SYSPRINT.
00022
```

FIGURE 9.3 The ENVIRONMENT DIVISION of the COBOL program written for Illustrative Problem 1. The SELECT statements identify the two I/O files used by the program. The double asterisks alert the programmer to the fact that statements 00020 and 00021 are not in sequence with the coding sheet numbers of previous statements.

consuming tasks of developing and testing programs. The second system is free to process a continuous stream of work.

The source and object computers used in Illustrative Problem 1 are the IBM 370. Thus the statements in the program identify this manufacturer and type of system. If a UNIVAC, National Cash Register, Honeywell, Burroughs, or other system were used, the source and object computer entries would so indicate.

The **INPUT-OUTPUT SECTION** identifies the files used by the program and assigns those files to specific I/O devices in the computer system. Both of the above are accomplished through the **SELECT clause** (statements 00020 and 00021). The first SELECT clause identifies the input card file by the name CARD-IN and assigns it to the card reader, which is defined by the characters UR-S-SYSIN. The second clause identifies the output file by the name PRINT-OUT and assigns it to the system's printer, indicated by the phrase UR-S-SYSPRINT.

The terms used to reference the card reader and the printer vary among computer systems according to their operating software. Two other common samples of SELECT clauses are

SELECT CARD-IN ASSIGN TO 'SYS005', UNIT-RECORD 2540R.
SELECT PRINT-OUT ASSIGN TO 'SYS007', UNIT-RECORD 1403.

In these statements, UNIT-RECORD 2540R and UNIT-RECORD 1403 are standard references to the card reader and the printer, respectively. The notations 'SYS005' and 'SYS007' refer to identification numbers assigned by the computer system to the card reader and printer devices.

Once the existence of the data files is noted in the SELECT clauses, the format of each file must be detailed. These definitions are provided in the DATA DIVISION.

DATA DIVISION   The DATA DIVISION details all data used in a COBOL program. The division uses two sections to accomplish this: the FILE SECTION and the WORKING-STORAGE SECTION. The **FILE SECTION** contains details related to every file identified by a SELECT clause by type, record format, and data fields in each record. The **WORKING-STOR-AGE SECTION** defines items of data not specified in any of the formats of the FILE SECTION. Figure 9.4 illustrates the DATA DIVISION of Illustrative Problem 1.

     The FILE SECTION contains the definition of all I/O files used by the program. The input card file, CARD-IN, is the first file defined. The letters **FD** (for **File Description**) always precede the file name. Care-

FIGURE 9.4   The DATA DIVISION of the COBOL program for Illustrative Problem 1. The FILE SECTION must always precede the WORKING-STORAGE SECTION in this division.

```
00026
00027   002010 DATA DIVISION.
00028   002020 FILE SECTION.
00029   002030 FD  CARD-IN
00030   002040     RECORD CONTAINS 80 CHARACTERS
00031   002050     LABEL RECORDS ARE OMITTED
00032   002060     RECORDING MODE IS F
00033   002070     DATA RECORD  IS  EMP-RECORD.
00034   002080 01  EMP-RECORD.
00035   002090     02 SOC-SEC-NO              PIC 9(9).
00036   002100     02 EMPLOYEE-NAME.
00037   002110        03 LAST-NAME            PIC X(15).
00038   002120        03 FIRST-NAME           PIC X(10).
00039   002130        03 MID-INITIAL          PIC X.
00040   002140     02 HOURS-WORK              PIC 99V99.
00041   002150     02 RATE-PAY                PIC 99V99.
00042   002160     02 FILLER                  PIC X(37).
00043   003010 FD  PRINT-OUT
00044   003020     RECORD CONTAINS 133 CHARACTERS
00045   003030     LABEL RECORDS ARE OMITTED
00046   003040     RECORDING MODE IS F
00047   003050     DATA RECORDS ARE PRINT-REC.
00048   003060 01  PRINT-REC.
00049   003070     02 FILLER                  PIC X(5).
00050   003080     02 SOC-OUT                 PIC 9(9).
00051   003090     02 FILLER                  PIC X(3).
00052   003100     02 LAST-OUT                PIC X(15).
00053   003110     02 FILLER                  PIC X(2).
00054   003120     02 FIRST-OUT               PIC X(10).
00055   003130     02 FILLER                  PIC X(3).
00056   003140     02 MID-OUT                 PIC X.
00057   003150     02 FILLER                  PIC X(2).
00058   003160     02 GROSS-OUT               PIC 9999V99.
00059   003170     02 FILLER                  PIC X(2).
00060   003180     02 FICA-OUT                PIC 9999V99.
00061   003190     02 FILLER                  PIC X(2).
00062   003200     02 NET-OUT                 PIC 9999V99.
00063 **003  0     02 FILLER                  PIC X(61).
00064   004010 WORKING-STORAGE SECTION.
00065   004020 77  GROSS-PAY                  PIC 9999V99. VALUE ZEROES.
00066   004030 77  FICA-DED                   PIC 9999V99. VALUE ZEROES.
00067   004040 77  NET-PAY                    PIC 9999V99. VALUE ZEROES.
00068
```

fully note that the file name used in the FD must be the same as that specified in the prior SELECT clause. Each statement of the FD following the file name is a standard COBOL entry and describes some aspect of the file.

The **RECORD CONTAINS clause,** statement 00030, specifies the number of characters in each record of the file. For the file CARD-IN, each record contains 80 characters, the equivalent of the number of columns on a standard punch card. If a different input medium were used, the number of characters in the incoming record would vary, and this would alter the RECORD CONTAINS clause. The number of characters specified in this clause depends on the file used.

The **LABEL RECORDS clause** relates to the file labels used in the program. The input file CARD-IN is a card file and does not use the type of file label that would be required by a tape or a disk file. Thus, the statement LABEL RECORDS ARE OMITTED is correctly specified for the CARD-IN file description. File labels would be necessary if tape or disk files were used, because such files are identified by labels. An example is the header label in a tape file. The header label is a required tape feature, identifying operational characteristics of the tape to be used in processing. The statement LABEL RECORDS ARE STANDARD is used when describing a disk or a tape file.

The use of a card file also fixes the size of each input record at 80 characters, because the standard punch card is limited to 80 columns of data. The statement RECORDING MODE IS F, where F represents the word *fixed,* notes the constant size of each incoming record. When tape and disk files are being processed, the record size occasionally varies; that is, one record might be 160 characters long and the next record 260 characters long. In this case, the **RECORDING MODE**[1] **clause** will read RECORDING MODE IS V. The letter V represents the word *variable* and handles the varying length of the records in that type of file.

The last statement of the FD defines the name of the individual record format of the file. In this program, the name EMP-RECORD is assigned to the record format of the file CARD-IN. The record is subsequently broken down into its component fields. Statements 00034 to 00042 depict the field-by-field breakdown of EMP-RECORD. The format described in these statements should be the same as the card format in the narrative of Illustrative Problem 1.

Statement 00034 provides a **level number** (01) and restates the record name (EMP-RECORD). Level numbers are an integral part of COBOL syntax because they show the relative importance of fields. These two digits are assigned to fields which compose the records

---

[1] In many computer systems, the RECORDS CONTAINS and RECORDING MODE clauses are optional because the system's operational software compensates for them. Programmers can learn about this option by checking their system's technical manuals.

defined in the DATA DIVISION. For example, the level number 01 is always assigned to the first statement of a record format (i.e., line 00034) and always begins at Margin A. The level number 01 identifies the name assigned to that record and represents the lowest level number which may be used. The level number 02 is assigned to the next level of fields that compose the record defined in the previous 01 entry. If any of the 02-level fields were subdivided, the level number 03 would be given to the smaller fields. Further subdivision of 03-level fields would require the level number 04. Essentially, each subdivision uses a higher level number. Always begin with the level number 01 and continue with 02, 03, and so on, as required. We further explain level numbers in the definition of EMP-RECORD.

The initial field in EMP-RECORD is the Social Security No., consisting of nine characters, columns 1 to 9. In the program, line 00035 represents this field as

<blockquote>

02   **SOC-SEC-NO**   **PIC 9(9).**

</blockquote>

The level number 02 notes that this field is a component field of EMP-RECORD. The name SOC-SEC-NO is the dataname selected for the Social Security No. field. Notice that hyphens are used to separate characters because blanks are not permitted in COBOL datanames. The last part of the 02 entry is the PICTURE clause, PIC 9(9). **PICTURE clauses** in COBOL identify the type and size of data contained in a field. The 9 outside the parentheses indicates that the field is composed solely of numeric data. The 9 inside the parentheses notes the size of the field; thus, SOC-SEC-NO is a 9-column numeric field.

The characters A and X are used in PICTURE clauses to define alphabetic and alphanumeric data fields, respectively. An alphabetic field of two characters could be correctly specified as PIC AA or PIC A(2). Similarly, a five digit alphanumeric field might be identified as PIC XXXXX or PIC X(5).

The alphanumeric PICTURE clause notation is used in the specification of the EMPLOYEE-NAME field. However, the PICTURE clause also indicates that this field is subdivided into three smaller fields. The first component field is LAST-NAME, identified as a 15-digit alphanumeric field, PIC X(15). The remaining two fields, FIRST-NAME and MID-INITIAL, are defined as alphanumeric fields of 10 and 1 characters, PIC X(10) and PIC X.

The three subfields for EMPLOYEE-NAME are also indicated by the level numbers used. The field EMPLOYEE-NAME is given a level number of 02; the three component fields are assigned the level number 03. In COBOL syntax, the type of field represented by EMPLOYEE-NAME is defined as a **group item,** and the subfields composing a group item are referred to as **elementary items** (i.e., LAST-NAME, FIRST-NAME, MID-INITIAL). Group items are not provided with PICTURE clauses, while elementary items must have them. One computes the size of a group item by adding the number of characters in its elementary items. In this case, EMPLOYEE-NAME is a 26-character alphanumeric field.

The next two fields, HOURS-WORK and RATE-PAY, are numeric fields. Both fields use a decimal point, and its position must be fixed in the PICTURE clause. The decimal point in these two four-digit fields is positioned using the clause PIC 99V99. The character V in a PICTURE clause implies the existence of a decimal point.

The position of a decimal point is not indicated in the data itself, because COBOL cannot accept input data containing decimal points. Thus the data 32.50 is actually input as 3250, with the decimal point omitted. Using PIC 99V99, COBOL interprets the data as 32V50, with V indicating the decimal point's position. In our sample program, the data items 37.50 hours worked and a pay rate of 03.50 are specified as 3750 and 0350 and understood to be 37V50 and 03V50, respectively.

The PICTURE clauses of SOC-SEC-NO, EMPLOYEE-NAME, HOURS-WORK, and RATE-PAY account for the first 43 card columns of EMP-RECORD. However, the RECORD CONTAINS clause originally defined this record size as 80 characters. The remaining 37 positions of EMP-RECORD are accounted for by the entry

02   **FILLER**   **PIC X(37).**

FILLER is a reserved word specifically for unused portions of I/O records. In input record formats, the FILLER entry ordinarily fills out the remaining portion of the record. In output records, the FILLER entry often separates items of data to create legible formats. In all cases, COBOL requires that the program account for every character specified in its I/O record formats. The use of FILLER simplifies this task.

The description of the output file PRINT-OUT employs the same clauses as the previous FD, with some modifications. The RECORD CONTAINS clause notes that each output record is 133 characters long. The record size of 133 characters is the fixed size of all records output by a printer (remember, a SELECT clause assigned this output file to UR-S-SYSPRINT).

The LABEL RECORDS ARE OMITTED clause is specified, because the output of printed data does not require special labels. Also, the fixed record length of 133 characters causes the use of the RECORDING MODE IS F clause. The last statement (00047) of the PRINT-OUT file description defines the record name as PRINT-REC.

The definition of PRINT-REC involves the use of FILLER to separate the output fields and provide an easily readable format. In addition to the output of the social security number (SOC-OUT) and the employee name, PRINT-REC contains the fields GROSS-OUT, FICA-OUT, and NET-OUT. These three fields relate to the results of processing.

Data fields composing output records are not ordinarily used in computations. Thus, all calculations must be performed in other fields and then moved to the output record. In this program, gross pay is computed using the variable GROSS-PAY. The data in GROSS-PAY is then transferred to GROSS-OUT just before the output of PRINT-REC. The same steps are followed for computing FICA-DED and NET-PAY and moving their data to FICA-OUT and NET-OUT.

The three fields GROSS-PAY, FICA-DED, and NET-PAY are all used in computations and are not part of PRINT-REC. Such fields are identified as **77-level entries** and are defined only in the WORKING-STORAGE SECTION.

Data fields defined by 77-level entries are an integral part of processing. Two examples of data items defined by 77-level entries are

1 Fields used in arithmetic operations that cannot be defined in input or output FDs (e.g., a counter)
2 Fields used to hold intermediate totals or subtotals (e.g., an accumulator)

Without 77-level statements, these types of fields could not exist. All 77-level entries let the programmer create any number of data items that are required for processing. A rule of thumb is, "Fields employed in arithmetic operations, not defined in input or output file descriptions, are established via 77-level entries." The fields GROSS-PAY, FICA-DED, and NET-PAY are all used in arithmetic operations and are not defined in the description of PRINT-REC. Therefore, each has to be defined by a 77-level entry to be used in Illustrative Problem 1.

A VALUE ZEROES statement is placed at the end of the three 77-level instructions. The **VALUE clause** lets the programmer initialize a 77-level entry and other data items within WORKING-STORAGE at any value desired. In this case, GROSS-PAY, FICA-DED, and NET-PAY have been initially set at zero to ensure that incorrect data is not included in any of these fields. The VALUE clauses must always follow the PICTURE clause and are only used in the WORKING-STORAGE SECTION.

Once all files, record formats, and 77-level entries are defined in the DATA DIVISION, the COBOL statements necessary to process this data may be detailed. The statements used to direct the computer's processing are in the PROCEDURE DIVISION.

PROCEDURE DIVISION

The PROCEDURE DIVISION is the only place in a COBOL program where statements related to the actual processing of data may appear. The logic of these statements should closely follow a flowchart. The flowchart and the PROCEDURE DIVISION for Illustrative Problem 1 appear in Figures 9.5 and 9.6. Refer to these figures during our discussion of Illustrative Problem 1.

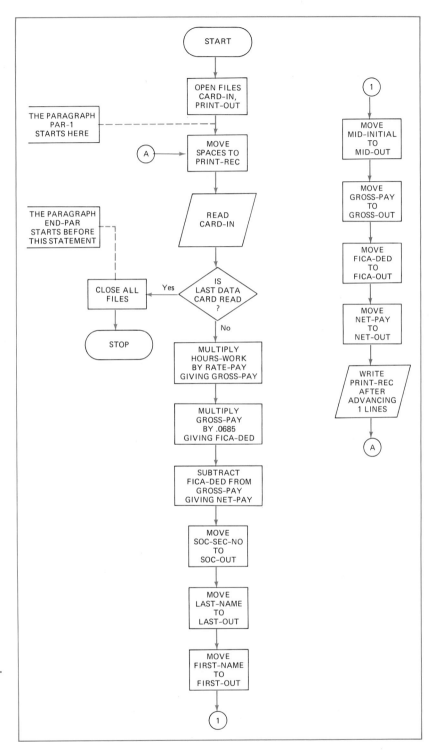

FIGURE 9.5 The flowchart depicting the processing of data in the PROCEDURE DIVISION of the COBOL program for Illustrative Problem 1.

```
00072
00073    004050  PROCEDURE DIVISION.
00074    004060      OPEN INPUT CARD-IN, OUTPUT PRINT-OUT.
00075    004070  PAR-1.
00076    004080      MOVE SPACES TO PRINT-REC.
00077    004090      READ CARD-IN AT END GO TO END-PAR.
00078    004100      MULTIPLY HOURS-WORK BY RATE-PAY GIVING GROSS-PAY.
00079    004110      MULTIPLY GROSS-PAY BY .0685 GIVING FICA-DED.
00080    004120      SUBTRACT FICA-DED FROM GROSS-PAY GIVING NET-PAY.
00081    004130      MOVE SOC-SEC-NO TO SOC-OUT.
00082    004140      MOVE LAST-NAME TO LAST-OUT.
00083    004150      MOVE FIRST-NAME TO FIRST-OUT.
00084    004160      MOVE MID-INITIAL TO MID-OUT.
00085    004170      MOVE GROSS-PAY TO GROSS-OUT.
00086    004180      MOVE FICA-DED TO FICA-OUT.
00087    004190      MOVE NET-PAY TO NET-OUT.
00088    004200      WRITE PRINT-REC AFTER ADVANCING 1 LINES.
00089  **004        GO TO PAR-1.
00090  **004    END-PAR.
00091  **004        CLOSE CARD-IN, PRINT-OUT.
00092  **004        STOP RUN.
```

FIGURE 9.6 The PROCEDURE DIVISION of the COBOL program written for Illustrative Problem 1.

The first statement of the PROCEDURE DIVISION, the **OPEN statement,** identifies CARD-IN as an input file and PRINT-OUT as an output file and opens these files. In COBOL, all files must be opened before they can be used in processing.

FILE NAMES

Correct file names are extremely important in COBOL. The programmer must check the assignment of file names in three strategic places of a COBOL program. The file names specified in SELECT clauses must match the file names defined by the FDs of the DATA DIVISION and those used in the OPEN statement of the PROCEDURE DIVISION. If these file names do not agree, the program will not run.

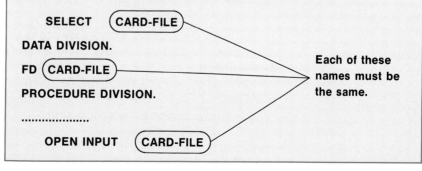

After the files are opened, processing can begin. The flowchart (Figure 9.5) shows only one program loop. This program loop is defined in the PROCEDURE DIVISION by statements 00075 to 00089 and is referred to as a paragraph. A **paragraph,** composed of any number of statements, is identified by a paragraph name. Paragraphs group related statements and make branching to them easier. In Illustrative Problem 1, PAR-1 is the paragraph name defining the program loop in which processing will occur.

Paragraphs are important to the structure of the PROCEDURE DIVISION, as they create modules in which specific programming activities are performed. For example, one paragraph may contain all the program instructions necessary to print headings at the top of a report. Other paragraphs may contain statements to handle incorrect input data, process data that has been segregated by a code number (e.g., one paragraph computes overtime pay, while another processes regular pay), or close all the files used by a program. Each paragraph has its own purpose and contains the statements necessary to complete a specific task. As data is processed, the program branches to the paragraph required to handle that type of processing. In completing one program loop, the number of statements used relates to the actual processing involved.

The initial statement of paragraph PAR-1 directs the computer to move SPACES to PRINT-REC. SPACES is a reserved word that defines one or more blank spaces. This statement places a string of 133 blanks in PRINT-REC and ensures that any unwanted characters accidentally positioned in PRINT-REC are not output.

The **READ statement** (00077) combines the input operation and tests for the last item of data. Initially, this statement directs the computer to read data from the input file CARD-IN. Because the file description for this file defined the input record as 80 characters, data is read one card at a time. The READ statement also defines the actions to be taken when the program runs out of data. Using the reserved words AT END GO TO, the READ statement causes the program to branch to the paragraph END-PAR when no data remains in the file CARD-IN. The END-PAR paragraph contains statements to close the files and end the program.

Though the READ statement is the primary means of inputting data from a file, COBOL offers a way to read individual card data without having to define that data using a File Description. The **ACCEPT instruction** allows the input of an individual card before data from a file defined by an FD is read. This technique is commonly used to enter card data on a date, control number, or department name and number that will be referenced in processing.

The fields composing the format to be input via the ACCEPT statement are defined in WORKING-STORAGE within an 01-level entry. The ACCEPT instruction used to read the specific card is positioned with

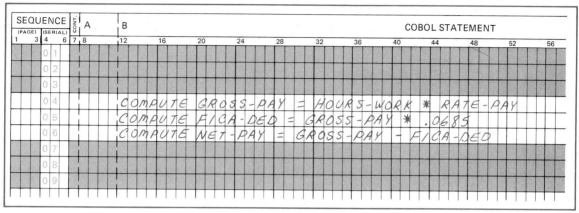

FIGURE 9.7   **The computation of GROSS-PAY, FICA-DED, and NET-PAY using COMPUTE statement. These statements begin at Margin B, as noted by the coding sheet.**

all other initial conditions (starting at Margin B), usually following the OPENing of files and preceding the printing of headings.

We should clarify one point about the ACCEPT statement. It is not designed to circumvent the *File Description* and READ statements. It should be used to enter a special data item which does not warrant a complete FD. All other file data should be properly defined with FDs and input via the required instructions.

Data input from CARD-IN is processed by statements 00078 to 00087. The statements compute amounts related to GROSS-PAY, FICA-DED, and NET-PAY, which are all 77-level entries of the WORK-ING-STORAGE SECTION. These three statements demonstrate the Englishlike format of COBOL. Each computation is represented by a sentence. COBOL also can represent these calculations as formulas through the **COMPUTE statement** (Figure 9.7).

The COMPUTE statement replaces words with mathematical symbols. The multiplication of HOURS-WORK and RATE-PAY is represented in the GROSS-PAY statement by an asterisk (*). Table 9.1 provides other mathematical symbols used with the COMPUTE statement. The option of using the COMPUTE statement or any other COBOL arithmetic statement remains with the individual programmer.

Table 9.1   Arithmetic Symbols

Symbol	Mathematical Operation
+	Addition
−	Subtraction
*	Multiplication
/	Division
**	Exponentiation

The statements following the computation of NET-PAY relate to moving data to the output format of PRINT-REC. The MOVE statement is usually used to transfer data in a COBOL program. The MOVE statement is required because of the way COBOL handles I/O operations.

SPACES SURROUNDING SYMBOLS

Adequate spacing must be provided for mathematical symbols in COBOL statements. For example, when using the COMPUTE statement, one space must be placed on either side of the equal sign. This spacing ensures that the statement will be properly processed.

COMPUTE GROSS-PAY = HOURS-WORK * RATE-PAY

Blank Spaces

COBOL establishes a separate area for input data, from which data cannot be directly output. Data in the input area must be moved to an output area. The MOVE statement is the principal means of making this transfer.

Seven MOVE statements are used to transfer data into the output record, PRINT-REC, in Illustrative Problem 1. For identification purposes, all the field names of PRINT-REC use the word OUT. Data from the input field SOC-SEC-NO is moved to SOC-OUT. Data held in the 77-level entries (i.e., GROSS-PAY, FICA-DED, and NET-PAY) must also be moved to their output fields. For example, data stored in GROSS-PAY is moved to GROSS-OUT.

The movement of data from NET-PAY to NET-OUT is indicated in the last MOVE statement and precedes the output of data. The **WRITE statement** contains the **AFTER ADVANCING clause,** which lets the programmer control the output of the program. The AFTER ADVANCING 1 LINES clause directs the computer to single space the output and print data one line at a time. The number preceding the reserved word LINES dictates the number of lines to skip. For double spacing, the WRITE statement might appear as

WRITE PRINT-REC AFTER ADVANCING 2 LINES.

The output of PRINT-REC completes data processing in this loop. The GO TO PAR-1 statement represents the unconditional branch to the start of the paragraph, PAR-1, where processing begins again. This looping continues until the program runs out of data.

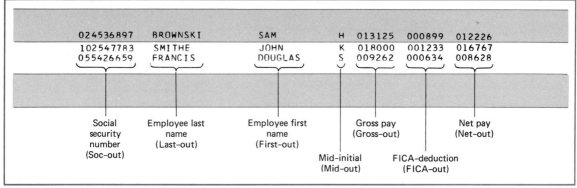

FIGURE 9.8   The line-by-line, single-spaced output produced by the first sample program. Each of the output fields is identified by its contents and the field name defined in PRINT-REC. The last three fields imply the existence of a decimal point to indicate cents. The gross pay amount 013125 should be considered to be 0131V25, where 131 is the dollar amount and 25 is the cents. The net pay is computed by subtracting the FICA amount from gross pay:

$$\begin{aligned}
\text{Net} &= \text{gross pay} - \text{FICA deduction} \\
&= 131.25 - 8.99 \\
&= 122.26
\end{aligned}$$

IMPROPER SYNTAX

Programmers must be careful not to alter the syntax of COBOL statements. A statement that might not appear grammatically correct could still be properly written. Examine the following statement:

WRITE PRINT-REC AFTER ADVANCING 1 LINES.

Though 1 LINES seems improper, it is correct. COBOL specifies the use of LINES in the AFTER ADVANCING clause.

9.3
The WORKING-STORAGE SECTION
Use in Creating Outputs

One advantage of COBOL is that it can print reports for management. Headings are an integral part of any report. With COBOL, headings can be easily constructed line by line in the WORKING-STORAGE SECTION. COBOL's **WRITE FROM clause** allows these headings to be output directly from the WORKING-STORAGE SECTION and thus eliminates the need to repeatedly move data to the output area. Illustrative Problem 2 demonstrates the use of the WRITE FROM clause and the WORKING-STORAGE SECTION to create report headings.

ILLUSTRATIVE PROBLEM 2

The overall problem deals with the output of lists of student grades. The card input to the program follows.

Card Column	Field Description
1–4	Student Number
5–29	Student Name
30–32	Grade 1
33–35	Grade 2

Student averages are computed from the two grades provided. The headings used in the output of this program are:

STUDENT NUMBER	STUDENT NAME	FINAL AVERAGE

Student data should appear beneath these column headings.

The program for Illustrative Problem 2 appears in Figure 9.9. The statements in the first two divisions of the program are consistent with prior discussions. The program's name is 'PROG2', and it is processed on an IBM 370 computer. The SELECT clauses identify two files as CARD-FILE and PRINT-FILE and assign them to the card reader and the printer, respectively. Of special interest, however, is how these files are defined in the DATA DIVISION.

The FD for CARD-FILE properly details an 80-column punch card as the input medium and identifies the record name as CARD-REC. The 01-level subdivision of CARD-REC is taken directly from the card format of the problem definition.

The FD for PRINT-FILE correctly specifies the record length of 133 characters required for the output of printed data. However, the 01-level description of PRINT-REC consists of only one statement describing an alphanumeric field of 133 characters. This statement is correct and represents the creation of a dummy print area to prepare for the WRITE FROM clause. The WRITE FROM clause allows data formats, created in the WORKING-STORAGE SECTION, to pass through this dummy area and to be printed directly. The programmer does not have to use a large number of MOVE statements to create the desired output format. The proper use of the WORKING-STORAGE SECTION is related to the successful use of the WRITE FROM clause.

Because no output formats are described in the FD of PRINT-FILE, they are detailed in the WORKING-STORAGE SECTION. Note in Figure 9.9 that three output formats are defined in that section.

```
00001    01   IDENTIFICATION DIVISION.
00002    02   PROGRAM-ID. 'PROG2'.
00003    03   ENVIRONMENT DIVISION.
00004    04   CONFIGURATION SECTION.
00005    05   SOURCE-COMPUTER. IBM-370.
00006    06   OBJECT-COMPUTER. IBM-370.
00007    07   INPUT-OUTPUT SECTION.
00008    08   FILE-CONTROL.
00009    09        SELECT CARD-FILE, ASSIGN TO UR-S-SYSIN.
00010    10        SELECT PRINT-FILE, ASSIGN TO UR-S-SYSPRINT.
00011
00012
00013
00014
00015
00016 ** 01   DATA DIVISION.
00017    02   FILE SECTION.
00018    03   FD  CARD-FILE
00019    04        RECORD CONTAINS 80 CHARACTERS
00020    05        LABEL RECORDS ARE OMITTED
00021    06        RECORDING MODE IS F
00022    07        DATA RECORD IS CARD-REC.
00023    08   01   CARD-REC.
00024    09        02   STUD-NUMBER     PIC 9(4).
00025    10        02   STUD-NAME       PIC X(25).
00026    11        02   GRADE-1         PIC 999.
00027    12        02   GRADE-2         PIC 999.
00028    13        02   FILLER          PIC X(45).
00029    14   FD  PRINT-FILE
00030    15        RECORD CONTAINS 133 CHARACTERS
00031    16        LABEL RECORDS ARE OMITTED
00032    17        RECORDING MODE IS F
00033    18        DATA RECORD IS PRINT-REC.
00034    19   01   PRINT-REC           PIC X(133).
00035
00036
00037
00038
00039    20   WORKING-STORAGE SECTION.
00040         77   FINAL-AVG           PIC 999V99.
00041         77   TOT-1               PIC 9(6).
00042 ** 01   01   HEAD-1.
00043    02        02 FILLER           PIC X(5), VALUE SPACES.
00044    03        02 ITEM-1           PIC X(7), VALUE 'STUDENT'.
00045    04        02 FILLER           PIC X(5), VALUE SPACES.
00046    05        02 ITEM-2           PIC X(7), VALUE 'STUDENT'.
00047    06        02 FILLER           PIC X(19), VALUE SPACES.
00048    07        02 ITEM-3           PIC X(5), VALUE 'FINAL'.
00049    08        02 FILLER           PIC X(86), VALUE SPACES.
00050    09   01   HEAD-2.
00051    10        02 FILLER           PIC X(5), VALUE SPACES.
00052    11        02 ITEM-4           PIC X(6), VALUE 'NUMBER'.
00053    12        02 FILLER           PIC X(6), VALUE SPACES.
00054    13        02 ITEM-5           PIC X(4), VALUE 'NAME'.
00055    14        02 FILLER           PIC X(22), VALUE SPACES.
00056    15        02 ITEM-6           PIC X(7), VALUE 'AVERAGE'.
00057    16        02 FILLER           PIC X(83), VALUE SPACES.
00058    17   01   STUDENT-LINE.
00059    18        02 FILLER           PIC X(5), VALUE SPACES.
00060    19        02 STUD-NO-OUT      PIC 9(4).
00061    20        02 FILLER           PIC X(8), VALUE SPACES.
00062         02 STUD-NAME-OUT         PIC X(25).
00063         02 FILLER                PIC X, VALUE SPACES.
00064         02 AVG-OUT               PIC 999V99.
00065         02 FILLER                PIC X(85), VALUE SPACES.
00066
00067
00068
00069
00070
00071 ** 01   PROCEDURE DIVISION.
00072    02        OPEN INPUT CARD-FILE, OUTPUT PRINT-FILE.
00073    03        MOVE SPACES TO PRINT-REC.
00074    04   PAR-1.
00075    05        WRITE PRINT-REC FROM HEAD-1 AFTER ADVANCING 1 LINES.
00076    06        WRITE PRINT-REC FROM HEAD-2 AFTER ADVANCING 1 LINES.
00077    07   PAR-2.
00078    08        READ CARD-FILE AT END GO TO END-PAR.
00079    09        ADD GRADE-1, GRADE-2 GIVING TOT-1.
00080    10        DIVIDE TOT-1 BY 2 GIVING FINAL-AVG.
00081    11        MOVE STUD-NUMBER TO STUD-NO-OUT.
00082    12        MOVE STUD-NAME TO STUD-NAME-OUT.
00083    13        MOVE FINAL-AVG TO AVG-OUT.
00084    14        WRITE PRINT-REC FROM STUDENT-LINE AFTER ADVANCING 1 LINES.
00085    15        GO TO PAR-2.
00086    16   END-PAR.
00087    17        CLOSE CARD-FILE, PRINT-FILE.
00088    18        STOP RUN.
```

FIGURE 9.9 The COBOL program written for Illustrative Problem 2.

HEAD-1 and HEAD-2 represent formats of the two lines used to create the column headings of the report. STUDENT-LINE describes the line format used for printing data on individual students. The STUDENT-LINE format contains the student's number, name, and computed average.

The lines HEAD-1 and HEAD-2 contain the literals for the headings. HEAD-1 contains the characters for the first line of the heading; HEAD-2, the second line. The literals in both lines are created through COBOL's VALUE clause.

PLACEMENT OF 77-LEVEL ENTRIES

All 77-level entries and 01-level descriptions of output formats are detailed in the WORKING-STORAGE SECTION. The order of these two types of statements is fixed. All 77-level entries must precede the 01-level record descriptions.

The VALUE clause, used solely in the WORKING-STORAGE SECTION, allows the programmer to initialize a variable at a numeric value or to create a literal. For example, the dataname ITEM-1 is assigned the characters STUDENT. These seven characters fit perfectly in the area defined by the clause PIC X(7). The VALUE clause is similarly used to create the literals STUDENT and FINAL for the variables ITEM-2 and ITEM-3. These three literals compose the first line of the heading (HEAD-1). The gaps between these three literals are defined as FILLER. The clause VALUE SPACES directs the computer to fill these gaps with blank spaces.

The second line of the heading, HEAD-2, uses the VALUE clause similarly. The literals printed beneath the first heading line are defined as NUMBER, NAME, and AVERAGE. The output resulting from these heading lines is shown in Figure 9.10.

Figure 9.10 illustrates how heading lines are aligned. The output of line HEAD-1 must immediately precede the output of HEAD-2. Their sequential printing is evident from the PAR-1 paragraph of the PROCEDURE DIVISION. The WRITE FROM clause allows both lines to be printed using their WORKING-STORAGE formats. No changes in their original formats were necessary, and it was not necessary to move data to PRINT-REC. The WRITE FROM clause caused the computer to pass the original formats through the dummy print area (PRINT-REC) and print them.

The WRITE FROM clause is also used in paragraph PAR-2 to output individual student data. After the computation of each student's grade, the data is moved to STUDENT-LINE. The output of the program is single spaced, because AFTER ADVANCING 1 LINES is used.

```
         STUDENT       STUDENT                      FINAL
         NUMBER        NAME                         AVERAGE
         1204          G. WASHINGTON                08000
         1458          J. WAYNE                     07400
         2459          A. HARRIMAN                  08050
         5837          H. FORD                      05050
```

FIGURE 9.10 The printed output produced by the program for Illustrative Problem 2. The overall heading consists of two lines and the three column headings STUDENT NUMBER, STUDENT NAME, and FINAL AVERAGE. Data for four students appears in this report. The proper use of FILLER made possible the alignment of the column headings and data printed beneath them.

The **READ INTO** form of the READ instruction parallels the WRITE FROM statement. Whereas the WRITE FROM governs output, the READ INTO instruction inputs data through a dummy input area to a specific record format defined within WORKING-STORAGE. Thus, for example, a dummy card-related input area would be initially defined in the FD with a PICTURE clause of PIC X(80); the actual formats identifying each field would be detailed within an 01 entry in WORKING-STORAGE. Datanames for both areas would be included in the resultant READ instruction, which might appear as

READ CARD-FILE INTO CARD-REC1 AT END GO TO END-PAR.

The name CARD-FILE identifies the input file defined in both the SELECT instruction and the FD entry. CARD-REC1 is the name assigned to the 01-level entry in WORKING-STORAGE which actually details all the fields composing that input record.

The READ INTO format is often used for processing multiple card formats. It offers programmers some flexibility in defining those input formats, since they can be described in WORKING-STORAGE and altered with a minimum of difficulty.

The Editing of Output Data

Not only can COBOL create headings, but it can also modify and enhance the output of data. COBOL can suppress unwanted characters, output dollar signs, place asterisks ahead of dollar amounts (as a protection against the fraudulent alteration of bank checks), and insert commas in numeric data. These special features allow the programmer to **edit** a program's output; that is, to arrange output data in a format that is correct, readable, and informative.

These edit features are defined in the WORKING-STORAGE SECTION and specifically in the PICTURE clauses of the datanames which will be edited. Each editing feature has its own format.

CLEANING THE PRINT AREA

The following statements may appear in some COBOL programs:

> **WRITE PRINT-REC AFTER ADVANCING 1 LINES.**
> **MOVE SPACES TO PRINT-REC.**

The computer is directed to print the contents of PRINT-REC and then move spaces to that print record. This sequence of statements ensures that unwanted characters are not carried over to the next output operation. Immediately after output, PRINT-REC is filled entirely with blanks, erasing its previous contents. Subsequent MOVE statements will transfer data into a clean PRINT-REC area. No characters are carried over from an earlier output operation.

Zero Suppression

Examine the output of Illustrative Problem 2 (Figure 9.10), and note the format of the data printed beneath FINAL AVERAGE. The student G. WASHINGTON has an average of 80.00. However, the printed average appears as 08000. The 0 preceding the digit 8, referred to as a **leading zero,** is unnecessary. COBOL lets you suppress leading zeros with the character Z.

The original PICTURE clause applied to the FINAL AVERAGE field is PIC 999V99. **Zero suppression** is accomplished with the clause PIC ZZZV99. This clause produces an output of 8000.

This output can be further enhanced by a decimal point. Though decimal points cannot be used in PICTURE clauses of data items associated with arithmetic operations (i.e., 77-level variables), they are permissible in their outputs. A PICTURE clause applied to the FINAL AVERAGE might be PIC ZZZ.99. This clause would accomplish zero suppression and insert a decimal point within the printed output. The 80 average of student G. Washington would appear as 80.00. Table 9.2 illustrates other examples of the zero suppression editing feature.

Table 9.2 Examples of Zero Suppression

PICTURE Clause	Data Involved	Printed Output
PIC ZZZZZ	00612	612
PIC ZZZ.9	001.6	1.6
PIC Z(6)	007100	7100
PIC ZZ.99	00.01	.01

The Floating Dollar Sign

COBOL can output dollar signs. Their positioning is directed by one or more $'s in a PICTURE clause. For example:

    02   GROSS-PAY   PIC $$$$$$.99.

The above PICTURE clause might appear as part of an output format in the WORKING-STORAGE SECTION. This clause will cause a $ to be printed ahead of the gross pay amount. The amount 219.78 would be printed as $219.78. Though six dollar signs are specified, the $ is not fixed; the computer will position it ahead of the data amount. Therefore, it is referred to as a **floating dollar sign.** Table 9.3 provides additional examples of the floating dollar sign.

Table 9.3 Floating Dollar Signs

PICTURE Clause	Data Amount	Printed Output
$$$$$$.99	00010.84	$10.84
$$$$$$.99	01634.57	$1634.57
$$$$.99	000.08	$.08
$$$$.99	609.45	$609.45

Insertion of Commas

Commas can highlight amounts of data. Commas in a numeric field can indicate quantities of data in the thousands or millions. COBOL allows commas to be inserted in numeric data through a PICTURE clause entry in the WORKING-STORAGE SECTION. The two sample entries below illustrate the combined use of commas, zero suppression, and the floating dollar sign.

    02   TOTAL-COUNT   PIC ZZZ,ZZZ
    02   GROSS-PAY   PIC $$,$$$.99.

Table 9.4 further illustrates the use of commas in PICTURE clauses.

Table 9.4 The Insertion of Commas in Selected PICTURE Clauses

PICTURE Clause	Data Amount	Printed Output
$$$,$$$.99	00064.38	$64.38
$$$,$$$.99	00564.38	$564.38
$$$,$$$.99	01453.67	$1,453.67
ZZ,ZZZ	00671	671
ZZ,ZZZ	01735	1,735

Check Protection Using the Asterisk

One of the primary uses of COBOL is in processing employee payrolls. An important aspect of any payroll is the preparation of employee paychecks. These checks must be safe from illegal alteration. COBOL provides a form of **check protection** with a series of asterisks.

The required string of asterisks is defined in a PICTURE clause in the WORKING-STORAGE SECTION. A typical format employing asterisks is:

> **02   NET-PAY-OUT   PIC $***,***.99.**

The above clause will cause a dollar sign to precede the string of asterisks protecting the amount of the check. Table 9.5 provides additional samples of PICTURE clauses involving strings of asterisks.

Each of the four editing features can be used in any COBOL program. They offer the programmer flexibility in creating formats for printed outputs.

Table 9.5 PICTURE Clauses Using Asterisks

PICTURE Clause	Data Amount	Printed Output
$***,***.99	001349.66	$**1,349.66
$***,***.99	000008.49	$******8.49
$****.99	1453.00	$1453.00
$**,***.99	00628.18	$***628.18

ACCOUNTING FOR CHARACTERS

Each of the 133 characters of the output area must be carefully accounted for. When computing the FILLER entry of the print area (i.e., PRINT-REC), the programmer must carefully examine editing characters. Commas, dollar signs, asterisks, and decimal points each assume one position in the total of 133 characters. The programmer must be certain to include these characters in that total.

9.4 Selected COBOL Features

The program written for Illustrative Problem 3 incorporates some of COBOL's additional features. From this solution, it is possible to examine the use of the following: a line counter to control the printing of headings and data on a page, the DISPLAY statement to output special messages, the PERFORM statement to direct the uninterrupted completion of a series of program instructions, and the conditional statement.

ILLUSTRATIVE PROBLEM 3

The overall problem relates to the output of a monthly inventory listing. Cards input to the program have the following format:

Card Column	Field Description	Data Format
1–6	Part Number	9(6)
7–26	Part Name	X(20)
27–30	Quantity on Hand	9(4)
31–36	Unit Cost	9999V99
37–80	Blank	X(44)

The program must compute the cost of each item in inventory and the total cost of the entire inventory. The program's output should appear as shown in Figure 9.11. A heading is required above each column of data, and a label should precede the output of the total inventory cost. The line limit per page is 50 lines of data, plus headings.

FIGURE 9.11   The printer spacing chart used for Illustrative Problem 3. The chart indicates the field descriptions, heading lines, summary lines, output formats, and editing used in the program.

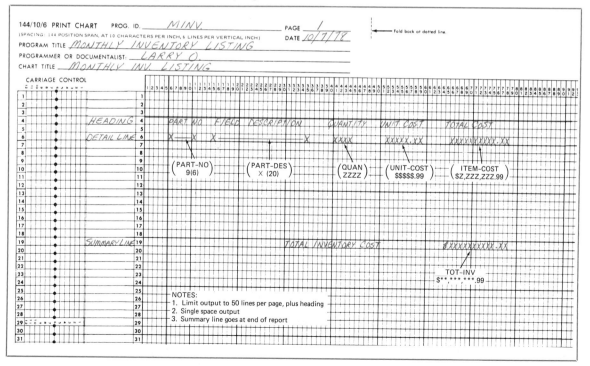

```
00001    001010 IDENTIFICATION DIVISION.
00002    001020 PROGRAM-ID. 'PROG3'.
00003    001030 ENVIRONMENT DIVISION.
00004    001040 CONFIGURATION SECTION.
00005    001050 SOURCE-COMPUTER. IBM-370.
00006    001060 OBJECT-COMPUTER. IBM-370.
00007           SPECIAL-NAMES.
00008               C01 IS TOP-OF-PAGE.
00009    001070 INPUT-OUTPUT SECTION.
00010    001080 FILE-CONTROL.
00011    001090     SELECT CARD-FILE ASSIGN TO UR-S-SYSIN.
00012    001100     SELECT INV-FILE ASSIGN TO UR-S-SYSPRINT.
00013    001110 DATA DIVISION.
00014    001120 FILE SECTION.
00015    001130 FD  CARD-FILE
00016    001140     RECORD CONTAINS 80 CHARACTERS
00017    001150     LABEL RECORDS ARE OMITTED
00018    001160     RECORDING MODE IS F
00019    001170     DATA RECORD IS CARD-REC.
00020    001180 01  CARD-REC.
00021    001190     02  PART-NUM        PIC 9(6).
00022    001200     02  PART-DESCRIP    PIC X(20).
00023    001210     02  QUAN-IN         PIC 9(4).
00024    001220     02  U-COST          PIC 9999V99.
00025    001230     02  FILLER          PIC X(44).
00026    002010 FD  INV-FILE
00027    002020     RECORD CONTAINS 133 CHARACTERS
00028    002030     LABEL RECORDS ARE OMITTED
00029    002040     RECORDING MODE IS F
00030    002050     DATA RECORD IS INV-REC.
00031    002060 01  INV-REC             PIC X(133).
00032    002070 WORKING-STORAGE SECTION.
00033    002080 77  INV-COST            PIC 9(7)V99, VALUE ZEROES.
00034    002090 77  TOT-COST            PIC 9(8)V99, VALUE ZEROES.
00035    002100 77  KOUNT               PIC 99, VALUE ZEROES.
00036    002110 01  HEAD-1.
00037    002120     02  FILLER          PIC X(5), VALUE SPACES.
00038    002130     02  ITEM-1          PIC X(7), VALUE 'PART NO'.
00039    002140     02  FILLER          PIC X(3), VALUE SPACES.
00040    002150     02  ITEM-2          PIC X(18), VALUE 'FIELD DESCRIPTION'.
00041    002160     02  FILLER          PIC X(6), VALUE SPACES.
00042    002170     02  ITEM-3          PIC X(8), VALUE 'QUANTITY'.
00043    002180     02  FILLER          PIC X(3), VALUE SPACES.
00044    002190     02  ITEM-4          PIC X(9), VALUE 'UNIT COST'.
00045    002200     02  FILLER          PIC X(5), VALUE SPACES.
00046    002210     02  ITEM-5          PIC X(10), VALUE 'TOTAL COST'.
00047    002220     02  FILLER          PIC X(59), VALUE SPACES.
00048    003010 01  INV-LINE.
00049    003020     02  FILLER          PIC X(5), VALUE SPACES.
00050    003030     02  PART-NO         PIC 9(6).
00051    003040     02  FILLER          PIC X(4), VALUE SPACES.
00052    003050     02  PART-DES        PIC X(20).
00053    003060     02  FILLER          PIC X(5), VALUE SPACES.
00054    003070     02  QUAN            PIC ZZZZ.
00055    003080     02  FILLER          PIC X(7), VALUE SPACES.
00056    003090     02  UNIT-COST       PIC $$$$$.99.
00057    003100     02  FILLER          PIC X(6), VALUE SPACES.
00058    003110     02  ITEM-COST       PIC $Z,ZZZ,ZZZ.99.
00059    003120     02  FILLER          PIC X(55), VALUE SPACES.
00060    003130 01  SUM-LINE.
00061    003140     02  FILLER          PIC X(30), VALUE SPACES.
00062    003150     02  ITEM-6          PIC X(20), VALUE 'TOTAL INVENTORY COST'.
00063    003160     02  FILLER          PIC X(14), VALUE SPACES.
00064    003170     02  TOT-INV         PIC $**,***,***.99.
00065    003180     02  FILLER          PIC X(55), VALUE SPACES.
00066    003190 PROCEDURE DIVISION.
00067    003200     OPEN INPUT CARD-FILE, OUTPUT INV-FILE.
00068    004010 PAR-1.
00069    004020     MOVE ZEROES TO KOUNT.
00070    004030     WRITE   INV-REC FROM HEAD-1 AFTER ADVANCING TOP-OF-PAGE.
00071    004040     COMPUTE   KOUNT = 1 .
00072    004050 PAR-2.
00073    004060     READ CARD-FILE AT END GO TO END-PAR.
00074    04070      IF QUAN-IN IS NOT NUMERIC OR U-COST IS NOT NUMERIC
00075    04071          GO TO ERR-PAR.
00076  **004080     MULTIPLY QUAN-IN BY U-COST GIVING INV-COST ROUNDED.
00077    004090     ADD INV-COST TO TOT-COST.
00078    004100     MOVE PART-NUM TO PART-NO.
00079    004110     MOVE PART-DESCRIP TO PART-DES.
00080    004120     MOVE QUAN-IN TO QUAN.
00081    004130     MOVE U-COST TO UNIT-COST.
00082    004140     MOVE INV-COST TO ITEM-COST.
00083    004150     WRITE INV-REC FROM INV-LINE AFTER ADVANCING 1 LINES.
00084    004160     IF KOUNT = 50, PERFORM PAR-1 ELSE ADD 1 TO KOUNT.
00085    004170     GO TO PAR-2.
00086    004180 ERR-PAR.
00087    004200     DISPLAY 'DATA ERROR CARD NUMBER', PART-NUM.
00088  **004         GO TO PAR-2.
00089    005010 END-PAR.
00090    005020     MOVE TOT-COST TO TOT-INV.
00091    005030     WRITE INV-REC FROM SUM-LINE AFTER ADVANCING 2 LINES.
00092    005040     CLOSE CARD-FILE, INV-FILE.
00093    005050     STOP RUN.
```

FIGURE 9.12 The COBOL program written for Illustrative Problem 3.

The COBOL program written for Illustrative Problem 3 is provided in Figure 9.12. Examination of the WORKING-STORAGE SECTION reveals that a heading line (HEAD-1), a detail line (INV-LINE), and a summary line (SUM-LINE) will be used by the file INV-FILE for output. The last two lines are edited so that they provide the desired output formats. In INV-LINE the PICTURE clause of UNIT-COST (line 00056) uses a string of floating dollar signs, and zero suppression is applied to ITEM-COST and QUAN (lines 00054 and 00058). A string of asterisks protects the TOT-INV item of SUM-LINE (line 00064).

The editing of each line is evident in the output of Illustrative Problem 3 (Figure 9.13). Zero suppression must have been performed on the data for QUANTITY, since no leading zeros are evident. Through the use of a floating string, every amount printed under UNIT COST is preceded by a dollar sign. The outputs beneath TOTAL-COST are zero suppressed and properly use commas. In the summary line, an asterisk properly fills the unused portion of TOT-INV. The editing of output data will occur on every page of the inventory report.

Note the output of headings at the top of each report page in Figure 9.13. Headings make reports more understandable by identifying columns of data. Often the number of headings closely parallels the amount of data printed on a page. In any case, the preparation of headings is an integral part of a program solution.

FIGURE 9.13   The printed output of the program for Illustrative Problem 3. The headings on top identify data printed on page 1. A label appears on the last page of the report, on which the total cost of the inventory is output.

PART NO	FIELD DESCRIPTION	QUANTITY	UNIT COST	TOTAL COST	
002357	GAUGES AIRGUN	25	$368.54	$ 9,213.50	
000312	METRIC HAMMERS	4	$125.62	$ 502.48	
050006	LEFTHANDED AWLS	206	$26.25	$ 5,407.50	
072847	SCREWDRIVERS	14	$8.95	$ 125.30	Page 1 of the
121977	3/4 INCH BOLTS	2550	$.98	$ 2,499.00	inventory
003414	AXLE WRENCHES	6	$209.53	$ 1,257.18	report
000014	ELECTRICAL AMPLIFIER	73	$1221.77	$ 89,189.21	
002049	CONTACT BOXES	630	$531.35	$ 334,750.50	
347660	LIGHT SOCKETS	6000	$310.08	$1,860,480.00	

PART NO	FIELD DESCRIPTION	QUANTITY	UNIT COST	TOTAL COST	
060104	WELDING PINS	8000	$428.04	$3,424,320.00	
004339	55 GALLON DRUMS	250	$95.62	$ 23,905.00	
000624	10 TON TRUCKS	6	$8995.95	$ 53,975.70	
096338	TARPAULINS 2000 SQFT	62	$614.57	$ 38,103.34	Last page of
324817	METAL RACKS	100	$1000.55	$ 100,055.00	the report
773800	LAMPLIGHTS 1000 AMP	2200	$783.66	$1,724,052.00	
	TOTAL INVENTORY COST		$**8,227,495.31		

Line Counters

Output in Illustrative Problem 3 is controlled with a **line counter,** which totals the number of lines printed on a page. When the desired number of lines has been printed, the line counter will cause the program to branch to the instructions necessary to print headings at the top of the next page of the report.

The line counter is defined as KOUNT, a 77-level entry (line 00035). KOUNT is set equal to one before the first line of data is printed beneath the headings (line 00071). The line counter is incremented by one (line 00084) after each line is printed. Line 00084 illustrates the format of a conditional statement. This format can be analyzed as follows:

IF	KOUNT = 50	PERFORM PAR-1	ELSE	ADD 1 TO KOUNT.
	Condition	Action to be taken if answer to condition is yes (equivalent of YES branch)	Reserved word	Action to be taken if condition is rated no (equivalent of NO branch)

In this problem, 50 lines of data are to be printed per page. Thus, if KOUNT is less than 50, then 1 is added to the line counter. When KOUNT = 50, the fiftieth line of data has been printed on the page and the program will branch to PAR-1.

Paragraph PAR-1 contains the WRITE statement necessary to output the report's heading line. The use of the term TOP-OF-PAGE ensures that the heading is always printed at the top of each page of the report. The printing of TOP-OF-PAGE on a new page is established by an entry in the SPECIAL-NAMES paragraph of the ENVIRONMENT DIVISION (line 00008). After the heading is printed, the line counter is set back to one, and the printing of individual data lines can continue.

The **PERFORM statement** used in the conditional statement enables a program to branch to a paragraph, complete the series of instructions composing the paragraph, and return to the point of departure. When KOUNT = 50, Illustrative Problem 3 branches from statement 00084, completes PAR-1, and returns to statement 00084. The next instruction completed is GO TO PAR-2, where the program loop and the output of data are resumed.

Class Tests

The initial conditional statement of PAR-2 does not compare an input item with a specific number; it tests whether the data entered is numeric. This type of comparison is referred to as a **class test.** Its purpose is to test data before it is used in processing. In this case, QUAN-IN and U-COST are tested to ensure that these inputs are composed solely of numbers. The use of the reserved word OR permits the programmer to use one instruction to test both fields. A statement that tests two or more data items is generally referred to as a *compound conditional statement.*

If either QUAN-IN or U-COST contains input data that is not numeric, the program unconditionally branches to the paragraph ERR-PAR. This paragraph will output information to alert the programmer or operator to the invalid data. This output, composed of a literal and a related part number, is accomplished via the **DISPLAY statement.** The DISPLAY statement creates a special output that can appear after all other data printed in the report or on another I/O device, depending on the computer system. The DISPLAY statement does not replace the output file defined by the SELECT clause in the DATA DIVISION.

If input data related to QUAN-IN and U-COST are deemed valid, then the computation of INV-COST proceeds. The reserved word **ROUNDED** at the end of this statement directs the computer to round off all computed amounts of INV-COST (e.g., .846 is rounded off to .85). This amount is then added to the accumulated inventory total cost (line 00077). The five MOVE statements that follow these computations transfer data to INV-LINE. The WRITE FROM clause (line 00083) outputs the contents of INV-LINE to compose each line of this inventory listing. The line-by-line printing of data will continue until no data cards remain. At that point, the program will branch to END-PAR. After moving TOT-COST to TOT-INV, the summary line (SUM-LINE) is printed. The amount printed in this line represents the total cost of every item listed in the inventory report. The closing of all files used precedes the end of the program.

PERFORM Statements

Illustrative Problem 3 used only one form of the PERFORM instruction. But the PERFORM statement can take many forms, each suited to a different role. For example, it can be used as an automatic looping statement being written as

PERFORM PAR-6   30 TIMES.

This will instruct the computer to repeat paragraph PAR-6 30 times.

Another form of the PERFORM statement directs the repeated processing of a series of paragraphs. An example appears below.

PERFORM PAR-1 THRU EXIT-PAR 10 TIMES.

This statement directs the computer to execute all instructions in paragraphs PAR -1 to EXIT-PAR. This technique is common with programs subdivided into many paragraphs, such as the one in Figure 9.14. After executing the 10 required loops, the program exits from the EXIT-PAR paragraph, returns to the PERFORM statement that started the looping sequence, and passes to the next instruction.

FIGURE 9.14 The PER-
FORM statement can be
used to execute a group
of paragraphs a speci-
fied number of times.
When branching out of
the looping sequence,
the EXIT instruction
must appear as the last
instruction. The instruc-
tions here show the
PERFORM instruction
under these conditions.

```
PROCEDURE DIVISION.
           :
      PERFORM PAR-1 THRU EXIT-PAR 10 TIMES.
           :

PAR - 1.
      READ CARD-FILE AT END GO TO EXIT-PAR.
      IF CODE = 1 GO TO EXIT-PAR.
           :

PAR - 2.
           :

EXIT - PAR.
      EXIT.
```

Though the EXIT-PAR contains only one instruction, it is critical to the looping sequence. If the program branched out of a PERFORM looping sequence without passing through the EXIT-PAR paragraph, the results would be unpredictable. Unless it recognizes the **EXIT instruction** of the EXIT-PAR paragraph, the computer does not properly close the looping operation and can inhibit further use of the PERFORM statement.

As Figure 9.14 shows, the program branches to the EXIT-PAR paragraph when the READ instruction runs out of data and encounters a code = 1. The branch to EXIT-PAR and the execution of the EXIT instruction let the computer properly exit from the looping sequence.

Another form of the PERFORM statement allows for a counter, its increment, and a limit on the number of loops to be performed. An instruction of this type appears below.

PERFORM PAR-1 THRU EXIT-PAR VARYING K
FROM 1 BY 1 UNTIL K = 30.

Defined as the **PERFORM with VARYING option,** this format has special features. It defines a counter variable K, a starting point *from 1,* and an increment *by 1* on each loop, and it dictates that looping should continue until K is equal to 30. Within the instruction, the variable follows the word VARYING and is defined as a 77-level entry. The number following the word FROM defines the start of the looping process, and the increment follows the reserved word BY. The condition on which looping should end, assuming no error states, follows the word UNTIL. This format is common for working with arrays of data stored within the computer or generated by the program.

Case Study One

Computers Answer to a Higher Authority

With the help of their computer, administrators at one of the West Coast's largest synagogues attend to the needs of their congregation. The Wilshire Boulevard Temple of Los Angeles uses a computer for informational mailings to members and for administration of the temple's religious school, summer day camp, and cemetery.

After years of doing all the temple's paper work by hand, in 1978 controller Mark Greenstein began investigating how to automate office procedures. He looked into service bureaus, time-shared operations, and other forms of DP services and ultimately chose an in-house computer system. The temple contracted with Quantel Business Systems for a system complete with the necessary hardware and software. The system Greenstein chose was the Quantel 1400, supported by 4 CRTs, a 12-megabyte disk, and a high-speed printer.

After several years, temple administrators are very pleased with their choice. Their decision to opt for a turnkey system, in which the manufacturer provides all components, appears to have been sound. Quantel designed all software specifically to meet the temple's needs. In effect, the temple installed a customized data processing system in which the manufacturer did all implementing, testing, and certifying. The temple accepted the system only when all components proved operational.

The Quantel system helps administer high holy day seating, the preparation of announcements for weddings and anniversaries, Yahrzeit (memorial) notices, and analysis of membership information. It also maintains school records, enrollment data on the 1000 children at the temple's summer camp, and operational data on the temple's cemetery. Billing data for each of these services is prepared monthly, and all other information is made available as it is needed.

As a sidelight, installation of the computer did not reduce the size of the office staff, but it did simplify the workload. The computer permitted the smooth reorganization of files and speeded access to data. Now accurate information is quickly available.

Summary

The following major points have been discussed in Chapter 9:

Point 1 All COBOL programs contain four divisions. The IDENTIFICATION, ENVIRONMENT, DATA, and PROCEDURE DIVISIONS must appear, in exactly that order, in every program. COBOL is primarily used in business applications. Its English-like format makes it relatively easy to understand, learn, and debug. The drawbacks of COBOL are the length of its programs and the necessity to run these programs on systems possessing sufficient main storage.

Point 2 The IDENTIFICATION DIVISION supplies general information on the program, including the program's name, the date the program was written, the programmer's name, and overall remarks. The two required entries are the IDENTIFICATION DIVISION and the PROGRAM-ID statements. Both statements are composed of reserved words, special terms that have predefined meanings and uses.

Point 3 Entries in the ENVIRONMENT DIVISION describe the hardware and assign the files used by the program. The SOURCE-COMPUTER

Case Study Two
Computers Help Mail Order Firm

For a mail order business, the adage that "time is money" has special truth. Accurate billing of customers is critical for them. Excello Press, a Chicago-based direct-mail-order firm, faced an untenable situation. Its manual bookkeeping techniques were leading to constant problems in estimating costs of new work, pinpointing billing errors, controlling inventories, and monitoring production costs. Excello chose a computer.

Excello's first move toward computerization was with an IBM System/32. Installed in 1978, the system provided general accounting data for accounts receivable and payable, payroll, and inventory. The software supporting these services was specifically developed for Excello, no existing software having been deemed appropriate. The computer's performance and company growth combined to convince Excello's management to switch to a larger computer within a year.

The newly installed computer, an IBM System/34, allowed for the concurrent handling of several jobs. Several users therefore could have online access to the computer, and data processing was speeded up. The improvements in performance were felt most strongly in the preparation of customer quotes for work to be performed. These estimates were not only more accurate, but available in one-third the previous time. Each itemized statement was a boon to both the customer and Excello. The customer knew exactly what services were being received and at what price, and Excello could properly monitor the cost of services and better plan its production.

Once the services were performed, expenses could be properly allocated to the correct accounts. The reconciliation of accounts was also simplified. Customers were pleased with the prompt response to their requests for mail order services and the promptness of the actual marketing.

Excello's management is planning to gear up its computer services once again. Software is being developed to schedule production, analyze cash flow, and prepare tax and financial statements. One might say that a computer is being made to order for Excello.

Consider this . . .

What aspects of a mail order operation lend themselves to computerization? Does most of the junk mail received at your home or office look computer-prepared?

---

entry identifies the system on which the program was tested. The OBJECT-COMPUTER statement notes the computer used to process the program. The INPUT-OUTPUT SECTION contains the SELECT clauses that associate data files with their I/O devices.

Point 4 The DATA DIVISION details all files, record formats, and constants used by the program. The file descriptions (FDs) define the composition of each file by field name, type of data, and size. PICTURE clauses are an integral part of these statements. The WORKING-STORAGE SECTION describes any necessary variables and I/O formats that were not defined in the previous FDs. Headings, totals, summary lines, counters, literals, and labels are normally specified in this section.

Point 5 All editing of output data must occur in the WORKING-STORAGE SECTION. The edit features available in COBOL include zero suppression, the floating dollar sign, the insertion of commas or decimal points, and asterisks for check protection. Zero suppression deletes leading zeros from the output of numeric data. Floating dollar sign strings enable the programmer to place a dollar sign before the output of any value representing a dollar amount. Decimal points and commas can be placed in numeric output formats. Though decimal points cannot be used when inputting data, they can be inserted when the same information is output. Check protection permits the placement of asterisks into any unused positions of numeric output. All editing is accomplished in the PICTURE clauses of data defined in WORKING-STORAGE. The VALUE clause can be used to set selected variables at specific numeric amounts or groups of characters.

Point 6 The PROCEDURE DIVISION contains the COBOL instructions that actually direct the processing of data. The logic used in the PROCEDURE DIVISION is normally detailed in the flowchart developed for the problem solution. Files are opened to permit their use. MOVE statements are employed to transfer data to output areas. Arithmetic operations are possible using the COMPUTE statement or instructions involving the reserved words ADD, SUBTRACT, MULTIPLY, and DIVIDE. Groups of related statements are defined in paragraphs, Printed outputs can be produced using the AFTER ADVANCING clause of the WRITE statement. The PRINT FROM instruction permits the use of output formats defined in the WORKING-STORAGE SECTION.

Point 7 Three illustrative problems introduce the structure of a COBOL program and specialized COBOL techniques. Class tests are conditional statements that verify the accuracy of input data. Line counters control the amount of data printed per page and facilitate the output of headings. Specialized outputs can be printed using the DISPLAY statement. The PERFORM statement enables paragraphs to be executed a predetermined number of times.

Glossary

ACCEPT instruction A specialized input instruction that permits the input of data without construction of an FD or use of a READ or SELECT instruction.

AFTER ADVANCING clause A clause used in a WRITE statement to control the line-by-line printing of data.

Check protection The editing feature that inserts asterisks into the unused positions of dollar amount fields.

Class test The conditional statement used to verify input data.

COMPUTE statement The statement that permits the use of formulas to perform arithmetic computations.

CONFIGURATION SECTION A section of the ENVIRONMENT DIVISION; it contains the SOURCE- and OBJECT-COMPUTER entries.

DATA DIVISION One of the four major divisions of a COBOL program; it defines the contents of files used by a program.

DISPLAY statement An output statement used to display specialized items of data that appear after all other report data.

Editing The term applied to the special effects used in a PICTURE clause to create printed formats.

Elementary items The subfields of a larger field referred to as a group item.

ENVIRONMENT DIVISION The second division of a COBOL program; it defines the hardware used by the program.

EXIT instruction The only instruction of the EXIT paragraph.

FD (File Description) Entries in the DATA DIVISION that define the contents of a data file.

FILE SECTION The DATA DIVISION section which defines the FDs.

Floating dollar sign   An editing feature that places a dollar sign immediately in front of output data.

Group item   A data item composed of two or more subfields (elementary items).

IDENTIFICATION DIVISION   The first division of the COBOL program; it supplies information related to the program.

INPUT-OUTPUT SECTION   A section of the ENVIRONMENT DIVISION; it includes the SELECT clauses.

LABEL RECORDS clause   A clause appearing in the FD of the DATA DIVISION; it indicates the use of standard labels.

Leading zeros   Zeros that appear before the first significant digit of a numeric data item (e.g., the three 0's preceding the digit 6 in the number 000614).

Level numbers   Numbers used to define the relative importance of fields and subfields or specific data items (e.g., 77-level items).

Line counters   A programming technique used to control the number of lines printed per page and the output of headings.

Margin A   The starting point of selected COBOL statements; the punched card equivalent of card column 8.

Margin B   The starting point of selected COBOL statements; the punched card equivalent of card column 12.

OBJECT-COMPUTER   The entry in the ENVIRONMENT DIVISION indicating the computer system on which the program is to be executed.

OPEN statement   The statement used to open data files; it appears in the PROCEDURE DIVISION.

Paragraph   A group of related statements identified by paragraph name.

PERFORM statement   A processing statement used to define the execution of a paragraph one or more times.

PERFORM with VARYING option   A form of the PERFORM instruction that incorporates a counterlike variable, its increment, and a conditional statement to control the looping process.

PICTURE clause   The DATA DIVISION clause used to describe the size, type, and format of data used in the program.

PROCEDURE DIVISION   The last division of a COBOL program, containing statements that actually process data.

READ statement   An input statement.

READ INTO clause   A clause used with the READ instruction to input formats defined in WORKING-STORAGE.

RECORD CONTAINS clause   A clause used in the FD of the DATA DIVISION to indicate the size of the record format employed by the file being described.

RECORDING MODE clause   A clause used in the FD of the DATA DIVISION to note whether a file uses fixed- or variable-length records.

Reserved words   Words or phrases with special, predefined meanings.

ROUNDED option   A term that directs the computer to round off the results of computation (e.g., .087 is rounded up to .09).

SELECT clause   The ENVIRONMENT DIVISION clause that assigns data files to selected I/O devices employed in the computer system.

77-level entry   The level number assigned to individual data items in WORKING-STORAGE that are not defined in FDs.

SOURCE-COMPUTER   The ENVIRONMENT DIVISION entry that identifies the computer used to compile and test the program.

SPACES   A reserved word used to define one or more blank spaces.

VALUE clause   A WORKING-STORAGE entry that is used with a PICTURE clause to initialize variables at specific amounts or establish character groupings.

WORKING-STORAGE SECTION   A section of the DATA DIVISION where records not defined with FDs are detailed (e.g., 77-level entries).

WRITE FROM clause   A clause employed with the WRITE statement to output formats prepared in WORKING-STORAGE.

WRITE statement   An output statement.

Zero suppression   The editing technique that suppresses leading zeros from the output of data (e.g., 0062 is output as 62).

Discussion Questions

1 Discuss the purpose and contents of each of the four divisions of a COBOL program.

2 Examine the PICTURE clauses and the data in the table below. Enter in the last column of the table the format the data would take if output.

PICTURE Clause	Data	Printed Output
PIC ZZZ.99	000.01	
PIC $$$,$$$.99	000673.84	
PIC $$$,$$$.99	001732.45	
PIC $**,***.99	16.75	
PIC $**,***.99	483.34	

3 Examine the card format given below. Write the entire file description for the card file from which this card was taken. The file is named CARD-FILE, and the record name is CARD-REC. Individual field names can be taken from the card.

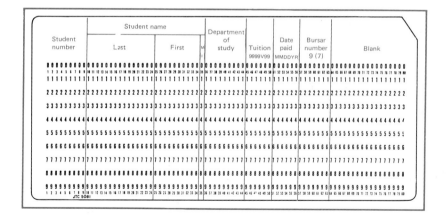

4 The data on the card in question 3 must be printed in a report. Write the file description that will allow the data to be output in printed form. Use a line length of 133 characters. Be sure that filler is placed between output fields to provide a readable format.

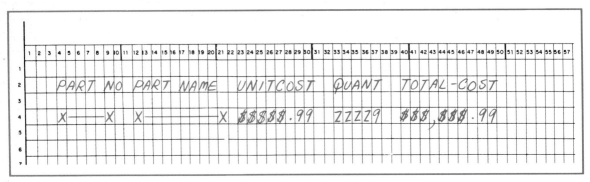

FIGURE 9.15

5 Write the WORKING-STORAGE entries necessary to define the heading line (HEAD-1) and the detail line (PRINT-REC) described in Figure 9.15. Be sure to account for all 133 characters in the print area.

6 Write PERFORM instructions to satisfy the following situations:

a Execute the paragraph OPEN-PAR just once.

b Execute the paragraph READ-RTE 25 times.

c Process all paragraphs from PAR-A to PAR-F seven times.

d Process the paragraphs PAR-1 to PAR-EXIT, until the variable COUNT equals 100.

e Process the paragraph READ-LOOP twenty times, using the counter CTR-1 to control the looping; it starts at a value of 51 and has an increment of 1.

f Process all paragraphs PAR-READ to PAR-EXIT 10 times, using a counter VCT that starts at 1 and has an increment of 5.

7 Using the flowchart of Figure 9.16, write the PROCEDURE DIVISION statements needed to satisfy the depicted solution. The overall problem relates to the printing of an employee listing of jobs. The input file used is TAPE-IN; the output file is named PRINT-OUT and has a dummy record format PRINT-REC. All output record formats used are actually defined in WORKING-STORAGE. Double space all lines printed.

8 Using the flowchart in Figure 9.17, write the PROCEDURE DIVISION statements to satisfy this solution. The general problem deals with listing and counting the number of accounts in an accounts payable file that are overdue for payment. The files used are ACCTS-IN for input and PRINT-OUT for output. A dummy output area called PRINT-1 is defined within PRINT-OUT. The detail line (LINE-1) and summary line (SUM-1) used in printing the actual data are defined in WORKING-STORAGE. Single space all lines printed. An accumulator totals the amount overdue in each account.

9 Using the flowchart in Figure 9.18, write the PROCEDURE DIVISION entries that might be used in a COBOL program. Begin with the PROCEDURE DIVISION statement and proceed through to STOP RUN. Remember to open and close the files. A card file, CARD-IN, is used for input, and the output file is PRINT-OUT. Don't forget to move data to the output area, PRINT-REC.

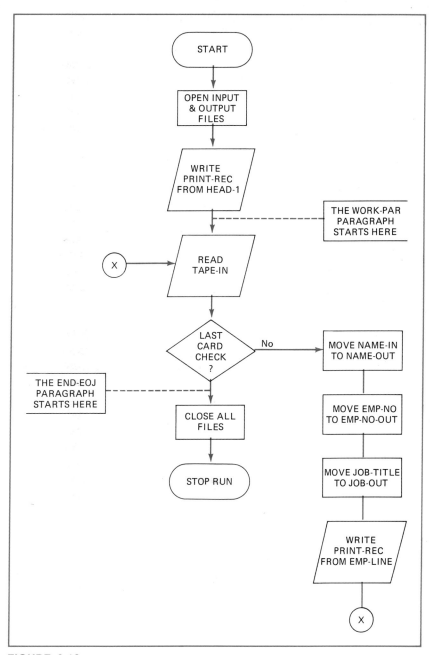

FIGURE 9.16

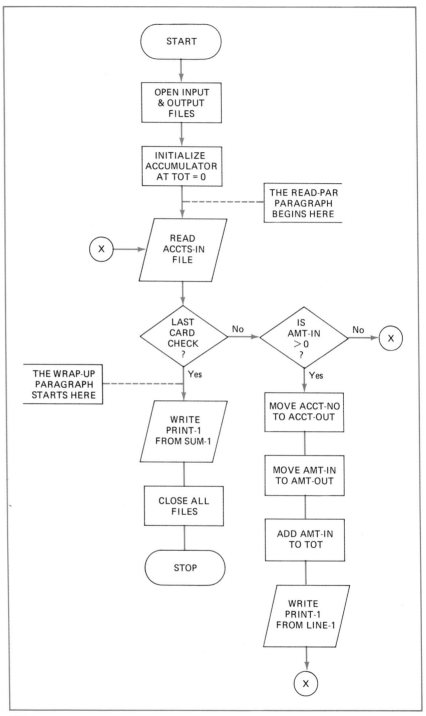

FIGURE 9.17

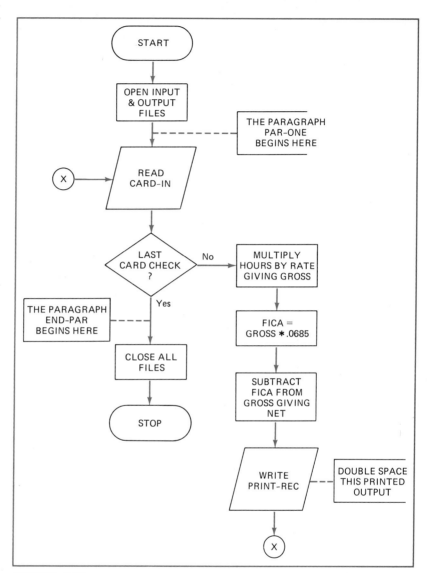

FIGURE 9.18

Summary Test

_____ **1** Picture clauses describing the output of printed data may appear in the PROCEDURE DIVISION.

_____ **2** The WORKING-STORAGE SECTION is contained in the ENVIRONMENT DIVISION.

_____ **3** The PICTURE clauses PIC 999 and PIC 9(3) are equivalent.

_____ **4** Margin A is equivalent to card column 12 on a punch card.

_____ **5** A line counter can be employed to control the number of lines of output printed per page.

_____ **6** The CONFIGURATION SECTION defines the computer systems used to process the program.

_____ **7** The statement WRITE PRINT-REC AFTER ADVANCING 2 LINES may be found in the DATA DIVISION.

_____ **8** The PICTURE clause PIC ZZZZ, when applied to the data 0041, will produce a printed output of 41.

_____ **9** The VALUE clause can only be used in the WORKING-STORAGE SECTION.

_____ **10** The WRITE FROM clause enables the output of formats directly from WORKING-STORAGE.

_____ **11** The clause LABEL RECORDS ARE STANDARD must be specified when processing data from card files.

_____ **12** Reserved words are terms or phrases in COBOL that have predefined purpose or meaning.

_____ **13** The PICTURE clause PIC $$$$$.99, when applied to the data 649.25, will produce a printed output of $$649.25.

_____ **14** In WORKING-STORAGE, all 77-level entries must precede 01-level descriptions of heading lines.

_____ **15** The term *paragraph* refers to a group of one or more related statements.

_____ **16** The PICTURE clause PIC $*,***.99, when applied to the data 19.42, will produce the edited output:

a	$19.42	**b**	$**19.42
c	$***19.42	**d**	$*,*19.42

_____ **17** The conditional statement that verifies the accuracy of input data is a:

a	class test	**b**	read check
c	data check	**d**	data test

_____ **18** FILLER must be defined by a(n):

a	A PICTURE clause	**b**	X PICTURE clause
c	9's PICTURE clause	**d**	a and b

_____ **19** The PICTURE clause PIC A(4) defines a(n):

a alphameric field

b field composed of 4As

c alphabetic, four-character field

d four-character numeric field

_____ **20** A required entry within the IDENTIFICATION DIVISION is:
  a the PROGRAM-ID statement
  b the DATE-WRITTEN instruction
  c an AUTHOR statement
  d all the above

_____ **21** The READ INTO statement involves:
  a an FD
  b a dummy input area
  c an 01-level entry in WORKING-STORAGE
  d all the above

_____ **22** The ACCEPT statement requires the use of:
  a an FD
  b a SELECT clause
  c an 01-level WORKING-STORAGE entry
  d a 77-level WORKING-STORAGE entry

For statements 23 to 25, use the following PERFORM statement:

**PERFORM PAR-A THRU PAR-EXIT VARYING K
FROM 11 BY 2 UNTIL K $>$ 30.**

_____ **23** The number of loops completed using this PERFORM statement is:
  a 19   **b** 30   **c** 10   **d** 15

_____ **24** The counter K would be originally defined as a(n):
  a 77-level entry in an FD
  b 77-level entry in WORKING-STORAGE
  c 01-level entry in WORKING-STORAGE
  d 01-level entry in an FD

_____ **25** The single instruction composing the PAR-EXIT paragraph is:
  a an END statement   **b** an EXIT statement
  c the STOP RUN statement   **d** a RETURN statement

Summary Test Answers

1 F	**2** F	**3** T	**4** F	**5** T
6 T	**7** F	**8** T	**9** T	**10** T
11 F	**12** T	**13** F	**14** T	**15** T
16 C	**17** A	**18** B	**19** C	**20** A
21 D	**22** C	**23** C	**24** B	**25** B

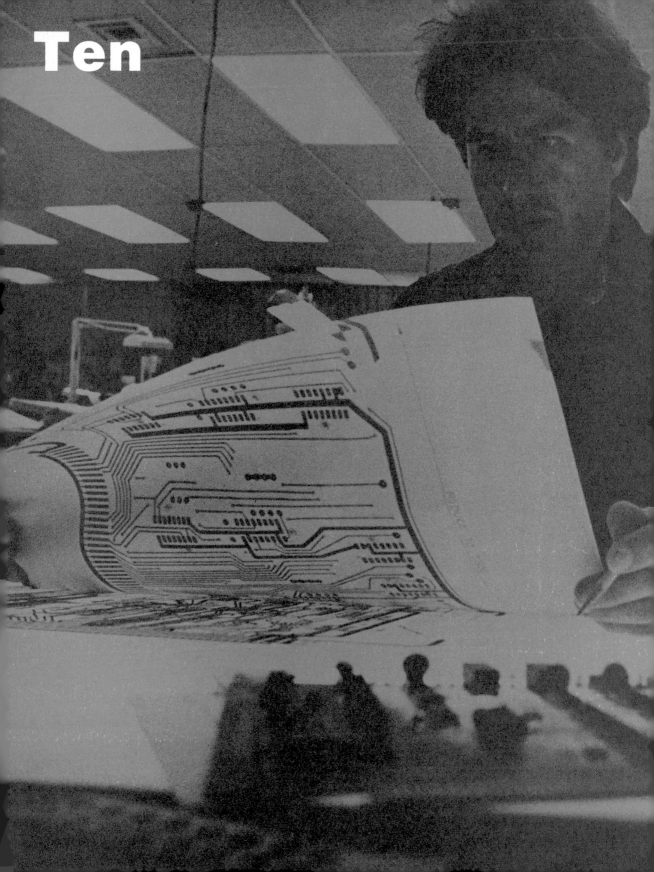

Ten

Structured Programming

Purpose of This Chapter

Introduction

10.1 The Concepts of Structured Design
Top-Down Design
Top-Down Programming and Testing
Reviewing the Structured Design
The Personnel Involved

10.2 Documenting the Structured Design
HIPO Documentation
Pseudocode

10.3 Structured Programming
Three Control Sequences
Other Flowcharting Symbols

10.4 Applications in BASIC

10.5 Applications in COBOL

10.6 Applications in PASCAL

Case Study

Summary

Glossary

Discussion Questions

Summary Test

FIGURE 10.1 Structured programming concepts are based upon the top-down design of modules which handle specific units of a solution. Many of these same concepts are applied to the design and construction of computer components. In this figure, an engineer examines the circuitry of a computer module under design. (*P. Arnold, Inc.*)

Purpose of This Chapter

This chapter introduces the topics of top-down design and structured programming. Sample programs in three programming languages illustrate the practical application of these techniques.

The chapter opens with a discussion of structured design. It explains the use of modules to represent major functions within a top-down solution and in structure charts. Programming and testing of top-down designs are also examined. The chapter explains structured walkthroughs and how the chief programmer team (CPT) is an important vehicle for implementing structured designs.

The major method of documenting top-down projects is the HIPO package, consisting of a visual table of contents, detail and overview HIPO diagrams, and other descriptive paperwork. A nonlanguage means of representing top-down program solutions is pseudocode, which uses a variety of terms to simulate actual program instructions.

The best application of top-down principles comes in structured programming, a technique that can improve the development of software, eliminate GO TOs, and increase programmer productivity. The three major control sequences, a process box, IF/THEN/ELSE conditional, and a looping sequence, are discussed. Other flowcharting symbols for documenting structured solutions are also reviewed.

The last three sections of Chapter 10 apply structured concepts in programs written in BASIC, COBOL, and PASCAL. Each illustrative problem implements a structured solution. Structured statements from all three languages are reviewed. These statements include the GOSUB, RETURN, IF/THEN/ELSE, PERFORM, BEGIN, and END instructions. Each program solution is carefully explained so that the reader can follow the logic employed.

After studying this chapter, you should be able to:

■ Discuss the concepts of top-down design.
■ Briefly discuss the implementation, testing, and review of structured designs.
■ Discuss HIPO documentation and the forms that compose the HIPO package.
■ Generally understand pseudocode.
■ Discuss the three control block sequences of structured programming.
■ Discuss the documentation of structured program solutions.
■ Understand and discuss the application of BASIC, COBOL, and PASCAL to problems involving structured programming.
■ Describe the use of the GOSUB, RETURN, BEGIN and END, PERFORM, IF, VARiable, and WRITELN statements.

■   Discuss how modules represent related groups of statements.

■   Understand the following terms:

BEGIN instruction	Predefined process symbol
Bottom-up approach	Processing and control module
Chief programmer team (CPT)	Processing module
Control block	Pseudocode
Detail HIPO diagram	RETURN statement
Dummy module	Structure chart
END instruction	Structured programming
Formal design review	Structured walkthrough
GOSUB statement	Subroutine
Hierarchy plus Input-Process-Output (HIPO)	Top-down design
	Top-down programming
HIPO package	Top-down testing
Informal design review	VARiable instruction
Main control module	Visual table of contents
Overview HIPO diagram	WRITELN instruction

Introduction

It has been estimated that if the automobile industry's progress had paralleled that of the computer industry, gas-powered cars would be getting over 550 miles per gallon. While many other computer-related costs have risen, hardware costs have decreased. Processing speeds have reached new highs. Today, it costs well under a penny to process 100,000 instructions. In almost 20 years, the work a computer can perform in one second has increased by 2700 percent, while the related cost has dropped to $\frac{1}{37}$ of what it was.

Yet while hardware-related costs have declined, computer personnel costs have risen dramatically. The high salaries paid to programmers have increased the costs associated with developing new software. This demand for the newest, most cost-efficient hardware has softened because the expense of developing the accompanying software is so high.

DP managers realize that software costs are composed of initial developmental costs and maintenance costs. If all programs ran on their first trial and never had to be modified, the problem of expense would be minor. But we know that this is not the case. The increasing demand for timely information results in the continual development of new software.

To produce better software and to monitor related costs, structured design and programming evolved. It was shown that the structured approach helped to develop more logically correct solutions and provided a vehicle for documenting the software. The net effect was better and less expensive software.

We must again caution the reader: this chapter is meant to introduce you to the structured approach; it will not make you a proficient structured programmer. If you want to learn more, we suggest that you read some of the many technical publications on the subject. This chapter should provide you with enough information to begin your investigation.

10.1
The Concepts of Structured Design
Top-Down Design

Breaking a complex problem into its component units, and analyzing each of these before formulating a solution, is a well-accepted problem-solving technique. A large problem is subdivided into a group of small problems which are easier to handle. This problem-solving approach offers the rationale used in developing top-down designs.

Top-down design provides a method for breaking down a total problem into its component units or modules. Other names applied to this technology are *modular approach, structured design,* and *composite design.* All describe the breaking down of the problem into its major functions, the subdividing of those functions into their subunits, and so on, until the final level is reached. This method lets you record the levels of complexity associated with each solution and the operational requirements of each subunit's processing.

Structured design avoids illogical solutions and solutions that deal with only part of the problem. The term generally applied to solutions such as these is the **bottom-up approach.** A small narrative will help explain the difference.

A programmer/analyst is directed to work with a manager to develop software for an inventory listing. In performing the analysis, the programmer focuses on one report, ignoring all other aspects of the problem and begins writing the program based solely on that report. The remainder of the program is forced into the solution. In effect, all other aspects of the solution were dictated by that one report rather than by the results of analysis or user needs. The solution was designed from the bottom up, not from the top down.

A top-down approach to this inventory problem would have defined the solution in a series of levels. The topmost level defines the overall, original problem. The second level divides the overall problem into its major components (i.e., input, processing, and output requirements). These major components are further refined on level 3 into their subunits to depict the type of inputs to be used, the nature of the processing to be performed, and the outputs that the program will provide. Level 4 would further redefine level 3's activities, detailing all aspects of the inputs, outputs, and processing incorporated into the solution.

You should have gathered by now that top-down design is a careful, sequential approach to problem solving. You must completely analyze one level at a time. The top-down technique forces you to examine and define all aspects of a problem before proceeding to the next lower level.

The relationship of each module in a top-down design may be graphically represented in a diagram called a **structure chart.** The structure chart looks much like an organization chart, which defines the relationships among a company's departments and personnel. Within the structure chart, however, each box or **control block** defines an activity associated with a particular level and subunit. The structure chart associated with our inventory example appears in Figure 10.2.

This structure chart shows how each level is assigned a number which establishes its relative position. The topmost level is assigned the number 0 and is called the **main control module.** It indicates the chart's overall objective. Each succeeding level receives a higher number, beginning with 1, until the last level of the chart is reached. Control blocks on this last level (i.e., level 3) are referred to as **processing modules.** All intermediary blocks are called **processing and control modules** (i.e., levels 1 and 2).

The use of numbered levels reinforces the top-to-bottom reading of the structure chart. The flow of control and data must proceed downward through the structure chart. Each block controls and provides the link to the module beneath it. Only at the lowest level of the structure chart, with the processing modules, does the subdivision cease.

For using top-down designs, certain general rules are suggested. These rules are:

1 Each module should be independent of all other modules.
2 The operational responsibility of each module should be concisely defined.
3 Each module should offer only one entrance and exit point.

The first rule addresses itself to the fact that a module's activities are undertaken only when control is passed to it from the preceding block. Similarly, when a block's operations have ceased, control returns to the module immediately above it. Rule 1 is aimed at eliminating the jumping around that occurs in ill-conceived solutions where program control travels continually among many statements rather than through a series of logical instructions.

Rule 2 suggests that each module of a structured design be designed to handle only one activity. Blocks should process one task and one task only. This rule offers three advantages: errors found in relation to a module are more easily identified and debugged; a module remains small enough that the amount of programming required is minimal; and the analysis of the block's operational activity is simplified.

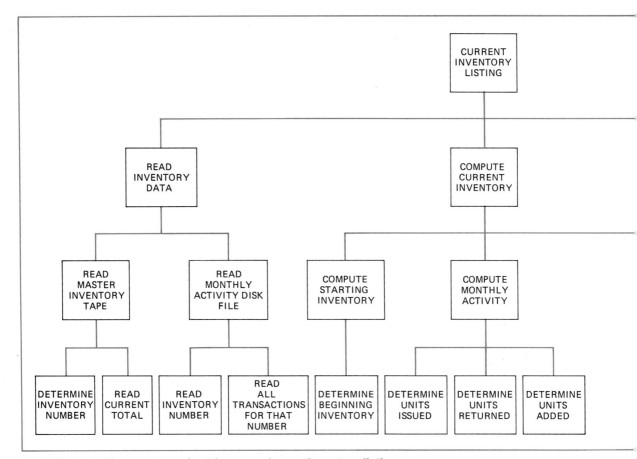

FIGURE 10.2   The structure chart for preparing an inventory listing.

Rule 3 addresses a technical detail, suggesting that a block have only one entry and exit. The rule lets you follow the control flow of a structure chart easily. Information flows down one leg of the chart and then back up. Control then passes to another leg of the chart. Again, the point is to eliminate the haphazard transfer of information. Note that the processing modules are the only blocks that do not contain exit points, as they represent the last level of processing.

Top-Down Programming and Testing

Once a top-down design is approved, its implementation may begin. **Top-down programming** identifies the development of software for that design. **Top-down testing** evaluates the efficiency of the implemented design.

At this point, we should clarify a possible misconception. The structured approach may be applied to both systems analysis and software design. In systems work, top-down designs detail the relationships among modules that dictate how data is handled in an organization. For example, one could lay out all the steps an accounts payable

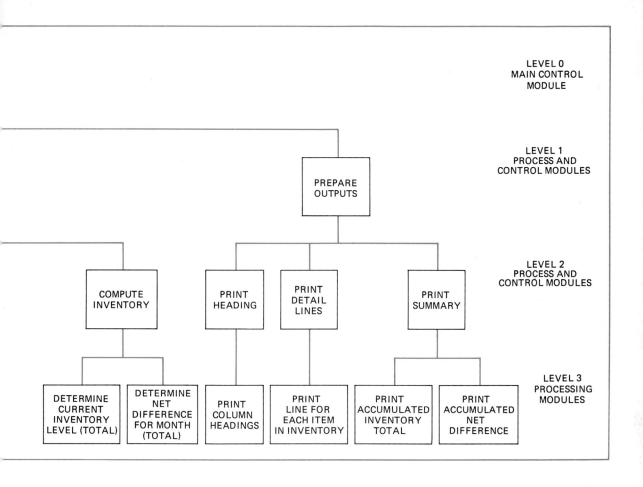

staff takes in paying vendors. This layout would indicate all the programs and steps necessary to support the processing of accounts payable data. The top-down systems design indicates the logical positioning of required programs in relation to the overall flow of information.

In programming work, the top-down design details the instructions that compose the actual program. The structure chart depicts both type and logical placement of each program instruction. Figure 10.2 shows blocks associated with a software effort. Usually, the top-down design of a system to handle the flow of organizational data precedes the structured design of the software necessary to support the processing of that data.

As top-down programming begins, each programmer is assigned a specific module, representing one program that must be written. Because each module represents a distinct program, programmers are free to develop their software independently. In top-down designs in which a series of program modules will interact, another activity is performed as the individual programs are being written. Other programmers write and test the operational software necessary to link these programs and permit their sequential execution and the access of data from required peripheral devices.

Because the relationship of the program modules is defined by the top-down design, it is possible to determine the control commands necessary to link their processing. The question asked is, "How can a series of programs be processed, using the required control commands, if the actual modules do not exist?" The answer lies in the use of a **dummy module.** Dummy modules are substitute modules that simulate the function of the module being replaced. They are inserted in place of the actual module and generate a sample of the data needed for the next module to commence its processing.

When dummy modules are in place, the JCL commands necessary to supervise the transfer of control between program modules may be tested. This procedure lets programming personnel find errors before the actual software is available and well before the final system is operational. Once the actual software has been written and tested, the dummy modules are replaced and the top-down design retested. Dummy modules enhance the continuity of software development.

This integrated approach is not the only way of implementing a structured design. Most DP professionals agree that no one approach is applicable in all instances. Although it is advantageous to develop all the modules on one level of a top-down design, it is not always necessary. Often, one leg of a structure chart will serve as prototype for the development of other modules, letting analysts and programmers find representative obstacles on a restricted scale.

In other cases, certain modules will be developed according to hardware constraints. If, for example, the required equipment is not immediately available, program modules dependent on that hardware will not be written. Other modules can be developed so that the staff does not remain idle.

DP professionals have not reached a consensus on the size of programming modules. No guidelines exist in this area, and programmers are free to develop their own standards. Some programmers believe that a program module should consist of 200 to 300 statements, or the number of instructions that can be printed on 1 page of output, or the amount of programming that can fit into a fixed amount of storage (i.e., 4096 bytes or 1024 words of storage). Generally, the approach to module sizes depends on the programming staff, their skill and experience, and equipment constraints.

Reviewing the Structured Design

Two reasons for top-down design are to produce an error-free system and to do so in a minimal amount of time. It is extremely desirable that errors be detected as early as possible so that corrections can be quickly made and costly delays avoided. A structured design may be evaluated on both a formal and an informal level.

An **informal design review** is often instituted during the early phases of a top-down design project. During this review, management and members of the project team examine all documentation and suggest possible changes. The informal design review usually precedes the development of software for the program modules. As a form of intermediary control, it prevents the project's straying from its intended goals.

A **formal design review** is rather different. Under this more formal review, detailed documentation on modules within the structured design is reviewed by a select team of two to four people. After the team has had a predetermined period to study this documentation, it meets with analysts and programmers who have worked on a particular module. Each reviewer evaluates the accuracy, thoroughness, logic, and general approach of that module's design. Formal review sessions of this type are commonly referred to as **structured walkthroughs,** because the responses to questions are intended to lead the reviewers through the logic of the design.

Structured walkthroughs are useful for evaluating the completeness of top-down designs but are especially valuable for reviewing the software developed for modules within the design. The structured walkthrough lets software designers desk-check their programs, validate their logic, trace the flow of data, and catch undetected errors. This formal review also lets others evaluate the error procedures of that software and whether the programmer has adhered to the established guidelines.

The structured walkthrough is a rigorous exercise. It is a very intense session at which a person's work is critically evaluated. Many individuals do not respond favorably under such conditions. It is vital that the person acting as moderator of the structured walkthrough maintain firm control of the session. Many DP organizations have instituted rules for conducting structured walkthroughs. These rules include limiting the length of any session to 1 hour, having no more than two sessions in one day, never conducting sessions immediately before or after lunch, and rotating the review members.

Errors or discrepancies detected during the structured walkthrough are recorded on the moderator's summary report. Coding of the software cannot begin until these errors are corrected.

The Personnel Involved

Teamwork is critical to top-down design because the size and scope of such projects usually require the efforts of many talented individuals. Programming teams have been used effectively for well over a decade. They have shown that they can produce a high volume of quality coding and software at economically attractive rates of productivity.

The team of data processors that programs a structured design is frequently called the **chief programmer team (CPT).** This team is normally composed of a small, select group of programmers under the coordination and direction of a chief programmer. The objectives of the chief programming team are simply to generate software that is accurate, reliable, and well documented. Their programs should be easy to maintain and modify as necessary. The CPT activities should keep the implementation of software on schedule (if not ahead of schedule), minimize the errors encountered during the writing and implementation of programs, and maintain a high level of programming output.

The chief programmer supervises and coordinates all aspects of the team's work. On large projects, a lead programmer/analyst works with the chief programmer. The distribution of work between them depends on their specialties, the demands of the project, the available resources, and time. The chief programmer is usually assigned an assistant who specializes in software and assists in coding the most critical aspects of the system. Other programmers within the CPT code the remaining software and integrate all programs into the overall system.

The CPT tests all modules within the top-down design, using techniques previously discussed or specially developed for the project. Because the CPT produces so much paperwork, a librarian is included on the team. The librarian is responsible for maintaining a complete and current library of all documentation associated with the project. The librarian frees programmers to develop software. Activities performed by the librarian include the preparation of coded input data, maintaining accurate and current source listings, collecting all program-related outputs and inputs, ensuring that the proper control statements are used during test runs, and maintaining complete files of documentation for all modules.

Good communication within the CPT is essential. Each team member must keep all the others informed of such matters as errors encountered and their probable causes or test data used and its results. Open communication advises the chief programmer of everyone's progress and helps control team costs.

10.2 Documenting the Structured Design
HIPO Documentation

An important aspect of the top-down approach is its documentation. In addition to detailing the components and logic of a solution, the structured approach dictates the documentation of all derived results. We have already seen one form of documentation used, the structure chart, Figure 10.2. A second form, similar in appearance to the structure chart, is the **visual table of contents.**

The visual table of contents derives its appearance from the structure chart but includes other descriptive data. Figure 10.3 shows the visual table of contents prepared from the structure chart of Figure 10.2. An important feature of the visual table of contents is the identification numbers assigned to each block in the diagram. These identifying numbers let the programmer refer to any block within the visual table of contents, and enable them to identify the various component legs (as well as their subdivisions) of that diagram.

We can see that the numbering scheme helps define each level of activity. The topmost control level receives the number 1.0; the subdivisions of this level receive the succeeding numbers 2.0, 3.0, and 4.0. Each number in effect defines a different and separate leg of the solution. Each of these legs then uses that identification number in assigning numbers to the lower levels on that leg. Thus, for example, the two blocks on the level beneath module 2.0 are assigned the identification numbers 2.1 and 2.2. The .1 and .2 in the code denote subdivisions of the 2.0-level block. This subdivision of blocks continues to the last level of the visual table of contents. This scheme is different from that used with a structure chart.

Figure 10.3 illustrates the breakdown of identification codes on the other legs. Using these digits, we can identify block 3.23 as the last block on the second leg of the diagram. Considering the many blocks in a visual table of contents, these numbers are handy references.

The visual table of contents is just one part of the papers in a HIPO package. The term **HIPO** refers to a documentation technique called **Hierarchy plus Input-Process-Output** that is used to record activities surrounding top-down designs. HIPO serves both as a documentation tool and as a design aid for the logical development of sound structural designs.

The **HIPO package** consists of a visual table of contents, overview HIPO diagrams, and detail HIPO diagrams. It can also contain non-HIPO documentation, such as printer spacing charts and card layouts, decision tables, systems and program flowcharts, and written narratives to detail any aspect of processing. **Overview HIPO diagrams,** used for higher-level modules, give readers a general understanding of a particular function. The **detail HIPO diagram** looks like the overview HIPO diagram but defines the specifics of lower-level modules, including datanames, branching factors, I/O operations, and all data handling activities. A practical example will illustrate how a HIPO package may be constructed and used.

Consider the payroll application depicted by the structure chart of Figure 10.4. Within this diagram, the steps necessary to process an individual's pay are represented as blocks within the structure chart. This structure chart defines three main legs that represent the input of employee data, computation of net pay, and output of payroll data (reading left to right).

The structure chart provides the basis for preparing the visual table of contents, the first component of a HIPO package. From the visual table of contents diagram of Figure 10.5, it is possible to identify the major components of the processing to be performed. Block 2.0 defines the input of payroll data for an employee. The middle leg of the diagram, topped by block 3.0, depicts the modules necessary to actu-

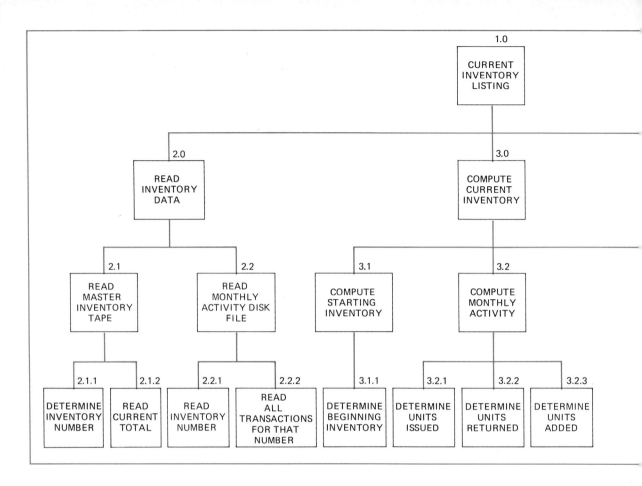

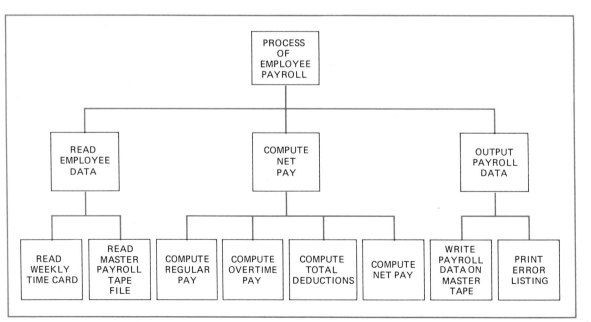

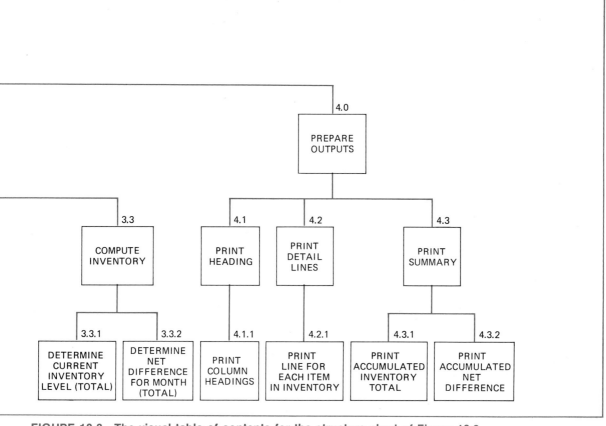

FIGURE 10.3 The visual table of contents for the structure chart of Figure 10.2.

ally compute the employee's net pay. The writing of payroll data on a tape file is identified by the modules under block 4.0. Each module of the visual table of contents is then further described within overview and detail HIPO diagrams.

The overview HIPO diagram, Figure 10.6, provides a general description of block 2.0, the Read Individual Employee Data module. Initially, note the information in the chart's heading. Identified are the person preparing the report, the name of the application, module number and name, date, and page number. The remainder of the overview diagram is divided into the three fundamental operations of input, processing, and output. Each region is defined to detail the specifics of that module in relation to those three operations.

Within the Input area are listed the inputs that relate to block 2.0. From Figure 10.6, note that the inputs specified are the weekly time card (block 2.1) and the master payroll tape (block 2.2). The use of these inputs is defined in the Process area, which shows the operations to be performed.

FIGURE 10.4 The structure chart defining the operations necessary to process one aspect of an employee payroll procedure.

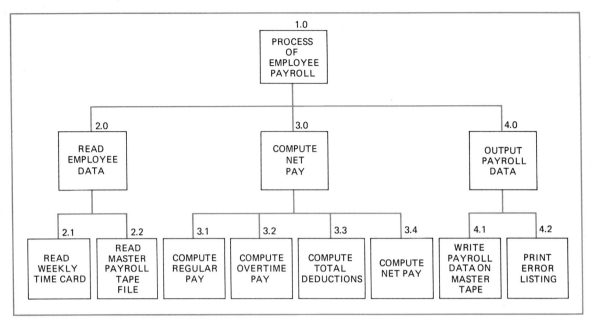

FIGURE 10.5 The visual table of contents developed from the structure chart of Figure 10.4.

The first task indicated is to match the employee time card against that employee's payroll record on the Payroll Master Tape. Task 2 notes that if a match exists, then that employee record should be made available for processing. The unmatched condition, task 3, will generate an error message which will be used by a payroll clerk to research the source of the unmatched time card data. The Process rectangle should describe all the processing steps related to that module.

The product of the Process area's work is revealed in the Output area. If a match exists, the tape record containing that employee's payroll data and weekly time card are made available for computation of net pay (block 3.0). An unmatched condition will generate the printing of an error message. Each of these three outputs will result from the actions initiated with module 2.0. Only outputs related to the module under discussion are listed in the Output area.

Generally, overview HIPO diagrams offer a broad understanding of the processing performed in higher-level modules, whereas detail HIPO diagrams specify actions undertaken with the lower-level processing modules. Figure 10.7 shows the detail HIPO diagram for module 3.2.

As we have stated, this HIPO diagram details specifics of the module's processing. The Input area describes the data entering by its general and field names, for both the time card and the master tape record. These datanames are an integral part of the processing to be performed. The input data is checked for accuracy after it is made

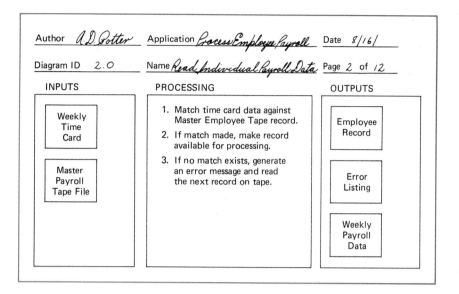

FIGURE 10.6 The overview HIPO diagram prepared from the visual table of contents shown in Figure 10.5.

available for processing. Valid data will be used to compute the total overtime pay (TOT-OT) due the employee. Incorrect input data will be flagged by a printed error message, using the label "BAD OT DATA". Note that datanames, formulas, literals, and any specifics related to processing are clearly defined within the detail listing.

The entire HIPO package is prepared with a visual table of contents, overview and detail HIPO diagrams, and any other pertinent forms. A properly prepared HIPO package simplifies subsequent programming.

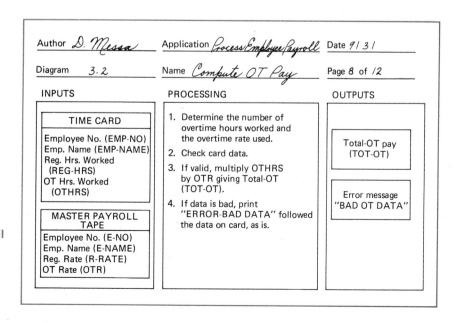

FIGURE 10.7 The detail HIPO diagram for module 3.2 prepared from the visual table of contents shown in Figure 10.5.

Pseudocode

Once the HIPO package is presented and a design approved, the writing of the software necessary to support that solution may begin. Usually the chief or lead programmer tries to distribute the work evenly, assigning the more difficult programs to senior programmers. Programmers develop solutions from flowcharts and materials in the HIPO package.

Larger, more complex programs are generally prepared using similar techniques but require more testing and time. If the complexity or length of a program warrants it, a technique called **pseudocode** may be introduced. Pseudocode is not a computer language, but an Englishlike description of a program's logic. In pseudocode, flowcharting symbols are translated into English equivalents of the program's logic. Many programmers use this technique when writing program instructions in the source language. They believe that pseudocode is an easy-to-read, logical form of the program that is well suited to top-down design.

Pseudocode has helped some programmers to analyze program logic within lengthy and complex flowcharts. Using key terms such as IF/THEN/ELSE, DOWHILE, and ENDIF, programmers can represent in pseudocode the conditional statements, automated program loops (e.g., FOR/NEXT, PERFORM statements), and last record checks in flowcharts. No strict or standard set of pseudocode instructions exists, creating a flexible state of affairs that leaves programmers free to adapt pseudocode instructions to their needs. Figure 10.8 shows a sample of pseudocode.

In Figure 10.8, we observe the pseudocode program and the flowchart from which it was developed. The flowchart depicts the processing and accumulation of sales commissions. After initializing the accumulator (T) at zero, the flowchart loop begins at the READ symbol. The input of an employee's sales data precedes the computation of a total sales amount. This total determines whether a 20 percent or 10 percent rate is used. The computed commission is added to the accumulator and output with the remainder of the individual's sales data. The looping will continue until the last record is processed. Then the accumulated total of commissions paid is output.

The pseudocode written for this flowchart closely parallels the solution diagramed. The start and initialization are easily associated with their flowchart counterparts. The pseudocode term DOWHILE defines the start of program looping and indicates that the looping should continue as long as data exists. Note that the DOWHILE visually denotes the start of the loop, as all statements within it are indented. This indentation is deliberately done to reinforce the logic of the solution.

Within the loop, the sales data is read, then the total sales amount is computed. The third pseudocode instruction is an IF/THEN/ELSE line, defining the comparison of total sales against $500. Note that the equivalent of the YES branch follows the word THEN, but that the NO branch equivalent comes after ELSE. Again, the indenting of both

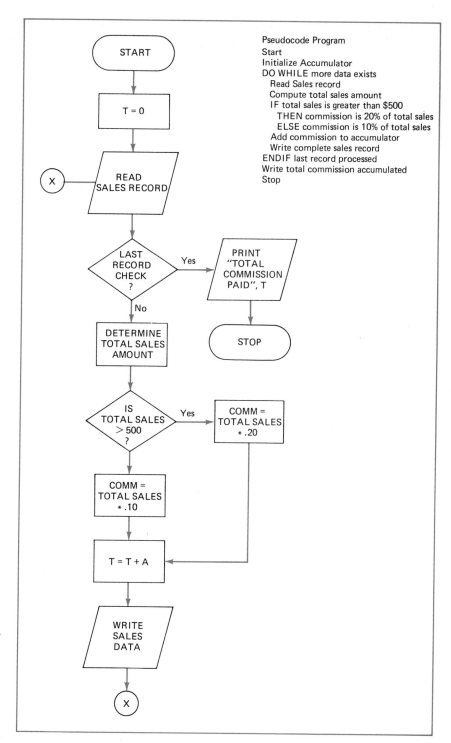

FIGURE 10.8 The pseudocode solution for the flowchart at left. Note that though the pseudocode terms are used, the solution parallels the logic of the flowchart.

THEN and ELSE highlights their logical position. The last two actions of the loop are the accumulation of the commission amount and the output of that individual's sales data.

The ENDIF pseudocode line has several purposes. It signals the loop's end, the point at which the flowchart unconditionally branches back to commence the next loop and the point at which the program should logically branch when the last record is processed. In the pseudocode solution, you can see how the processing loop is framed by the DOWHILE and ENDIF codes.

The processing of the last record indicates that no additional data exists and that the total held within the accumulator can be output. The pseudocode solution ends at stop.

The sample solution offered in Figure 10.8 illustrates how pseudocode may be applied to a flowchart solution. The complexity of the flowchart will be reflected in the pseudocode solution. Though we will not illustrate them here, pseudocode can be used to simplify many complex problems. Better understanding of a problem's logic produces better written code, more concise logic, and better documentation. If you understand what you're doing, your work should be clearer and more informative.

10.3 Structured Programming
Three Control Sequences

Structured programming represents the ultimate application of top-down concepts to software. Structured programming combines a modular design with written statements in a logical and sound program. Structured programming can achieve the following results:

1 Sound, well-thought-out program solutions whose logic is easily followed
2 Reduced testing and debugging time
3 Increased programmer productivity
4 Less complex programs that are readily maintained and modified

Structured programming emphasizes the design of logically correct, well-thought-out programs. The logic should be clear and easily followed, avoiding indiscriminate unconditional branching (GO TOs) between the various parts of a program. If the logic is sound, the debugging process is greatly simplified. Because debugging takes less of the programmer's time, the result is greater productivity. Similarly, changes to software are more easily accomplished because maintenance programmers do not have to waste time mastering faulty logic.

Structured programming is neither a recent development nor the product of only one person's imagination. In 1965 a Dutch professor named E. W. Dijkstra suggested the elimination of the GO TO statement from all programming languages. He theorized that eliminating it would stop the unwarranted branching between program modules that resulted from poor logic or technique or from expedience. In

1966, a paper presented in Italian (and later translated into English) by C. Bohm and G. Jacopini defined the theoretical framework for structured programming. The paper stated that any program solution can be expressed in three fundamental control blocks: a processing box, a decision symbol of the IF/THEN/ELSE type, and some form of looping procedure. These three components provide the basis for structured programming solutions.

These three control blocks in Figure 10.9 are represented using flowchart symbols. The simple sequence, Figure 10.9(a), shows a process box used for two consecutive instructions. The IF/THEN/ELSE control sequence, shown in Figure 10.9(b), lets the programmer perform a logical operation and two types of processing tasks on either branch exiting the decision. Although only one process box is represented in Figure 10.9(b), many processing operations may be placed on either branch, depending on the source language. This allows for the processing of many statements that depend on a decision.

Figure 10.9(c) represents the looping procedure associated with structured programming. We can see that the looping sequence is continued in the TRUE conditional branch of the decision. If the answer to the decision is YES, the looping continues. Each of these control sequences may be incorporated into a flowcharting solution, as shown in Figure 10.10. Though this flowchart segment is not related to a specific problem, it illustrates how the three fundamental control operations may be put together.

The point of Figure 10.10 is to show the similarity to a conventional flowchart. Before the start of the loop is a process box. After two processing blocks, an IF/THEN/ELSE sequence is indicated. On its

FIGURE 10.9   The three fundamental control blocks in structured programming.

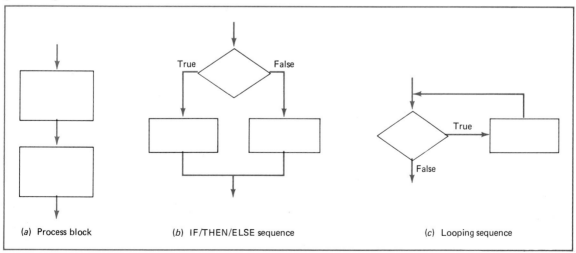

(a) Process block   (b) IF/THEN/ELSE sequence   (c) Looping sequence

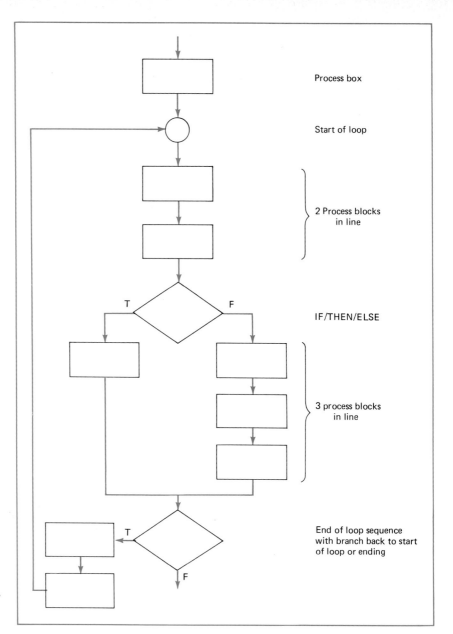

FIGURE 10.10 The use of the three fundamental control blocks in one solution. Note that this figure looks like a flowchart. The three control operations may be combined in any way to document the logic of a solution.

Labels in figure: Process box; Start of loop; 2 Process blocks in line; IF/THEN/ELSE; 3 process blocks in line; End of loop sequence with branch back to start of loop or ending; T; F

false branch are three process boxes, whereas on its true branch only one process box appears. The loop is closed at the end of the IF/THEN/ELSE sequence. Two processing tasks are indicated on the true branch's return to the start of the looping operation. The false exit from that decision indicates the end of the looping sequence.

Other Flowcharting Symbols

In addition to the control sequences diagramed, other flowcharting symbols are used in structured solutions. Figure 10.11 depicts them.

The **predefined process symbol,** Figure 10.11(*a*), represents a group of related instructions that handle specific types of processing.

This symbol is frequently used with the IF/THEN/ELSE sequence to represent many instructions on a branch exiting the decision. An example of a predefined process symbol is the representation of a paragraph in a COBOL program that handles one processing task.

The newly introduced symbol in Figure 10.11(*b*) represents a looping sequence. The symbol is broken into three parts to show the value at which the looping variable is initiated (K = 1), the increment of the loop (K = K + 1), and the decision used to test for the loop's end (K > 25?). The NO branch from this symbol indicates entry into the loop; the YES branch defines an exit from the loop. Though this symbol is not standard, many programmers use it to define a looping operation. This symbol is often used to represent a FOR/NEXT statement in BASIC or a COBOL PERFORM instruction.

10.4 Applications in BASIC

Though it was not designed for structured programming, BASIC programs may be written advantageously using many of the benefits associated with that technique. With a logical design, the dependence

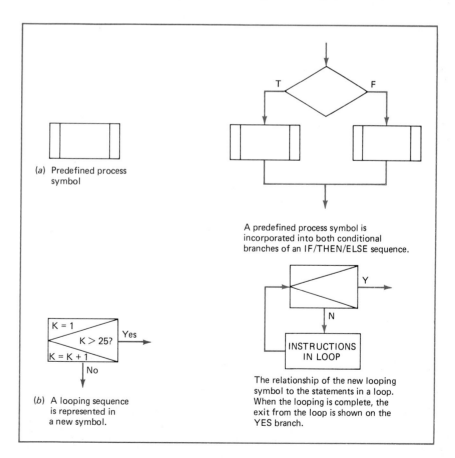

(*a*) Predefined process symbol

A predefined process symbol is incorporated into both conditional branches of an IF/THEN/ELSE sequence.

K = 1
K > 25?   Yes
K = K + 1
No

(*b*) A looping sequence is represented in a new symbol.

The relationship of the new looping symbol to the statements in a loop. When the looping is complete, the exit from the loop is shown on the YES branch.

FIGURE 10.11 Two symbols often used in the representation of structured flowchart solutions.

on GO TO statements can be minimized, resulting in a well-structured program. A discussion of these principles is assisted using Illustrative Problem 1.

ILLUSTRATIVE PROBLEM 1

The problem is to compute grades by two formulas. Input to the problem are a student's name, class code, and four test grades, the last being the final exam grade. The professor wants to use two different marking formulas to determine the student's grades, because they are drawn from two different courses. If the class code is 1, the final is 40 percent of the grade and the three other tests 60 percent of the grade. If the class code is 2, all grades are totaled and divided by 4 to derive an average score. In class 1, if the final grade is above 70, the student gets a grade of P. If not, the grade is a U. In class 2, the grade assigned is the average of all four grades. Output each student's name, class code, and final grade beneath the respective headings "NAME", "CLASS", and "FINAL MARK". The data for this problem are:

NAME	CODE	3 GRADES	FINAL EXAM
Jones	1	87, 60, 75	69
Hennen	2	56, 67, 78	81
Black	1	80, 90, 95	96
Marti	2	70, 54, 57	65
Stanx	1	63, 82, 89	76

Use a FOR/NEXT statement to create the looping sequence.

The flowchart for Illustrative Problem 1 is shown in Figure 10.12. In the flowchart, the loop is framed by processing symbols with the FOR and NEXT narrative. Following the READ symbol for the input of student data is the decision for class code. The major change is in the branches of that decision. Instead of having all statements necessary to compute and output the student grade, the flowchart shows one process box. This block represents the statements required to compute individual grades for either class 1 or class 2, and their respective outputs. Note that one class receives a letter grade of P (Pass) or U (Unsatisfactory) and the other a numeric grade. Each requires its own PRINT statement.

The vehicle for a group of related statements, since BASIC does not have COBOL's ability to create individual paragraphs, is the **GOSUB statement.** The GOSUB statement lets the program leave a certain point, branch to and execute an entire set of instructions, return to the exact point at which it left, and continue processing. It lets us test for the class code, branch to the instructions for the particular class, complete the proper grade, print it, and return to the main flow of processing.

After the column headings are printed via line 20, the FOR statement (line 30) initiates the looping sequence. The input of student data

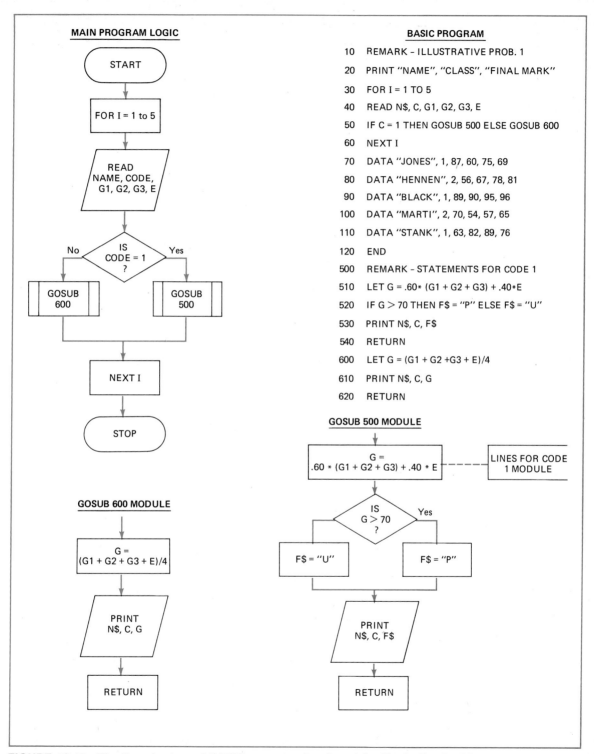

MAIN PROGRAM LOGIC

START

FOR I = 1 to 5

READ
NAME, CODE,
G1, G2, G3, E

IS
CODE = 1
?

No → GOSUB 600

Yes → GOSUB 500

NEXT I

STOP

GOSUB 600 MODULE

G =
(G1 + G2 + G3 + E)/4

PRINT
N$, C, G

RETURN

BASIC PROGRAM

```
10    REMARK – ILLUSTRATIVE PROB. 1
20    PRINT "NAME", "CLASS", "FINAL MARK"
30    FOR I = 1 TO 5
40    READ N$, C, G1, G2, G3, E
50    IF C = 1 THEN GOSUB 500 ELSE GOSUB 600
60    NEXT I
70    DATA "JONES", 1, 87, 60, 75, 69
80    DATA "HENNEN", 2, 56, 67, 78, 81
90    DATA "BLACK", 1, 89, 90, 95, 96
100   DATA "MARTI", 2, 70, 54, 57, 65
110   DATA "STANK", 1, 63, 82, 89, 76
120   END
500   REMARK – STATEMENTS FOR CODE 1
510   LET G = .60* (G1 + G2 + G3) + .40*E
520   IF G > 70 THEN F$ = "P" ELSE F$ = "U"
530   PRINT N$, C, F$
540   RETURN
600   LET G = (G1 + G2 +G3 + E)/4
610   PRINT N$, C, G
620   RETURN
```

GOSUB 500 MODULE

G =
.60 * (G1 + G2 + G3) + .40 * E

LINES FOR CODE 1 MODULE

IS
G > 70
?

F$ = "U"

Yes → F$ = "P"

PRINT
N$, C, F$

RETURN

FIGURE 10.12 The flowcharts and BASIC program developed for Illustrative Problem 1.

at line 40 precedes the test for class code. The choice of the IF/THEN/ELSE at line 50 was deliberate because it lets us handle the two class codes. If the class code = 1, the program goes directly to line 500. If the class code = 2, it branches to line 600. The branching operation is directed by the GOSUB 500 statement. No line number precedes the word GOSUB because it is placed within another statement. A line number defining where to branch to must always follow GOSUB.

The program temporarily leaves the loop and branches to line 500. The computation of a final grade for class 1 is performed at line 510. Once the grade is computed, a decision to determine whether G > 70 is made. Note that to assign an alphabetic grade of either P or U requires a string variable name. Because either a P or U must be assigned, the program goes from line 520 to 530 to print the student's grade.

Line 540 denotes the **RETURN statement** necessary with the GOSUB instruction. The RETURN statement directs the program back to the instruction from which it originally branched. It is always last in the GOSUB group of statements. The return to line 50 completes all operations related to the YES condition, and the program continues to line 60. The Next I instruction returns control to line 30 to continue the looping sequence for each remaining student. When the last student has been processed, the program will go from line 60 through the used DATA statements (lines 70 to 110) and stop at line 120, the END statement.

A class code of 2 is as easily handled. When C is tested for at line 50 and does not equal 1, the decision will direct it toward the equivalent of the NO branch, the instruction following the word ELSE. The GOSUB 600 statement causes the program to branch to line 600 for the computation of class 2's grade. Because only a numeric grade is required, its computation and output are performed at lines 600 and 610. The RETURN statement, line 620, directs the program back to the IF/THEN/ELSE instruction at line 50 and the looping sequence is resumed.

The important facts to see from this application are the presence of GOSUB and relative absence of GO TO statements in the program solution. The GOSUB let us group related statements and treat them as one unit, a technique sometimes called a **subroutine.** If changes are made in the grading formulas, the programmer need only modify the instructions in the subroutines. The main program will remain unchanged.

The absence of GO TOs is a result of sound logic and the presence of the GOSUB instruction. The looping sequence created by the FOR/NEXT meant that no GO TOs were required to restart the looping sequence. The GOSUB instruction made it possible to employ the statements in a subroutine without unconditionally branching to and from those statements.

Figure 10.13 offers two alternative versions of the flowchart dia-

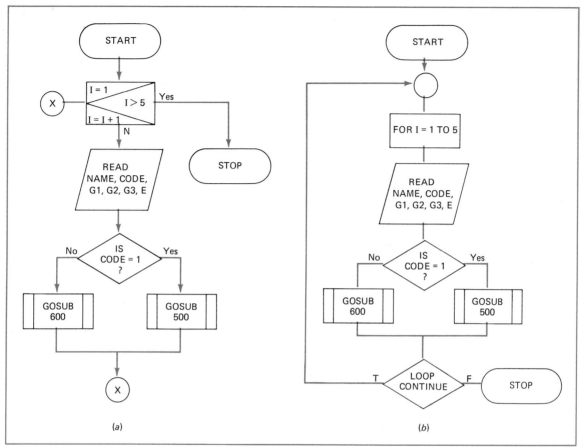

(a)   (b)

FIGURE 10.13 Two alternative versions of the flowchart solution developed for Illustrative Problem 1. (a) The special form of the looping symbol defines the loop, its increment, and its end. (b) The looping sequence control block used with structured programming is incorporated into the diagram.

gram employed for Illustrative Problem 1. In Figure 10.13(a), the specialized looping symbol is incorporated in the flowchart. It depicts all processing related to the looping sequence. The remainder of the flowchart is the same as in Figure 10.12. Figure 10.13(b) uses a format similar to the three control block diagrams associated with structured programming. Again, its similarity to the original flowchart is evident. Unless dictated by flowcharting policy, the format chosen is usually up to the individual programmer.

10.5
Applications in
COBOL

The syntax of COBOL is better suited to structured programming than that of BASIC. The use of paragraphs to group related statements and the many types of PERFORM statements that generate looping sequences make COBOL ideally suited to the structured approach. COBOL's IF statements let the programmer apply the IF/THEN/ELSE control sequence and branch to paragraphs under the direction of a

PERFORM statement. Illustrative Problem 2 will let us expand on COBOL's structured aspects.

ILLUSTRATIVE PROBLEM 2

The overall problem is to print an accounts payable listing. Vendor data is read from a file called ACCTS-MASTER. Three vendor rates for three payment plans are used to compute the discounts earned by paying bills promptly. Accumulate the total of discounts earned and the total of all accounts due. Compute the difference between these sums. Output vendor data and data relating to the amounts due for each record on one line. After all vendor records are processed, print on separate lines the two accumulated totals and their difference.

The PROCEDURE DIVISION of the COBOL program related to Illustrative Problem 2 appears in Figure 10.14. We have omitted specific details about I/O formats because they are not necessary here. What the statements show is the modular structure of COBOL paragraphs. In the PROCEDURE DIVISION, we see the use of six paragraphs to support processing. The function of each paragraph will be explained as the program unfolds.

The first statement of the PROCEDURE DIVISION opens the ACCTS-MASTER and PRINT-FILE files as input and output files, respectively. The format of these files and the record formats used with them are detailed in the DATA DIVISION and its WORKING-STORAGE SECTION. The next three PERFORM statements dictate the logic of the program and its structured design.

The PERFORM HEADING-ROUTINE statement (line 003) creates the two-line headings for our accounts payable report. The two heading lines, TITLE-1 and TITLE-2, were detailed in WORKING-STORAGE and output using the PRINT FROM instruction. A line counter called KOUNT records the number of lines printed on each page. Once a value of 1 is moved to KOUNT, that paragraph is completed and program control returns to the line following the PERFORM that initiated the execution of HEADING-ROUTINE.

The PERFORM statement of line 004 represents the main module of this solution because it contains the data handling statements. The PERFORM THRU instruction directs the program to line 016, where the input of accounts payable data is begun. The READ instruction (line 017) inputs each account record, from which individual data items are chosen. Vendor name and number are moved into their output fields (lines 019 and 020), before discount codes are input.

Three discount codes, of 1 percent, 2 percent, and 5 percent, are defined as Plans A, B, and C, respectively. To simplify the computation of the discounts, each code is tested for with an individual IF statement. When a match is made, the program is directed to the appropriate paragraph by the simple PERFORM instruction. The three discount codes are handled within paragraphs DIS-1, DIS-2, and DIS-3, which start at line 033, 038, and 043, respectively. Each paragraph computes

Line Number	Statements composing the PROCEDURE DIVISION
001	PROCEDURE DIVISION.
002	OPEN INPUT ACCTS-MASTER, OUTPUT PRINT-FILE.
003	PERFORM HEADING-ROUTINE.
004	PERFORM READ-APFILE THRU AP-EXIT UNTIL EOF = 1.
005	PERFORM SUMMARY-ROUTINE.
006	CLOSE ACCTS-MASTER, PRINT-FILE.
007	STOP RUN.
008	HEADING-ROUTINE.
009	MOVE SPACES TO PRINT-REC.
010	WRITE PRINT-REC FROM TITLE-1 AFTER ADVANCING
011	TO TOP-OF-PAGE.
012	WRITE PRINT-REC FROM TITLE-2 AFTER ADVANCING
013	1 LINES.
014	MOVE SPACES TO PRINT-REC.
015	MOVE 1 TO KOUNT.
016	READ-APFILE.
017	READ ACCTS-MASTER AT END MOVE 1 TO EOF
018	GO TO AP-EXIT.
019	MOVE VENDOR-NAME TO V-OUT.
020	MOVE VENDOR-NO TO VNO-OUT.
021	IF DISCOUNT-CODE = 1 PERFORM DIS-1.
022	IF DISCOUNT-CODE = 2 PERFORM DIS-2.
023	IF DISCOUNT-CODE = 3 PERFORM DIS-3.
024	ADD AP-AMT TO AP-TOTAL.
025	ADD DISCOUNT-MADE TO DIS-TOTAL.
026	WRITE PRINT-REC FROM DISC-LINE AFTER ADVANCING
027	2 LINES.
028	MOVE SPACES TO PRINT-REC.
029	IF KOUNT = 50 PERFORM HEADING-ROUTINE
030	ELSE ADD 2 TO KOUNT.
031	AP-EXIT.
032	EXIT.
033	DIS-1.
034	COMPUTE DISC = AP-AMT * .01
035	COMPUTE DISCOUNT-MADE = AP-AMT - DISC
036	MOVE DISCOUNT-MADE TO DISC-OUT.
037	MOVE "PLAN A" TO DIS-OUT.
038	DIS-2.
039	COMPUTE DISC = AP-AMT * .02
040	COMPUTE DISCOUNT-MADE = AP-AMT - DISC
041	MOVE DISCOUNT-MADE TO DISC-OUT.
042	MOVE "PLAN B" TO DIS-OUT.
043	DIS-3.
044	COMPUTE DISC = AP-AMT * .05
045	COMPUTE DISCOUNT-MADE = AP-AMT - DISC
046	MOVE DISCOUNT-MADE TO DISC-OUT.
047	MOVE "PLAN C" TO DIS-OUT.
048	SUMMARY-ROUTINE.
049	MOVE AP-TOTAL TO AP-TOT-OUT.
050	MOVE DIS-TOTAL TO DIS-TOT-OUT.
051	SUBTRACT DIS-TOTAL FROM AP-TOTAL
052	GIVING DIFF-AP.
053	MOVE DIFF-AP TO DIFF-AP-OUT.
054	WRITE PRINT-REC FROM SUM-LINE1 AFTER
055	ADVANCING 2 LINES.
056	WRITE PRINT-REC FROM SUM-LINE2 AFTER
057	ADVANCING 1 LINES.
058	WRITE PRINT-REC FROM SUM-LINE3 AFTER
059	ADVANCING 1 LINES.

FIGURE 10.14 The COBOL program solution for Illustrative Problem 2.

the discount figure using the appropriate rate, moves the result to its output record field, and defines a literal of either PLAN A, B, or C. After completion of the discount paragraph's instructions, the program will return to one of the 3 IF statements which lead to line 024.

The accumulation of total accounts payable and the discounts made (lines 024 and 025) precede the output of vendor data relating to that record. Note that each detail line is double-spaced because the AFTER ADVANCING clause dictates 2 LINES. The conditional statement (line 029) indicates that only 50 lines are printed per page of output. After 50 lines, the PERFORM HEADING-ROUTINE is initiated, printing a new heading at the top of the next page. If not, KOUNT is incremented by 2.

At this point, you may ask, "What is the purpose of the AP-EXIT paragraph?" This paragraph was indicated in the original PERFORM statement (line 004) and is used when the last record on the ACCTS-MASTER file is read and processed.

The precipitating PERFORM instruction (line 004) directs the program to process all instructions through the READ-APFILE to AP-EXIT paragraphs. When no records are left in the ACCTS-MASTER file, the READ statement (line 017) causes a value of 1 to be moved to an EOF (a 77-level item) and unconditionally branches to the AP-EXIT paragraph. This approach is a form of safeguard to prevent the program from incorrectly branching to the wrong statement when data is exhausted or improperly branching out of a PERFORM statement, causing an error condition and the program's cancellation.

When no data is found, EOF = 1, and the program branches to AP-EXIT. No further processing is performed within the READ-APFILE paragraph, and the program branches to line 005. Line 004 denotes another safeguard written into the statement. The PERFORM instruction directs the computer to execute paragraphs READ-APFILE through AP-EXIT until EOF = 1. EOF will equal 1 when no other accounts payable data is read, at which point the program will switch to line 005 and print out a summary of accounts payable data.

This output of data, initiated by the PERFORM on line 005, is controlled by the statements in the paragraph SUMMARY-ROUTINE (line 048). The accumulated totals of discounts made and all accounts processed are printed, and the difference between those amounts is computed (line 051) and output on a third line (line 058). The printing of SUM-LINE3 completes the PERFORM begun by line 005, and the program returns to execute line 006.

The closing of the files ACCTS-MASTER and PRINT-FILE completes processing and precedes the STOP RUN instruction ending the program. Note that even though the STOP RUN is written within the text of the program, it is logically positioned at the end of processing and will cause the program to stop.

We can gather some interesting points from this program solution. Note the absence of GO TO statements and the integrated use of PER-

FORM statements. The modular approach used the PERFORM to branch to paragraphs which actually accomplished the required processing. There was no haphazard branching between paragraphs because the program's logic dictated branching only under specific conditions.

Using paragraphs in this fashion has other advantages. When changes are made in the program, the programmer need work only with the paragraph in question. Likewise in debugging, when an error is noted, programmers can focus their attention on a particular paragraph.

The paragraph structure also allows for additions to the program. For example, let's say that a fourth code were introduced. It could be added readily to the program. An IF statement could be added to test for a code = 4, along with a paragraph (DIS-4) to handle that rate.

Similarly, the paragraph structure allows for deletions. For example, the removal of statements regarding code-3 requires the removal of its IF statement (line 023) and the paragraph DIS-3 (lines 043 to 047). Otherwise the program remains unchanged.

Structured programs in COBOL will not cure all programming problems, but they offer some real advantages. A structured program is one of the many tools a programmer has for developing sound, logical, and manageable programs.

10.6 Applications in PASCAL

PASCAL is a recently introduced language specifically designed for structured programming. Its syntax is more structured and detailed than BASIC's. This drawback is more than compensated for by PASCAL's ability to perform complex manipulations on both numeric and alphameric data. For purposes of comparison and discussion, we have coded the solution for Illustrative Problem 1 in PASCAL (Figure 10.15). This solution involves a structured design and permits a discussion of PASCAL's syntax.

This solution to Problem 1 shows a PASCAL program, which has an appearance that we have not seen before. Its indented statements are designed to help you to understand the logic and to highlight structured concepts. As we discuss the program line by line, we will use the line numbers in Figure 10.15 as a means of identification.

The $JOB instruction that opens the program assigns it the name SAMPLE PROG3. Line 2 marks the start of the program and causes the computer to start processing. Lines 3 and 4, like BASIC'S REMARK statement, add descriptions or advice without incurring any I/O operations. Note that these statements are indented and placed in parentheses and that asterisks mark their beginning and end.

The **VARiable instruction** at line 5 defines the types of data used in the program. PASCAL's syntax requires that you specify numeric data as being either real or integer and different from alphameric

Line	PASCAL STATEMENTS
001	$JOB "SAMPLE PROG3"
002	PROGRAM PROB (INPUT, OUTPUT);
003	(* ILLUSTRATIVE PROBLEM 1 - DEFINES MARKING FORMULAS *)
004	(* SOLUTION DEPICTED IN FIGURE 10.15 *)
005	VAR C, G1, G2, G3, E : INTEGER;
006	G : REAL;
007	NAME: PACKED ARRAY [1 . . 18] OF CHAR;
008	FGRADE: PACKED ARRAY [1 . . 2] OF CHAR:
009	BEGIN
010	FOR I: = 1 TO 5 DO
011	BEGIN
012	READ (NAME, C, G1, G2, G3, E);
013	IF C = 1 THEN
014	BEGIN
015	G: = .60* (G1 + G2 + G3) + .40*E;
016	IF G 70.0 THEN
017	FGRADE: = "P"
018	ELSE
019	FGRADE: = "U";
020	WRITELN (NAME, C, FGRADE)
021	END
022	ELSE
023	BEGIN
024	G: = (G1 + G2 + G3 + E)/4;
025	WRITELN (NAME, C, G)
026	END;
027	END
028	END.
029	$DATA
030	JONES 1 87 60 75 69
031	HENNEN 2 56 67 78 81
032	BLACK 1 89 90 95 96
033	MARTI 2 70 54 57 65
034	STANK 1 63 82 89 76

FIGURE 10.15 The PASCAL program solution for Illustrative Problem 1.

data items. The variables specified in line 5, G1, G2, G3, and E, are defined as integer variables because they will represent that type of data. In line 6, G is specified as a real variable. Lines 7 and 8 define variable names, NAME and FGRADE, that represent alphameric data items. NAME can represent a maximum of 18 characters; FGRADE, 2 characters. The numbers in the brackets of lines 7 and 8 define the respective size of each data item.

We should point out a piece of PASCAL punctuation. Lines 5 to 8 end with a semicolon to note the end of a statement. Though only line 5 contains the op code VAR, it is assumed to carry through for all following statements until another op code appears. The statements before line 9 do not manipulate data. They specify processing variables and ready the program for execution.

The **BEGIN statement** at line 9 identifies the start of the processing loop. Note that it is aligned with the VAR of line 5 and that many loop-related statements will follow it. The BEGIN and **END statements** help define the PASCAL equivalent of loops, paragraphs, and modules. Aligning the BEGIN and END statements highlights the loops. The BEGIN of line 9, here associated with the END of line 28, defines all processing within the main loop of the program.

The FOR statement of line 10 defines the automated looping sequence with variable I, beginning at I = 1 and ending at I = 5. Five loops are necessary because five data items are supplied. The BEGIN and END statements of line 11 and 27 help define the FOR's looping. The BEGIN instruction implies that the loop contains many instructions. The line 27 END statement defines the end of the loop and the point at which the program will branch back up to its companion BEGIN (line 11) and start the next loop.

If we momentarily stop and examine the entire program, we may note that an equal number of BEGIN and END statements appear. Each pair tends to frame a related grouping of statements. The attempt here is to create the effect of a module within these statements.

The READ statement of line 12 begins the input of data. Note that the variable names in parentheses define the order in which data is read from lines 30 to 34. Coordinating line 30 with line 12, we can see that JONES is assigned to NAME, 1 to C, 87 to G1, 60 to G2, 75 to G3, and 69 to E. Because no punctuation appears in line 30, we may wonder how these assignments are made. Figure 10.16 will supply some answers.

If you recall, NAME was defined in line 7 as 18 characters long. Thus, 18 consecutive characters are set aside for NAME's data. Even if all 18 characters are not used, they must be blocked out. Four positions are then allocated to each of five integer data items that follow the name date. Each integer is right-justified in that field. The computer reads that grouping of four characters and takes whatever data is found within them. If you override the boundaries between data items, data errors will ensue.

Once C is read in line 12, the IF statement used to test for a code = 1 is initiated at line 13. Because separate computations are necessary for each code, an IF/THEN/ELSE format is used. Because we will not branch to a separate paragraph or subroutine (via a GOSUB), the processing for each code will be handled in a branch of the decision. The YES branch of line 13 is noted in statements 14 to 21, and the NO state (a code = 2) in lines 23 to 26. Note that each grouping is framed by BEGIN and END statements.

FIGURE 10.16 The relationship between line 30, the data line of the PASCAL program of Figure 10.15, and the variables noted in the READ statement of that program, line 12.

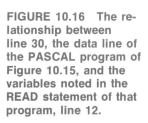
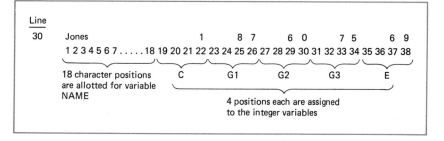

Within the YES option, line 15 computes the actual grade using G, a real numeric data item. Line 16 determines whether $G > 70$ and a letter grade of P should be awarded as final grade (FGRADE). No BEGIN and END statements are used within branches of this IF statement because only one statement is positioned on the YES and NO branches. The **WRITELN instruction** of line 20 results in the printing of a line of output containing the student's name and code and the letter grade of P or U. Note that the entire processing of the YES branch is framed by line 14, a BEGIN statement, and line 21, its companion END statement.

The equivalent of a code $= 2$ is handled after the ELSE on lines 23 to 26. The computation of G, a numeric grade, is accomplished on line 24. The output of that grade is performed on line 25. At this point, we may notice that equations require that you place a colon (:) immediately after the variable defined on the left of the equal sign. The END instruction, line 26, contains a semicolon to indicate the end of the IF/THEN/ELSE started at line 13.

Line 27's END frames the looping sequence associated with line 11 and begun at line 10 via the FOR instruction. This END does not require a semicolon because it precedes the END statement, line 28, that closes the program.

Lines 30 to 34 define all the data in the problem. Note that the five sets of data match the data originally used in our BASIC program of Illustrative Problem 1 (Figure 10.12). This data is specified differently in PASCAL syntax than in BASIC syntax.

We have not covered every rule associated with PASCAL. We suggest that interested students invest many more hours of research as they study structured design and programming.

Summary

The following major points have been presented in Chapter 10:

Point 1 Top-down design is a technique for breaking a problem into its component units or modules. Concepts are completely developed at all levels of a solution, from top to bottom, rather than from the bottom-up.

Point 2 A diagram used to represent the relationship among modules at different levels is the structure chart. The topmost level defines the main control module, intermediate levels define processing and control modules, and the lowest level defines processing modules. Rules associated with formulating top-down designs are: each module should be independent, have its opera-

tional responsibility clearly defined, and possess only one exit and entrance.

Point 3 Top-down programming is the writing of programs for top-down designs. Top-down testing evaluates the success of these programs. The modular approach allows programmers to write programs independently and then integrate them. The top-down design can be tested with dummy modules and the required control commands.

Point 4 Two methods of evaluating structured designs are the informal and formal design reviews. The informal design review is an intermediary control undertaken before programs are written. The formal design review is a required

Case Study One

Tracking Tornadoes Via Computer

One of the more interesting applications of computers to weather forecasting occurs in the Midwest. In a region called Tornado Alley, from northern Texas through Oklahoma and as far north as Iowa, a computer has become indispensable in monitoring rapidly changing weather conditions.

Weather specialists rely on information from the computer at the U.S. Severe Storm Center (USSSC) in Tulsa, Oklahoma, which has analyzed mountains of data on the formation and habits of tornadoes. Tornado profiles are retained in online files for immediate access. This data provides a basis of comparison for developing weather fronts.

The USSSC computer communicates constantly with weather stations throughout Tornado Alley and monitors the continuous flow of data for weather conditions that indicate a brewing storm. Preliminary warnings are issued when the computer confirms the potential start of a tornado.

At that point, the team on duty pinpoints the location of the front. Its major source of information and analytic tool is the USSSC computer. Data is presented in both hardcopy and softcopy format. Printed reports are used in post-analysis studies. CRTs display weather data as it is received and analyzed. The relationship of hot and cold weather fronts and their altitude, direction,

movement, and intensity are displayed. The computer also offers early estimates of the severity of the developing tornado.

Once the tornado's existence is confirmed, the second phase of operations begins. Local radio stations alert residents to the tornado's likely path. Weather teams are dispatched in vans to the tornado area to gather meteorological data during the storm. This data is later analyzed and compared against computer projections to substantiate computed results.

At USSSC headquarters, the staff and computer continuously monitor the tornado. CRTs display data on the tornado's winds, intensity, and

movement. At the tornado's peak, the system scans all weather conditions for other tornadoes because several tornadoes on the same day are common in Tornado Alley.

The USSSC computer is an invaluable asset. Early prediction of oncoming tornadoes has saved many lives and minimized loss of property. The information gathered from analyzing tornadoes has been used in other meteorological studies and confirmed theories on how violent windstorms behave. Further studies are underway to predict the erratic behavior of tornadoes and the atmospheric conditions that spawn them.

Consider this . . .

The computer's ability to amass and analyze data was invaluable to the forecasting of tornadoes. In what other fields are these powers applied?

Could doctors, scientists, geologists, or stockbrokers advantageously use these analytic properties?

---

evaluation during which the total design and its documentation are carefully scrutinized. A structured walkthrough is a type of review session used with formal design reviews.

Point 5   The team of programmers that implements a top-down design is called the chief programmer team (CPT). The chief programmer may be assisted by a systems analyst and programming specialist. A librarian is a critical member of the CPT, handling clerical and related paperwork activities.

Point 6   An extension of the structure chart is the visual table of contents. It assigns identification numbers to modules within the diagram. A HIPO package can document all aspects of a structured design. The overview HIPO diagram provides a general understanding of a module's purpose. The detail HIPO diagram specifies the processing within a block.

Point 7   A general, hypothetical language used in software design is pseudocode. Though it is not a computer language, it can represent statements in an actual program. Terms often used with

pseudocode are DOWHILE, IF/THEN/ELSE, and ENDIF.

Point 8   The three major control block sequences associated with structured programming are the process box, IF/THEN/ELSE decision, and looping sequence. Structured programming is designed to produce sound, well-conceived programs that are easy to debug and modify, are readily maintained, and increase programmer productivity. Other flowcharting symbols employed in documenting structured program solutions are the predefined process symbol and the special form of the automated looping/processing symbol.

Point 9   Structured concepts may be applied through the IF/THEN/ELSE and GOSUB statements. They allow for grouping related statements and branching to them via a conditional statement. The RETURN statement is used with the GOSUB statement.

Point 10   COBOL is well suited to structured programming. COBOL permits the construction of paragraphs which may be accessed via PERFORM statements. Paragraphs offer flexibility in developing or modifying structured solutions and relate to the concept of a subroutine. COBOL's IF statement supports the IF/THEN/ELSE control sequence and allows branching to paragraphs via PERFORM statements.

Point 11   PASCAL was designed for struc-tured programming. It frames modules within pro-grams using BEGIN and END statements and in-dents them to highlight their placement. Instructions available in PASCAL are the IF/THEN/ELSE, VARiable, WRITELN, and FOR statements.

Glossary

BEGIN instruction   A PASCAL instruction that defines the start of a module of instructions.

Bottom-up approach   A nonstructured strat-egy in which the solution is developed from the lowest level of logic.

Chief programmer team (CPT)   The team of programmers that writes and implements a top-down design.

Control block   A unit, module, or subunit within a structure chart.

Detail HIPO diagram   A form within the HIPO package that specifies the processing related to a module.

Dummy module   A mock-up module, used in testing a top-down programming solution, that replaces an actual module and permits the evalua-tion of control statements that connect program modules before the actual software is written.

END instruction   A PASCAL instruction to denote the close of a program module.

Formal design review   The formal review of the documentation and design of a top-down de-sign solution, which may include a structured walkthrough.

GOSUB statement   The BASIC statement that enables a program to branch to a group of related statements.

Hierarchy   plus   Input-Process-Output (HIPO)   A documentation technique that rec-ords activities related to top-down designs.

HIPO package   A top-down documentation package consisting of a visual table of contents, overview and detail HIPO diagrams, and non-HIPO paperwork that details aspects of the problem so-lution.

Informal design review   An informal review of the logic in a top-down design made before the start of the writing of programs.

Main control module   The topmost module of a structure chart.

Overview HIPO diagram   A form in the HIPO package that explains the module's purpose.

Predefined process symbol   A flowcharting symbol that defines a related group of statements that are accessed to handle a specific processing problem.

Processing and control module   Intermedi-ary-level modules within a structure chart.

Processing module   The lowest level of con-trol blocks in a structure chart.

Pseudocode   A non-programming language that uses structured techniques to simulate state-ments in an actual program.

RETURN statement   BASIC's companion statement to the GOSUB instruction, used to re-turn the program to the point at which it left the main program.

Structure chart   A diagram that documents the component modules of a top-down design.

Structured programming   The application of top-down programming techniques.

Structured walkthrough An evaluation in formal reviews of top-down designs in which a committee of specialists evaluates program and design specifications.

Subroutine The term occasionally applied to a group of related statements in a program that handles one aspect of processing.

Top-down design The modular, structured approach in which a design is divided into its component units and the logic of the solution is developed from the topmost level downward.

Top-down programming The programming and implementation of component modules within a top-down design.

Top-down testing The testing of a top-down design's implementation to make sure that it is functioning within limits.

VARiable instruction The PASCAL instruction used to define the variables in a program and the data they represent.

Visual table of contents The HIPO package form which identifies the modules contained on a structure chart by numbers and level.

WRITELN instruction A PASCAL instruction used to print a line of data.

Discussion Questions

1 Identify and discuss the three main control block sequences associated with structured programming. Use flowchart symbols to represent each.

2 Convert the structure chart in Figure 10.17 to a visual table of contents.

3 Draw the HIPO diagram for module 3.0 in the visual table of contents shown in Figure 10.5.

4 Write a pseudocode program for the flowchart of Figure 10.18.

5 Write a PASCAL program for the flowchart of Figure 10.18. Use the following information:

    a Inputs to the problem are part number (I), number of units kept at warehouse 1 (I), number of units kept at warehouse 2 (I), and average number of units of this part number normally stored (R). I identifies integer quantities; R identifies reals.

    b Quantity (Q) equals the sum of the units kept at warehouses 1 and 2. The reorder level (L) equals one-fourth of the average number of units ordinarily kept on hand for that part.

    c The printed output consists of part number and quantity only, per line. Use the WRITELN instruction.

    d Accumulate the number of parts reordered, and print that total after processing all other records. Use an increment of 1 as the program notes that a part is reordered.

    e Because no data is supplied, no DATA statements are necessary.

6 Write a flowchart and BASIC program, using structured concepts, to satisfy the following narrative:

The problem is to compute and accumulate union dues. Input to the problem are employee's name, job title, hourly rate, and union code. Only two union codes exist, 1 or 2. If the code = 1, the union dues are 15 percent of the hourly rate plus $2.00. Separately accumulate the total of dues paid by code 1

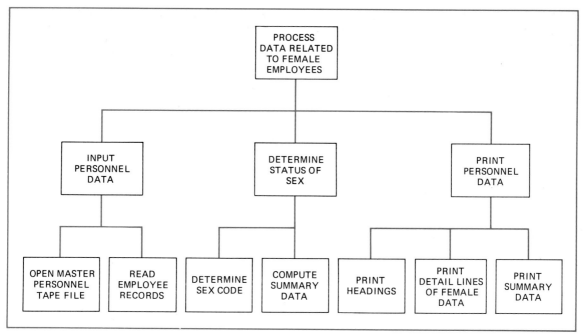

FIGURE 10.17   An initial structure chart for computing personnel data.

employees. The code 2 employees are divided into two categories, and each type must be handled differently. If the hourly wage is greater than $5.00, the union dues are 40 percent of the hourly rate plus $3.50. If a code 2 hourly rate is $5.00 or less, the dues are 25 percent of the hourly rate plus $1.00. Accumulate the total of dues paid by code 2 employees. Print out each employee's name, union code, job title, and union dues. Use the column headings "NAME", "CODE", "TITLE", and "DUES PAID", respectively. After processing all data, print on two lines the accumulated totals of code 1 and code 2 dues, preceded by the labels "CODE 1 DUES =" and "CODE 2 DUES =". The data for this problem are:

Employee Name	Job Title	Hourly Rate	Union Code
E. Marino	Supervisor	10.60	2
G. Shortell	Accountant	26.00	1
C. Stewart	Writer	4.50	2
B. Hirsch	Clerk	3.30	2
B. Cronin	Programmer	22.50	1
T. Lione	Broker	18.75	2

7   Using the flowcharts in Figure 10.19, write the COBOL statements necessary to compose the PROCEDURE DIVISION. Assume the input file's name is ACCTS-IN, where the output file is PRINT-OUT using a print record of PRINT-

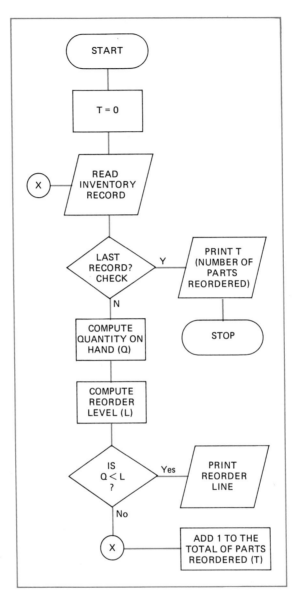

FIGURE 10.18 The flowchart solution for preparing a list of inventory items to be reordered.

REC. Individual printed record formats are previously defined in WORKING-STORAGE as 01-level entries and are noted in the flowcharts.

The overall problem relates to the reading and printing of data from a transaction file of bank deposits and withdrawals. A bank code of 1 identifies a deposit; withdrawals are a code 8. As all bank transactions are read, accumulate the net total of all transactioins completed by the bank. Whenever possible, use the PERFORM to handle processing. Statements composing each PERFORM are flowcharted.

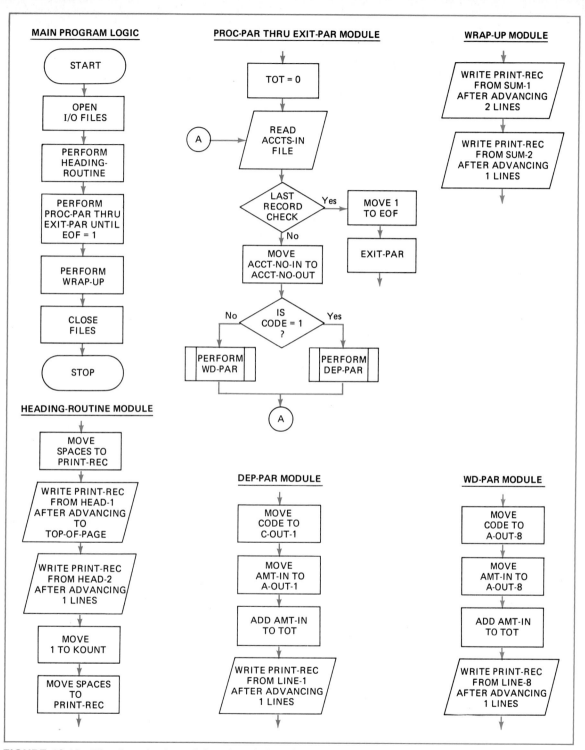

FIGURE 10.19 The flowchart modules that define the processing of a COBOL program. Each module represents a paragraph used in processing.

Summary Test

_____ **1** The module on the highest level of a structure chart has an identification number of 1.0 and is referred to as the main control module.

_____ **2** A HIPO package is composed solely of a structure chart, visual table of contents, and HIPO diagrams.

_____ **3** Modules in top-down designs can have only one entrance and one exit point.

_____ **4** In the top-down testing of structured software, programmers must wait until the entire system is complete before testing the control statements that tie the related modules together.

_____ **5** The coordination and handling of documentation within the CPT are handled by the librarian.

_____ **6** Rules about pseudocode are standard and allow uniform structured designs.

_____ **7** Structured walkthroughs are restricted to checking structured programs.

_____ **8** Within a flowchart, a group of related statements may be defined with a PERFORM symbol.

_____ **9** The PERFORM and GOSUB instructions are alike in that they both branch to a group of statements, process them, and return to the same point at which they left the main program.

_____ **10** The PERFORM and RETURN statements must be paired in a COBOL program.

_____ **11** The VARiable statement in PASCAL identifies names as representing either real or integer data.

_____ **12** While executing a PERFORM statement, it is impossible to execute another PERFORM and process another item of data.

_____ **13** In the CPT, chief programmers generally share the writing of the major program modules with their software specialists.

_____ **14** Both BASIC and PASCAL were specifically designed to support the application of structured program concepts.

_____ **15** An overview HIPO diagram provides a general explanation of a module's purpose and is normally employed with the lower-level modules in a visual table of contents.

_____ **16** In most cases, a module identified by the number 2.1 in a visual table of contents would be positioned at:

    a level 2   **b** level 3

    c the lowest level   **d** b and c

_____ **17** The preliminary evaluation of a top-down design before programs are written is referred to as a(n):

    a informal design review

    b formal design review

    c structured walkthrough

    d scheduled review

_____ **18** A desired result of structured programming is:

    a less complex solutions

    b sound, well-thought-out software

c   increased programmer productivity

d   all the above

_____ **19**   A control block associated with structured programming is:

a   a GO TO branching sequence

b   an I/O control sequence

c   some form of looping sequence

d   all the above

_____ **20**   In a BASIC program, the automatic branching to and from a group of related statements set aside from the main program is accomplished via the:

a   PERFORM statement

b   GOSUB statement

c   BEGIN statement

d   IF/THEN/ELSE statement

_____ **21**   The PASCAL statements that highlight the relationship of two or more related instructions are the:

a   BEGIN and END statements

b   PERFORM and RETURN statements

c   GOSUB and RETURN statements

d   FOR and DO statements

_____ **22**   The IF/THEN/ELSE statement in COBOL:

a   does not exist in that form

b   permits the simultaneous test for two variables

c   branches to two or more program modules

d   creates two concurrent looping sequences

_____ **23**   Within the structure chart, modules on the lowest level are called:

a   program control modules

b   process and control modules

c   processing modules

d   program modules

_____ **24**   A substitute module used in testing top-down designs is the:

a   test module   **b**   dummy module

c   submodule   **d**   stub module

_____ **25**   A group of related statements may be defined within a:

a   paragraph   **b**   subroutine

c   program module   **d**   all the above

Summary Test Answers

1 F	**2** F	**3** T	**4** F	**5** T
6 F	**7** F	**8** F	**9** T	**10** F
11 T	**12** F	**13** T	**14** F	**15** F
16 B	**17** A	**18** D	**19** C	**20** B
21 A	**22** A	**23** C	**24** B	**25** D

Eleven

Mass Storage Files

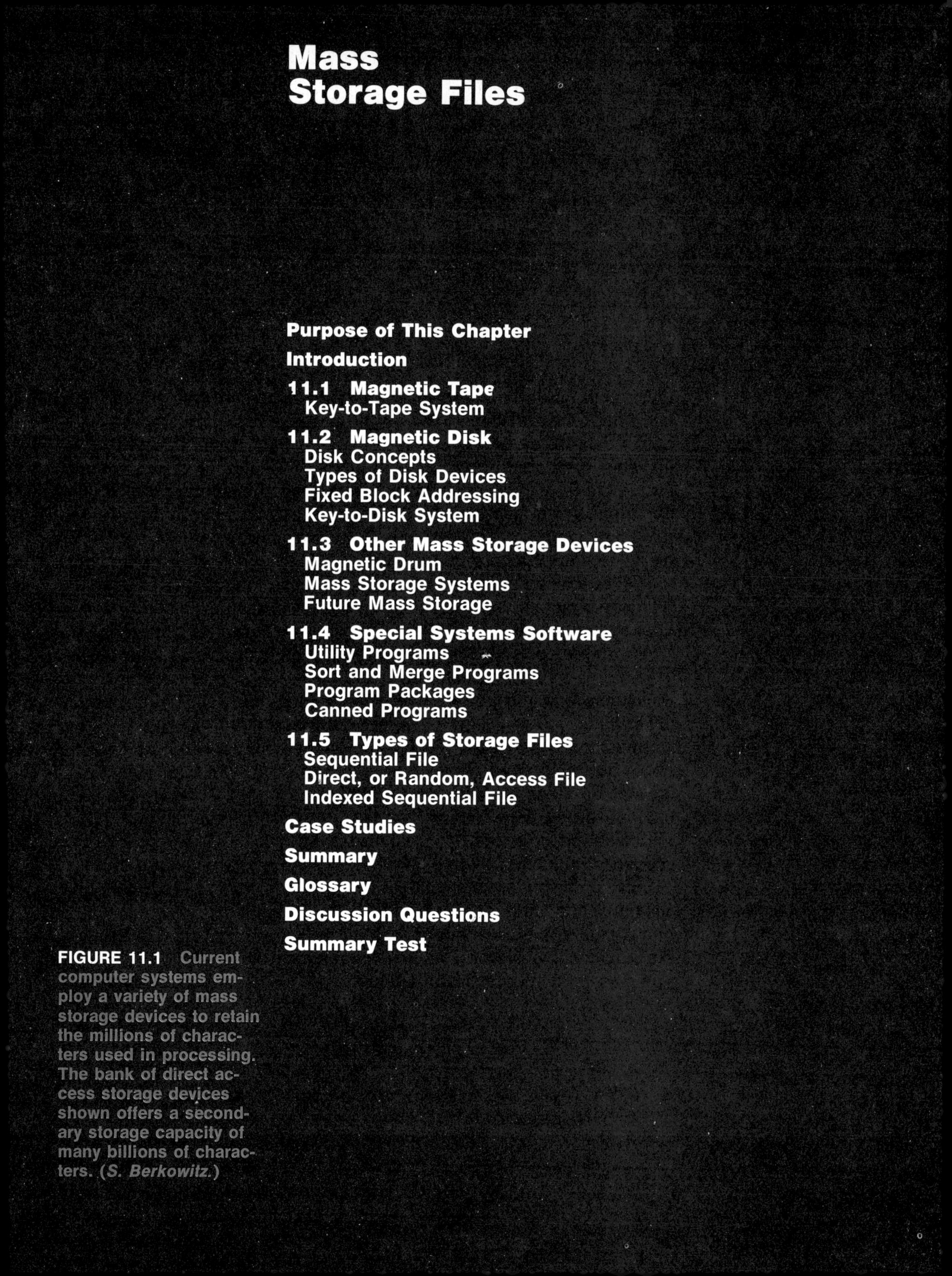

FIGURE 11.1 Current computer systems employ a variety of mass storage devices to retain the millions of characters used in processing. The bank of direct access storage devices shown offers a secondary storage capacity of many billions of characters. (*S. Berkowitz.*)

Purpose of This Chapter

In this chapter we further develop the subject of secondary storage media. We explain additional concepts related to the use of magnetic tape and disk, and we also explain technical terms such as IBG, BPI, "no ring, no write," and header label, used with magnetic tape. We describe a tape peripheral device, the key-to-tape system.

The terms *cylinder, track, sector, rotational delay,* and *recording surface* are explained in relation to their use with magnetic disk. Concepts related to staggered addressing and fixed block addressing are developed in terms of disk storage. Devices used for the random access and storage of data are reviewed, as are key-to-disk systems.

We examine the magnetic drum and mass storage system, also devices currently employed in data processing. Storage systems currently under development including laser beams, photographic storage, charge-coupled devices, electron-beam storage, and cryogenics are explored.

We describe special software designed to assist the computer's processing of data, and we review utility programs, sort and merge programs, and program packages. This manufacturer-supplied software allows data processing to be performed without specially written programs. This prewritten software speeds processing and saves many hours of work. Canned programs provide the same advantages for specific problems.

We discuss the storage of data in computer files, describing the three fundamental file structures—sequential, direct access, and indexed sequential. The merits of each type of file structure are reviewed.

After studying this chapter, you should be able to:

■ Discuss the major aspects of storing data on magnetic tape and magnetic disk

■ Describe the types of peripherals used with magnetic disk storage

■ Describe the purpose of utility programs, sort and merge programs, and program packages

■ Describe the concepts and merits of sequential, direct access, and indexed sequential data files

■ Discuss many of the advanced storage techniques currently under development

■ Understand the following terms:

Access arm
Access time
Bits per inch (BPI)
Block
Blocking factor
Bytes per inch (BPI)
Canned programs
Charge-coupled devices (CCD)
Check bit
Cryogenics
Cylinder
Data transfer rate
Direct access file
Direct access storage facility
Disk
Disk module
Disk pack
Electron-beam-addressed memory
  (EBAM)
End-of-reel marker
Expiration date
File protection ring
Fixed block addressing
Fixed disk
Header label
Head positioning
Head selection
Holographic memory storage
Indexed sequential (ISAM) file
Interblock gap (IBG)
Interrecord gap (IRG)
Josephson tunneling device
Key field
Key-to-disk system
Key-to-tape system

Label checking
Load-point marker
Magnetic bubble memory storage
Magnetic drum
Mass storage system
Megabyte
Merge program
Millisecond (ms)
Nanosecond (ns)
Nine-track tape
Nonremovable disk
"No ring, no write"
Optical memory storage
Parity bit
Photodigital storage
Picosecond (ps)
Program package
Random access file
Removable disk
Rotational delay
Sector
Sequential files
Seven-track tape
Sort program
SPSS
Staggered addressing
Storage density
Table
Tape mark
Tape pooler
Track
Trailer label
Utility program
Volume number

Introduction

While waiting for your airline reservations to be confirmed, have you ever wondered where the information displayed on the CRT is maintained? The terminal displays flight information data, but it must be tied to a computer system that maintains this data. From the discussions in Chapter 5, you may recall that additional online storage is provided by secondary storage devices. In those discussions, we briefly described the storage media of magnetic tape and magnetic disk. This chapter offers an in-depth study of these topics.

11.1
Magnetic Tape

Magnetic tape was developed in the 1950s as an alternative to punched cards for storing and processing data. It was clear then that standard punched cards could not satisfy the growing needs of the industry and were limited in their use. Magnetic tape could store millions of characters of data, the equivalent of over 500,000 cards, on one reel. One magnetic tape could contain all the data related to one card file and eliminate the handling, preparation, and bulky storage of cards.

Tapes were a milestone in data processing. They were the first mass storage medium that could store millions of characters in one physical device.

Standard reels of magnetic tape are 2400 feet long, with a plastic coated magnetizable surface, and can store over 4 million characters of data. As the tape passes beneath the read/write heads of the tape drive, data is sequentially written directly on the surface or read from it. These operations resemble the way sound is recorded or played back on a home tape recorder. The tape must pass directly beneath the read/write head for any data to be properly written on the tape or read from it.

Each read-write head has a specific storage density. The term **storage density** refers to the number of characters stored on 1 inch of magnetic tape. Storage density is measured in either **bits per inch** or **bytes per inch,** depending on the manufacturer. The terms may be used interchangeably when describing density and are represented by the initials **BPI.** A high BPI indicates a high concentration of characters per inch. A low BPI indicates that the characters on a tape are more loosely packed. In this measurement, the terms *character, byte,* and *bits* are equal because each represents exactly one character of data.

The BPI rate is normally a function of the hardware available at the data processing installation. Common storage densities are 800, 1200, and 1600 BPI. More recently, rates of 3200 and 6250 BPI have been developed and applied in daily operations. The actual BPI rate is not important to the programmer coding programs, although it may be used to estimate whether the storage of a particularly large file will require two reels of tape. It becomes important, however, when a tape recorded on one computer system is to be used on another system.

Simply put, a tape recorded at 1200 BPI cannot be read and used at 1600 BPI. The level must be consistent. Thus, before any actual production runs, a programmer must know a tape's BPI rate. This knowledge can save time and money and prevent embarrassment. Many business people have bought information stored on tape, only to discover that it is incompatible with their computer system.

The original use of magnetic tape was closely related to the 80-column punched card. Thus magnetic tape initially stored data following the unit record concept; that is, one record represented one com-

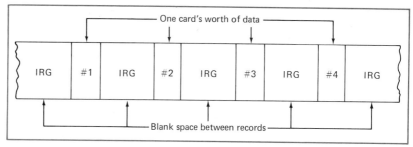

FIGURE 11.2 The format of data originally stored on magnetic tape when an operational concept, similar to the unit record concept, was used. More blank space existed on the tape, in the form of interrecord gaps (IRGs), than data. Note that the space required for an IRG is almost double the space for one card's data.

plete transaction and contained all required data. Furthermore, data was originally stored on tape one card at a time.

The configuration depicted in Figure 11.2 was conceptually correct because each record was followed by a blank space. This space, called an **interrecord gap (IRG),** served two valuable purposes. First, IRGs separated one record from the next. Second, they helped maintain the correct speed for reading data. The tape drive read its data in a stop-and-go fashion; that is, the tape sped up so that data could be read at the proper speed, then stopped. The IRGs before and after each record provided for this acceleration to and deceleration from the correct reading speed. In turn, the correct reading speed meant that the correct BPI rate was used during the reading or writing of data on tape.

Data processors were quick to notice faults in this initial use of magnetic tape. As Figure 11.2 illustrates, the tape had more blank space than data. If we compare the space necessary to store one card's data and the size of one IRG, we can see, with sample measurements, that an IRG used .75 inch of tape whereas the card data required much less space. Approximately two cards could be stored in one IRG. Storing an equal number of card records and IRGs would result in a tape almost two-thirds blank. Another problem was that the tape continuously stopped and started, inefficiently accessing only one record at a time and placing unneeded wear and tear on the equipment.

The solution to these problems was to group similar records or **blocks** on magnetic tape. The concepts of blocking and the **interblock gap (IBG),** represented in Figure 11.3, were developed.

The blocking of records permits a more efficient use of magnetic tape. The tape drive does not have to stop and start so often to access data, and more data is available for processing at one time. In blocking, the IRG is replaced by the IBG. The IBG separates blocks of data

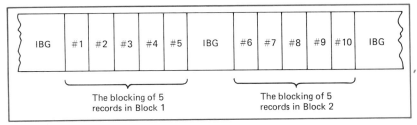

FIGURE 11.3 The blocking of records on magnetic tape reduces the amount of stop-and-go movement of the tape drive and permits the efficient access of data. Five records are blocked together in the illustration. Each block is separated by an interblock gap or IBG. The blocking factor in this case is five.

and lets the tape speed up to and slow down from the proper reading speed.

The number of records in a block of data is identified by a number called a **blocking factor.** In Figure 11.3, the blocking factor is five. The programmer chooses the size of the blocking factor according to the computer's ability to store data and the size of each record in the block. For example, not all computers can read a block of 100 records (a blocking factor of 100) in which each record contains 1000 characters. Blocks of 100,000 characters each are too large for the storage capacity of many CPUs. The size of a block must be tailored to the system on which it is used. COBOL is one programming language that regularly uses a blocking factor as part of its syntax, when tape storage operations are involved.

IBGs and the blocking of data ensure the efficient use of magnetic tape as a storage medium. Safeguards have also been devised to minimize the chance of error with magnetic tape.

One early problem with magnetic tapes involved the writing of data on previously recorded tapes. Often, through confusion or error, the wrong tape would be mounted onto a tape drive, and data written on it. The new data completely would overlay the existing information, destroying it and rendering that tape file useless. The entire file would have to be rerun, at added expense, to recapture the lost information.

This type of error was solved by use of the **file protection ring.** This plastic ring, shown in Figure 11.4, is never put on the tape reel except immediately before tape-writing operations.

When a tape is mounted on a tape drive without a file protection ring, the tape can only be used for input operations; that is, data can only be read from the tape. Nothing can be written on a tape without the insertion of the ring. Thus the computer cannot be accidentally directed to write anything on the tape, and the files stored on the tape are protected. The phrase **"no ring, no write"** was created to remind computer operators about the file protection ring.

The file protection ring is an external form of tape security that prevents tapes from being written on accidentally. However, another safeguard is needed to ensure that the wrong tape file is not used in processing. This feature, incorporated into the structure of tape files, is the header label. The **header label** appears at the beginning of a file stored on a magnetic tape and contains data relevant to that file. The file's identification number and expiration date, along with other data, are included on the header label.

During the processing of any tape, the program must identify the file number of the specific tape to be used. The tape file number specified in the source program is compared with the tape identification number read from the header label of the tape just accessed. If these numbers match, processing can continue. If the numbers are different, the computer operator is alerted to remove or check the tape in use, and processing is suspended. This technique is sometimes referred to as **label checking** and helps prevent the needless destruction of tape files.

A second part of the label-checking sequence involves the **expiration date** of a tape's header label. A file's expiration date indicates the last day that a file can be used. For example, consider a tape file that has an expiration date of 09/30/82. It can be used in processing until that date with no difficulty. However, the system will reject the file if an attempt is made to use it on 10/01/82. The system is designed to prevent the use of files that have exceeded their expiration date. This aspect of the label-checking procedure ensures that only timely information and the proper tape files are employed in processing, thus minimizing costly processing errors.

FIGURE 11.4 A file protection ring used on a tape reel. This plastic ring is only inserted into the center of the tape reel when data is to be written on a tape. At all other times, the ring is not inserted. The ring means that even though a tape is mounted on a tape drive, nothing can accidentally be written on it. The phrase "no ring, no write" describes this condition.

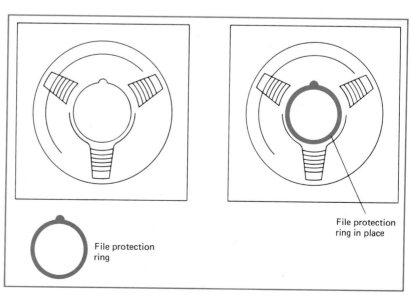
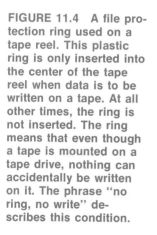

File protection ring

File protection ring in place

FIGURE 11.5 The relationship of the header label to other physical features of magnetic tape.

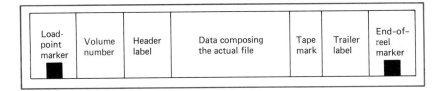

Load-point marker	Volume number	Header label	Data composing the actual file	Tape mark	Trailer label	End-of-reel marker

The relationship of the header label to other physical features of magnetic tape is illustrated in Figure 11.5. These other factors are vital in actual tape processing operations. The **load-point marker** and **end-of-reel marker** are reflective strips sensed by the read/write head that appear on the underside of the tape's surface. The load-point marker at the beginning of the tape indicates the point at which data storage can begin. The end-of-reel marker at the end of the tape indicates the end of the usable storage area. The writing of new data cannot continue past this point.

Whereas the end-of-reel marker denotes the end of the tape reel, the **tape mark** indicates the physical end of a data file stored on tape. The tape mark is not a reflective strip; it is a special code character actually recorded on the tape's surface. The tape mark always appears at the end of each file stored on a tape. When many files are written on one reel of tape, they are separated by individual tape marks.

The speed at which data is transferred to the CPU is referred to as the **data transfer rate.** In magnetic tape operations, the data transfer rate depends on the speed with which the tape passes beneath the read/write head and on the tape density used. A high BPI rate plus a large blocking factor will produce high data transfer rates.

The **volume number** is the identification number of a reel of tape. This number is frequently included in label-checking procedures to ensure that the proper tape is mounted on the tape drive. A **trailer label** must follow any file stored on magnetic tape. The trailer label contains the same data as the header label and also specifies the number of blocks of data in the file. This number is used as a check on the quantity of records processed. It is always output and checked at the end of all processing operations involving magnetic tape. Using this number, the programmer or DP supervisor can quickly determine whether the proper number of records were processed.

Another way to make sure that data stored on magnetic tape cannot be permanently lost is to maintain a tape generation. Despite precautions, tape records may become unusable and have to be re-created. A copy of the tape file from which the original tape was written is kept to assist in the re-creation process. All data used in updating the original file is also kept. With both these inputs, it is possible to re-create any tape file.

Some data processing centers retain two prior versions of an existing file, as a form of *backup.* They can then return to two previous processing cycles to regenerate a file. The three versions of the file are referred to as the *grandfather-father-son tape generation.* The term *son* describes the existing file, *father* the tape file from which the existing file was updated, and *grandfather* the file preceding the father tape. These backup files allow for the regeneration of unusable files.

File protection rings, label checking, and tape generations are precautions against the misuse or destruction of tape files. The computer system employs a different device for internal checking. Computers use a **parity bit,** or **check bit,** to protect against inaccurate recording of data on tape.[1]

All data must pass through the CPU. Data may be transferred one character at a time between the CPU and its peripheral devices at speeds in excess of 500,000 characters per second. To ensure that data is properly transferred, the computer attaches a parity bit to each character. The computer can determine whether the data was correctly input to, or output from, the CPU using the parity bit. Parity errors rarely occur. However, when they do occur, the computer alerts the operator to this condition, processing ceases, and corrective measures are taken.

The addition of the parity, or check, bit means that the computer has to account for 9 bits of information each time a character is transferred between the CPU and the tape drive (1 bit for parity and 8 bits for EBCDIC, for example). All 9 bits are accounted for via the read-write head during I/O operations. The use of 9 bits per character resulted in the development of **nine-track tape,** now used in most magnetic tape processing. One track is reserved for each of the 8 bits of an EBCDIC or ASCII character, and one is for the parity bit. Nine-track tape effectively handles the storage of all information and its accompanying parity bit.

Seven-track tape is similarly constructed, with 6 bits reserved for character code configurations and 1 bit for parity. Seven-track tape has recently become more popular because of its use with newer, smaller computer systems.

Key-to-Tape System

One difficulty with magnetic tape is the time required to place data on the tape. For many years, the most common method of creating a file on tape involved 80-column cards. Data destined for a tape file was keypunched onto cards. These cards were then processed by the computer to create the original magnetic tape file. A considerable delay was inherent in this process because of the handling and use of the cards. The entire process was time-consuming and created the problem of what to do with the used cards.

Computer designers developed a device that eliminated the inter-

---

[1] The concept of a parity bit was introduced in Chapter 5.

mediary use of punched cards. Card handling and storage were no longer a problem, and large amounts of data could be easily handled. The device that made this improvement possible was the **key-to-tape system,** illustrated in Figure 11.6.

The key-to-tape system is an offline device that looks like a keypunch because of its keyboard. However, it keys data onto small reels of magnetic tape instead of punched cards. Cards are eliminated. Data is keyed directly onto magnetic tape at a storage density of 20 BPI. A counter on this device keeps track of the number of records keyed onto the tape.

Verifying tapes produced by the key-to-tape device involves rekeying the same source data. The rekeyed data is compared with the data originally keyed onto the tape. The operator makes corrections by reentering the correct data onto tape.

After the tapes are verified, they must be converted into computer-compatible formats, a step made easy by the **tape pooler.** The tape pooler converts the smaller 7-inch reels of magnetic tape prepared by the key-to-tape device into the larger reels normally employed with magnetic tape storage. The tape pooler converts the original 20 BPI rate to the storage density of the computer system in which the new tapes will be processed (e.g., 800 BPI, 1200 BPI, 1600 BPI).

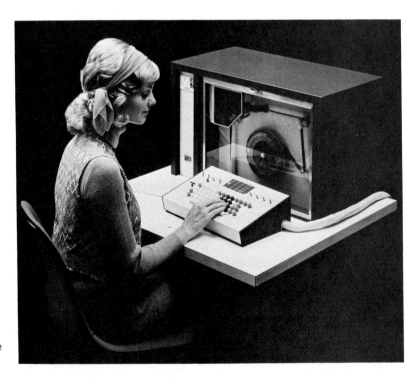

FIGURE 11.6 Data entered via key-to-tape devices are stored on smaller magnetic tapes, which are subsequently merged into regular tape reels.

This final tape contains the contents of many of the smaller reels of magnetic tape prepared using the key-to-tape system.

Key-to-tape systems are invaluable assets to companies that depend on magnetic tape. Insurance companies are examples of organizations that benefit from key-to-tape devices. Data on policyholders is perfectly suited for magnetic tape. Because of the volume of this information and its periodic processing, magnetic tape is the most economical storage method available. Because thousands of reels of tape are required to store the data, an efficient method for placing it on the tapes is the key-to-tape system.

11.2
Magnetic Disk
Disk Concepts

Though magnetic tape has had a profound effect on data processing, the storage medium that has revolutionized the industry is magnetic disk. Magnetic disk as a peripheral device allows for forms of processing not possible with magnetic tape. The random, or direct, access of data stored on magnetic disk is the mainstay of today's computerized processing. Current computer configurations rely heavily on the direct access storage capabilities of disk. Airline reservation systems, time-sharing computers, motor vehicle registration systems, and retail point-of-sales systems are possible only with the support of magnetic disk.

Each item of data in a direct access file stored on magnetic disk can be accessed independently in milliseconds. A **millisecond (ms)** is one-thousandth of a second. The great speed of magnetic disk comes from its construction and storage concept.

Magnetic disk is composed of a series of circular storage surfaces called **disks.** These disks are stacked vertically, one on top of the other, in configurations called **disk packs.** Figure 11.7 shows one type of disk pack, composed of six disks, as it is situated during actual use. Note in this figure, the physical relationship of the recording surfaces to the read-write heads. Though there are only six disks, there are 10 recording surfaces. The top and bottom surfaces are not used to hold data; they serve as protection for the entire disk. The interior disks store data on both their upper and lower surfaces. Magnetic disk storage allots one read/write head to each of these recording surfaces.

Each disk is exactly the same size in diameter (14 inches) and holds the same amount of data. Data is stored on the surface of each disk in a series of concentric storage areas called **tracks.** Figure 11.8 illustrates the relationships among these tracks. Each track has its own number. The outermost track is always identified as track 000, and the inner tracks are numbered 001, 002, and so forth. These numbers are vital when storage or access of data is undertaken. Each track is also subdivided into **sectors,** with each sector capable of

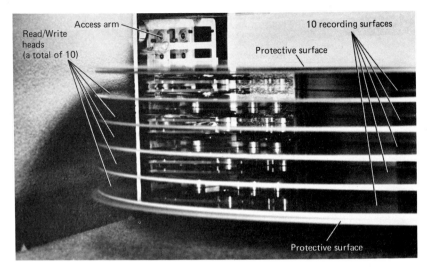

Access arm

Read/Write
heads
(a total of 10)

10 recording surfaces

Protective surface

Protective surface

FIGURE 11.7 This illustration is a side view of a disk pack in use. Note that the 10 read/write heads are positioned between the 10 recording surfaces. The top and bottom surfaces of the six disks are protective covers and are not used to store data. (*IBM.*)

storing one record or item of data. Figure 11.9 shows how data is actually stored on magnetic disk.

The relationships among the read/write heads, recording surfaces, and tracks on a disk pack are illustrated in Figure 11.9. It is important to recognize these physical relationships because they define the manner in which data is stored on a disk or removed from it. The items below relate to the actual storage of data on magnetic disk:

FIGURE 11.8 A disk is composed of a series of concentric recording surfaces called tracks. The number of tracks on each disk varies according to the disk used. It is not uncommon to find disks composed of 100, 200, or 400 tracks. Each track is subdivided into sectors. Each sector is capable of storing one record.

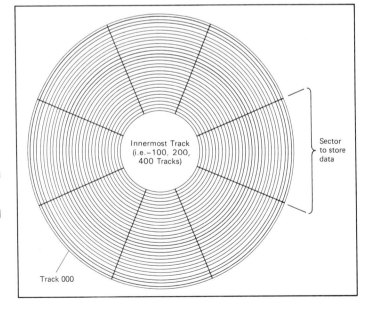

Innermost Track
(i.e.–100, 200,
400 Tracks)

Sector
to store
data

Track 000

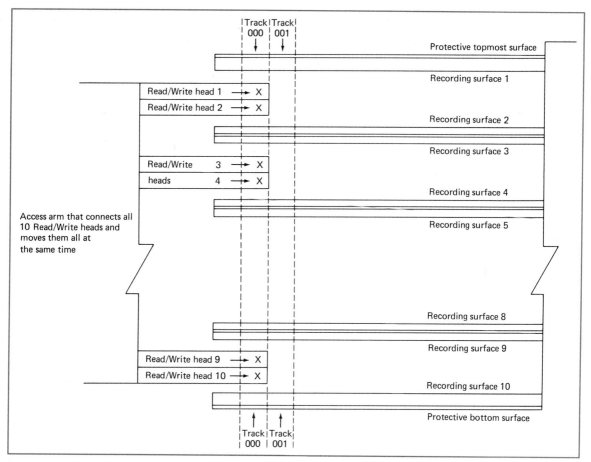

FIGURE 11.9 An illustration of the relationship among read/write heads, tracks, recording surfaces, and the access arm that simultaneously moves all 10 read/write heads.

1 Each read/write head is identified separately by its own number and associated with its own recording surface. Thus, read/write head 1 reads or writes data on recording surface 1, and read/write head 2 is associated with recording surface 2. This relationship exists for all recording surfaces and read/write heads.

2 Each surface begins with track 000.

3 All read/write heads are attached to one **access arm.** Thus, the read/write heads move together; none can move independently.

Employing these points, the next paragraph conceptually describes how data is stored on magnetic disk.

The first track filled with data is track 000, recording surface 1. Read/write head 1 completely fills this track with data as the entire disk revolves. Once track 000 is filled, the next track must be determined. One might consider moving to track 001, surface 1. Design engineers realized that this would not be efficient, because the entire access arm would have to move. Instead of filling track 001, surface 1, they theorized it would be more efficient to fill track 000, surface 2, because the access arm is already positioned above that track and would not have to move. Thus, in a fraction of a millisecond, the computer directs read/write head 2 to write data on track 000, surface 2. When track 000, surface 2, is filled with data, read/write head 3 is directed to record data on track 000, surface 3.

This sequence of filling tracks continues to the last surface (track 000, surface 10). Only at that point does the access arm move. From track 000, surface 10, the storage of data continues on track 001, surface 1. Ten recording surfaces are made available for the entry of data with that one move of the access arm. The tracks on all 10 surfaces are systematically filled with data using read/write heads 1 to 10. This process is continued until the required amount of data has been stored.

On a magnetic disk, each group of tracks with the same track number is called a **cylinder.** Thus cylinder 000 is composed of all tracks numbered 000 on all 10 recording surfaces. Similarly, cylinder 001 consists of track 001 on each of the 10 recording surfaces. Cylinders can be identified for the entire disk. We can therefore state that data is systematically stored cylinder by cylinder, from cylinder 000 to cylinder 001, cylinder 002, and so forth, until all data is stored. Data is always recorded on cylinders, never on a continuous string of tracks on the same recording surface.

The cylinder-by-cylinder method of disk storage also contributes to the speed with which data is accessed. It minimizes the movement of the access arm and lets the read/write heads do most of the work, an arrangement that means the retrieval of data is 1000 times faster than if the access arm were moving back and forth.

Specific terms are applied to the various components of disk storage. For example, the switching between read/write heads to access data is defined as **head selection.** As with magnetic tape, the speed at which data is transferred to the CPU is called the data transfer rate. The access arm's placement of the read/write heads over the proper tracks is referred to as **head positioning.** Finally, because the disk is spinning, there is an occasional wait for a particular item of data to rotate beneath the desired read/write head. This wait is termed **rotational delay.** Each of these factors affects the speed with which data is accessed using magnetic disks. Thus, the **access time** for data on magnetic disk depends on the head selection, data transfer rate, head positioning, and rotational delay of the device.

New technology has sped up the cylinder-by-cylinder method of disk storage. A new technique called **staggered addressing** uses essentially the same relationships among cylinder, track, and sector, but staggers the starting point of the initial sector on each succeeding recording surface to overcome the effect of rotational delay.

In most conventional disks, cylinders are aligned, as are the initial sectors on each recording surface. Thus when data is written on one cylinder, the disk must rotate completely before writing can begin on the first sector of the succeeding surface. The rotation of the disk wasted time and slowed the retrieval of data.

By staggering the starting addresses of the first sector on each successively lower recording surface, it was possible to compensate for and minimize the rotational delay. With staggered addressing, the disk could write data on the top surface, electronically shift to a new read/write head, and write a new record on the next lower surface without the disk revolving completely. Staggered addressing has reduced data retrieval time from an average of 75 milliseconds to 27 milliseconds.

We should point out that disk access times are generally expressed as averages, not to confuse people, but in an attempt to compensate for rotational delay. In some cases, the data being accessed is close to the read/write head, and the disk rotates only slightly. But sometimes a full rotation is necessary to access another record. Because these extremes tend to balance out, access times can be expressed as an average time. Average access time is a fair representation of a disk's performance.

HOW SMALL IS SMALL?

One of the questions students often asked is, "How much space is there between the read/write head and its recording surface when data is being accessed?" Even though the actual answers vary only slightly, most students are confused by the variations because they have no basis for comparison.

Although the size may vary by the disks' manufacturer, there is approximately 20 microinches of space between the read/write head and the recording surface. That's 20 millionths of an inch between the spinning disk and the moving read/write head. By comparison, a smoke particle is almost 100 microinches across, and human hair has a diameter of about 800 microinches. Disk units operate under very tight tolerances.

When a disk is improperly mounted or defective, the disk may wobble and smash into the read/write head. This type of accident is referred to as a *head crash* and usually destroys the disk and all data contained on its surfaces. Head crashes are relatively rare, and the tolerances maintained by these devices are indeed remarkable.

**Types of
Disk Devices**

The types and capabilities of magnetic disks vary among manufacturers. For example, storage capacity can range from 2.8 million to almost 800 million characters, depending on the manufacturer. This section will introduce many of the disk devices currently available.

Essentially, magnetic disks are divided into two categories: **removable disks** and **fixed** or **nonremovable disks.** Their structure is the same, but they are used differently. A removable disk can be removed from its disk drive, whereas a fixed disk cannot. Figure 11.10 shows two types of removable disk. Figure 11.10*a* shows a conventional disk pack, one that is mounted in a disk drive unit. The read/write heads in the drive unit position themselves between the recording surfaces to access data. The **disk module,** Figure 11.10*b*, is also a removable disk but has its own access arms and read/write heads. This unit is positioned within a different type of disk drive unit.

Both the conventional disk pack and the disk module offer a random access capability and some operational flexibility. Both types of removable disk may be changed whenever a different file is needed.

Fixed disks offer the same direct access features as removable disks, but they are permanently fixed within their disk drive units. They cannot be interchanged with other disks, but must have new data read into them. Fixed disks were developed to speed access times by minimizing the seek time necessary to access records on disk files. Nonremovable disks do not use access arms, but position read/write heads above each track containing data. They are generally referred to as *head-per-track devices.* Fixed disks generally offer less storage than removable disks, but provide slightly higher data access speeds.

FIGURE 11.10 Removable disks allow for random access in retrieving data from computerized files. (*a*) A conventional disk pack, one that is inserted into a disk drive unit. (*b*) Another form of removable disk, where the disk module possesses its own read/write heads and access arms. (*IBM.*)

(*a*)   (*b*)

FIGURE 11.11   The direct access storage facility combines many disks into one physical unit capable of storing billions of characters of data. (*IBM*.)

The type of disks in a computer system usually relate to the system's resources and operational needs. Some systems use a series of disk drives to provide a large, online, direct access storage capacity. The number and type of disk devices in that series will reflect the system's needs. Many systems combine fixed and removable disks to take advantage of the best features of each.

An alternative to multiple disks is the **direct access storage facility,** which combines several disks into one unit with a large storage capacity. Figure 11.11 shows a storage facility that can hold over 2 billion characters of data. Although this device uses removable disks, direct access storage facilities may also use fixed disks.

As we have stated, individual disk packs can store from 2.8 million to 800 million characters. The term **megabyte** helps data processors describe these vast amounts of data. One megabyte is the equivalent of 1 million characters of storage. Thus 2.8 million characters of storage are correctly represented as 2.8 megabytes.

Fixed Block Addressing

Introduced with staggered addressing was **fixed block addressing,** a concept that describes how data is stored on magnetic disk. As we know, data is stored on disk according to cylinders, tracks, and sectors. Fixed block addressing simplifies access to that data.

The fixed block concept relies on fixing the size of the blocks of storage on the disk. This standardization solves problems created when different types of hardware and software dictate different block sizes. Compatibility between what programs could run, in relation to what devices were employed, has always been a consideration. With a standard block size, data processors can be sure of working within the same set of constraints.

With fixed block addressing, the contents of each disk appears to the computer as a series of consecutive fixed-size storage areas. The blocks begin at 0 and are numbered consecutively upward. This numbering simplifies reference to a series of data items, because one can actually count the number of blocks which hold that data. This numbering provides an external reference, though the disk actually uses cylinder, track, and sector information to locate records. Software built into the disk and computer system translates the fixed block identification numbers into equivalent cylinder, track, and sector coordinates. This software also verifies that the correct record location was accessed, before the data is transferred.

The IBM 3310 direct access subsystem, composed of four individual disk drives, exemplifies the use of fixed block addressing. Each disk within the 3310 subsystem appears to the computer to consist of 126,016 512-byte blocks of storage. The blocks on each disk are referenced from block 0 on that disk.

Key-to-Disk System

The **key-to-disk system** is an offline peripheral device similar to the key-to-tape system. The key-to-disk system, illustrated in Figure 11.12, permits the entry of data directly onto magnetic disks. Data is input to the disk in the exact format required by computers. Thus no intermedi-

FIGURE 11.12   The Inforex System 3300, a key-to-disk system, permits data to be entered onto magnetic disks, one of which is shown behind the operator. The printer to the left of the disk can print data for subsequent verification. (*Inforex.*)

ary device, such as a tape pooler, is required to convert the data into a usable form.

The key-to-disk system can verify as well as monitor all data entered from the device's keyboard. The operator can define the format to be used for entering data. Thus the operator is immediately alerted to errors during the input of data, and corrections can be quickly made. Key-to-disk systems are extremely advantageous to installations that handle a high volume of data via magnetic disks.

11.3 Other Mass Storage Devices

Magnetic tape and magnetic disk are the two major means of secondary storage employed with most of today's computer systems. However, these storage devices occasionally are not adequate. For example, sometimes even magnetic disk cannot supply data fast enough for a computer system. Furthermore, it is not possible to store large amounts of data on tape or disk without overtaxing the resources of the system.

Magnetic Drum

Magnetic tape and disk can transfer data to the CPU at over 500,000 characters/second. However, even these data transfer rates are sometimes insufficient. During the processing of simulated space flights, national defense communications, or business statistics, some data must be accessed faster than is possible with normal secondary storage devices. The device capable of transferring data at speeds as high as 1 million characters per second is the **magnetic drum.**

The magnetic drum is a direct access storage device that can randomly select any item of data from a file. The drum's ability to access and transfer data is related to its method of storage. Data is stored on the surface of a continuously spinning drum rotating at speeds as high as 3500 revolutions per minute. As it spins, the drum continuously places its data beneath a string of fixed read/write heads. Any item of data is therefore quickly accessible to the entire computer system. Magnetic drums are used in larger computer systems to hold key items of data such as those necessary for starting the processing of other jobs or for allowing the continuous processing of programs.

Though magnetic drum devices have high data transfer rates, the amount of data they can store is limited. For example, the magnetic drum illustrated in Figure 11.13 can store only 4 megabytes of data. Many of the largest drums can store only over 20 megabytes. In contrast, magnetic disks can average in excess of 200 megabytes of data.

The use of magnetic drum devices has been declining as the data transfer speeds of disk devices improve. Recently introduced disk devices have a combined instantaneous data transfer rates of over 3 million bytes per second and a storage capacity in excess of 800 megabytes. As disk devices improve, they may eventually replace the magnetic drum.

FIGURE 11.13 A magnetic drum device with direct access storage that can randomly access data from part of a file. (*IBM.*)

Mass Storage Systems

Mass storage systems are those that provide access to billions of characters of stored data. One such system, the IBM 3850 Mass Storage facility, can store 472 billion characters of data, the equivalent of over 188,000 reels of magnetic tape or 5900 disk units. It is enough to store a 100-character record on almost every person in the world or to store 27 million newspaper pages.

The heart of this mass storage system is a magnetic cartridge upon which data is stored. Figure 11.14 shows the retrieval mechanism for selecting cartridges from their honeycomb of storage areas. The access time for mass storage systems is 2 to 3 seconds rather than milliseconds. This relative slowness (compared to disk or drum) results from the movement of the selection mechanism. Despite this minor disadvantage, the mass storage system is an inexpensive, effective way to store vast quantities of data. Mass storage systems with capacities of trillions of characters will soon be available.

Future Mass Storage

Researchers are always attempting to improve the means for storing data and lessen its cost. Future storage media will probably employ a somewhat different technology, yet provide an effective, low-cost means of storing vast quantities of data. Two promising advances are **optical memory storage** and **magnetic bubble memory storage.**

One optical memory technique under development uses laser beams. This technique, referred to as **photodigital storage,** uses the laser to record data on small chips of film. Storage densities can reach 13 million BPI. A prototype of this technique, called the UNICON Laser Mass Storage system, was developed at the University of Illinois. The system records data on the film surface of a continuously rotating drum. It has an equivalent storage capacity of approximately 1 trillion characters.

Another optical memory technique, developed by RCA, is **holographic memory storage.** This technique uses a laser to etch images into the surface of a heat-sensitive plastic plate. These etchings of data, called holograms, are reread by another type of laser. The

FIGURE 11.14 The components of a mass cartridge storage system. Here we see an array of cartridges, each of which contains a magnetic strip storing millions of characters. (*Control Data Corp.*)

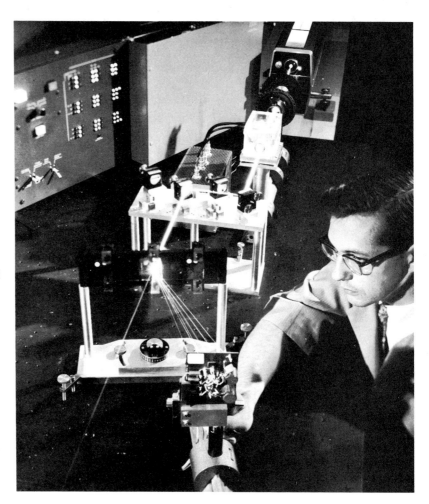

FIGURE 11.15   The light beams generated by a laser can be directed to holographic plates in an optical memory system. Data can be transmitted in ten-millionths of a second and made available 1000 times faster than with conventional secondary storage devices. It is estimated that more than 100 million bits of information can be stored on a holographic plate 9 inches square. (*IBM*.)

impulses created by the second laser are then employed by the computer. This technique holds promise as a means of storing vast quantities of data.

The magnetic bubble memory technique makes use of microscopic spots, or bubbles, on the surface of a magnetic film. These bubbles are magnetized so that they stand out from the surface of the film, and they provide the means for storing and accessing data. Magnetic bubble technology is currently used in the manufacture of hardcopy printers, point-of-sale terminals and automated telephone systems that redirect improperly dialed telephone numbers.

Charge-coupled devices (CCD), electron-beam-addressed memory (EBAM), and **cryogenics** are among the advanced memory techniques currently under development. Charge-coupled devices are

HOW FAST IS FAST?

Most people have difficulty imagining a tenth of a second, much less the billionths of a second that current computers operate in. The following comparisons may provide a frame of reference for the fantastic speeds attained by modern computer systems.

Consider the nanosecond, which is one billionth of a second in duration. If you could stride one yard every nanosecond, you could circle the planet Earth **23 times** in just **1 second.** You would be traveling at almost 575,000 miles each second.

A similar ratio tells us that a nanosecond is to a second what a second is to 30 years. The relationship to a picosecond, which is one trillionth of a second, is even more astounding. One picosecond is to a second what one second is to almost 31,710 years.

semiconductors that use electronic particles contained within their crystallized surface to represent the bits of data stored. CCD technology, although it offers faster access times than bubble memory, has not advanced at the same pace. Currently, CCDs are used in the design of main and secondary storage units.

Electron-beam-addressed memory technology was rediscovered during the search for faster memory speeds. Used in the construction of early computers, EBAMs were replaced by then-superior core memory devices. EBAM designs are now more efficient. In EBAM storage, data are written via an electron beam on a semiconductor chip inside a tube. Bits are recognized by the absence or presence of positive charges on the chip's surface. An electron beam of one-millionth of a meter in diameter allows rapid and concise data storage on the chip's small surface. Although EBAM's potential for storing vast quantities of data is great, no breakthroughs in its technology seem imminent.

Cryogenics involves superconductive circuits that operate at temperatures of −450°F. Under experimental conditions, access times of under a **nanosecond** (one billionth of a second) have been achieved with cryogenic systems. However, problems in the development of refrigeration systems to support this technology have impeded the progress of cryogenic devices.

One successful experimental cryogenic system using supercold circuitry is the **Josephson tunneling device.** In memory devices, it has produced arithmetic operations in a few nanoseconds and bit-switching operations in **picoseconds** (one trillionth of a second equals 1 picosecond). Test computers constructed using Josephson technology are quite small and possess extremely high processing

FIGURE 11.16 A technician sets up the equipment to test a Josephson tunneling device. This technology employs cryogenics, the supercold freezing of supersensative wires. (*IBM.*)

speeds. Technicians estimate that such computers will offer hundreds of times more processing potential than current systems at a fraction of their cost, projecting the cost for one million bits of storage at under $50. Figure 11.16 shows a researcher preparing the experimental circuitry that uses the Josephson tunneling principle.

11.4 Special Systems Software
Utility Programs

Because of improved disk storage, more computers include magnetic disks. But magnetic disk storage has several problems. The amount of data it can store is limited. Data processors also realize that it is uneconomical to store all data on disk. Thus, infrequently used data is often maintained on magnetic tape until it is required for processing. This data is then transferred from tape to disk and processed. After processing, the updated data is transferred back to tape for storage.

Computer manufacturers were quick to recognize that this type of operation was an integral part of day-to-day computer room activities and so have developed software to support it. Their programs are easily incorporated into a computer's operating software and make it unnecessary for programmers to write special programs for this purpose. Using simple JCL commands, programmers can request the use of this software in their programs.

For example, one JCL statement can direct the computer to transfer data from a magnetic tape to a disk pack. At the end of processing, another JCL statement calls on the software necessary to transfer data to tape from its disk storage. The general name applied to this type of software is a **utility program.**

Utility programs perform routine processing activities in a computer system. Since they are manufacturer-supplied programs, they make individual programming efforts to obtain them unnecessary. Utility programs are regularly used to transfer data from one tape to another tape, from a disk to a tape, from a tape to a disk, or from one disk to another disk. There are also utility programs used to print the contents of secondary storage devices. This type of program is referred to as a tape-to-printer or a disk-to-printer program.

Utility programs are not restricted to the transfer of data between secondary storage devices. Specialized utility programs perform the specific tasks of sorting and merging data.

Sort and Merge Programs

Frequently, when working with files of data, programmers find it necessary to sort data before it can be used. Without the assistance of utility software called **sort programs,** the programmer would not be able to readily perform this task. Individual programmers might have to write sort programs every time a new file of data was encountered. This repeated effort would be considerable, tedious, and expensive.

Manufacturer-supplied sort programs enable the easy sorting of data files. The programmer specifies the sort program and the details by which the file should be sorted. The sort utility program does the rest. It takes this file and sorts the data exactly as directed. The result is a completely sorted file of data.

A similar type of utility program combines files of data. Referred to as a **merge program,** it combines two similar files of data into one. Programmers need only specify the two files and request the merge utility program. Again, utility programs save a considerable programming effort.

Program Packages

Occasionally, during the development and implementation of a company's computer system, DP managers realize that they do not have enough programmers to complete a project on schedule or that the staff cannot program a particular application. Faced with this type of problem, many DP managers turn to program packages.

A **program package** is a group of programs that completely handles a specific application. A program package offers a complete solution to a particular problem. Program packages are supplied by computer manufacturers or private companies that specialize in writing this type of software.

Consider a company developing its first computer system to process the employee payroll. The company is faced with writing all its own software, a task projected to cost $30,000 and require at least 6 months. The DP manager, investigating other approaches, finds that a payroll package can be purchased for about $20,000. This package provides all the software necessary to print payroll checks, maintain employee payroll records on tape files, and produce the required tax statements. The package is totally operational, requires no alteration, and is available for immediate use. Purchasing this package will possibly save a 6-month programming effort and free three programmers for other activities. The DP manager must now weigh this alternative against writing the necessary program software.

Program packages are complete sets of software. They perform specific tasks for particular applications. A word of caution is necessary, however, about purchase of a program package. Prior to certifying any program package, carefully examine the conditions under which the programs are guaranteed and can be used. Also, make a complete and exact duplicate of the original software contained in the package. Thus, if the programs are subsequently destroyed, a copy of them is always available.

Canned Programs

Another form of prepared software is the **canned program.** Canned programs are specially designed software that can be added to a computer system to handle one type of problem. Generally, canned programs are written to satisfy a need faced by many companies. For example, canned programs can handle sophisticated statistical analyses in business and mathematics, prepare marketing data and related results, and solve standard engineering design problems. In almost all cases, canned programs offer a standard, well-documented solution.

A prime example of a canned program is **SPSS** (**S**tatistical **P**ackage for the **S**ocial **S**ciences). The SPSS software offers a set of standard statistical analyses which social scientists (or anyone else) can use to evaluate experimental results. SPSS directions define how data must be prepared for input to the program and for the desired analysis. The rules tell the user how to obtain the desired analysis without the need for having to develop a detailed knowledge of programming or having to actually write the software. Most canned programs do require that users take the time to master most of the intricacies of the software in order to obtain the desired results. Canned programs grant users access to specialty software that would normally not be available to them, because of its expense or their lack of programming skill.

**11.5
Types of
Storage Files**

In earlier chapters, we have discussed two types of files. First, we presented the random access files used in an airline reservation system. Second, we described the sequential files used to maintain payroll data. These files represent only two of the three types of data files principally employed with computer systems. In this section, we will define the three types of file structures used for almost all computerized storage of data, and discuss the merits of each.

The three types of file structures are

1 The sequential file
2 The indexed sequential file
3 The direct, or random, access file

We can best explain the differences among these files with a simple analogy.

Imagine that you are using a reference text and that the material you want is on page 100. If you open the text exactly to page 100, you've paralleled the operation of a direct, or random, access file. In accessing the desired data, you had no intermediary assistance. You went directly to the desired page and data. If instead you read every page from 1 to 100, you've operated like a sequential file. If you examine the table of contents, note the start of the chapter containing the desired data (say, page 93), then turn to that page, sequentially read the seven pages to page 100, and find the information, you've operated like an indexed sequential file.

In a **sequential file,** records are accessed one after another in sequence. A **direct,** or **random, access file** lets the computer go directly to a desired record. An **indexed sequential** file is a combination of the other two file types. It accesses a particular point in a file by using an index, then sequentially accesses the desired data.

Sequential File

All the records in a sequential file are maintained in ascending or descending order employing a common **key field.** This key field must appear in every record of the file.

Sequential files can use numeric or alphabetic key fields. For example, a personnel file might be based on employee social security numbers or on last names. Either type of data serves the purpose.

After the key field is assigned, the remainder of the fields in the record format of the file can include any combination of data. Consider the record format illustrated in Figure 11.17. The key field of that record is social security number. This field appears in every record in the file. The entire employee file is sorted by social security numbers. With the key field fixed, the rest of the record format is composed of any combination of data fields desired. All records in the file will follow exactly the same format.

Sequential files are usually used with magnetic tape. (An exception is a card file.) Most are updated via batch processing, because it is the most efficient method for sequential files. First all update data is

Social security number	Employee name Last, First, MI	Address	City	S t a t e	Zip code	Job title	Fields with additional employee data

FIGURE 11.17 The beginning of a record used in a file composed of employee personnel data. The key field is Social Security No. The file is ordered in ascending numbered sequence by social security numbers.

sorted. During batch processing, the update data and the sequential file data are alternately read and processed. After scanning each incoming record, the computer determines which records require updating. After all the changes are made, the update is complete. Sequential files can also be constructed on magnetic disk, but this does not take advantage of the direct access capabilities of disk.

Overall, the advantages of a sequential file are its low cost (resulting from the use of magnetic tape) and its overall efficiency as a batch-processing medium. The drawbacks of a sequential file are the need to process the entire file to update it and its incompatibility with online processing.

Direct, or Random, Access File

The direct, or random, access file is the file organization compatible with online data processing activities. Direct access files enable data to be processed randomly. Unlike sequential files, data for direct access files can be processed as it is encountered. Each record in a direct access file is independently accessible without reading intermediate records. The access of data is valuable in updating direct access files. Data used in the update does not have to be sorted because each record, and thus all data, is handled independently.

Random access files are maintained on magnetic disk devices. With these peripherals, records in direct access files can be stored or read without having to search the entire file. This random access relates to the files' structure. Direct access files use an identifying key to store their data. This identifying key relates a record to its actual storage position in the file. The computer works out this relationship and performs all the necessary computations to find a particular record and relate it to its actual storage location. This approach permits the computer to go directly to any specific record.

Overall, the advantages of direct access files include their compatibility with online and real-time processing and their coordinated use of multiple files. The disadvantages of direct access files are the time lost in computing the actual storage location, the duplication of some storage addresses when computed, the incomplete use of storage locations, and the special security precautions required to ensure that only authorized people can get to specific files.

FIGURE 11.18 Many companies have a large library of magnetic tape. The number of stacks may be astonishing. (*Minnesota Mining and Manufacturing.*)

Indexed Sequential File

Sequential and direct access files are considered each other's opposites. The **indexed sequential file** is a synthesis of the two and combines their positive aspects. In an indexed sequential file, records are stored sequentially on a direct access device (e.g., magnetic disk), and data is accessible either randomly or sequentially. The sequential access of data occurs one record at a time until the desired item of data is found.

For the random access of data, the indexed sequential file must construct a **table** of storage locations. This table is an index of selected records and their respective storage locations in the file. The computer continually refers to the table during the random access of data. It examines the index, determines the storage location immediately preceding the desired item of data, and proceeds to it. From that location, the system sequentially searches upward through the file for the exact item of data desired. This procedure is followed for each record randomly accessed from an indexed sequential file. Though it seems lengthy, the entire process is performed in a few milliseconds. In computer slang indexed sequential files are often called **ISAM** (**I**ndexed **S**equential **A**ccess **M**ethod) files.

The indexed sequential file structure is quite popular because of its ease of usage and its higher access rates. COBOL programmers often employ the file structure when updating files because of its features.

Case Study One

Bubble Memories Keep Growing

People always seem to need more and more storage space, and computer users are no exception. Computer manufacturers are trying to meet this need by developing ever larger storage capacities. Bubble memories, magnetized ovals one-sixteenth the diameter of a hair which store binary digits, have huge potential storage capacities.

Computer experts think that a minimum density of 1 million bits of storage will be needed to make bubble memory devices practical. Present bubble devices can store only about one-quarter of that amount, and the largest random access semiconductors can store only about 64,000 bits.

With technological improvements, bubbles may eventually replace disk storage. But bubbles will first be used where people need inexpensive, compact, reliable storage. Individual calculators, "intelligent" computer terminals, electronic cash registers, telephone switching devices, and computerized production lines are likely applications

for bubble memories. Bubbles for cash registers will store inventory depletion and sales tax data as clerks ring up sales. This data could then be transmitted at evening telephone rates over telephone lines to a central computer for processing. Unlike semiconductors, bubbles do not lose their contents when the power goes off, and so users can avoid expensive battery or other power backup systems. Bubbles are also unaffected by dust or temperature variations, assets that suit them for use in factories.

Manufacturers are racing to put out bubble memories with ever greater storage capacities. One California company, Intel Corporation, estimates that the capacity of bubbles will increase fourfold every 3 years or so. By 1982, Intel itself expects to offer a 4-million-bit bubble memory.

Source of data: Peter J. Schuyten, "Bubble Memory Competition," *The New York Times,* May 3, 1979, p. D2.

Consider this . . .

For many, the all-knowledgeable ship's computers on the TV series, *Star Trek,* were fantasy. With the advent of newer storage technologies,

in your opinion, how long will it be before these storage data banks become reality? What will be the effect of having all that data available?

Summary

The following major points have been presented in Chapter 11:

Point 1 Magnetic tape is a sequential storage medium. Data is stored as blocked records, with each block of data separated by an interblock gap (IBG). IBGs enable the tape to attain the proper speed to read or write data as the tape passes directly beneath the read/write head. Specific storage densities are used for tape I/O operations, and the term *BPI* is applied to the storage

densities. A file protection ring precludes the accidental destruction of tape data. The check of tape header labels assures that only the current tape is mounted. The key-to-tape system was devised to facilitate the input of large quantities of data on magnetic tape.

Point 2 Data stored on magnetic disk is accessed randomly in milliseconds. Data is actually stored on the surface of magnetic disks in a series of concentric storage areas called tracks.

These tracks are subdivided into sectors to store data. Data is written on or read from tracks by individual read-write heads adjacent to each recording surface. The term *cylinder* is applied to groups of tracks identified by the same number on every record surface. The first track on the recording surface is always numbered 000.

Point 3   The components of accessing data on magnetic disk are identified by various terms. Head selection refers to the choice of the read/write head used to access data. Head positioning applies to the movement of the access arm to position the read/write heads. Data transfer time denotes the speed at which data is transferred to the CPU. Rotational delay refers to the time required for the data to rotate beneath the proper read/write head. These four aspects determine the amount of access time necessary to read or write data using magnetic disk. New storage concepts associated with magnetic disk are staggered addressing and fixed block addressing. Both are designed to speed access to data stored on disk devices.

Point 4   Many devices are used for the random storage of data. These include disk packs, disk modules, and removable and nonremovable disks. Single-disk devices can store up to 800 megabytes of data. Mass storage systems have a storage capability as high as 472 billion bytes. The key-to-disk system was developed to speed the input of data on magnetic disk.

Point 5   Mass storage devices are peripheral devices for storing vast quantities of data. The magnetic drum is a device that stores large amounts of data and has extremely high data transfer rates. The direct access storage facility combines many disk packs into one physical unit with a capacity of many billions of characters. Mass storage systems can use a cartridge-oriented system to provide random access to large quantities of data in a few seconds. Future mass storage devices will use optical memory, bubble memory, charge-coupled devices (CCD), electron-beam-addressed memory (EBAM), and cryogenic techniques to store data.

Point 6   Special software was developed to improve secondary storage devices. Utility programs readily enable the transfer of data among magnetic tape, magnetic disk, and printer devices. The sequencing, ordering, and combining of data files are accomplished using sort and merge utility programs. A program package provides a group of programs to perform one complete task. A payroll package is a good example of a set of programs used for one task. Canned programs offer users specialty software for common problems. SPSS is an example of a canned program used for statistical analyses.

Point 7   Three types of files support data processing operations. A sequential file stores and reads data on records one at a time. A random access file handles data on an independent-record basis, going directly to the desired item of data. An indexed sequential file combines the best points of the other two files. Each type of file uses a key field when accessing data. A sequential file uses this field to order and access its records. A direct access file converts this key field into the storage location of each record. An indexed sequential file uses the key field to construct a table of key storage locations, which it refers to when accessing a record from its files.

Glossary

Access arm   The disk drive component to which all the read/write heads are attached and which is used to position them during the access of data.

Access time   The amount of time necessary to locate and retrieve an item of data from secondary storage.

Bits per inch (BPI)   A term used to denote the density with which data is stored on tape.

Block   A grouping of data records on magnetic tape.

Blocking   The technique used to group records of data on magnetic tape to improve the efficiency of tape operations.

Blocking factor   The factor that indicates the number of records contained in one block of data on magnetic tape.

Bytes per inch (BPI)   Another term used to describe the density with which data is stored on tape.

Canned programs   Specialty software designed to handle commonly encountered problems using standard techniques and requiring a minimum knowledge of programming.

Charge-coupled devices (CCD)   An advanced storage technique in which data is stored as charged particles within the crystallized surface of a semiconductor.

Check bit   Another term for a parity bit.

Cryogenics   An advanced storage technique that uses the superconductivity of metals at extremely low temperatures to speed data access.

Cylinder   A group of tracks that have the same number, comprising one track on each of the recording surfaces of a magnetic disk.

Data transfer rate   The speed at which data is transferred between the CPU and its secondary storage devices.

Direct access file   A computerized file of data in which each record is randomly and independently accessible.

Direct access storage facility   A disk device that combines several disks into one physical unit to increase the amount of data stored.

Disk   A recording surface in a disk pack or magnetic disk storage device.

Disk module   One type of magnetic disk pack.

Disk pack   One type of magnetic disk storage device, composed of multiple disks from which data can be randomly obtained.

Electron-beam-addressed memory (EBAM)   An advanced storage technique in which data is written on semiconductors using an electron beam.

End-of-reel marker   A reflective strip at the end of a reel of magnetic tape that indicates the physical end of that tape.

Expiration date   The part of a header label which indicates the date until which a file can be used in processing.

File protection ring   A plastic ring that must be inserted onto a reel of tape to enable the writing of data on that tape.

Fixed block addressing   A storage concept used in current disk devices in which standard-size storage areas are addressed as a consecutive series of blocks of data.

Fixed disk   A nonremovable disk that is permanently fixed within its drive unit; generally one read/write head is assigned to each track.

Header label   The identification label placed at the beginning of a data file stored on magnetic tape.

Head positioning   The term describing the movement of the access arm used with magnetic disk to position the read/write heads over the proper track to access data.

Head selection   The selection of the proper read/write head to read or write data in a magnetic disk operation.

Holographic memory storage   An advanced data storage technique involving the use of lasers to store data images on plastic plates.

Indexed sequential (ISAM) file   A type of data processing file that combines random and sequential access of data and uses a table to identify key storage locations of the file when accessing data.

Interblock gap (IBG)   A blank space between blocks of data on magnetic tape which enables the tape to accelerate to the proper reading speed and decelerate from that speed.

Interrecord gap (IRG)   The predecessor to the IBG; used to separate individual records on magnetic tape.

Josephson tunneling device   An advanced storage technique involving supercold circuitry that has experimentally shown high processing speeds.

Key field   The field on which a computerized file of data is constructed and which is used to identify and access items of data from the file.

Key-to-disk system   A peripheral device possessing a keyboard that enables the easy recording of data on magnetic disks to be used with the computer.

Key-to-tape system   A device similar to the key-to-disk system, used with magnetic tape.

Label checking   A technique used during processing of magnetic tapes to check the number of the tape file (from the header label) against the file number specified in the program.

Load-point marker   A reflective strip at the beginning of a reel of tape, indicating the physical point at which data can be recorded on that tape.

Magnetic bubble memory storage   An advanced data storage technique in which microscopic magnetized bubbles, representing data, are stored on the surface of a magnetic film.

Magnetic drum   A mass random access storage device which stores data on its drumlike surface and possesses a high data transfer rate.

Mass storage system   A mass storage device that stores its data in an array of magnetic cartridges and can store up to 472 billion bytes.

Megabyte   The term used to represent 1 million characters of storage.

Merge program   A prewritten, manufacturer-supplied utility program used when two similar files of data are to be merged into one combined file.

Millisecond (ms)   One-thousandth of a second.

Nanosecond (ns)   One-billionth of a second.

Nine-track tape   The type of magnetic tape used in most current tape operations; each of eight tracks represents 1 of the 8 bits of an EBCDIC or ASCII character, and the ninth track is assigned to the parity bit.

Nonremovable disk   One of the two types of magnetic disk used in disk operations; it is physically fixed into the disk drive.

"No ring, no write"   A phrase associated with the file protection ring, indicating that no tape writing operations are possible without the insertion of that ring.

Optical memory storage   An advanced data storage technique that uses laser beams to record data on film chips or light-sensitive plastic plates.

Parity bit   A bit that is assigned by the computer to every EBCDIC or ASCII character configuration as it is transferred between the CPU and all secondary storage devices.

Photodigital storage   One of the new technologies associated with optical memory storage, in which lasers record data on chips of film.

Picosecond (ps)   One-trillionth of a second.

Program package   A group of programs that completely satisfies and handles an entire computer application (e.g., a payroll package).

Random access file   A file structure in which data is independently accessed.

Removable disk   A magnetic disk which can be removed from the disk drive.

Rotational delay   The time necessary for the magnetic disk to spin and place the desired data beneath the proper read/write head.

Sector   One of the subdivisions of a track (on a disk's recording surface), into which data is stored.

Sequential file   A file structure in which data is written, read, and accessed one record at a time.

Seven-track tape   A type of magnetic tape on which 7 bits are used to represent a character of data, 6 bits for the character's code plus 1 parity bit.

Sort program   A manufacturer-supplied program used to sort the data employed by a program undergoing processing; available in the computer for general use.

SPSS   A canned program applied to social science problems involving statistical testing of test results.

Staggered addressing   Disk storage in which the starting points of records on succeeding surfaces are staggered to minimize the time lost by rotational delay.

Storage density   The density with which data is stored on the surface of magnetic tape; represented by BPIs.

Table   An index of selected records and their storage locations used with indexed sequential files to access data from the file.

Tape mark   A special code character placed at the end of each data file stored on tape.

Tape pooler   A peripheral device used with key-to-tape systems to convert smaller tapes of 20 BPI to large tape reels of 800 to 6250 BPI, which can be processed on the computer.

Track   One of the concentric recording surfaces on a magnetic disk.

Trailer label   The identification label placed at the end of a data file stored on magnetic tape.

Utility program   A prewritten, manufacturer-supplied program used to perform specific processing operations involving secondary storage and peripheral devices (e.g., a tape-to-disk program, a tape-to-printer program).

Volume number   The data, preceding the header label, that identifies a specific reel of tape by a unique identification number.

Discussion Questions

1   Briefly discuss the three types of file structures used in data processing (sequential, random access, and indexed sequential).

2   Describe the use of interblock gaps and the blocking of records on magnetic tape (use your own illustrations).

3   Describe the relationships between tracks, cylinders, read/write heads, and recording surfaces when data is stored on magnetic disk (use your own illustrations). Briefly explain how staggered addressing might speed the access of data on a disk.

4   Visit the computer room at your school. Examine the secondary storage devices that are used. Ask how, when, and what type of utility programs are used.

5   Scan the data processing and computer journals in your library for articles related to the development of new storage techniques. (Ask the librarian for assistance, if necessary. Look up the use of lasers, bubble memory, charge-coupled devices, EBAM storage, and cryogenic technology in the index of periodicals.)

6 Discuss the use of utility programs, sort and merge programs, program packages, and canned programs.

7 Discuss how the file protection ring and label-checking techniques are used to protect tape files.

Summary Test

_____ **1** The storage density of magnetic tape is measured in IBGs.

_____ **2** On magnetic disk, tracks are subdivided into cylinders that are used to store individual items of data.

_____ **3** Indexed sequential files employ a table, which is an index of selected storage locations in the file.

_____ **4** A file's expiration date indicates the last date the file can be used.

_____ **5** Header labels contain information about a file and appear at the end of the file.

_____ **6** A magnetic drum is a direct access storage device with a data transfer rate as high as 1 million characters per second.

_____ **7** The file protection ring is an important part of the label-checking operation to protect tape files.

_____ **8** Optical memory storage techniques involve the use of lasers to store data.

_____ **9** Utility programs are supplied by manufacturers and can perform routine processing activities.

_____ **10** IBGs enable the tape drive to accelerate the tape to proper reading speeds, but they do not separate blocks of data.

_____ **11** The parity bit is assigned by the programmer to ensure that data is properly transferred between storage areas.

_____ **12** Three terms that completely describe the access of data via magnetic disk are head positioning, track selection, and rotational delay.

_____ **13** A cylinder is a grouping of the same-numbered tracks on all the recording surfaces of a magnetic disk.

_____ **14** Sequential and indexed sequential files are similar and are employed in the same way.

_____ **15** With a fixed disk, the term fixed block addressing identifies the fact that the disk cannot be removed from the disk unit.

_____ **16** A complete set of programs for one specific data processing application is called a:

    a utility application
    b canned program
    c program package
    d b and c

_____ **17** A characteristic generally associated with a fixed disk device is:

    a simultaneous movement of all read/write heads
    b one read/write head per track
    c slower access times than removable disks
    a all the above

_____ **18** The number of records contained within a block of data on magnetic tape is defined by the:

    a record per block factor

    b block definition

    c record contains clause

    d blocking factor

_____ **19** The reflective strip noting the physical end of a tape is the:

    a load-point marker

    b tape mark

    c end-of-reel marker

    d tape end marker

_____ **20** The Josephson tunneling device illustrates principles associated with the advanced storage technique:

    a cryogenics   **b** CCD

    c EBAM   **d** holographing

_____ **21** A mass storage system is a direct access device capable of storing within its array of cartridges:

    a over 500 megabytes of data

    b almost 16 billion characters

    c 2000 megabytes of data

    d 472 billion characters

_____ **22** One disadvantage of a direct access file is:

    a the delay in computing the storage address

    b duplication of address locations

    c unused, but available, storage locations

    d all the above

_____ **23** The recently introduced disk concept for reducing time lost from rotational delay is:

    a fixed block addressing

    b cylinder, track, sector data

    c staggered addressing

    d graduated block identification

_____ **24** The optical technique that uses lasers is:

    a photodigital storage

    b EBAM storage

    c CCD storage

    d cryogenic storage

_____ **25** A billionth of a second is defined as a:

    a millisecond

    b microsecond

    c nanosecond

    d picosecond

Summary Test Answers

1	F	2	F	3	T	4	T	5	F
6	T	7	F	8	T	9	T	10	F
11	F	12	F	13	T	14	F	15	F
16	C	17	B	18	D	19	C	20	A
21	D	22	D	23	C	24	A	25	C

Twelve

Information Processing Systems

FIGURE 12.1 The computerized handling of data extends into many fields. The transmission of sporting events via satellite and microwave stations is computer assisted to improve reception. (*Ellis Herwig/Stock, Boston, Inc.*)

Purpose of This Chapter

In this chapter, we present additional material on advanced data processing. We have briefly introduced many of these concepts in previous discussions. The chapter opens with a presentation of data communications systems and focuses on the online processing of data. We review online batch processing, real-time, and time-sharing systems.

Current modes of data communication are discussed, including two of the most common telephone services, leased lines and dialed service. We also present newer means of data communication, such as satellites and microwave stations. We explain the use of simplex, half-duplex, and full-duplex lines, as well as multiplexer devices.

A computer system's ability to handle multiple programming assignments is examined in a discussion of multiprogramming and multiprocessing. Multiprogramming involves the concurrent processing of programs, whereas multiprocessing defines the simultaneous execution of two or more program statements. The use of partitions is also explained.

The concepts related to multiprocessing lead to a discussion of distributed processing systems. We review three types of distributed systems. These systems are supported by a group of computers that process vast amounts of data generated at widely dispersed points within an organization. Such computers can independently process data or pass data to an online database, which is controlled by a larger computer system. We also present a special form of distributed system, a distributed data entry system.

After studying this chapter, you should be able to:

- Discuss and differentiate among the various types of online processing systems
- Understand the types and classes of data communications services
- Discuss the differences in simplex, half-duplex, and full-duplex lines
- Discuss the concepts of multiprogramming and multiprocessing
- Discuss distributed processing systems and their overall purpose
- Understand the structure of spider, ring, and hierarchical networks with distributed systems
- Understand the following terms:

Background partition	Dedicated line
Concentrator	Dialed service
Conversational mode	Distributed data entry system

Distributed processing

Foreground partition

Full-duplex line

Half-duplex line

Hierarchical network

Leased line

Multiplexer

Multiprocessing

Multiprogramming

Narrowband channels

Online batch processing

Online real-time processing

Partition

Polling

Private line

Remote batch processing

Ring network

Simplex line

Slave computer

Spider network

Time-sharing

Voice-grade channels

Wide Area Telephone Service (WATS)

Wideband channels

Introduction

Social scientists have concluded that by the year 2000, the merging of computer and telecommunications technologies will have revolutionized the manner in which we collect, process, and distribute information at all levels of society. They also believe that in the workplace of the future, a continuous flow of data will be available for managerial decision making. Computers will massage the data, and telecommunications hardware will distribute this information to users at all types of offices.

This projection is based upon an evaluation of the future direction of the computer field. We can measure the impact that data communications systems are having on the DP field by the current and future spending on data communications equipment. According to an industry-wide marketing survey, spending on data communications equipment increased by 20 percent in 1980 and should continue to do so during the early 1980s. Expenditures for terminals to support telecommunications activities are expected to exceed $600 million, and over $1 billion will be spent on communications lines of all types to connect computer systems regionally, nationally, and internationally. These increases coincide with the projected growth of the data processing field and future work force requirements.

The increased use of these modes of processing has resulted from the technological ability to develop and support data communications activities coupled with the online processing of data. Banks, hospitals, factories, credit card companies, government agencies, and many other organizations have recognized the operational efficiency of these modes of processing and converted to them. Online processing makes data readily available and allows for the immediate distribution of this data. Online processing and data communications will probably dominate among the future modes of data processing.

12.1
Data Communications Systems
Online Batch Processing

Many computer systems can separately support both batch and on-line processing of data. This dual capability permits users to choose the processing mode most suited to their operational needs. Some data processing tasks, such as payroll processing, are best suited to batch processing. In contrast, immediate access to medical data is easier with online processing. In some cases, users want to combine both techniques, and the resulting operational mode is termed **on-line batch processing.**

In a typical online system, data is telecommunicated to a computer and processed. However, an online batch-processing system must also perform the activities involved in batch processing. Data is accumulated over a period of time and transmitted to the computer at regular intervals. The actual processing of these batches of data may take place immediately or be delayed until the computer system is free. In either case, the acceptance of the batched data will signal the computer that processing is ready to begin. An illustration of an online batch-processing system is provided in Figure 12.2.

Figure 12.2 shows a situation in which inventory data, in the form of punched cards, is accumulated throughout the day at a company's warehouse. This batch of data must be posted daily against the company's inventory files. Because the warehouse is miles away from the company's data processing center, the data must be transmitted to the main computer over telephone lines. Thus every afternoon at a specific time, inventory data stored on punched cards is telecommunicated to the company's computer. Once received, this data is processed, updating the inventory file.

FIGURE 12.2   The online batch processing of inventory data.

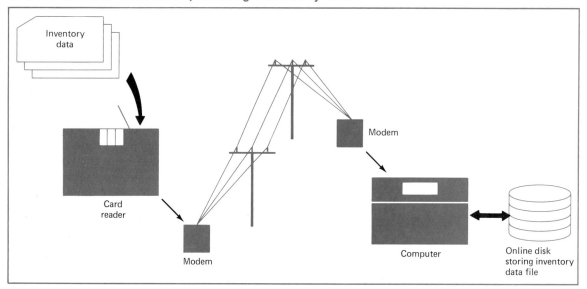

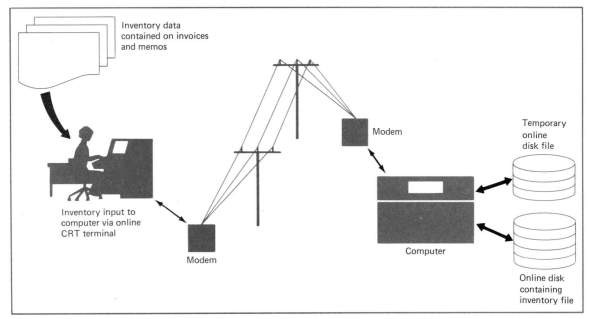

FIGURE 12.3   The online batch processing of inventory data. Data is input via an online terminal. The clerk enters one item of data at a time to the system, using a conversational mode.

Online batch processing may also involve terminals, as depicted in Figure 12.3. In this case, however, the accumulation and transmission of the data to be processed are somewhat different. A clerk accumulates inventory data in the form of invoices and memos. This data is not in a machine-acceptable format and cannot be directly input to the computer. The problem of converting the data into an acceptable input format is solved with an online terminal.

The batch of inventory data will be processed according to the following procedure: After establishing an online link to the system, the clerk will use predefined computer commands to create a temporary online disk file. This temporary file will receive and store all the inventory data entered through the terminal. One item of data will be input at a time. The computer will scan each item of data and reject any incorrect items. These items can be reentered once they have been corrected. The interactive mode in which data statements are individually transferred between the terminal and the computer is referred to as the **conversational mode.**

The conversational mode of inputting data will continue until the entire batch of inventory items has been entered. At that point, the clerk will direct the computer to process the data contained in the temporary file against the inventory file. The updating of the inventory file will then begin, completing the online batch processing of the data.

The common term for this version of online batch processing is **remote batch processing.**

In online batch processing, the delays normally associated with batch processing are minimized, since data does not have to pass through a time-consuming conversionary process. Batches of data are keyed directly into the system and processed. Retailers commonly use another form of online batch processing.

Throughout the day, retailers may use terminals to interrogate computer files for information on customer accounts. Corrections to these accounts are keyed directly into intelligent terminal devices equipped with limited storage buffers. Regularly throughout the day, the main computer sequentially accesses each terminal and pulls in for processing all data held within the buffered storage areas. When each batch of stored data has been input, the main computer returns to normal processing. Depending on the computer's workload and capacity, the batched data may be processed immediately or later in the day. If processing is to come later, a temporary file will be established to hold the batched data until it is processed.

The above retail example represents another method of handling online batch processing using currently available hardware. The addressing of each intelligent terminal, controlled by the system's operating software, is referred to as **polling.** It is said that each terminal is *polled* as to the availability of data.

Online Real-Time Processing

The **online real-time processing** of data is best illustrated by the airlines' computerized reservations systems. Real-time computer systems provide almost instantaneous responses to customer requests for flight information, since there is virtually no delay in processing. Customer reservations entered via online terminals are teleprocessed and matched immediately against ticket data maintained in direct access files. Normally, CRTs are used in real-time systems because they can visually display information more rapidly than hardcopy terminals can print it. Once a reservation is confirmed, however, a ticket can be printed by a hardcopy terminal at a ticket counter. Figure 12.4 diagrams an online real-time reservation system.

Online real-time systems are useful when processing and reaction to processed data are critical. The Stock Exchange uses a real-time system to monitor the millions of shares of stock bought and sold each day. The defense industry and NASA also use this type of system. In each of these examples, a large volume of data must be immediately processed, and all data enters the system on an online basis.

Real-time systems are highly specialized and are often prohibitively expensive. Their development and use require large amounts of time, money, and human energy.

Time-Sharing

Time-sharing is a special form of online processing in which several users share the resources of an online computer system. Terminals let

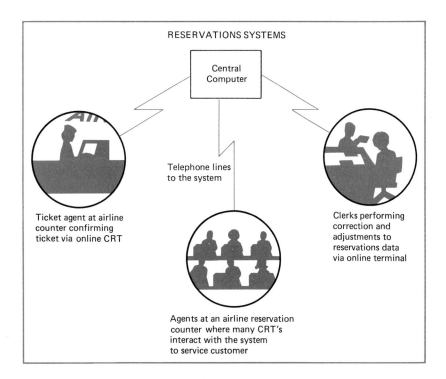

RESERVATIONS SYSTEMS

Central Computer

Telephone lines to the system

Ticket agent at airline counter confirming ticket via online CRT

Clerks performing correction and adjustments to reservations data via online terminal

Agents at an airline reservation counter where many CRT's interact with the system to service customer

FIGURE 12.4 An on-line, real-time system handling passenger flight reservations.

users interact with the system in a conversational mode. Instructions flow to the computer one at a time and are executed when directed. Because the system is so fast, users are seldom aware that many people are sharing the same computer resources.

Many users can share a system without long delays in processing. Most time-sharing systems respond to users' instructions in seconds. On occasions when the number of terminals being used approaches the limit of the system (e.g., when 20 users are sharing a system designed for 25 online terminals), users may notice a small delay in the execution of their programs.

Time-sharing systems are often used in business, engineering, science, and education. Many schools and universities use them for their student programming courses. Students use online terminals to interact with the system and develop programming skills. The computer language BASIC was developed primarily for time-sharing purposes. Other interactive languages have been developed for use in a variety of time-sharing applications (e.g., interactive forms of COBOL, FORTRAN, and PASCAL).

Many businesses use time-sharing systems for their daily data processing operations. A manager might interrogate an online file for information on past sales performances. An accounts receivable clerk might enter corrections to customer charge accounts before monthly statements are issued. A programmer/analyst might enter research data to forecast and analyze future inventory levels. An accountant might process audit data to develop an analysis of a company's financial position. All these activities could be conducted concurrently in a time-sharing system.

The advantages of time-sharing systems have made them extremely popular. Their online capability means that users can obtain an immediate response to file interrogations and computations. Time-sharing systems are flexible in that they can offer access to a central computer via telephone lines and portable terminals. By concurrently handling many jobs, time-shared systems achieve higher levels of utilization and therefore are more cost effective, an advantage that recommends itself to many users.

The disadvantages of time-sharing include its vulnerability to faulty telephone service or breakdowns. Processing is often hampered by marginally operating equipment or interference in communication lines. Data security is always a consideration in time-sharing. Overall, for the average user, the advantages of time-sharing far outweigh its drawbacks.

FIGURE 12.5 A time-shared computer system capable of performing a range of DP activities, but primarily designed for time-sharing activities.

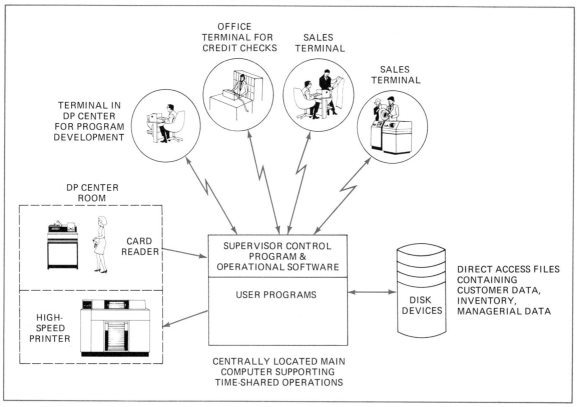

12.2
Modes of Data
Communications
**Communications
Lines**

The illustrations accompanying the discussion of online systems depicted the transfer of data through telephone lines. This method of telecommunications is only one possible mode of data communications. Telephone lines used with online systems must be leased from a common carrier such as AT&T. This type of service is divided into **leased lines** and **dialed service.**

Leased lines, sometimes referred to as **private** or **dedicated lines,** are telephone lines that are strung between the user and the supporting online system and are exclusively available to the user on a 24-hour basis. Usually a monthly flat rate is charged for this service. No message units are charged for each minute the lines are used. Once connected to the system, a user can stay online as long as necessary. A good rule of thumb for estimating the monthly cost of a leased line is approximately $1 per month for each mile of telephone line between the terminal and the online system.

With dialed service, message units are charged each time the line is used for online processing. Users must dial a specific telephone number to gain access to the computer. In dialed service, users are competing for access to the computer because only a certain number of input lines exist. When all lines are being used, a busy signal will indicate the unavailability of free lines and the inability to gain access to the system.

In dialed service, the user is charged only for the time the line is used. The actual rate varies according to the distance involved and the day and time at which the lines are used. A dialed service used by many users is the **Wide Area Telephone Service (WATS).**

LASER TRANSMISSIONS VIA SATELLITE

In August 1980, two IBM researchers working in Zurich, Switzerland obtained a U.S. patent. This patent lets IBM transmit data via laser beams from satellites to receiving stations on the ground. Data communications activities will be controlled by holographs inside the satellites. Holographs are laser-coded images on photographic plates; they represent one of the newer computer-related storage technologies.

Satellites will contain several holographs that will control laser communications to the various ground receiving points. Inclement weather will present no obstacles, as the holographs may be accessed by remote control and directed to transmit their communications to the ground station in question. IBM plans to incorporate holographs and laser transmissions into the communications satellites in which it has joint ownership. Researchers believe that these techniques will greatly enhance the speed and performance of the communications satellites which orbit 22,000 miles above the earth.

The relative advantages of leased or dialed service depend on the user's needs. If a high level of online activity is anticipated, a leased line could prove more economical. Generally, leased lines provide better quality transmission of data, because they are dedicated to a single user. Dialed service is better suited to a lower level of online activity and provides the user some flexibility. Dialed service users gain access to computer systems through any number of telephone lines.

The data communications services available from common carriers can be classified into three categories: **narrowband, voice-grade,** and **wideband channels.** Dialed and leased line services are available in all three categories.

Narrowband channels offer the lowest data transfer rates and support the transmission of data through telegraph lines. Western Union is the largest common carrier to offer this type of service. Voice-grade channels represent the middle range of data communications classes and are used to handle the bulk of online processing activities. Private telephone and WATS lines are examples of voice-grade service. Wideband channels have the highest data transfer rates, with data communications through coaxial cables and microwave transmission.

Technology has not stopped at these levels in the support of data communications. Research is continually underway to develop new and more reliable means of online data transfer. Currently, researchers are testing the effectiveness of lasers and light beams in transferring data. Though much of this work is still experimental, data communications involving lasers holds great promise.

XTEN—A SATELLITE MESSAGE SERVICE

A highly imaginative satellite-related data communications system was developed by the Xerox Corporation. This electronic message switching service, called Xten, will combine radio signals, microwave transmissions, and a satellite to provide a national digital transmission system. Anyplace that can receive radio signals can be serviced by Xten. Xten will support conventional data communication services, teleconferences among distant users, and the online distribution of printed matter between two locations. The Xten system will use satellite and microwave signals, but its innovation is the use of radio-based signals. Radio signals should offer an alternative vehicle for data communications to customers plagued by spotty or faulty telephone service.

The Xten has caused much comment. Its detractors state that it is not a sound form of national message system, that data security will be a major problem because radio signals are so easily intercepted, and that

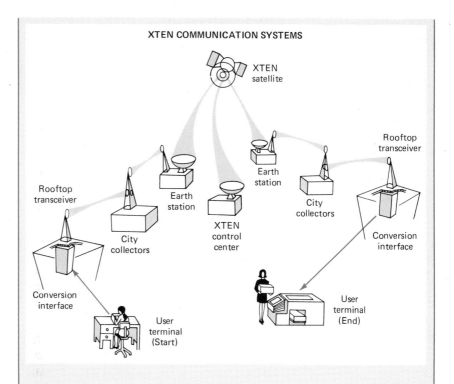

XTEN COMMUNICATION SYSTEMS

Xten has inadequate growth potential. Xten supporters note its use of technology to solve the pressing problem of insufficient data communications transmission capacity, its avoidance of bad telephone lines, and its provision of an alternative national common carrier for electronic messages.

A representative Xten hookup appears in the accompanying figure. It can help us understand how the Xten transmits data. The user keys data via an online device connected to a unit that converts that data to radio signals. These signals are transmitted via microwaves by rooftop transceivers to the Xten satellite. The process is reversed for transmitting data to a receiver. The receiving hardware outputs the data as desired. The handling of data in the Xten system is a series of actions. Users feed messages to local transceivers. These feed into city collectors, which in turn feed into earth stations which beam data to the satellite. The Xten satellite is controlled via a computer located at the Xten control center.

The Xten system is certainly innovative. It provides a glimpse of the time when computer and communications technologies will have been integrated.

Source of data: "Looking beyond XTEN," *Infosystems*, November 1979, p. 72.

The Bell System is developing a national digital data service that will connect more than 100 cities. As envisioned, this system will transmit only computer-related data and will virtually eliminate the need for modems. The leased service will permit data transfer rates of 2400 to 120,000 bits per second, well above the existing voice-grade levels of 600 to 2400 bits per second.

Other specialized companies have been given permission by the FCC to construct data communications systems and compete with AT&T. Special carriers provide their services only in high-user-density areas where competition among carriers is possible and where networks of microwave stations to transmit data are available. In addition, they may offer users special rates. These factors give special carriers marketing advantages, help them avoid low-profit markets, and reduce their operating expenses. It is estimated that the increased competition among carriers will result in lower costs and improved service to users in general. Some of these special common carriers are Western Tele Communications, Inc. (WTCI), Data Transmission Co. (DATRAM), and Microwave Communications, Inc. (MCI).

The most glamorized form of data communications uses communications satellites. Satellites have been successfully used for international communications since 1961. In April 1974, the first domestic communications satellite was launched under the sponsorship of Western Union. This satellite, called Westar 1, could transmit data at speeds in excess of 8 million words per second. Western Union now operates a data communications system composed of a series of satellites which services the entire United States.

IBM, Aetna Insurance, and Comsat have joined forces to sponsor a digital communications satellite that supports a variety of computer-related activities. Even with the additional capacity it offers, experts predict that full transmission capacity will be reached by 1983 or 1984. The demand for satellite data communications has grown faster than anticipated. Many experts recommend the development of additional satellites to support worldwide computer activities.

Transmission Lines   Communication lines are classified by their manner of transmitting data. Data can be transmitted through a line in only three ways. These three modes are the **simplex, half-duplex,** and **full-duplex lines,** each with its own operational characteristics.

A simplex line transmits data in one direction only. Simplex lines are often used for individual I/O activities. Simplex lines are used to connect data collection terminals to distant computer systems, thus speeding the flow of data from these online input terminals.

The half-duplex line permits data transmission in two directions, although the flow of data in one direction must stop before data may flow in the opposite direction. The direction may change any number of times, but the integrity of the directional flow must be maintained.

Half-duplex lines are often used in time-sharing operations, where the interactive mode dictates a one-way flow of data at any one time.

The most versatile transmission line is the full-duplex line. It can concurrently handle the flow of data in two directions. Full-duplex lines allow I/O operations to be undertaken and completed simultaneously. Full-duplex lines are integral to any complex computer system that handles a vast array of I/O activities. A real-time system, which must concurrently handle a large volume of I/O transmissions, depends on full-duplex lines to interact with its remote terminals and peripheral devices. The transmission of data, in both directions, over these lines is critical to the rapid distribution of information in this type of system.

Multiplexing Devices

We have referred many times to attempts to increase the computer's overall efficiency. Two hardware units developed to enhance I/O operations are **multiplexers** and **concentrators.** Both are designed to increase the number of terminal devices a communication line can support.

Multiplexers solve the problem of online I/O devices not fully using the resources of a communication line. It is inefficient for a line to remain underutilized for any period of time. A multiplexer is designed to accept data from several terminal devices, combine that data into one unified stream, and transmit it over one communication line. In this fashion, one channel can handle a large amount of data that was formerly input via many channels.

The concentrator works somewhat differently. It lets only one terminal device access a particular communication channel. The concentrator controls access to a limited number of channels by polling each terminal connected to it. If a terminal device has an I/O operation to perform, the concentrator grants access to the channel. When all available channels are in use, the concentrator establishes a queue of requests, sequentially assigning jobs to channels as they free up.

Concentrators and multiplexers are integral components in online processing systems. Their type and quantity depend on the capacity of the computer system in which they operate.

12.3 Handling Multiple Jobs Multiprogramming

Online time-sharing usually encompasses the concurrent execution of two or more jobs held in main storage. This kind of execution is called **multiprogramming** and allows for more efficient use of the computer. The concept of multiprogramming is related to overlapped processing, which we discussed in Chapter 5.

The CPU can only execute one program instruction at a time. The CPU cannot simultaneously execute two instructions, whether from two programs or the same program. However, as you learned from the discussions of time-sharing, the computer can handle a statement in one program, jump to a different program and execute another statement, then return to the first program and process still another statement. Switching between programs lets the system concurrently process two or more programs. This is the fundamental principle on which multiprogramming is based.

With manufacturer-supplied systems software, main storage can be divided into compartments called **partitions.** Individual programs that are concurrently processed are stored in them. Partitions reserve a specific number of storage locations and do not permit other programs to write or store data in them. Partitions also help define the order in which programs are executed, as individual programs will be assigned to specific partitions dependent on their operational needs.

Partitions in main storage are designated as **foreground** or **background partitions** (Figure 12.6). High-priority programs, which must be processed ahead of other jobs, are placed in the foreground partition. These programs normally exhibit a high level of I/O activity and require some form of online processing support (i.e., time-sharing or real-time processing). Low-priority jobs, typically involving batch processing, are assigned to the background partition. Low-priority programs are generally characterized as having a minimum of I/O operations and requiring a large number of computations.

The reasoning used in allocating programs to either partition is simple. The CPU can initiate I/O operations for programs in the foreground partition and release them to channels for completion. While these I/O activities are underway, the CPU is free to turn to programs stored in the background partition. Because of its speed, the CPU can alternate continuously between partitions and execute a large number of jobs.

In Chapter 7, we alluded to the importance of an operating system, noting its impact on the flow of processing. The assignment of jobs to the various partitions is one responsibility specifically administered by the operating system. During the initial phases of processing, with the aid of the proper JCL commands, the operating system will assess the

FIGURE 12.6 The relationship of foreground and background partitions to the supervisor control program in the CPU.

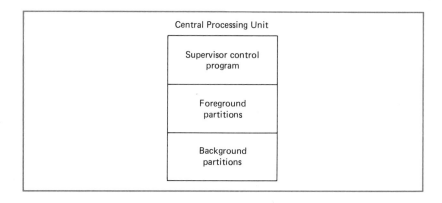

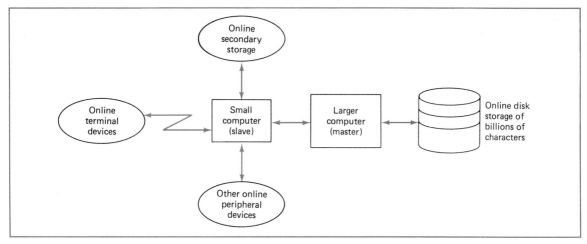

FIGURE 12.7 A multiprocessing system involving a larger (master) computer and smaller (slave) computer which does all the preparatory work. The online disk storage is often a database made of many files. The smaller computer is sometimes referred to as a pre-processor or front-end computer.

operational needs of the program and the available system's resources, and assign that job to the proper partition. If these assignments are properly made, the flow of jobs passing through the computer is maximized, thus improving the efficiency of the entire system.

Multiprocessing

Despite the similarity in labeling, multiprogramming and multiprocessing are operationally different. Whereas multiprogramming uses one CPU, **multiprocessing** uses two or more CPUs. Multiprocessing effectively increases the speed with which data is processed, because it permits the simultaneous execution of two or more different programs.

Multiprocessing is a very powerful data processing tool. It dramatically increases the speed with which data is accessed and made available for processing. During multiprocessing, the CPUs can communicate with each other, one CPU can support another CPU's processing when needed, several CPUs can share the processing load (i.e., one handles a real-time system, and the others support online batch processing), and a group of CPUs can have access to the same vast database.

Multiprocessing systems are extremely expensive. They require large expenditures in human energy, time, and equipment. Special systems software must be developed and written for each overall system. Multiprocessing is frequently incorporated into online real-time systems. Two possible configurations of multiprocessing systems are given in Figures 12.7 and 12.8.

The multiprocessing system illustrated in Figure 12.7 depicts a relationship between two computer systems. The smaller computer is

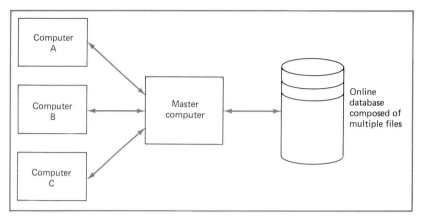

FIGURE 12.8   A multiprocessing system composed of a master computer and three smaller systems. Each small system is free to process data independently using online terminals, secondary storage, and a variety of peripheral devices. Their access to data in the database is through the master computer. Computers A, B, and C are remotely located from the master system and transfer data using some form of data communication.

referred to as the **slave computer,** because it performs all the initial processing activities required of the total system. All data entered into the overall system is initially handled by the slave computer, which interfaces with all secondary storage devices, terminals, and peripheral devices. The slave computer prepares all data processed by the larger (master) computer. It handles the slower preparatory tasks necessary to initiate and maintain a smooth flow of processing. These responsibilities include compiling programs, opening and closing data files on tape or disk, accessing systems software essential to processing, and providing the data required by the master computer. The slave computer leaves the master computer free to process data in the system's vast amount of online storage. The real-time nature of this system is related to the master computer's facility to process data against that database and make it available to users via the slave computer.

Figure 12.8 illustrates a different system with the same multiprocessing capability. In this case, three computers interact with a larger system. The three smaller systems can independently process their own data and, when necessary, interface with the larger system. The larger system accepts data from all three systems and controls access to the vast files of data maintained by the larger system. Data accessed from this database can be made available to any user via the three smaller systems.

Communications Handling

Multiprocessing configurations have taken on added importance with the current and anticipated growth of data communications operations. Some computer systems possess the hardware to handle adequately both data communications tasks and the processing of all the data related to those transmissions. They can monitor all I/O requests from online devices, process programs relating to those requests, and output data over communications lines.

But as the volume of data communications has increased and grown more sophisticated, many computer systems have not remained operationally efficient. They have spent more time on handling data communications and have been able to perform only a minimum of the required processing. This problem has been common with online processing systems handling a high volume of I/O activity from an array of online peripheral devices. A typical example of this situation might result from a dramatic increase in customer sales activity in a retail organization, originally designed for a much lower sales volume.

In many instances, simply using a larger or faster CPU was not sufficient. A separate computer was necessary. This slavelike computer would undertake all data communications activities. It would coordinate the use of all communications lines, monitoring which devices were tied into what lines, and assume responsibility for both input and output operations. The level and complexity of data communications activities accomplished by some systems require a computer to handle those requests adequately and speedily.

FIGURE 12.9 Two multiprocessing configurations in which a computer is assigned the responsibility of handling data communications.

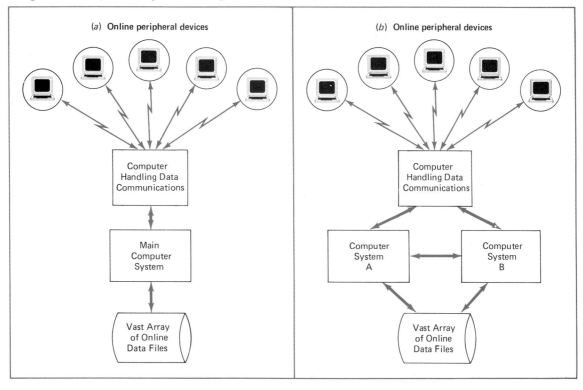

Two examples of a separate data communications computer appear in Figure 12.9. In Figure 12.9*a*, a single computer fronts the main computer and handles all data communications initiated by the system's online peripheral devices. As the smaller CPU handles all data communications, the larger, main CPU is responsible for processing and access to the vast array of files in the system's database.

Figure 12.9*b* shows a slightly different configuration. In this case, two larger CPUs share processing activities and a vast array of online files. The system's volume of activity requires the support of a separate computer to handle data communications. One example of this configuration is the combination of two IBM 370 model 158s for processing and an IBM 3033 Processing Unit for data communications. Such a configuration is typically quite expensive, for it involves three CPUs and hundreds of peripheral devices. This vast system might support the sophisticated data processing of a large corporation or municipal agency.

Despite the expense of a configuration of three CPUs, it does offer some operational advantages. Its vast data communications capability can support a variety of online processing applications. Many users with a variety of tasks can concurrently access the system. These tasks may assume some form of file manipulation or interrogation with a high level of I/O activity. The two main CPUs can also back each other up. If one CPU is inoperable, the other can assume all essential processing until full service is restored.

One CPU may also be held in reserve until the level of processing requires its services. The operational software would direct the second CPU to begin processing jobs the first CPU could not handle. The second CPU also could be assigned special jobs that might otherwise tie up the system for hours. Many organizations use their system that way to process a high-priority task without interfering with other routine but critical jobs.

An organization must carefully examine the cost of such an elaborate multiprocessing system, which can be several million dollars per year. The vast processing and data communications potential that such a system can offer a large organization may fully justify its installation.

**12.4
Distributed
Processing
Distributed
Processing
Systems**

The concept of **distributed processing** was developed employing principles of multiprocessing. In a distributed processing system, computers are strategically distributed throughout the organizational structure of a company to handle data generated by the organization. Each of these computers must be able to interact with a centrally located computer which oversees the activities of the entire system. Branch computers initially handle the data generated at lower levels. Once this data has been processed, pertinent information can be transferred into a database maintained by the main computer. The

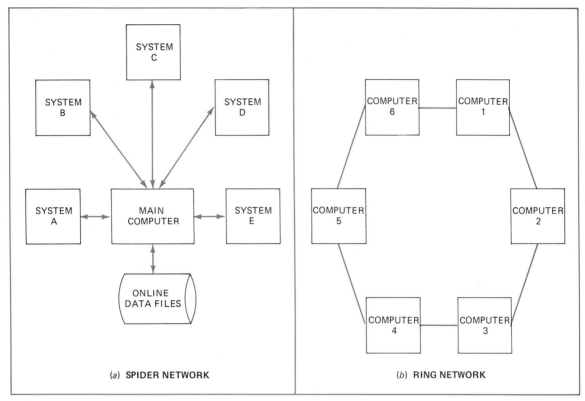

(a) **SPIDER NETWORK**

(b) **RING NETWORK**

**FIGURE 12.10   Two possible distributed data processing configurations
are (*a*) the spider network and (*b*) the ring network.**

branch computers handle the bulk of the preliminary work, and the
main computer is free to monitor the entire system.

Distributed data processing systems may assume several configurations. The differences lie in how the main computer is placed in relation to its satellite systems. One configuration, which uses a large central computer ringed by smaller systems, is called a **spider network.**
In a spider network, the main computer is the focal point of all processing, with all communications routed through it. The branch systems
interact with the main computer or teleprocess data with other
branches via the central computer. Figure 12.10*a* shows a spider network.

A disadvantage of the spider network is its vulnerability to a malfunction in the central computer. If the main system goes down, the
interactive capability of the total distributed data processing network
is canceled for as long as the main system is inoperative. An alternative to the spider network is the **ring network,** Figure 12.10*b*, in which
a series of computers handle processing activities. The ring network is
similar in principle to a parallel circuit in an electrical system. If one of
the computer systems fails, the ring network continues to function by

bypassing the failed system. The other systems pick up the work of the nonfunctioning member. The ring network can continue to function and serve its users.

A slightly more sophisticated setup, using several principles of structured design, is the **hierarchical network.** It divides the overall distributed data processing structure into levels of support. The lowest level of computer support supplies users with their DP services and corresponds to the lowest level of the hierarchal network. Computers at the next higher level assume a supervisory role, handling communications activities and the interaction of the systems beneath them. They, in turn, are overseen by computers at the next higher level. The refinement continues to the highest level of the network, where one system controls the entire network.

A hierarchical network is usually reserved for large systems that both need and can afford it. Though smaller systems may be used at the lower levels of a hierarchical network, each higher level requires a slightly larger, more sophisticated machine with more complex operational software. The expense of installing and running multiple systems with differing levels of operational software can run into millions of dollars.

Consider a distributed data processing network used by a retail corporation with four major stores and one corporate headquarters. Figure 12.11 shows a spider network in which each store has a smaller computer to support its data processing needs. The larger main computer oversees the entire system, monitors the retail data produced by each small computer, makes this data available to the corporate database, and coordinates the interaction of the individual computers at each store.

The four smaller systems support the day-to-day operation of the stores. Each system records all sales, credits, and returns issued by a given store and updates inventory on an online basis. Each store computer has a sizable disk storage capacity, terminals for online data handling, and peripheral devices for conventional data processing I/O operations (e.g., card reader, printers, etc.). These four systems must not only fully support the data processing needs of each store but must also supply data relevant to the retail database maintained by the main corporate computer.

The corporate database is composed of online files which contain data relating to all customer charge accounts, a composite total of the inventories maintained by all four stores, profiles of all sales performances, and financial data on the entire corporation. The interaction of the main computer and the individual smaller systems is illustrated in the following examples.

Each store monitors its own inventory levels. Changes in inventory are online batch processed daily, with each store maintaining this data in its own files. These changes are also transmitted to the retail database, where they are processed against the joint inventory file, which

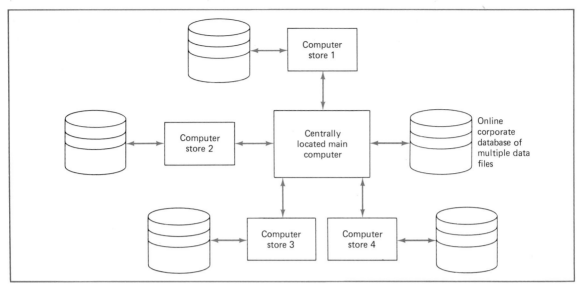

FIGURE 12.11   **A retail distributive processing system. Four smaller systems interact with a centrally located main computer which maintains the corporate database and provides access to that data. Each of the computer systems located in each store possesses its own online disk storage and a full complement of peripheral devices, such as terminals, printers, card readers, etc.**

reflects the total inventory held in all four stores. One of management's prime goals is to maintain an accurate accounting of inventory levels.

The overall inventory data compiled in the retail database is of value to management. It helps them distribute the inventory among the four stores to maximize their potential profit. If a major sale is considered to attract customers, managers are aware of the level of goods the stores must sell. One advantage of a distributed processing system is its ability to access data and make it available for use.

In a distributed processing system, the availability of sale items is easily determined. If a particular item has been sold out at one store, it can be quickly determined whether or not the item is in stock at another store. Using an online terminal, a sales clerk can request that the larger system scan the composite inventory file (maintained in the retail database) for that item. If the item is in stock, the system will respond with the location of the item and the number of units currently held in inventory. The clerk can then access the inventory file of the store in which the item is available, confirm its availability, and reserve it for the customer. In a distributed processing system, component systems can interact and access data from each other's files.

The interactive nature of a distributive processing system is even more apparent as it deals with retail charge sales. The file on all customer charge accounts is maintained in the retail database and is therefore accessible to all stores. The online availability of charge data permits any clerk to verify a charge sale and offers some protection against the fraudulent use of credit cards. It is a storewide policy to check each credit account prior to the completion of a charge sale.

The sales clerk enters the credit card into an online terminal device which reads the account number off the card's surface. This device transfers the acount number, via the store and main computer, to the retail database and verifies the status of the account. If the account is valid, the charge sale is completed. If not, the sales clerk seeks the assistance of the floor manager. The credit card check takes only seconds and can save the store a considerable sum of money.

The decision to maintain customer charge account data at the database level is an advantage to the customer also. Shoppers can use their credit card at any one of the four stores because all of them have computerized access to customer charge data. Overall, a distributed processing system permits management to exercise tighter control over a widely dispersed, dynamic operation.

Distributive processing delegates control to the local branches of a company and enables these branches to tighten their own operations. If accurate and timely data is developed at these branches, the data made available to the centralized computer is of greater value. Though branch distributive processing centers operate independently, they are responsible to higher management and must adequately support the main computer. This type of system allows for tight financial and administrative procedures and can produce potentially large cost savings. A disadvantage of a distributed processing system is its cost. Two or more computers must be purchased, along with the peripherals necessary to support the system. Also, sufficient time must be allocated to train the personnel that operate the system.

As managers recognize how well they process data and give information, distributed data processing systems are growing increasingly popular. Manufacturers now supply program packages to support distributed data processing in retailing, manufacturing, education, inventory distribution, and marketing. These packages can save organizations software development expenses.

Distributed Data Entry System

A special form of distributive processing system is the **distributed data entry system.** This type of system employs small computer systems to prepare input data for entry to a vast database controlled by a large computer system. The smaller systems act as data collection points, verifying the accuracy of all data entered into the system. Once checked, the input data is stored on disk and subsequently transferred to the database.

Consider how a key-to-disk system might help to monitor data in a vast parts inventory. A key-to-disk system would be placed at key con-

RETAIL DISTRIBUTED PROCESSING SYSTEM

Dillard Department Stores, Inc., operating a chain of retail stores located throughout the Southwest, offers a practical example of a distributed processing system. Sales data generated by individual stores is telecommunicated to Dillard's main computer in Little Rock, Arkansas.

Stores in the Dillard chain are supported by NCR 280 retail computer systems. These independent systems let each store's computer operation be tailored to its data processing needs. Throughout the day, the 280 system supports the processing of retail sales data for each store. At the end of the business day, pertinent sales data retained by the 280 system is transferred to Dillard's central computer in Little Rock. The data received is processed against a retail database maintained by the central computer, containing sales data relating to the entire Dillard chain. Data retained in the retail database is used to plan sales strategies, consolidate the purchase of inventory for all stores, control customer accounts, reduce waste and lost inventory, and provide management with the type of information necessary to effectively run the entire chain of stores.

Source of data: Training publication, Dillard Department Stores, Inc., Little Rock, Ark.

trol points where inventory data is collected. This data would be input to the overall inventory system via terminals connected to the key-to-disk computer. Using programs stored in its CPU, the computer would check input data, verify its accuracy, and store it in online disk files.

All the key-to-disk computers in the entire data entry system would input their data to a central database under the control of one large system. In this distributive system, these smaller systems would be used as data entry points that have online access to a vast database. They would continually input correctly verified data to the system's database. Essentially, the data entry computers would be distributed throughout the system.

A slight variation of the distributed data entry network involves small computer systems that accept input data and support normal processing. These systems accept data from online terminals situated at major stations, where clerks key data directly into the system. The data is processed and retained in the system's disks. Once processed, these data are forwarded to the main computer. The system's design dictates whether the data are fed to the central system at regular intervals, as necessary, or when polled by the main (receiving) system.

FIGURE 12.12 The IBM 8100 Information System was designed specifically for distributed data processing activities. This system can accept data from various peripheral devices, up to a maximum of 24 terminal devices. The 8100 can retain or input data to a larger, controlling system. It can manipulate data to conform to any file structure of the local system or main computer. (*IBM.*)

Large airline and automobile companies use distributed data entry systems. Both of these industries have widely scattered work centers which generate large quantities of service data that must go immediately into their computers. Workers can use online terminal devices to input data into their local systems. The local systems in turn feed data to overseer systems. The system's main computer uses all this data to create work and service schedules, plan for equipment needs, verify the existence of materials, and evaluate workers' performance.

Distributed data entry systems allow for the speedy and accurate entry of important data into a vast computer system. Without them, companies might suffer long waits before data became available for processing and planning.

The improved flow of data resulting from a distributed data entry system is readily converted into real savings. Inventory resources are more readily distributed to where they are needed, managers have the data they need to operate, and the computer has the most current data for use in its update and planning activities.

Case Study One

Companies Get the Word Electronically

Though most managers are unaware of electronic mail, they could probably profit from its use. Electronic mail represents one of the newer aspects of office automation that could revolutionize all forms of written communications.

The fundamental idea behind electronic mail is point-to-point communications. Essentially, data keyed at an origination point is electronically transferred in minutes through an online distributed network to a reception point. Messages, letters, drawings, or any other form of document can be sent electronically, relieving the secretarial staff of their preparation and handling. The electronic mailing of documents also reduces the risk of loss from postal delays.

Distributed data processing systems can easily incorporate electronic mail capabilities. Many manufacturers offer the necessary operational software. Savings on secretarial costs may be considerable. Costs for electronic mail are estimated at about 50 cents by 1982. Many users also believe that electronic mail can provide them with a competitive marketing edge.

Electronic mail services have been classified into five major categories. The first category is composed of carrier-based systems provided by major organizations such as the U.S. Postal Service and Western Union. The second category is provided by private and public teletypewriter companies and focuses on the TWX or Telex message network. The transfer of document images defines category three. These services would be available from private or commercial computer networks. ITT's FAXPAK is an example of this type of service.

The application of electronic mail in offices is covered by category four, which describes the transfer of messages between offices via many forms of data communication. Computer-based message systems are the fifth category. These systems, similar to large time-sharing networks, offer an expanded communication system in which to transmit electronic mail. The costs of these systems are currently quite high.

Competition appears to be developing in this market as manufacturers recognize the potential offered by electronic mail systems and as technology reduces the associated costs. Four companies, ITT, IBM, Wang, and Rolm, have recently introduced electronic mail systems with a promise of more on the way. Office managers will have to be educated about the benefits of electronic mail. Until then, ignorance will inhibit its growth. Electronic mail has the potential to completely revamp future office structure and procedures. Messages and important memos will go between electronic offices in seconds. The adage "Bad news travels quickly" may take on a new meaning.

Summary

The following major points have been presented in Chapter 12:

Point 1 Data communications systems are used for the online transfer of data to computer systems. Online batch processing involves the online communication of batches of data, which have been accumulated over a period of time, to a distant computer system where that data is proc-

Case Study Two

Distributed Processing Helps Canadian Firm Cash In

Distributed data processing systems often can perk up not only a company's DP operation but its finances as well. Such has been the case for Domtar, Inc., a Montreal-based manufacturer of construction materials which it distributes throughout Canada. Domtar's switch from batch processing to an online distributed data processing system sped up the distribution of accurate managerial data and improved customer service and cash flow—the latter a critical factor considering the construction industry's high financing costs.

Domtar operates from three regional centers in Canada. It used to collect data at these centers and forward it to Montreal for processing. But the information which was mailed back to the centers was weeks out of date. The company could not respond fast enough to customers' needs, daily operational data often was incorrect, and inventory control was difficult.

Domtar's new distributed data processing system continues to rely on the three regional centers, but now these centers can support local DP needs, provide timely information, and telecommunicate data to the main computer at corporate headquarters. Relying on its own computer support, each office has become its own sales and profit center. The data each center needs for competitive selling is now available via its own computer.

Domtar chose the Hewlett-Packard HP 3000 Series system for each regional center and an IBM 370 System for the Montreal office. The computers were installed in stages. This approach let management monitor the installation, train employees, and test the system under actual con-

essed. Remote batch processing is a special type of online batch processing in which a temporary data file is constructed at the receiving computer system and filled with batched data. Data is transferred to this file one record at a time, employing a conversational processing mode.

Point 2 Online real-time processing and time-sharing require the direct support of the CPU. Real-time processing involves instantaneous processing of data entering the system. Real-time systems rely on data communications to perform their I/O functions. Time-sharing systems enable many users to share resources of an online computer. Using data communications, users employ terminal devices to interact with a time-sharing computer.

Point 3 Data communications can be accomplished via telephone lines, which are either leased lines or lines providing dialed service. Leased, or dedicated, lines are specially strung lines tied directly to the computer. Dialed service uses regular telephone lines that provide access to the computer and are dialed in the same way that a phone call is made. A WATS line is a type of dialed service. Other modes of data communication include the use of satellites, microwave transmission, cables, and telegraph lines.

Point 4 Data communications services can be classified into three categories: narrowband, voice-grade, and wideband channels. Narrowband channels offer the lowest data transfer rates, wideband channels the highest. Voice-grade

ditions. As one leg was accepted, another was begun.

The regional HP 3000 systems have CPUs of 512K and support two 50-megabyte disks, a low-speed printer, tape drives, and up to 17 CRTs. The centrally located 370 System possesses a CPU size of 1024K, 9 disks, 5 tape drives, and a high-speed printer. CRTs attached to the 370 are used for programming and correcting data.

Domtar's new configuration has already been judged a success. Customer orders, which used to take almost 15 days to process, now go through in under a day. Processing which once took 4 to 8 weeks now takes minutes and returns to the requesting center the same day via telecommunications. The costs for the network's communications lines are two-thirds of those for messengers and mailing.

The distributed system has also improved Domtar's finances. Because customers receive their invoices quickly, they pay their bills sooner to gain the discounts offered. In the system's first month of operation, the Montreal center's cash flow improved by more than $500,000.

The system provides other benefits as well. It automatically flags customers who exceed their credit limit. The returns on this service alone equal almost 50 percent of the cost of the HP 3000 systems. Similar savings are anticipated for inventory control, projections of market and consumer needs, and improvements in collecting money owed to the company. The system lets each center communicate with the others and with the main computer. Centers can now pool their resources, share information on customers or markets, and shift inventory items to satisfy market needs.

Source of data: "DDP Strategy Aids Canadian Firm's Cash Flow," *Computerworld*, March 3, 1980, pp. 54–56.

Consider this . . .

How might a distributed data processing system assist management of a transportation company? Could it help manage their resources, if materials were shipped between major industrial cities in the Sun Belt?

---

channels have the middle range of data transfer rates and handle the bulk of data communications activities.

Point 5 Communications lines are also classified by the manner in which they handle data. In a simplex line, data can travel in only one direction. Data can move in two directions in a half-duplex line, but not at the same time. Full-duplex lines can support the concurrent flow of data in two directions. Multiplexers and concentrators enhance a computer's ability to perform I/O operations.

Point 6 Multiprogramming systems offer the ability to concurrently handle two or more programs residing in main storage. During multiprogramming, the CPU is divided into compartments called partitions. Programs having a high I/O activity, simple computations, and a high online priority are placed in the foreground partition. Programs having complex computations and low I/O activity are positioned in the background partition.

Point 7 Multiprocessing involves the simultaneous execution of two or more programs in an equal number of CPUs. Multiprocessing systems enable two or more computers to interact. When a small computer feeds data to a larger computer, the smaller machine is referred to as the slave computer. The slave computer performs all the slower, preparatory tasks required by the overall system and leaves the other computer system free to interact with a database, or vast number of online files. Multiprocessing may also involve the use of many smaller computers to feed data to one larger computer that handles the access of information from a database. The smaller systems are free to handle all forms of processing, as well as interface with the larger system.

Point 8 Distributed processing systems involve the operation of multiple computer systems distributed throughout an organization. Three distributed data processing structures are the spider, ring, and hierarchical networks. Individual computers support their own processing and interact with a centrally located system that oversees the function of the entire system. Distributive processing systems are employed by vast, widely dispersed organizations to efficiently monitor, process, and control their flow of data and create a database composed of data useful to management. Distributed data entry systems employ small computers as data collection points. These computers interact with a larger computer, which controls access to an online database.

Glossary

Background partition The partition of main storage CPU, during multiprogramming, that contains lower-priority programs requiring a low I/O activity and complex computations.

Concentrator A communications device that permits a terminal to access a specific communication channel.

Conversational mode An interactive mode used in online batch processing or remote job entry, in which individual statements are transmitted to an online computer.

Dedicated line Another term for a leased line.

Dialed service A data communications line that requires the user to dial the computer in a manner similar to using a telephone.

Distributed data entry system A distributed processing system in which small computers are employed as data collection points to transfer data to a larger system controlling access to a database.

Distributed processing A network of computer systems that fully support the data processing needs of one organization, interacting with each other and a vast database generally via larger computers that oversee the entire system.

Foreground partition The partition of the CPU, during multiprogramming, that contains higher-priority programs involving a high I/O activity and simple calculations.

Full-duplex line A communications mode in which data can concurrently travel in two directions within the same line.

Half-duplex line A communications line in which data can move in two directions, but not at the same time.

Hierarchical network A distributed data processing configuration distributing computer systems throughout the various levels of its structure, with users' computers at the lowest level and supervisory systems at higher levels.

Leased line A data communications line that is dedicated to one user and is strung directly between users and supporting online computer systems.

Multiplexer A communications device that combines transmissions from multiple devices into one communications line.

Multiprocessing The simultaneous execution of two or more instructions employing two or more CPUs.

Multiprogramming The concurrent execution of two or more programs residing in partitions of the same CPU.

Narrowband channels The classification of data communications services that offers the lowest rates of data transfer, using telegraph lines.

Online batch processing The batch processing of data transmitted over data communications lines to an online computer.

Online real-time processing   An online computer system in which there is no delay in the processing of data.

Partition   A compartment of the CPU set aside by the systems software during multiprogramming.

Polling   One process by which a controlling computer system contacts the systems that it oversees and requests the input of data.

Private line   Another term for leased line.

Remote batch processing   The online batch processing of data in which the user and the computer interact using a conversational mode.

Ring network   A distributed data processing configuration in which a series of computers are interconnected, sharing the processing load, and do not depend on a centrally located computer system.

Simplex line   A communications line that supports the flow of data in only one direction.

Slave computer   The smaller of two computers in a multiprocessing system, which performs all the preparatory and slower tasks required to permit processing.

Spider network   A distributed data processing configuration in which the main computer system is ringed by a series of smaller systems and all processing activities function through the main system.

Time-sharing   An online system in which users, via terminals, share the resources of the same computer system.

Voice-grade channels   The middle range of data communications services, used to support the bulk of online processing operations.

Wide Area Telephone Service (WATS)   A special type of dialed service used for data communications with online systems.

Wideband channels   The data communications classification offering the highest data transfer rates (i.e., coaxial cables and microwave transmission).

Discussion Questions

1 Discuss multiprogramming and multiprocessing.

2 Examine the concepts related to multiprocessing and distributed processing. Describe the similarities that exist between these two methods of processing.

3 Discuss the differences between online batch processing, online real-time processing, and time-sharing.

4 Discuss the differences among simplex, half-duplex, and full-duplex lines.

5 Examine the list of data processing applications given below and define the method of processing employed. Discuss how data might be processed in each application.

Offtrack betting (OTB)   Motor vehicle registration system
Airline reservation system   Retail sales in a chain of stores
Savings bank   Ticketron sales of theater tickets

6 What might happen in a distributive processing system if the individual systems could not interact during charge sales involving credit cards?

7 Examine data processing periodicals for examples of new and different forms of data communications. Compile articles on satellites, transmission lines or cables, national wire services, and microwave stations.

8 Briefly discuss why a national sales organization (e.g., Sears, Roebuck, and Co.) might use a distributed processing system to handle its sales data and make it available to corporate headquarters.

9 Would a banking institution use a distributed processing system or distributed data entry system to process customer deposits and withdrawals? Briefly describe and illustrate a banking system using either approach. Describe the method by which a bank might use both types of distributed processing systems to serve its customer accounts.

Summary Test

_____ 1 The remote batch entry of data employs a temporary online file to accumulate data prior to its processing.

_____ 2 The online interaction of a user and a computer system, via terminals, when processing individual data statements is referred to as the conversational mode.

_____ 3 A time-sharing system does not employ any of the principles of multiprogramming.

_____ 4 The use of a leased line requires the user to dial the computer system to be used during processing.

_____ 5 Data communications activities are restricted to the use of telephone lines.

_____ 6 Microwave transmissions are classified as voice-grade channels.

_____ 7 Multiprogramming requires the use of multiple CPUs.

_____ 8 Multiprocessing enables the simultaneous execution of two program statements.

_____ 9 The foreground partition normally contains high-priority programs involving highly complex computations and a low level of I/O operations.

_____ 10 Many of the principles of multiprocessing are incorporated into a distributive processing system.

_____ 11 A distributed data entry system utilizes small computers to scan, collect, and transmit input data to an online database.

_____ 12 A distributed data entry system is a good example of an offline batch processing system.

_____ 13 A simplex line lets data flow through it one direction at a time, switching the direction of the flow as I/O operations are performed.

_____ 14 A multiprocessing configuration may use a small computer for preparatory data handling, but it will never use that computer to control data communications activities because that responsibility is always assigned to the large central computer.

_____ 15 A hierarchical distributed data processing system will position local computing systems at its lower levels and assign supervisory systems to the higher levels.

_____ 16 A subdivision of main storage created by operational software is referred to as a:

a	compartment	b	time-shared program
c	divided core	d	partition

_____**17** An anticipated result from multiprogramming operations is:
   a   reduced computer idle time
   b   the handling of more jobs
   c   better scheduling of work
   d   all the above

_____**18** Most data communications involving telegraph lines use:
   a   simplex lines   **b**   wideband channels
   c   narrowband channels   **d**   dialed service

_____**19** A distributed data processing configuration in which all activities must pass through a centrally located computer is called a:
   a   ring network   **b**   spider network
   c   hierarchical network   **d**   data control network

_____**20** A communications device that combines transmissions from several I/O devices into one line is a:
   a   concentrator   **b**   modifier
   c   multiplexer   **d**   full-duplex line

_____**21** A characteristic of a multiprogramming system is:
   a   simultaneous execution of program instructions from two applications
   b   concurrent processing of two or more programs
   c   multiple CPUs
   d   all the above

_____**22** Which of the following communications lines is best suited to interactive processing applications?
   a   narrowband channels   **b**   simplex lines
   c   full-duplex lines   **d**   mixedband channels

_____**23** A remote batch-processing operation in which data is solely input to a central computer would require a:
   a   telegraph line   **b**   simplex line
   c   mixedband channel   **d**   all the above

_____**24** A required characteristic of an online real-time system is:
   a   more than one CPU   **b**   offline batch processing
   c   no delay in processing   **d**   all the above

_____**25** The systematic access of small computers in a distributed data processing system is referred to as:
   a   dialed service   **b**   multiplexing
   c   polling   **d**   conversational mode

Summary Test Answers

1 T	**2** T	**3** F	**4** F	**5** F
6 F	**7** F	**8** T	**9** F	**10** T
11 T	**12** F	**13** F	**14** F	**15** T
16 D	**17** D	**18** C	**19** B	**20** C
21 B	**22** C	**23** B	**24** C	**25** C

Thirteen

Management Information Systems (MIS)

FIGURE 13.1 The focal point of any MIS is the distribution of decision-making information to management. (*Copyright © 1978 Herb Levart/ Photo Researchers, Inc.*)

Purpose of This Chapter

This chapter focuses on how computers prepare data to service managements' informational needs. The chapter first presents concepts about management information systems (MIS) and an overview of a retail MIS organization. It describes the use of MIS data for the various levels of management.

The chapter reviews the four output formats associated with MIS and the MIS structures a management system can assume. Samples of each type of output and MIS structure are illustrated. The chapter also explains how operations research techniques can create and test mathematical models of business activities. Two simulation languages, GPSS and SIMSCRIPT, and management control techniques, PERT and CPM, are introduced.

The purpose and function of a database are examined. A database represents a group of integrated data elements and is vital to the efficient access of data in a large computer system. Because of the required size and complexity, the costs of a database are often prohibitive. Two principal methods of ordering data within a database are described. The management of a database, both administratively and using operational software, is discussed. Characteristics of database management systems (DBMS) software and the role of the database administrator are detailed.

A discussion of information management systems (IMS) closes this chapter. The use of customer information control systems (CICS) software to enable access to databases is presented. The structure of a DC/DB system is examined, as are its computerized data communications activities.

After studying this chapter, you should be able to:

■   Discuss the general concepts of management information systems and the organizational uses of the information they provide
■   Discuss the uses of regularly scheduled, exception, on-demand, and forecasting reports in MIS
■   Describe the four MIS structures that management systems can assume
■   Understand the role that operations research techniques may play in MIS activities
■   Discuss the use of a database and its organization of data
■   Briefly describe the role of the database administrator
■   Discuss the purpose of DBMS and CICS software and IMS and DC/DB systems
■   Understand the following terms:

Centralized MIS structure
Chaining
Critical path method (CPM)
Customer information control
  system (CICS)
Database
Database administrator
Database management systems (DBMS)
Data communications/database
  system (DC/DB)
Data Language/1 (DL/1)
Decentralized MIS structure
Distributed MIS structure
Exception listings

Forecasting reports
General purpose system
  simulation (GPSS)
Hierarchical MIS structure
Information management
  system (IMS)
Inverted structure
On-demand reports
Operations research (OR)
Program evaluation and review
  technique (PERT)
Regularly scheduled listings
Simple structure
SIMSCRIPT

Introduction

Advances in computer technology often parallel advances in business. Distributed data processing systems were developed to help business people collect and organize data within a widely dispersed organization. Distributed systems helped many companies to expand their business, offer customers many new services, and monitor the data produced by such activities. Vital to these distributed operations is the computer with its ability to process data input to a company and give managers the data they need for managing. Managers in many companies turn repeatedly to computer personnel for operational data vital to active and successful management.

Just as no two companies function in exactly the same fashion, most data processing services are also unique, with each organization reflecting its own needs. A term often applied to describe the comprehensive systems that provide management with its operational data is *management information system* or simply *MIS*. An MIS functions to supply managers with the information they need to govern an organization and to make decisions. Though the MIS was originally developed for large businesses, it has applications in all organizations. It is most successful where a diverse collection of data must be managed to provide the required decision-making information.

Current MIS projects accomplish the same objectives as their predecessors, but are markedly more complex. For example, international companies use online real-time processing systems and satellite communications in their international management information systems. These sophisticated systems provide all levels of management in a multinational organization with the most current information.

Management information systems for small organizations are less elaborate than those in larger organizations, but they offer the same decision-making potential. All businesses require accurate and timely information, and management information systems can provide that information.

It is important to recall that an MIS is designed to produce both routine data and highlights on conditions to which management must react. MIS outputs are in directly digestible formats and need no detailed manipulations. Thus, instead of merely noting that an item is out of stock, an MIS report will highlight that fact and generate a purchase order for the item. Instead of scanning a personnel file for people to fill a particular job, the MIS approach would have the computer develop a set of criteria for that job, apply them to all candidates, evaluate their qualifications, and output a list of acceptable candidates ranked by their qualifications. Management information systems are designed to provide data that management can act on.

13.1
MIS Concepts
An Operational Overview

Management information systems are one of the most controversial data processing topics. Almost all data processors agree in principle to the overall concept; however, few people agree on the exact nature of an MIS. A **management information system (MIS)** will be defined here as a computer system, integrating equipment, procedures, and personnel, that develops and provides information used by management for decision making. The key requirement for the proper functioning of an MIS is an effective *combination* of personnel, equipment, and computer system. No single factor is sufficient to carry the entire system. A few examples will clarify this relationship.

Most management information systems are supported by fairly large computer systems. This vast processing capacity is wasted when employees provide faulty or incomplete input data. On the other hand, the most accurate data is useless if the receiving output device is inoperative or if it malfunctions. Users poorly trained on peripheral devices completely negate the effect of an MIS. Though the computer is a vital component of an MIS, many tasks can be performed manually. The computer's speed will therefore have little effect, because it too depends on the workers' skills.

All these examples highlight the integrated nature of a management information system. People, machines, and the computer must be organized to produce the desired results—information that management can use in decision making.

An MIS is useful to all levels of management. Executives can use the information provided to formulate yearly corporate strategies, establish financial goals, and create broad economic policies for future years. Middle management can use MIS-generated information to develop administrative plans, establish operational policies, and initiate sales or manufacturing campaigns to attain specific management goals.

Lower levels of management can benefit from MIS information in their daily operations. Managers and supervisors must evaluate the effectiveness of the MIS information and provide necessary feedback. A management information system cannot operate in a vacuum. The system must be capable of evaluating its performance. It needs low-level managers to analyze its effectiveness.

Management information systems are designed to improve the flow of information in an entire organization and enable managerial personnel to perform their jobs more efficiently. Ideally, an MIS is designed to make the total organization interact more effectively. An MIS can reduce waste, increase corporate profits, improve employee wages and morale, and improve the flow of information throughout the organization.

The informational flow of an MIS-based organization is depicted in Figure 13.2. It shows how all the organizational units in an MIS are operationally related. Data generated in one part of the MIS will affect other units in the system.

Management must formulate the overall plans by which the whole organization operates. These plans are converted into sales estimates, inventory levels, and operating budgets. Data input to the MIS provides starting points and guidelines for the overall system. The units of the system can interact as follows:

Marketing/Sales will conduct surveys to determine if the direction and estimates generated by management are valid. These results will be analyzed and computer prepared for presentation to management. Once reviewed and approved by management, these results will trigger a series of MIS-related actions.

FIGURE 13.2 All the component systems in a management information system interact through the computer. Data generated in one part of the MIS can affect another component. The MIS is designed to analyze input data, alert management to developing trends, and help in decision making.

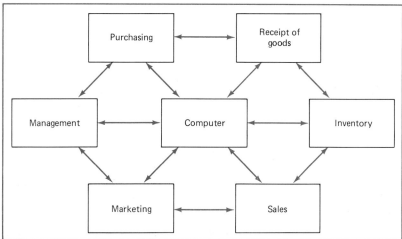

The MIS will generate purchase orders for items required by inventory. The orders will reflect current levels of inventories, sales projections, market conditions or cycles, and the best terms on which to buy goods. This data is accumulated and retained in the system's online storage.

As orders are filled and merchandise received, the MIS will monitor and record all inventory-related transactions. The system will reflect all changes in inventory levels and costs incurred. Vendor payments and data on whether operating budgets have been exceeded will be generated.

Sales performance will produce data that affects inventory and the market sales group. Every item sold will reduce the inventory. Sales patterns will indicate whether the company's marketing strategies have been effective or need revision. The MIS will automatically adjust inventory totals when processing sales data and will prepare sales analyses for the marketing unit and management.

The MIS data will alert management to current operating conditions and can dictate necessary changes. The data may reveal a smoothly running system or units that need immediate intervention. In any event, MIS data serves as a bench mark for these activities.

The computer is an integral part of MIS, preparing almost all the data employed by the system. Most MISs need a large computer to support their processing and online data requirements. This computer may be used to directly record sales data; analyze sales data; prepare market surveys; adjust inventory totals; produce purchase orders, credit memos, and return invoices; prepare vendor payments; and complete other tasks, including the preparation of all managerial reports. The data can be output in a variety of printed and visual formats. Input data can be collected via any number of online data collection devices and terminals. The objective of MIS is the efficient collection and presentation of data for management use. The computer system acts as the vehicle for processing MIS-related data.

Organizational Characteristics

We can see that an MIS causes many levels of management to interact. Information may be communicated from the top to the bottom of an organization. It is important that an MIS provide the right people with accurate data when they need it.

Not all management people use the same information. Thus analysts must tailor reports to their users' needs. To do this, they must distinguish not only each user's informational needs but the needs at each managerial level. As a general rule of thumb, the higher managers are in the organization, the more planning and supervisory their roles. Lower-level managers ordinarily are responsible for day-to-day operations.

Analysts generally distinguish three types of decision making for MIS purposes:

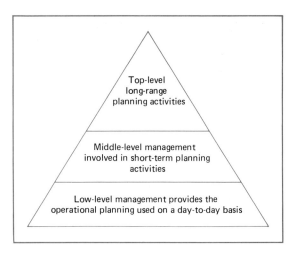

Top-level
long-range
planning activities

Middle-level management
involved in short-term planning
activities

Low-level management provides the
operational planning used on a day-to-day basis

FIGURE 13.3 Planning goes on at all levels of management. The pyramid illustrates how the levels of planning relate. The broadest base of operation is at the lowest level of an organization. Relatively few people formulate plans at the highest level.

1 Long-range planning
2 Short-term planning
3 Operational planning

Their interaction is depicted in Figure 13.3

As its name implies, long-range planning relates to future operations which fall directly into the sphere of top-level management. They are the individuals responsible for governing the organization's activities for many years ahead. These activities provide a general direction in which the organization desires to move, with the immediate year's goals implementing steps in that direction.

But as the old saying implies, even the best laid plans go astray. Plans for future activities are subject to uncertainty, as a variety of factors can widely fluctuate. One merely has to recall the first oil embargo of 1973–1974 to observe the impact that an unforeseen event can have on planning activities. The revision of executive planning strategies must be based on the information supplied by the MIS.

Although unforeseen conditions usually have their greatest effect on day-to-day operations, they also affect long-term plans. In such cases, computer-developed strategies can provide invaluable assistance to corporate planning sessions. It is possible to simulate a number of corporate strategies and computer test them for effectiveness under a wide range of economic conditions. Using the data derived from these analyses, management can devise contingency plans should these factors occur. Though these plans might not provide immediate solutions, they offer a vehicle for dealing with a problem. The computer can develop and test corporate strategies for new products; corporate takeovers; the purchase of equipment; construction of plants or production facilities; financing for expansion; and the elimination of costly product lines and loss-prone divisions. Data drawn from MIS files can be used in these simulations, with computerized printouts detailing the results of the applied strategies. Results from this form of MIS analysis give management a basis for long-range planning.

Once top management makes long-range plans, middle-level management must implement them. Most short-term decisions are tactical and must be implemented within a year. Examples of short-term plans are annual and quarterly financial and production budgets; production schedules; annual forecasts of inventory requirements; staffing projections; and resource distribution in an organization. Information from these plans lets middle management control their organizational groups, administer short-term projects, and make decisions confidently.

Computers can greatly help middle management implement short-term plans. In MIS, computers are an integral part of the budget preparation cycle. They plan the budget, record expenses related to budget items, and monitor each department's performance in light of budgetary limits. The computer can project costs on a quarterly, semi-annual, or annual basis and observe the development of trends. If an MIS report projects that a specific department will exceed its budget, its manager may elect to take corrective action to avert the problem. Similarly, the computer can prepare reports for managers that highlight exception conditions where budget limits have been exceeded (e.g., monthly overtime in one area). The computer can save managers much work and direct their attention where it is needed.

The administration and control of day-to-day operations, which proceed from operational planning, occur at the lowest level of the organization. Supervisors and other first-line people make sure that employees do their jobs and maintain schedules. Their supervision of recordkeeping activities is critical, since it is this data that is input to and used by the MIS. First-line supervisors implement the policies and plans of higher management.

Computerized data at the operational planning level focuses on daily administrative details. Decisions at this level are about preparing invoices, sales receipts, or shipping orders; determining items necessary for daily production or items out of stock; analyzing daily sales and credit figures; and scheduling employee shifts. The computer's ability to rapidly collect current data and prepare reports for the next day is essential to MIS. These daily reports are critical to low-level managers, because they dictate their actions.

The objective of a management information system is to provide the proper manager with the data necessary to perform his or her function. It is easy to observe that the three levels of planning and decision making within the MIS structure require different types of data. The complexity of MIS derives from its concurrent preparation of information for each of these levels. The computer is invaluable in this work, because only it can operate at the speeds necessary to make the MIS useful.

The reports, data, or information prepared from MIS activities must be timely, accurate, and of value to their users. They are the true measures of a management system's efficiency. An MIS responsive to organizational needs should incorporate the following characteristics:

1 All outputs are decision-oriented.
2 All data is user-oriented
3 Adequate growth potential is provided.

MIS outputs must be timely, complete, and directly usable. Above all, they must be accurate. If any of these qualities is lacking, the usability of the output is questionable. Decisions made with partially accurate data are not desirable.

Outputs must also be usable. Hardcopy and softcopy outputs must offer users the information they need to manage their people and make decisions. MIS are not successful if they cannot satisfy their users.

Last, MIS must be designed to accommodate growth. Without room for expansion, a system is operationally limited from the start. Most management systems use a growth factor of 25 percent or the growth estimated in 2 years. This characteristic offers MIS users flexibility in responding to changing needs and new sets of conditions.

13.2 Deriving MIS-Related Data
Reports to Management

The outputs derived from the manipulation of MIS data are critical to the effectiveness of management information systems. Because each level of management requires a different type of operational data, reports must be tailored to their needs. Four report formats are associated with MIS:

1 Regularly scheduled listings
2 Exception listings
3 On-demand reports
4 Forecasting reports

Regularly scheduled listings are prepared at regular intervals and are the most widely distributed type of report. Regularly scheduled outputs provide users with information for the routine performance of their jobs. Examples are payroll listings, inventory reports, personnel listings, mortgage or bank loan summaries, and summaries of credit card accounts. These reports contain a large amount of data to satisfy their many users. Regularly scheduled listings are most frequently used by the lower levels of management, because they ordinarily reflect the daily activities of an organization.

Whereas regularly scheduled listings will usually print data relating to a majority of transactions, **exception listings** are selective in the material printed. These reports highlight conditions which deviate from normal results. Thus instead of printing all customers who have made payments against their bills, the computer outputs customers

---

OLIS: A POWERFUL NEW TOOL FOR LEGISLATORS

The Oregon Legislative Information System (OLIS) is an MIS system developed for the state's legislature. Using the OLIS system, any state senator or representative can access information on any pending bill. It is possible to determine the status of a bill; when and where committee meetings are scheduled; what recommendations, amendments, and parliamentary actions have been made regarding the bill; and when a bill may be acted upon by each house of the Legislature. All this information is kept in a vast file called Measure Status, one of two databases employed by OLIS. The second database, Oregon Revised Status (ORS), contains complete transcripts of all Oregon statutes and bills pending before the legislature. The OLIS system can print any law or bill retained in the ORS database at any time. This type of printing service has saved the Oregon legislature over $300,000 per year in printing costs.

---

who have made no payments. Such reports let supervisors focus their attention on abnormal events and their causes. Exception reports may be produced on a regular basis or when exception conditions necessitate their use. Because they deal with abnormal conditions, exception reports are employed by all levels of management for decision-making purposes.

On-demand reports are generated only as specifically mandated or requested. On-demand reports often take the form of softcopy displays when online terminals are used to interrogate files. They generally have limited usefulness and are selectively distributed. An on-demand report may be used when a credit clerk is keying corrections onto customer charge account files via an online terminal. An on-demand report summarizing all changes made by the clerk can be produced after processing all corrections.

Top and middle management rely heavily on on-demand reports when monitoring a developing trend. This is frequently the case when a doctor is monitoring a critically ill patient and wants periodic reports. The on-demand reporting feature can increase the cost of MIS, but the rapid response to inquiries justifies the cost. It lets management get specific items of data for making decisions on a timely basis.

Outputs that detail projections about the future are defined as **forecasting reports.** These reports, generally used for planning, play an important part in the decision-making process. Top and middle management use forecasting reports as analytic tools. For example, they can use these reports to determine whether the organization will meet projected financial goals.

Forecasting reports can also help in the plotting of alternative strategies. Different sets of data can be input to the computer, and management can analyze the projected results. Their analysis can indicate which strategy will be most effective under what circumstances. Forecasting reports are helpful in developing marketing strategies for different product lines in various regions.

Each of the formats we have described can be used effectively within an MIS to help management at all levels. Of course, they cannot guarantee the success of decisions made employing such data. Decisions grow from a synthesis of computer-generated data, experience, and intuition. Management would be just as foolish to ignore computer-prepared data as to base their decisions solely on them.

Management must monitor the decisions that evolve from an MIS. An MIS can develop manufacturing schedules, plan manpower requirements, automatically reorder inventory items, or project levels of financing. But managers must check each of these actions before they are implemented. This form of managerial check ensures that computer-generated decisions, based upon quantitative data, do not ignore other contributing factors. Actions dictated by MIS-related decisions should be based on sound logic and knowledge of conditions at hand.

MIS Structures

The structure of management information systems closely resembles that of distributed data processing systems. As both systems are designed to effectively handle data at many levels, the similarity is not surprising. Four MIS designs are the centralized, hierarchical, distributed, and decentralized structures.

The **centralized MIS structure** positions the computer at the focal point of all data processing services, as Figure 13.4a illustrates. In a centralized approach, online communications pass through a central computer system which also controls access to the system's files. The advantages of a centralized approach are simplicity, low cost, elimination of duplicate computer hardware, and efficient use of data processing resources. All informational needs are handled by a central computer. This structure is most efficient, but often slow in responding to the needs of a multilevel organization.

A **hierarchical MIS structure** (Figure 13.4b) distributes its resources through an organization according to particular needs at various levels of management. Each managerial level receives the computing power its informational needs require. Requests for data are handled within each unit of the structure, and a minimum of information is transferred between units. Each leg of the hierarchy essentially operates independently, although under the control of a main system.

In a hierarchical design, the type of computing depends on managerial level. The lowest level of support corresponds to the lowest levels of the hierarchy. As one climbs through management levels on an organizational leg, computer support increases. Data files are usually distributed only within organizational levels, and each maintains its own file data. Because interaction between legs is minimal, it is essen-

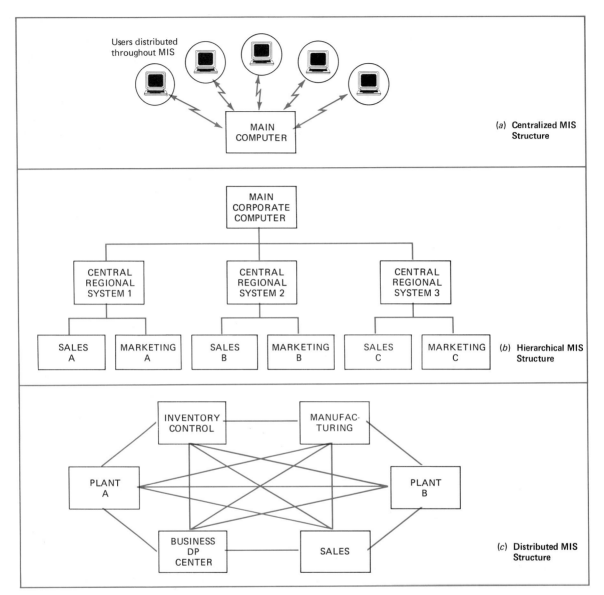

Users distributed
throughout MIS

MAIN
COMPUTER

(a) **Centralized MIS Structure**

MAIN
CORPORATE
COMPUTER

CENTRAL
REGIONAL
SYSTEM 1

CENTRAL
REGIONAL
SYSTEM 2

CENTRAL
REGIONAL
SYSTEM 3

SALES
A

MARKETING
A

SALES
B

MARKETING
B

SALES
C

MARKETING
C

(b) **Hierarchical MIS Structure**

INVENTORY
CONTROL

MANUFAC-
TURING

PLANT
A

PLANT
B

BUSINESS
DP
CENTER

SALES

(c) **Distributed MIS Structure**

FIGURE 13.4   Three forms of MIS structures.

tial that the proper data be maintained. Managers within a leg of an MIS design have access to that leg's data files.

The **distributed MIS structure** is also a multiprocessing system in which separate computers support independent centers (see Figure 13.4c). This ringlike distributed system places the computing power where it is needed and is well suited to widely dispersed organizations. Computers supporting regional centers may interact, perhaps sharing a workload or a common set of files. This type of MIS structure is expensive because an organization needs multiple systems with separate staffs and communications lines. On the other hand, it provides localized computing support for on-site managerial decision-making activities.

The **decentralized MIS structure** is really a divisional breakdown of computing resources. Each division handles its own DP needs and does not generally interact with any other division. This structure is very responsive to users' needs within each division, as it is solely responsible to that management. It is well suited to a decentralized management scheme in which organizational autonomy is important. For example, research divisions of large corporations may adopt the decentralized MIS structure to provide data security for their work. The decentralized structure prevents outsiders from having access to the MIS computer, thus compromising their security.

The decentralized structure is somewhat expensive because it requires duplicate facilities and files. However, security and other informational needs may require the implementation of this type of management system.

Operations Research

Management information systems provide a way to plan and to monitor data, as it is generated and flows through the organization. The ability to generate forecasts of operational conditions is quite advantageous. Managers may then plan alternative strategies to counter adverse situations well in advance of their occurrence.

Computer specialists working within the MIS structure can develop mathematical models that simulate forecast economic conditions and provide an experimental basis for testing alternative management strategies. Results of tests run on these models can be presented to top and middle management, so that they can incorporate them into their long- and short-term plans.

Operations research (OR) is the management science that provides many of the techniques for integrating the mathematical, computer, and business principles required to develop and test these theoretical models. Computer models that simulate an organizational activity are usually the result of many months' work by a team of analysts. Because procedures usually are unique to an organization, it is not normally possible to purchase canned software. As a result, analysts must collect data, develop the desired model, and fine-tune its performance.

Once analysts develop the basic relationships, it is possible to computerize the model rather than developing test results on a manual basis. Two problem-oriented languages used to construct simulated business models are **SIMSCRIPT** and **GPSS (General Purpose Systems Simulation).** With these languages, variables in the mathematical model may be assigned values and tested using time frames ranging from minutes to years. Results can be projected over time and trends uncovered.

OR techniques are especially helpful because they synthesize many variables into one cohesive model. They allow specialists to create a mathematical model of an entire organization and observe the effect of changes in one or several areas. Thus, we can create corporate divisions, adjust their budgets, build in inflation factors, generate sales data tied to federal or cyclic economic factors (e.g., GNP or the stock market), include personnel salary data, and test the model within any desired time frame. Consider how effectively management could use such a model in developing budgets for individual departments, projecting the need for corporate financing, the effects of increasing sales, or determining the effects of an acquisition or a recession.

OR techniques are principally used in business-related problems, but they have also been effectively applied to the design of office space, inventory distribution problems, the analysis of traffic patterns, and urban planning. Computerized linear programming techniques have been used in inventory distribution problems where companies want to distribute their resources to maximize production and minimize expenditures of time and effort. This problem is often referred to as the classic transportation problem. As the linear programming involved is easily converted to a computerized format, the analysis of this type of transportation problem has been simplified greatly.

Two other common OR planning tools are **PERT (program evaluation and review techniques)** and **CPM (critical path method).** Both techniques were developed by the U.S. Navy to control a missile program which involved over 2000 contractors. Each uses the concept of a network to detail a project's activities. Figure 13.5 illustrates a simplified PERT network.

In this network, each major step is identified and an estimate of

FIGURE 13.5 A PERT diagram indicating the network of activities necessary to plan a project. PERT and CPM are planning and control techniques used by analysts and OR specialists.

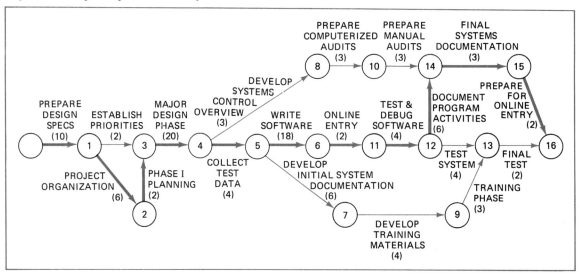

the time needed for its completion is assigned. Using these time estimates, the path of critical tasks is detailed and the time computed. In Figure 13.5, the critical path is highlighted by a solid line. We can see that a total of 77 days is necessary to complete the critical tasks of the project. Because PERT and CPM are rather complex, readers interested in learning more about them should consult technical manuals.

Not all organizations use operations research methodology in their planning activities. Large corporations which can afford the extra staff and hardware often use OR. These studies take time to prepare, and management must patiently wait through the development stage. The advantages of having valid forecasting information, alternative strategies, and tighter organization control can more than compensate for the extra costs. Small organizations interested in OR techniques may wish to contact independent software houses that specialize in the development of that type of software.

13.3
Databases
Purpose and Use

Two factors have contributed to the development of the database concept: first, the unprecedented growth in the amount of data handled by the computer in business-related applications; and second, the unwillingness of organizations to plan ahead and check the proliferation of files in their computer systems.

Table 13.1 shows increases in transactions in selected industries. These figures reflect the tremendous growth of the informational needs of business. Computers have aided this growth, because data processing systems can store millions of characters of data and make it available in seconds. Continuous pressure is on the computer field to develop technologies to meet growing information needs.

Many growing businesses and organizations opted to use the computer to support their processing of information. Often data processing organizations developed a day-to-day operational philosophy, with no plans for future growth. Whenever new informational requirements arose, the immediate solution was to develop a new file. This proliferation of files to support new informational needs tied many computer systems into economic and processing knots. Files developed with no cohesive or integrated philosophy clogged the effective processing of data. Many files were duplicates of one another, wasting valuable storage resources, programming efforts, and DP dollars.

It was evident that a cohesive, integrated approach to the construction of files supporting a large volume of data was required. It was out of this need that the concept of a database was developed.

A **database** is a collection of data elements grouped together as one entity and structured to fit the informational needs of an organization. Although the data is connected by a series of tables and indexes to simplify access to it, items of data are independently retrievable. The database is not structured to support solely one type of applica-

Table 13.1 Annual Transactions in Selected Industries

Type of Transaction	1940	1955	1970	1980
Social security payments	222,000	8 million	26 million	57 million
Airline passengers	3 million	42 million	171 million	310 million
Motor vehicle registrations	32.5 million	62.7 million	108.4 million	226 million
New York Stock Exchange transactions	283 million	821 million	3.2 billion	9.1 billion

tion, but is designed to service transactions throughout an organization. Because of the integrated structure of a database, one transaction may trigger updates in other files. This integration means that data can be entered just once, simplifying the stream of input data and improving the overall system's data handling capabilities. Data input to the database is available to the entire organization.

A database avoids the duplication of files, the reprocessing of data items, and the repeated handling of data. It is designed to improve the overall efficiency of a computer system that handles sizable amounts of data. The savings attributed to the use of a database result from the computer sharing of records, reduced processing times, reductions in the use of software and hardware, more efficient use of data processing personnel, and an overall improvement in the flow of data.

The disadvantages of a database are its size, its cost, and the time required to implement such a system. A database requires the use of a large-scale computer system. A large full-time staff is also required to design, program, and support the implementation of a database. The time involved for a project of this scope is a minimum of one to two years. The overall price of a vast database project starts at $1 million and goes upward. This cost is prohibitive for many organizations. Database-oriented computer systems are not luxuries, however, and are undertaken when proven economically justifiable.

Data Organization Within a database, data must be arranged for easy retrieval and use. Generally, direct access storage devices, such as magnetic disk and disk storage facilities, provide these storage capabilities. Magnetic tape does not offer comparable direct access storage and is primarily used for backup storage. Direct access devices are necessary because of the intricate nature of data handling operations in a database. Inquiries may require the computer to rapidly access a series of records in order to satisfy a user's informational needs. Though database designers try to anticipate the relationships among data elements, databases often must be restructured.

Two methods of ordering data within a database are the **simple structure** and the **inverted structure.** Within the simple structure, all records are of equal importance and are sequentially ordered by a common logical relationship. Thus, in effect, we have a linear sequence of records as might appear in a sequential file. Data elements involving employees, customer orders, inventory control data, and even parking tickets may be maintained in this way.

Data elements in a simple structure can also be subdivided into groups. We might have a major record in the logical sequence of the file and a series of subrecords related to that major record. A good example of this structure is a monthly customer accounts receivable file in which each customer record is the major element in the overall customer file, and all new monthly transactions follow the record. Each new transaction is a complete record in itself, but is accessed via the customer's records.

Though a simple structure is sound, it sometimes slows the retrieval of data at peak periods. The slowness results from having to access many subrecords through their major records. Many more comparisons are required, lengthening the time needed to find a data item. The inverted structure was introduced to overcome this problem.

The inverted structure does not focus its activity on one major record, but employs lists of key data items within records to access data. Thus, data items in a file are cross-referenced to other items by means of an index. This linkage of one item to another is sometimes called **chaining.** The advantage of the inverted structure is its ability to quickly handle inquiries into a database. Its disadvantage is the complexity of the linking structure that permits such rapid retrieval.

An example will help illustrate how the simple and inverted structures work. Examine the data in Tables 13.2 and 13.3. Table 13.2 contains data as it might be ordered in a simple structure, and Table 13.3 shows the same data in an inverted structure.

Although Tables 13.2 and 13.3 may look dissimilar, they present the same data. The visible difference is in access to the items of data. In Table 13.2, access is keyed to ascending location number only. Data is not ordered by any other characteristic. This is not the case with

Table 13.2 Data Defined in a Simple Structure

Location	Last Name	Job Title	Department	Salary Code
019470	Karter	Engineer	Tech/Support	Bi-Weekly
019484	Reagun	Sales Mgr.	Sales	Weekly
019502	Anders	Engineer	Tech/Support	Bi-Weekly
019542	Randisi	VP-Adm.	Administration	Monthly
019576	Bushey	Engineer	Tech/Support	Bi-Weekly
019600	Cronin	Sales Mgr.	Sales	Weekly

Table 13.3 Data Defined in an Inverted Structure

Last Name		Job Title		Department		Salary Code	
Item	Location	Item	Location	Item	Location	Item	Location
Karter	019470	Engineer	019470	Admin.	019542	Weekly	019484
Reagun	019484		019502	Sales	019484		019600
Anders	019502		019576		019600	Bi-Weekly	019470
Randisi	019542	Sales Mgr.	019484	Tech/Support	019470		019502
Bushey	019576		019600		019502		019576
Cronin	019600	VP-ADM	019542		019576	Monthly	019542

Table 13.3. Here, access to data is possible via the four categories of last name, job title, department, and salary code. Data items accessed in one category provide a location number for access to all related items.

This point is illustrated by examining the data items circled in Table 13.3. Note that each relates to REAGUN and is identified by the location 019484. Thus, if an inquiry is made regarding sales managers, the computer will access the locations 019484 and 019600, and access the data recorded at those locations.

Simple and inverted data structures are just two of the file structures associated with databases. Other more complex designs exist, many assuming hierarchical or network structures depending on the needs of their computer hardware and organizational needs.

Managing a Database

Management of a database may be divided into administrative and operational functions. This division acknowledges the importance of the people and equipment that contribute to the successful use of a database.

Database Administrator

The programmers, analysts, and technicians who maintain and monitor database operations are usually coordinated by a **database administrator.** This administrator needs both technical and managerial skills. The size of the database administrator's staff will depend on the scope of the organization's data processing operation.

Key functions of the database administrator are:

1 Interaction with users and all levels of management
2 Supervision of all database maintenance
3 Design and coordination of data security measures to restrict unauthorized access
4 Design of database files and supervision of their implementation
5 Preparation and maintenance of a database dictionary and/or user's manual which offers standardized procedures for access to the database

6 Responsibility and control over all database documentation
7 Oversight of all database activities to ensure prompt system response, satisfactory user support, and data security

The database administrator's position requires an individual with both technical and managerial savvy, as he or she must deal with many levels of management. That person also needs political sensitivity, since the database administrator effectively controls access to, and what data is maintained on, the database. The database administrator may be part of the data processing department, report to a vice president or higher, or act as a consultant.

Database Management System (DBMS)

Operational control over a database is exercised through software called a **database management system (DBMS).** DBMS is a set of programs which facilitate the creation and arrangement of data to minimize duplication, the modification of data within the database, and the interrogation of files and provide ready access to data. The DBMS software acts as the vehicle for accessing information from the database and simplifies the task of the computer's operating system.

Whereas DBMS software once had to be specially written for each system, it is now available from manufacturers and private software specialists. DBMS programs are used in large and small computer systems to increase the speed with which data items are accessed in a large array of files. In small systems, DBMS software helps organize data elements and simplify access to them. These characteristics are extremely important to users where the predominance of their work relates to the actual interrogation of, and interaction with, data files.

DBMS software interacts with programs undergoing execution, simplifying their access to the data elements of the database. When the program requests specific items of data, the DBMS software assumes the responsibility of accessing that data. Reference to the data is independent of the file structure in which it is contained. The DBMS software compensates for that fact and eliminates the need to detail such requirements. This feature of DBMS software, the physical independence of applications software from the database, greatly simplifies the programmer's work and minimizes the modifications written into existing programs when changes in the database are accomplished.

DBMS software reflects user needs and operational aspects of the hardware involved. Most DBMS software exhibits the following characteristics:

1 The capability to store the vast amount of data necessary to satisfy user's needs. This data is stored on direct access devices for online support.
2 The operational capability of concurrently interrogating data files, retrieving and modifying data, and recording all changes.

3 The development of data elements which integrate data into operational units that minimize the duplication of data and maximize access to all data within the database. If data items are interrelated according to conventional associations, access to data items is simplified and more readily understood by users.

4 Sufficient controls must be incorporated into the overall system to limit access to the database files and assure the confidentiality of all data maintained within those files. Users are restricted to files they are authorized to use.

5 Provides sufficient growth potential for the addition of data and programs to the system.

The design, implementation, and maintenance of a database requires a highly trained staff. Projects of this type generally require 6 to 24 months to implement and need constant supervision. DBMS software must be written to facilitate access to information in the database.

13.4 Information Management System (IMS)

Though its initials are similar to MIS, an **information management system (IMS)** is designed for more specific objectives. Whereas MIS has a decision-making orientation, IMS focuses its attention on the management of information generated within the computer system. IMSs are concerned with the distribution of data through a system, data communications activities, access to a database, and user information needs. A major function of an IMS is to provide large quantities of information to organizational personnel for their use in answering questions and in problem-solving activities.

An IMS is perfectly suited for an organization that must provide large quantities of information to the public, such as a college, rental agency, public utility, or statewide motor vehicle bureau. These organizations are continually dispensing information to the public upon demand, with much of it accessed from databases. The focal point of these IMS activities is the online distribution of this information to users.

IMS support may form part of a larger MIS. Consider the previously discussed retail MIS. IMS support could easily be incorporated into that MIS structure, for the sole purpose of handling customer informational requests. Changes resulting from these inquiries could be handled by IMS and incorporated into the analysis of data when management-oriented strategies are developed. The IMS would handle access to the database and simplify the distribution of information. Other operational aspects of the retail MIS would also have access to the database.

STATE CONTROLS WAGERING VIA COMPUTER

The computerized management of financial data can take many forms. An unusual online database to manage sales-related data was initiated on September 1, 1980 when New York State computerized its lottery. Terminals at each lottery outlet were connected to the statewide computer and began recording ticket purchases. The wagers are immediately telecommunicated to the state lottery database in Albany.

The purpose of these computerized activities was not to speed winning payoffs, but to monitor data generated by statewide wagering. The online retrieval of lottery data let state officials oversee all betting revenue. They could uncover unusual betting trends or possibly fraudulent betting schemes.

The lottery database lets state officials assess and validate all ticket sales, distribute payoffs to winners, and improve financial accountability. They can rapidly account for lottery revenues and determine the lottery's cash flow statewide and at each sales outlet. The system reduces tampering with ticket sales and the time necessary for receiving and validating.

State officials are pleased with the performance of the lottery database system and plan to expand it. They plan to continue training all sales agents who may interact with the system. Data management and software analysis go on continually.

An integral part of an IMS is the DBMS software used for accessing information from the corporate database. Whether user-written or manufacturer-supplied, DBMS software simplifies access to the database files and enhances IMS performance.

At this point, it may prove wise to again restate differences between MIS and IMS objectives. An MIS is a broad-based system which coordinates personnel, equipment, procedures, and a computer to generate decision-making data for all levels of management. An IMS is primarily concerned with the distribution of data. It is quite conceivable that an IMS will be incorporated into an MIS to distribute information, should the MIS warrant its use. It is also possible to have an MIS that does not incorporate an IMS, and vice versa. An organization might require only the computerized distribution of information to its users, without other managerial constraints. Similarly, another organization could require MIS support for the implementation of corporate strategies and have limited need for IMS services. In both organizations, however, DBMS software might be used to facilitate access to the online database. How might a brokerage house incorporate one or all three of these techniques in its computer services?

Customer Information Control System (CICS)

An example of IMS-related software is a set of programs referred to as **customer information control system (CICS).** CICS was originally developed for the public utility Consolidated Edison to support the interrogation of customer account files. Con Ed found it economically unjustifiable to employ conventional approaches to process the thousands of daily inquiries it receives regarding customer accounts. CICS supports online terminal access to a database containing millions of customer accounts.

The CICS software was designed to do two jobs:

1 Provide access to customer information within the database
2 Oversee the data communications generated by requests for customer information

Con Ed had a problem because customer inquiries generated such a high level of I/O activity that existing software could not satisfactorily perform both of the tasks listed above. The system was overloaded. But CICS solved Con Ed's problem. Residing in one partition of the CPU, the CICS software could monitor which terminals were requesting access to the database, schedule their use of available data communications resources, and facilitate their access to the database. CICS supported these activities for both the input and output of customer data.

The actual handling of data within the database and other processing activities were supported by programs written in other programming languages (e.g., COBOL). Thus, in effect, CICS turned over the request for data to the applications software, which accessed and manipulated the customer information drawn from the database. The resulting data was recaptured by CICS for transmission to the requesting user's terminal.

In addition to supporting inquiries into customer files, CICS also lets authorized users modify customer records and correct data. CICS provides access to the database, but additional software must be written to accomplish these modifications. Some people consider this need for additional software a drawback to CICS.

Data Communications / Database Systems (DC / DB)

CICS represented the successful coordination of data communications and database interrogation. But in some quite complex systems, CICS and its operational software proved inadequate. It was incapable of handling the extremely high volume of inquiries, the volume of processing generated by these requests, and the variety of data communications services supported by these larger systems. The complexity of processing exceeded the limits of the CICS software, especially in the area of data communications. In many of these larger configurations, the system devoted most of its resources to supervisory data communications activities, inhibiting the performance of processing activities.

To overcome these conditions, the concept of a **data communi-**

cations/database system (DC/DB) was introduced. The DC/DB configuration is a multiprocessing configuration in which two computers, each with a different operational objective, work together. The first system handles all *DC* or data communications activities for the total system. It monitors all channels, multiplexers, and related hardware, fielding transmissions from online devices through the total system. This DC system records how requests entered the system, the device the message originated from, the nature of the request, and where in the database that request is handled. This data is retained for the input and output of data for every inquiry.

The second computer system supervises access to the database and performs the necessary processing. This DB system accepts the inquiry data, handles it, and returns it to the DC system for transmission to the user. This second system manipulates data within the database.

This combined DC/DB configuration has its advantages. The division of data communications and database activities improves processing speed and efficiency. Delays from improperly handled data communications are minimized.

DC/DB also has improved on CICS in the database operational area. A specialized language, **Data Language/1 (DL/1),** was developed by IBM to facilitate manipulation of and access to database information. It eliminated the need to use different languages when working within the data base and helped standardize the software written for these purposes. Database maintenance was thus simplified.

The most impressive result of the DC/DB configuration was the dramatic increase in processing speed and capacity. The separate systems used to handle data communications and database processing let each computer focus its full resources on these activities.

DC/DB systems are designed to support large, complex international data processing operations. Their cost is prohibitive except for those organizations that require that type of system. A large, well-educated, and continually trained staff is normally on hand to support the DC/DB system.

Summary

The following major points have been discussed in Chapter 13:

Point 1   Management information systems (MIS) are designed to provide management with decision-making data. MIS integrate equipment, procedures, and personnel to develop and provide the information used in the decision-making process. MIS are designed to improve the flow of information throughout an organization and help managers perform their jobs.

Point 2   Managers need information for long-range, short-term, and operational planning. The first two categories support planning activities undertaken by top and middle management, respectively. Long-range plans project company needs into the future and focus on the upcoming year's corporate objectives. Short-term planning is used by middle managers to evaluate monthly, quarterly, and semiannual performance. Day-to-day needs are handled with operational planning

(*continued on page 556*)

A DC/DB MIS Supports County DP Operations

To support the variety of services supplied to its almost 1.5 million residents, the General Services division of Nassau County, Long Island, New York, uses a large centralized computer system and vast database. This system serves over 40 county agencies and is a distinct change from the practice of each agency having its own system. The new configuration represents a major saving in staff and equipment, and a reduction in duplicated services, funded by only .4 percent of the total county budget.

Centralized facilities mean that smaller agencies get services they normally would not have. Larger agencies also benefit from the more sophisticated system. The four major users of the county's DP services are its medical center, social services department, law enforcement, and general administration. Figure 13.6 shows the agencies in the Nassau system.

The key to the centralized DC/DB configuration is its multiprocessing capacity, supported by two IBM/370 158s to handle processing and an IBM 3033 Processor for data communications. This DC/DB setup was incorporated when online activity by all county agencies increased and the county wanted to speed up its service.

To improve its services and stay within budget, the county combined in-house written programs and software packages. A sample of the IBM software products used include CICS software for data communications; DL/1 for file handling and interrogations; TSO software for interactive, time-shared services; and operating control software JES3 and OS/MVS (for a multiple virtual storage capability). An examination of selected agencies will help us to understand the system's potential.

The social services agency handles over 30,000 cases, representing almost 60,000 people. Online access to all cases and both hardcopy and softcopy outputs are available. Data is derived from a database. Previously, inquiries took from 5 minutes to 5 hours to handle. Better control over caseloads and better data have improved services and reduced active cases by 30 percent. The system's security protects the privacy of all social service recipients. Conversely, to protect against fraud, the system can interact with New York State motor vehicle, unemployment, and social service files.

The Nassau County Medical Center also receives DP services. It provides emergency and routine clinical medical help to over 30,000 patients a year. When a patient enters the NCMC, computer tracking of that patient's records begins. A database of over 40,000 patient records is maintained and updated interactively. All services provided to the patient are recorded via online terminals and posted against that patient's bill. All medical insurance claims are computer prepared to include Medicare and Medicaid statements. Considerable savings have been achieved by eliminating unnecessary secretarial work and improving the accuracy of medical records.

The county police use a database composed of warrants, hazardous addresses, arrest and detention records, and court-related data. The law enforcement agencies also have online access to all state and federal police and motor vehicle files. The computer system also actively supports over 70 volunteer fire departments. Nassau's court system's 4000 cases are monitored and scheduled by computer. The court database maintains case data, names, calendar dates, and other data. The system is designed to track cases through all phases of law enforcement.

The General Services Agency is the monitoring division of Nassau County's government. It prepares all fiscal reports, monitors all payments made by county agencies, develops budgets, assesses property taxes, oversees purchasing, and controls county inventories, vendor files, and tax records. The computer analyzes budgets, maintains timely data on all county expenditures,

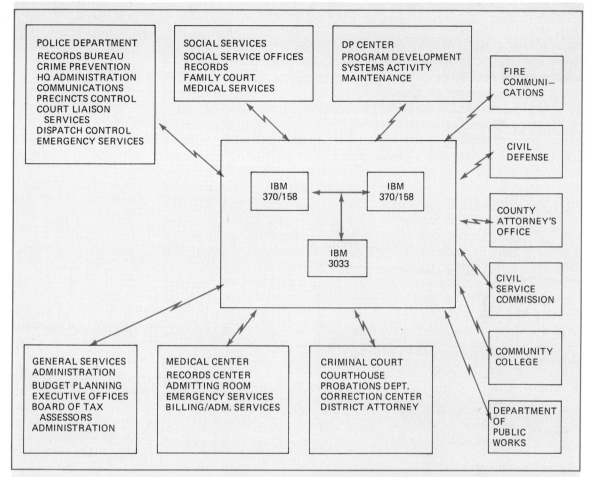

FIGURE 13.6 The many activities supported by the Nassau County computer center require a vast computer system. The DC/DB system depicted offers an MIS orientation and efficient data communication. The online access capabilities of this dynamic system offer each department timely DP support.

and provides county officials with the data they need to make decisions. The General Services Agency benefits greatly from the centralized MIS-oriented system.

The range of services offered by the vast computerized system requires that it incorporate data communications, database, and MIS technologies. This multiprocessing, database-oriented, DC/DB system is economically justifiable. F. X. Murphy, Director of DP services, emphasizes, "The central computer concept makes it possible to assess each agency's requests as they relate to the overall county government. Thus, priorities can be set, exchange of information between related agencies can be facilitated, and the duplication of effort minimized."

Consider this . . .

Why would a large municipal organization desire a large centralized DC/DB system? Does this system reflect the needs of government and provide real service to its constituents?

Pan American Airways Operations/Maintenance Data Base

As an international airline, Pan American flies to virtually every corner of the world. It needs maintenance and service facilities throughout the world. The costs of supporting these operational facilities are quite high, up to $300 million a year. This worldwide network of maintenance facilities must service a fleet of well over 100 aircraft and a total inventory costing in excess of $1 billion. Because of the size, scope, and expense of such a vast system, the information needed to control it must be timely and accurate. One mistake might send millions of dollars worth of equipment thousands of miles away from its proper destination.

To coordinate maintenance, Pan Am must monitor the flights of all aircraft, ship spare parts, and provide equipment to all service centers. When an aircraft lands, the necessary service equipment has to be available.

The control of resources and the data generated to support maintenance services is the responsibility of the Operations/Maintenance Data Base System. This system is the result of a 3-year project supported by 40 professionals. The multiple-file database is designed to collect, store, and provide data related to all maintenance activities. Data is collected via online CRTs and terminals. The point of this database is to provide parts, equipment, and service crews to service any aircraft in the Pan Am fleet. Each aircraft must be properly serviced before it is certified and released for departure.

The key to the files in the database is related to the numbers on all equipment and parts. The database identifies all activities using part numbers. Transactions or interrogations of files are accomplished by individual part numbers. The database uses the part number as its key to the largest file of the system, the inventory file, which maintains records on all equipment or parts necessary to service any aircraft. It is estimated that for every five jets flying, the equivalent parts of two planes are held in readiness on the ground.

Information produced from the database can be used for the construction of budgets, fixed-asset assessments for tax purposes, and projections for future budget and maintenance expenditures. The database maintains files for all the above data.

The database also maintains an extensive inventory control file. This file accounts for all parts and equipment throughout the maintenance system. It defines the status of each part and its location. Obviously, a part cannot be assigned into service if it is not available at the maintenance center, is not in working order, or does not exist. A file of completed and serviceable parts is maintained, as well as a work-in-progress file. The work-in-progress file details all parts and equipment currently undergoing repair and servicing. These inventory control files provide up-to-data information on the location and use of all equipment and components.

One benefit of the database is the timely and accurate reporting of data to all maintenance centers. The same data is available and distributed to everyone. Before the database system, data ranged from 1 day to 3 months old, contributing to the operational confusion.

The database maintains files on any work assigned to outside service centers. Many parts are repaired by the vendors from whom they were purchased. Data is maintained on parts shipped to vendors and parts outstanding from inventory. Data relating to the guarantees and warranties of individual vendors is also stored in the database.

The operations database also records the hours that parts are actually used. Because of strict federal regulations, logs related to the number of hours flown by specific aircraft and hours of use for critical aircraft parts are maintained. These logs are maintained, by part numbers and plane number, in the database. At regular intervals, selected aircraft and parts must be serviced. The database scans the flight time files, indicates which aircraft or parts require service, and schedules the location and type of service necessary. The database ensures that the appropriate personnel and equipment are on hand for the service.

The flight-hour logs are also used to develop reliability files. These files maintain and develop records on how long particular components and parts can be used before they require service or become inoperative. These statistics are used to develop inventory levels for specific parts and determine the number of parts that must be kept on hand for actual use. Because it is possible to project the length of time that parts are used before needing service and replacement, the database system can indicate when replacement parts and equipment must be purchased. Data on any purchase order, part, or vendor is recorded in the file.

Information in the database also establishes work standards. A task management file, which establishes the time required to perform specific service tasks, is used for planning purposes. The time needed to repair or service an aircraft or part is estimated using the file. These estimates are employed to predict the work force required to service aircraft or meet production schedules. This time will eventually be used in determining the development cost and accounting ratios for personnel, service, and budget purposes. Data from this task file is applied to the work-in-progress file.

The overall effect of the operations database is improved control over all inventory items, tighter scheduling of services, reduced levels of nonessential inventory and equipment, and more accurate and timely data. The savings anticipated from the database are estimated at 30 percent of the annual maintenance budget. Initial savings resulting from the system are in the millions of dollars, with projected savings on target. Specific savings will accrue from reduced parts inventories, improved work and production schedules, better parts repair, efficient scheduling and use of personnel, and tighter control over the use of equipment and aircraft. It is estimated that these improvements will permit Pan Am to bid on contract service work for other airlines, which will provide additional revenues for the company. This service work is possible without overtaxing the company's personnel and equipment resources.

The Pan Am database has been designed with an eye toward the future. Eventually it will support sophisticated cost accounting systems, budget preparation by service centers, flight scheduling, and production scheduling projections. The planning, scheduling, and projection of all maintenance activities will be coordinated through the database. Considering the flight activities of the future, Pan Am's choice of a database to support its operations/maintenance activities appears wise. Figure 13.7 depicts the component files of this database.

An important point to be gained from this case is the integrated structure of the Maintenance MIS. Because of the size and interrelated nature of this maintenance data, it was imperative that these facts interfaced. The MIS structure facilitated the ready management of the mountain of data generated by this system.

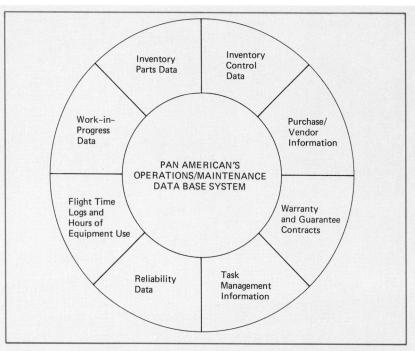

FIGURE 13.7 The files composing the Pan American Operations/Maintenance Data Base. Data is made available through the interacting database. Thus one entry is sufficient to input data to a group of related items. The savings created by this system run into the millions of dollars.

data. Control activities are immediate, implemented on a daily basis. An MIS should be user-oriented, provide data for decision-making activities, and possess adequate growth potential.

Point 3 Four MIS report formats are regularly scheduled listings, exception listings, on-demand reports, and forecasting reports. Regularly scheduled listings, prepared at set intervals, are the most widely used type of report. Exception listings highlight abnormal conditions for managerial review. On-demand reports are made available when specifically requested by a user. Forecasting reports are planning vehicles that project future conditions. Information derived from forecasting reports will often play a vital role in management's decision-making process.

Point 4 Four possible MIS configurations are the centralized, hierarchical, distributed, and decentralized MIS structures. The centralized

structure places a computer at the focal point of its activities, whereas the decentralized MIS structure enables each corporate division to use its own system independently. A hierarchical structure has computer support at each level of management and feeds data up to the next level. The distributed MIS structure employs a ringlike configuration of interacting computers to distribute managerial information and share the operational workload.

Point 5 Operations research (OR) represents specialized techniques incorporated into MIS structure to solve complex problems or derive special types of data. OR techniques are frequently used to develop computerized simulations of business activities. Two languages used in these simulated designs are GPSS and SIMSCRIPT. Two supervisory planning techniques, PERT and CPM, are used to control large projects.

Point 6   A database stores large amounts of data in interrelated files or data elements. Database structures avoid the duplication and waste associated with multiple files. Data elements and files are more efficiently employed on a database because it is designed to simplify access to this information. Two methods of organizing data within a database are the simple structure and the inverted structure. In a simple structure, all records are of equal importance and are ordered by a logical relationship. The inverted structure uses keys to organize and permit the cross-reference of data.

Point 7   Database management requires people and operational software. Database administrators usually oversee database operations and control planning, procedures, and access to the database. Database administrators need both managerial and technical expertise. Database management systems (DBMS) are operational software for managing a database's resources.

DBMS software is available for both large and small systems and may be written from scratch or purchased from manufacturers. DBMS software must be capable of storing vast amounts of data, interrogating files, integrating data elements, controlling access to sensitive data, and permitting growth.

Point 8   Information management systems (IMS) manage vast amounts of data within a computer system. DBMS software may be incorporated into a system to enhance IMS performance. Customer information control system (CICS) is a software package that lets many users concurrently interrogate data in a database. DC/DB systems are large systems in which one computer is solely assigned data communications activities and another system handles processing and access to the corporate database. The language DL/1 is used to write the software necessary to support these latter processing activities.

Glossary

Centralized MIS structure   An MIS organization with a computer system at the center of all DP services.

Chaining   A term used when working with a database that refers to the cross-referencing of data items via a key or index.

Critical path method (CPM)   A management planning technique, associated with operations research, used to monitor and control the completion of a large project.

Customer information control system (CICS) A set of operational programs used to facilitate access to a database and control the data communications services related to those activities.

Database   A vast amount of data stored within a group of totally integrated and interactive computerized files or data elements.

Database administrator   The individual responsible for controlling and supervising all activities, administrative and technical, of a database.

Database management system (DBMS) The set of operational programs that facilitate the use of a computerized database.

Data communications/database (DC/DB) system   A database-oriented system in which a computer handles all data communications.

Data Language/1 (DL/1)   A computer language designed to support access to, and manipulation of, data within a database.

Decentralized MIS structure   An MIS structure composed of totally independent units which possess self-contained systems and do not interact with each other.

Distributed MIS structure An MIS structure in which widely dispersed computer systems supply local DP services and interact to share the workload, often assuming a ringlike multiprocessing configuration.

Exception listings An MIS report format in which abnormal conditions are highlighted.

Forecasting reports An MIS report format, used for managerial planning and decision making, which details projected results derived from data input for test purposes.

General purpose system simulation (GPSS) A specialized programming language used to construct and test simulated models of business systems or activities.

Hierarchical MIS structure A highly structured MIS organization in which computers are positioned at all levels of the organization to handle data, monitor processing, and report to the next higher level.

Information management systems (IMS) Computer systems which manipulate data and permit access to it.

Inverted structure A method of organizing data within a database which cross-references data items via indexes or keys.

Management information system (MIS) A computer system that integrates equipment, procedures, and organizational personnel to develop information for managerial decision making.

On-demand reports An MIS report format produced only when requested.

Operations research (OR) A management science field that uses computers to develop simulated business models.

Program evaluation and review technique (PERT) A managerial planning technique, associated with operations research, used to oversee the implementation and completion of large projects.

Regularly scheduled listings An MIS report format produced at regular intervals (i.e., weekly, monthly, quarterly).

Simple structure A method of data organization for a database in which data is ordered using one common key.

SIMSCRIPT A specialized computer language used to construct and test simulated models of business activities.

Discussion Questions

1 Discuss the three types of planning activities used with MIS, and identify the levels of management associated with each type. Cite examples of reports that might be used in each planning activity.

2 Examine the following list of reports and specify whether each is long-range, short-range, or operational.

Out-of-stock report	Employee absence report
Quarterly budget report	Monthly manpower report
Annual sales projection report	3- to 5-year sales estimate
Christmas sales estimate	Quarterly estimated tax returns
Monthly aircraft availability report	Daily sports report

3 Could an MIS be implemented in the smaller system of a distributed data processing system? If so, what would be the advantages to management or other users?

4 Examine the following lists of people and reports received, and indicate which of the four types of management reports is illustrated.

User	Report Received
Credit Manager	List of overdue accounts
VP—Marketing	Annual sales estimates
Personnel Manager	List of personnel with Masters degree only
Student	Course outline
Inventory Clerk	CRT display of parts data
Payroll Clerk	Weekly payroll listing
Inventory Control Supervisor	Out-of-stock parts reports
College Registrar	Individual student grade profile (on terminal)
Mortgage Manager	Government estimate of inflation report
College student	Transcript of grades
Motor Vehicle Bureau Clerk	Display of previous traffic violations

5 Briefly discuss the organization of the four MIS structures. What advantages does each possess? If you were the DP manager of a sales organization with outlets in four major cities, which MIS structure might you adopt? Give the reasons for your selection.

6 Discuss the differences between inverted and simple structures of data in a database. Illustrate your explanation with an example.

7 Discuss the purpose of:
 a   An information management system
 b   DBMS software
 c   CICS software
 d   A DC/DB system

Summary Test

_____ **1** The interaction of computer systems in separate corporate divisions is a primary goal of a decentralized MIS structure.

_____ **2** CICS may be considered an example of IMS-related software.

_____ **3** Forecasting reports are primarily designed to serve the lower levels of management because they provide projections of day-to-day activities.

_____ **4** A major objective of MIS is to provide management with data on which to make sound decisions.

_____ **5** Cross-referencing data with an inverted structure is sometimes called chaining.

_____ **6** A monthly inventory control report on all inventory items is an example of a regularly scheduled, exception listing.

_____ **7** In a DC/DB system, one computer is assigned the responsibility of handling all data communications activities, processing data, and interacting with the database.

_____ **8** CICS is a software package employed solely to simplify access to a database; it does not monitor data communications activities within that system.

_____ **9** A disadvantage of CICS software is that programs using data accessed from the database must be written independently.

_____ **10** Information generated via OR techniques would generally fall into the area of forecasting reports.

_____ **11** PERT is a planning tool for monitoring the completion of projects that bases its evaluation of performance on the time needed to complete a series of critical tasks.

_____ **12** A database would not normally be an integral component of an MIS and usually stands alone.

_____ **13** File interrogation capabilities are not important in DBMS software.

_____ **14** DBMS software is only available for large computer systems to support their high level of data communications activities.

_____ **15** A language associated with the handling of database items in a DC/DB configuration is DL/1.

_____ **16** The MIS structure with one main computer system is called a:

    a distributed MIS structure   **b** hierarchical MIS structure

    c centralized MIS structure   **d** decentralized MIS structure

_____ **17** Administrative supervision of the activities relating to a database is the responsibility of the:

    a DP manager   **b** Database administrator

    c VP—DP Administration   **d** DB manager

_____ **18** A language for simulating models of business activity is:

    a SPSS   **b** DL/1

    c GPSS   **d** COBOL

_____ **19** The online, softcopy display of a customer's charge account to respond to an inquiry is an example of a(n):

    a regularly scheduled report   **b** on-demand report

    c exception report   **d** forecasting report

_____ **20** Within a database, the sequential organization of data by a common key is called:

    a logical structure   **b** inverted structure

    c simple structure   **d** all the above

_____ **21** Long-range planning reports produced in an MIS are primarily designed for:

    a top management   **b** middle management

    c lower management   **d** a and c

_____ **22** A characteristic of a distributed MIS structure is:

    a computers supporting local DP operations

    b a multiprocessing environment

    c interactive sharing of the workload

    d all the above

_____ **23** A characteristic of an MIS is:

    a   user-oriented information

    b   restrictions on the system's size to inhibit future growth

    c   priority for data handling over the output of decision-oriented information

    d   all the above

_____ **24** Which of the following statements is true?

    a   Most analysts agree on the structure and organization of MIS.

    b   Operational planning reports are a primary informational tool for middle management.

    c   An IMS focuses on managing information generated within a computer system.

    d   The cross reference of data items is an integral feature of the simple structure used in database organization.

_____ **25** A condition that led to the development of databases was:

    a   the proliferation of data files

    b   an increase in the amount of data handled by organizations

    c   a demand for more data to support informational needs

    d   all the above

Summary Test Answers

1 F	**2** T	**3** F	**4** T	**5** T
6 F	**7** F	**8** F	**9** T	**10** T
11 T	**12** F	**13** F	**14** F	**15** T
16 C	**17** B	**18** C	**19** B	**20** C
21 A	**22** D	**23** A	**24** C	**25** D

Fourteen

Systems Analysis and Design

FIGURE 14.1 Systems analysts concern themselves with the flow of information through an organization. To ensure the accuracy of systems that they have designed and installed, analysts will continuously recheck the results provided by the computer. This information will provide a basis for evaluating the overall systems performance. (*STOCK, Boston.*)

Purpose of This Chapter

This chapter presents many of the concepts related to business systems, systems analysis, and systems design. Initially, we learn that a system is an organized method of achieving a goal.

The chapter focuses on business systems, which are combinations of policies, personnel, equipment, and computer facilities, operating according to specific guidelines and organized to attain goals established by management. These goals become the objectives of the system. We review five business systems: payroll, personnel, accounts receivable, accounts payable, and inventory.

The purpose of a systems analysis, that is, an evaluation of a system's operation, is explained. Factors that lead to the decision to evaluate a system are pointed out, and the various ways a systems analysis is initiated are described. The role of the systems analyst in this evaluation is discussed. The most common techniques for collecting data for a systems analysis are listed, including an examination of the organization manual, personal observations, personnel interviews, and a comparison of comparable systems.

The need to document the data collected by the analyst is emphasized. The uses of printer spacing charts, multiple card layouts, and record layout forms in documentation are described. In addition, the purpose of a systems flowchart is discussed. This type of diagram represents the flow of data through a system much as a program flowchart details the processing of data in a program. A sample systems flowchart is analyzed.

The implementation of a feasibility study is discussed in detail. This study, accomplished by a feasibility committee, is a thorough analysis of every aspect of a business system to determine whether a proposed change is warranted and economically justifiable. The four types of individuals ordinarily included on the feasibility committee are a top executive, departmental representatives, a senior analyst, and an outside consultant. The specific role of each member is summarized.

The major objectives of a feasibility study are listed, and the types of recommendations a feasibility committee may make are discussed. The preparation of cost estimates for a proposal is described, and a sample cost comparison of two proposed computer systems is provided. In addition, an example of a manufacturer's bid to implement a new computer system is given. The process of selecting an alternative is discussed briefly.

The steps involved in designing a new system are presented. The proper sequence of these steps is emphasized; for example, a system's outputs must be defined before the required input forms and file structures can be prepared. Methods for making rough estimates of file sizes and the system's storage capacity are explained. The development of program specifications for the new system and the subsequent writing of the required programs are discussed briefly.

Testing and implementing the new system are described. We also describe the staging of a parallel run, that is, having the new system and the existing system independently process the same set of live data and comparing the results of each system. We also discuss three other systems conversions: the phased, pilot, and crash conversion.

The contents of the final report, which must document every aspect of the new system, are outlined, with several tips on the proper preparation of the report. The chapter closes by presenting factors for management to consider when adopting a computer system.

After studying this chapter, you should be able to

- Understand the purpose and objectives of a business system
- Describe the five fundamental business systems
- Discuss the role of the analyst in system analysis and the methods of data collection he or she can employ
- Understand the use of the record layout form and the systems flowchart
- Discuss the purpose, objectives, and personnel involved in a feasibility study
- Discuss the overall approach to designing a proposed system
- Briefly discuss factors management should consider before adopting a computer system
- Understand the following terms:

Accounts payable system	Phased conversion
Accounts receivable system	Pilot conversion
Business system	Program specifications
Crash conversion	Prooflisting
Feasibility committee	Record layout form
Feasibility study	Subsystem
Inventory system	System
Manual system	Systems analysis
Organization manual	Systems flowchart
Payroll system	Written narrative
Personnel system	

Introduction

The systems analyst is responsible for examining the total flow of data through an organization. Analysts may examine almost any aspect of an organization's operation: forms used and the methods of completing them, personnel interactions, procedures for handling problems, or the computer being used.

The term **system** is generally applied to the group of actions, personnel, and procedures used to support the processing of data. Thus, in an organization, the group of procedures, forms, and equipment used to handle payroll data can be referred to as a *payroll system*. Similarly, an *inventory system* represents all people, forms, machines, and procedures used to process inventory data. It is the analyst's responsibility to study each of an organization's systems.

In general, a system is a set of related activities. It may or may not involve computers. The term **manual system** applies to a non-computer-oriented group of activities. The component parts of a large system are referred to as **subsystems.** Subsystems let the analyst work with a smaller group of tasks. Though the concept of a system can be applied to a wide range of activities, it has particular impact in business.

14.1 Business Data Processing Systems

What Is a Business System?

Business systems are the means by which business organizations achieve their stated goals. A **business system** combines policies, personnel, equipment, and data processing facilities, in a prescribed set of procedures to coordinate the activities of a business organization. Essentially, a business system represents an organized way of achieving the stated goals of a business and establishes the rules and actions which govern that organization.

Business systems define how data must be handled. Input data, entering these systems in a variety of ways, will be methodically processed through an organized series of steps. Procedures for processing data and displaying the resulting information are dictated by a business system. For example, systems may be designed to automatically order parts for an inventory, monitor future corporate profits, or post credit card sales against online customer accounts. The type, scope and overall nature of a business system will reflect the ingenuity and resourcefulness of its designers. Most business systems share certain common characteristics.

Objectives of a Business System

Before any system is designed, its objectives must be clearly defined. These objectives will reflect goals established by management for the entire organization. The system must be designed to meet the needs of the organization or it will be of little value. For example, monthly inventory information may be of little value to a business with an inventory that turns over every 2 weeks. Data indicating a negative cash flow should be available to management so that a company does not go bankrupt.

Objectives are the short-term plans used by an organization to achieve management's stated goals. They are the operational measures used to run the organization. The goals from which these objectives are derived represent the results of management's future projections. Goals are broadly stated, long-term plans which management will employ to guide the organization in upcoming years. Objectives are the vehicles for achieving them.

Though most business systems are unique to the organization for which they were designed, their objectives are quite similar. The objectives of a business system are:

1 To handle data efficiently and provide management with timely information
2 To establish the most desirable distribution of data, services, and equipment throughout an organization
3 To meet user and customer needs
4 To minimize operating costs and maximize savings
5 To eliminate duplicated, conflicting, and unnecessary services
6 To define orderly methods of handling business activities
7 To smooth the flow of data through the various levels of an organization
8 To speed up access to and availability of reliable data in a system

The successful administration of objectives depends on the motivation, intelligence, and responsiveness of analysts and management.

Five Business Systems

The five business systems found in most businesses are:

1 Payroll
2 Personnel
3 Accounts receivable
4 Accounts payable
5 Inventory

Though each has a specific purpose, these five systems share general objectives. (Differences develop in a given system as it is "personalized" to fit the needs of its users.)

A **payroll system** is designed to handle and provide all the information relating to the processing of an employee payroll. This system must incorporate all the paperwork necessary to pay each employee and record personal taxes and deductions, maintain files on all past individual earnings, provide up-to-date totals of amounts, print all outputs detailing payroll information, and conform to all tax regulations. In addition, the system must incorporate checks and controls that prohibit the fraudulent use of payroll funds.

A **personnel system** is designed to process data on the people employed by an organization. This system uses input documents to collect employee data for storage in the personnel data files. The type and number of personnel system outputs are closely tied to the needs of a particular organization. Personnel systems vary extensively among companies. Whereas payroll information is frequently generated weekly or semimonthly, personnel systems may be geared to a monthly timetable. Companies use personnel information to develop employee mailing lists, maintain employment and promotion histories, evaluate primary and secondary work skills, and qualify for federally funded work programs. Personnel data have been used as evidence in court cases involving women's rights and minority employment.

An **accounts receivable** and an **accounts payable system** are similar in that both monitor the flow of money through a business. However, an accounts receivable system monitors the people who owe money to a business and an accounts payable system monitors the organizations to which money is owed. Most businesses use variations of each type of system.

An accounts receivable system provides the means to process all data related to the use of credit cards and other kinds of charge accounts. Charge sales may enter the system directly via online terminals or be batch processed. These charges are processed against files of customer accounts, which are updated daily. The files are composed of individual customer data, including names, addresses, credit references, credit limits, account numbers, previous balances, current charges, finance charges, and payments received. This information appears on the monthly statements issued to each customer. Other outputs of this system provide control information for management's use (i.e., invalid accounts, accounts exceeding their credit limit, a listing of all existing accounts, etc.).

An accounts payable system may use almost the same file structure and I/O formats as the accounts receivable system. A major exception is that the accounts payable system issues checks to vendors at the end of its billing cycle. Its data files contain the accounts of vendors to whom money is owed. Inputs relate to goods and services received by the company, whereas outputs will issue payments and management reports.

An **inventory system** essentially monitors the contents and changes made in an inventory. Supporting files detail all items contained in the inventory and related cost data. Vendor invoices and memos of goods received, returned, or transferred and requests for stock provide the bulk of input data. Listings of all inventory items, stock on order, specially ordered goods, critical stock items, and cost data are included in the system's outputs. Considering the amount of money that can be tied up in an inventory, management must have reliable information.

14.2 Systems Analysis
The Role of the Analyst

Business systems are designed to function efficiently and provide accurate management information. When they perform erratically, the systems analyst must determine why. The careful scrutiny of all aspects of a business system is called **systems analysis.** It is a methodical, step-by-step investigation. The analyst must pinpoint the problem before suggesting a solution. Because there are often many alternative solutions, the analyst must recommend the most economically justifiable one.

The decision to investigate a system may result from many factors. A specific administrative request for data processing support, a scheduled review, or an analyst's own curiosity may initiate a systems analysis. The resulting analysis will examine and evaluate the system's ability to handle the flow of data. A formal request for a systems analysis may come from any level of management. Normally, the request is made in a memo directed to the manager of the systems group, identifying the system to receive the analysis. The memo generally defines the particular problem and suggests an initial meeting date. Preliminary discussion defines the scope of the problem and orients the analyst to the system to be studied. Once the systems group manager approves, the analysis can begin.

The individual analyst may sometimes prove to be the catalyst to a systems analysis effort. While working on a project, analysts may often be intrigued by a particular aspect of a system or notice that a subsystem requires modification. The request to begin an analysis may then come from the individual analyst. The decision to undertake this project will be made by the systems manager. The speed with which analysis projects are started depends on the existing workload, the priority of the system in question, and financial resources.

Business systems are designed to undergo periodic evaluation. These check-ups ensure that a system is performing up to standard. No formal request is required for a periodic review, and the analyst assigned to the specific system is permitted to initiate his or her own evaluation.

Operational policies in some systems groups mandate that existing systems be evaluated every 12 to 24 months. Newer systems may be evaluated every 6 months after their completion. In these cases, it is the analyst's responsibility to maintain a time log for each system, record the start of the analysis, and report the results of the study.

In organizations without a separate systems group, the request for a systems analysis may originate in a similar fashion to that described above, the study being performed by a team of employees that management selects. Most smaller DP organizations have a more informal systems approach, although no less quality appears in their systems. Here too, a team of analysts and programming personnel actually analyze the systems.

Collection of Data

The analyst may go after evidence for the analysis in many ways. Some of the most common methods of collecting data are:

1 A review of available organizational material
2 Personal observations
3 Interviews with personnel working with the system
4 A comparison with similar business systems

ZIP CODE GOES TO 9

Often the basis of systems study is a change in operating conditions, thus affecting the data used within a computerized system. Generally, this type of change is felt on an individual organizational basis. However, a change envisioned by the U.S. Postal Service will virtually affect everyone.

The Postal Service is introducing a nine-digit ZIP code which it originally hoped to have fully operational by February 1981. This change is the result of a study begun back in September 1978 to expand the existing five-digit code. The four additional digits designate streets, blocks, buildings, and business zones to which mail is delivered. Officials believe that the new codes will speed mail deliveries. It is estimated that the nine-digit code will enhance the automated sorting of mail and enable 7 workers to perform the sorting currently assigned to 20 clerks.

A test of the new nine-digit codes was authorized for early in 1979 in Wilmington, Delaware. Preliminary steps in this test study required the preparation of a citywide coding scheme, development of a ZIP code database, and modification of existing ZIP code software to support the use of the nine-digit code. Initial test results showed the nine-digit code to be effective, buoying the spirits of postal officials about its eventual usage across the country. Plans are currently under way to convert operational software to handle these nine-digit operations.

This shift to a nine-digit code will have considerable inpact on the DP industry. Though it will occur gradually over many years, the shift to the new codes has DP management already concerned. DP installations face the tedious task of revamping the software, operational procedures, and forms used to accommodate ZIP codes. The conversion effort will require many hours of work and great detail. It is expected that by 1985, 80 percent of all organizations will have adopted the new codes.

The scope of this effort is quite large, as both the private and public sector are involved. Systems analysts will be in the forefront of the design and implementation of these new ZIP code systems.

Most large companies or agencies maintain a volume of documents about their daily operation in an **organizational manual.** This manual, often called a *policy and procedures manual,* describes the function and procedures used in most departments of the organization. The procedures are described step by step, informing personnel of the actions to be taken to complete specific tasks. For example, a manual could detail how an employee should complete a change-of-address form, the codes used on the form, where to send the completed request, and its initial handling at the DP center.

The procedures included in the organization manual generally describe the proper methods for handling data generated by the organization. Thus they provide a basis for the comparison made by the investigating analyst. The analyst can observe how data is handled, evaluate how it should be handled, and draw conclusions on the system's effectiveness. Employee reluctance to adhere to a written procedure might be the reason for a system's inconsistent operation. If a system's performance is satisfactory, then the actual procedure used should replace the one described in the organization manual. Another alternative open to the analyst is to scrap both procedures and redesign the entire system. This alternative, often the most costly, is sometimes the only rational solution.

The organization manual is a starting point, but the analyst must gather practical information on a system. One of the analyst's most valuable tools is the personnel interview. It gives the analyst information about a system from the people who use it on a daily basis. Interviews often correct misconceptions held by the analyst and fill in information gaps. Even though analysts may watch the operation of a system, they may not fully understand it. A brief interview with the right clerk could clarify any question or misconceptions.

Practical knowledge from an interview can provide valuable information on a system and potential solutions to problems. Often, interviewees have developed solutions that, with refinement, can be implemented into a system, thereby saving the analyst time and effort and improving the system's efficiency.

Another time-saving avenue open to an analyst is the examination of similar systems used by other organizations. Frequently, other companies that have encountered a similar problem have attacked it in unique ways. Conversations with employees of these companies provide immediate access to the results of solutions attempted by other analysts. Essentially, the analyst can gain valuable information through the experience of others.

The analyst performing a systems analysis should also collect copies of all documents used in the system under study. These forms will detail the current I/O data employed by the system and enable the analyst to evaluate their effectiveness. Occasionally, errors found in a system are the result of improperly developed I/O forms.

In summary, analysts should use any means at their disposal to investigate and collect data necessary to their analyses. Though these efforts may require many months for a large project, the information gathered will ensure the accuracy of the analysis performed. Once the analysis effort is firmly under way, the analyst must record data in an orderly fashion. The need for documentation is vital. Documentation becomes a measure of the progress achieved and provides orderly access to the information gathered.

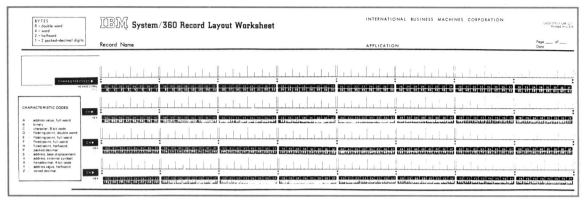

FIGURE 14.2   A record layout form used to detail the format of records composing data files.

14.3
Systems
Documentation
Record Formats

Data collected during analysis includes copies of all I/O forms, charts detailing softcopy outputs used with CRTs, layouts of data files, and written narratives of all procedures developed for the system. All these items refer to how the system uses data and supports the analyst's conclusions.

In Chapter 7, you were introduced to two forms used with systems analysis: the printer spacing chart and the multiple card layout form. The card layout form indicates the contents (fields) of cards used in processing, whereas the printer spacing chart details the formats of outputs resulting from the system.

Another form available to the analyst is the **record layout form,** illustrated in Figure 14.2. This form is used to describe the format of records stored on data files constructed in the system. The format of any record in a file may be detailed character by character. Figure 14.3 illustrates the combined use of a multiple card layout form, a printer spacing chart, and a record layout form for one data processing application.

The formats of two data cards used to input employee data appear in Figure 14.3a. Two cards are required since more than 80 characters of data are involved. The fields composing each card are indicated on a multiple card layout form. Note that a Social Security No. field, columns 1 to 9, appears on each card. This lets the computer properly identify the two cards for every employee. To distinguish between the two cards, a 1 is punched into column 80 on the first card and a 2 is punched into that column on the second card.

Once input, the card data is stored in a file controlled by the computer. The storage format used in that file is illustrated in Figure 14.3b. In this format, the Social Security No. field appears only once, at the

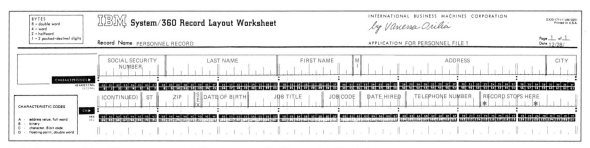

FIGURE 14.3(a) A multiple card layout form showing the format of input cards with personnel data.

FIGURE 14.3(b) The contents of the two cards illustrated in (a) are stored in a file according to the format on the record layout form shown.

start of the record. Under the direction of its program, the computer will take the data input from the second card and place it immediately after the data of the first card. The second social security number is used solely for card control purposes and will be eliminated from the file format.

The printer spacing chart, Figure 14.3c, indicates the output format used to display the contents of the personnel file discussed above. This format contains all the file data that will be printed. This output, referred to as a **prooflisting,** will be used to check the actual data stored in the file. Data written into the file will be printed in the prooflisting.

FIGURE 14.3(c) The printer spacing chart depicting the prooflisting of data written into the personnel file.

Systems Flowcharts

Documenting input, output, and record formats is only one aspect of the analyst's task. The analyst must also detail the sequence of steps involved in a procedure. The analyst may describe the sequence in a written narrative, a systems flowchart, or both. A **written narrative** is a step-by-step breakdown of all operations involved in completing a procedure. Each step of the procedure is given in one complete sentence; hence each sentence defines a specific task.

The **systems flowchart** defines the same series of operations, except in pictorial form. The systems flowchart is quite similar to the program flowchart in that it portrays a logical series of operations. Although the program flowchart is restricted to describing programming logic, the systems flowchart can depict any organization procedure.

The symbols used in a systems flowchart are somewhat different from their programming counterparts. Each symbol describes a specific task and thus has its own operational significance. Figure 14.4 shows the symbols for systems flowcharts. An example of a systems flowchart and its written narrative appears in Figure 14.5.

This systems flowchart opens with a document symbol representing the job applications which are received daily. The label in this symbol indicates that job applications are being handled. The next symbol, a manual operation symbol, indicates that the applications are time-stamped by a clerk. Their temporary storage in a holding file is noted by the triangular symbol (point down) for offline storage.

The next two symbols indicate that the batch of applications (documents) is to be keypunched and verified. The results of these operations are the cards which will be held for processing and the original applications which are returned to the personnel department.

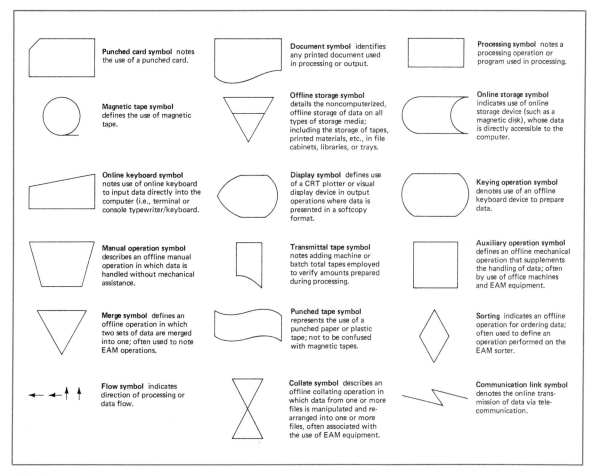

FIGURE 14.4 The symbols used in preparing systems flowcharts.

The batch processing of these cards is accomplished using program LATV and is represented by the rectangular processing symbol. The flowchart illustrates that the program interacts with an online storage capacity which holds the applications file. Note that only the program identification is indicated in the processing symbol. A program flowchart may accompany the systems flowchart; however, no program instructions will appear.

The results of processing are an updated applications file and the cards which are retained in a DP card file cabinet. A prooflisting prints all the applications data added to the file and the applicants who were rejected.

A systems flowchart describes all the actions of a procedure using a sequence of symbols. Each symbol identifies an action and contains a narrative that defines the action taken or data involved. Figure 14.6 offers another example of a systems flowchart and written narrative.

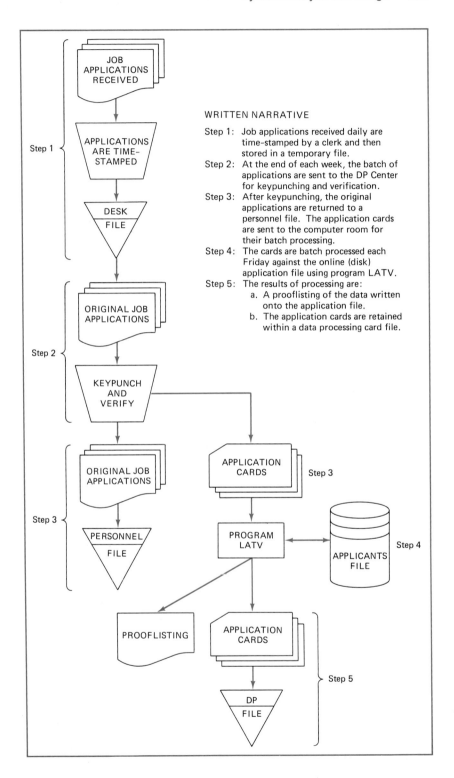

WRITTEN NARRATIVE

Step 1: Job applications received daily are time-stamped by a clerk and then stored in a temporary file.
Step 2: At the end of each week, the batch of applications are sent to the DP Center for keypunching and verification.
Step 3: After keypunching, the original applications are returned to a personnel file. The application cards are sent to the computer room for their batch processing.
Step 4: The cards are batch processed each Friday against the online (disk) application file using program LATV.
Step 5: The results of processing are:
   a. A prooflisting of the data written onto the application file.
   b. The application cards are retained within a data processing card file.

FIGURE 14.5   A systems flowchart and written narrative, describing one procedure for handling job applications.

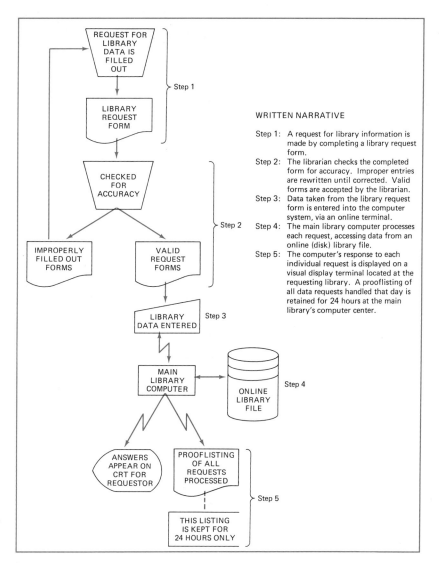

FIGURE 14.6 The systems flowchart and narrative describing the handling of a request for data from a library information system.

WRITTEN NARRATIVE

Step 1: A request for library information is made by completing a library request form.

Step 2: The librarian checks the completed form for accuracy. Improper entries are rewritten until corrected. Valid forms are accepted by the librarian.

Step 3: Data taken from the library request form is entered into the computer system, via an online terminal.

Step 4: The main library computer processes each request, accessing data from an online (disk) library file.

Step 5: The computer's response to each individual request is displayed on a visual display terminal located at the requesting library. A prooflisting of all data requests handled that day is retained for 24 hours at the main library's computer center.

14.4 Feasibility Study

The results of the analyst's preliminary analysis will affect later decisions regarding the system. For example, the analysis may reveal that the system under study is operating satisfactorily and requires only minor modification. The recommended changes would be designed to fine-tune the system so that it operates at peak performance. Adjustments of this type can be accomplished relatively quickly.

On the other hand, the initial analysis may reveal that the system is operating below par and substantial changes must be made in policies, procedures, or equipment. The analyst might suggest purchasing a new computer. Vast system changes usually take at least 6 months and may take up to 3 years to complete. The costs of this type of effort are substantial, often totaling well over $100,000.

An analysis may also reveal that although current systems are operating satisfactorily, phases of new business operations may over-burden existing resources. New and rapidly growing business activities often outstrip existing, and projected, DP facilities. This increased demand may require a major conversion in computer facilities—after an extensive systems study. Such a project also requires a heavy expenditure of time and money. Major system modifications are carefully considered because they cost so much. Before any vast system change, management normally requires a confirmation of the original analysis. This detailed analysis is called a **feasibility study** and is performed by a select group of people referred to as the **feasibility committee.**

The feasibility study will determine whether it is economically justifiable to purchase and maintain a new computer and make other suggested system modifications, and will develop cost estimates for every alternative receiving consideration. The operation of the total system will be examined in the feasibility study. The feasibility study provides management with enough information to make a sensible decision.

The Feasibility Committee

The feasibility committee collects all data related to the feasibility study. Its research must be comprehensive, delving into many areas of the organization. The members of the feasibility committee should be able to reach into any level of management to obtain the required information.

Most feasibility committees consist of the following individuals:

1 A senior-level management person
2 A member of each department that may be affected by changes resulting from the study
3 A senior systems analyst
4 An outside consultant

Each member of the committee represents a specific area of interest and brings a unique operational viewpoint to it.

The senior management officer represents the organization's top management. As a corporate executive, he or she can advise the committee on management's goals, objectives, and ability to provide financial support. This individual can also tell management about directions taken, the progress made, and the conclusions drawn by the feasibility committee.

The individual department members provide a broad base of support for the study and represent the eventual users of the proposed system. Members bring their knowledge to the committee and provide collective views of the entire organization. They are also sources of information for the committee, and they can furnish any required departmental data. With this representation, each department can monitor the study's progress. Each department has input to the committee and can offer advice on specific trouble spots.

Departmental representation is often vital to the success of the committee's work. It prevents employees from feeling that changes are being forced on them. They can willingly accept these changes and work toward their implementation. Broad representation helps create an atmosphere for successful systems analysis and design.

The senior systems analyst, drawn from the systems group, is familiar with the existing computer system and the company's operating procedures. This representative thoroughly understands the organization's data processing operation and supporting facilities.

The outside consultant offers a special type of expertise that company members may not possess. The consultant advises the committee of the current technology, systems approaches used in other companies, and potential economic pitfalls associated with each approach. The consultant should serve as the independent voice of the committee and render impartial, but tactful, opinions. Frequently, committee members do not criticize a suggested solution because of its political impact in the company. Consultants can offer negative comments when necessary, without the fear of reprisal. Of course, if the committee is sufficiently autonomous, a consultant may not have to perform this function.

The top-level executive, the department members, the senior systems analyst, and the consultant are the individuals normally assigned to the feasibility committee. However, any member of an organization possessing a particular expertise may be added to the committee to bolster their information gathering capabilities. A cross section of views improves the committee's ability to develop a comprehensive feasibility study.

Objectives of the Study

The major objectives of a feasibility study are:

1 To analyze the current system
2 To determine whether a new computer system is needed or the existing computer system can adequately support suggested modifications
3 To prepare a list of computer hardware that will be used in the new system and request manufacturer bids on this equipment
4 To evaluate all bids received and compile a list of recommended equipment
5 To devise a plan to implement the newly purchased computer equipment and the proposed system

The feasibility committee's detailed examination of the existing system is a major systems analysis project. The system is evaluated for its ability to meet the information needs of the organization. The feasibility committee, through a series of management directives, is free to enter most levels of an organization and perform its analyses. All areas are evaluated for their current ability to handle and accelerate the flow of information through the organization.

The feasibility committee amasses data and formulates ideas that will be incorporated into the proposed system. Its recommendations may range from sweeping changes in the existing system to minor modifications in current data-handling techniques, forms, or procedures.

Suggesting a major change in computer hardware affects the physical appearance of the system. The decision to change computer equipment must be economically justifiable. Comparing the estimated costs of the existing and proposed systems would be essential.

The comparison should include costs of designing the proposed system, writing and testing new programs, buying and renting computer equipment and systems software, training personnel slated to work with the new system, and costs of supplies and overhead for the computer center. In addition, potential savings accrued from either system should be estimated. Comparing estimated costs and savings helps the feasibility committee understand each system's potential. Table 14.1 provides an example of cost estimates for two proposed systems.

Once the major portion of the analysis is completed, the feasibility committee will evaluate the alternative systems. From this group a few systems will be selected for further development. This selection enables the committee to focus their attention on the limited group of alternative systems that will eventually be presented to management.

Management's selection of a specific alternative will dictate the type and scope of computer involvement in the system's data processing capability. After these factors have been refined, a list of required computer hardware and software can be prepared. The list will generally describe the type of computer equipment, peripheral devices, and manufacturer-supplied software which the proposed system will require.

The list will then be sent to computer manufacturers for their consideration, with a request that cost quotations be prepared for the equipment indicated. Manufacturers will have to reply by a fixed deadline and detail all costs, relating to equipment, services, and financial terms. Table 14.2 provides a sample of a manufacturer's bid.

Once the manufacturers' bids have been received, the feasibility committee can begin evaluating. Computer hardware and software described in the bids will be evaluated for their ability to support the needs of the organization and the activities of the proposed system. The costs of operating the proposed computer system are always considered.

Table 14.1 A Cost Comparison of Two Computer Systems*

Budget Items	System A—Existing Computer, New System			System B—New Computer, New System		
	Year 1	Year 2	Year 3	Year 1	Year 2	Year 3
System costs:						
System design	$100,000	$ 15,000		$150,000	$ 5,000	
Programming	50,000	20,000		50,000	15,000	
Employee training	10,000			10,000		
Physical plant	20,000			15,000		
Conversion, testing,						
& implementation	10,000	5,000		10,000	5,000	
New personnel	20,000	40,000	$ 45,000	20,000	24,000	$ 32,000
Computer rental	36,000	42,000	48,000	12,000	18,000	20,000
Supplies	12,000	14,000	15,000	10,000	11,000	12,000
Overhead	6,000	8,000	10,000	6,000	8,000	10,000
Total costs	$264,000	$144,000	$118,000	$283,000	$86,000	$ 74,000
Savings from each system:						
Personnel reassignment	$ 35,000	$ 42,000	$ 24,000	$ 50,000	$ 36,000	$ 30,000
Reduced overtime	35,000	70,000	90,000	35,000	70,000	90,000
Inventory reductions	50,000	100,000	150,000	50,000	100,000	150,000
New sales	12,000	12,000	16,000	12,000	12,000	16,000
Total savings	$132,000	$224,000	$280,000	$147,000	$218,000	$286,000
Annual net savings (loss) (total savings − total costs)	($132,000)	$ 80,000	$162,000	($136,000)	$132,000	$212,000
Accumulated net savings (loss)(each year carried forward)	($132,000)	($ 52,000)	$110,000	($136,000)	($ 4,000)	$208,000

*The comparison is given on an annual basis, projected for 3 years. System A involves using the existing computer system but with major changes. System B incorporates a new computer and major system modifications. System A will result in an estimated savings of $110,000; System B, $208,000.

After reviewing all the manufacturers' bids, the feasibility committee recommends which computer equipment should be purchased. This recommendation will highlight for management the factors considered and reasons for the choice. Management's decision is based on the organization's economic position. Though it rarely happens, management may select a cheaper system.

After management's selection of computer equipment, the feasibility committee is free to recommend an overall design strategy for use during the development of the proposed system. This approach should reflect the results derived from the feasibility study and guidelines established by the organization's management. It usually includes a timetable for installing, implementing, and testing both the computer hardware and system being designed. Once this timetable is established, the detailed designing of the proposed system can begin.

Table 14.2 XYZ Computer Corp. Estimate of the Costs Associated with the Computer Equipment Requested on Bid No. 628-1801, Johnson Associates, Inc.*

Item	Purchase Price	Monthly Maintenance	Monthly Rental Cost
XYZ System 1228 Series, CPU size 64K, 20 megabytes of fixed disk storage, 260 line printer, basic supervisor	$ 82,000	$ 400	$1,200
40 megabytes of additional disk storage (removable), Model XYZ 728	18,000	210	720
4 visual display terminals, Model 930	12,800	120	400
4 adapters for CRTs (Model 930) Model XYZ 66ADR	4,000	50	200
4 modems, Model 66YAN	4,000	50	250
2 diskettes, Model TK02	1,800	180	580
Diskette interfaces, Model X3	260	30	140
Software package (COBOL, RPG)	820	100	50
Total costs	$123,680	$1,140	$3,540

Additional notes:
1. The above prices do not include transportation expenses.
2. Costs do not include telephone line costs for leased lines.
3. Costs valid until 30 days after quotation date.
4. Monthly rental costs include maintenance fees. Monthly maintenance fees listed related to equipment purchased outright.

*These costs provide the feasibility committee sufficient data to compare this system with those offered by other manufacturers.

14.5 Designing the Proposed System

Management's choice of computer hardware means that the systems staff can begin designing the new system. Because there is often a 6- to 12-month delay in the delivery of computer equipment, the design effort may proceed in its development of I/O formats, files, and procedures for handling data generated throughout the system. Any of the information compiled by the feasibility committee will be made available to systems people working on the project. To familiarize all analysts with the proposed system, an orientation period of a few weeks should be planned. Project personnel should attend seminars and research the aspects of the system in which they are involved. For the purpose of continuity, the departmental representatives who have served on the feasibility committee may be included on the systems staff. Again, these representatives will act as liaisons to their departments and as information specialists.

Outputs, Inputs, and Processing

The design effort normally begins with a definition of outputs generated by the new system. It is important to develop a firm understanding of the information the system will provide to its users. These outputs represent the results of the system, and if they are not of value, the effectiveness of the system is negligible. These informational requirements must be clearly established before any other aspects of the system are designed.

After the system's outputs have been defined, the design of input and file formats can begin. In addition, the definition of the information to appear on the system's outputs (visual or printed) enables the analysts to establish the input data required for their preparation. Record sizes for each file can also be determined.

A crude estimate of the size of the system's files can then be developed. The number of characters a file holds can be found by multiplying the record size by the number of records in the file. For example, if an employee record size consists of 1500 characters and the number of employees is approximately 2000, then that employee file holds almost 3 million characters of data. By adding the estimates for each file, the analysts can estimate the storage capacity the system must possess. Thus, if 10 files of 3 million characters each are envisioned, then the system must have a minimum secondary storage capacity of 30 million characters. Moreover, if the data is used in online processing activities, magnetic disk storage is a possibility. Normally, estimates of file sizes and the amount and type of secondary storage are developed during the feasibility study. These crude estimates help analysts confirm their initial estimates and prevent glaring errors.

Definitions of I/O and file formats do not preclude later changes. Minor changes are made continuously as the system is completed. Naturally, as the system comes together, the number of modifications will be restricted to those considered essential.

With the determination of the input, output, record, and file formats, the analysts can develop **program specifications** for writing the software required for the system. The specifications will include file names, record names and sizes, field names and sizes, types of data used, special codes, formulas, computer control statements, and special remarks to the programmer. Good program specifications decrease the probability of error and speed the writing of necessary software. They also make it possible for programmers to monitor their work with a minimum of changes and delays. The period of time set aside for the programming phase will vary between projects. A general rule of thumb is 6 to 24 months for the completion of software.

Testing and Implementation

All aspects of a system must be operationally tested prior to their use. Applications software must be certified before it can be accepted. Newly designed input forms are generally used by clerks to test their effectiveness and permit any necessary redesign. Outputs will be repeatedly refined after discussions with their intended users. Online files must be created and filled with test data to ensure their accurate storage of data. When these individual parts prove satisfactory, the components of a system can be integrated. The total system can then be tested in much the same manner that a computer program is tested.

Initially, the entire system's performance is evaluated with test data. All the system's outputs are generated with input data fed into files. Every aspect of the system is checked and verified to ensure its operational accuracy.

This preliminary test period gives the designers a chance to train the employees destined to work with the system. Because test data can be repeatedly processed, these individuals may perform a procedure any number of times until they have mastered that facet of the system. This training increases the overall cost of the project since the personnel must be relieved of their regular duties to develop skills related to the new system. This extra expense is more than offset by the speed with which employees operate and adapt to the system.

When solid results are derived from the use of test data the entire system is reinitialized to handle *live data*. During this phase of testing, the proposed system runs concurrently with the existing system, processing exactly the same data. This test procedure is referred to as a *parallel run*. If the new system has been properly implemented, its results should be identical to the results of the existing system. The parallel run should be conducted for a complete processing cycle. For example, if a payroll system was implemented, the parallel run should process a weekly, biweekly, semimonthly, and monthly payroll. An accounts receivable system, used with credit cards, should process a minimum of 1 month's charge data.

The maintenance of dual systems during a parallel run adds expense to the project. However, the consequences of an untried system may be more expensive in the long run. During a parallel run, many of the quirks and trouble spots in the new system will be resolved. The advantage of this type of test is that the organization is protected from relying on untested information. Another advantage is that the original system is still providing necessary information.

Parallel tests are desirable but not always possible. Actual conditions may dictate a different implementation schedule. Although details may vary slightly, according to the particular organization and application, here are three major conversion techniques.

A gradual systems conversion is a **phased conversion.** In this approach, components of the new system are implemented one at a time into the old system, and the old system is phased out piece by piece. When all the new subsystems are operational, the whole new system provides the projected computer support. The advantages of phased conversion are that the organization always has some form of computer support, the conversion is gradual, and costs associated with operating two systems in parallel are minimized. The disadvantages of a phased conversion are that it is time-consuming and the relationship among subsystems is continually undergoing change.

In the **pilot conversion,** one subsystem is chosen as the lead or prototype system and implemented before all others. Only when that subsystem is completely operational can conversion of the next system be considered. If five subsystems were to be implemented, each would be treated as a separate project. Each subsystem is treated as the stepping stone to the next part of the system. The pilot approach permits analysts to experience development problems and prepare test solutions, minimize losses associated with parallel runs, and gradually retrain concerned employees. The pilot conversion takes more time and money than other approaches.

The most drastic systems implementation is the **crash conversion.** Within this approach, an entire new system is installed. The old system is completely dismantled, leaving the organization suddenly to rely on the new system alone. A crash conversion has merit when the old system is seriously inadequate or radically different from the new system and when the conversion will be so rapid that it will not severely disrupt operations. The crash approach is risky, for even a minor problem can seriously delay the implementation schedule. Careful planning and attention to detail are necessary for a successful crash conversion. Organizations that need continuous DP support or are doing their first systems conversion do not ordinarily undertake crash conversions.

Final Documentation

The design project ends with the final documentation of the new system. A final report on the new system must document every aspect of its operation. The report should contain the following:

1 An overview of the entire project, describing the general purpose of the system and the information available.

2 Printer spacing charts, accompanied by detailed narratives, describing each of the system's outputs. Card and record layouts should detail inputs and files used to prepare any output.

3 Systems flowcharts which describe any procedure or series of steps used in the processing of data.

4 A financial analysis of the proposed and the existing systems, projecting current and future costs, as well as potential cost savings.

5 A description of the computer system and its peripheral equipment.

The final report should be professionally typed and bound, contain clear illustrations, and be concisely written. Nothing should detract from the appearance of this important document. Technical jargon should be kept to a minimum. If management can grasp the concepts of the new system, they are more likely to convey their appreciation and support future projects. Obviously, management will readily support projects they understand and agree with in scope, if they are sponsored by people with a proven record of achievement.

HOW FIRMS JUDGE NEED FOR COMPUTER   Brian Moss

Small business, big problems? Maybe a computer is the answer. On the other hand, maybe it isn't. How can you know for sure?

Several managers of stores that sell microcomputers, the small kind selling in the $8,000 to $15,000 range typically used by small businesses, talked recently about how they decide whether a potential customer really needs one.

"It's not just one question," explained Bob Price, manager of the Digital Computer Store in Garden City. "It's a series of questions. What we do is look at the customer's type of business, and he outlines his problem."

At the Radio Shack Computer Center in Bethpage, the process is similar. "We sit with him," Steve Radzinski, the store manager, said. "We don't talk about a computer. We talk about his business. At that point, we can intelligently make recommendations."

Bill Barton, the president of Datel Stores of New York, which operates a store in Rockefeller Center, said a business owner can ask: "This is what I want to do. Can the computer do it for me?"

Sometimes it can't. Price said that a sailboat salesman wanted to put a computer in his showroom. He had a high sales volume—more than $500,000—but as few as 10 sales over several months. To invoice and keep track of those few items could be done as simply, manually.

"I could have sold the guy a computer system, but he didn't need one," Price said. "What we try to do is determine: Does the guy really have a need? And then, is the cost justifiable?"

Price said, in general, that a business with more than 15 employees, 300 items in inventory, 30 accounts payable or any one or combination of these, is a likely candidate for a computer, as is a company with more than 100 accounts payable.

14.6 Managerial Considerations Regarding Computer Systems

The management of many an organization has been troubled about the best way to process data and the best computer system to choose. Many firms must choose between using a service bureau and running an in-house computer system. In either case, management must answer many questions before it decides. If it wants its own DP center, it needs a study of available hardware. The evaluation process is tedious and time-consuming because so many different kinds of equipment are available. Management should try to answer the following questions during the evaluation process:

Buying a computer makes the most sense, the sales representatives said, for help in two troublesome areas: keeping track of accounts receivable—money owed the businessman—and inventory.

"Many businessmen have accounts receivable out in the thousands and thousands of dollars," Radzinski said. "They have no idea—maybe a ballpark figure—but they don't specifically know who has what out and for how long. And these people are using *his* money."

He added, "When he's looking for money to increase his inventory and he doesn't have the money, the purpose of the computer is to allow him to go in and immediately access those kinds of information. Sometimes it comes as a very rude awakening."

"If he can take his accounts receivable and cut them in half, that's money he can reinvest in his own business," Radzinski continued. "By buying more intelligently and knowing his stock and flow of merchandise with a computer, he can effectively turn his inventory over much more times a year and turn his stock into cash assets much faster."

Radzinski and Price agreed that a customer should shop around, for price, service and programing help.

Companies tend to look cautiously at expenditures during recessions, and Datel's Barton said he is feeling this already. The time between tentative orders and company approval of them has begun to lag. But all agreed that a recession makes a computer even more important for small firms.

"In order for a business to stay profitable, it's got to have a handle on costs at all times," Radzinski said. "A businessman can't borrow money, he's going to have to find money from his own product sales. He's going to have to stop indiscriminately buying inventory and buy what's moving. He needs to have hard facts to make hard decisions."

Source: This article appeared in the Business Section of *Newsday*, June 1, 1980, p. 90. Reproduced by permission.

---

1   What type of data processing is right for the organization?
2   What CPU size and speed are needed?
3   What purchase or rental costs accompany the system?
4   What kind of peripheral devices are needed?
5   What software is needed?
6   What kind of vendor maintenance is available, and what does it cost?
7   What staffing and training will the DP center need?

Thoroughly answering each question will provide management with a good basis for its decision. Once a choice of batch processing, time-sharing, or online processing is made, management can decide on hardware. The complexity of the operations will, of course, determine the complexity of the hardware.

A major consideration is the size and speed of a system's CPU. A real-time system needs a large and fast CPU, as do online systems that take data from a broad array of files. Batch processing can use smaller CPUs because the flow of data is not critical and tends to be minimal. Once, the rule of thumb was that the larger the CPU, the more expensive. But recent technological improvements have rendered this rule inaccurate. Many new systems have CPUs that once would cost three times as much for half the processing speeds. Technology is improving processing and reducing the size and cost of CPUs.

Management must examine from many angles the question of whether to buy or rent a computer system. Renting or leasing offers several advantages. Leasing lets the DP shop stay up to date without the problems associated with disposal of old equipment. Rental fees are usually tax deductible and avoid the outlay of a large purchase price. Four to five years of rental fees usually are necessary to match a system's purchase price. In that period, most organizations have outgrown their systems and are looking for new hardware.

The type of peripheral devices a company wants relates to all the factors we have already discussed. If, for example, online support is necessary, a terminal will also be necessary. The decision then becomes which type of terminal is best suited to the applications at hand. Management must decide on price, model, shape, color, capability, discounts offered for quantity orders, and the like. Many organizations buy all equipment from one manufacturer to ensure compatibility within a system. Recent advances have made it possible, however, to mix different manufacturers' equipment into a smoothly operating system. Competitive pricing by certain smaller manufacturers has made their equipment quite attractive. All these considerations come into play when people are deciding on what equipment to use.

Software for a system will depend on what is available, on processing needs, on compatibility with hardware, and on ease of modification. A totally new system requires careful thinking about matching software. Existing systems can sometimes accommodate modified software. Sometimes more people must be hired or consulted with to develop the necessary software for a company. Management may also decide to develop software as needed rather than buy it all at once. Here, too, costs for either alternative will affect management's decision.

Service is another important consideration. Most manufacturers include service in a rental contract. When computers are bought outright, maintenance is contracted for separately. Although users are free to shop around for service, many buy service from the manufacturer.

The people who will work with the computer must be adequately trained, and management must train enough people so that work is done efficiently. Employees have to understand their job and how it relates to others in the DP department. Many manufacturers offer sound training programs to their equipment users at no or a nominal charge. Employees are scheduled into training sessions before the computer arrives and before they assume their new duties.

To answer the seven questions at the beginning of this section requires thorough investigation by management. There are no standard answers, no answers that are correct for everyone. If management cannot answer the questions, it should hire consultants to help. Although consultants may be expensive in the short run, they can help a company avoid expensive mistakes over the long haul.

Summary

The following major points have been presented in Chapter 14:

Point 1   A system is an organized method of achieving a goal. Systems can be broken down into components called subsystems and normally involve the use of computers. A non-computer-oriented system is called a manual system.

Point 2   A business system can be defined as a combination of policies, personnel, equipment, and computer facilities, operating according to sets of procedures, which coordinate the activities of a business organization. Business systems are designed to improve the flow of data through an organization by eliminating waste, providing the best distribution of resources, efficiently handling data, and responding to user needs.

Point 3   Five fundamental business systems are payroll, personnel, accounts receivable, accounts payable, and inventory systems. A payroll system handles data on the processing of an employee payroll. The accurate maintenance of employee-related data is accomplished through a personnel system. An accounts receivable system monitors the people and organizations that owe a business money, whereas an accounts payable system keeps track of the money owed to others. An inventory system monitors the status of an inventory of goods and the adjustments made in that stock.

Point 4   Systems analysis involves the careful scrutiny of all aspects of a business system. The systems analyst is the individual assigned the operational task of systems analysis. The decision to investigate a system may evolve from a formal administrative request, a scheduled review of that system, or an analyst's observation.

Point 5   The collection of data represents one of the first tasks performed in a systems analysis. Four methods of collecting data for systems analysis are a review of organizational material, personal observations, personnel interviews, and a comparison to similar systems. The organization manual is often a good place to begin the analysis effort. Personal observations and personnel interviews give the analyst firsthand information on the functioning of any system. Systems comparisons enable the analyst to examine solutions to similar problems.

Point 6   Formats used to store data in files can be shown on record layout forms. Systems flowcharts can pictorially represent a series of operations involved in the processing of data. Symbols are used to represent specific operations in a procedure. A written narrative normally accompanies a systems flowchart.

Point 7   The detailed analysis of whether a new computer system and a major system revision are required is called a feasibility study. The feasi-

Case Study One

Computers Provide Another Form of Insurance

Because insurance agencies, like other small businesses, generate so much paperwork, many are computerizing. Two insurers who have converted to computers are the Maryland Casualty Insurance Co. of Baltimore and the Aviation Insurance Center, Inc. of Carbondale, Ill.

At one time, quoting rates and issuing policies at Maryland Casualty (MC) was a lengthy and involved process, requiring many phone calls among three or more agents for even the most basic policy. To handle the special peril policies that MC specializes in, an IBM software package called Commercial Policy Quote (CPQ) was purchased and incorporated into an IBM 5100 computer. The CPQ software allowed one agent to issue a policy in minutes without any phone calls. The CPQ software prepared all the necessary quotes.

The 5100 system and CPQ software let Maryland Casualty simplify its office procedures. The old, manual system required agents to read through bulky rate tables to develop policy premiums. The process took one to five people at least 4 hours. The computerized preparation of the same policy takes one person 2 hours or less.

Selecting the hardware (each national office has a CPQ system) and converting from the old manual system took MC months. MC management finally decided that the combination of equipment and readily available CPQ software met their immediate objectives of rapid conversion at each branch office at the lowest cost. Another consideration was the possible networking of the 5100 system into a distributed data processing system that could speed the entry of data to the corporate headquarters in Maryland from throughout the country. The new system allows for this kind of future expansion.

The implementation schedule called for the installation of a 5100 computer at one office, with a parallel test of the CPQ software and equipment. Once all bugs were worked out, the other systems were installed, which allowed for training of agents without a substantial change in customer services.

The new system provides faster access to quoted rates, simplifies computation of premiums, and offers better service to clients. Agents may now obtain policy and premium information from their local office and do not any longer have to go

bility committee accomplishing this study is normally composed of a top-level executive, departmental representatives, a senior systems analyst, and an outside consultant. The objectives of a feasibility study are to analyze the existing system, determine the need for a new computer, compile a list of the computer hardware needed for the proposed system, evaluate bids received from manufacturers, and devise a plan to implement the new system.

Point 8   System design usually starts with a definition of its outputs. This information enables the analysts to determine the inputs and data files required to support the system. The confirmation of I/O and storage formats lets them write program specifications for the necessary software.

Point 9   Once all aspects of a system have been individually certified, the total system can be assembled and tested. A parallel run tests the new system, using live data. The results of the new sys-

through corporate headquarters. Each branch 5100 system can prepare quotes. In competitive sales situations, rates are easily recomputed. The 5100 can also print sample policies. Agents believe the 5100 systems give them a real selling edge by freeing them from tedious manual calculations and letting them concentrate on selling.

Aviation Insurance Center, Inc. (AIC) has different needs. As independent agents and brokers, they face ever higher costs which erode profits. AIC must also monitor their clients to ensure prompt service and policy retention. AIC insures over 300 aircraft, from private jets to cropdusters. Both Bob and Bernadette Zimmer, who run AIC, believe that without their IBM System 34 computer, they would have been buried in paperwork. The 34 has let AIC keep its employees and double its sales.

Management felt that converting to a computerized broker system was imperative for reducing paperwork and helping brokers on every aspect of selling. CRTs give agents access to policy information and rates, and they can offer prompt service to clients and prospects.

When prospects call AIC, an agent requests policy information and records it with an online CRT. The system quickly estimates a policy cost for the customer. The system can be told to pre-pare a personalized letter for a client, as well as a policy, a statement, and mailing labels for correspondence.

The System 34 offers other features. It will generate reports advising agents to contact prospects who did not accept a quote or call AIC. It can prepare personal diaries for salespeople on overdue policies, upcoming due dates, renewal dates, and sales leads. The old, manual system offered none of these services. The cost of a staff to provide such services would probably pay for the computer's installation and service.

The new system has improved both sales and customer relations. Before, the entire AIC staff was very pressured. Getting data was an arduous task. The new system records all transactions and prepares monthly accounting reports and premium notices.

The system also prepares management reports on market penetration, sales by state or region, budget forecasting, competitor quotes, and claim responses. This type of data, not previously available, helps the company monitor its performance and keeps it competitive. The computer has allowed AIC to eliminate unwarranted overtime, to increase operating efficiency, to open new markets, and to increase profits.

Consider this . . .

Systems conversions not only change data processing procedures, but how a business operates. Could a system alter a company's marketing approach or distribution of information to its customers?

---

tem are compared with those of the old system. When both are correct, the new system can assume total operational control. In addition to the parallel run, other systems conversion approaches include the phased conversion, pilot conversion, and crash conversion.

Point 10 Before adopting a computer system, management must evaluate several factors: the best data processing approach for the organization, the type of CPU required, whether to rent or buy a system, necessary peripheral devices, software requirements, availability of maintenance, and staff needs. Data on all these considerations must be compiled and carefully evaluated.

When planning for the installation of a new computer system, staffing computer personnel is *not* a management consideration although their training is.

Glossary

Accounts payable system   A business system that maintains records of all the individuals and organizations to which money is owed.

Accounts receivable system   A business system that monitors the individuals and organizations from which money must be collected.

Business system   A combination of policies, personnel, equipment, and data processing facilities, operating according to a defined set of procedures, which coordinates the activities of a business organization.

Crash conversion   A systems conversion technique where the new system replaces the old system immediately with no overlapping period.

Feasibility committee   The committee assigned the task of accomplishing a feasibility study.

Feasibility study   A detailed analysis of the factors related to the purchase of a new computer and/or the modification of an existing system.

Inventory system   A business system designed to maintain a status on the current level of, and adjustments made to, an inventory.

Manual system   A noncomputerized method of processing data.

Organization manual   A manual that contains documents describing the day-to-day operation of an organization.

Payroll system   A business system which monitors the entire processing of an employee payroll.

Personnel system   A business system that maintains complete files of data on the employees that work in an organization.

Phased conversion   A systems conversion technique in which new subsystems gradually replace the old systems.

Pilot conversion   A systems conversion technique in which one new subsystem is completely developed prior to all others.

Program specifications   The detailed list of specifications which describe the software required to support the processing of data in a system.

Prooflisting   The systems output which is a printout of all the data stored in a file of a secondary storage device.

Record layout form   A form used to depict the contents of the records making up a data file.

Subsystem   Any of the smaller components of a system.

System   An organized way of accomplishing a stated goal or objective.

Systems analysis   A careful examination of all aspects of a business system.

Systems flowchart   A pictorial representation of a series of operations composing a system or a procedure.

Written narrative   A statement-by-statement breakdown of all operations related to the completion of a procedure.

Discussion Questions

1 List and discuss the objectives of the following:
  a   A business system
  b   A feasibility study

2 Briefly discuss the four techniques of collecting data for a systems analysis project. In addition, do the following:
  a   List other sources of information concerning a business system.

b Prepare a list of questions you might ask an employee during an interview to uncover information related to his or her job. As an exercise, interview parents, friends, and coworkers about their jobs and ways of improving their handling of data. Compile these comments in report form.

3 Visit local computer manufacturers and collect information on the types of business systems their equipment can accommodate. Many manufacturers have pamphlets on specific systems that have been adapted to their computer systems.

4 Briefly discuss each of the five fundamental business systems. If possible, cite examples of each type of system, drawn from your own experience.

5 Discuss the purpose and composition of the feasibility committee. What members would you consider adding or eliminating from that group?

6 Discuss the reasons for designing a system's outputs before its inputs and files. Could the reverse order be feasible? Discuss that point of view.

7 Using the following card formats, design a record format that could be used to store this data in a file.

	Card 1		Card 2
Card Columns	Field Name	Card Columns	Field Name
1–8	Part Number	1–8	Part Number
9–28	Description of Part	9–34	Vendor Name
29–35	Quantity in Inventory	35–59	Address
36–42	Quantity on Order	60–72	City
43–48	Order Date	73–74	State
49–55	Delivery Date	75–79	Zip
56–64	Purchase Order No.	80	(Coded as a "2")
65–79	(Blank)		
80	(Coded as a "1")		

Describe the card formats on a multiple card layout form and the storage format on a record layout form. Design an output format that could be used for a prooflisting of the data written into the inventory file. Show this output format on a printer spacing chart.

8 Draw the systems flowcharts representing the flow of data described by the written narratives that follow.

Narrative 1:

a Precoded inventory cards are removed from parts as they are issued from inventory.

b The stock clerk collects these cards and at the end of each week sends the batch to the computer center.

c Inventory cards received have control data keypunched onto them.

d The completed cards are batch processed against an online inventory file and stored on disk. The program used is INVUP6.

e The outputs produced from processing are

(1) A listing of parts issued from inventory that week.

(2) A listing of the complete current inventory.

(3) A listing of parts that must be purchased because their inventory levels have fallen below their reorder point.

f All reports are sent to the inventory department. The inventory cards are retained for 1 week in a temporary data processing card file.

Narrative 2:

a Requests for new employees are coded on a personnel request form.

b When received, this form is checked and verified by a personnel clerk.

c Data on the form is transmitted over a telephone line to the main computer, using an online terminal.

d The computer accesses an online file of potential applicants and telecommunicates the information back to the report clerk, via a hard-copy terminal.

e Using data from the printout, the clerk types a letter to each of the individuals listed, requesting that he or she contact the company for a job interview.

9 Discuss the five items that should appear in the final documentation of a system.

10 It is often stated that a personnel system is really an inventory system of people. Take a position for or against this statement and defend it.

11 Discuss the differences among phased, pilot, and crash systems conversion techniques.

12 If you were a manager considering the purchase of a computer system, what criteria would you use for deciding? Compare your criteria to the seven questions asked in Section 14.6. Are they similar? How would you defend your criteria?

Summary Test

_____ **1** A system is an organized way of achieving a goal without any consideration of the people involved.

_____ **2** A manual system excludes the use of people and computers in its operation.

_____ **3** The feasibility committee is responsible for devising a plan to implement both the new computer hardware and the proposed system.

_____ **4** An accounts payable system monitors the businesses that must pay a firm money, whereas an accounts receivable system monitors the organizations that are to receive the firm's payments.

_____ **5** A cost comparison is not essential to management's evaluation of proposed computer hardware, because they must accept the feasibility committee's recommendation.

_____ **6** Once a new system is completed, no subsequent evaluation of its performance is undertaken.

_____ **7** A parallel run involves the concurrent operation of the existing system and the new system.

_____ **8** Analysts can gain all the knowledge they need regarding a system from the organization manual.

_____ **9** During the analysis phase, fellow analysts can provide insights into solutions that have been applied to similar systems problems.

_____ **10** The final documentation of a system must clearly and concisely present all aspects of the newly designed system.

_____ **11** The training of employees destined to interact with a system must be part of a design strategy.

_____ **12** The writing of program specifications which define the types of programs employed in a system, precedes the start of the feasibility study.

_____ **13** The detailed information necessary to support an analyst's initial evaluation of a system can be gathered in a feasibility study.

_____ **14** The outside consultant on the feasibility committee must concur with all decisions reached.

_____ **15** The feasibility committee should compile a list of needed computer equipment immediately prior to the analysis of the system in question.

_____ **16** The document listing all procedures and regulations that generally govern an organization is the:

    a   personal policy book
    b   organization manual
    c   administrative policy manual
    d   procedures log

_____ **17** The initiation of a systems investigation may result from:

    a   a manager's formal request
    b   an analyst's investigation
    c   a scheduled systems' review
    d   all of the above

_____ **18** The fields composing a file's record format which will be stored on tape are detailed on a:

    a   multiple card layout form   **b**   tape spacing chart
    c   record layout form   **d**   all of the above

_____ **19** A statement-by-statement description of a procedure is detailed in a:

    a   procedure's log   **b**   written narrative
    c   systems flowchart   **d**   record layout

_____ **20** Samples of the data written onto a tape or disk file may be recorded in a report form described as a:

    a   printer spacing form   **b**   softcopy ledger
    c   manager's run report   **d**   prooflisting

_____ **21** The first items defined for a new system are its:

    a   inputs   **b**   processing requirements
    c   outputs   **d**   file formats

_____**22** On the feasibility committee, department representatives serve as:

a direct users of the new system
b liaison to their departments
c ready sources of information
d all of the above

_____**23** The systems conversion technique of totally removing the existing system and immediately implementing the new system is called a:

a	crash conversion	**b**	phased conversion
c	pilot conversion	**d**	parallel run

_____**24** A consideration evaluated by management when planning to convert to a computer system is:

a	CPU size and speed	**b**	available software
c	vendor maintenance	**d**	all of the above

_____**25** Management's decision to rent a computer system may be based upon:

a tax advantages
b desire to avoid a large one-time payment
c operational flexibility in changing hardware
d all of the above

Summary Test Answers

1 F	2 F	3 T	4 F	5 F
6 F	7 T	8 F	9 T	10 T
11 T	12 F	13 T	14 F	15 F
16 B	17 D	18 C	19 B	20 D
21 C	22 D	23 A	24 D	25 D

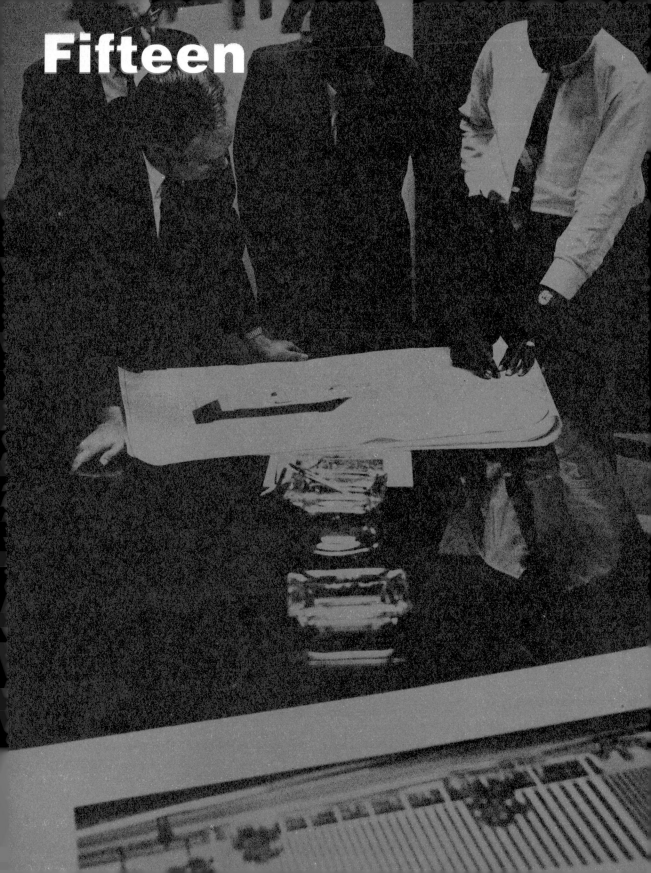

Fifteen

Documentation of a System

FIGURE 15.1 The documentation of systems activities is performed at all levels of the project. Sound documentation provides a basis of evaluation for the existing system and a starting point for design of a new system. (*Magnum Photos.*)

Purpose of This Chapter

This chapter continues our discussion of systems analysis and design by examining systems documentation in greater detail. The first section of the chapter presents a general introduction to the material contained in a systems documentation report. This documentation must include an analysis of the existing system, a problem definition, and a description of the newly designed system. We discuss the contents of each of these major parts of the report.

The second section of the chapter presents a practical example of a systems documentation report written for a payroll system. This example shows how an actual report might appear if presented to management. The report describes the existing and the new system, including outputs, inputs, storage layouts, and systems flowcharts. Comparisons of tentative costs for both systems are also provided. Thus, a representative sample of a systems documentation format is presented.

After completing this chapter, you should be able to

- Discuss the purpose of systems documentation
- Describe the contents of a problem definition
- Understand how the descriptions offered by a systems overview, objectives, constraints, outputs, processing, inputs, feedback, controls, and costs are used in the documentation of a system
- Understand the sample systems documentation report
- Understand the following terms:

Backup file	Feedback
Constraint	Problem definition
Control	Systems overview
Exception reporting	

Introduction

Though the systems staff is intimately aware of the overall care and the attention to detail required in the analysis and design of a system, other personnel may not have this understanding. Corporate management especially may have little knowledge of the painstaking care exercised in the development and completion of a systems project. They judge a project only by the systems documentation with which they are presented. Therefore, this set of documents must be carefully prepared and must fully describe the new system.

The completeness, clarity, and accuracy of the systems documentation powerfully influence management's acceptance of a project. Many good systems have been poorly received because documentation failed to present them properly and emphasize their fine points. Conversely, a mediocre system may receive managerial acclaim because of superior documentation. Well-prepared systems documentation is readable. You cannot expect a manager who does not understand the function of a system to support it.

Before entering into the discussion of systems documentation, we must point out that the sample documentation presented here represents formats used in data processing organizations. The actual format used by a systems staff will reflect the needs and past practices of that organization. The systems documentation here generally introduces a format which you may encounter.

15.1 Components of Systems Documentation

Systems documentation represents the collective efforts of the systems staff in their analysis, design, and development of a new system. The documentation should clearly define the overall nature of the system. The systems documentation is divided into three parts:

1   An analysis of the existing system
2   A problem definition
3   The design of the new system

Each part describes a specific facet of the system.

This portion of the systems documentation report presents an in-depth analysis of the existing system. This discussion should include

1   An overview of the system
2   The managerial objectives and constraints under which the system is operating
3   An analysis and description of the outputs, inputs, processing, and storage formats used in the system
4   A development of cost factors related to the existing system's operation

Analysis of the Existing System

The **systems overview** offers both a pictorial and a written description of the inputs and outputs in the current system. It shows the input and output documents used in processing data. Because each I/O document is defined by its name, the reader can determine the types of data generated. The systems overview is designed to provide a general introduction to the existing system and enable the reader to develop an understanding of its overall purpose.

A list of the stated objectives of the existing system provides a review of the system's intended function. This list identifies the general goals of the system, and the efficiency of the system is judged by these goals. Often when a system is not meeting its intended goals, an analysis may be in order.

Thus, if the stated objectives of a payroll system are the payment and maintenance of payroll-related records, and the system cannot properly account for vacation or sick days, then it must be considered for analysis. Similarly, an inventory system that cannot account for damaged merchandise returned to manufacturers cannot meet its goal of monitoring the status of an inventory and may need revision.

Equally important are the constraints applied to a system. A **constraint** is a specific limitation or condition within which a system must operate. Time, budgets, and computer equipment are types of constraints that affect a system. For example, an accounts payable system that must pay vendors within 15 days to gain discounts and must operate within a monthly budget of $25,000 is limited by those constraints. The same system might be forced to function with existing computer hardware, because management has limited the purchase of new equipment. Hardware and software constraints are just as restrictive as monetary constraints. During their analysis, analysts must fully understand the constraints that affect a system's ability to handle data.

The descriptions of outputs, inputs, processing, and storage formats define the fundamental elements of a system. Each aspect of I/O, storage, and processing activities details the exact nature of how data is processed through a system. Many of the computer-related forms previously discussed are employed for these purposes. Multiple card layouts, record (storage) layouts, printer spacing charts, and systems flowcharts pictorially represent a system's capacity to process data and provide useful information.

Many analysts collect duplicates of all forms used in the existing system and include them in the systems documentation. This simple chore saves them the effort of redrawing hardcopy outputs. Visual outputs should be described on a printer spacing chart. Data entered via a terminal should be detailed in a written narrative or any pictorial format the analyst deems appropriate. Procedures used in handling data should be noted in systems flowcharts. These diagrams will help management understand the system's purpose.

Controls in the existing system that prevent the improper or fraudulent use of data, supplies, or money must be detailed. The control procedures indicate a system's level of security. Often these descriptions provide initial points of investigation for the analyst and lead to the discovery of flaws in a system.

Controls are essential to any system in which dollar amounts, checks, or monetary exchanges are handled. Management will always carefully examine the controls built into payroll, accounts receivable, accounts payable, and related systems. Examples of the types of controls employed in a system are:

1 The necessity of having a supervisor approve all payments on exchanges of merchandise in excess of $10. All payments over $10 will be sent to the customer's home address in the form of a bank check.

2 The rule that payroll checks must be processed twice. Totals in each run are to be compared with the payroll supervisor's tabulation of the total payroll amount. All checks must be picked up and signed for personally by each employee. The total number of employees receiving checks must match the total number of checks processed. Both amounts must match exactly with the number of checks processed by the bank handling the payroll funds. All discrepancies between these amounts must be accounted for and approved by the controller.

The above procedures are only selected examples of the many controls used in systems. A common misconception is that only computer-related controls are needed. Although the computer does the bulk of processing, someone must audit its performance and use manual procedures in doing so.

These regular manual checks monitor the system's performance and may include the processing and verification of accounts due or payable, checks cashed and issued, credit checks and charge account adjustments, payroll vouchers, inventory and purchase invoices, and personnel data. Generally, these periodic audits are distributed among the accounting staff so that no one person always performs them. Although manual procedures are tedious, they are vital. They may often uncover fraudulent expense claims, improperly computed taxes, improperly prepared vouchers or bills, and misappropriated checks. They are instrumental in properly closing the books at the end of an accounting period. A balance of both manual and computerized checking procedures should be incorporated into any system. Controls help the analyst judge whether a system is performing satisfactorily.

The last and often most vital aspect of a system's documentation is a description of its operating costs. For many managers costs denote a system's true efficiency, independent of all other factors. Excessive costs offer one of the strongest arguments for redesigning a system. Although they may overlook the fine points of systems design and analysis, most management personnel are keenly aware of budgets and the necessity to adhere to them. Thus, the development of costs must be accurate and truly representative of the system. The decision to commit an organization's resources to a systems project may rest solely on the economic factors involved.

ALBANY COMPUTERS
HELP CUT RELIEF FRAUD

Systems projects often originate when administrators want to solve financial problems. The article below discusses New York State's effort to develop a system to identify people who fraudulently receive duplicate welfare payments, a practice that costs taxpayers over $10 million per year.

Any study must carefully balance the administrative objectives of eliminating fraud and tightening control of welfare payments against the individual's right to privacy. The problem of fraud came to light after an analysis determined that about 7000 of New York's 372,000 recipients of aid to dependent children had higher incomes than officially acceptable.

ALBANY, Feb. 11—A project using computers to weed out fraud by matching the Social Security numbers of welfare recipients with those of wage earners will save the state, local and Federal governments $10 million a year, the state's Social Services Department said Thursday.

The results of the project—believed by the state to be the first to match welfare rolls with Federal Social Security records—come as the Legislature considers whether to require New York companies to report wage information to the state for a welfare-fraud detection system here.

"Privacy Safeguards" Promised

The legislative proposal has the strong support of Governor Carey, who made it part of his legislative program for this year, and is backed by legislative leaders in both houses. But it is drawing sharp criticism from civil-liberties groups, which fear possible abuse of another large accumulation of data on private citizens, and is meeting some resistance from businessmen, who do not want to have to file yet another set of forms with yet another government bureaucracy.

Barbara Blum, the Acting Social Services Commissioner, praised the system as a "tool which could greatly enhance" welfare-fraud control. She said that this system would have "strict privacy safeguards" to assure that, other than monitoring welfare and unemployment fraud, "there would be no other probing into the financial affairs of New Yorkers."

The Social Security matches cannot be continued, she said, because the Federal Government is switching to an annual wage-reporting requirement that would make the data too dated to be useful for this purpose.

A sample of the project's results noted that 7,000 of the state's 372,000 recipients of aid to families with dependent children had higher incomes than they should have had to receive the grants they were getting.

The state's program would include not only recipients of aid to families with dependent children—the largest welfare program—but also recipients of home relief and unemployment-insurance benefits.

Problem Definition   The specification of the costs related to a system's operation normally comes last in a systems analysis. With the description of the existing system complete, the report can focus on the major problems uncovered by the analysis. A brief description of the existing problems is compiled in a section of the system documentation called the **problem definition.** Point by point, the problem definition identifies major problem areas and provides information, developed through analysis, to support these claims.

The problem definition lists what is wrong with a system, defines all aspects of a system that need revision, and provides the rationale for such changes. Systems revisions often result from one or more of the following:

1 Changes in the laws governing data handled by a system
2 A desire to regain lost business or increase sales
3 The need for newer, more up-to-date information
4 Changes in management's goals and objectives for the system

A few years ago, the credit card industry made extensive changes after consumer protection legislation was passed. Methods of computing finance charges, assessing charge sales, and many other aspects of credit cards were governed by law. Accounts receivable systems involving charge cards had to be revised to conform to the new laws and avoid serious legal penalties.

Frequently, the need to remain competitive in the marketplace provides the incentive for systems revisions. A prime example of this can be seen in the airlines industry. The development of an online reservation system by one airline forced other airlines competing for the same market to develop their own systems of this type.

Management's desire for more timely information may result in a systems revision. The need for immediate inventory information may result in the replacement of a batch-processing system with an online inventory system. The online processing of data can provide management with the most current inventory status.

The switch from batch processing to online processing may also reflect a shift in managerial objectives and goals. Management's desire for current information may signal an attempt to either improve customer service or develop tighter controls over inventory costs. Remember that management's objectives virtually dictate the allocation of resources, including the computer, within the organization. Their wish to use the computer in support of a specific system must be honored.

The problem definition must detail problem areas in a system, as revealed by the analysis effort. The severity of the problems described will indicate the extent to which the existing system must be modified.

Design of the New System

The new system must be described in the same detail as the old system. All aspects of the new system must be carefully presented because only a few people will have a thorough knowledge of its function. Sufficient documentation can reduce the amount of uncertainty associated with the function of the new system. It can also reduce the number of errors and ease the adoption of new procedures.

The design section of the systems documentation packet will parallel the analysis portion of the report. The new system must be defined in terms of an overview, managerial objectives, constraints, outputs, inputs, storage formats, controls, and costs. Each component carefully defines an aspect of the new system.

Another item in the new system is feedback. **Feedback** represents the system's ability to evaluate its performance. An organization needs some vehicle to observe and rate the new system's operation and ensure that it is meeting its stated objectives. Feedback must be both immediate and long term. Immediate feedback can affect the daily operation of the system by recording and correcting minor problems as needed. Long-term feedback is obtained by evaluating the total system from 6 months to 2 years after its implementation. This scheduled review helps analysts eliminate rough spots and stabilize the system's operation. The review is also designed to assess the necessity of a major systems revision.

Questions that should be asked during the evaluation of a system include:

1 Is the system meeting its planned objectives and delivering the anticipated results?

2 Is the system providing the anticipated savings?

3 Has the new system been completely implemented and are users satisfied with the results?

4 Do employees need more training to interface more effectively with the new system?

5 Are the new system's inputs, outputs, and controls functioning and providing the necessary information?

6 Does management know about and support the system?

7 Has all the required documentation been prepared?

In answering these questions, analysts can evaluate the new system's performance and prepare recommendations for management. It is important to remember that the systems evaluation is continuous. A project is not finished once it is implemented. Auditing a system ensures that management receives timely and accurate information. Without feedback, a system could not respond to changes in an organization. A detailed schedule of planned systems' reviews is critical to an effective informational system.

GSA AUDITORS UNCOVER $95,000 ERROR

Systems audits are one way to check how effective a system's controls actually are. Auditors constantly look for loopholes which give people access to a system so that they can enter false data without being detected. These security violations can bankrupt an organization.

Because it handles vast amounts of federal funds, the General Services Administration (GSA) uses a variety of computerized audit techniques to monitor its computer financial systems and ferret out such loopholes. On a recent check of systems controls, GSA auditors were able to issue a $95,256 check to a fictitious vendor without the payment being recorded. A GSA report to the Senate documented this security problem and noted that the lack of adequate controls creates opportunities for other similar violations. The report detailed how the auditors were able to enter the GSA database, generate the $95,000 payment, and erase any record of the check. No subsequent audit trails, prepared specifically for the report, showed any record of the payment. Controls were clearly inadequate.

The episode raises several questions. How could such a vital financial system have been operationally approved without tests of control features revealing these deficiencies? Were the original safeguards bad, or did the controls become ineffective as the system changed? Were the controls sabotaged? Only an investigation can provide the answers.

Source of data: "Faulty DP Data Tricks GSA into $95,000 Payment," *Infosystems*, December 1979, p. 22.

The section describing the new system may contain any graphs, diagrams, or written explanations that the analysts consider useful. Graphs are often helpful in depicting the time necessary for developing a new system. Estimates of the time required to initiate a system help management plan ahead.

15.2 Documentation of a Payroll System

This section provides a sample of a systems documentation package in the format described above. The report presents the analysis of a payroll system and the proposed design for a new system. The systems documentation is presented as it would actually appear in a report to management.

<u>Systems Documentation--Payroll System</u>

<u>Table of Contents</u>

   I. Analysis of the Existing System
       A. Overview of the Existing Payroll System
       B. Objectives of the Existing Payroll System
       C. Constraints of the Existing System
       D. Outputs of the Existing System
       E. Processing in the Existing System
       F. Inputs to the Existing System
       G. Controls Employed in the Existing System
       H. Costs Related to the Existing System

  II. Problem Definition

III. Design of the New System
       A. Overview of the New System
       B. Objectives of the New System
       C. Constraints of the New System
       D. Outputs of the New System
       E. Processing in the New System
       F. Inputs Used in the New System
       G. Feedback for the New System
       H. Controls on the New System
       I. Costs for the New System

I. <u>Analysis</u> <u>of</u> <u>the</u> <u>Existing</u> <u>System</u>

   A. <u>Overview</u> <u>of</u> <u>the</u> <u>Existing</u> <u>Payroll</u> <u>System</u>

      Johnson Associates is a small business firm
      providing consulting and literary services to
      its customers. Currently, Johnson Associates
      employs 150 people full-time and upwards of 40
      people on a part-time basis, who are hired as
      needed. The existing payroll system offers a
      fundamental payroll system, involving only the
      deduction of federal taxes. A pictorial
      overview of the existing payroll follows.

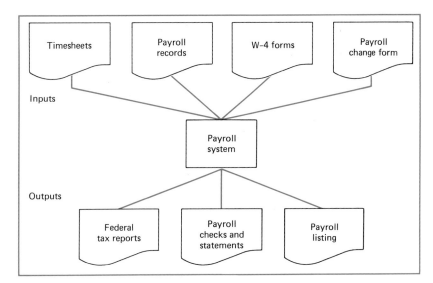

FIGURE 15.2 An overview of the existing system indicates that three types of outputs and four types of inputs are involved in the processing of payroll data.

   B. <u>Objectives</u> <u>of</u> <u>the</u> <u>Existing</u> <u>Payroll</u> <u>System</u>

      1. To provide a vehicle for the payment of all
         employees and the collection of federal taxes

      2. To maintain accurate records of the payments
         made to all employees and the updating of
         these records each pay period

      3. To maintain accurate and current records that
         comply with federal and state legislation

C. Constraints of the Existing System
1. All employees are paid biweekly, on alternate Thursdays.
2. Equipment used in the computation of the payroll includes
    a. Five desk calculators.
    b. One electrical accounting machine which employs a specialized form of magnetic tape.
    c. One offline printer.

    The accounting machine is employed to compute the payroll amounts for each employee. The offline printer is employed to actually print all checks and payroll-related outputs. Both devices have operated satisfactorily for the past year. The accounting machine has recently had mechanical problems, however.
3. All employees are required to take their vacation in August, when the company closes for 2 weeks.
4. Each full-time employee is entitled to 10 paid sick days annually.
5. Federal W-2 forms, indicating monies withheld from each employee's pay, must be issued by January 29.
6. An annual budget for these services is set at $70,000.
7. All employees are paid by check.

D. Outputs of the Existing System

The outputs of this system, listed above in the system overview, are the following:

1. Paychecks and Statements--All employees are paid by check on alternate Thursdays. Payroll checks and statements printed using the offline printer are illustrated below. The statement contains information relating to the current pay period and provides year-to-date totals of gross pay earned and federal and social security taxes withheld.

JOHNSON ASSOCIATES NO. 18076

PAY TO THE ORDER OF:

M. B. BELL $ **368.48

THREE HUNDRED SIXTY EIGHT AND FORTY SIX

BAY TRUST CONTROLLER

0628-715664 00036846

DETACH STATEMENT NO. 18076

M.B.BELL

STATEMENT OF DEDUCTIONS

EARNINGS	GROSS	FED. W/H	FICA	NET
CURRENT	477.25	72.57	36.20	368.48
YEAR-TO-DATE	7663.50	1439.29	717.60	5506.61

JOHNSON ASSOCIATES-STATEMENT-DO NOT CASH

RETAIN FOR YOUR RECORDS

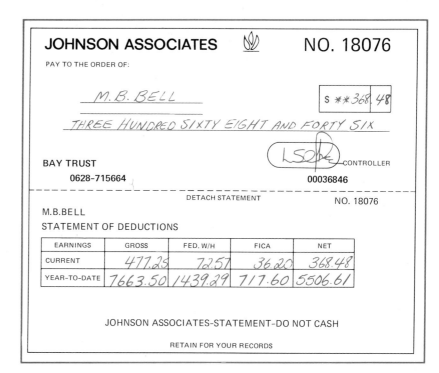

FIGURE 15.3 The check and statement currently used by Johnson Associates to pay all employees.

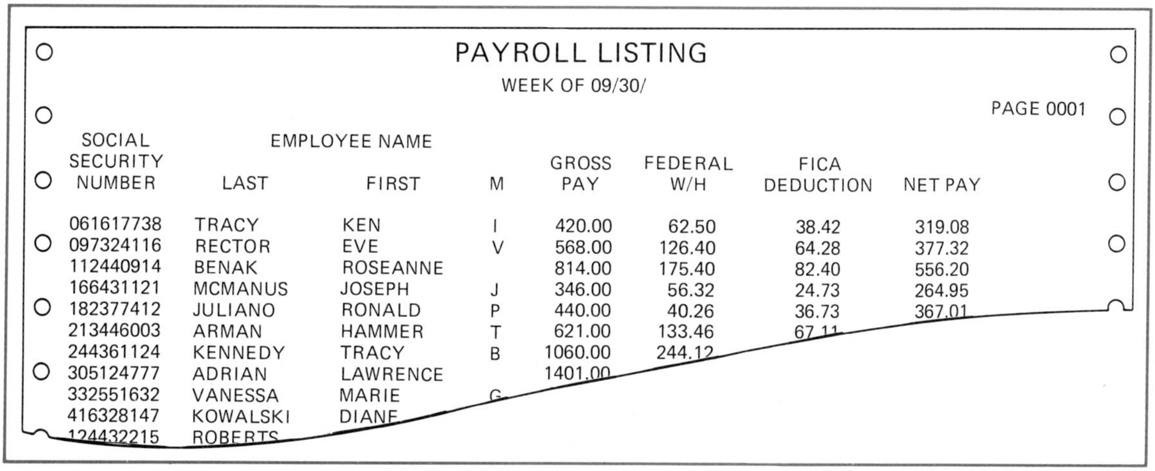

2. Payroll Listing--The payroll listing is a printed document which contains data related to each employee paid during that pay period. The listing contains each employee's name, social security number, gross pay, federal withholding tax, FICA deductions, and net pay. In this output, employees are listed in ascending order by social security number. A sample of the payroll listing follows.

FIGURE 15.4 The payroll listing for all employees in the existing payroll system.

PAYROLL LISTING

WEEK OF 09/30/

PAGE 0001

SOCIAL SECURITY NUMBER	EMPLOYEE NAME LAST	FIRST	M	GROSS PAY	FEDERAL W/H	FICA DEDUCTION	NET PAY
061617738	TRACY	KEN	I	420.00	62.50	38.42	319.08
097324116	RECTOR	EVE	V	568.00	126.40	64.28	377.32
112440914	BENAK	ROSEANNE		814.00	175.40	82.40	556.20
166431121	MCMANUS	JOSEPH	J	346.00	56.32	24.73	264.95
182377412	JULIANO	RONALD	P	440.00	40.26	36.73	367.01
213446003	ARMAN	HAMMER	T	621.00	133.46	67.11	
244361124	KENNEDY	TRACY	B	1060.00	244.12		
305124777	ADRIAN	LAWRENCE		1401.00			
332551632	VANESSA	MARIE	G				
416328147	KOWALSKI	DIANE					
124432215	ROBERTS						

FIGURE 15.5 These
two forms are required
by federal tax regula-
tions. The W-2 form pro-
vides annual earning
data for each employee.
The 941 form provides a
quarterly summary of
employee withholding
taxes.

3. Federal Tax Reports—Payroll tax information must be made available to both the individual employee and the federal government. Employees must annually receive a W–2 form indicating earnings information which will be used in the computation of their personal income tax. Every 3 months the Internal Revenue Service must receive a 941 form which lists the federal taxes withheld from all employees and a check equal to that amount. Currently, both forms are manually prepared by payroll clerks. The W–2 form is prepared annually during the month of January, whereas work on the 941s must begin 2 weeks prior to the end of each quarter. Copies of both forms follow.

FIGURE 15.5 These two forms are required by federal tax regulations. The W-2 form provides annual earning data for each employee. The 941 form provides a quarterly summary of employee withholding taxes.

Wage and Tax Statement 19

For Official Use Only

Type or print EMPLOYER'S name, address, ZIP code and Federal identifying number.

Copy A For Internal Revenue Service Center

Employer's State identifying number

21 ☐

| Employee's social security number | 1 Federal income tax withheld | 2 Wages, tips, and other compensation | 3 FICA employee tax withheld | 4 Total FICA wages |

Name ▶

Type or print Employee's name, address, and ZIP code below. (Name must aline with arrow)

5 Was employee covered by a qualified pension plan, etc.?	6 *	7 *
8 State or local tax withheld	9 State or local wages	10 State or locality
11 State or local tax withheld	12 State or local wages	13 State or locality

* See instructions on back of Copy D.

Form W–2   See instructions on Form W–3 and back of Copy D.   Department of the Treasury—Internal Revenue Service

---

Form **941**
(Rev. April 1978)
Department of the Treasury
Internal Revenue Service

Employer's Quarterly Federal Tax Return

1 First Quarter Only.—Number of employees (except household) employed in the pay period that includes March 12th . . . . ▶

2 Total wages and tips subject to withholding, plus other compensation . . . . ⟶

3 Total income tax withheld from wages, tips, annuities, gambling, etc. (see instructions) . . . .

4 Adjustment of withheld income tax for preceding quarters of calendar year . . . .

5 Adjusted total, of income tax withheld . . . . ⟶

6 Taxable FICA wages paid . . . . $................ multiplied by 12.1%=TAX . .

7 Taxable tips reported . . . . $................ multiplied by 6.05%=TAX . .

8 Total FICA taxes (add lines 6 and 7) . . . . ⟶

9 Adjustment of FICA taxes (see instructions) . . . .

10 Adjusted total of FICA taxes . . . . ⟶

11 Total taxes (add lines 5 and 10) . . . . ⟶

Deposit period ending:
Overpayment from previous quarter. . . . .

| I. Tax liability for period | II. Date of deposit | III. Amount deposited |

E. Processing in the Existing System

This section of the documentation describes the processing used in the system to produce the outputs previously discussed. Written narratives will be used to complement the systems flowcharts in selected cases.

1. Preparation of Paychecks and Statements

a. Payroll data in the form of timesheets is received from each supervisor. This data is manually checked and verified by a payroll clerk.

b. Corrected payroll data is keyed into the electrical accounting machine on an individual-employee basis, in ascending order by social security number. This data is processed against previous payroll data stored on magnetic tape using program PAYUP. The original unprocessed tape is referred to as the old master payroll tape and catalogued in the DP library.

c. The updated master payroll tape is produced by this processing and contains current payroll data, year-to-date earnings, and deductions for employees.

d. The updated tape is processed through an offline printer to produce the actual checks and statements. Data drawn from this tape is printed on both outputs.

e. Completed checks and statements are sent to Payroll, where they will be validated prior to distribution. The updated master payroll tape will be retained in a DP file until the processing of the next payroll. Then it becomes the old master payroll tape and is used for input.

The flowchart depicting this processing, as well as the record layout form detailing the storage format of the master payroll tape, follow.

FIGURE 15.6 The record layout of the payroll record used to maintain payroll data for each employee.

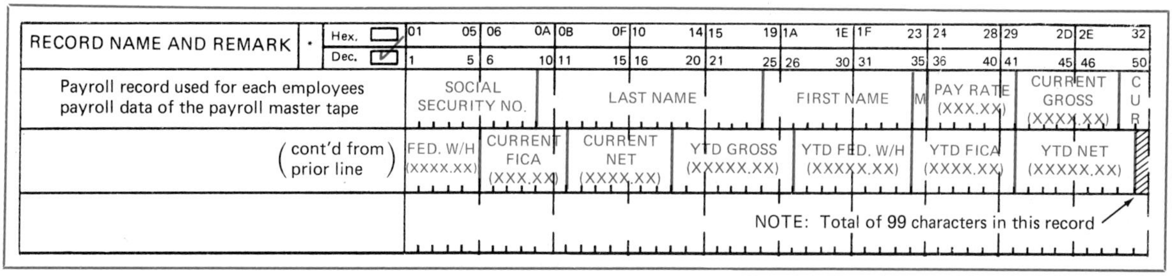

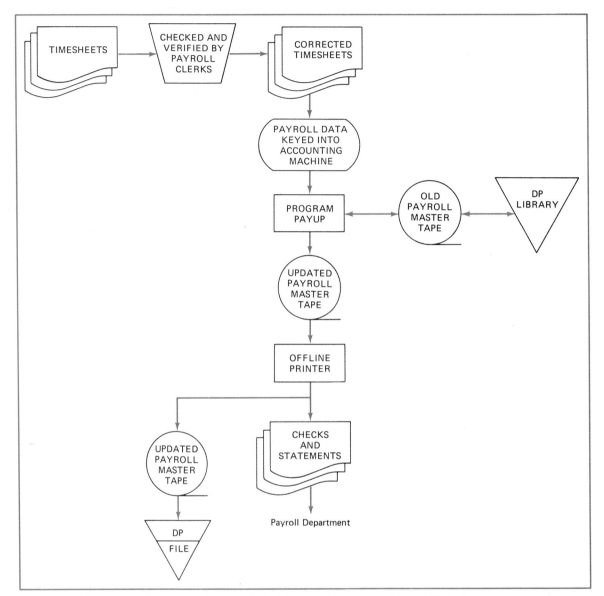

FIGURE 15.7 The systems flowchart depicting the processing of payroll data to produce employee checks and statements.

2. <u>Preparation</u> <u>of</u> <u>the</u> <u>Payroll</u> <u>Listing</u>
   a. The updated master payroll tape is taken from its DP file and processed through the offline printer.
   b. The result of processing is the payroll listing, which is sent to Payroll. The updated master payroll tape is then returned to its DP file.

The flowchart depicting this processing is presented in the diagram that follows.

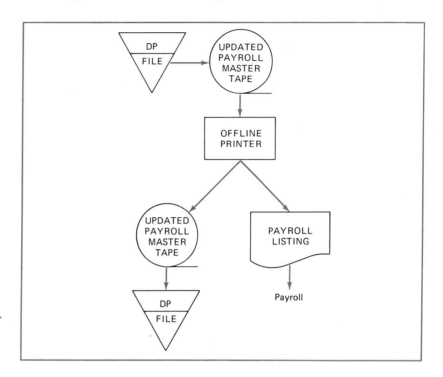

FIGURE 15.8 The preparation and processing of the payroll listing in the existing system.

3. <u>Preparation of Federal Tax Reports</u>
   These forms are manually prepared by payroll clerks immediately prior to their due dates. Payroll data is drawn from the payroll listings, which are retained in the Payroll area. Both the W-2 and the 941 forms are typed by the two payroll clerks. W-2 forms are mailed to each employee's home, while the 941 forms are sent to the nearest IRS office.

4. <u>Monitoring of Sick Days</u>
   Each full-time employee is entitled to 10 paid sick days per year, as of January 1. The use of sick days is recorded by the individual supervisor on the employee's timesheet. When the timesheets are received, a payroll clerk records the number of sick days taken on the individual's payroll record. When an employee exceeds the limit of 10 days, subsequent sick days are taken at the employee's expense. Sick days not used may be converted into a cash bonus at the end of the calendar year. Sick days may not be accrued from year to year. Part-time employees receive no sick days.

F. <u>Inputs</u> <u>to</u> <u>the</u> <u>Existing</u> <u>System</u>

The following inputs are employed in the payroll system:

1. <u>Timesheets</u>—Employee timesheets are prepared by each area supervisor. The names of the employees are written on the timesheet in ascending numerical order by social security number. The total number of hours worked that week, overtime hours worked, sick days used, days of absence without pay, and remarks by the supervisor are items of payroll data included on the timesheet. A copy of a completed timesheet is shown below.

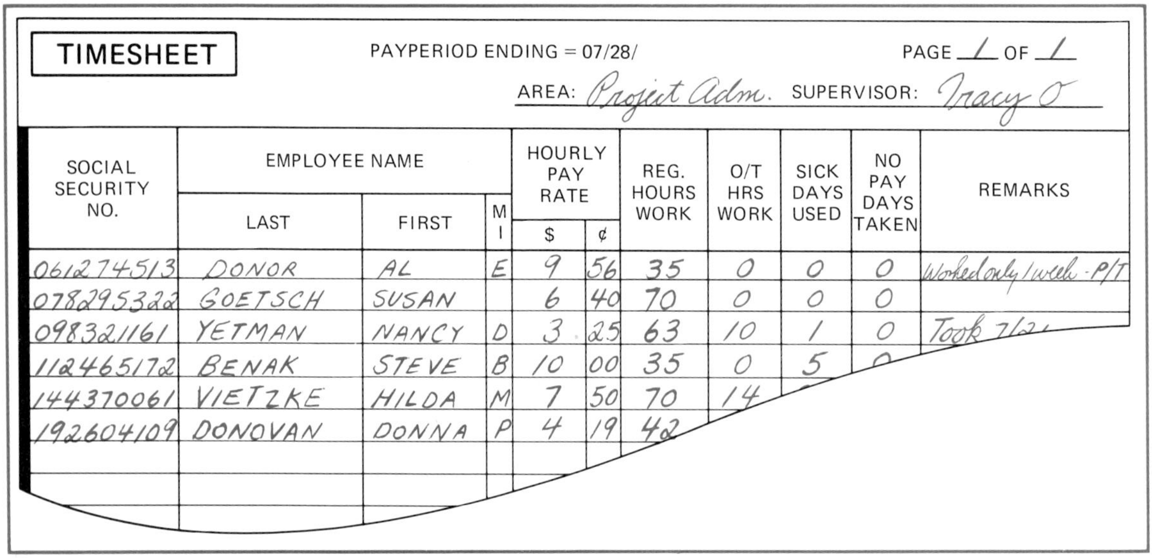

TIMESHEET		PAYPERIOD ENDING = 07/28/							PAGE _1_ OF _1_	
		AREA: *Project Adm.*				SUPERVISOR: *Tracy O*				
SOCIAL SECURITY NO.	EMPLOYEE NAME			HOURLY PAY RATE		REG. HOURS WORK	O/T HRS WORK	SICK DAYS USED	NO PAY DAYS TAKEN	REMARKS
	LAST	FIRST	M I	$	¢					
061274513	DONOR	AL	E	9	56	35	0	0	0	Worked only 1 week - P/T
078295322	GOETSCH	SUSAN		6	40	70	0	0	0	
098321161	YETMAN	NANCY	D	3	25	63	10	1	0	Took 7/21
112465172	BENAK	STEVE	B	10	00	35	0	5	0	
144370061	VIETZKE	HILDA	M	7	50	70	14			
192604109	DONOVAN	DONNA	P	4	19	42				

FIGURE 15.9 The timesheet used in the current payroll system. Note that the biweekly payroll is reflected in the total number of hours worked (2 weeks at 35 hours per week). Thus, 70 hours is the total number of hours for the normal employee work period.

2. <u>Payroll</u> <u>Change</u> <u>Form</u>—Changes in an employee's payroll status are recorded on a standard memo form sent to the payroll supervisor. The memo will be placed in the employee's payroll record. Both the payroll clerk and the employee's immediate supervisor will record this change in their pay records. Because a standard company memo is used, a copy of this form is not included.

3. <u>Payroll</u> <u>Records</u>—Payroll data for each employee is maintained in a payroll record. This form is used to monitor an employee's payroll history and maintain his or her annual payroll statistics. These records are retained for a total of 6 years. A sample payroll record follows.

069-33-4108 Darkski, Tony							

QRTLY. FED. W/H		QUART. FICA		JOB HISTORY			PROMOTION DATA
				DATE	CURRENT JOB		
4/1	639.26	4/1	264.32	2/1/61	Drafting Clerk		Works hard, slow
7/1	1278.52	7/1	480.75	8/91	Draftsman		but good. Reliable,
							conscientious. Promoted
T O T		T O T					for work on Proj #1063.

SICK DAY USAGE		PAYROLL DATA		FICA CONTRIBUTIONS	
DATE USED	AMT. REMAIN'G	YEAR	ANNUAL GROSS	YEAR	AMOUNT
3/9	9	1976	8906 –	1976	462.69
4/20	8	1977	10200 –	1977	512.08
4/28	7	1978	11000	1978	563.47
				1979	603.45
					711.57

FIGURE 15.10 A portion of the employee payroll record prepared for each employee. The employee's name and social security number appear on the tab of the folder (filed in personnel records) for easy identification.

4. Employee Withholding Form (W-4)—Federal tax regulations require that each employee file a W-4 form indicating the number of deductions to be used when computing federal withholding taxes. A copy of the W-4 form follows.

FIGURE 15.11 A copy of the employee withholding form, W-4.

Form **W-4**
(Rev. May 1977)
Department of the Treasury
Internal Revenue Service

Employee's Withholding Allowance Certificate
(Use for Wages Paid After May 31, 1977)
This certificate is for income tax withholding purposes only. It will remain in effect until you change it. If you claim exemption from withholding, you will have to file a new certificate on or before April 30 of next year.

Type or print your full name

Your social security number

Home address (number and street or rural route)

Marital Status
☐ Single ☐ Married
☐ Married, but withhold at higher Single rate

City or town, State, and ZIP code

Note: If married, but legally separated, or spouse is a nonresident alien, check the single block.

1 Total number of allowances you are claiming . . . .
2 Additional amount, if any, you want deducted from each pay (if your employer agrees) . . . . $
3 I claim exemption from withholding (see instructions). Enter "Exempt" . . . .

Under the penalties of perjury, I certify that the number of withholding exemptions and allowances claimed on this certificate does not exceed the number to which I am entitled. If claiming exemption from withholding, I certify that I incurred no liability for Federal income tax for last year and that I anticipate that I will incur no liability for Federal income tax for this year.

Signature ▶ . . . . Date ▶ . . . . , 19 . . . . .

For Company Payroll information, please supply the additonal information: Date of Birth . . . . Sex: ☐ Male ☐ Female

— Detach Along This Line — — — — — — — — — — — — — — —

G. <u>Controls</u> <u>Employed</u> <u>in</u> <u>the</u> <u>Existing</u> <u>System</u>

In this payroll system, controls have been applied to four specific areas:

1. <u>Payroll</u> <u>Changes</u>—All changes in an employee's payroll status must be approved by the controller.

2. <u>Paychecks</u>—Prenumbered checks are issued by the payroll supervisor, prior to their processing, in batches of 50 checks. After processing, the number of checks printed are counted. The number of checks used must match the total number of employees paid. Discrepancies must be noted and verified in writing by the payroll supervisor before the payroll may be released for distribution. Unused checks are returned to the payroll supervisor and locked in a cabinet.

3. <u>Limits</u> <u>on</u> <u>Check</u> <u>Amounts</u>—All checks are personally signed by the controller, after the payroll supervisor has verified the amount of each check. All check amounts in excess of $500 are individually recomputed to ensure their accuracy and accountability.

4. <u>Batch</u> <u>Totals</u>—The total payroll amount is computed by the controller and payroll supervisor through the addition of each check. These totals should match the summary total produced by the accounting machine immediately after its processing of the payroll.

H. <u>Costs</u> <u>Related</u> <u>to</u> <u>the</u> <u>Existing</u> <u>System</u>

The monthly costs for the existing payroll system are as follows:

Equipment rental	
Offline printer	$ 200.00
Electrical accounting machine	450.00
Supplies	500.00
Payroll supervisor	1800.00
Payroll clerks (2 @ $1000 ea.)	2000.00
Total	$4950.00
Overhead	800.00
Total	$5750.00
Avg. overtime expense (10%)	575.00
Monthly total cost	$6325.00

The actual monthly cost for the payroll system is $6325, which means an annual cost of $75,900. The amount of overtime has been increasing by approximately 5 percent over the past year. The anticipated inflation rate is 10 percent per year for the entire budget. It is estimated that in less than three years, expenses related to this system will exceed $100,000.

II. Problem Definition

An analysis of the existing system and the objectives expressed by management reveals the following problem areas:

A. The existing payroll system is exceeding the budget by about $6000, and future cost overruns are estimated to grow by 10 percent. One of the reasons for exceeding the budget is overtime resulting from the preparation of payroll data, W-2 forms, and 941 forms and the overall inefficiency of the entire payroll system.

B. The electrical accounting machine and offline printer duplicate services. A computational device which can process payroll data, update employee payroll records, and print all payroll-related outputs would be highly desirable. The elimination of the offline printer could save $200 per month. A computer system that could provide equivalent services must be considered as an alternative.

C. The initiation of a state income tax requires that the payroll system maintains records of these deductions. The current system is not equipped to handle the processing of state taxes. The payroll supervisor estimates that an additional clerk is needed to handle the computation and recording of these new taxes, at an additional annual cost of $10,000. The new state deduction will necessitate the revision of the payroll listing.

D. Management desires to reduce or maintain the same number of payroll personnel. They feel that a new computer system might provide a trade-off to hiring additional clerks. It is felt that an additional clerk will not speed the processing of the payroll and will further complicate the existing system.

E. The manual preparation of W-2 and 941 forms is time-consuming, expensive, and wastes talent. Weeks are spent preparing these forms, whereas a computerized device would take minutes to complete the task, at a savings of over $5000.

F. Management wants the development of tighter controls over its payroll records. Many checks have been improperly issued for the wrong amounts and the processing of payroll data on part-time employees has been erratic. Estimated work levels for the upcoming year indicate that an increase in part-time workers may be required. It is vital that an efficient method of maintaining these records be found. The issuance of invalid checks must stop.

III. Design of the New System

A. Overview of the New System

The new system will involve the use of a
minicomputer system to support the processing
of the payroll. The new system will automate
the entire processing of the payroll. The
system will maintain complete employee payroll
records on disk files and process all federal
and state tax information. All W–2 and 941
(quarterly) tax forms will be computer
prepared, as well as all other payroll–related
outputs. A pictorial overview of the system
follows.

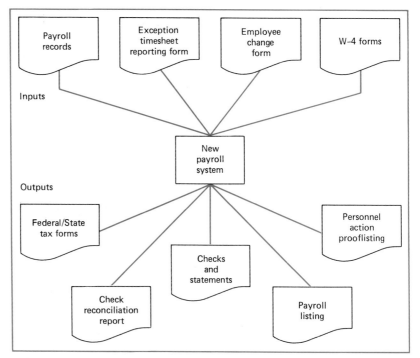

FIGURE 15.12 The systems overview for the new payroll system.

B. Objectives of the New System
1. To provide for the computerized processing of the company's payroll
2. To maintain and update employee payroll records with the assistance of a computer
3. To comply with all federal and state tax regulations
4. To act as a prototype for other business systems which the company is considering for conversion to computerized processing
5. To reduce costs related to the payroll system and streamline the processing of payroll information
6. To enable management to exercise tighter controls over the issuance of payroll funds

C. Constraints of the New System
1. All employees will continue to be paid on a biweekly basis by check, on alternate Thursdays.
2. The computer hardware supporting the new payroll system consists of the following:
   a. A minicomputer system with a CPU capacity of 64K
   b. An online disk storage capacity of 10 million bytes where files will be kept (5 million fixed disk and 5 million removable disk)
   c. Two diskette drives with a capacity of 500,000 characters
   d. One line printer printing approximately 120 lines per minute
   e. Two CRTs for I/O operations
3. All full-time employees receive 10 paid sick days per year. Part-time employees receive no sick time.
4. Employees must take their 2 weeks of vacation during the first 2 weeks of August.
5. W-2 forms must be sent to all employees prior to January 29 and 941 forms must be prepared quarterly.
6. An operating budget of $70,000 is provided.
7. Federal, state, and FICA taxes must be withheld from all employees' pay.
8. Management will allow 1 year for the complete installation and implementation of the new payroll system.

D. Outputs of the New System

The newly designed system will employ the
following outputs:

1. Federal Tax Forms--Payroll tax information
    will be provided via the output of W-2 and
    941 forms. The W-2 is produced annually,
    the 941 form quarterly. The format of both
    forms will remain unchanged, since they are
    fixed by the federal government. Copies of
    the W-2 and 941 forms were shown in Part I
    of this report.

2. Checks and Statements--All employees will
    be paid by check every other Thursday. A
    new check and statement format are being
    used. The new statement must reflect the
    new state tax deductions and all prior
    payroll information. A sample of the new
    paycheck and statement follows.

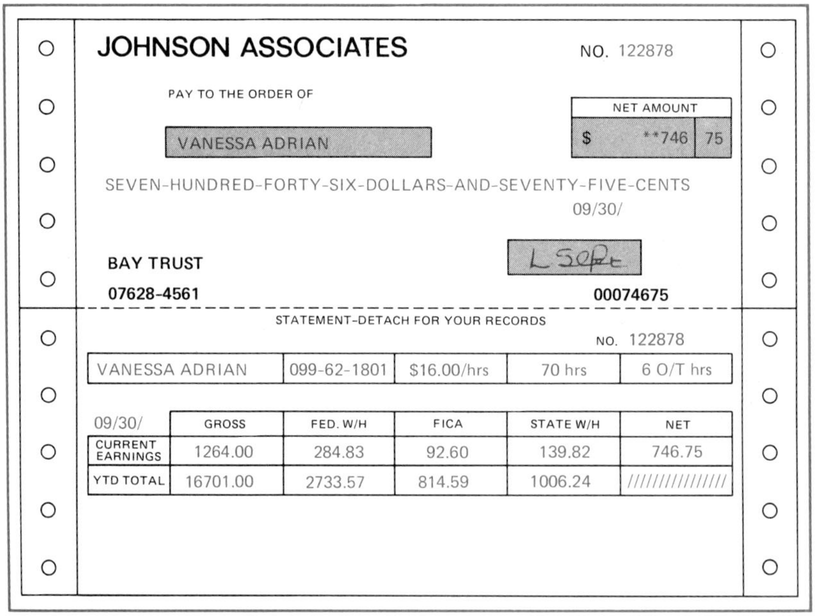

JOHNSON ASSOCIATES   NO. 122878

PAY TO THE ORDER OF

VANESSA ADRIAN

NET AMOUNT

$ **746 | 75

SEVEN-HUNDRED-FORTY-SIX-DOLLARS-AND-SEVENTY-FIVE-CENTS

09/30/

BAY TRUST

07628-4561   00074675

STATEMENT-DETACH FOR YOUR RECORDS

NO. 122878

| VANESSA ADRIAN | 099-62-1801 | $16.00/hrs | 70 hrs | 6 O/T hrs |

09/30/	GROSS	FED. W/H	FICA	STATE W/H	NET
CURRENT EARNINGS	1264.00	284.83	92.60	139.82	746.75
YTD TOTAL	16701.00	2733.57	814.59	1006.24	//////////////

**FIGURE 15.13 The new check and statement design for the proposed
payroll system. This statement now has a more legible format, provides
state tax information, and possesses sufficient space for the output of
additional deductions.**

3. Payroll Listing—This printed output is essentially a duplicate of the check statement, presenting all the payroll information on each employee. This report is a cumulative listing of all employees and the amount paid to them on the current payroll and all prior pay periods. It also shows the check number assigned to each employee's paycheck. The report is output in two formats. One format is sorted alphabetically by the employee's last name, and the other is sorted in numerical ascending order by the employee's social security number. A sample of the payroll listing follows.

PAYROLL LISTING
WEEK OF 04/28/

PAGE 0001

SOCIAL SECURITY NO.	EMPLOYEE NAME LAST	FIRST	M I	HRS WORKED REG	OT	GROSS PAY	FEDERAL W/H TAX	FICA W/H	STATE W/H TAX	NET PAY	SICK DAYS USED	REM
062403662	EMMI	THOMAS	J	70	10	965.00	208.41	86.43	75.08	601.08	0	10
CHECK NO = 18126			YTD TOTALS			8720.00	1762.39	712.78	692.44	—		
079231490	DECKER	EUGENE	C	35	0	700.00	106.39	45.56	39.80	508.25	1	8
CHECK NO = 18150			YTD TOTALS			6342.00	1160.98	486.32	401.79	—		
080364857	SYLVESTER	JOHN	S	70	0	626.00	96.80	35.42	28.70	465.08	2	7
CHECK NO = 18162			YTD TOTALS			4865.00	728.24	242.36	203.57	—		
109361998	BASSI	SANDY		64	4	1224.00	286.92	106.53	98.60	731.95	0	9
CHECK NO = 18199			YTD TOTALS			15816.00	2964.08	926.11	1109.55	—		

FIGURE 15.14   A sample of the payroll listing produced by the new system. This output is sorted by social security number. The payroll listing is also output in alphabetical order by last name.

4. <u>Check</u> <u>Reconciliation</u> <u>Report</u>—This output specifically identifies by number all checks that have not been cashed or received by the bank handling the company's payroll account. The bank prepares a diskette of the checks processed by their DP center and supplies this file to Johnson Associates. This information is processed against the current payroll file to identify the checks which have not been processed by the bank. This form is used by the payroll clerks to balance cash accounts and to alert company management and the bank to any discrepancies.

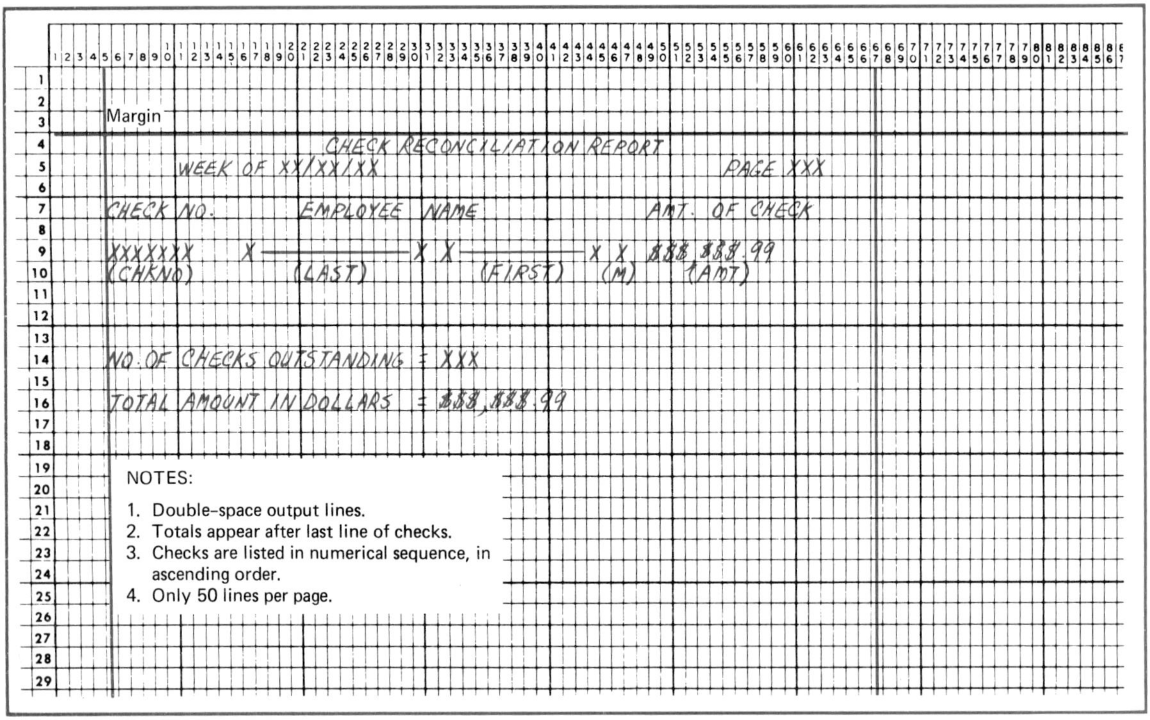

FIGURE 15.15 An excerpt of a printer spacing chart which describes the format of the check reconciliation report.

5. <u>Personnel</u> <u>Action</u> <u>Prooflisting</u>--Often it is
    necessary to alter an employee's payroll
    record to reflect an increase in salary, a
    change in title, or a correction of
    existing data. This prooflisting is
    produced whenever any payroll record is
    modified. It prints the previous record
    format, the change of data input, the
    revised record format, and the name of the
    clerk performing the modification. This
    prooflisting is used by the payroll
    supervisor to ensure that only proper
    entries are processed against individual
    payroll records and that all requested
    changes are made. The prooflisting's
    output assumes the same pattern as the
    payroll file format which is shown below.
    An excerpt from this output follows.

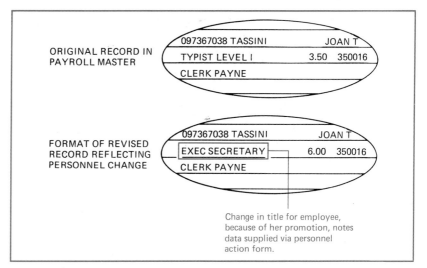

ORIGINAL RECORD IN PAYROLL MASTER

097367038 TASSINI   JOAN T
TYPIST LEVEL I   3.50   350016
CLERK PAYNE

FORMAT OF REVISED RECORD REFLECTING PERSONNEL CHANGE

097367038 TASSINI   JOAN T
EXEC SECRETARY   6.00   350016
CLERK PAYNE

Change in title for employee, because of her promotion, notes data supplied via personnel action form.

FIGURE 15.16 The type of data revealed through the personnel action prooflisting notes all changes made to individual employee records. All changes will be noted in the prooflisting.

E. <u>Processing in the New System</u>

The processing developed for the new system focuses on the creation and maintenance of the master payroll file and the outputs which are derived using that file. The narratives and systems flowcharts that follow describe the processing.

1. <u>Creating the Master Payroll File</u>

   a. Employee payroll data drawn from payroll records is checked by clerks before it is entered into the computer via an online terminal.

   b. The data is used to construct the master payroll file. Program PAY1 is employed to perform the task.

   c. Data entered via the terminal appears on a CRT screen as it is input and entered into the master file. All data from the master file is printed on a prooflisting.

   d. Program PAY1 also produces a diskette version of the master file. This diskette is a copy of the original file and could be used to regenerate the file if anything happened to the original magnetic disk. The diskette copy makes it unnecessary for the payroll clerks to rekey the original payroll data and is referred to as a backup file.

The illustrations that follow show the record layout of the master payroll file and the systems flowchart describing its creation.

FIGURE 15.17 The record layout describing the format of the master payroll file. This format accounts for all the data required for the preparation of the payroll. With an eye toward the future, the analysts have designed into the storage format room for payroll deductions other than taxes. These may be used for a proposed credit union, profit-sharing plan, payment of a medical insurance plan being considered, or U.S. savings bond deductions. The incorporation of these four deduction areas will make it easier to redesign the format at a later date.

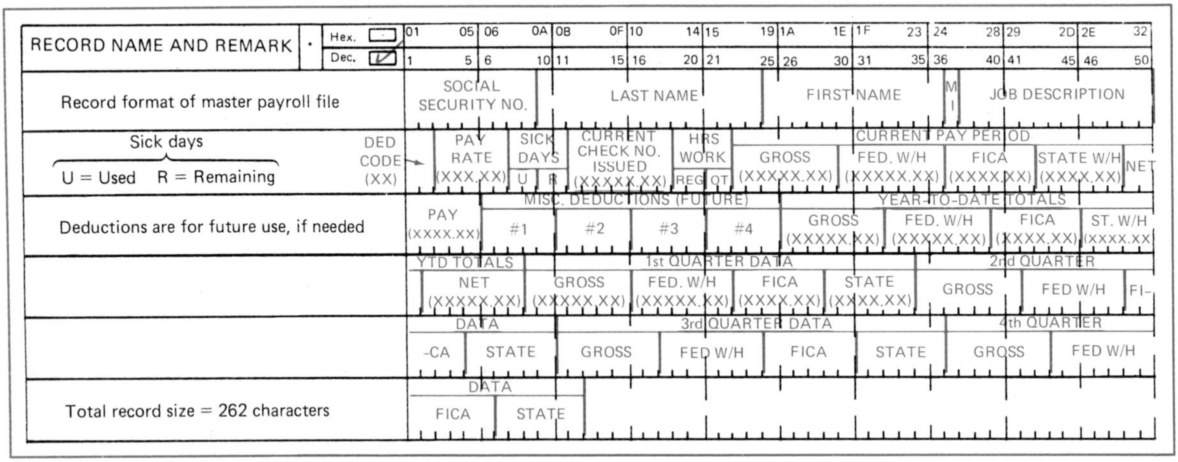

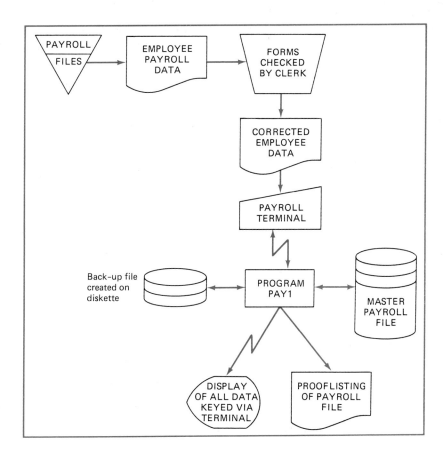

FIGURE 15.18 A systems flowchart describing the creation of the master payroll file.

2. <u>Updating the Master Payroll File</u>--Once the master payroll file is created, each processing of the payroll will update the contents of the file. In the master file, current work week data will reflect the previous 2-week pay period, while year-to-date figures will provide cumulative totals of payments and taxes incurred by each employee. All updating occurs under the direction of program PAYUP1. The following narrative describes the update of the master file.

   a. All employees are assumed to work a 35-hour week (7 hours per day, 5 days per week). Supervisors are required to report only those individuals who do not work 35 hours, i.e., people using their sick days or working overtime, on the exception timesheet reporting form.

   b. This form, received at Payroll, is verified for completeness and validated to ensure that each employee name and number listed are correct.

c. A payroll clerk enters this data into the PAYUP1 program prior to the actual processing of the payroll. Current payroll data is computed and posted in the master payroll file. A diskette copy of the master file is produced for back-up.

d. The master file is then used to produce the payroll listing. This listing is checked by a payroll clerk and approved by the payroll supervisor before the checks and statements can be run. All changes in payroll data will appear in the payroll listing.

The flowchart describing this procedure follows.

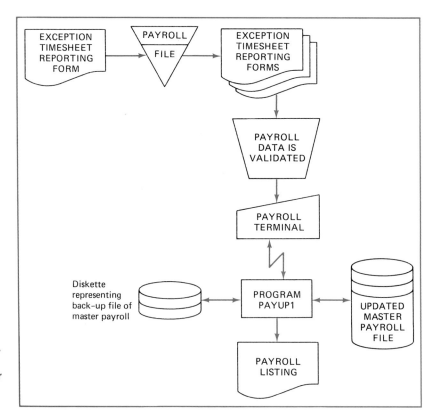

FIGURE 15.19 The systems flowchart detailing the update of the master payroll file and printing of the payroll listing.

3. <u>Processing</u> <u>Checks</u> <u>and</u> <u>Statements</u>––Once the payroll listing is verified, the actual production of checks and statements can begin. Current payroll data stored in the master payroll file is printed on individual checks and statements via program PAYCK. The completed checks and statements are delivered to Payroll for their subsequent distribution. The systems flowchart describing this sequence of operations follows.

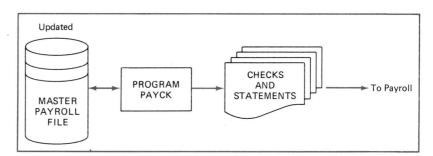

FIGURE 15.20 The systems flowchart describing the preparation of employee checks and statements. Checks are sent to payroll prior to their distribution.

4. <u>Processing</u> <u>Federal</u> <u>Tax</u> <u>Forms</u>––W–2 and 941 forms are prepared from the master payroll file, using program PAYFED. The program is designed to prepare either output, since the operator is able to select the desired format. This program reads the necessary data directly from the master payroll file in the preparation of the W–2 and 941 documents. The output of these federal tax forms is depicted in the following flowchart.

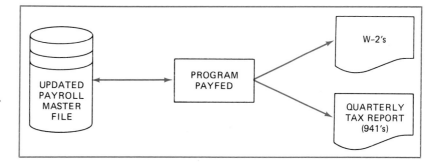

FIGURE 15.21 The systems flowchart detailing the processing related to federally required tax forms.

5. <u>Processing for Check Reconciliation</u>--The
purpose of this processing is to account
for all payroll checks issued by the
company and determine which checks have not
been cashed. This accounting enables the
company to balance its books at the end of
each month and quarter. The bank handling
the payroll account delivers a diskette
containing a file of the numbers of all
checks cashed. The file is processed
against the master payroll file using
program CKREC, which matches the number on
the diskette against employee paycheck
numbers. Numbers which do not appear on
the diskette file represent uncashed
checks. The flowchart depicting this
process follows.

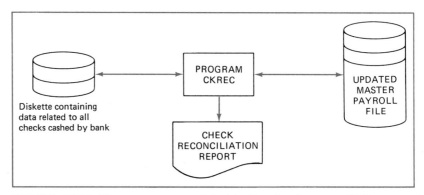

**FIGURE 15.22 The processing related to the check reconciliation report
is depicted in this flowchart. Note that the diskette is prepared and sent
to the company by the bank handling its payroll funds.**

6. <u>Processing Employee Payroll Changes</u>--
Changes in employee payroll data may be
initiated by either the employee or
management, using the employee change form.
Any field in an employee payroll record
can be altered. All modifications made to
the master file, using program EMPCHG, are
recorded in the system and output for the
payroll supervisor's review and
certification. This output, the personnel
action prooflisting, shows the previous and
revised record and the name of the clerk
processing the change. This online form of
processing is described by the following
systems flowchart.

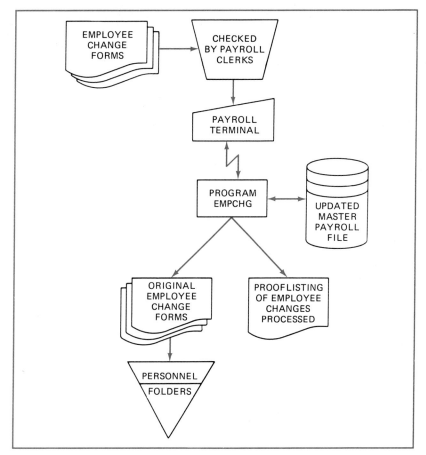

FIGURE 15.23   The flowchart defines the operations involved in the processing of employee changes.

F.   <u>Inputs</u> <u>Used</u> <u>in</u> <u>the</u> <u>New</u> <u>System</u>

The following forms are employed to input
payroll data into the new system:

1.   <u>W-4</u> <u>Forms</u>--This form is a government-
supplied document which identifies the
number of dependents the employee wishes to
claim in the computation of his or her
payroll deduction. The form illustrated in
the review of the existing system will be
used.

2. Exception Timesheet Reporting Form--All employees are assumed to work a full 35-hour week. Supervisors need only report personnel who do not meet that requirement by using sick days or working overtime. This type of reporting is referred to as exception reporting, since only the exceptions to normal activity are reported. The exception timesheet reporting form used for this type of payroll data is shown below.

EXCEPTION TIMESHEET REPORTING FORM

SUPV. TKO AREA Accounting WEEK OF 09/30/xx PAGE 1 OF 1

SOCIAL SECURITY NUMBER	LAST NAME	FIRST NAME	MI	DAYS WORKED WEEK 1							DAYS WORKED WEEK 2							CODE
063409972	TASSINI	ALEX	J			10			X	X					9	10	X	1
099325860	DEVINS	KORINE		X				X	X	X	X				X	X	X	3
112467008	NIMBLE	JACK	B	X		X		10	X	X	X		X		10	X	X	2
120426619	LIONE	THOMAS	P						X	X		S	S			X	X	4
144817523	CHRISTMAN	THOMAS	A		U	U			X	X						X	X	3
145263308	HIRSCH	JOANNE	S	4	4	4	4	4	X	X	4	X	4	4	4	X	X	3

CODES USED:

1 = 35 hrs + O/T
2 = < 35 hrs + O/T
3 = < 35 hrs
4 = 35 hrs, sick day taken

INSTRUCTIONS:

1. Cross out days of week when no work was done.
2. Enter S for sick days used.
3. Enter U for unauthorized sick days that are taken at employers expense.
4. When working O/T enter total number of hours worked that day (7 + O/T)
5. If a full day (7 hours) is not worked, enter only total number of hours worked that day.

FIGURE 15.24 The exception timesheet reporting form used to identify all employees not working a regular 35-hour week. The use of boxes in which data must be placed improves the preparation of input data, because each character is individually written in one box. This format permits the legible entry of payroll data on the form.

3. Employee Change Form--Changes in the Master Payroll File are accomplished using the employee change form (illustrated below). Employees may correct information such as social security number, spelling of last name, or job description. Data relating to payroll changes (i.e., changes in pay rate, gross pay totals, etc.) must be initiated by a payroll clerk. Most of the changes anticipated for the master file will relate to promotions, changes in pay rate, the hiring or firing of an employee, and the temporary inactivation of records of part-time employees. Again the principle of exception reporting is evident. The clerk processing a change will alter only that field of the record needing modification. All changes will be accomplished via an online terminal. A prooflisting of all changes must be read and approved by the payroll supervisor.

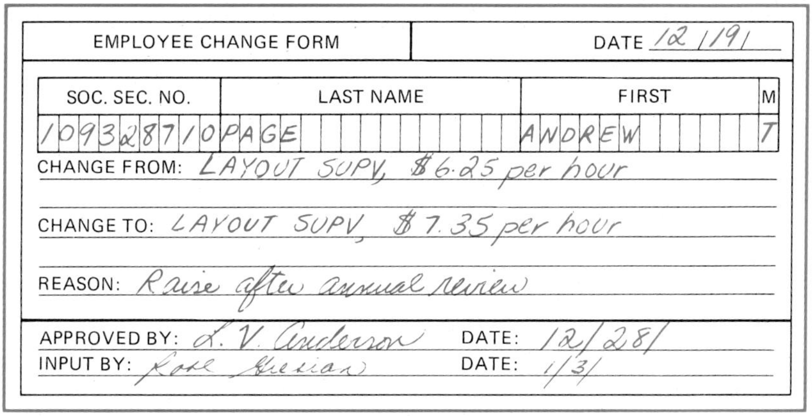
EMPLOYEE CHANGE FORM — DATE 12/1/91

SOC. SEC. NO.	LAST NAME	FIRST	M
109328710	PAGE	ANDREW	T

CHANGE FROM: LAYOUT SUPV, $6.25 per hour

CHANGE TO: LAYOUT SUPV, $7.35 per hour

REASON: Raise after annual review

APPROVED BY: L. V. Anderson DATE: 12/28/

INPUT BY: DATE: 1/3/

FIGURE 15.25 The employee change form which is used to make changes in individual employee records maintained in the Master Payroll File.

4. Payroll Records--These records are folders in which payroll data relating to individual employees is kept. These folders are permanent sources of all employee pay data and are created when an employee is added to the master payroll file. No change is anticipated in this current form of the folder. The folder is illustrated in the prior discussion of the existing system.

G. Feedback for the New System

Management has allotted 1 year for the completion of this project. During this time it is hoped that many of the problems encountered will be overcome. The systems staff will have monthly meetings during the first 3 months of the project and weekly meetings thereafter. Four quarterly reports will be issued. The final systems report will completely document the new system.

Six months after completion of the system, one analyst will be assigned to evaluate the new system. All recommendations resulting from that review will be evaluated and implemented as deemed necessary.

The systems staff undertaking this project consists of three people, all currently employed by Johnson Associates. The payroll supervisor and the payroll clerks will be participating adjuncts to the staff. When the systems review is underway, these individuals should be available for consultation. The payroll personnel will provide firsthand information as to the system's operational efficiency. They will alert the analyst involved to any glaring errors which become evident in the new system. All major modifications will be accomplished after the 6-month review.

H. Controls on the New System

The following controls have been incorporated into the new system to ensure the efficient, accurate, and proper use of the information generated:

1. All checks in excess of $500 must be personally approved by the payroll supervisor.

2. All check numbers will be assigned in order and printed next to each employee's name in the payroll listing. When being issued a check, an employee must verify the amount of the check and its check number and initial the copy of the payroll listing retained in the payroll office.

3. The payroll listing will contain the total amount of the payroll issued. The payroll clerks will individually verify the amount of each check. The batch totals from the payroll listing and the clerk's tabulation should match. Any discrepancy must be reported to the payroll supervisor before the paychecks can be released.

4. An audit from an outside CPA will be performed annually at the end of the fiscal year in July.

5. The following checks have been instituted in the program that prepares the payroll:

   a. The program must verify that the employee is in an active status before computing a payroll amount.

   b. Two checks cannot be issued to the same employee.

   c. All modifications to the master payroll file must be recorded on a protected file for output to the company controller.

I. Costs for the New System

The estimated monthly costs of the new system in its first year of operation are the following:

Minicomputer rental and all peripherals	$1500.00
Supplies	500.00
Payroll supervisor	1800.00
One payroll clerk	1000.00
Total	$4800.00
Overhead	600.00
Total	$5400.00
Anticipated overtime expense	100.00
Monthly total cost	$5500.00

The monthly cost for the new system is $5500, which means an annual cost of $66,000. This cost provides an initial savings of more than $10,000 over the existing system. A significant reduction has been made in the area of overtime, which has been reduced by an estimated $475. The overtime rate is now considerably less than 1 percent. Also, an additional clerk was not hired and the second payroll clerk, currently involved in payroll activities, has been reassigned to another administrative position.

The overall budget for the new system is expected to grow at only 4 percent per year, owing to the stability offered by the new computer system. A 3-year projection of the existing and new systems follows.

Existing System

Item	Yr. 1	Yr. 2	Yr. 3
Equipment rental	$ 7,800	$ 8,580[1]	$ 9,440
Supplies	6,000	6,600	7,260
Payroll supervisor	21,600	23,760	26,140
Payroll clerk (2 @ $12,000 ea.)	24,000	26,400	29,040
Additional clerk	--	12,000	13,200
Overhead	9,600	10,560	11,620
Overtime ($575 per mo.)	6,900	7,590	8,350
Total	$75,900	$95,490	$105,050

[1]Increases are estimated at the rate of 10 percent annually.

New System

	Yr. 1	Yr. 2	Yr. 3
Total computer system[2]	$ 18,000	$18,720	$18,720
Supplies	6,000	6,240	6,490
Payroll supervisor	21,600	22,460	23,360
Payroll clerk[3]	24,000	12,480	12,980
Overhead	10,000	7,490	7,790
Overtime	3,500	1,200	1,250
Systems staff	20,000	--	--
Programming	15,000	5,000	5,000
Training	3,000	--	--
Total	$121,100	$73,590	$75,590
Net annual difference (loss) (old - new)	(45,200)	21,900	29,460
Cumulative annual difference	(45,200)	(23,300)	6,160

[2]Includes all peripheral devices.

[3]Number of clerks reduced to one after first year.

The net savings anticipated for the new
system, after 3 years, is approximately
$6,000. First—year costs of the new system
reflect the additional costs of a parallel
run, in which both systems will be used. The
savings may be accelerated if the new computer
can be delivered in less than six months,
enabling the new system to go into operation 3
months sooner.

A tentative timetable for the implementation
of the newly designed payroll system is given
in the graph which follows.

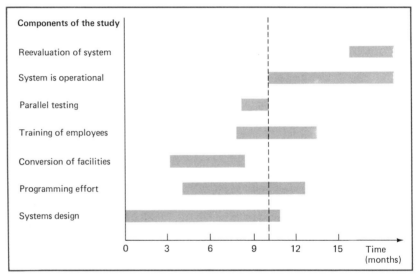

**FIGURE 15.26 A graphic representation of the time frame estimated for
the complete implementation of the new system. Note that the system
becomes operational within the 12 months allotted by management. The
reevaluation of the new system is initiated 6 months after the system becomes operational.**

Summary

The following major points have been presented in Chapter 15:

Point 1   Systems documentation presents all facets of a systems analysis and design project to management. Systems documentation should be given in a clear, concise, well-written report.

Point 2   Systems documentation is usually divided into an analysis of the existing system, a problem definition, and a description of the design of the new system. The analysis segment of the report normally includes a systems overview; managerial objectives and constraints applied to the system; a description of the system's outputs, inputs, processing, and storage formats; and a development of the costs relating to the existing system. The problem definition is a brief explanation of specific problem areas discovered from the analysis of the existing system. The description of the new system defines all aspects of the new system, in much the same manner that the existing system is detailed.

Point 3   Specific points are important in the composition of the systems documentation. The systems overview depicts the I/O documents used in the system. Objectives detail the stated purpose of the system. Constraints are limitations or conditions under which a system must operate. I/O and storage formats, as well as procedures employed in a system, can be defined through the use of printer spacing charts, multiple card layouts, record layouts, and systems flowcharts. The detailing of costs related to any system provides management with a viable form of systems comparison and is an important factor in the documentation of a system.

Point 4   The need to revise a system may result from changes in the laws that govern a system, business's desire to maintain control over its resources, a need for currently unavailable information, and changes in management's goals and objectives. A systems revision may also result from the feedback designed into a new system. Feedback represents an attempt by the system to monitor its own effectiveness.

Glossary

Constraint   A limitation or condition under which a system operates.

Controls   Checks and procedures in a system which protect against the improper or fraudulent use of resources and data.

Feedback   The vehicle by which a system attempts to evaluate its own performance.

Problem definition   The segment of the systems documentation which defines all the problem areas in the existing system, as determined by an analysis effort.

Systems overview   A written and pictorial representation of the inputs and outputs employed in a system.

Discussion Questions

1   Assume that you are a junior analyst assigned to investigate a dating system being developed for a nearby university. The system's project name is Date-a-Match.

Students will complete an application which describes their attributes, interests, qualities, and objectives in dating. These applications will be converted to an input medium for entry into the computer, which will compare data on each applicant. The system will output the names of applicants with similar attributes who might get along. It is anticipated that a fee of $5 will be

(*continued on page 640*)

Case Study One

New York Police Act to Bar the Sale of Confidential Data in Computers

It is very important that adequate safeguards and controls be incorporated into any computer system. The news article below highlights the kind of difficulties that may arise when unauthorized individuals obtain access to computerized files containing highly confidential data. A year-long systems study revealed that inadequate controls in police informational systems enabled the unauthorized removal of data in relation to criminal activities. The security measures designed into the new system include restrictions on the conditions under which selected individuals may have access to police data. Also, all inquiries from and responses to computer terminals will be recorded on an unerasable storage tape. This tape will indicate the data requested, time, place, and person requesting the information.

The New York City Police Department has taken measures to prevent any members of the force from selling confidential information in computerized data banks to criminal figures and others.

Although authorities say that they knew of or suspected only a few such acts of corruption in the past, the matter was regarded as serious enough to be pointed up as a "hazard potential" in a recent report by the department's Corruption Assessment Task Force. The force consisted of high-level anticorruption and intelligence officials.

The new precautions were ordered after a study by the Inspectional Services Bureau found that many station houses were lax in maintaining record books intended to help protect the system against unauthorized use.

Last July the United States Drug Enforcement Administration introduced new security measures after two narcotics agents were arrested for allegedly trying to sell secret information from the agency's computer.

Extent of Operation

The New York City Police Department's computerized communications system—now in operation in all 73 precincts, the seven area commands, and certain headquarters units—can provide information on wanted and missing persons; stolen vehicles, license plates, boats, and guns; vehicle ownership by registration and other data.

Access to such information, officials said, could enable an unscrupulous person to discover whether, for example, an acquaintance or neighbor was a scofflaw and use this information to perhaps extort money or otherwise abuse him. Or it could enable a shady dealer to learn that the car being offered for sale was stolen and use this knowledge to buy the car cheaply.

In some instances, legitimate businesses are known to have tried to obtain "name checks" on prospective employees. And in one case, an underworld figure supposedly sought information about the car owned by his potential victim so he could "do a job on it."

Restriction on Access

The new security measures include restrictions on who can have access to the system and under what circumstances, according to Capt. Philip J. Bowden, executive officer of the Management Information System Division at headquarters.

In the station houses, he noted, the terminals are supposed to be situated within view of the desk officer but not in a position where they are overly accessible. The station houses are also required to maintain records showing who used the system and when. All inquiries as well as responses are also recorded on a computer tape.

Source: Leonard Buder, *The New York Times*, Feb. 12, 1978, p. 44. © 1978 by The New York Times Company. Reprinted by permission.

Case Study Two

Systems Conversion Helps Park District Spruce Up

A desire to tighten its budget and improve services to the community led the Wilmette Park District, Wilmette, Illinois, to install its own in-house computer system. An extensive systems study revealed that an in-house system could improve the efficiency of administrative operations, let the park agency offer better community programs and trim its escalating data processing costs.

Originally supported by a service bureau, the Wilmette district watched its DP budget grow by $2.3 million in 6 years as services declined. The study's problem definition pointed toward poor turnaround times between the company and service bureau, increasing clerical costs, unusable reports containing marginal data, and a system unresponsive to organizational needs. The decision to convert to the in-house system was made in 1975. A BASIC/FOUR Model 400 was bought and installed by 1976. Software was specifically written to meet the needs of the park district.

Because the park's programs were so diverse, the computer was a necessity. Having the system on-site just made the job easier. The Wilmette district consists of 20 parks, an 18-hole golf course, a shopping mall, tennis courts, pools, skating rinks, and a community center. Over 500 different recreational programs are administered during one year.

After the scheduled review and evaluation of the initial system, a BASIC/FOUR Model 410 was installed in 1979. The review also revealed that the existing software could be used with only minor modification. The 410 system has a CPU of 96K, a disk capacity of 42 megabytes, 5 CRTs, a low-speed printer, and a backup tape system. The online terminals permit the immediate entry of data, thus speeding data handling activities. This feature was highlighted in the systems study as particularly desirable, because it could improve the processing of administrative and community service-oriented information. Currently, the new district system monitors $5 million in programs for the 32,000 plus residents of this lakeside community and processes personnel data for 700 district employees.

The in-house 410 system helps the park's management administer the many programs offered. A major problem of the old service bureau was the lack of timely administrative data. The in-house system now provides reports which include financial and accounting statements, residential registration materials, statistical data on park use, and program planning data. Trends in attendance and participation in various activities are now easily recognizable, and the agency can modify programs accordingly.

The 410 system's word processing capability produces advertising and informational materials. The computer has simplified registration for activities and is credited with increasing enrollment by 10 percent. The new system was designed to accommodate this expansion. The park agency now provides services to Wilmette's handicapped. Data for administering these services is maintained in the 410 system. The in-house 410 system has allowed the Wilmette park district to provide a wide range of services to the community and to administer 1500 classes annually.

Consider this . . .

Why does a systems conversion generally result in an improved use of a company's resources? Does having better information really help, and how can we convert this advantage into real dollars?

charged for the service, with all monies entering the student fund. Approximately 10 percent of the student body of 20,000 has expressed an interest in such a project. The school is willing to devote its computer facilities to this project for a nominal fee of $100 per month.

From this general description, you must recommend the following:

   a   An overview of the new system

   b   Objectives of the system relating to its use, purpose, or service to students

   c   Constraints within which the Date-a-Match system should operate

   d   The types of outputs this system will produce, including receipts for student fees, accounts for the transfer of funds, letters that will be sent to students, and a method for correcting student data on file

In addition, you are to prepare the following:

   e   A systems flowchart of how data will be generally handled by the system to produce the above outputs

   f   A list of the data to be stored in the Master Student File that will contain all dating information

   g   Designs for the inputs, including the student application, receipts for payments, forms for entry of data into the system (or cards), and other inputs that you feel are required

   h   A description of the type of feedback and control that the system must have to evaluate its performance and ensure student privacy; also, the controls required for the accurate accounting of the student fees collected.

In performing all these activities, use any analyst's tools you feel appropriate. Put your recommendations in the form of a report.

2 Visit the data processing center in your organization and ask the systems manager to explain their systems documentation format.

3 Select a procedure used in the DP center of your organization. Document this procedure, initially describing inputs, outputs, etc. Draft ideas on how you believe it might be improved. Present your findings and ideas using the format of the systems documentation package.

4 Describe the registration procedure at the school you attend. Can it be improved? Briefly outline the existing system and your proposed improvement using a systems documentation format. Collect copies of existing documents used in the registration process and include them in your report. Design new forms that suit your proposed system.

5 As an analyst working for a toy company, you have been asked to participate in the design of an inventory system. The company produces and handles over 2000 types of toys and maintains a total inventory of over 20,000 toys. Currently, 10 employees are involved in inventory-handling activities. Management wants to maintain this number of employees, as well as the operating budget of $100,000. One month's lead time is required for the purchase of all toys. Special seasons, such as the Christmas and Easter sales cycles, require a 120-day order time. These times enable the company to accumulate adequate levels of stock.

For this new system, develop the following:

a   A systems overview
b   Objectives for the system
c   Constraints under which the system should operate
d   Outputs that will assist in the control of the inventory and provide knowledge of those inventory items that have very low or zero stock levels
e   Written narratives and flowcharts showing how inventory data will be entered, handled, and processed through the system
f   Inputs that will describe all items entering the inventory, removed from stock, issued for sale, or returned to other manufacturers
g   Feedback and controls to ensure that the system is operating satisfactorily and that nothing is being stolen from inventory.

Use any analyst's tools you feel are necessary, e.g., printer spacing charts, card and record layouts, etc. Put your recommendations in the form of a report, and present them to the class.

Summary Test

_____ **1** Systems documentation is composed only of the analysis of the existing system and a problem definition.

_____ **2** Systems documentation formats vary extensively from company to company, because one standard format is not recognized.

_____ **3** A systems overview offers only a written narrative describing the system.

_____ **4** Normally, systems overviews are applied to the new system, not to the existing system.

_____ **5** When describing the updating of tape files in systems flowcharts, the original and newly created files are referred to as the _old_ and _updated_ files, respectively.

_____ **6** In cost analyses, savings are developed for the existing system only, since savings in the new system are only estimates and are unreliable.

_____ **7** Controls are vital to almost all systems, except money-related systems, in which banks assume control responsibility.

_____ **8** The development of costs is an integral part of a systems evaluation and should appear in its documentation.

_____ **9** The major problems uncovered by analysts in their investigation are revealed in the section of the systems documentation report stating their analysis of the existing system.

_____ **10** Management has often little or no effect on the objectives of a system, new or old.

_____ **11** Business systems must be responsive to changes made in laws governing selected industries.

_____ **12** The need for more timely information frequently provides the reason for revising a system.

_____ **13** All studies result in the purchase of a new computer system.

_____ **14** Feedback is designed into a new system so its performance can be evaluated.

_____ **15** The scheduled review of a system 6 to 24 months after its full implementation can be regarded as a form of feedback.

_____ **16** The principle of detailing data that does not conform to normal conditions is referred to as:

a	abnormal reporting	**b**	exception reporting
c	highlight listings	**d**	singular reporting

_____ **17** A duplicate copy of a file, used to regenerate the file if it is rendered unusable, is called a:

a	duplicate file	**b**	grandfather file
c	backup file	**d**	all of the above

_____ **18** An annual budget amount reserved for systems implementations is considered a:

a	management objective	**b**	future cost
c	reason for a systems study	**d**	constraint

_____ **19** To ensure that available resources are properly distributed, a system will implement:

a	constraints	**b**	controls
c	limit factors	**d**	a and b

_____ **20** The element of documentation that offers both a pictorial and written description of a system is:

a	problem definition	**b**	systems narrative
c	systems overview	**d**	systems abstract

_____ **21** Which of the following can result in a systems revision?

a	a need for more timely data	**b**	a desire for more business
c	changes in laws	**d**	all the above

_____ **22** A brief description of the troublespots in a system is called the:

a	problem definition	**b**	systems overview
c	current analysis	**d**	problem overview

_____ **23** When initiated, controls are:

a planned and only manually administrated
b implemented and computerized only
c implemented either manually or by computer
d applied to financial areas only

_____ **24** The item of documentation added to the description of the new system is:

a	control review	**b**	problem overview
c	I/O analysis	**d**	feedback

_____ **25** When reviewing a new system's performance, the analyst should determine if the new system is:

a	meeting its objectives	**b**	satisfying its users
c	in need of additional employee training	**d**	all the above

Summary Test Answers

1 F	**2** T	**3** F	**4** F	**5** T
6 F	**7** F	**8** T	**9** F	**10** F
11 T	**12** T	**13** F	**14** T	**15** T
16 B	**17** C	**18** D	**19** B	**20** C
21 D	**22** A	**23** C	**24** D	**25** D

Sixteen

Minicomputers, Microcomputers, and Other Computer Systems

FIGURE 16.1 Minicomputers and microcomputers have opened new vistas to the field of education. Students, even at the lower grades, are now using the computer as a valuable learning tool. (*Courtesy of UPI.*)

Purpose of This Chapter

Minicomputers, microcomputers, and other current computer systems are introduced in this chapter. Minicomputers, which reflect one of the fastest developing sales trends in the industry, are initially compared with larger systems. The three classes of minicomputer systems—the mini-, the midi-, and the maxi-system—are discussed. We also present an overview of many models of minicomputers.

Many specific aspects of minicomputer systems are provided, including their CPUs, peripheral devices, and software. The concepts of random access memory (RAM) and read only memory (ROM) are developed, and the role that microprocessors play in ROM memory is detailed.

Microcomputers, the smallest of all computer systems, are discussed. These systems are constructed of miniaturized integrated circuits called chips, which make the systems' small size possible. We also discuss home and office microcomputers.

Word processing applications using minicomputer and microcomputer systems are explained with examples. Peripheral devices for word processing systems are discussed, as is the dissemination of data in a distributed word processing system.

A comparison is made of the four classes of computer systems: small-scale, medium-scale, large-scale, and supercomputer systems. The comparison is presented in terms of CPU size, cost, and operational capabilities, and it is intended to help the reader distinguish between the types of computers. Examples of selected systems are included in the discussion.

After studying this chapter, you should be able to

■ Discuss the three classes of minicomputer systems and processing operations of each
■ Distinguish between minicomputers and larger computer systems
■ Describe the difference between RAM and ROM memory
■ Describe the peripheral devices used in minicomputer and microcomputer systems
■ Discuss word processing operations and their hardware
■ Briefly discuss microcomputer use in the home or office
■ Discuss the four categories of computer systems and cite examples in each category
■ Understand the following terms:

Applications software
Applied Text Management System
  (ATMS)

Automatic typesetter
Board
Chips

Diskette
Distributed word processing
   system (DWPS)
Erasable programmable read only
   memory (EPROM)
Floppy disk
Intelligent printer
Large-scale computer systems
Maxi-minicomputers
Medium-scale computer systems
Microcomputers
Microprocessors

Midi-minicomputers
Minicomputers
Mini-minicomputers
Modules
Programmable read only memory (PROM)
Random access memory (RAM)
Read only memory (ROM)
Small-scale computer systems
Supercomputers
Systems software
Tape cassettes
Word processing (WP)

Introduction

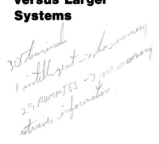

Minicomputers were first developed and manufactured by the Digital Equipment Corporation in the early 1960s. They have replaced much larger computer systems in many cases. Sales of minicomputers exceeded $3 billion in less than a decade and will double again in the 1980s. Many financial and computer analysts believe that minicomputers will revamp the appearance and direction of data processing.

16.1
The Concept of Minicomputers
Minicomputers versus Larger Systems

The data processing needs of businesses in the mid-1960s explain the development of the minicomputer. Most experts then believed that large, conventional computer systems could provide all the data processing support an organization might require. As a result, companies purchased large computer systems to provide centralized data processing services. These systems were designed to handle any type of computer problem.

Though many organizations effectively used these large, centralized systems, others realized that these vast systems were too large. They required small, compact, task-oriented computers, not large systems. They therefore bought minicomputer systems, which were physically smaller but large enough to handle the needs of these companies. Minicomputers were designed to handle a specific set of jobs and did not require a vast array of peripheral or secondary storage devices and a large CPU. The reduction in size and equipment necessary to support the system brought about considerable savings in cost.

Consider the case of an organization that wanted a time-sharing computer system for its research activities. A few years ago, a general-purpose computer for time-shared data processing might have required the equivalent of at least 256,000 bytes of CPU storage and cost more than $500,000. By comparison, a minicomputer system with a CPU of 64K could have provided the same time-shared support and cost approximately $100,000. The marked difference in CPU size and cost resulted from the fact that the minicomputer was specifically designed to support time-sharing. The minicomputer's potential to perform other, more sophisticated data processing tasks may have been sacrificed, but the minicomputer was more suited to the company's original need.

Minicomputer systems have cost less than conventional computer systems for many years. Though it is estimated that the overall cost of computer systems will drop, minicomputers will continue to enjoy a distinct price advantage.

Classes of Minicomputers

The diversity among minicomputers led some data processors to believe that these systems should be assigned into three operational classes. Each classification would suggest how each type of system could be used. To this end, the classes of mini-, midi-, and maxi-minicomputers were created. Table 16.1 details operational characteristics associated with each category.

Though this categorization was initially successful, people drifted away from these limits as technology improved. Users were more interested in what minicomputers could do than in their category. Technical improvements also blurred the distinctions among categories.

As a result of this confusion, most data processors now employ the three classes of minicomputers as guides to their operational potential. We will do likewise. Each minicomputer classification generally defines the type of processing it is capable of supporting. We will discuss the capabilities of each category and give examples of various types of minicomputer.

The **mini-minicomputer,** the smallest type, has a limited set of operational features. It has the smallest CPU capacity, supports one or two visual display terminals, and averages the lowest cost. An example of a mini-minicomputer system is the WANG 2200 SVP computer, illustrated in Figure 16.2.

Table 16.1   Classes of Minicomputer Systems

	Mini-	Midi-	Maxi-
Capacity:			
CPU storage, in bytes	4000–128,000	128,000–512,000	512,000–2,000,000
Online disk storage, in millions of bytes	1–40	40–100	over 100
Other peripherals:			
Speed of printer	30–165 CPS	200–600 LPM	600–1,200 LPM
Magnetic tape	Not normally used in system	Limited use	Limited use
Card reader	Not normally used in system	Used in system	Used regularly in system
Number of CRTs the system can support	1–2	3–16	4–33
Price range, in $1000	8–50	50–100	100–300

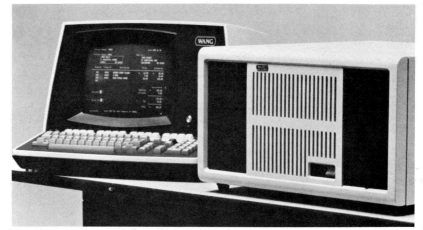

FIGURE 16.2 The WANG 2200 Series small business computer provides single-user support for a variety of fields. Diskettes let the 2200 retain data on a direct access basis. (WANG)

The 2200 SVP system is a task-oriented, single-user computer for various applications. It features a CRT, a CPU which may be expanded to 64K, and limited disk storage. A low-speed thermal or impact printer can provide hardcopy outputs.

The 2200 system has been used for structural engineering problems. Using special software packages, the 2200 aids in the design of steel beams and girders and can analyze the stress developed in multistory steel structures. The 2200 can analyze factors such as beam length, structural span, wind force, gravity, and the live load on a girder, and can recommend types of beams appropriate under such conditions. All recommendations are viewed on the CRT screen, and may be output via the 2200's printer.

Mini-minicomputers are successfully used in financial planning, processing accounts receivable or accounts payable data, and in auditing and engineering. Despite their effectiveness, however, mini-minicomputer systems are normally applied to one type of problem and do not have the capabilities of larger systems.

Midi-minicomputers can be applied to a wider range of data processing activities. They offer larger CPUs and more terminals and other peripheral devices. Midi-systems also incorporate online disk storage of up to 100 million characters in some models. These features expand the usefulness of midi-minicomputers.

One objective of most minicomputers is to provide a teleprocessing capability in a small computer system. But minicomputer systems must also batch-process data. The midi-system handles both tasks extremely well. It can handle one large problem or several smaller ones at the same time.

Consider a company that maintains a vast inventory and needs an inventory control system to monitor stock. Because of the activity and

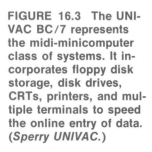

size of this inventory, the inventory control system receives the full support of the midi-minicomputer The focal point of the system is inventory control. Terminals distributed throughout the company tele-process data to continuously update the inventory. However, the midi-system is not restricted to teleprocessing. It can also batch-proc-ess the employee payroll and its related data, prepare and print monthly statements, and print inventory-related reports. When the sys-tem is not fully occupied with online processing of inventory data, it can batch-process other data. The system cannot perform teleproc-essing and batch-processing operations at the same time, however.

Midi-minicomputer systems offer another advantage. Different users can independently access separate online files from the sys-tem's magnetic disk units. Using terminals, users can interact with on-line files and access data from their contents. This is a real advantage, because it permits a clerk to work on one file and a manager to inquire and draw data from another file.

The concurrent use of online files draws attention to the problem of data security. Terminals give users direct access to any of the data files maintained in a computer system. Without adequate security, users could improperly access data critical to a business. Thus, con-trols must be established in online systems to restrict the use of data files and permit only authorized personnel to access files. A simple example will point out the importance of securing data files.

Consider an online file containing the accounts of customers that owe money to a company. Without some form of data security, an unauthorized user could access this file, apply credits to an account, and erase the amount due to the company. Through these actions, the account would be cleared, the owed money would be lost, and no one would know about it. Proper data security prevents this kind of misuse.

Examples of midi-minicomputer systems are the NCR 8250 and UNIVAC BC/7 systems (Figure 16.3). The basic NCR 8250 has a CPU

FIGURE 16.3 The UNI-VAC BC/7 represents the midi-minicomputer class of systems. It in-corporates floppy disk storage, disk drives, CRTs, printers, and mul-tiple terminals to speed the online entry of data. (*Sperry UNIVAC.*)

size of 48K, which can be increased by increments of 16K to a maximum of approximately 128,000 bytes. Similarly, the online storage capacity of the 8250 begins at 10 million bytes and can be increased to 80 million bytes. Most minicomputer systems have a basic CPU and online storage configuration which can be increased according to the needs of the users. The 8250 system can support a maximum of seven terminals. It can teleprocess and batch-process data, although not simultaneously, since only one CPU is available. The 8250 system is supported by a full complement of peripheral devices.

The UNIVAC BC/7 is a midi-minicomputer with a CPU size of 48 or 64K. The peripheral devices available with the BC/7 include terminals, printers, and magnetic disk and tape devices. It has an online disk storage capacity of 40 million bytes. The BC/7 can support the online and batch processing of data related to all types of business applications. This system has been successfully applied to inventory control, accounts payable or receivable, payroll, and the projection of future sales.

Maxi-minicomputers have even greater operational capabilities. They use larger CPUs, support more terminals, and have greater online storage than midi-mini-systems. Maxi-systems can perform online and batch processing concurrently. For example, users seated at terminals can interact with an online file while the system concurrently batch-processes other data.

This concurrent processing is possible because of the operating system incorporated into maxi-minicomputers. Let us say that a user is interacting with a specific online file, via a CRT. A delay normally exists between the processing of requests made via the terminal. However, the system is not permitted to remain idle. Instead, it may be directed to batch-process a job. When the system is not processing requests received from the terminal, it will turn to batch processing. When an inquiry is received from the online terminal, the system will momentarily suspend batch processing to handle the request and then continue batch processing. Because of the computer's speed, the system seems to be performing both tasks simultaneously. In reality, the computer is efficiently handling one type of processing at a time. The ability to concurrently support batch and online processing is an important addition.

It should be noted that minicomputers are not the only systems capable of this type of concurrent processing. Many non-minicomputer systems also possess this capability. However, they may require much larger CPUs and more sophisticated operating systems and cost much more. Although the cost of a minicomputer that performs this type of processing may exceed $100,000, a comparable conventional system may cost three to four times that amount. On the other hand, a larger conventional system may have an online storage capacity of billions of characters, support more terminals than maxi-minicomput-

FIGURE 16.4 The BASIC-Four 730 computer is one of the larger mini-computer systems with a CPU of 512K, an online disk storage capacity in excess of 800 megabytes, and online access to many terminals. (*Basic Four/Corp.*)

ers, and support more complex forms of online processing. The type of system chosen depends on user needs and financial resources.

Two systems classified as maxi-minicomputers are the BASIC-Four and Burroughs B 900 systems. The BASIC-Four system, illustrated in Figure 16.4, possesses a CPU which can be built up to 512K and an online disk storage capacity of 800 million characters. It can support 32 terminal devices. The BASIC-Four system can perform batch processing, online processing, and a combination of both. This system permits the online access of separate files and the concurrent batch processing of other data.

The B 900 system, illustrated in Figure 16.5, has similar operational capabilities. It may have a CPU of 64K or larger, maintain an online storage capacity well in excess of 500 million characters on magnetic disk units, and support teleprocessing via 33 terminals. The vast online storage capacity of the B 900 and BASIC-Four systems enables them to handle the large amounts of information that are associated with a database. Both the B 900 and BASIC-Four systems can be applied to almost all forms of business data processing. Each can handle the online update of files as well as the batch processing of data for any organization.

The systems discussed in this section are representative of minicomputers manufactured by a group of independent companies. Each configuration illustrates just one of a group of available models. The actual minicomputer purchased by any organization will reflect its needs and resources. The cost of any minicomputer will depend on its peripheral devices and the computer model selected.

FIGURE 16.5 The B 900 is another maxi-minicomputer capable of supporting teleprocessing operations with concurrent terminals. (Burroughs Corp.)

16.2 Minicomputer Systems
CPU Storage

The processing speeds attained by minicomputer CPUs are comparable to those of larger, more expensive systems. In many minicomputers, data is stored in the CPU on a fixed-word basis, employing 16 or 32 bits per word in the ASCII code. CPU sizes and storage formats depend on the model and manufacturer of the minicomputer.

As in conventional computers, the CPU is the heart of the minicomputer. In discussions of minicomputer CPUs, two terms frequently used are **random access memory (RAM)** and **read only memory (ROM).** Random access memory, or RAM memory, defines primary storage as an organized series of storage areas into which a continuous flow of data can be stored and subsequently read during processing. Each item of data stored in RAM memory is independently accessible. Thus, data written into RAM memory can be used in processing and output without affecting other storage positions. Data created during processing can be stored in previously used RAM memory and becomes immediately available. However, when this occurs, data previously stored in RAM positions is overlaid and destroyed. Data is transferred in and out of RAM memory as required by the computer.

Read only memory, or ROM memory, consists of storage areas from which data can be read only. No data can be entered or stored in ROM memory because of the way ROM memory is constructed. ROM memory is composed of a series of miniaturized integrated circuits called **chips** (see Figure 16.6). Each chip is permanently wired to perform a specific function. This permanent wiring prevents data from being entered into these chips and leaves the contents of ROM memory unaltered.

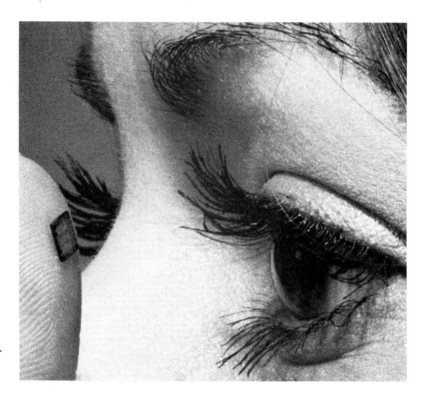

FIGURE 16.6 A read-only memory chip is a completely miniaturized integrated circuit permanently wired for one task. (*NCR.*)

Normally, the ROM chips are grouped together in configurations called **modules** or **boards.** These modules are supplied by the manufacturer and can be constructed to perform predefined computerized tasks. Modules are employed to process certain types of programming statements, perform numeric computations, assist in the editing and correction of input data, and execute selected JCL commands. At the users' request, modules may be added to minicomputers as well as conventional computer systems. In both types of systems, ROM modules assume specific operational responsibilities to facilitate processing.

Two new types of storage recently introduced are **PROM** (**p**rogrammable **r**ead **o**nly **m**emory) and **EPROM** (**e**rasable **p**rogrammable **r**ead **o**nly **m**emory). Both PROM and EPROM expand the capabilities of smaller systems and offer users more operational flexibility. PROM storage is essentially a blank ROM chip onto which a set of instructions are stored. Once filled, the contents of PROM storage cannot be altered.

EPROM chips are operationally similar to RAM, in that data can be written onto and read from it. EPROM is also initially blank and can have a series of instructions written onto it. However, the contents of

EPROM are erasable, permitting a change in those instructions stored within the chip. Thus, it is possible to start with one set of instructions and eventually change them. The ROM aspect to EPROM storage is that once instructions are stored, they are protected and accessed as a unit.

Peripheral Devices

As you may have concluded from the discussion of classes of minicomputers, these smaller systems can support a full range of peripheral devices (see Figure 16.7). Minicomputer systems support card readers, hardcopy and visual display terminals, magnetic tape and disk devices, and printers. However, the advent of minicomputer systems has given rise to many new types of peripheral devices. Figure 16.8 shows some of them.

FIGURE 16.7 Minicomputer systems support a variety of peripheral devices. The Honeywell minicomputer system includes a hardcopy terminal, card reader, magnetic tape cassette unit, magnetic disk, and printer. The operator is placing a magnetic disk unit into the system. (*Honeywell Inc.*)

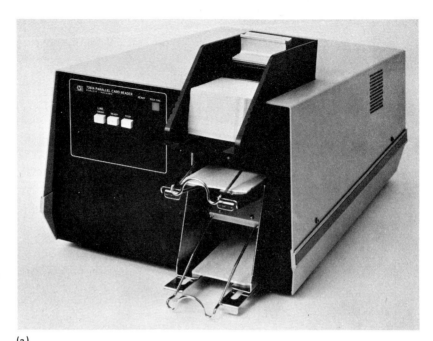

FIGURE 16.8(*a*) Peripheral devices developed for use with minicomputer systems: card reader. (*Hewlett-Packard.*)

(*a*)

FIGURE 16.8(*b*) Magnetic tape cassette unit. (*NCR.*)

(*b*)

The card reader shown in Figure 16.8a can read data not only off punched cards but also off mark-sense cards. The input process is accelerated by the direct reading of mark-sense data.

Minicomputer systems can use magnetic tape as a secondary storage medium. They can also use **tape cassettes** similar to those used for home tape recordings. Figure 16.8b shows one of these small cassettes in a tape cassette unit. This unit both reads and writes data on cassette. A tape cassette is a portable means of storing approximately 250,000 characters of data.

Manufacturers have developed smaller disk drives for use with minicomputer systems. The compact disk drive illustrated in Figure 16.8c contains a removable disk capable of storing more than 80 million characters of data.

FIGURE 16.8(c) Magnetic disk drive. (*Cal Computer Products.*)

(c)

FIGURE 16.9 The use
of floppy disks or disk-
ettes adds a direct
access dimension to
the use of minicomput-
ers. Diskettes are man-
ually inserted by the
operator and may be
switched with other disk-
ettes to gain access to
data in different files.
(*Digital Equipment
Corp.*)

Apple IIe is soft sector → it
writes on the sectors for you
Hard sector → the sectors
are already written on diskette

A more specialized means of disk storage is the small magnetic
disk called a **diskette** or **floppy disk.** As shown in Figure 16.9, this
small disk is manually inserted into a disk drive unit and provides a
low-cost, random access capability of up to 1 million characters.
Diskettes provide an online and backup storage medium similar to
magnetic tape. The storage of data on both sides of a diskette is now
possible with floppy disks called **dual-density diskettes.**

New peripheral devices are also being developed to enhance the
output capabilities of minicomputer systems. The receive-only printer,
illustrated in Figure 16.10a, offers a stand-alone printing capability that
may be attached to a CRT or used as a remote hardcopy printer for
limited output activities. The plotter shown in Figure 16.10b allows the
reproduction of diagrams of up to 7 inches × 10 inches, for under
$800. This desktop unit is compatible with all classes of minicomputer,
produces crisp nonlinear diagrams, and requires no extensive
training for its use.

These newer peripheral devices broaden the operational capabilities of minicomputer systems. They offer users great flexibility in satisfying their data processing needs. These devices are not meant to replace standard peripheral devices, but to complement them. Although the floppy disk has its advantages, a standard magnetic disk drive will probably be the primary means of direct access storage in a minicomputer system.

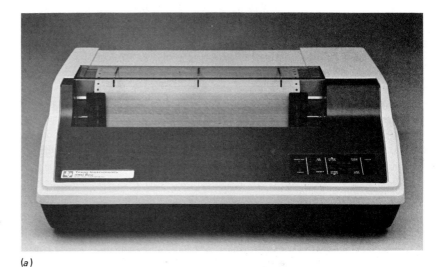

FIGURE 16.10(a) The Model 810 receive-only printer provides a remote hardcopy printing capability to a minicomputer. (*Texas Instruments.*)

(a)

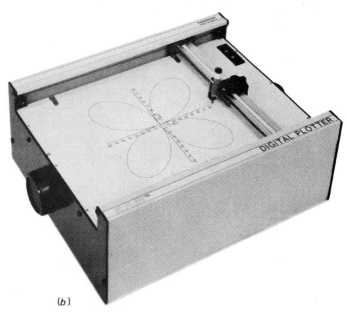

FIGURE 16.10(b) The HI PLOT is a portable plotter for the lower levels of minicomputers. This plotter is ideal for small drawings that must be reproduced. (*Houston Instrument.*)

(b)

Software

Minicomputer software can be divided into the broad areas of systems software and applications software. **Systems software** are manufacturer-supplied programs for controlling the operations of the system. This software includes any of the supervisor control programs, operating systems software, utility programs, and language compilers. Systems software can also establish and manage a database in a minicomputer.

Applications software are user-written programs for specific data processing tasks (e.g., processing a payroll, updating an inventory, or preparing customer monthly statements). They use the languages BASIC, FORTRAN, COBOL, PASCAL, and RPG. Most minicomputer companies clearly identify the languages their systems use, a factor that may affect the choice of minicomputer.

16.3 Microcomputers
An Overview of Their Use

Computers on chips.

Microcomputers are small, inexpensive computers that are sometimes referred to as "computers on a chip." This reference is derived from the fact that the components used to construct microcomputers are chips similar to those employed with ROM memory. These chips are miniaturized integrated circuits referred to as **microprocessors.** They can also provide the operational capabilities of the computer system. Thus it is possible to simulate the operation of a CPU, control I/O operations, and create a primary storage area for a microcomputer. The microcomputer (on a single chip) shown in Figure 16.11 possesses a CPU, ROM memory, RAM memory, and the ability to initiate I/O operations.

Microcomputers are essentially miniaturized computer systems with a limited range of uses. Each microcomputer can input, process, and output data. Storage in microprocessors is composed of ROM, RAM, PROM, and EPROM memory modules.

Current technology has made the microcomputer relatively simple to use. Most microcomputers are programmed on an interactive basis, and most programs are entered via CRT keyboard. Program packages are also available for microcomputers, with these programs retained on a magnetic tape cartridge or floppy disk. The transfer of the desired software from these media is accomplished, with a few control statements, in minutes.

Improvements in the microcomputer hardware have been continuous. Once limited to CRT and tape cassette, current microcomputers use multiple diskettes, bidirectional printers, plotters, graphics terminals with multicolor capabilities, and voice I/O units.

An example of these features is the WANG PCS-III microcomputer, illustrated in Figure 16.12. This desktop unit can support two diskettes for 280K of random access storage, a 32K CPU, and a low-speed printer. PCS-III programs are in BASIC, using over 110 types of in-

FIGURE 16.11 The Intel 8748 is a microcomputer contained on a single chip measuring 0.221 by 0.261 inches. The 8748 contains the equivalent of a CPU, RAM memory, and ROM memory in which program instructions are stored, and it can initiate input/output operations. (*Intel.*)

structions. Data may be manipulated in the disk files, which are readily available during processing for file interrogations. A wide range of canned software is readily available for engineers, researchers, small-business owners, and students.

Microcomputers are usually applied to highly specialized tasks and have been effectively used to process business, laboratory, hospital, statistical, and financial data. They are the major components in many of the video cartridge games attached to television sets. Many commercial electronic outlets offer kits for building microcomputers.

FIGURE 16.12 **The WANG PCS-III is a microcomputer that offers a personal computing. Its CRT, floppy disks, and printer support small business activities and research projects. The interactive use of BASIC provides online access to all data stored in files and the immediate update of those files. (*WANG.*)**

Home and Office Computing

Though microcomputers have had an effect on business, their greatest impact has been on the home computing market. Microcomputers have made it possible for individuals to bring the computer into their home and actually benefit from its use. These small systems are used in tax preparation, balancing checkbooks, recording recipes and important family dates, preparing lessons for children prohibited from engaging in normal schooling, and developing an interest in computers.

Two leaders in the expanding home market are the TRS-80 by Radio Shack and APPLE microcomputing systems, shown in Figures 16.13*a* and 16.13*b*, respectively. It was the initial success of the TRS-80 that launched the microcomputer into prominence at a cost of under $600. The TRS-80 Model III can support a CPU of 64K, four diskettes, and many models of printers and color terminals.

The APPLE microcomputer, equally as proficient, supports a comparable CPU, diskette storage, color CRT with graphics capabilities, and a low-speed printer. Both the APPLE and TRS-80 are used in businesses and homes.

The rapid expansion of the home computer and small business market has attracted the larger computer manufacturers. Two recent entrants are the Digital and IBM 5100 series systems. Figure 16.14*a* shows Digital's system with features comparable to those described

(a)

FIGURE 16.13(a) A TRS-80 Model III microcomputer. (Radio Shack.)

FIGURE 16.13(b) Apple computer system. (Apple.)

(b)

above. A full version of this microcomputer costs under $9000 and handles a full range of business problems. Software packages and training classes are available for new users.

The IBM 5120, Figure 16.14b, has a vast CPU of 512K, diskette storage of over 1 million characters, bidirectional printers, and an assortment of management-oriented program packages. This system may be used as an offline, independent computer or linked to a larger system for telecommunications.

Microcomputers offer a limited processing capability and cannot approach the internal speeds achieved by larger computer systems. However, these devices are not meant to compete with the larger systems in either scope or price. Current prices of microcomputers start at $400, with future prices expected to drop. The long-range outlook for microcomputers is good, because technology continues to decrease the size requirements for computer systems. More and more

(a)   (b)

FIGURE 16.14(*a*) A digital **microcomputer**. (*Digital Equipment Corporation.*) (*b*) An IBM 5120 micro-computer. (*IBM.*)

processing potential can be squeezed into ever smaller compart-ments. Thus, future microcomputers will possess capabilities that sur-pass existing computers of the same size. The microcomputer may well become the computer found in every home.

16.4 Word Processing (WP)
Office Applications

Minicomputers and microcomputers are having a marked impact on word processing operations. **Word processing (WP)** may be defined as the computerized preparation and handling of an organization's paperwork. Word processing systems accomplish these tasks in a vari-ety of ways. Let us examine two word processing applications.

Case 1

A secretary must individually type the same letter to 25 people. Nor-mally, it would be manually typed 25 times with increasing fatigue. But a new word processing system has simplified the process. The original letter is keyed into the WP system along with commands to control margins, tab settings, and the indexing of lines. A sample letter, output when the keying operation is complete, lets the secretary visually check its contents. The word processing system can then automati-cally prepare 25 original letters.

Case 2

A company must print an insurance form that will be distributed to its almost 1800 employees. Because the form must have three print sizes, use of a conventional hardcopy printer is not feasible. A word process-ing system equipped with a special printer can help complete this task. The form and directions for printing it are keyed into the WP computer. The computer will transmit an image of the document to the WP-directed printer and will output the 1800 letters in under an hour. The

A CHICKEN IN EVERY POT,
A COMPUTER IN EVERY CAR.

Not satisfied with just a computer at home, a New York businessman had an APPLE microcomputer system installed in his car. The computer is programmed to accept business data and provides an array of computerized games for those long drives. Consider how advantageous a mobile computer would be for children on a long cross-country trip?

(Photo courtesy of Newsday.)

final form will have the three print sizes and the name of the employee receiving it. These names are drawn from a disk incorporated into the system and are fed to the printer as each form is printed.

Both examples illustrate the advantages of word processing systems. The WP system assumes the drudgery of repeatedly preparing a document. Word processing systems can rapidly prepare many copies of conventional and computer-generated outputs.

WP Hardware

As you might imagine, word processing systems vary in type and configuration according to manufacturer and application. Figure 16.15 offers a glimpse of two word processing devices. In the foreground of Figure 16.15 is a magnetic card system; in the rear is a specialized printing device.

The IBM Mag Card II Typewriter system represents one of the most fundamental word processing systems. It is designed to handle a moderate level of office correspondence. Data entered via the typewriter is stored on magnetic cards, one of which is being inserted by an operator in Figure 16.15. The insertion of this card at a later date permits the repeated printing of that correspondence. Thus, it is possible to recall copies of letters at any time and have them reprinted as needed.

The magnetic card system can be used alone or attached to the special printer shown in the background of Figure 16.15. The device is

HATE MEMOS? THEN CONSIDER THIS

Philadelphia (AP)—An insurance office without paperwork? That's what the Reliance Insurance Co. tried to achieve during a "Paper Free" day at corporate headquarters.

Vice president Raymond E. Hafner sprang the surprise exercise on his 225-member Corporate Systems and Administrative Support staff Tuesday. At an early morning meeting, the employees were told to try to do all their work without generating new pieces of paper to read or file.

"The response was better than we expected," Hafner said yesterday. "People worked hard at finding creative ways to get their work done without paper."

It became a day of no memos, no dictation notes, no photocopies. Workers were encouraged to deliver information by telephone and to store it in computers.

The effort was a step toward realization of the company's "Paper Free in '83" program. By then, the firm hopes to be almost completely reliant on computers. Hafner said that the exercise will be repeated for longer periods in the future and will include more of the company's 1,100 headquarters employees.

John W. Folk, Reliance's deputy chairman and chief executive officer, said the idea of halting the use of paper grew out of studies. They showed that 25 per cent of the company's 5,400 workers nationally spend their entire workday creating, storing or looking in files for information written on paper. They also showed that about 80 per cent of the paper filed wasn't looked at again until it was retrieved to be destroyed or microfilmed.

With the advent of computers for recordkeeping, "we believe that we can achieve a reduction of 75 per cent in our use of paper records," Folk said. The experiment ran into a few problems. For example, workers still had to jot down telephone messages for fellow employees who were out. But Hafner was undaunted. "The tool to handle that situation isn't available yet," he said.

Guiding the day's activities were seven monitors wearing "Paper Free" buttons and blue baseball caps.

Hafner said he selected people who were "most creative" at coming up with no-paper ideas to help the rest of the staff.

Hafner, who estimates that he usually handles about 120 pieces of paper a day, said he managed to break the habit. "I struggled, it slowed me down, but I found I could get the job done without generating new pieces of paper," he said. And he acknowledged: "The insurance industry probably proliferates more paper than any other except banking."

Hafner added: "While other companies seem to focus on clerical workers as a source of paperwork, we've begun with the executive offices and management. It's an idea whose time has come."

Source: Associated Press, New York, N.Y., July 31, 1980.

FIGURE 16.15 Word processing operations incorporate many devices. In the foreground, the MAG Card II Typewriter system lets users key and store letters on magnetic cards. These cards may be used with the Mag Card unit or with the IBM 6670 Information Distributor shown in the background. The 6670 has a variety of printing specialties and is sometimes called an intelligent printer. (*IBM.*)

the IBM 6670 Information Distributor, a laser printer capable of printing 1800 characters per second, or 36 pages per minute. The 6670 may be used as an online printing unit, connected to a magnetic card system, or operated as a stand-alone word processing printer. It offers great flexibility to organizations with a high volume of printed correspondence.

Data may be keyed into the 6670 from a magnetic card typewriter or CRT. It can also accept data stored on magnetic cards. A special control language called Operator Control Language (OCL) controls the system's text-editing features such as margin setting, line indexing, and use of up to four different kinds of printed characters.

Used as an online printer, the IBM 6670 accepts data from a computer and outputs it as directed. It can print, collate, and prepare reports directly from computer outputs without incurring any intermediate delay. Reports appear on $8\frac{1}{2}$ inch $\times$ 11 inch sheets and look professionally printed. The 6670 can also prepare transparencies, gummed labels, and offset printed materials. Because of its special features, the 6670 is sometimes called an **intelligent printer.**

The 6670 has other advantages as an online printer. Data transmitted over ordinary telephone lines in a distributed DP system can be printed in various formats. Letters may be electronically transmitted and printed between offices, speeding their arrival. Manuals or text pages can be printed at their point of distribution. The 6670 offers great flexibility to organizations with diverse word processing needs.

FIGURE 16.16 The WANG Office Information System (OIS) 145 offers word processing for an office. It uses both floppy and conventional disks. It can retain approximately 300,000 pages of material. (*WANG.*)

Word processing systems also incorporate CRTs and disk storage, as shown in Figure 16.16. The Wang Office Information System (OIS) 145 supports 32 peripheral devices, 24 of which may be input terminals. It can store approximately 334,000 pages of material on disks and uses diskettes for offline storage. The OIS 145 can support one or two 275-megabyte disk units. Many forms of operational software and utility programs are also available for the 145 system.

The OIS 145 lets users key in, store, recall, and print pages of data as necessary. Standard memos, forms, or letters may be output without rekeying. Disk storage means that long manuscripts or letters can be retrieved in their entirety and rapidly printed. Features of this type make the 145 attractive to publishers, law firms, or organizations that handle many printed documents.

Word processing now also extends to automatic typesetting. Figure 16.17 shows an **automatic typesetter** which produces galleys, in a variety of type styles and sizes, which are used in printing manuscripts, reports, or books. The Wang Typesetter 48 in Figure 16.17 first prints material on film and then on galleys on paper.

The Typesetter 48 may be attached directly to a word processing system, such as the OIS 145, to automate the preparation of galleys. The computer sends the material directly to the automatic typesetter, and it produces the required film. This set up eliminates the need for printing and rekeying the data in order to produce galley pages.

FIGURE 16.17 Another peripheral device that may be added to a word processing system is the automatic typesetter. The WANG Typesetter 48 shown here photographs information and produces film from which reports are actually printed. This typesetter can mix different sizes and fonts of type. (*WANG.*)

Distributed Word Processing

Word processing now spans the distance between various offices within an organization. **Distributed word processing systems (DWPS)** speed the transfer of documents between distant offices.

The method of transfer depends on the systems resources available. Two current DWPS configurations are illustrated in Figure 16.18. In Figure 16.18*a,* the main computer is online to word processing systems at regional offices. The regional WP systems have online CRTs, disk storage, and intelligent printers. Messages from one office are telecommunicated through the central system to other offices. Memoranda, letters, forms, or inquiry responses go rapidly between offices and avoid postal delays. Information is printed at the office in which it is needed rather than at the computer center. This type of centralized DWPS provides immediate access to another office's files. Copies of correspondence needed at one office, if recorded in the system, are instantaneously telecommunicated for output at the requesting office. The possible savings in paper-handling, mailing, and duplication costs are great.

Similar word processing operations are possible with the slightly different online configuration detailed in Figure 16.18*b.* In this system, word processing terminals are tied into one vast, central system. All documents are retained in the main database, to which any office may gain access via the main computer.

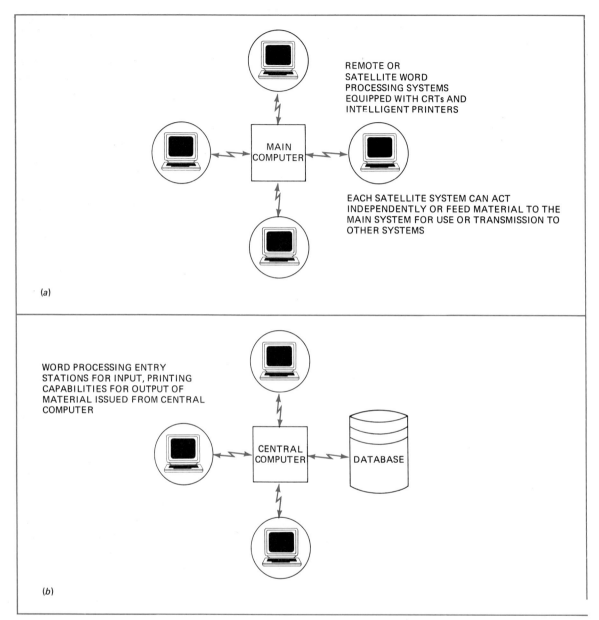

REMOTE OR
SATELLITE WORD
PROCESSING SYSTEMS
EQUIPPED WITH CRTs AND
INTELLIGENT PRINTERS

MAIN COMPUTER

EACH SATELLITE SYSTEM CAN ACT
INDEPENDENTLY OR FEED MATERIAL TO THE
MAIN SYSTEM FOR USE OR TRANSMISSION TO
OTHER SYSTEMS

(a)

WORD PROCESSING ENTRY
STATIONS FOR INPUT, PRINTING
CAPABILITIES FOR OUTPUT OF
MATERIAL ISSUED FROM CENTRAL
COMPUTER

CENTRAL COMPUTER

DATABASE

(b)

FIGURE 16.18 Two distributed word processing configurations.

This configuration permits tight security at the main computer over the system. It is designed primarily for organizations that distribute large amounts of information to field offices. The DWPS described above (and illustrated in Figure 16.18a) is better suited to heavy interoffice activity. Savings here, too, accrue from the reduction in paper-handling. Information is rapidly distributed throughout an organization as needed. Printers are installed at strategic points to provide hardcopy outputs.

Software packages are available for these distributed word processing operations. One such package is the **Applied Text Management System (ATMS)** from IBM. It is designed for the large organization which handles vast amounts of paperwork.

ATMS is an interactive system. Users seated at terminals may prepare and store letters, memos, reports, or other documents. As directed, ATMS will establish margins and hyphenate words at a line's end, carry lines to a new page, and properly space, indent, or index each line. Corrections may be inserted at any time. ATMS will insert the correction and adjust all following lines. ATMS software lets users:

1 Key in a message ahead of time and have it printed at a particular time, at a specific terminal

2 Prepare a written report to be copied in a certain quantity by a specified date and in a particular format

3 Retain memos for fixed periods of time

4 Gain access to standard letters which can be printed in seconds and include the recipient's name and address

Organizations which must handle their paperwork efficiently will eventually turn to word processing systems for their savings in time and money. Offices of the future will use WP systems for internal communications. Today's distributed word processing systems and software packages are just the first stages of the revolution in the computerization of office paperwork.

16.5
A Comparison of Computer Systems

Have you ever considered what the record is for the fastest computer? According to the *Guinness Book of Records,* the fastest computer is the Control Data Corporation's Star-100, which performed an astounding 97.9 million operations per second. Speed records are set under ideal conditions and represent a minor measure of a computer's efficiency. The true measure of a computer's effectiveness is its day-to-day performance.

Computer systems possess their own operational capabilities which set them apart from other systems. It is important that a user considering adoption of a computer system understand its operational characteristics. This knowledge may prevent the purchase of a system totally unsuited to an organization's data processing needs.

It is difficult to assess a computer's capabilities. Because the industry advances so rapidly, this assessment is ongoing. Knowledge comes only with time, practical experience, and continued exposure.

To help people, the data processing industry has classified computer systems into the following four categories:

1 Small-scale computer systems
2 Medium-scale computer systems
3 Large-scale computer systems
4 Supercomputer systems

These general categories are useful for evaluating different models of computers and for comparing one manufacturer's computer with other models in that category.

Like automobiles, computers range in cost and complexity. The most sophisticated systems fall into the category of supercomputers, while the least expensive computers are the small-scale systems. The cost and complexity of a computer system are closely related to the size of its CPU and its peripheral devices.

Small-Scale Computer Systems

Small-scale computer systems are exactly that: smaller-sized computer systems. These computers have the same capabilities as their larger counterparts, except on a smaller scale, with CPU sizes generally ranging from 4 to 64K. Many of these smaller systems can support batch and online processing, including teleprocessing. Many minicomputer and microcomputer systems fall into this category. Small-scale computers are designed for use in small businesses, manufacturing and production companies, public and private schools, financial and banking institutions, and small government or municipal organizations. Examples of small-scale computer systems are the UNIVAC 90, IBM System/34 and /38, Honeywell 60, Burroughs 90, Digital Equipment Corporation's PDP-11, and Data General Corporation's Nova series. Let's discuss two systems that are representative of this category.

The IBM System/38, illustrated in Figure 16.19, is a small-scale computer designed for a business that uses both batch and online processing. Its primary language is RPG, and it is unique in using the 96-column card. The System/38 can support many types of peripherals.

The Hewlett-Packard 3000 computer, illustrated in Figure 16.20, is a minicomputer with a CPU size of 64K, which can be enlarged to 2 megabytes of storage. The HP 3000 uses the normal complement of I/O devices (card reader, printer, disk and tape drives, etc.), and it can also support CRTs and other terminal devices. This system is capable of batch processing, online processing, and teleprocessing, and it can function as a remote job entry (RJE) station. A variety of computer languages are used with the 3000, and a large selection of systems

FIGURE 16.19 The IBM System/38. (*IBM.*)

software is available from the manufacturer. The purchase price of the HP 3000 is approximately $100,000. The addition of peripheral devices may add anywhere from $25,000 to $200,000 to the price. The NCR 8450, PDP 11, and Burroughs 900 are comparable to the HP 3000.

Medium-Scale Computer Systems

Medium-scale computer systems provide users with a wider range of activities. These systems provide a larger storage capacity and can use more I/O devices. These additional features increase teleprocessing support and enlarge the system's capability to handle tasks. Medium-scale computers have CPU sizes of 64 to 512K, but may range up

FIGURE 16.20 The Hewlett-Packard 3000 computer is capable of batch processing, online processing, and teleprocessing, and it can function as an RJE. (*Hewlett-Packard.*)

to 2 million bytes of storage and have uses similar to those of small-scale systems. Medium-scale computers are effective for colleges, government and military installations, manufacturer facilities, retail stores, and defense plants. Examples are the IBM System 4300 series, UNIVAC 1100/10, Burroughs 4900, Honeywell 62/60, and many models of maxi-minicomputers.

Each of these computer systems is a general-purpose machine, capable of processing information for all types of applications. Each system usually has a card reader, a card punch, multiple tape and disk drives, and a high-speed printer. Medium-scale systems support a wide range of peripheral devices and typically rent for approximately $2000 to $20,000 per month.

Large-Scale Computer Systems

The jump from medium-scale computers to **large-scale computer systems** is considerable. Medium-scale computers can support data processing in most corporations, but large-scale computers are required by organizations that handle a sizable quantity of data. Primarily, these larger systems are employed by vast domestic and international corporations and government agencies.

The New York Stock Exchange is an organization which needs the tremendous processing potential of a large-scale computer. The Exchange handles all the data generated by the daily sale of 45 million or more shares of stock.

The largest brokerage house on Wall Street, Merrill Lynch, Pierce, Fenner & Smith Inc., has a large-scale computer system to handle its high daily volume of stock transactions. Merrill Lynch uses a total of five IBM 370/168s for its data processing. This number of 168s is necessary to process the volume of data produced during the prompt and accurate servicing of the firm's clients. Four computers are assigned to handle the amount of data generated from all transactions. The fifth computer oversees the other four. This configuration ensures the most effective use of Merrill Lynch's system. The overseer computer efficiently controls and apportions the work to the four subordinate computers.

Municipal and county governments in densely populated areas require the support of larger systems. Nassau County, New York, uses a large-scale system for its court and tax system and welfare and social services departments. In addition, its IBM 370/168 system supports all other areas of administration for a county of over 2 million people. The volume of data handled by most large city or county governments requires large-scale computers. It would prove inefficient and extremely costly to process this amount of data by any other means.

Because of the enormous amounts of data they process, large-scale systems need vast CPUs. CPU sizes for this type of computer begin at 512K and often run into the millions of characters. Accord-

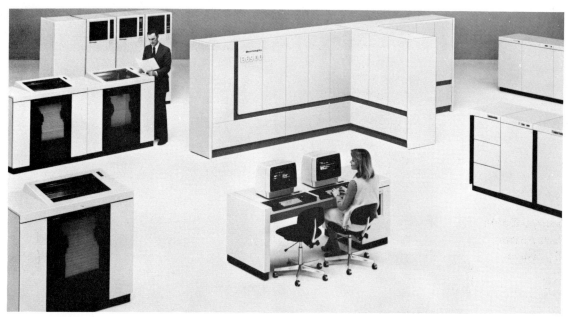

FIGURE 16.21   The Burroughs 6900 is a large system with many peripheral devices. A system of this size requires a large DP staff. (*Burroughs.*)

ingly, the cost of these systems is quite high, with monthly rental costs approaching $75,000.

Large-scale systems can accommodate a variety of peripheral devices, including many tape and disk drives, disk storage facilities, optical character readers, plotters, printers, CRTs, RJEs, and many types of communication terminals. Online processing is an earmark of most large-scale computers. However, these systems can fully support time-sharing, batch processing, and all forms of teleprocessing. Examples of large-scale systems are the IBM 370/Model 168, Burroughs 6900 (illustrated in Figure 16.21), Honeywell 66/80, Control Data Cyber 175, and Amdahl V5.

Supercomputer Systems

Relatively few companies or organizations require the extraordinary capabilities of a **supercomputer.** Supercomputers are the largest, fastest, and most expensive computer systems. These systems are capable of storing well over 5 million characters in their CPUs and operate two to five times faster than large-scale computers. The cost of a supercomputer begins at $10 million.

Scientific laboratories involved with space exploration and simulated space flights are an example of organizations that require the tremendous processing speed and storage capacity of supercomput-

FIGURE 16.22 The CDC Cyber 7600 supercomputer can store well over 5 million characters in its CPU. (*Control Data Corp.*)

ers. Similarly, international corporations with large, sophisticated time-sharing systems among their corporate offices need the processing potential of supercomputers. Many national defense systems are currently supported by supercomputers.

One highly visible user of a supercomputer is the United States Weather Service, which requires this capability to process weather information received from throughout the country. The service receives regional data, analyzes it, and issues its forecasts. The process of monitoring existing weather conditions and preparing new forecasts is continuous. The weather supercomputer must issue both short- and long-range forecasts as well as hurricane, tornado, and other natural disaster warnings. The volume of data handled is staggering when you consider that the origination of data never stops. New conditions are always arising, and therefore, the weather must continuously be monitored, analyzed, and reported.

Examples of supercomputers are the CDC Cyber 7600 (illustrated in Figure 16.22), the CRAY-1, and the CRAY-2. Each of these systems is capable of tremendous processing speeds, potentially up to 15 times the speed of a large-scale system.

Case Study One
Word Processing Operations Help Triple Output

The installation of a word processing system at Ciba-Giegy Corp., at Ardsley, N.Y., has speeded their processing of written materials and increased their productivity by 300 percent. A diversified drug manufacturer, Ciba-Giegy determined that a word processing center would efficiently handle its paperwork. All jobs, including letters, memos, lengthy reports, research data, statistical surveys, and mailing lists, are handled by the C-G word processing center. Conventional typewriters are rarely used.

Conversion to the word processing system took a few years. In 1973, 12 mag card typewriters replaced a large clerical staff that had handled documents generated by offices in 32 states. A substantial increase in sales created a paperwork crisis, and C-G switched to Vydec WP systems. Six Vydec systems replaced the 12 mag card units. Each contained a CRT with a 4096 character

buffer, disk drive, and low-speed printer. Three additional Vydec systems, added in 1976, allowed the WP center to increase its output from 150 to 250 documents weekly. By the end of 1977, the center was producing 450 documents a week.

Materials come to the WP center in hand-written documents and on dictation tapes and tape cassettes. Operators are trained to handle these media. C-G conducts extensive training to ensure the continued success of the WP operations. New operators, selected for their mechanical aptitude and grammatical skills, receive 24 to 40 hours of training.

Ciba-Giegy management is exploring the conversion to a distributed word processing system to further speed the word processing. It is also examining the feasibility of incorporating automatic typesetting equipment and intelligent printers.

Consider this . . .

Word processing operations are in their infancy. To what other office tasks could word processing be applied? Could you use this technology in your home? Under what conditions and where?

Summary

The following major points have been presented in Chapter 16:

Point 1 Minicomputers are small, task-oriented computer systems which may be applied to a variety of jobs. Minicomputers possess the operational capabilities of larger, conventional systems in that they employ a CPU and peripheral devices to process data. Their smaller size results in cost savings to their users.

Point 2 Minicomputer systems are divided into three classes according to their CPU sizes and operational potential. Mini-minicomputers can have CPUs of 4 to 128K, have a maximum disk storage of 40 million bytes, are limited to the use of one or two CRTs, and cost $50,000 or less. The middle range of minicomputers, midi-minicomputers, possess CPU sizes of approximately 128,000 to 512,000 bytes. The midi-systems support peripherals to provide a disk storage up to 100 million bytes, use of 3 to 16 terminals, and high-speed printers. The cost of midi-systems ranges between $50,000 and $100,000. Maxi-minicomputers are

Case Study Two

WP Systems Replace Secretaries

What does a $350 million corporation which writes $7 billion in insurance, employs 3200 agents, and services people in 60 countries do when it faces a document bottleneck? It certainly doesn't hire more employees! It switches from manual, clerical operations to a word processing system.

That is exactly what the American Life Insurance Company (ALICO) did in 1976. Unhappy with hiring temporary clerical personnel who were unable to handle an ever-increasing workload, ALICO bought a Vydec Text Editor system. Feasibility studies evaluated ALICO's needs and the operational characteristics of competitive word processing hardware. ALICO wanted a CRT-oriented system with high-speed printers that produced crisp hardcopy. It wanted a system that was reliable and had a history of minimal downtime.

Six Vydec systems now support ALICO's word processing operations. They have allowed ALICO to balance its workload and staffing requirements and to eliminate part-time clerical help. Analysts estimated that one word processing system is the operational equivalent of 18 clerical employees. A 2-day training seminar helps operators maintain their skills.

The ALICO word processing system outputs policy applications and proposals, advertising brochures, newsletters, management advertising bulletins, and various other publications. The word processing center has recently assumed the preparation of financial statements for distribution to stockholders as well as annual reports and balance sheets. Special programs allow the system to prepare and print these double-width reports. Because the Vydec system has been so successful, ALICO management is considering expanding its word processing services throughout the company.

the largest minicomputers, with CPUs of 512 to 2000K. These systems perform all types of batch and online processing and can support 4 to 33 terminals. The disk storage capacity of the larger minicomputers ranges up to 800 million characters. These systems cost from $75,000 to $300,000.

Point 3 CPU sizes of minicomputer systems range between 4 and 512K. Many minicomputers store data in the CPU on a fixed-word basis, using the ASCII code. Two types of CPU storage can be employed in minicomputer systems. Random access memory (RAM) consists of storage areas into which data can be randomly processed. Read only memory (ROM) consists of storage areas from which data can be read only, remaining unaltered. ROM memory is composed of chips, or microprocessors, which can be collectively grouped into boards, or modules. PROM enables the storage of instructions onto a blank chip, where it remains unaltered. EPROM chips can have instructions written onto them, or erased with new data stored in its place.

Point 4 Minicomputers support a full range of peripherals and have encouraged the development of newer devices. These systems can employ card readers, magnetic tape and disk units, and printers. Newer peripheral devices such as the tape cassette unit, diskette, and floppy disk increase the operational flexibility of these systems.

Point 5 The software in minicomputer systems is compatible with software in larger systems. Programmers may use BASIC, FORTRAN, RPG, or COBOL, as well as other languages developed for specific systems. Generally, minicomputer software is broadly divided into systems and applications software.

Point 6 Microcomputers are small computers constructed of microprocessors, or chips. These intregated miniaturized circuits provide microcomputers with operational capabilities that approximate the functioning of larger computer systems. BASIC is frequently used to write programs for microcomputers. Microcomputers offer a personalized computer capacity for a wide range of activities.

Point 7 The computerized preparation of paperwork is the goal of word processing systems. Word processing permits the distribution of documents throughout an organization with a minimum of clerical activity. Word processing hardware may include mag card typewriter systems, intelligent printers (for example, IBM 6670), and automatic typesetters. Word processing units may be distributed through an organization or operate through a main computer. ATMS is a word processing software package which offers a range of services to its users.

Point 8 Computer systems can be generally classified into four categories: small-scale, medium-scale, large-scale, and supercomputer systems. Computer systems are categorized according to their CPU sizes. Supercomputers have the largest CPUs and are the most expensive systems.

Glossary

Applications software   A term applied to user-written programs employed with computer systems.

Applied Text Management System (ATMS) A word processing software package which simplifies the preparation and distribution of documents in a distributed word processing system.

Automatic typesetter   A photographic printer that produces galleys for printed matter in a word processing system.

Boards   A group of ROM microprocessors (chips) wired together to support a specific computerized task.

Chips   Miniaturized integrated circuits which compose ROM memory.

Diskette   A small magnetic disk enclosed in a plastic envelope, used with minicomputer systems to provide a disk storage capacity.

Distributed word processing systems (DWPS)   A distributed system in which word processing activities are employed to distribute documents to various users.

Erasable programmable read only memory (EPROM)   Blank chips onto which sets of instructions may be written and then changed.

Floppy disk   See diskette.

Intelligent printer   A peripheral device that may be attached or may stand alone as a printer in a word processing system, with special features which enhance the output of printed data.

Large-scale computer systems   The third category of computer systems, consisting of computers that possess CPUs of up to 5000K.

Maxi-minicomputers   The largest type of minicomputer system, having a CPU size of 512 to 2000K.

Medium-scale computer systems   The second category of computer systems, consisting of computers that generally have CPUs of 64 to 512K.

Microcomputers   Small, highly specialized computer systems constructed using miniaturized integrated circuits (chips).

Microprocessors   Same as chips.

Midi-minicomputers   The middle range group of minicomputer systems, possessing CPUs of 128 to 512K.

Minicomputer   Small, compact, task-oriented computer systems possessing the potential of larger systems, but to a limited degree.

Mini-minicomputer   The smallest type of minicomputer, employing CPU sizes of 4 to 128K bytes of storage.

Modules   See boards.

Programmable read only memory (PROM)   Blank chips onto which instructions are written at the factory and never altered.

Random access memory (RAM)   Primary storage used with many minicomputer systems, in which data can be randomly stored and accessed.

Read only memory (ROM)   Storage created using microprocessors from which data or instructions are read only; nothing can be written into ROM memory.

Small-scale computer systems   The first category of computer systems, consisting of systems having CPUs of 4 to 64K.

Supercomputers   The fourth category of computer systems, possessing CPUs of 5 million bytes or more; the largest type of computer.

Systems software   The term applied to manufacturer-supplied programs used in computer systems.

Tape cassettes   Small magnetic tape reels used with minicomputer systems, providing limited sequential storage.

Word processing (WP)   The computerized processing and distribution of printed materials and paperwork in an organization.

Discussion Questions

1   Discuss the differences between mini-, midi-, and maxi-minicomputers.

2   Visit the office of a computer manufacturer and collect information relating to their minicomputer systems. Compile a list of all the types of peripheral devices and software which may be used with the systems. Prepare a brief report on a specific minicomputer, describing the business applications it can support.

3   Discuss the differences between ROM and RAM memory. Discuss an advantage associated with using either form of memory.

4   Define in your own words the following terms:

Chip	Tape cassette
Module	Diskette
Microprocessor	Minidiskette
Floppy disk	Applications software
Intelligent printer	Distributed WP systems

5   Discuss the four categories of computer systems. Complete the table that appears on page 681.

6   Discuss the advantages of a word processing system. How could it help the organization in which you are employed? Cite possible savings from word processing.

7   Cite examples of how a microcomputer might be used in the average home. Would you consider purchasing a microcomputer? Why?

	Type of System			
	Small Scale	Medium Scale	Large Scale	Super-computer
Range of CPU sizes				
Price ranges				
Type of peripheral support				
Examples of computers falling into this category				

Summary Test

_____ **1** Cost savings associated with minicomputers result solely from their use of smaller CPUs.

_____ **2** The three classes of minicomputers are mini-scale systems, medium-scale systems, and maxi-minicomputer systems.

_____ **3** Some maxi-minicomputer systems fall into the category of medium-scale computer systems.

_____ **4** Different models of computers can be compared using the three classifications of computer systems.

_____ **5** Large-scale computer systems are not restricted to batch-processing operations and can perform all types of online processing.

_____ **6** Maxi-minicomputer systems possess the capability to concurrently support the online access of data from a disk file and the weekly processing of a payroll.

_____ **7** Except for large-scale computers, supercomputers are the largest and most expensive types of computers.

_____ **8** Concurrent batch processing and online processing are possible in all minicomputer systems.

_____ **9** Magnetic tape cassettes are the same size as conventional tape reels and provide an effective means of sequential storage.

_____ **10** Compilers employed with minicomputer systems are classified as applications software.

_____ **11** ROM memory enables data to be read from and stored in every one of its storage areas.

_____ **12** Data is stored in minicomputers using the ASCII and ROM computer codes.

_____ **13** Modules composed of chips can be added to minicomputer systems to increase their operational capabilities.

_____ **14** Microcomputer systems may be used in homes as well as offices.

_____ **15** Word processing operations are restricted to the computerization of clerical tasks and do not permit output distribution throughout an organization.

_____ **16** Because it can function in more ways than a line printer, the IBM 6670 is sometimes referred to as a(n):

    a plotter   **b** mag card printer

    c intelligent printer   **d** photostatic copier

_____ **17** An I/O device which provides photographic outputs for printing galleys is the:

    a camera printer   **b** automatic typesetter

    c radix printer   **d** all of the above

_____ **18** An IBM System/38 represents the computer class of:

    a small-scale computer   **b** medium-scale computer

    c large-scale computer   **d** supercomputer

_____ **19** A term used interchangeably with diskette is:

    a disk cartridge   **b** disk pack

    c floppy disk   **d** packette disk

_____ **20** A characteristic normally associated with a large-scale computer system is:

    a real-time processing   **b** a complex array of I/O devices

    c a CPU of 1000K   **d** all of the above

_____ **21** A software package generally used within a distributed word processing system is:

    a ATMS   **b** DWPS   **c** RPG   **d** DBMS

_____ **22** An advantage of a distributed word processing network is:

    a increased number of reports handled

    b less delay in interoffice communications

    c greater corporate control over outputs

    d all of the above

_____ **23** Which of the following is true?

    a Plotters are not available for microcomputer systems.

    b Microcomputers are not programmed like conventional computers.

    c Minicomputers are task-oriented.

    d The contents of ROM are easily changed.

_____ **24** ROM is composed of:

    a magnetic cores   **b** microprocessors

    c photoelectric cells   **d** floppy disks

_____ **25** A peripheral device used in a word processing system is:

    a floppy disk   **b** magnetic card reader

    c CRT   **d** all of the above

Summary Test Answers

1 F	**2** F	**3** T	**4** F	**5** T
6 T	**7** F	**8** F	**9** F	**10** F
11 F	**12** F	**13** T	**14** T	**15** F
16 C	**17** B	**18** A	**19** C	**20** D
21 A	**22** B	**23** C	**24** B	**25** D

Appendix

Most of our arithmetic operations are performed with decimal numbers. The computer, however, does not use the decimal numbering system. It uses the binary numbering system, which is based on the number 2. This base 2 system uses only the digits 0 and 1 to represent numerical values, and thus when completing computations involving decimals, the computer must essentially perform three steps:

1 It converts numeric data input from its decimal format into its binary equivalent.
2 It performs the desired arithmetic manipulations in binary.
3 It converts the binary results into their decimal equivalents for output.

Why does the computer do this? The reason is simple. It is easier and faster for the computer than for people to accomplish the required conversion. Furthermore, the accuracy of the results is more certain.

Often, however, programming personnel must simulate the computer's performance of arithmetic operations and work problems in computer-related numbering systems (e.g., base 2). This need may arise when a programmer is verifying the results of processing or debugging a program. Computer personnel normally develop a familiarity with numbering systems other than base 10.

In computerized data processing, the numbering systems most commonly encountered are the binary (base 2), octal (base 8), and hexadecimal (base 16) systems. The structure of these bases, methods of converting from one base to another, and the unique relationships among bases 2, 8, and 16 will be discussed in this appendix.

The Expansion of a Number

All numbering systems provide a ready means of representing quantities. However, each numbering system represents a given amount in a different way. A quantity of fourteen sheep is expressed as 14 in the decimal system but 1110 in the binary system. The amount of sheep remains constant; only the means of representing the amount changes. Because of the way we have been educated, we readily identify the number 14. The computer uses the equivalent 1110 in its computations.

Each numbering system uses different digits. For example, in the decimal number system, the digits are

$$0, 1, 2, 3, 4, 5, 6, 7, 8, 9$$

Each can be used individually, or they can be grouped to form a numeric value. The decimal number 14 is composed of the digits 1 and 4, and the positioning of each digit is important. The 1 is placed in the 10's column, while the 4 is positioned in the 1's column. Essentially, one 10 and four 1's have been added to equal 14. This relationship is represented symbolically as follows:

$$14 = \underbrace{1 \times 10} + \underbrace{4 \times 1}$$
$$= \quad 10 \quad + \quad 4$$
$$= \quad 14$$

In the following example, the same analysis is made of a larger value:

$$2847 = \underbrace{2 \times 10^3} + \underbrace{8 \times 10^2} + \underbrace{4 \times 10^1} + \underbrace{7 \times 10^0}$$
$$= 2 \times 1000 + 8 \times 100 + 4 \times 10 + 7 \times 1$$
$$= \quad 2000 \quad + \quad 800 \quad + \quad 40 \quad + \quad 7$$
$$= \quad 2847$$

The first line of the above expansion represents a breakdown of the number 2847 into its base 10 components. The quantity 2000 is the equivalent of 2×10^3, where $10^3 = 1000$. The values 800 and 40 represent the amounts 8×10^2 and 4×10^1, where $10^2 = 100$ and $10^1 = 10$.

The last component in the expansion, 10^0, normally causes some confusion because of its exponent. The expression 10^0 is always equal to 1. In fact any number taken to the zero power equals 1 (i.e., $n^0 = 1$). For example:

$$1000^0 = 1 \qquad 6^0 = 1 \qquad -18^0 = 1$$

The breaking down of the number 2847 into its base 10 components is referred to as the *expansion* of the number. This type of breakdown can be applied to any value in any positional numbering system. This analysis provides the basis for a computative technique, referred to as the *expansion method,* which can be used to convert a number written in any base to its decimal equivalent. Thus, using the expansion method, a binary number can be converted to its equivalent base 10 value.

The Binary (Base 2) Numbering System

The decimal system uses the digits 0 to 9 to represent numeric quantities, whereas the binary numbering system uses the digits 0 to 1. All values represented in binary will contain only 0's and 1's. A comparison of decimal digits 0 through 9 and their binary equivalents is provided in Table A.1.

Table A.1   The Binary Equivalent of
Decimal Numbers

Decimal Number	Binary Equivalent	Decimal Number	Binary Equivalent
0	0000	5	0101
1	0001	6	0110
2	0010	7	0111
3	0011	8	1000
4	0100	9	1001

The Expansion Method

The expansion method can show the equivalence between the decimal number 9 and the binary number 1001 as follows:

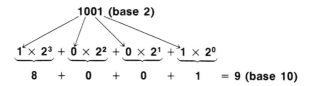

$$1001 \text{ (base 2)}$$

$$1 \times 2^3 + 0 \times 2^2 + 0 \times 2^1 + 1 \times 2^0$$

$$8 \quad + \quad 0 \quad + \quad 0 \quad + \quad 1 \quad = 9 \text{ (base 10)}$$

The following points can be observed from the above expansion:

1   The digits (0's and 1's) in the original binary number individually precede each of the components of the expansion.

2   The base of the number undergoing conversion is consecutively raised to a power, starting with the zero power on the extreme right. In this case, we begin with 2^0 and use the powers 2^1, 2^2 and 2^3, with 2^3 being the highest power used.

3   The result obtained from the expansion is a decimal (base 10) number.

Applying the expansion method to an earlier problem, we can demonstrate that the binary number 1110 equals 14 in base 10.

$$
\begin{aligned}
1110_2 &= 1 \times 2^3 + 1 \times 2^2 + 1 \times 2^1 + 0 \times 2^0 \\
&= 1 \times 8 + 1 \times 4 + 1 \times 2 + 0 \times 1 \\
&= 8 + 4 + 2 + 0 \\
&= 14
\end{aligned}
$$

Note that the original binary number 1110 has a suffix associated with it. The suffix 2 following the digits 1110 indicates that the number is given in base 2. The suffix 5 indicates a base 5 number. The suffix 16 indicates a base 16 value. The following examples further demonstrate the use of the expansion method in the conversion of binary numbers to base 10.

$$101100_2 = 1 \times 2^5 + 0 \times 2^4 + 1 \times 2^3 + 1 \times 2^2 + 0 \times 2^1 + 0 \times 2^0$$
$$= 1 \times 32 + 0 \times 16 + 1 \times 8 + 1 \times 4 + 0 \times 2 + 0 \times 1$$
$$= 32 + 0 + 8 + 4 + 0 + 0$$
$$= 44$$

$$11010_2 = 1 \times 2^4 + 1 + 2^3 + 0 \times 2^2 + 1 \times 2^1 + 0 \times 2^0$$
$$= 1 \times 16 + 1 \times 8 + 0 \times 4 + 1 \times 2 + 0 \times 1$$
$$= 16 + 8 + 0 + 2 + 0$$
$$= 26$$

The Remainder Method

The expansion method can be used to convert any number, in any base, to its equivalent in base 10. The remainder method provides the opposite capability; it is used to convert a decimal number to its equivalent value in any other base. Thus, using the remainder method, it is possible to convert a decimal number to its binary equivalent. The discussion that follows outlines the use of the remainder method to convert 14 to its binary equivalent.

```
2 | 14    R
```

Step 1 Position the decimal number being converted into base 2 as illustrated. The 2 to the left of the 14 represents the binary numbering system to which we are converting. Note, if we were converting to base 8 or 16, the value 8 or 16 would replace 2, respectively. The R indicates the use of the remainder method.

```
2 | 7     0
```

Step 2 Divide 2 into 14. Place the result, 7, on the line below 14, and the remainder of that division, 0, on the line beneath the letter R. Set up another line (and position the 2) for the next computation.

```
2 | 3     1
```

Step 3 Repeat the division procedure of step 2. Here, 2 goes into 7 three times, with a remainder of 1.

```
2 | 1     1
```

Step 4 Continue the division by 2. Two is divided into 3 once, with a remainder of 1.

```
2 | 0     1
```

Step 5 Continue the division by 2. In this case, 2 cannot be divided into 1 and result in a whole number. We say 2 goes into 1 zero times, leaving a remainder of 1. When this result occurs; the division process ends.

```
2 | 14    R
2 | 7     0
2 | 3     1
2 | 1     1
2 | 0     1
```

Step 6 The digits beneath the letter R are read upward (from bottom to top) to obtain the binary equivalent of 14. The equivalence can be expressed horizontally as

$$14 = 1110_2$$

The suffix 2 indicates that the digits 1110 are represented in base 2.

The following examples illustrate the use of the remainder method.

EXAMPLE 1

```
2 | 26    R
2 | 13    0
```

Determine the base 2 equivalent of the number 26.

Step 1 Set up the format of the remainder method.
Step 2 2 goes into 26 thirteen times, with a remainder of 0.

```
2|   6   1
2|   3   0
2|   1   1
2|   0   1
26 = 11010₂
```

Step 3 2 goes into 13 six times, with a remainder of 1.
Step 4 2 goes into 6 three times, with a remainder of 0.
Step 5 2 goes into 3 once, with a remainder of 1.
Step 6 2 goes into 1 zero times, with a remainder of 1.
Step 7 Reading up the list of remainders, we state that the decimal number 26 is equal to the binary number 11010.

EXAMPLE 2

What is the base 2 equivalent of 127?

```
2|  127   R
2|   63   1
2|   31   1
2|   15   1
2|    7   1
2|    3   1
2|    1   1
2|    0   1
127 = 1111111₂
```

Step 1 Set up the format for the remainder method.
Step 2 2 goes into 127 sixty-three times, with a remainder of 1.
Step 3 2 goes into 63 thirty-one times, with a remainder of 1.
Step 4 2 goes into 31 fifteen times, with a remainder of 1.
Step 5 2 goes into 15 seven times, with a remainder of 1.
Step 6 2 goes into 7 three times, with a remainder of 1.
Step 7 2 goes into 3 once, with a remainder of 1.
Step 8 2 goes into 1 zero times, with a remainder of 1.
Step 9 Reading up the list of remainders, we state that the decimal number 127 is equal to the binary number 1111111.

The Hexadecimal (Base 16) Numbering System

Whereas the decimal system and the binary system use 10 and 2 digits, respectively, the hexadecimal (base 16) numbering system uses 16 digits to represent data. Because our standard numbering system has only the 10 digits 0 to 9, it has been necessary to create 6 more digits for base 16. Table A.2 gives the six additional hexadecimal digits and their decimal equivalents.

Table A.2
Hexadecimal Digits and the Base 10 Equivalents

Base 16	Base 10
A	10
B	11
C	12
D	13
E	14
F	15

In base 16, alphabetic characters are used to represent numeric quantities and are used with the remainder or the expansion methods like any other number.

Consider the expansion of the hexadecimal number 1AF:

$$1AF_{16} = \underline{1 \times 16^2} + \underline{A \times 16^1} + \underline{F \times 16^0}$$
$$= 1 \times 256 + 10 \times 16 + 15 \times 1$$
$$= 256 + 160 + 15$$
$$= 431$$

Note that in the expansion of the number, the digits A and F represent 10 and 15, respectively. Each is used like any number to represent a numeric quantity. For ease of understanding, A and F were converted to 10 and 15 before multiplying.

The application of the remainder method to hexadecimal digits offers a somewhat different problem. Reversing the prior example, and using the remainder method, we should be able to show that 431 equals 1AF (in base 16).

This use of the remainder method is illustrated below:

$$
\begin{array}{r|rl}
16 & 431 & R \\ \hline
16 & 26 & F \\ \hline
16 & 1 & A \\ \hline
16 & 0 & 1 \\ \hline
\end{array}
\qquad 1AF_{16} = 431
$$

After setting up the problem, divide 16 into 431. From this division, note that 16 goes into 431 twenty-six times, with a remainder of 15. However, because 15 cannot be used in base 16, its equivalent, F, must be specified. In the next line, 16 can be divided into 26 once, with a remainder of 10. Again, since 10 cannot be written, its base 16 equivalent, A, is used. Finally, 16 cannot be divided into 1, so enter a 0 and note a remainder of 1. Reading upward in the column of remainders, note that 1AF (base 16) equals 431 (base 10).

From this example, the conclusion can be drawn that any remainder larger than 10 and less than 16 must be represented by its base 16 equivalent. Other illustrations involving the use of hexadecimal numbers follow.

EXAMPLE 1

$$
\begin{array}{r|rl}
16 & 172 & R \\ \hline
16 & 10 & C \\ \hline
16 & 0 & A \\ \hline
\end{array}
$$

What is the hexadecimal equivalent to the decimal number 172?

Step 1 Set up the problem.
Step 2 16 goes into 172 ten times, with a remainder of 12, or C.
Step 3 16 goes into 10 zero times, with a remainder of 10, or A.
Step 4 Reading up, we state that $AC_{16} = 172$.

EXAMPLE 2

$$
\begin{array}{r|rl}
16 & 4261 & R \\ \hline
16 & 266 & 5 \\[6pt] \hline
16 & 16 & A \\[6pt] \hline
16 & 1 & 0 \\ \hline
16 & 0 & 1 \\ \hline
\end{array}
$$

What is the base 16 number equal to 4261?

Step 1 Set up the problem.
Step 2 16 goes into 4261 two hundred and sixty-six times, with a remainder of 5.
Step 3 16 goes into 266 sixteen times, with a remainder of 10, or A.
Step 4 16 goes into 16 once, with a remainder of 0.
Step 5 16 goes into 1 zero times, with a remainder of 1.
Step 6 Reading up, we state that $10A5_{16} = 4261$.

**Base 2 versus
Base 16**

A unique relationship exists between the binary and the hexadecimal numbering systems because both are based on multiples of the number 2. Because of this relationship, it is possible for one hexadecimal character to represent four binary digits. The correspondence between the base 16 digits and base 2 is shown in Table A.3. The equivalent decimal numbers, 0 through 15, are also listed.

Table A.3   Decimal, Binary
and Hexadecimal Numbers

Decimal	Binary	Hexadecimal
0	0000	0
1	0001	1
2	0010	2
3	0011	3
4	0100	4
5	0101	5
6	0110	6
7	0111	7
8	1000	8
9	1001	9
10	1010	A
11	1011	B
12	1100	C
13	1101	D
14	1110	E
15	1111	F

Observe from this table that the binary equivalent of the number 12 is 1100, whereas the base 16 equivalent of 12 is the number C. The table illustrates the 4 to 1 relationship between binary and hexadecimal numbers. This 4 to 1 ratio makes it possible to convert base 2 numbers directly to base 16 numbers and vice versa.

Consider the base 2 number 111101101110_2. By dividing this number into groups of four, from right to left, it is possible to convert these binary groupings directly into their hexadecimal equivalents, as follows:

$$1\ 1\ 1\ 1 \quad 0\ 1\ 1\ 0 \quad 1\ 1\ 1\ 0 \quad \text{(base 2)}$$
$$\text{F} \qquad\qquad 6 \qquad\qquad \text{E} \qquad \text{(base 16)}$$

The group on the right, 1110, is the equivalent of the hexadecimal digit E. Similarly, 0110_2 and 1111_2 are the equivalents of 6_{16} and F_{16}, respectively. After determining these relationships, we can state that 111101101110_2 equals $F6E_{16}$.

In the above example, it was possible to go directly from base 2 to base 16 without using base 10 because of the special relationship between base 2 and base 16. Additional examples illustrating the conversion of base 2 to base 16 follow:

EXAMPLE 1

Convert 1011000101_2 to a base 16 number.

$$\underbrace{1\ 0}\ \underbrace{1\ 1\ 0\ 0}\ \underbrace{0\ 1\ 0\ 1}\quad \text{(base 2)}$$

$$\quad\ 2\qquad\ \ \text{C}\qquad\quad\ 5\qquad \text{(base 16)}$$

The original binary number is divided into groups of 4, from right to left. In doing this, note that the grouping on the extreme left contains only 2 digits. When this condition occurs, the 2 unfilled positions are filled with zeros. These leading zeros do not alter the value, yet they complete the required grouping of 4 digits. Thus 10_2 becomes 0010_2 and is assigned the correct value of 2_{16}.

EXAMPLE 2

Convert 110001101_2 to a hexadecimal number.

$$\underbrace{1}\ \underbrace{1\ 0\ 0\ 0}\ \underbrace{1\ 1\ 0\ 1}\quad \text{(base 2)}$$

$$\ 1\qquad\ \ 8\qquad\quad\ \text{D}\qquad \text{(base 16)}$$

The initial binary number is divided into groupings of 4 binary digits, which are assigned their equivalent base 16 values.

EXAMPLE 3

Convert 1011011_2 to its base 16 equivalent.

$$\underbrace{1\ 0\ 1}\ \underbrace{1\ 0\ 1\ 1}\quad \text{(base 2)}$$

$$\quad 5\qquad\quad\ \text{B}\qquad \text{(base 16)}$$

The binary value of 1011011 is $5B_{16}$.

Just as it is possible to go directly from base 2 to base 16, the reverse is also possible. However, in the conversion from hexadecimal to binary numbers, 4 binary digits are substituted for each base 16 digit. Consider the following conversion:

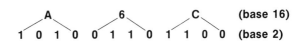

Each hexadecimal digit is assigned its binary equivalent. These binary equivalents are connected, in sequence, to form the final answer. Thus, $A_{16} = 1010_2$, $6_{16} = 0110_2$, and $C_{16} = 1100_2$, and each is sequentially positioned to form the answer 101001101100_2.

EXAMPLE 4

Convert $6DC_{16}$ to its binary equivalent.

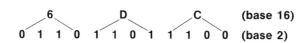

After the conversion of the individual base 16 digits into their binary equivalents, notice that the binary grouping on the extreme left has a leading zero. In supplying the answer, this leading zero can be dropped without affecting the solution. Thus, the following may be stated:

$$6DC_{16} = 11011011100_2$$

EXAMPLE 5

Convert $14E_{16}$ to binary.

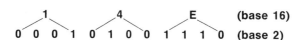

The binary equivalent of $14E_{16}$ is 101001110_2.

The Octal (Base 8) Numbering System

A third numbering system used with some computers is the octal (base 8) numbering system. The octal system uses the digits 0 to 7 and can be employed with either the remainder or the expansion method. The sample problems that follow will easily illustrate this use.

EXAMPLE 1

Using the remainder method, determine the octal equivalent of the decimal number 728.

8	728	R
8	91	0
8	11	3
8	1	3
8	0	1

$728 = 1330_8$

Step 1 Set up the format for the remainder method.
Step 2 8 goes into 728 ninety-one times, with a remainder of 0.
Step 3 8 goes into 91 eleven times, with a remainder of 3.
Step 4 8 goes into 11 once, with a remainder of 3.
Step 5 8 goes into 1 zero times, with a remainder of 1.
Step 6 Reading up the list of remainders, we state that the decimal number 728 is equal to the octal number 1330.

EXAMPLE 2

Demonstrate by the expansion method that the octal number 1330 is equal to the decimal number 728.

$$
\begin{aligned}
1330_8 &= 1 \times 8^3 + 3 \times 8^2 + 3 \times 8^1 + 0 \times 8^0 \\
&= 1 \times 512 + 3 \times 64 + 3 \times 8 + 0 \times 1 \\
&= 512 + 192 + 24 + 0 \\
&= 728
\end{aligned}
$$

Octal numbers are readily employed with either method and are somewhat easier to use than base 16 digits, because they do not involve the use of characters A through F. The two examples above also illustrate how the remainder method and the expansion method can be used to verify computations made in any base. The conversion and reconversion of any number enables users to check their results and create and solve their own homework problems. Other illustrative problems involving the use of base 8 numbers follow.

EXAMPLE 3

What is the octal equivalent of the decimal number 346?

8	346	R
8	43	2
8	5	3
8	0	5

$346 = 532_8$

Step 1 Set up the problem.
Step 2 8 goes into 346 forty-three times, with a remainder of 2.
Step 3 8 goes into 43 five times, with a remainder of 3.
Step 4 8 goes into 5 zero times, with a remainder of 5.
Step 5 Reading up the list of remainders we state that the octal number 532 is the equivalent of the decimal number 346.

EXAMPLE 4

What is the decimal equivalent of the octal number 2314?

$$2314_8 = 2 \times 8^3 + 3 \times 8^2 + 1 \times 8^1 + 4 \times 8^0$$
$$= 2 \times 512 + 3 \times 64 + 1 \times 8 + 4 \times 1$$
$$= 1024 + 192 + 8 + 4$$
$$= 1228$$

The decimal number 1228 is the equivalent of 2314_8.

Base 2 versus Base 8

Because base 8 numbers are derived from multiples of the number 2, a relationship exists between the octal and the binary numbering systems. This relationship is similar in many ways to the relationship noted between base 2 and base 16 numbers. However, instead of a 4 to 1 ratio, only three binary digits are related to one octal number. The base 8 digits and their base 2 equivalents are given in Table A.4.

Table A.4
Decimal, Binary, and Octal Numbers

Decimal	Binary	Octal
0	000	0
1	001	1
2	010	2
3	011	3
4	100	4
5	101	5
6	110	6
7	111	7

From this table, we can note the 3 to 1 relationship between binary and octal numbers. For example, 111 in base 2 equals 7 in base 8. This relationship enables the direct translation of base 2 numbers to base 8 numbers and vice versa, in a manner similar to the conversion of hexadecimal and binary digits. The difference, of course, is that instead of creating groups of four binary digits, only three binary digits are required to create one octal digit. Thus, the conversion of the binary number 101110 to octal is as follows:

$$1 \ 0 \ 1 \ \ 1 \ 1 \ 0 \qquad \text{(base 2)}$$
$$5 \qquad \ \ 6 \qquad \text{(base 8)}$$

Initially, the digits are grouped by three, from right to left. The binary groupings 110 and 101 are converted to their octal equivalents, 6 and 5, respectively. Thus, 101110_2 equals 56_8.

By applying the same procedure, the conversion of the binary number 1011100 produces the octal digits 134.

$$1 \ \ 0 \ 1 \ 1 \ \ 1 \ 0 \ 0 \quad \text{(base 2)}$$
$$1 \quad 3 \qquad 4 \qquad \text{(base 8)}$$

The conversion of octal to binary numbers requires the reversal of the above process. Three binary digits are provided for each octal digit, from right to left. The following problems illustrate the conversion technique.

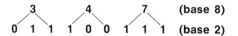

The binary equivalent of the octal number 347 is 11100111. Note that we can suppress the leading zero, because it does not affect the answer. Initially, however, the zero is included to ensure that three binary digits are substituted for each octal number. The conversion of 531_8 to base 2 can be performed as follows:

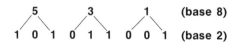

Discussion Questions

1 Convert the following decimal numbers to base 2, base 8, and base 16 numbers, using the remainder method.

a	216	b	47	c	1313
d	28	e	823	f	511

2 Convert the following numbers into their decimal equivalents:

a	101101_2	b	10111_2	c	1101101001_2	d	10110011_2
e	$4D_{16}$	f	$13A_{16}$	g	$F7E_{16}$	h	$2BED_{16}$
i	14553_8	j	427_8	k	1024_8	l	36_8

3 Convert the following binary numbers into base 16 and base 8 numbers:

a	1011101001_2	b	101101_2	c	101101110_2	d	1101_2
e	110100_2	f	10111000_2	g	10000110111_2	h	10110_2

4 Convert the following base 16 numbers to their binary and octal equivalents:

a	$F4_{16}$	b	$A06_{16}$	c	$2D69_{16}$	d	$3E_{16}$
e	793_{16}	f	BAD_{16}	g	$13C8_{16}$	h	$5A6F7_{16}$

5 Convert the following base 8 numbers to their binary and hexadecimal equivalents:

a	62_8	b	11156_8	c	432_8	d	6123_8
e	124_8	f	3006_8	g	1313_8	h	24635_8

Index

Page numbers in **boldface** indicate definitions of entries appearing in glossaries at the end of each chapter.